Becoming Elizabeth Arden

ALSO BY STACY A. CORDERY

Alice

Juliette Gordon Low

Becoming

Elizabeth Arden

THE WOMAN BEHIND THE
GLOBAL BEAUTY EMPIRE

Stacy A. Cordery

VIKING

VIKING
An imprint of Penguin Random House LLC
penguinrandomhouse.com

Image credits can be found on pages 493–495.

LIBRARY OF CONGRESS CATALOGING-IN-PUBLICATION DATA
Names: Cordery, Stacy A., author.
Title: Becoming Elizabeth Arden : the woman behind the global beauty empire /
Stacy A. Cordery.
Description: [New York] : Viking, [2024] |
Includes bibliographical references and index.
Identifiers: LCCN 2024016805 (print) | LCCN 2024016806 (ebook) |
ISBN 9780525559764 (hardcover) | ISBN 9780525559771 (ebook)
Subjects: LCSH: Arden, Elizabeth, 1878-1966. |
Businesswomen—United States—Biography. | Cosmetics industry—United States.
Classification: LCC HD9970.5.C672 C67 2024 (print) |
LCC HD9970.5.C672 (ebook) | DDC 338.7/66855092 [B]—dc23/eng/20240514
LC record available at https://lccn.loc.gov/2024016805
LC ebook record available at https://lccn.loc.gov/2024016806

Printed in the United States of America
1st Printing

DESIGNED BY MEIGHAN CAVANAUGH

To Simon, Gareth, and Sophie—

because, lucky me, the most beautiful thing

in my life is my family.

Contents

Preface

This is where the story begins: steely determination, unshakable certainty in her own abilities, passionate belief in her ideas. Businesswomen—at least successful, high-profile ones—were an anomaly well into the twentieth century. In 1955, *Big Business Leaders in America* included not a single woman among the nearly nine thousand executives listed—except in the index, under "wives of business leaders." When Elizabeth Arden opened her first salon in 1910, she entered an unusual field, one run by women who hired women and catered to women. Beauty and skin care required trust, and women knew best how to minister to one another. But by the late 1920s, the enormous potential for profit attracted male graduates of the new business schools who applied cutting-edge theories to women's beauty needs. They bought out female-owned companies and redefined success. Across all industries, men simply disregarded women. Businessmen shrugged at the idea of bias against their female counterparts: "There is no prejudice here against women. They just don't get to the top." As the landscape changed, successful women became chameleons, learning to adapt.[1] Business culture, federal laws, and social mores stacked up against them.

Elizabeth Arden, impervious, maintained her own path, straight to the summit.

Arden's entire life was an entrepreneurial success story that, at every juncture, ran counter to expectations. Born in rural Canada, raised without a mother, lacking a high school education, an immigrant with barely a penny in her pocket, she was perceptive, creative, street-smart, hardworking, self-confident, thick-skinned, and intrepid. She was un-afraid of risks. If her name was connected to a product, it had to be per-fect, damn the cost. She could be imperious, commanding. Her style was not everyone's. Yet what she achieved in the many and varied moving parts of the global business she created was astonishing—whether mea-sured in profits, brand-name recognition, number of imitators, longevity, or reputation. Elizabeth Arden was a woman self-taught in the masculine world of business. Her feminine appearance, little-girl voice, and demure public demeanor cloaked a driving ambition.

Competition thrilled her. She took on all comers with a certain glee. Arden early defined her client base as wealthy white women and those who aspired to their status. She guarded that sales segment tenaciously. There is a persistent fable that Helena Rubinstein was Arden's most bit-ter adversary, and that they never met. It does make a good story, but it is not true. Arden and Rubinstein were titans in a small field, battling for the same sliver of customers. Yet they shared membership in two professional organizations. They worked together on federal programs in the 1930s. They attended the same industry gatherings, spoke to the same beauty columnists, and had overlapping friendship circles. Helena Rubinstein was a competitor—at some moments *the* competitor—but never her only opponent.

Arden's financial and personal goals were intertwined. Starting with nothing, she aspired to recognized social status. Victory meant acquir-ing wealth and cornering the market of sophisticated patrons while gaining entrance to their society. She succeeded at both, in a staggeringly short time. Of course, Arden could never become a member of America's old money club—that was impossible. The company she loved hindered her social acceptance because Elizabeth Arden was a woman "in trade." The fact that she worked for a living and upper-class women did not was a barrier that took years to overcome. But astute study of her customers followed by decades of philanthropic work opened the doors of high society to her on two continents. She could have given up her trade at any moment and joined the idle rich. She would not do it. Arden rejected seven-figure offers for the business that was more important to her than everything else. She enjoyed it too much. Elizabeth Arden—the company—defined her as thoroughly as she defined it. They were one and the same.

Her greatest goal was to make women beautiful. As a girl, she substituted a romantic and flowery view of the world for the dingy reality of her childhood. When she discovered how to create beauty, she determined to give that gift broadly. She believed, and often repeated, that "the woman does not live who cannot be made pleasant to look on."[2] Arden knew that beauty equaled strength, and that a woman who felt beautiful could conquer the world. The creation of beauty drove her. Beauty was behind every business decision she made, and it brought her wealth, acceptance, and international fame.

Arden was a public figure whose private life is opaque because she wrote no memoir and did not commit her thoughts to paper beyond a few letters. If she kept diaries they are not preserved in any archive. Associates and acquaintances left word pictures that described a complicated woman with unexpected talents, a picture reinforced by articles and interviews in newspapers, popular and fashion magazines, trade journals, and periodicals from the thoroughbred horse racing world. Friendships, fame, and media coverage grew steadily, and each decade further illuminated Arden's character.

How a young, uneducated, working-class Canadian struck out for

New York, changed women's relationship with cosmetics, and transformed herself into a global business magnate is an extraordinary tale. It rests on what Americans like to think of as their very best qualities: grit, determination, hard work, common sense, honest dealings, and a deep belief in unlimited opportunity. Here is how she did it.

Becoming Elizabeth Arden

One

Beginnings

For a woman who dedicated her life to beauty, Elizabeth Arden had an unprepossessing start. Born in the Canadian hinterland, she was the third daughter and the fourth child of immigrant parents who never could quite gain a solid footing in their new home. Luxuries were few. Poverty and uncertainty made for a childhood steeped in deprivations, indignities, and obstacles. Yet that hardscrabble upbringing fueled impassioned dreams of a better life, for even as a very young girl, Elizabeth Arden was as determined as she was industrious. She was always busy, first from necessity and then from a ferocious longing to make something of herself.

Her birth, on the last day of 1881 in rural Woodbridge, Ontario, was unremarkable. Elizabeth's mother, Susan Pearce Tadd Graham, had grown up in a fairly well-to-do maritime family in Cornwall, on the southernmost tip of England. Susan's parents, Jane Pearce and Samuel Tadd, were not best pleased when she fell in love with William Pierce Graham, a rough, working-class Scotsman from a Lanarkshire cotton mill family. Parental censure caused the nearly penniless pair to immigrate—unwed—to Toronto in June 1870. Two years later, they married, and Graham found a job as a clerk. A difficult crossing, harsh Canadian winters, and penury caused by Graham's small salary weakened Susan's constitution. She developed a cough that never left her.[1]

Christine (1873), Lillian (1875), and William (1878) preceded Elizabeth, and in 1884, the Grahams' last child, Jessie (always called Gladys), was born. With each birth, Susan's frailty increased. Unable to contribute to the family income and worried that her five offspring would lack schooling, Susan persuaded her favorite aunt to send money to educate the children so they could better themselves. It was her last grand gesture. The chronic cough signaled tuberculosis, and she wasted away slowly and painfully at home until her death in July 1888. Elizabeth was only six years old.

At Susan's insistence, Elizabeth had been christened Florence Nightingale Graham. This honored the famous nursing pioneer who had defied mid-nineteenth-century gender constraints to pursue her calling, first with the battlefield nursing corps she organized during the Crimean War in the 1850s, then in a lifetime of public service in healthcare reform. With Nightingale as a namesake, Susan gave young Florence—as she was known for the first three decades of her life—a resolute and nonconformist role model, one that influenced her in profound ways.

The Graham children labored hard, cooking, cleaning, sewing, keeping the fire going, growing and preserving food. Their existence was little better than hand to mouth. William Graham, after a series of short-term jobs, found work as an itinerant peddler.[2] This was a common occupation, "born of poverty and misfortune . . . the last, desperate resort of the unskilled, the unemployed, the very young and the very old, the sick, the injured and the victimized."[3] There was no shop, no storefront. He took his wares around on his back or with a horse and wagon to hawk to neighbors nearby and strangers farther afield. Florence learned firsthand from her father the importance of a good reputation, an effective sales pitch, and an appealing product presentation, as well as how to sell what customers wanted and gauge the price they would pay. She also saw plainly that peddling seldom led to upward mobility.

Today, Woodbridge is a thriving suburb of the city of Vaughan, itself now a northern suburb of Toronto. But when the Grahams—William, Susan, and baby Christine—moved there in 1875, it was barely forty years old. To thank Rowland Burr, the owner of the thriving gristmill and sawmill, citizens named the village Burwick. The tiny settlement relied on a hardy immigrant workforce. As houses went up, British settlers evoked their heritage in street names like Cheltenham, Landsdowne, and McKenzie. And when the appellation "Burwick" had to be abandoned because the newly opened post office didn't want its stop mistaken for another Burwick farther west, community members rechristened it Woodbridge, after the town in Suffolk, England.[4]

By the time Susan died and Christine, Lillian, Bill, Florence, and Gladys were performing the incessant chores to keep the home together, Woodbridge was bustling. Two newspapers chronicled the increased production of the prizewinning tractors of Abell Agricultural Works, the comings and goings of guests at the Gilmour Commercial House or the Inkerman Hotel, and the everyday business of Maynard's Machine Shop and the Wallace Brothers General Store. Woodbridge added three churches, a library, a doctor, a pharmacist, a printer, and a butcher to its booming building trade. The Graham children attended the brick grammar school, and the younger ones moved into the new "continuation," or high school, when it was built around 1896.

The stubbornness of railway executives hampered Woodbridge when the Toronto, Grey and Bruce Railway refused John Abell's request to run a spur to his agricultural implements factory. Stymied, he moved his plant and his workforce to Toronto. As a result, the population of almost fifteen hundred fell sharply to a little over six hundred by 1901. The rush of modernity paused. Roads went unpaved. Sidewalks and electricity were pushed further into the future. Thus, while Florence was born at a promising moment in her little town's history, she grew up during a long-term recession that bit at her family's already pinched circumstances.[5]

Her comfort was horses. She was born, she later said, "with a whinny in my ear," thanks to her father. Stories about William Graham lack trustworthy sources, and he has been identified variously as a jockey, a trainer, a horse trader, the owner of "a horse which finished second in the Queen's Plate," and—more likely—a man whose peddler's wagon was drawn by a series of knock-kneed mares barely up to the task.[6] Regardless, Florence's happiest duties involved horses. If she traveled the sales route with her father, then she spent even more time with them. Florence dearly loved all animals, but a lifelong equine bond developed early.[7]

By 1901, the four sisters had given up trying to make ends meet in Woodbridge. There were no jobs to provide economic independence and no potential husbands. Together they moved to the nearest big city, Toronto, where they hoped to indulge their passion for beautiful clothes and life at a faster clip. Christine found work as a dressmaker. Lillian became a china painter. Florence, who had not completed high school, was a "machine operator." At $275 a year, she earned more money than her sisters.[8]

Factory work proved tedious, and Florence soon cast about for something else to do. Looking toward her eponym and what she believed was their shared gift for healing—she had treated the various ailments of siblings and horses—Florence enrolled in nursing school. That field of endeavor had previously fallen to Catholic orders in Canada. Nuns did not have to worry, as other women did, that their reputations would be compromised by the intimate act of nursing men. This changed in 1874, when Ontario doctors began the nation's first secular training program with the help of nurses who had been instructed by Florence Nightingale herself. The "Angel of the Crimea" made nursing a respectable career for all women. Florence probably matriculated at St. Michael's Hospital School, which opened in 1892 and required only a ninth-grade education. A three-month probationary period preceded commitment to the full two- or three-year program of study.[9] Students learned how to dispense medicines and assist doctors in the care of wounds, accidents, and fevers. But her zeal to serve the sick faded quickly and she dropped out. Decades later, she explained that "nursing wasn't enough. I not only wanted to make people well, I also wanted to make them beautiful."[10]

At twenty, Florence Graham was ambitious, resourceful, and hard-working, but unsure about her destiny. She was also quite pretty. Only an inch or two over five feet tall, with blonde hair, blue eyes, and a quick wit, she turned heads. She inherited her peaches-and-cream complexion from her mother and never looked her age. She adored films, poetry, and novels. Intensely competitive with her older sisters, Florence was best friends with the younger, Gladys, who admired Florence and stuck with her through thick and thin. Both women were animated and personable and found it easy to speak with strangers and adapt to changing situations.

Seeking a more congenial occupation, the two turned optimistically to a new business: the home manufacturing of skin creams. Women had been making their own moisturizers, toothpastes, hair dyes, and cosmetics for centuries, using recipes handed down from female relatives or printed in domestic manuals. Ingredients such as oils, waxes, lanolin, eggs, orange water (an astringent), lavender, and rose water were readily available. Briefly back in Woodbridge, Florence and Gladys hoped to create beauty aids to peddle or sell to drugstores.

The sisters began their venture at a propitious moment. Industrialization in North America was well under way. That meant many more choices for women, who were turning from producers into consumers.

Greater discretionary income gave them an important role in the emerging economy. Every mass-produced item appearing on store shelves provoked a desire for more.[11]

Florence and Gladys planned to grow rich selling their creams. They tinkered doggedly. One day, their trial-and-error mixing resulted in the mephitic smell of rotten eggs. Mistaking the odor of an unsuccessful science experiment for destitution, their concerned Unitarian minister hurried to the Graham home bearing a fresh dozen.[12] Even though these initial beauty attempts came to nothing, they would later prove to be time well spent.

Back in Toronto, Florence worked as a receptionist for an establishment that produced wearable athletic and surgical supports, learning about the types of help that some people's bodies required.[13] Next was a job as a dental assistant. There she honed the gentle art of persuasion learned along her father's peddling route. She found creative ways to convince patients of the benefits of brushing their teeth—including terrifying them with worst-case scenarios. Though not in her job description, her efforts resulted in marked growth for the dentist's practice. For a time she held a position in a bank, which she later credited with teaching her the basics of finance and making her "a whiz at bookkeeping." Florence sought better wages and more knowledge with each job. She left only one position involuntarily. A real estate firm fired her because she never aced the necessary typing.[14]

Whether it was the sting of being fired, impatience with the string of dismal jobs, or the fact that the first of her sisters—Christine—had married, Florence considered a radical break. Her older brother, Bill, had initially stayed behind in Woodbridge to help their father, but decided there was nothing for him in Canada. As restless and driven as his sisters, he immigrated to New York in 1895. It wasn't long before he had a fine sales job and a secure future.[15] Bill found New York a vibrant, thrilling, expansive city and no doubt told his sisters of its immense potential. Disliking the cold and grime of Toronto and the thought of more dead ends, Florence resolved that she, too, would escape the grinding poverty of her childhood. She would apply the lessons she learned and seek the material comforts her mother had described from her own youth. Immigration had not improved her father's economic situation, but she was not her father. She would succeed where he had failed. In 1908, Florence Nightingale Graham left Canada for New York City and never looked back. She set out to replace the shame and uncertainty of being poor with something better—something only dimly glimpsed at the time that she would turn into reality with spectacular speed.

New York was—then as now—a city of contrasts. Atop society's summit sat old money families—the Van Rensselaers, Astors, Roosevelts, Schermerhorns—whose roots stretched back to the country's founding. Sometimes eclipsing them in size of fortune, but never reaching their social status, were the nouveaux riche: Rockefellers and Carnegies, among others, who had begun more recently to build business empires from nothing. Just below the small middle class of professionals—physicians, attorneys, architects, successful business owners—were skilled artisans. At the bottom of New York's economic and social strata, the very poor lacked basic housing, sanitation, food, clothing, health care, and job security. Their streets were paved with despair. If they could climb, overcoming entrenched racism, antisemitism, sexism, anti-immigrant hostility, and simple bad luck, they might land jobs that paid a bare subsistence. Banding together with family or friends and pooling resources could help.

Florence Graham's precise New York destination is unclear, but her brother's place was a likely spot. As she explored the mammoth city, marveling at the skyscrapers, the streetcars, the sheer variety of life and experiences, Florence surely compared herself to those around her. She could retrim her old hats and dresses to make them appear less rural and more stylish as New York defined it. She was fortunate that Bill already knew the city and could help her locate work. Her first job was a bookkeeping position at E. R. Squibb & Sons Pharmaceuticals in Brooklyn. It was an auspicious start.

Edward R. Squibb was a surgeon and a former U.S. naval officer. In 1892, he went into business with his sons, opening a laboratory to produce drugs and other chemical compounds. Squibb was a perfectionist, impatient with inferior medicines. He made purity and standardization the goals of his laboratory, and that is the reputation it had when he died in 1900. His fellow physicians demonstrated their respect by calling him "incarnated honesty," committed to "medical ethics," and personally responsible for replacing "haphazard and rule-of-thumb methods" with "technical accuracy."[16] Squibb's sons retained the public's faith by staying true to his high standards. Florence learned the value of pure ingredients and a good name.

Although hired as an office worker, Florence was drawn to Squibb's extensive, modern laboratories where both testing and production occurred. What could she discover there that had eluded her when she and Gladys so disastrously cooked up facial creams in their kitchen? To find out, she sweetly pestered Squibb's top-notch chemists. Some measure of charm and determination saw her slip past her desk and into the lab to learn from the experts.[17]

TORONTO HAD A FEW HAIRDRESSERS, but no manicurists, beauty salons, or cosmeticians—only druggists who sold the supplies needed for homemade toiletries and probably rice powder, which women used sparingly on their faces.[18] The city's newspapers contained occasional discreet advertisements for mail-order products to improve one's looks. But in New York, Florence walked daily by storefronts of the emerging and daring field of "beauty culturists," all of whom made wonderful promises. Skin and hair care had only recently moved from the hands of female relatives and attendants in the privacy of the boudoir to commercial establishments run by strangers. It was not long before Florence found a job in the salon of international beauty culturalist Eleanor Adair.

Born Eleanor Hanley in Liverpool, England, in 1864, she had become Eleanor Adair by 1904. She billed herself as an exclusive beauty professional with salons in New York, London, and Paris, and a thriving mail-order trade as well.[19] Very little is known about Adair's actual business, except that she borrowed significantly from the hapless Harriet Hubbard Ayer, creator of Récamier Toilet Preparations.[20]

Ayer's life was blemished by bad decisions and worse luck. Arden was only a child when Ayer began Récamier Preparations in 1886, but as an adult, she, like Adair, would have heard of her, for Ayer's beauty products were just as famous as the mayhem of her life. Ayer's heartbreaks included a husband who became an obstruction, a business partner who deceived her, deep indebtedness, accusations of product impurity, charges of personal madness fueled by addiction, the death of her child, the loss of her company, and terrible poverty at the end of her life.[21]

Yet for the seven years she ran her company, Ayer was a leader. Her business blueprint included charmingly packaged products with a signature color sold at high prices (and high profit) under her own name, clever marketing campaigns, and the 1899 publication of *Harriet Hubbard Ayer's Book: A Complete and Authentic Treatise on the Laws of Health and Beauty*.[22] Ayer faced significant barriers to the men's club of business, even though she was in a woman's field. Her life "reveal[ed] the iron wall facing women who would not settle for a waged or salaried position and who demanded access to the resources available to their class."[23] While Ayer could not climb that iron wall, her groundbreaking techniques provided a blueprint followed closely by other beauty culturalists.

Eleanor Adair probably hired Florence in 1908 as a receptionist or cashier in her midtown Manhattan salon. The address aimed explicitly at affluent clients, as did Adair's two European salons—in London's Mayfair district and just off the Place de la Concorde in Paris. To reinforce this message, her advertisements in magazines such as *Vogue* and *The Smart Set* stated boldly that she was "patronized by royalty" and by "young women and matrons of high social position, refinement and character." Such customers sought well-appointed salons, and hers had floral wallpaper, potted plants, comfortable furniture, and large picture windows.[24]

Patrons also expected refined personnel. Because any tie to an international fashion capital suggested high style, Adair claimed she employed "English Experts." It is true that Canada was part of the British Empire in 1908, so perhaps that was close enough, but Florence certainly did not meet the other requirement Adair touted publicly: that her employees had all been "thoroughly drilled in the London Establishment."[25] Florence had never been to England and did not consider herself refined—but she longed to be. And in lieu of expert training, she had other skills. There was an art to pleasing this sort of patron, Florence quickly discerned, and she determined to master it. She scrutinized the way Adair's clients spoke, dressed, and moved, as well as how the best of the treatment girls (as they were called) conducted themselves.

Florence craved insight about how to make women beautiful. Adair referred to herself as "Europe's leading skin Specialist," and insisted that "it is a woman's duty to study the best means of caring for her face." Florence asked to do just that.[26] She persuaded her new employer to unlock the mysteries of skin care and train her as a treatment girl. Florence acquired the Adair technique—not "steaming and old-fashioned massage" but "oil to remove lines," "tonic to remove puffiness," cream as "a face cleanser and a skin food," and "Bandelettes for tired eyes."[27]

Treatment girls wrapped Adair clients in comfort and tranquility. Wrinkles, double chins, enlarged pores, crow's-feet, scrawny arms, unsightly neck hollows, even freckles and dandruff could be cured—sometimes "instantly"—with the correct procedures. Learning how to coddle customers was surpassingly important. Adair eschewed tradi-

tional massage for fear it would stretch the skin, but she did utilize a
sort of bodywork that all the treatment girls applied and that produced,
at the very least, a relaxed and happy customer. Florence became so
good at this, and so many women asked for her by name, that she negotiated a raise from Mrs. Adair.[28]

There was much more to learn. Adair's "scientific method" had two
elements: "tapping" the facial muscles and "strapping" the forehead and
chin. Tapping was complex, but it was key to Adair's method and could
be done by a technician or by the customer herself. To begin, one had
to "brace the muscles of the neck, then half close the hands and press
the backs of them very firmly against the throat kneading towards the
side muscles; then, close the hands and knead up the middle of the cheek
toward the temples doing this about twenty times." Adair's technique
entailed gently grasping and pulling the skin under the eye away from
the face—a step Arden would later skip for fear it stretched that delicate
skin—before tapping it. Having moved from neck to temples, Adair
finished by tapping the forehead and eyelids.[29] Tapping could be done
with a "patter," which resembled a large spoon or spatula with cotton
pads holding an astringent or a cream.

Muscle strapping entailed wearing one or both of two straps that Adair
had invented and patented.[30] The forehead strap "obliterated" wrinkles,
Adair promised, while the chin strap eliminated a double chin and the
"lines running from nose to mouth." It also "induces correct breathing
while sleeping," by which she meant it stopped a woman from snoring.
She later devised an "extra strong" chin strap for habitual snufflers.[31]
The straps could be used at the salon or purchased for overnight wear at
home. Adair was not the first to promote strapping, but she became a recognized proponent of it.[32] Florence added tapping and strapping to her
toolbox, a fervent convert to their wrinkle-reducing powers.

Adair taught Florence about another emerging beauty technique: electricity. The thrill of electrification lay in its novelty and its rarity. Few
American homes were electrified in 1908. Electricity had seemingly

magical properties. When applied to the body, electrical pulses were supposed to rejuvenate the skin, thicken follicle growth, remove unwanted hair, and decrease signs of aging.[33] Adair's "Hygienic Face Massage and Electrical Face Treatments" were given at the salons where employees like Florence applied the Adair Electro-Coil Battery, a small tubular instrument soaked in a preparation, to the customer's face, neck, shoulders, or hands.

The entire Adair method rested on her broader product line called "Ganesh," named for a Hindu god. She claimed to have lived and studied in India, where she "learned that . . . production of muscle and tissue by [my muscle] strapping treatment is the only remedy" for fading beauty. To work in the salon, Florence had to memorize the properties and uses of many preparations, from Ganesh Eastern Oil ("the Greatest Skin Food in the World") to Lily Sulphur Lotion. Ganesh was meant to connote exoticism and mystery, and thereby convince women that Adair's toiletries must be superior to anything concocted in the United States. Through the lens of this all-encompassing, trademarked name, Florence glimpsed the potential of selling an entire product line and branding it for a memorable appearance.[34]

Should clients who longed for these exciting treatments find travel to her salon inconvenient, Mrs. Adair would attend them at their residence. For those living far from New York City, she sent her booklet *How to Retain and Restore Youthful Beauty of Face and Form.* She pledged a return letter with a solution to every woman's specific beauty concern. And all her products could be ordered by mail. Florence noted how such strategies expanded the pool of potential patrons well beyond shop visitors.

One other thing she gleaned must have seemed strange at first. Each Adair salon treatment cost a phenomenally expensive $2.50 at a time when the average female garment worker made $10.00 a week. The counterintuitive idea that increased cost equals increased demand for an item was not new to commerce. Exclusivity breeds desire, as Harriet

Hubbard Ayer knew. Eleanor Adair's "Home Treatment" line, sold in decorative, lacquered boxes for travel, retailed for $35 in 1908, about $1,200 today. Her Ganesh Forehead and Chin Straps cost $5.00—or $6.50 for the "extra strong" chin strap.[35] These were prices—and profits—that Florence Graham could barely imagine, but the message sank in quickly. She was smitten with the elegant salon and inspired by the glamorous lives of Adair's clients. But Florence also saw opportunities to improve Adair's preparations. To improve herself. To realize more directly her dream of making people beautiful.

She first sought a better face cream than the Ganesh product. When she found it at Elizabeth A. Hubbard's, Florence considered: to quit Adair and strike out on her own would be double the work and twice the cost. Instead, she proposed a partnership. Florence and Hubbard combined forces in December 1909. Florence had the vision, as well as treatment experience and the understanding of promotion and sales that began in her childhood. She thought they could be financially successful selling Hubbard's toiletries to the same class of women who had responded so well to Adair's.

They leased two expensive rooms on the second floor at 509 Fifth Avenue—a five-minute walk from Adair's—kitty-corner from the New York Public Library. They decided to call their salon after "Mrs. Elizabeth Hubbard" rather than "Miss Florence Graham" because a married woman suggested greater respectability. Hubbard's name went on the door but not on the product. For that all-important sales influencer, Florence invented something new, or new again: Grecian. It was close enough to Ganesh to gain from a customer's confusion, but unlike Ganesh—which could have been made up as far as most American women knew—the word *Grecian* conjured up gorgeous blue seas and magnificent architecture from a noble civilization. It allowed them to weave in that legendary beauty Helen of Troy (who was, of course, Greek, not Trojan). Their first advertisement, in the December 4, 1909, issue of *Vogue*—one of the earliest fashion magazines—tempted women

with a listing of their "famous Grecian" products: Chin Strap, Daphne
Skin Tonic, Muscle Oil, Skin Food, and Japonica Lotion.[36]

As a conventionally attractive, bare-shouldered woman wearing the
Grecian Chin Strap smiled faintly at readers, Mrs. Hubbard trilled that
"the springtime of a woman's life should be all the time." "Age is no
barrier," the ad assured readers, and "those charms of youthful beauty . . .
may be possessed by every woman, young or old." The advertisement
invited women to join the other "strictly high-class clientele" whom
Hubbard "has long served" in the new "elaborate and beautifully appointed" salon. The partners were unafraid of hyperbole: "The privacy
and charming surroundings will appeal to you; its equipment surpasses
anything heretofore attempted. Mrs. Hubbard's assistants are the most
competent on this side of the Atlantic, having been thoroughly trained
in 'Beauty Culture' methods in the leading foreign schools." Grecian
products by mail order could go anywhere in the nation. Advice about
"beauty, health and hygiene," as well as their booklet, *Beauty, How Acquired and Retained*, were free to all who asked.[37] By their second ad, not
quite two months later, the partners were claiming a salon at 267 rue
Saint-Honoré in Paris, and a third in London with an unspecified address. These were almost certainly fictional. They had also added a
Grecian Forehead Strap, Cleansing Cream, and Cream of Velvet, plus a
Home Treatment Box. Their prices were just below what Eleanor Adair
charged.[38]

The creative duo of Graham and Hubbard faced unspecified "business troubles," as the *New York Times* headline read, by August 1910. They
held their business together for barely eight months before landing in
court. The salon was turned over to a receiver when Florence, who had
provided "the experience in beautifying," sued Hubbard, who had furnished "the money." The partnership dissolved.[39] Hubbard kept the name
"Elizabeth Hubbard Beauty Salon" and the rights to the Grecian line.
Florence kept their quarters at 509 Fifth Avenue.[40]

This, Florence knew, was not failure. It was an invitation to reinvent herself. At not quite thirty years old, she had loyal customers and a salon space at a tony address. She had some savings, for she had been moonlighting steadily as a manicurist in the evenings.[41] If she were honest with herself, she had never been fully satisfied with Hubbard's Grecian products. She knew she could improve on them. Her familiarity with sales, promotion, bookkeeping, and salon design had grown, as had her understanding of how to entice her targeted clientele. She took elocution lessons to sound more like them.[42] She set the right tone in the salon foyer by purchasing an expensive Persian rug and an antique reception desk.[43] Convinced that she could do more and do better than Adair and Hubbard, Florence Graham struck out on her own.

Two

The Beauty Culturalist

lizabeth Arden rose from the rubble of the Graham-Hubbard partnership. In the fall of 1910, Florence Graham created Elizabeth Arden—first the salon and then the woman. The business she rechristened almost immediately. The new name she adopted for herself over time until few knew there had ever been a Florence Nightingale Graham.

Developing fictional business personas was an American pastime and it was no different in the beauty field. Indeed, an astonishing number of people in the industry changed their names.[1] For example, François Coty began life as Joseph Marie François Spoturno. Italian immigrant Angelo Siciliano became the great American bodybuilder and trainer Charles Atlas. After he left Poland, Maksymilian Faktorowicz took the Hollywood makeup industry by storm as Max Factor. Helena Rubinstein kept her last name but changed Chaja to Helena. Estée Lauder was originally Josephine Esther Mentzer. Many immigrants live between their old and new lives. They juggle two worlds, two cultures, often two languages. Some immigrants change themselves to fit in, soften their accents, learn a new language, alter the way they dress or eat or celebrate holidays. It's perhaps no surprise, then, that Graham/Arden was very good at moving between identities, hiding parts of herself and modifying her biography, even as she excelled at the business of disguise, of providing women with another face. It was "a very American act of self-creation."[2]

Exactly how Graham settled on the name Elizabeth Arden is a matter of debate. Arden herself offered several creation stories. The simplest explanation was that she borrowed Elizabeth from Hubbard, and slid from Adair to Arden. The confusion in the consumer's mind would serve her well, to start. Another theory is that she simply saw and liked the name. Several Elizabeth Ardens appeared in newspapers of her day.[3] A third tale has Florence, sadly contemplating an empty salon and a nearly empty cash drawer, deciding to keep the name Elizabeth because it was already stenciled in gold on the front door. Repainting only one name would save money. In 1960, she told an interviewer that she had never liked the name Florence, especially when shortened to Flo: "I didn't want my customers to say, 'I had a treatment at Flo Graham's today.'" She also said she had been reading *Elizabeth and Her German Garden*, and that gave her the idea for the first name. The author of that very popular novel was Elizabeth von Arnim—almost a homophone![4]

She often suggested that she took the last name from Alfred, Lord Tennyson's poem "Enoch Arden." This was not as far-fetched as it seems. Tennyson was famous in Florence's youth and young adulthood, and "Enoch Arden" is a highly romantic poem about the triumph of selfless love in a seaside community. "Enoch Arden" may seem treacly and overwrought today, but to a girl born into a humble family with sailors for relatives, the romance would have been unforgettable.[5] However she came to it, Elizabeth Arden turned out to be a magnificent choice, both for her and for her salon. And she appreciated the aesthetics. She addressed an envelope to "Elizabeth Arden" and sent it to herself at the salon address. When it arrived, looking classically elegant, she knew it was perfect.[6]

Unable to market "Grecian" products, Arden had to think up another name. The same short steps that turned Harriet Hubbard Ayer to Eleanor Adair to Elizabeth Hubbard to Elizabeth Arden turned Ganesh into Grecian into Venetian.[7] Italy, like Greece, called up images of sophistication and glamour in potential clients. Picturesque, romantic Venice, the "Queen of the Adriatic," famous for its canals and gondolas, the Bridge of Sighs, the Doge's Palace, and the Piazza San Marco. The warm colors, the breathtaking art, and the transcendent music drew cultured visitors from around the globe to a city associated with luxury. Choosing "Venetian" as a brand gave Arden reason to create a lavish salon and to use Italian art in her advertisements.

Shop design underwent extraordinary changes between 1890 and 1915, and businesses with poorly lit, grimy store interiors had to up their game to remain competitive. Out went wooden floors and counters. In came sumptuous carpets, marble and bronze accoutrements, murals, mosaics, chandeliers, and glass—frosted, opal, iridescent, colored, and clear. Artists and theater set designers suddenly had second jobs when shop owners vied to demonstrate their good taste to patrons. Painter Joseph Cummings Chase developed an entire color theory that enabled proprietors to determine the precise yellow or blue to tempt shoppers to linger longer and purchase more.[8]

Arden chose pink. It was her favorite color, and she believed that pink best set off every woman's beauty. She decorated her salon herself, putting her past client observations to good use and calculating what would appeal. Pink dominated the tasteful interior, and she dressed her packages in a distinctive pink and gold. Arden's love affair with pink was permanent, and it was not long until merchandisers and customers instantly recognized what came to be called "Arden Pink."[9]

The Venetian theme pervaded the booklet she prepared for all Elizabeth Arden Salon clients in 1911.[10] *The Quest of the Beautiful* remained in use through the 1930s, updated frequently and eventually augmented by others geared to specific topics. Beauty culturalists' pamphlets were generally product guides with a philosophical preface about why women should seek beauty. Arden obsessed over the details in her booklet, as she did all aspects of her business. The earliest extant *Quest of the Beautiful* is from 1920. It measured a convenient four by five inches, easily held or tucked into a dressing table drawer for ready consultation. The cover featured a slender white woman, basket on her arm, picking pink and white roses. She wore a tall pale wig and a pink-accented mid-eighteenth-century gown that spilled out of the frame and onto the embossed gold border. The overall effect was of wealth, serenity, and conventional feminine beauty. This same illustration (although in a more stylized version by the 1930s) adorned the front of every subsequent edition.

The Quest of the Beautiful indoctrinated women into the evolving Arden philosophy, including the importance of muscle strapping. It was particularly helpful for the aspirational customers she astutely courted. "The desire to be beautiful is older and stronger than the desire to be either modest or comfortable," Arden wrote reassuringly. "Vanity . . . is natural. It is a sub-conscious putting-your-best-foot-forward." Then came a history of skin care products that, she asserted, were "as old as Egypt." She recounted the use of natural ingredients in Greece, Rome, Italy, central Africa, China, and Japan, and cautioned that some contemporary treatments were harmful. But not her Venetian line. It was based on science, "composed of the purest ingredients from a chemist's formula." Her message was that science undergirded every cream and lotion she sold and guaranteed their purity. The use of science to increase credibility was nothing new in the beauty field. Poisonous preparations were the stuff of gruesome urban legends, all the more chilling when true. Like the reference to sites of classical beauty, invoking science reassured customers, and virtually every entrepreneur did it.[11]

How Elizabeth Arden found the funds to secure a product line, rent her salon, decorate it lavishly, and advertise widely in magazines and newspapers is unclear. She may have saved enough from her salary, tips, and evening manicures. Most accounts of Arden's beginnings state that she secured a loan, anywhere from $100—about $3,300 today—to an implausible $6,000, which would be closer to $200,000.[12] If she did have a loan, she was unlikely to have received it from a bank, as few then did business with single women. She might have turned to money lenders, some of whom advertised their willingness to assist women.[13]

Family members were a more likely source of capital. Uncle J. Liberty Tadd was a possibility because he was well established in his career by 1910. Liberty Tadd was Arden's mother's brother who emigrated from England to make his name as a proponent of the industrial arts. Tadd was a professionally trained painter, who, with Renaissance man Charles G. Leland, began a forward-thinking, hands-on art program for children and adults at the Public Industrial Art School of Philadelphia.[14]

A much more probable source was her brother, Bill, who had already made a success of himself by the time Arden reached New York. Three years older than his sister, Bill had immigrated to the United States at age sixteen. He worked as a salesman before enlisting in the 1898 Spanish-American War. He married Ada Frazee in 1901, and four years later the couple had taken in Bill's sisters Lillian and Gladys. Lillian continued as a china painter while Gladys was a stenographer. In 1907, Patricia, the first of Bill and Ada's three daughters, was born. The second, Virginia, followed one year later. Beatrice arrived in 1915. By then, Lillian and Gladys had moved out, and Bill had been importing and selling china dinnerware for at least five years.[15]

By 1913, Bill was cofounder and president of Graham & Zenger Inc. Capitalized at $50,000, the glass and china dealer was located in the business district a block from Union Square.[16] Carl Zenger mostly remained in New York and managed the retail side of the company, including salesmen across the United States. Graham traveled often to Europe, Canada, China, and Japan, stopping at factories that produced the glassware sold to individuals and to institutions such as hotels.[17] Bill Graham's business grew and prospered. Over time, he dealt with changing governmental regulations, international clients, overseas travel, the upheaval (and discounted currency) of global instability, and matters of product shipment and promotion.[18]

Bill had money, but just as important he had the experience to advise and assist his sister. There were many good reasons to do so. The loan may have earned him interest when she repaid it. Helping her strike out on her own meant that he and Ada wouldn't be saddled with a third relative in their home. He may simply have felt duty bound to aid a family member. But most likely of all, Bill saw in his kid sister Florence an echo of his own ambition.

THE FORMULA FOR a successful salon was complicated. Location mattered. This is why Arden and Elizabeth Hubbard had paid the high rent for the ultrafashionable Fifth Avenue address. Arden knew where social elites shopped. Drawing foot traffic was every bit as important as advertising. Turn-of-the-twentieth-century New York boasted the famous "ladies' mile," a shopping district centered on Broadway, from Park to Sixth Avenues between Union and Madison Squares. Elizabeth Arden knew that commerce was moving uptown because more than two dozen prestigious retailers relocated to choice spots between Thirty-Fourth and Fifty-Second Streets by 1910.

Shopping in these exclusive districts was an event. The public admired the ornate architecture while strolling past small storefronts. Women wishing to see and be seen could spend freely on French kidskin shoes and Tiffany necklaces while socializing on "Gotham's golden shopping strand."[19] Aspirants who came to study the beau monde purchased more cautiously while dreaming of the day they would make their own fortune. The real draws were the colossal department stores:

Siegel Cooper, Lord & Taylor, and B. Altman. Architectural wonders, with whole worlds of merchandise under one roof, they daily enticed hundreds of New Yorkers and out-of-towners to part with their money.

Social critics fretted that department stores filled with marvelous goods would tempt women beyond rationality; they would lose themselves in a frenzy of unseemly consumption. They were also the seed nurseries for the patrons Elizabeth Arden hoped to cultivate. It would be wonderful if Roosevelts and Vanderbilts frequented her salon, but more realistically, she was angling for shoppers seeking upward mobility through Fifth Avenue purchases they could show off in their homes. Frequently changing display windows planted in pedestrians an irresistible desire for the goods they spied. Through her location and her advertisements, Arden focused on women yearning for an elevated life. She taught them to start with affordable luxuries such as her face creams and muscle strapping. And she promised that only her knowledge and products could transform them. She could erase wrinkles, slenderize bodies, and make them into the women they longed to be.[20]

The best location drew in pedestrians, but the only way to reach beyond those who shopped in midtown Manhattan was to advertise. And "the time to advertise," as Arden well knew, "is all the time."[21] She was a savvy student of copy. From her earliest days, she stressed her trustworthiness, expertise, top-notch clientele, and scientific grounding. She especially emphasized the vital importance of following her program. Her guidance was free, and she swore she "never loses interest in those she personally advises by mail."[22] This was very much in keeping with Hubbard and Adair. And, like them, in these early days, Arden unapologetically boasted of her "wonderful ability in progressive Beauty Culture" and the efficacy of her products.

Advertising is an ancient human activity. Newspaper ads are nearly as old as newspapers themselves, dating to late-sixteenth-century Europe. Merchants proclaimed the arrival of new objects, from books to wigs, but when they began to trumpet certain aspects of those items (it makes teeth "white as ivory"), or to make claims about their abilities ("the Only True Plague-water"), or to provide real or fictitious endorsements ("Mrs. Hollingsworth, aged 68, about a year ago was inclined to Dropsy . . ."), announcements then became advertisements.[23] Eighteenth- and nineteenth-century ads made claims every bit as astonishing as Arden's. They featured poetry, riddles, descriptions chockablock with adjectives, paragraphs that read like novels, puzzles, repetition, varying font sizes, clever slogans, illustrations, and fine art. Arden aimed for a romantic, idyllic femininity—even in her time it was more fantasy than reality. She avoided the most outrageous of her competitors' claims as a point of honor. Critics focused on her flowery copy: "And like a garden is the beauty of woman. Tended, it sings with glory; one catches his breath at the sight of it, he becomes a poet, and life is a poem. Neglected, weeds creep in, and not only is the garden no longer a romance and a delight, but one grieves over it—that a rose should have a weed choking out its beauty—that lovely eyes should be marred by lines, a charming mouth by a double chin or a 'scraggly' throat beneath."[24]

Advertisers recognized that women both single and married did much of the purchasing for the home. *Godey's Lady's Book*, the *Ladies' National Magazine* (later renamed *Peterson's Magazine*), and *Leslie's Illustrated Weekly* were among the earliest magazines directed at American women. By the time Elizabeth Arden sought the best places to advertise, there were more choices. *Vogue, The Smart Set, Harper's Bazaar,* and *House & Garden* aimed at patrician readers. *Ladies' Home Journal, Woman's Home Companion, Good Housekeeping,* and *McCall's* sold mainly to middle-class women. *Women's Wear Daily* (*WWD*) was a trade journal that routinely covered fashion, mostly from the United States and western Europe. Arden began with *Vogue* and New York newspapers, but it was not long before her ads appeared in dozens of periodicals, crossing the nation and generating significant mail-order business.[25]

By October 1910, she had taken out quarter-page advertisements in

Vogue, which called itself "a dignified authentic journal of society, fashion, and the ceremonial side of life." She penned them herself, often in the first person.[26] The phrase "Elizabeth Arden Says" suggests that she wanted "Elizabeth Arden" to be understood as an actual person. "I can tell you how," she wrote, "these blemishes can be Entirely Obliterated and the Freshness and Beauty of Youth coaxed back with the aid of my Facial Treatment Methods and Famous Venetian Toilet Preparations."[27] Such "personalism" in ads had been in use since Arden's childhood. It built a connection between seller and buyer and suggested a bond of trust.[28]

A fortnight later, another quarter-page *Vogue* ad demonstrated Arden's command of all she had learned thus far. It stressed her authority as one who understood the "delicate beauty most admired in a woman." This ideal could not be achieved "by hap-hazard concoctions or widely advertised 'creators of beauty.'" Only Elizabeth Arden, holding the "pre-eminent position in her profession," could deliver what was "heretofore unattainable in *Beauty Cultivation*," as "attested to by a numerous clientele of women of the highest social standing in the United States and Europe."[29] As her friend writer Fannie Hurst later put it, Arden "wrote gorgeous ballyhoo." And, Hurst emphasized, "her copy was weighed with the quality of conviction uncoated by even the priceless veneer of a sense of humor."[30] Business was no laughing matter to Elizabeth Arden.

CLEANSE. TONE. NOURISH. Arden's three simple foundational skin care steps were not entirely new, but as her fame increased, she received credit for creating them. Her 1910 Venetian product line consisted of Cleansing Cream, Velva Cream, Muscle Oil, and Lilli (later spelled Lille) Lotion.[31] By February 1911, Ardena Skin Tonic (an astringent) and Skin Food appeared. In March, she branched beyond cleanse, tone, and nourish with Adona Cream to plump the neck, arms, and shoulders, and Bleachine Cream "for removing tiny wrinkles around and under the eyes, and discolorations and puffiness beneath them."[32]

Skin-whitening lotions had been sold for decades and were used by both white and Black women. Arden occasionally advertised Venetian Lilli Lotion, Ardena Skin Tonic, and Bleachine Cream to "firm, clear, and whiten" age spots, liver spots, and freckles. Arden never sold the highly caustic skin lighteners common in the late nineteenth century marketed to African American women. Neither she nor any white beauty entrepreneur purposefully sought Black customers. Beauty products for white and Black women were almost hermetically sealed off from each other. Advertising did not cross the racial divide. In all but a few places in the United States, Jim Crow segregation meant that Black women could not enter salons or stores where such toiletries would be sold. Arden, like other white purveyors, never considered women of color in developing products or clientele. Her Venetian Lilli Lotion, for example, came in "colors to suit all skins. Pink, Cream, White."[33] Nevertheless, as historian Kathy Peiss pointed out, even if billed to lighten spots or freckles, such products always had "class and racial overtones" because darker skin then was anathema to the "genteel white lady" whose pale complexion marked her as a lady of leisure.[34]

Throughout Arden's life, the understanding of beauty widely held by the upper-class white women she wanted as her clients came from classical art. The beautiful female figure was symmetrical, graceful, possessed of soft curves and white skin. These were the sorts of women frequently painted from the fifteenth through the nineteenth centuries by artists such as Leonardo da Vinci and Peter Paul Rubens. In the United States, during the nineteenth and most of the twentieth centuries, the dominant beauty standards privileged conventional, heteronormative, white ideals.[35]

Thus, Arden chose for her initial advertisements the image of a white bare-shouldered woman clad only in a gossamer wrap and a Venetian Chin Strap. She resembled a Renaissance version of the Napoleonic-era drawing of "Madame Récamier" used by Harriet Hubbard Ayer and the depiction of "Helen of Troy" displayed in the Graham-Hubbard ads.[36] It was less homage to Ayer and more the fact that Arden knew what customers were used to seeing. Part of Arden's genius was identifying and improving on an already effective technique.

The Elizabeth Arden Salon was a success from the start. She had found the proper formula: the right location, a simple and elegant name, a presentation of eternal beauty through the word *Venetian* with an appropriate female image, the shrewd use of science and her own reputation to promote trust, the decision to invest early and often in advertising, a signature color and packaging, and her relentless hard work. In her small office, she later hung a hand-made sign that took up most of one wall. On it she wrote: "Nothing Succeeds Like Success."[37]

She was used to exertion and economizing. She became adept at multitasking. Arden personally welcomed clients to the salon she had decorated herself. She did the treatments. She managed the salon, kept the books, wrote the advertising copy, and procured her products. She probably created the creams herself in a kitchen turned lab from several readily available recipe books. She may have also purchased products from a large chemical or drug firm and then rebottled and labeled them herself. Arden stayed late after hours to clean and lock the salon. In four months, she attracted enough customers to hire three assistants. From that moment forward, Arden trained treatment girls herself. She made them practice their massage skills on their own knees before graduating to one another's faces.[38]

At that juncture, Arden found a way to expand her potential patron base by inviting two hairdressers to rent space in her salon. Arden had been impressed to learn that Jessica and Clara Ogilvie told their clients that the best hat for their new hairstyle could be found at the millinery shop owned by their sisters Gladys and Georgina, and that Gladys and Georgina sent their customers to Jessica and Clara's for the ideal hairstyle to match their new hats. It was a charmed circle, and Arden wanted in. The Ogilvies agreed; they benefited by moving from Thirty-Fourth Street to Arden's more upmarket address. Women conveniently saw to their skin care, hair care, and millinery needs all in one location—Arden's.

Like Arden, the Ogilvies were just starting out. The loss of a parent forced all seven Ogilvie sisters to find an occupation. As customers increasingly patronized Arden's, every Ogilvie sister eventually migrated from San Francisco to enter the business in New York. Elizabeth Arden was responsible for launching what would become the highly successful, global Ogilvie hair products corporation, a brand still in existence today.[39]

The Ogilvies were part of a burgeoning industry. Historically, women did their hair at home with the help of female relatives, friends, or servants, using regular soap. Nothing like modern shampoo appeared in the United States until the early twentieth century. In the late nineteenth century, as hairstyles became more elaborate, hair salons began to dot urban landscapes. In Europe, by 1910, Eugène Schueller had invented a nontoxic, long-lasting hair dye, marketed as L'Oréal, and German hairdresser Karl Nessler had perfected a workable permanent wave. Nessler and François Marcel—for whom the iconic Marcel wave was named—moved hairdressing into the salon and made it respectable.[40] This transformation opened the field to female entrepreneurs, and the number of woman-owned hair salons skyrocketed.

Two American women made their mark in short order: Annie Turnbo Malone and Sarah Breedlove (better known as Madam C. J. Walker). Both successfully marketed products to an African American clientele at the start of the twentieth century. Walker began by selling the hair-strengthening products of Malone's successful Poro Company before she left to develop her own. Both businesses included the hiring, training, and deployment of door-to-door saleswomen into Black communities. Malone and Walker established beauty schools, sold by mail order, and became important philanthropists. Competitors in the beauty business, both women ceaselessly battled racism and sexism. Malone was among the first Black female millionaires, and Walker was not far behind her in wealth. Respected and beloved, the two entrepreneurs broke stereotypes and established lasting legacies, including a business model that many others—Black and white—would follow.[41]

IN 1911, ARDEN made another solid business decision by hiring Florence G. Delaney as bookkeeper. "Laney" became a trusted lieutenant who worked side by side with Arden in various roles until her retirement more than three decades later.[42] Delaney respected her boss. She recalled the early days and her astonishment at Arden's optimism and energy: "I used to marvel at her. She never thought she might run out of money. She never worried about anything. She just worked all the time, from morning till night."[43] Delaney matched Arden's pace, and they made a good team.

Then came Arden's audacious expansion idea: to follow wealthy women on their summer vacations. Arden easily located the watering holes of the very rich because they were reverently and extensively covered in magazines. So, although she'd never vacationed in Bar Harbor, Maine, Arden knew who did. In 1911, she opened a salon for the summer colony created by physicians, bankers, and businessmen wishing to escape the heat and noise of New York, Boston, and Philadelphia.[44] The 221 families who sojourned there in 1910 created their own social register that included America's most prominent captains of industry: Morgan, Bowdoin, Pulitzer, Rockefeller, Ford. Their "cottages"—George W. Vanderbilt's boasted nine living rooms on the first story and eight bedrooms on the second—felt the magic touch of famous designers such as Frederick Law Olmsted and Beatrix Farrand. The summer residents united in their goal to preserve their caste and traditions. "A 'hard, bold Northern landscape' . . . combined with racial purity proved irresistible to an elite fleeing the city and its immigrant population," a Bar Harbor scholar wrote. The *Boston Advertiser* extolled the "diplomats and society leaders of the old school, persons eminent in literature, professional life, and the arts," in short, "the best to be found at any American resort."[45]

Narragansett, Rhode Island, was a similar enclave where Arden trusted her advertisement would be opportune news: "Elizabeth Arden, the eminent beauty culturist of New York, whose progressive methods are similar only to those of beauty specialists of note abroad, announces to the many of her clientele who will be at Narragansett Pier and neighboring resorts throughout the summer season that she will locate at the Mathewson Hotel . . . to make appointments for the VENETIAN FACIAL TREATMENTS, to be given either at residences or at Mrs. Arden's Salon. . . . *Ladies only received.*"[46] The "Mrs." was a polite fiction connoting respectability.

Newport was the biggest prize. In the epicenter of East Coast affluence Arden rented a space in the legendary Newport Casino, a club whose members included Astors, Goelets, Van Rensselaers, and Belmonts. Alongside her salon were branch shops from "many of the great firms on Fifth Avenue, Madison Avenue, and Fifty-seventh Street." The casino was the central gathering spot for the moneyed. Understated and exclusive, it had a ballroom designed by Stanford White, the best tennis courts in the nation, and a gorgeous, members-only piazza into which the locals peered with wonderment.[47] Arden cannily took her beauty aids right to the heart of the nation's highest concentration of moneyed white women, for, she was pleased to announce later, "a most successful season."[48]

WHILE UP-AND-COMING BUSINESSWOMAN Elizabeth Arden sat in her New York office contemplating further expansion, different plans— for a woman suffrage parade—were under way half a mile south in the Women's Political Union (WPU) headquarters. Even though this would not be the first such demonstration in New York, women marching in public spaces on behalf of their controversial demand for the vote was still so unusual that it sent newspapers into paroxysms. Such participation broke social taboos. Stepping off the curb and into the street was crossing a line into a radicalism difficult to imagine today but searingly provocative then.

A year of concerted effort on the part of suffrage organizations resulted in an estimated ten thousand people setting off down Fifth Avenue at 5:00 p.m. on May 4, 1912, in an overwhelming display of women's desire to vote. Women on horseback, mothers pushing strollers, Black women, girls, college students—even men took part. Prominent suffragists who lined up that day included WPU president Harriot Stanton Blatch, Inez Milholland, and Alva Vanderbilt Belmont. Many women wore white dresses decorated with ribbons in the suffrage colors of yellow, purple, and green. The marchers took two hours to pass onlookers, some of whom, inspired, impulsively entered the parade.[49]

Elizabeth Arden may have joined their ranks that afternoon. As she seems not to have confided her thoughts to paper, it is impossible to know how strongly she felt about suffrage. A cynical read of her involvement in the parade would suggest that she gauged the size of the crowd, saw in it thousands of potential clients, and wanted to claim an honest involvement in the movement. Or that Arden joined in because she knew that several well-heeled women had come out in support of suffrage that day.

A more pragmatic analysis would consider the fact that Arden was a single woman trying to establish and grow a business with most of the laws of the land stacked against her. That she was not a U.S. citizen made a tough legal and economic situation more difficult. Seeing herself as an independent entrepreneur, surrounded by the Ogilvies and others like them, and listening daily to the talk of the women she served and the women she hired, could have persuaded her to move boldly into the suffrage movement and commit to its promise of equal citizenship.[50]

The new century eviscerated many old ways of thinking even among the class most staunchly wedded to tradition. Social elites began their assault on convention by promoting and funding the suffrage campaign. They sought "not the moral suasion of motherhood or the indirect power of social standing, but the political influence . . . long denied them because of their gender." "Gilded suffragists" numbered in the hundreds, and their influence was outsize thanks to their money and status. Female Rockefellers, Belmonts, Vanderbilts, Whitneys, Astors, Tiffanys, and Harrimans participated in nearly every aspect of the suffrage fight, including parades, speechmaking, and public relations.[51] Even the reliably anti-suffrage *New York Times* knew that "women who are supposed to be authorities on dress and manners, who are at home in the most exclusive social circles, are bound to influence others."[52]

Rich women helped remove the hateful stereotype of the unfeminine, boorish suffragist that men used to belittle women's political efforts. In 1911, *The Washington Post* summarized the "popular belief" that "suffragettes are a set of hoodlum-like women, mannishly or sloppily dressed, and thoroughly untidy in every way." Beating back that trope became the new suffragist tactic. *The Post* editorialized that, according to suffragists themselves, "the well-groomed, attractive matron or maid . . . has more influence over both sexes on the speakers' platform or in personal conversation than her out-at-elbows sister."[53]

This Elizabeth Arden fervently believed. She may or may not have been a suffragist. She may or may not have actually marched in a suffrage parade. But her belief that all women could be beautiful is behind the persistent myth that she dashed out of her office during the 1912 suffrage parade with a basket full of red lipstick to hand out to every suffragist. It was red, as the story goes, to symbolize women reclaiming the Jezebel stigma, red to shock men into understanding that women would no longer be defined by rules dictated by their fathers and husbands, red as a banner of independence from the past and a promise of the liberty and equality to come.

This is wishful thinking. [54] Arden was neither making nor selling lipstick in 1912! She would not have had a single lipstick to hand out, let alone basketfuls. Even had it existed, red lipstick would have been a step too far, causing backlash, not support. Suffragists worked to present themselves as socially acceptable to be taken seriously. They would not jeopardize that with the harlot's red lipstick.

Elizabeth Arden appreciated the fine lines of appearance and behavior that divided the social classes. She had studied them closely, and the proof was that her business was attracting women of means. In under two years, Arden had established a successful salon, developed and marketed a line of products with a signature color and look, opened summer salons for the well-to-do, and begun a mail-order department. She found a dependable right-hand woman, hired and personally trained assistants, and made a commercial connection with hairdressers and hatmakers. It was a formidable start. But it was only the beginning. Arden's next big idea lay across the Atlantic.

Three

Changing the Face of America

In July 1912, with less than two years of business experience, Elizabeth Arden set out to unearth Europe's beauty secrets. Eager to enhance her salons, she sailed for London and Paris to immerse herself in Western refinement. She planned to fill her days with appointments at every possible salon. How better to memorize new techniques than to put herself in the treatment chair? Arden understood the basic human craving for something different, something original and unique, and logically she knew that if she succeeded, the result would be greater publicity and profit.[1]

Bond Street was London's buoyant center of beauty culture. Many female entrepreneurs, including a handful of American expats, provided facial peels, massage, "dynamic electrical processes," and antidotes to aging. Since the early 1890s, for example, Missouri-born Anna Ruppert had operated a salon described as "One of the Sights of London." Her "Palatial Reception Rooms" gave "A Glimpse of Fairyland. Electric Lights, Palms, and Tapestry." The interior design concepts alone merited Arden's attention. She also could glean much from Jeannette Pomeroy or any of the other nearly two dozen Bond Street specialists. Opposition research may have taken her to her former employer, Eleanor Adair, whose shop enjoyed a stellar reputation and whose treatment experts were unlikely to recognize her.[2]

The beauty culturalist then becoming all the rage was rising star Helena Rubinstein. Relatively recently arrived in London, Madame Rubinstein and her Maison de Beauté Valaze had already achieved a toehold among the cognoscenti. To them and to Americans traveling abroad, she advertised the youth-preserving properties of her Valaze Face Cream and her "new methods" to reduce the telltale wrinkles of, as Rubinstein coyly styled it, the *cou de dindon*—the turkey neck. If these promises didn't raise Arden's competitive hackles, Rubinstein's spectacular self-descriptions certainly would. Madame called herself "the famous Complexion Specialist of British Fashionable Society," "the noted London Face Spécialiste," and "the noted Viennese Face Specialist." Rubinstein unashamedly proclaimed her booklet *Beauty in the Making* an "epoch-making treatise."[3]

In 1912, the two beauty mavens were not yet the competitors they would become. A decade older than Arden, Rubinstein was born in 1872 in Kraków, Poland, and grew up in a large working-class Jewish family. In 1896, she fled to Australia, as she recounted in her memoir, because her parents disapproved of the man she loved. There she worked in a restaurant before opening a beauty salon in 1902 at age thirty-one. Helena Rubinstein & Company was likely established with the financial help of businessman James H. Thompson, whom she may have met while waitressing. The origins of her Valaze products are obscure, and she put forward many stories about how she invented them. Rubinstein, like Arden, undoubtedly ladled her toiletries into bottles herself, added labels, and oversaw publicity. Success crowned her efforts. By 1905, Rubinstein had moved into a larger salon, was selling in local drugstores and by mail, and had returned to Europe in search of new ideas.[4]

That trip galvanized her. In the next few years Rubinstein opened two more salons in Australia before pronouncing her adopted country an "apprenticeship." Her desire for "a larger scope" took her to London's posh Mayfair district, where she received the first visitors to her new salon at 24 Grafton Street. She deemed it a "sensational success" thanks to her "incessant, and often drudging work," and her familiarity "with the needs and the temperament of the Englishwoman."[5] The heterodox Margot Asquith, wife of Prime Minister Herbert H. Asquith, became an early client who brought along her socialite friends and helped to launch Rubinstein. Also useful was the man she met in Melbourne and married in London, Edward Titus. He played a guiding role in Rubinstein's business.[6] Pleased with her growing family (the couple would have two sons), her salon, and her emerging London customer base, in 1909, Rubinstein opened her Clinique de Beauté at 255 rue Saint-Honoré in Paris, which she felt was just as popular as the London salon.

Her first journey abroad affected Arden the way Rubinstein's had. Once back in New York, Arden intensified her efforts, doubling her salon space, hiring more treatment specialists, purchasing more equipment, increasing her bookings, expanding her mail-order business, and creating new preparations. She even renamed her store. It became the more European-sounding "Arden Salon d'Oro."[7] The whole experience made Arden brave—brave enough to bring to American women the most controversial and daring new trend she had seen abroad: makeup.

The respectable woman in 1912 did not wear cosmetics. While it was common knowledge that ancient Egyptians employed kohl to emphasize their eyes, European women applied powder to lighten their skin, and anyone could stir up a rouge to tint cheeks or lips, in the United States, makeup was the mark of a deceitful woman presenting a false face to the world. American culture, steeped in a religiosity unknown in most of Europe, decreed that only God-fearing women who never descended to gossip, gluttony, self-indulgence, impiety, sloth, or selfishness could be beautiful. In the late nineteenth and early twentieth centuries, a woman's external beauty resulted from her internal goodness.

Those who cared for others, responded tranquilly to the day's troubles, and put their own needs below their family's concerns could, these social dictates held, be assured of a visage that reflected such inner grace. Powder or rouge hid the true self. What man would ever marry such a dishonest woman? Who knew what she was covering up? If she lied about her looks, where would her dissembling stop? A woman in makeup was by definition an untrustworthy wife and an unfit mother.

Women who stooped to makeup were excoriated. *Godey's Lady's Book*, a popular magazine, reported in 1865 the distressing news of "painted angels." These daughters of the eastern gentry were seen at Newport and Saratoga Springs "daubed all over with paint, and most shockingly disfigured . . . to gratify a prurient taste to be in the extreme of fashion." They had "disfigured" (the word was used twice for emphasis) themselves with "blue-black paint on the lower eyelids." *Godey's* lamented the deception: "It is bad enough to wear paste diamonds and [costume] jewelry; but when earth's angels begin to paint about the eyes, wear false busts, and false hair in a bag behind their heads, to what extremes may we not expect the dear creatures to go! . . . What is republican America coming to?"[8] This moral orthodoxy ruled for decades, during which polite society practiced self-control and rigid rules of deportment.[9] In the United States, as the twentieth century dawned, only sex workers wore makeup.[10]

Despite ongoing warnings, by 1912 inexpensive rice powder for the face had become available in drugstores across America, without instigating a moral panic. Arden sensed that the time was right. Evenings in Paris had taught her that a little bit of color magic could go a long way to complement a woman's beauty. She began selling a translucent "Venetian Face Powder" that fall.[11] The next year, she introduced Poudre de Lilac, "a delicately mauve tinted powder."[12] This "Flower Powder" imparted "a soft bloom" to hide "defects." This was a shrewd first step. Powder barely qualified as makeup and was becoming acceptable for those who would never consider themselves "painted women." Besides, the soft glow of gaslight was slowly being replaced by blazingly bright electric light bulbs that revealed every complexion flaw.[13] Poudre de Lilac was practically a woman's only defense.

Anything past powder was imprudent, but even before her European trip, Arden sold "Venetian Eyelash Grower."[14] It had a similar effect to mascara—which was highly improper for decent women. At the time, "mascaro" was used only on the stage for tinting men's facial hair and women's eyebrows. Actors moved it from eyebrows to eyelashes and from stage to street. Actress turned beauty columnist Lillian Russell recommended petroleum jelly for darkening eyelashes.[15] She warned women in 1911 to put "dark brown mascara on . . . eyebrows," not eyelashes.[16] A year later, Russell suggested that mascara could also be used for darkening eyelashes if a woman didn't want to use Vaseline for that purpose.[17] In 1913, the *Chicago Tribune* quoted a successful chorus girl who emphasized that it was "not necessary . . . to . . . put mascaro on her eyelashes."[18] The association of mascara with theater fakery remained, and even a chorus girl understood that wearing it meant public disdain. That is why Arden marketed "Eyelash Grower" rather than mascara.

Arden fully understood that the addition of visible color might cross a line. But she could not shake her admiration for the rubescent lips and smoky eyes she had observed on Paris's most beautiful women. She began slowly, with Venetian Lip Salve in "an absolutely natural color," in April 1913. She premiered a liquid tint for cheeks that year in "Rose," and new shades soon followed for lips and cheeks.[19]

In 1914, Arden unveiled a second innovation: eye shadow. She called hers "Yamina," and described it as "an extremely unique evening make-up for the eyes."[20] Eye shadow, with or without the darkening properties of Venetian Eyelash Grower, was so novel and racy that Arden has been called "the first to introduce eye makeup to America."[21] Hers became the only salon catering to social arbiters who wanted to try the new Parisian look for eyes. It made them part of a "transnational elite," an imagined community into which one entered by purchasing

what European aristocrats wore. Arden had an unfailing ability to approach exactly the right society leaders, women who were equally ad-
venturous and beautiful. And once such women gave cosmetics their
imprimatur, they became "figureheads" for others a little less brave or
a little less wealthy.[22] Arden's friends marveled. Methodically, deliber-
ately, Elizabeth Arden made wearing eye makeup respectable for all
women.

The key to cosmetics as European women wore them was moderation. Yet learning how to apply dark colors to light skin took practice.
This Arden did incessantly, on herself, on all the Ogilvie sisters she
could waylay, on each of her employees, and on her tittering but willing
customers. Her lifelong perfectionism served her well, as did her gift
for color combinations. Arden achieved a natural look that became her
hallmark. Understated shades and a light touch with color that repudi-
ated any hint of harlotry worked best. Women newly made up felt the
frisson of excitement from engaging in a radical act. And they loved the
look. Rather than appearing "painted," Arden's artistry somehow elevated their best qualities. People noticed. Clara Ogilvie recalled that
"her clients would go to parties, and other women would ask them what
they'd been doing, they looked so well. She got quite a few new clients
that way."[23] Arden's was a conservative "non-look" that disguised the
fact that makeup was worn.[24] Her minimalist palette may have promoted or reflected the era's classism based on a rejection of "the influx
of Southern and Eastern European immigrants, with their bright peas-
ant costumes [which] fueled nativist sentiments, which in turn fed the
mainstream reaction against colors with 'punch' and 'pizzazz.'"[25] Considered refined and sophisticated, it was known as "the Arden look." A
prosperous, middle-aged, white, conservative customer base—and those
who aspired to join that group—emphatically preferred it.

Elizabeth Arden was the first successful beauty culturalist to devise
and sell an entire makeup line (colored base powder, eye shadow, a prototype mascara, blush, lip color, eyebrow pencil, finishing powder) in

America, but her innovations transcended that. By marketing to trend-setters, drawing them to her salon, demonstrating how wearing makeup could be stunning, and teaching them to apply it with confidence, she converted them to cosmetics use. Arden thus smashed the social belief that women who wore makeup were disreputable, "fast," or "disfigured." *Mais non*, they were simply following the chic Parisian trend. Ingeniously, she gave out free samples of Venetian Rose Color rouge and Flower Powder at her salon. She made sure that no one transgressed by purchasing makeup openly if one bought her oh-so-handy Travelers' Box.[26] Inside, there it was, nestled in pink silk, just waiting to be tried on. These were the ways Arden made cosmetics first acceptable and then appropriate. She literally changed the face of America, as most women took to wearing makeup with abandon. Arden taught them that makeup was stylish and fun. At exactly the time when women's political, professional, and public options expanded, makeup made them feel both beautiful and liberated.

Not everyone approved. When *The Baltimore Sun* asked its readers in 1912 "Should Women Paint?," the majority of the forty-four respondents gave a resounding no. Cosmetics "stamp the average woman as silly and vulgar in the eyes of refined and cultured people," Ella Durkee thought. Nellie Lieberman blamed rising divorce rates on makeup, but even worse, she found wearing makeup "an act of servile subordination." Women made themselves inferior to men by using such "extraordinary means to please" them. One man cautioned that cosmetics were "an invitation to a flirtation. Every painted or flashily dressed woman is deemed by most strange men to be of questionable character."

A minority of readers pushed back. Mrs. William Pimes thought that "women are justified in making themselves as attractive as possible." Mrs. W. S. Farmer took a Darwinian view: "Today the beautiful and attractive things are admired more than ever before in business as well as the social world." Thus it followed that cosmetics were "necessary." Those who replied affirmatively underscored, though, that "they must not be botchers in the art" of makeup application.[27] This is where Arden saw great opportunity: makeup instruction.

The acceptance of and demand for makeup remained low before the end of World War I. Women in small towns and rural areas generally avoided it. Some larger department stores sold cosmetics, but outside of fashion centers such as Paris, London, and New York, colored lips, cheeks, and eyes were still considered "barely respectable."[28] Even those who grudgingly accepted makeup as part of the future began by asserting that diet and exercise were the true foundation of beauty, and that if a woman believed she had to wear makeup, she should first learn how to apply it well.[29] Arden emphatically agreed.

She preached throughout her career that makeup could never substitute for well-being, which was always the best guarantee of beauty. "To be beautiful," she asserted, "one needs only to obey the laws of health, as applied to skin and muscle and hair cell."[30] She frequently downplayed makeup, protesting, for example, that "cosmetics are but a make-shift. They deceive no one."[31] Without attention to one's complexion, without the use of her products to cleanse, tone, and nourish skin, makeup would fail. Even after makeup sales increased, her priority remained skin care. This derived from her deep conviction about the importance of healthy skin, a good diet, and a robust body—a belief that would strengthen over time.

VISITING EUROPE ALSO convinced Arden to change her marketing style. Before traveling, she had pursued nationwide sales by advertisement in newspapers beyond northeastern metropolitan centers. These ads were simpler in design than those in her East Coast periodicals. Starting in November 1912, she ran an ad for several consecutive months in Sunday newspapers from Buffalo to San Francisco.[32] This was in addition to her notices in New York and Washington newspapers and in magazines aimed at wealthier readers, such as *Cosmopolitan*. The new ads encouraged mail-order sales. Some regional newspaper ads displayed her name in all capital letters rather than the usual flowery cursive, and showed a good-time factory girl peeking flirtatiously into the newspaper frame instead of the distant Renaissance Madonna who graced New England newspapers. She slowly phased out this variety after her return from Europe. Her advertising took on a consistent look, echoing the continuity of her packaging.

While similar, the ads were never identical. She knew instinctively that different markets required different sales techniques. In *Vogue*, where she regularly advertised to a more select readership, Arden utilized an ongoing campaign—as later advertisers would call it—meant to attract and educate. Each episode kept readers looking for more. One month the emphasis was on Arden's new method to banish a double chin. The next explained how skin could be kept "soft and fresh" even in late winter. Like a serialized story, each ad brought an entirely new problem to readers' awareness—along with Arden's entirely new solution. She sprinkled her narrative with reassurances about her expertise, the science guiding her treatments, and reminders about free demonstrations at her salon. Mentioning a lecture on skin care she had just given to the "Congress of American Women," for example, provided outside validation of her credentials.[33] She made sure readers understood that it was she who invented the "Arden Hydro-Firmo Chin Perfector," which she described as "a scientific appliance (operating upon an entirely new principle)." The tone of the ad stressed her genuine concern for her customers. She made them feel special and that their Arden purchases put them in an exclusive group of women with discriminating cultural tastes.[34]

Arden grasped the power of marketing earlier than other beauty culturalists.[35] On this she spent as much as she could afford of her company's budget because she believed it paid handsomely in cultivating and keeping customers. She learned the efficacy of promotional campaigns for Listerine, Lysol, Luden's cough drops, and other major brands in

Collier's, Cosmopolitan, and *Ladies' Home Journal.* "When you have a good product, find out the best way to advertise it, to tell the truth about it, and once you have found the best of the best, hold on for dear life," she once urged an audience of business leaders. "Yes, repetition makes reputation and reputation makes customers."[36] Always happiest when in control, Arden wrote ads with an unerring understanding of women's curiosity about her and her products. She forged many different emotional and intellectual hooks to catch customers. She advertised early, extensively, and nationally. These were three important ways in which she was an innovator in the field that she was helping to create.

The ads generated demand, yet she had only one retail outlet—her New York salon. The next logical step was to hire people who could sell Venetian Preparations to department stores and drugstores: "Agents wanted: Will be given exclusive territory. We cater to the best class of people only."[37] She was not asking for, and never employed, door-to-door salespeople as had other beauty culturalists. She sought wholesalers, the sort brother Bill utilized, who would locate smart retail establishments to carry Arden goods. Little seems to have come from this attempt, and she appears to have included those two sentences in tiny print at the end of only one *Washington Post* ad in late November 1912. She sidelined this plan for the moment.

But she had more and more products to sell! She designed four new travel boxes, likely inspired by her own overseas journey. They may have been modeled on something she sold when working for Eleanor Adair, but her boxes would become an Arden signature product—and more, an art form. Elizabeth Arden herself invented and patented dozens of box, bag, and kit designs over the course of her career. Her 1913 versions were far superior to others being sold. Constructed not of cardboard but from sturdy metal with a decorative, rosy, toleware finish, Arden's cosmetics boxes came lined in pink satin. Her "Travelers' Box" contained Cleansing Cream, Velva Cream, Skin Tonic, Lille Lotion, Muscle Oil, Eye Drops, and the makeup she tucked in for timid women to try: a liquid blush and a "brush and pencil for eyebrows and lashes." It sold for $10—approximately $320 today. The larger "Boudoir Box," meant for the dressing room table, came with fifteen preparations and was sealed with a lock, presumably to keep one's maid from dipping into the precious unguents. A smaller, compartmentalized "Skin Treatment Box" sold for $3 and held four Venetian creams.[38] Boxed cosmetics in a matching set appealed to women who detested the chaos of makeup thrown higgledy-piggledy into a drawer or onto a dressing table. The high prices of the travel and boudoir boxes suggested that such serenity could be achieved only by very few.

Arden's approach to pricing was simple and consistent. She knew that the more women paid, the greater their belief in the products. That axiom drove her marketing, her packaging, and her financially risky ventures such as opening summer salons in Newport. High prices, unforgettable wrapping, gorgeous interiors, endless new products, and selling exclusivity—coupled with national advertising—would guarantee success. Advertising also increased mail orders and built a desire on the part of women far beyond the Big Apple to visit her salon. "I'm so excited!" she exclaimed jubilantly to the Ogilvie sisters. "The orders I'm getting in! If it goes like this, marvelous!"[39]

It did go like that. It was time to expand. She looked toward the nation's capital, and laid careful groundwork. She watched the national luxury goods market—Steinway pianos, Packard automobiles, and Cartier jewelry—increase exponentially as her business took off. For three years she advertised in *The Washington Post*, patiently building a mail-order clientele there. Finally, in April 1914, Arden opened her Washington, D.C., salon at 1209 Connecticut Avenue NW. Nine months later, she moved 350 feet closer to the White House, to 1147 Connecticut Avenue NW. She chose this address, less than half a mile from Dupont Circle, where the nation's political elite mingled with the city's social elite, just as judiciously as she had selected Fifth Avenue.[40]

Arden was the first beauty culturalist to appear at the center of

Washington's newest commercial district, hard by the mansions of ambassadors, financiers, editors, and social leaders. Throwing open the
doors, she announced: "Washington society women now have a wonderful opportunity." Her salon manager hailed from London, where,
she exaggerated, she had "practiced Miss Arden's methods continuously
in the capitals of the continent."[41] Once she had the idly curious inside,
admiring the splendid interior, Arden could turn them into lifelong
customers. She reiterated assurances that scientific study informed her
methods, that "beauty is one part nature and three parts care," and that
she was personally available to assist "Washington society women."[42]
She visited the salon regularly, preceded by headlines proclaiming
"Miss Arden Will Be Here Tomorrow." She promised "elimination of
deep lines and markings and sagging flesh."[43] Like a dear friend, she
empathized with their concerns: "Too busy—too hurried—too many
engagements—that is why so many Washington society women neglect
their complexions during the Fall and Winter months." She understood
the rhythm of capital life. As Lent approached and the social season
wound down, her relaxing muscle-strapping treatments were the antidote for wrinkles and blemishes caused by the hectic but necessary political entertaining and social calling.[44]

Adept hiring freed Arden from being tied to her salons. When she
was not in Washington, her British manager "kept customers satisfied."[45] Florence Delaney knew exactly how to run the Salon d'Oro, and
Arden relied on her when she left once again for Europe in the fall of
1914, hungry to know more. The great French designer Paul Poiret, she
learned, had begun to pair specific perfumes with his fashions. She
tucked that idea away.[46] Before departing, she studied French from phonograph records to communicate better with Parisians.[47]

Retracing her steps from two years earlier, investigating new salons,
taking the treatment à la mode, and meeting new people rejuvenated
her, but she was shocked to see firsthand a continent six months into the
horrifying world war. Around her, British and French women were join-

ing the Red Cross, volunteering at enlistment centers, knitting and sewing for soldiers, learning first aid, and conserving food for the long winter ahead. Uncertainty descended on the world like a chill, damp fog. There was much for the businesswoman to contemplate on the return journey, but not all of it concerned her business.

Four

Building a National Beauty Brand

Falling in love was definitely not part of the plan. It is impossible to know precisely when and how they met, but by 1914 Elizabeth Arden and Thomas Jenkins Lewis were sweethearts.[1] Handsome in a hail-fellow-well-met way, gregarious, and companionable, Lewis was the son of Welsh immigrants Anne Jenkins and Robert Lewis. The couple had five children who lived to adulthood, and Tom, born in 1875, was second youngest. Before he was twenty-five, Tom and his little brother, Henry, had embarked on banking careers. After a decade in that business, culminating in his service as a vice president of the National Reserve Bank, Tom Lewis resigned in 1911 to "associate himself," as *The Wall Street Journal* put it, with stockbrokers E. R. Chapman & Company. Later that year Tom, Henry, and three other men formed the Union First Mortgage Company. They intended to "do the business of a mortgage, loan, and investment company, buying and selling bonds secured by mortgage on real estate," *The New York Times* announced.[2]

Elizabeth Arden's business success might have been off-putting to Lewis, but apparently he found her unusual occupation charming. She also happened to be a blonde, beautifully made-up, well-dressed woman who conveyed a sense of refinement and style. As a banker and possibly a real estate investor, he ranked above her socially. Few details of their wooing exist, but when she said yes to Tom Lewis, she married up—and became a U.S. citizen.[3]

The Reverend George Clarke Houghton, rector of the Episcopal Church of the Transfiguration, performed the ceremony on November 29, 1915. One story has it that—like the robber baron John D. Rockefeller who, when he wed, "lost not a day from his business"—Arden left the salon at 5:00 p.m. and returned thirty minutes later as Mrs. Lewis. She lost not even an hour from her business. Mr. Lewis's thoughts have not been recorded.[4]

Their courtship had occurred against the backdrop of Arden's expansion into larger quarters farther uptown to 673 Fifth Avenue and the corner of Fifty-Third Street.[5] The move was such a sizable financial risk that Florence Delaney admitted to being "scared to death."[6] Arden planned carefully, though, throughout the summer of 1915, while business at 509 Fifth Avenue continued. She located the perfect space, studied decorating trends, and calculated the timing, among a thousand other details. Arden treatment specialist Sally Bulkley remembered the rush to ready new employees: "We'd grab a sandwich and train until midnight, and on Sundays and holidays."[7] Putting her products on sale to decrease the inventory to be moved, Arden iterated the impending change for weeks in her advertisements. She carefully announced that "a rapidly growing clientele, today the largest of its kind in New York," necessitated the relocation. In the new site no one would suffer the frustration of having to wait for services, not even women who dropped in unscheduled, thanks to more equipment, employees, and space—especially for her muscle-strapping treatments.[8]

Tuesday, September 7, 1915, finally arrived. An imposing entrance greeted customers. Walking up stairs flanked by potted plants, they passed between two Ionic columns toward the doors she had painted a bright and happy red. Arden's Red Door would become her enduring symbol, a shorthand for her salons and then her entire product line.[9] Smiling doormen stood beneath the gold-lettered sign reading ARDEN BUILDING, grandly ushering visitors into a world of luxury. No element went unplanned. As the backdrop for the beauty she drew out of her clients, her salons had to radiate a tasteful understatement that also felt inviting. A single jarring note—a foyer too bright or cluttered, treatment girls too zealous or gossipy—might violate the class codes and drive away her most desired customers. Selling her treatments and lotions *dans un milieu magnifique* conveyed respectability—but it also had to suggest a certain *je ne sais quoi*.

Borrowing from Europe added cachet and subtly nodded to status. The new Salon d'Oro centerpiece was, as she described it, "an exquisite oval room called the 'Camera Cornaro,'" after the erudite fifteenth-century Venetian beauty Caterina Cornaro. Arden herself did the interior design for the Camera Cornaro, and the rest of the salon. She was proud of it. To see it, she rhapsodized, "is to be stirred with desire to express beauty not only in one's personality but in one's whole environment."[10]

Relaxing in an Arden salon had to be worth every minute and every penny. Like Cornelius Vanderbilt, she began in New York as a rank outsider, and many years would pass before her arriviste status fell away. Like him, she was "in trade" and eventually became extremely rich. Unlike Vanderbilt, however, she did not have a wife or daughters to locate openings into high society or oversee lavish soirees where her nascent wealth could be quietly but efficiently displayed. Instead, Arden had to communicate her position through her salons.[11]

They had to deliver a complex array of messages to clients: indulgence is good; you are among your fellow sophisticates; change is possible with my system; we will hold old age at bay; we will guide you through the work you must do; this place dampens all troublesome feelings, difficult people, and mundane thoughts; trust me. "Beauty is power," Arden always preached. "It opens doors that nothing else can open. It lets one out of the prison that shyness, awkwardness, self-consciousness build about one. It opens locked doors into romance, love, depth of living."[12] The place to embrace this power was the Salon d'Oro. She was quick to remind those unable to visit that they should take advantage of mail order and remain true to her adage: "Don't Neglect Yourself."[13]

UNTIL THE UNITED STATES entered in 1917, the war overseas made nary a dent in the world of the New Yorkers Arden pampered. Nevertheless, she kept a wary eye out, and no doubt compared notes with her brother, Bill, recently returned from a business trip abroad. The war did affect international transportation, and many materials across the globe were diverted from their peacetime purposes. Arden feared that naval blockades, predatory submarines, and wartime shortages would reduce her access to the imported raw materials required for her face creams. Hoping to avoid this, she asked the scientists at her supplier, Parke, Davis & Company in lower Manhattan, about domestic substitutes. They suggested she try Stillwell & Gladding, a chemical testing laboratory founded in the 1870s.[14] Arden consulted there with Axel Fabian Swanson. Arden and Swanson worked so efficiently together that she soon made him her chief chemist. Onboarding this expert helped save her from utilizing dangerous or inferior ingredients. She thus avoided harming clients and being tarnished by bad publicity, as was Harriet Hubbard Ayer, whose toiletries routinely contained toxins such as mercury chloride.[15] Throughout her career, Arden justifiably boasted of the purity of her products, and this was due in part to Swanson's guidance. His talent for turning Arden's vision into reality facilitated the company's extraordinary early success.[16]

Swanson carefully analyzed the toiletries Arden carried back from Europe. She was searching for an improved face cream. Every brand, including hers, was hard, oily, heavy, and difficult to smooth on the face. She asked Swanson to devise something with the consistency of a light and airy whipped cream that would feel good on the fingers as they dipped into her pink container, and go on the skin softly, without dripping off or having to be rubbed in so vigorously that it would damage delicate facial skin. He set to work, either in the Stillwell & Gladding lab or in the new laboratory Arden created at 665 Fifth Avenue, just a stone's throw from her salon.[17] By April 1914, Swanson invented what Arden called her Venetian Cream Amoretta, with an exquisite "foamy consistency."[18] Arden adored it. It was Swanson's first test, and he passed spectacularly. He built a forty-year career with Arden, working closely with her on product development and enhancement.

The chemist's knowledge allowed new preparations to roll out in 1914: Vantie (later Vanité or Vanitie) Cream ("for red or shiny noses"), Bathodomes, Orange Skin Food, Ideal Bath Salts, Almond Skin Food, Special Eye Lotion, and Beauty Sachets.[19] Product proliferation continued into 1915: Special Astringent, Special Bleach Cream, Freckle Cream, Hand Cream, and Dermatex Depilatory. There were new makeup items, too: more Flower Powder colors—Blanche, Naturelle, Brunette, Marechal Neil, and Verdè Ophelia—and "Shading Powder." This latter item—eye shadow—was still so unusual that Arden had to specify that it was used "around" and not in the eyes. It should be "applied over the eyes, [where it] gives most exquisite light-and-shade effect; fascinating and popular." She couldn't help adding that it was "wonderful for day use as well," nudging its sales potential upward. It came in a neutral brown, softer and subtler than common black kohl. "Shading Powder" may have been her Yamina eye shadow from a year earlier, rebranded, as she never seems to have used "Yamina" again. Finally, Arden introduced a Venetian Atomizer made of "Bohemian glass," and a lockable Beauty Box for fifteen toiletries with a separate traveling case lined in pink silk.[20]

Success bred success. In late September 1916, Elizabeth Arden opened a third permanent salon, in Boston, the birthplace of Founding Fathers and Mothers. The city boasted a long line of sensible, duty-driven civil servants as well as writers, intellectuals, artists, and clergymen. Taking skin care and makeup there may have seemed rash, but many Bostonians already appreciated Arden's line from her earlier gamble with holiday summer shops. They patronized her salon as she knew they would.[21]

Developing loyal customers was imperative. A salon opening occasioned novel advertising campaigns, which were effective thanks to Arden's design eye. The better the advertising, the easier the product placement. As more women clamored for Arden toiletries, store buyers had to respond. Whole departments devoted to skin care were just starting to appear in America and shopping in them was becoming fashionable. Women who tried Arden products at her salon or by mail helped drive the development of these departments when they begged retailers to stock Arden goods.

An enormous step forward occurred in 1914 when Stern Brothers, a fashionable New York department store, approached her about selling her products. This was a phenomenal achievement. Other retailers soon followed suit. For example, businesses as disparate as the Steinbach Company of Asbury Park, New Jersey, which sold sewing machines and Philippine-made "undermuslins," added Arden's line, as did Jacobs' Pharmacy in Atlanta, the Joseph Horne Company in Pittsburgh, and the Philadelphia and New York Bonwit Teller department stores. The latter presented under the heading *"Haute Nouveauté,"* its "complete collection of Elizabeth Arden's Venetian Toilet Preparations."[22]

In Los Angeles, the J. W. Robinson Company opened its deluxe, seven-story headquarters store at Seventh Street and Grand Avenue with an entire department of toiletries from "Elizabeth Arden of New York."[23] This partnership would turn out to be long-lasting and mutually profitable. While some Californians already knew of Arden products because of her nationwide mail-order campaign, Robinson's was her gateway to the burgeoning West Coast market. Skin creams far outsold makeup in

1916, even in large cities, but when Hollywood became the center of the growing film industry around that time, wearing makeup grew more common, especially by the "starlets" who graced the covers of the first movie magazines.[24]

Thanks to Swanson, Arden had little difficulty keeping her customers happy, despite the war in Europe. Her raw ingredients were primarily domestic, and Bill had cautioned her early about potential shortages. Since Arden's business was creating beauty, she concentrated on reminding women of the importance of their health and the many wonderful treatments she offered to keep them looking young and fresh. Yet as the fighting continued abroad, some Americans urged preparedness—getting ready in case the United States entered the war—and uniformed Girl Scouts, Boy Scouts, Red Cross workers, and soldiers marched in preparedness parades to inspire men to enlist and women to plan for home-front exigencies.

As more women educated themselves about the European war and threw themselves into war-related fundraising, Arden reflected these changes back to them: "Tired? Does your face show it?," her December 1915 ad asked. "No chance to relax now!"[25] In a series of advertisements featuring archetypal society women, Arden described their ever-busier lives: one "called at the Arden Salon d'Oro," ready to drop because "she had presented an only daughter to society, she had espoused three new charities, [and] she had been untiring in Red Cross work."[26] So desperate for rejuvenation were these flagging females that Arden had "to again double the floor space . . . and to enlarge the corps of highly specialized workers" at 673 Fifth Avenue.[27] "The modern woman is practical," Arden philosophized. "She is quick to recognize any deficiency, and to overcome it. She makes no exception in the care of her skin and the preservation of a youthful contour. Society women have learned that my methods . . . are eminently successful and practical."[28]

Preparedness paid off when the United States officially entered the Great War on April 6, 1917. Tom Lewis immediately volunteered. Like

so many others ready to join the fight, he trained at Plattsburgh, in up-
state New York. He was formally inducted on November 27, 1917—
almost two years to the day since he and Arden had married. He joined
the U.S. Army Signal Corps and began training in the brand-new field
of aviation. As a first lieutenant, Lewis went to the School of Military
Aeronautics at the University of Illinois in Champaign. From there he
was sent for more training to Camp Mills on Long Island, which included the Aviation General Supply Depot. Lewis never served overseas. His age—he was in his early forties then—meant he would probably not be a pilot. Instead, the army moved him to Washington, D.C.,
where he worked for the War Department in preparation for duty at
Princeton, where he was stationed at war's end. Princeton's School of
Military Aeronautics, like its counterparts at a handful of other universities, provided an eight-week program with courses that included Principles of Cross Country and General Flight, Aerial Observation, Care
of Aeroplanes, and ground target training. Exactly what Lewis did at
any of his postings is unclear. His banking background could have made
him useful in any Air Service job concerning mathematics or bookkeeping.[29]

Being the wife of a military man made the European war more tan-
gible to Arden. Her advertisements reflected this change. She might
have been thinking of her own situation when she asked rhetorically,
"When the Man Who Is Absent thinks of you, does he see a vision of
your favorite hat? Absurd! It is *your face* he pictures in his mind's eye—
and it should be an inspiration to him. Yet you probably spend much
more time and money on your hats than on your complexion." Arden
had a talent for making her sales pitch relevant. She understood that
"since Society has decreed simple gowning for the duration of the war,
women will be dependent on personal charm as never before in this
generation, and"—Arden commiserated—"to engage in serious pur-
suits without becoming haggard and faded will necessitate extra care."
Her muscle-strapping treatments, she promised, were the best remedy

for endless volunteer work. She encouraged economizing housewives to conceal "our self-denials" from the world and to let Arden solve a complexion "faded, wrinkled and worn" by home-front concerns. And to those courageous few women who signed up with the military, Arden had a special message: "Even though you may have enlisted in a branch of service which precludes the wearing of delicate, lacy things, you can still be 'the eternal feminine' in the roseate freshness of your face," by following the Arden Method and using Venetian Preparations.[30]

Arden wrote a lengthy "Special Editorial" for *Vogue*'s November 1917 issue aimed specifically at wartime workers. She referenced the Italian Renaissance to state that her products were based on centuries' worth of tested beauty secrets used by legends like Caterina Cornaro, but scientifically modernized. She applauded "the up-to-date, progressive American woman" for shouldering "new responsibilities and anxieties," but regretted that too many women neglected their looks. A woman in wartime had to remain mentally and physically alert, while making sure that "the cares she has assumed do not perpetuate themselves upon her face. . . . The wisdom of beauty and the power of beauty are never underestimated by the wise woman." Who were these wise women? Why, New Yorkers, of course, "celebrated the world over for their wonderful freshness, youthfulness and charm of appearance; and it is a fact that a very large number of these are my regular clients— women in exclusive social coteries and clubs, famous singers and actresses noted for their beauty, to which in some degree I have contributed. They make frequent visits to the wonderful SALON D'ORO."[31]

In 1916, Elizabeth Arden boldly styled herself "America's leading authority" on skin care, as she invited women to join her for a free targeted assessment and "the privilege" of learning from her: "Her enthusiasm, her charming personality and her surprising skill have made Miss Arden a pronounced favorite with people of refinement and discrimination." Her ads routinely stressed that the "society leaders in every city" were her clients. One year later, she promoted herself to "the international authority on the scientific care of the skin" with "the LARGEST EXCLUSIVE CLIENTELE IN THE WORLD."[32]

The claims intensified because of escalating competition in the beauty world. Since nearly anyone could concoct a cream and flog it through the newspaper or perhaps in a drugstore, Arden was just one of hundreds of people—still mostly women—who offered skin, hair, and nail improvements. In addition to Arden's Rose perfume, for example, Bonwit Teller carried Houbigant, Coty, and Guerlain fragrances. Maybell Labs opened in 1915 and began selling colorless "Eyebrow-Ine" and petroleum-based "Lash-Brow-Ine" by mail order a year later. In 1917, pharmacies across America stocked their Maybelline products, including cake mascara.[33] Eleanor Adair products could still be found, and there were always lesser-known names, such as the Dr. J. Parker Pray's Toilet Preparations Company, as well as imported brands such as Dorin, from France. Dorothy Gray launched her beauty business in 1916 by selling "Russian Bleach Cream" in a tiny classified *Vogue* ad and at her salon at 2 West Fifty-Seventh Street.[34] Gray would be the first of many former Arden employees who used their intensive Arden training to start their own businesses. Gray copied Arden's signature colors, face patter, advertisements, and packaging, and targeted Arden's clientele.[35]

The biggest threat was Helena Rubinstein—at least according to Helena Rubinstein, who believed herself a match for every other beauty culturalist. Reluctantly leaving Europe for New York in the early months of World War I, Rubinstein was unimpressed with American women. Their noses were "mauve with cold," their lips "oddly grayish," and their skins too white. This did create, she admitted, "a huge new market for my products."[36] Rubinstein's first American Maison de Beauté Valaze opened at 15 East Forty-Ninth Street, between Fifth and Madison Avenues, in early February 1915. With a flourish she proclaimed herself "the accepted adviser in beauty matters to the Royalty, Aristocracy and the great Artistes of Europe; whose position as a scientific Beauty Culturalist and whose unique work on exclusive lines have created for her a world-wide fame; whose [European] establishments . . . are well-known landmarks in the itinerary of the ladies of high society of both Continents." Her salon, the oversize ad continued, "radiates the Spirit of Beauty," but it did so with a very different ambience than Arden's.[37]

Rubinstein collected modernist art in strong, saturated colors and placed it throughout the Maison. The walls, she described, "were covered in dark-blue velvet, with rose-colored baseboards." Streamlined statues by Polish sculptor Elie Nadelman accented the rooms.[38] Rubinstein's had a chic edginess very unlike the calm, airy, pastel pink confection that was Arden's salon. The two women embodied contrasting definitions of sophistication. Rubinstein's obvious connection with contemporary European artists attracted women drawn to the avant-garde. Arden appealed to those seeking a more conservative, classic look, based on her modernization of the traditional, white, Western beauty ideal.

Rubinstein's salons offered a broader array of services than did Arden's at that time, including massage done by hand, with a roller, and with an electrical wand, "electrolysis to treat superfluous hair, warts and other blemishes," cream depilatories, anti-wrinkle paraffin wax injections, facial peels, and a "vacuum suction treatment to remove wrinkles." Elizabeth Arden observed or tried many of these when she visited Europe. Rubinstein began selling makeup in her salons in 1908, seven years before she came to America, and she owned at least one factory. Salon and mail-order income underwrote her expansion to New York, and then beyond: in 1916 to San Francisco, Philadelphia, and New Orleans; in 1917 to Chicago; and to Atlantic City in 1918.[39]

Madame Rubinstein may have been a threat greater in her own mind than in reality. Between 1915 and 1920, according to an industry insider, Arden "introduced a larger number of preparations, of greater diversification of use, than any other cosmetics manufacturer in the world."[40] Arden's advertising blanketed the entire East Coast. Department stores sold her pink packages to the carriage trade and to those who aspired to buy like them. Her New York, Washington, and Boston salons served customers year-round, many of whom loved the availability of Arden products at their summer vacation spots.[41] Sally Bulkley believed that by 1917 Rubinstein had not overtaken Arden; rather, Arden "had worn down all her early competitors" and "was getting the younger women."[42]

World War I finally ended in mid-November 1918, and Tom Lewis returned home on the day after Christmas.[43] Reunited, the couple looked ahead to the postwar years. They could not have foreseen the speed with which women flung away the old rules to dance to the new tempo of the Jazz Age, nor the nearly unlimited business success that accompanied that transformation.

Five

The New Woman
and the Arden Look

E lizabeth Arden welcomed her soldier husband back home with a proposition—a business proposition. Would he quit his job as a stockbroker and come work for her? It would be the world turned upside down. Businesswomen were anomalies in the 1920s, a minuscule fraction of industrialists, and only a very small percentage of shop owners. Few female bosses existed then, and even fewer supervised their husbands as that reversed gender roles.[1] But Arden adored her salons, the beauty she created there and the interesting women she encountered. She loved dreaming up new products, designing her distinctive line, and making personnel and advertising decisions.

Wholesaling, stocking, and distributing her goods she found far less interesting. Still, business was thriving. Profits continued to increase. The war's effect on women's opportunities had been surprising so far, and who knew where the 1920s would take them? If Lewis became her general manager, he could apply his logistical skills to the complicated task of seeing that all retail outlets received sufficient supplies, on time and in good condition. Arden preferred to concentrate on product development, marketing, design, and above all, improving her salons at this exciting moment.[2]

Tom agreed. He began by hiring Gladys. Elizabeth's little sister was now a beautiful woman in her early thirties. On May 4, 1918, she had married Edward J. G. Baraba, a blue-eyed, black-haired sales manager living in Philadelphia.[3] Almost exactly nine months later, on February 6, 1919, she gave birth to John Graham Baraba. Unhappy in her marriage, Gladys soon divorced. She returned to New York City seeking sororal solace and something to do with herself. Listening to Arden's shoptalk, Gladys had an idea: she should join the company. She felt she could locate stores not currently selling Arden products and persuade them to do so. Petite, pretty, persuasive—and every bit as ambitious as her sister—Gladys believed she could expand profits by increasing orders. She knew how to administer salon treatments; she promised to memorize the entire catalogue. Her own marvelous complexion would go a long way toward convincing store owners. Gladys just needed her sister to stop worrying about her traveling alone. She enlisted her brother-in-law's support. Tom divined great potential and proclaimed it an excellent plan. Outnumbered, Arden relented.

An ebullient Gladys packed Arden-designed travel boxes full of Arden products and set out to improve on the already impressive $25,000 in orders the firm averaged annually. She was among the first cosmetics demonstrators to go on the road. Gladys systematically called on department stores and drugstores where she set up a table or commandeered a counter. Natural inquisitiveness did the rest. As Gladys showed women how to apply Arden products, they made purchases, and delighted store managers signed on.[4] Goodwin's Drug Store in Hartford, Connecticut, for example, proudly set fifteen "high-class [Arden] articles . . . in a very elaborate case in the center of our main store."[5] Boston's elegant women's clothier E. T. Slattery hoped to draw customers with Arden "preparations for the skin and complexion, neck and arms, the hair and eyes [plus] Manicure articles, exquisite perfumes and toilet waters, soaps and bath requisites."[6]

"SEX O'CLOCK" BEGAN in earnest in the wake of World War I.[7] Cosmetics, automobiles, cigarettes, big-city fashions, and Hollywood films reshaped people's perceptions of their world and of one another. Even rural states such as Iowa and South Dakota proved unable to withstand the temptations of modern consumer society. Emblematic of the new age were flappers. The word *flapper* first appeared around 1910 to describe a self-absorbed, rather silly young woman who dressed to be noticed.[8] By the time war broke out in Europe, a flapper had become "a modern girl," who smoked and tangoed and wore makeup, someone with "half-portion clothes and ideas to match."[9] As the 1920s dawned, flappers were easily identifiable by their short skirts, bobbed hair, and enviable sense of freedom. They even felt at liberty to discuss topics heretofore forbidden to women, such as sports, sex, and the stock market.

Flappers and their rebellion against conventional gender strictures were part of a larger upheaval. Independent women of all backgrounds—"New Women"—began living alone or with friends and working for pay in fields that included beauty, advertising, retail sales, the telephone industry, clerical work, the arts, publishing, and fashion-related occupations like apparel buyers, designers, seamstresses, and journalists. Above all—especially if she was white—the New Woman seized her opportunity to vote after the Nineteenth Amendment was ratified on August 18, 1920. Like flappers (who might not be quite so independent), they wore makeup and marcelled hair, and bared their legs, arms, and necks. Dr. Beatrice Hinkle, a neurologist, identified the source of the changes happening around her: "In the general disintegration of old standards, women are the active agents in the field of sexual morality and men the passive, almost bewildered accessories to the overthrow of their long and firmly organized control of women's conduct."[10] This modern creature was something truly new—and Arden had seen it. Before the war ended, she applauded and appealed to this decisive, educated New Woman who was, as her advertisements cheered, "quick to recognize any deficiency—and to overcome it."[11] Arden artfully intended a double entendre: deficiencies in women's rights and in their complexions.

While some Americans considered the actions and appearance of New Women shameful, others hoped to emulate them. Arden understood this, too. At war's end, she was selling eye shadow and nail polish to women from Manhattan, New York, to Manhattan Beach, California. Her reading of cultural trends revealed that rural women yearned to be in step with their fashionable urban sisters. Newspapers, magazines, and her *Quest of the Beautiful* booklet carried Arden's promises of health, youth, and beauty to the countryside, made possible by the U.S. Postal Service. Tradition dictated marriage and motherhood, but enlightened parents approved of their daughters pursuing college degrees and working, at least until they wed. Rural women were expected to remain close to home, but in part because of wartime changes, young women and men moved from the countryside to the city in numbers large enough to turn America into an urban nation by 1920.

Sex seemed to be everywhere: in the movies, in novels, on campuses, in conversations, in the theater. Even in magazines aimed squarely at the middle class, among the ads for Elizabeth Arden and Tiffany, Cutex and Campbell's Soup, readers could send away for books with titles such as *Sexual Knowledge* or *Sexology*.[12] Women's sexuality went on display as fashion changed. When the war began, the ankle-length, aptly named hobble skirt went out of style, and a fuller, shorter skirt that rose as high as mid-calf came in. Fashion dictates had hidden women's legs for decades, but once skirts shortened and white or black cotton stockings gave way to tan silk stockings, manufacturers warned, "Look to your ankles: everyone else will."[13] "War crinoline" gowns tucked in at the

natural waist. Under them, women began to replace their old boned corsets with more flexible ones, or even an early version of the bra.[14]

Talented fashion photographers such as Edward Steichen, Adolph de
Meyer, and Cecil Beaton brought high fashion to a broader swath of
Americans through *Vogue, Harper's Bazaar,* and *Vanity Fair,* generating
a widespread desire to replicate the look of glamorous haute couture
models. This proved possible as America's economic fortunes rose at
war's end. The middle class, gaining more disposable income and more
leisure time, could share the upper-class obsession with appearances.[15]
As many Americans grew wealthier, fashion became accessible to everyday women. Helped along by new industrial technologies, marketplace
competition, and an explosion in chain stores catering to middle incomes,
haute couturiers such as Coco Chanel turned their attention to understanding their lifestyles.[16]

Other changes also contributed to the very different silhouette: increasing numbers of women in the workforce across Europe and the
United States, the class leveling that occurred in Great Britain, and
the acceleration of pre-wartime trends—including young women's desire for greater ease of movement. From the hourglass figure of the
1890s to the straight up-and-down flapper profile seemed an enormous
shift to those who lived through it. The ideal woman was now thinner,
leaner, athletic. Casual clothing revealed more, and the modern flapper
"project[ed] a *'soignée'* sophistication that implied a certain sexual availability."[17] The real distinction was the use women made of their new
look. They demanded "the right of self-expression, the celebration of
sexual desires, and the possibility of economic independence." The transformation under way was sweeping. For Black flappers, "freedom also
meant refuting degrading racist stereotypes" and "promoting claims for
inclusion in White society."[18] Arden makeup played an important role
in the new image for white women, which was thrilling or threatening—
or both—depending on one's point of view.

Disillusionment accompanied excitement. Veterans in particular often felt that the war had robbed them of their optimism. F. Scott Fitzgerald's novel *This Side of Paradise* described those whose youth had been scarred by the carnage of the trenches, now "grown up to find all Gods dead, all wars fought, all faiths in man shaken."[19] Bitterness over what appeared, in hindsight, to have been a senseless conflict with brutal new weapons, a horrifying number of victims, and no obviously positive outcome swept across the nation. Isolationism, the resurgence of the Ku Klux Klan, nativism, Prohibition, and nostalgia for an older, somehow better America resulted. In that misty past, women wore neither uniforms nor cosmetics. The new world was confusing. One young man recalled feeling unbalanced after having spent the war in Europe. Returning, he wrote, "Two years before . . . handbags didn't contain lipstick; girls didn't smoke; the hemline was lower; hair stayed the same tint; a kiss was tantamount to a proposal. And now—?"[20] As Helena Rubinstein put it, "Puritanism and Victorianism crumbled when America entered the war, and American doughboys returned from Europe with a new concept of emancipated women."[21] Not all of them liked what they found.

Elizabeth Arden balanced successfully on the knife's edge of change. Even though flappers often wore visible makeup with lurid circles of rouge and bright red lipstick, her color palette remained muted. It was only yesterday, after all, that Americans associated makeup with prostitution, and for many citizens, that psychological connection remained. Those who did not think it deceptive or immoral found it scandalous. Well into the 1920s, writers warned of the demoralizing effects of cosmetics. Novelist Irving Bacheller, for instance, wrote in 1924, "If women are to be respected, they must satisfy the notion of men as to what constitutes a respectable woman. No matter what they pretend, men hate the look of paint and powder on the face of youth. To many it is a bid for insult; to all," the sexagenarian concluded, "it is the flag of folly."[22] Nevertheless, flappers rebelled through makeup. Society women wore it because it was European chic. Other women used a little powder and blush

discreetly, more often at night than during the day—and with each passing year, makeup sales rose. Arden's consistent message that cosmetics
enhanced a woman's healthy appearance rather than *disguised* her looks
sanctioned its use.

Americans focused resolutely on the future. No more glancing back
to a past that included the horrific war. There was too much to antici-
pate. Travel increased exponentially as the world became auto-friendly.
Leisure sports were all the rage. Americans rushed to buy radios. They
fell in love with Hollywood films and emulated the dress, makeup, and
behavior on the silver screen. Wartime technology applied to civilian
products expanded the electric industry, and soon no middle-class
kitchen was complete without toasters, waffle irons, and refrigerators.
Consumers could buy items on credit, putting a little money down and
paying a little each week. This tempted even those who could not instantly afford the new gadgets, so that they, too, could be defined by
what they bought rather than what they produced or who they were.

The 1920s saw the full flowering of the consumer goods revolution.
Happiness came from buying things as the definition of "the good life"
shifted. In the nineteenth century, to live a good life meant to live mor-
ally, honorably. In the 1920s, the good life came to mean "abounding in
material comforts and luxuries."[23] And in that decade, the high-priced,
prestige brand of Elizabeth Arden became *the* cosmetics to acquire.

The war also knocked affluent, middle-aged matrons off the top of
society. They lost their status to their offspring.[24] Women themselves
felt it. Great Britain's Lady Troubridge admired the flapper as "slim,
beautifully proportioned, agile, active, able to play games, a perfect machine moved by the marvellous elixir of youth," but bemoaned that "no
one is allowed to be middle aged."[25]

Arden took advantage of this cultural shift. When the youth rebellion began, she pivoted to emphasize the perils of aging. Adroitly attuned to women's fears—and, herself nearing forty, possibly sharing
them—Arden promised to help women "turn back the clock!" Her

muscle strapping would "keep your face young, your skin clear and your eyes bright." She made alluring promises: "Whatever defects Time has wrought in your appearance, I can banish." She was, she reminded women, "the most successful specialist in the world" who had proven formulas—for skin care and for physical fitness—to shave years off a woman's appearance.[26]

Thanks to the youth rebellion, a "vogue for health" swept America. Suntans came into high fashion in the 1920s, reaffirming societal ideals equating wealth with leisure, but adding the ability to be healthily active outdoors.[27] Arden was among the first cosmeticians to capitalize on the trend. As was her way, she created several new products connected to a single idea: one cream to help a woman achieve the fashionably sporty golden hue, one to protect from burning, another to help maintain and preserve the perfect tan, and yet another to help remove it at the end of the season.

Then as now, physicians warned about "sun poisoning," and Arden was prepared for that, too. Her Protecta Cream, as journalist Regina Kelley described, had "the consistency of Hollandaise sauce, which one spreads on the skin with a little wooden paddle, for all the world like the application of mustard to a ham sandwich." It allowed a tan but not a burn. "This stuff," Kelley continued, "is a lovely flesh tint and has been proved waterproof."[28] To avoid the poisonous sunshine altogether, Arden offered Ardena Bronze, a colored lotion that worked like today's self-bronzers.[29]

To smooth out or diminish a tan there was her "enemy of tan" team: Anti-Brown Spot Ointment and bleaching creams.[30] Indeed, at the height of the fad, Arden created six different creams and tonics to help skin make the transition from summer to fall. If you needed the "pink and white complexion" (still the reigning measure of Beauty), which would, Arden reminded women with sincerity, look much better than a tan with the new fall fashions, she could help. And "anybody who continues to sport a tan . . . through the fall and winter days, just hasn't got her

fashion sense under control or doesn't know how quickly and satisfactorily an Elizabeth Arden Treatment removes the damage of summer and
creates the loveliness of the fall vogue."[31] At the forefront of tanning
products, Arden sold health and youth. She was also becoming an important arbiter of taste by establishing herself as the authority behind a
whole set of new rules: when to tan, how dark to tan, which shade was in
style, and when tanning season was over.

Arden instructions and products reached beyond the East Coast
thanks in part to Tom Lewis. He was, in the opinion of an industry insider, "an utterly brilliant salesman." Lewis persuaded the best department stores—such as Scarbrough's in Austin, Texas, and J.L. Brandeis
& Sons in Omaha, Nebraska—to commit to the dedicated Arden counter upon which his wife insisted.[32] In return, Lewis promised exclusive
sales rights in their geographical region. In big cities, he worked out
amicable divisions, as he did, for example, between Carson Pirie Scott
and Mandel Brothers in Chicago.[33]

Tom and Elizabeth deployed a dozen attractive demonstrators across
the country.[34] Their job was to amplify Arden's glamour, unsullied by
cash; they left the counter clerks to ring up sales. Arden took the selection and training of her demonstrators extremely seriously, hiring only
poised, attractive women with flawless complexions. She required them
to dress well and sound upper class. She drilled them on Arden products and rehearsed them on makeup application and sales techniques.
"Love that face. *Love* that face!" she commanded.[35] Their wages reinforced their importance. It cost her approximately $750 to hone them
"to a perfection of smart hauteur," and she paid them salaries between
$5,000 and $7,000 annually (or $355,000 to $500,000 today).[36] As Arden's beauty empire spread, demonstrators could vie for postings almost
anywhere in the world, a thrilling opportunity available to few women
in any career at that time.

Demonstrator Joyce Godsall recalled the rigorous education at the
Elizabeth Arden Schools. "For the first few weeks," she attested, "the

trainee's time is spent in hand and arm exercises, preparing the hand and fingers to give the treatment. One of the most difficult aspects . . . was to train the left hand to the same proficiency in the treatment as the right." "To attain perfection in rhythmical patting," Godsall "sat for hours going through hand movements to the strains of the 'Merry Widow' waltz." Students practiced on their knees and on plaster models before trying their new skills on one another's faces. Arden required attendance at lectures on musculature, skin types and conditions, aging, skin care, makeup colors, and the extensive Arden product line.[37] The expertise of Arden demonstrators was legendary.

Perfumed, coiffed, exquisitely made-up, these women dropped in like fairy-tale princesses or Hollywood celebrities from another, lovelier world. Arden evangelists, they spread her good news throughout the land, bestowing the "Arden look" on housewives from South Carolina to Idaho. Few women understood why or how to use a product line and even fewer understood the art of makeup application. Demonstrators shaped desires and guaranteed higher sales at every stop.[38]

To continue the magic after their departure, Arden burnished the old idea of the Home Course.[39] Since 1910 she had offered to reply to women who wrote to her with their skin complaints. In 1912, she had begun advertising her self-help beauty course.[40] In 1920, she revised *The Quest of the Beautiful*. The free booklet contained nine pages of advice such as how to avoid toxic and "crude chemical compounds" as well as the "obvious artifice" her competitors hawked. In prose calculated to comfort, Arden explained how she "developed the most wonderful, the most scientific and *effectual* methods for cultivating and retaining youth, beauty and charm." Copious illustrations assisted the woman ready to embark on the home correction of double chins, brown spots, acne, wrinkles, and weight. Arden's information-rich manual taught women how to "cultivate" their complexion, eyes, hair, hands, neck, shoulders, or bustline.[41]

Salon building sped up. Plans came to fruition quickly in those heady, lucrative times. By November 1920, Arden's Red Door salons operated in New York, Washington, Boston, Newport, Palm Beach, Detroit, and San Francisco. She selected her salon managers wisely, trained them herself, and stayed in close touch. To guarantee her exacting level of service, Arden made frequent unannounced visits. Most exciting of all, she had broken into the overseas market.[42]

Earlier that year, with orders still on the increase and her salons in good hands, Elizabeth and Tom sailed to Europe. Seeing an opportunity to knock a few years off her age, Elizabeth moved her birth year ahead to 1886 and claimed to be thirty-four years old on her passport application. Gladys, now suddenly her *older* sister, traveled with the Lewises.[43] Gladys was firmly part of the business, invested in its success and a true believer in the Arden system. The siblings looked forward to visiting French and British salons, but they had a much bigger goal in mind: European expansion. The trio wanted to place Arden products at exclusive beauty counters and hang the ELIZABETH ARDEN sign above red salon doors. They were ready to go toe-to-manicured-toe with beauty culturalists across the pond.

Elizabeth, Tom, and Gladys plotted strategy from the comfortable luxury of Brown's Hotel in Mayfair. They dined well and frequented the theaters. By day, the sisters scouted interesting treatments and captivating items to sell in their American salons. Mostly, though, the three tried to persuade Bond Street boutiques and central London department stores to sell their line. To their chagrin, not one showed any interest. There seemed to be too many beauty products with established reputations selling well. Arden was just another American import in an already crowded field.

Their luck turned when they met the head toiletries buyer for Harrods, London's very best department store.[44] Edward "Teddy" Haslam placed a small order. Then he gave them something of greater worth: good advice. Haslam, a pharmaceutical chemist with fifteen years' experience in the retail business, told the Lewises to "find some sales representatives. English. We don't really trust foreigners, you know. Have them take your merchandise around to the provincial cities. Start to build a reputation out there. The landed gentry often purchase your sort of thing locally. If you're any good, they'll bring word of you down to London, and the shops here will be forced to stock Arden."[45] Tall, distinguished, and honest, Haslam did right by Arden. *Harrods News* soon announced that "these Famous Toilet Preparations have won such an extraordinary measure of success in the United States, that Harrods offer them to their discriminating clients with every confidence."[46] Elizabeth Arden never forgot Teddy Haslam's kindness. It was the root of a lifelong friendship.

Meanwhile, Gladys, who, unlike her sister, spoke French fluently, took the lead in Paris. She worked quickly, and they had much greater success from the start. She discovered that Frenchwomen did not buy luxury beauty products at druggists. She called instead on department stores and perfume shops and, with a skill honed as a demonstrator, convinced them to stock Arden products. Her persuasive abilities won the rights to open an Arden kiosk under the stunning glass dome of the world-famous Galeries Lafayette department store.[47] But the goal was always a stand-alone salon, and by November, she had done it. The Elizabeth Arden Salon opened at 255 rue Saint-Honoré, at the center of city life. According to the "annonce légale" in the Paris legal press, the business was capitalized at 400,000 francs. Arden and Lewis headed a five-person board of directors, and Gladys ran the French operations.[48]

Advertisements quickly flew into service: "Elizabeth Arden, the great American dermatologist whose staggering successes have revolutionized all America, is coming to open a Salon in Paris where all whose complexions . . . are defective will be able to find an instant remedy. . . . She has discovered an infallible method for cultivating and retaining youth, beauty, and charm."[49] On such sensational promises, business increased rapidly, augmented by American visitors to Paris and émigrés who already knew and loved Arden products. Gladys secured retail outlets across France. With business booming from orders well beyond the capital city, she then sought to decrease the cost and the delay in shipping toiletries from New York. Guided by an entrepreneurial streak worthy of her sister, Gladys rented laboratory and factory space, and hired chemists and other experts—including fourth-generation *parfumeur* Louis Amic—to replicate the American products and create new ones. Fine European raw materials, as well as lower production and shipping costs, helped the French Arden concern to profits high enough that within months Gladys opened a second French salon in Nice, conveniently close to Monte Carlo and Cannes, both playgrounds of the rich.[50]

Elizabeth and Tom returned to the United States in September 1920. Thereafter Arden journeyed to Europe yearly to stay *"en rapport* with everything worth while." Assuaging concerns from American clients who missed her when she was abroad, Arden hoped they understood the "'fair' exchange" of helping Parisians while locating luxury products and tips from "French . . . masters in the art of 'make-up.'" While there, she also created partnerships with French *parfumeurs* and "Parisian surgeons."[51] Overall, her annual visits to oversee operations and nurture good relationships with suppliers, employees, and clients were a worthwhile highlight of Arden's year. She valued time with her sister. She loved the immersion in Europe's cultural milieu and delighted in rubbing elbows with European nobility. To her delight, that was happening more and more frequently.

Six

An Empire of Health

P roximity allowed Elizabeth and Tom to maintain close ties to her siblings. Lillian lived near them in New York while Bill, Ada, and their three daughters resided on the Upper East Side. Brother Bill Graham had been through some challenging times. He had been very ill, he'd lost a longtime employee, and his storefront had been badly damaged by a terrible fire.[1] Nevertheless, his globe-trotting on behalf of his company continued. Undoubtedly Bill and Elizabeth talked shop, but she also enjoyed visits with her nieces. Only the eldest Graham sibling, Christine, remained in Canada. She lived there with her husband, Elsworth J. Breese, and their two children. Christine looked after their father, William Graham, now in his early seventies and retired.[2]

Gladys had settled very happily into her position as head of the Arden operation in France. Though the farthest away geographically, she was spiritually Elizabeth's closest sibling. They shared the same aesthetic, a passion for entrepreneurship, and a knack for identifying market needs. But while Gladys loved Paris, it was London and its "social prestige and affluence" that Elizabeth preferred.[3] In a chatty 1921 ad, she confided "a bit of news that I've been keeping a secret: *there will soon be an Arden Salon . . . In London.* And for my European manager I've secured a man who has been at the head of one of London's more important retail establishments."[4] One of the most significant accomplishments of Arden's 1920 trip abroad had been convincing Teddy Haslam to leave Harrods "to take charge of her London salon, from whence he would spearhead her plans for European expansion." In this way, she implemented the advice he had given her. Haslam received training at the New York headquarters. He toured the salon, met Florence Delaney and the other managers in the Arden office, and admired the new, larger Arden warehouse and factory on Fifty-Second Street.[5]

Haslam returned to London with his new boss and her husband. Together, they searched for the ideal salon location. Haslam approved of Arden's choice of 25 Old Bond Street, near complexion specialists she had visited when she was starting out.[6] As usual, Arden trained the treatment staff herself. She hired women whose fingers were "of almost even length placed close together, and without a pronounced cushion at the base of the thumb, which would be apt to drag across a client's face and irritate her."[7] She made sure they understood the mechanics and the rationale behind her muscle strapping and patting, and the logic linking the items in her Venetian skin care line. Trainees practiced repeatedly, on her and on one another, until everyone who donned a pink smock could apply Arden products precisely and beautifully to clients who would, after all, be her walking advertisements in London.

She began by asking Britons "Who is Elizabeth Arden?" and answered her own question in *The Illustrated London News*: "a creator of beauty." It would be imperative, she insisted, for London's upper crust "to make acquaintance with Elizabeth Arden without delay."[8] They did so. The salon was a tremendous success, as was Ronald Hills, her chief chemist. Tom Lewis helped locate the perfect factory site—five minutes away at 25 Coach and Horses Yard—to keep the salon well stocked.

Elizabeth gave Haslam full power of attorney and the ability to act as her agent in Europe, then sailed home to New York.[9]

Arden's next salon opening was in West Palm Beach, a delightful world of iridescent blue waters and sparkling new friends. Florida's warm breezes beckoned vacationers and investors of all backgrounds who arrived on the Florida East Coast Railway. Arden capitalized on it early— by November 1919—taking, as *Women's Wear Daily* announced, "space for the winter season" at Beaux Arts, the "West Palm Beach Home of Fashion." She joined distinctive perfumeries, dressmakers, children's clothing shops, antique dealers, and interior decorators.[10]

Palm Beach was a calculated gamble. Listening carefully to her clients' conversations, Arden had noted that people were taking fewer overseas holidays after the war. Florida had been growing slowly since Henry Flagler, John D. Rockefeller's business partner, had traveled there in the 1870s. Flagler's luxury hotels, including the Royal Poinciana and the Breakers, made Palm Beach a destination for those in the know. By 1919, an expanding New England tourist trade propped up Palm Beach's small population from the end of Florida's hurricane season in late autumn to the blooming of the Washington cherry blossoms. Arden thought a seasonal salon was worth the risk, even though it was expensive to open, stock, staff, and close. Because a costly storefront lease made profits elusive, she invited New York society milliner Christine to share the space. Besides, beautifully styled hats, she had learned from the Ogilvies, looked best on beautifully made-up faces. She promoted her salon in northern and southern newspapers and national magazines, looking to lure customers both old and new.[11]

Arden was well ahead of the great Florida land rush, which took off in 1923. Miami was soon bursting with millionaires and their just-completed mansions. The money that industrialists such as Harvey Firestone, J. C. Penney, William H. Luden, and T. Coleman du Pont spent in Miami was considerable. Land speculators followed, as

developers—honest and dishonest—began to talk up Florida's potential. Rumors spread of cabdrivers making $1 million in a week buying
and selling land unseen, and of New York nobodies rich overnight as
land prices climbed astronomically. More "pioneers de luxe" came seeking
riches in Florida than had flooded California during its gold rush, *The
New York Times* claimed. A British journalist described "hatless, coatless
men rush[ing] about the blazing streets, their arms full of papers, per-
spiration pouring from their foreheads. Every shop seemed to be combined with a real-estate office." One reporter figured that 7,200 people
dashed to Florida daily in the boom years, many of them in cars, thanks
to the just-completed Dixie Highway.

Even Arden was swept into the frenzy. How could anyone resist when
land that had fetched $30 an acre in 1910 was selling for $75,000 an acre
in 1925? She invested in the ill-fated development plans of brothers Addison and Wilson Mizner. A Renaissance man who once starred in Alva
Belmont's 1916 woman suffrage operetta, *Melinda and Her Sisters*, Addison became the favorite architect of well-off Palm Beach citizens. He
then set his sights on developing Boca Raton.[12] Wilson was a different
sort: an opium-smoking, cocaine-sniffing, self-absorbed playwright and
filmscript writer, a gold digger (literally—in the Canadian Klondike), a
confidence man, "a womanizer," "a high-rolling gambler, roisterer, and
big spender."[13] Lamenting Prohibition, trying to shake his drug addiction, and on the lookout for quick cash, Wilson joined Addison in the
Florida land game. Together, they partnered with international playboy
Paris Singer, illegitimate son of the Singer sewing machine inventor
and the erstwhile paramour of dancer Isadora Duncan. Singer provided
the financial backing necessary to turn Boca Raton into an even more
select destination than Palm Beach. To do so, Singer and the Mizners
sought financial buy-in from leading lights to convince others to invest.
Elizabeth Arden fell in line behind a parade of luminaries including a
couple of Vanderbilts, Irving Berlin, Rodman Wanamaker, Charles
Spencer-Churchill, and actress Marie Dressler. Dressler later regretted

"the first big mistake of [her] life": helping to convince others to join the speculative buying fever. She lamented: "Not only was I a sucker, but . . . I was making suckers of those who bought through me."[14] The Mizners' creative financing and heated land transactions meant that very little came of their original vision for Boca Raton.[15] Addison did erect several now-iconic buildings, including the Via Mizner, the elegant Spanish-style shopping enclave on Worth Avenue in Palm Beach where Arden situated her salon.[16] But the get-rich-quick Florida land boom died a startling death in early 1926, bringing the Great Depression to the Sunshine State early. How much money Arden and the others lost is unclear, but she never gave up on Florida. She made good friends in Palm Beach, and her salon enjoyed a steady clientele who sought antidotes to sunburned skin and wind-tossed hair.[17]

NOT ONE TO DWELL ON DISASTER, Arden kept working. Her beloved salons were the locus of intimate connections among women. As female technicians patted, applied muscle strapping, removed facial hair with the Venetian Electra Eradicator treatment, and taught the art of lifelong skin care, connections formed. Among the workers. Between staff and clients. With patrons new and old. Laughter rang out and friendships deepened throughout the delicately scented pink-and-gold rooms. Women raised eyebrows. Kept secrets. Decoded men. Worried over children. Shared fears. Celebrated joys. Granted forgiveness. And gave one another courage. "An hour spent in a soft lounging chair in one of Miss Arden's charming treatment rooms is an hour of revelation!" her advertisements promised.[18]

This was Arden's empire. Her salons empowered women—not just to look their best, but to be their best. Her face-patting methods, massage techniques, manicures, and makeup application tips brought about an inner calm, a sense of rejuvenation, and a belief that one had done something good—but not selfish—for one's health. Arden knew that her treatments improved blood circulation, decreased stress, and increased basic well-being. She sincerely believed that women who looked their best also felt their best and would thus function their best whether they worked, volunteered, raised a family, or all three. She called her salons places of "love and luxury, repose and re-creation" and said that "to see women more beautiful, happier, more out-going . . . is my reason for being."[19]

Salons were also good business. That's why Arden unwaveringly pursued more locations. San Francisco opened the same year as Palm Beach. No land boom happened there, but economic growth was steady after the 1906 San Francisco earthquake and fire, and increased once the 1915 Panama-Pacific International Exposition turned a global spotlight on the city's recovery. In 1923, Arden worked with the J. W. Robinson department store in Los Angeles, already successfully selling her products, to create an in-store salon. From the pale gray woodwork to the pastel-clad beauticians, everything about the Arden salon on Robinson's top floor suggested exclusivity. Six stations kept the number of clients to a minimum. These special customers accessed a "private roof garden sun room" where Arden experts plied their skills. Those less fortunate frequented Robinson's "regular beauty parlor" on the second floor. In sharp and intentional contrast, it had thirty-eight stations and sixty-nine stylists taught by Robinson staff. The store promoted the Arden salon with a window display that reproduced one of her six chintz-covered booths, and with several full-page advertisements in the *Los Angeles Times*.[20] The only Arden salon in the city was, Robinson's verified, "under the direct management of Miss Arden and her New York Staff," and offered "the same specialized treatments which have made the other Arden Salons internationally known." This in-store salon put Arden ahead of another trend. Every Los Angeles department store was preparing to enlarge its beauty salon, because managers swore that women would cut back on their clothing budget to "keep properly manicured and marcelled."[21]

Detroit, the nation's fourth-largest city in 1921, was next. America's love affair with the thousands of cars being churned out daily at its factories was under way, and the metropolis was booming. Arden's salon was on the ground floor of the Book Building. Built in 1917 and decorated with twelve remarkable, naked caryatids, it was the linchpin of the Motor City's attempt to establish a lavish commercial district on Washington Boulevard. City fathers welcomed Arden's Red Doors as a marker of sophistication.[22]

The Newport salon became permanent by the end of 1921 as the vacation season lengthened. Farther south, Atlantic City's newly opened Ritz-Carlton hotel drew Arden's attention. The manager protested it was "not a mere haven for millionaire plutocrats," yet that is precisely what it became. Brimming with modern conveniences, including fresh- and salt-water taps and a "wireless radiophone system," the Ritz-Carlton became *the* gathering place for celebrities, politicians, and industrialists. Society patriarchs found it eminently suitable for their offspring's debutante balls and weddings. President Warren G. Harding and First Lady Florence Harding took over the fifth floor and dined on the hotel's "solid gold dinner service." The nation's first Miss America pageant was held there that fall of 1921. An Arden salon for weary sophisticates needing a quick makeover, for debutantes, brides-to-be, First Ladies, and beauty contestants, was bound to succeed, and it did.[23]

By 1922, Arden directed a thriving business of eleven salons, nine in the United States and three in Europe, each characterized by the distinctive pink interior, strong female managers, well-trained staff, and spotless reputation. Satisfied customers remained the key to Arden's business growth. Women left her holistic salons feeling luminous and returned with eager friends. "It is a profound truth," Arden held, "that if you look your best, you are your best, physically, mentally, yes and spiritually."[24]

Though Arden adored her salons, retail sales produced the highest returns. Maximizing those profits was Tom Lewis's job. In mid-1921,

Arden goods could be found in 188 stores in the United States, including her salons, and in fourteen outlets abroad. It was an extraordinary accomplishment to have placed her toiletries so widely, success that revealed demand among women well beyond the upper classes. Among their retail outlets were those less prestigious, such as Mrs. Mae West in Thermopolis, Wyoming; specialty stores like the Hat Shop in Wymore, Nebraska; independent druggists like Lincoln Pharmacy in Massillon, Ohio; and small department stores such as E. B. Colwell & Company in Monmouth, Illinois.

Lewis and Arden desired a shift, though, to truly grand department stores like Wanamaker's in Philadelphia, selling her complete line from a dedicated counter. Promising to limit the number of outlets in their region meant higher profits and cachet. The mass market was never Elizabeth Arden's goal. Lewis thus pulled Arden toiletries out of stores that they considered a less-than-perfect fit. He canceled contracts to provide their chosen stores a local monopoly. As he had done in Chicago, he rationalized the number of retail sites in Boston, Washington, Louisville, Detroit, St. Paul, and Rochester, where there had been three in each city, and halved the number in smaller towns such as Joplin, Missouri, and Chattanooga, Tennessee.[25] At the same time, he extended sales when upmarket shopping areas opened or established stores built new branches. Twelve months after implementing this two-pronged strategy, "368 exclusive shops" carried the full Arden line of Venetian Preparations.[26] At the same time, Haslam's work bore fruit. British women could purchase Arden cosmetics in forty-seven different villages and towns across the United Kingdom.[27]

Word-of-mouth demand by American women traveling and living overseas meant that Arden products became available elsewhere: Australia, South Africa, Canada, Bermuda, Peru, Brazil, Argentina, Uruguay, Cuba, and El Salvador. Zealous advertising also helped, especially as magazine readership increased dramatically. In 1900, only two magazines had a circulation of more than a million. By 1925, twenty-five did.[28] Retail stores were better than no sales outlets, but Arden longed to see her salons encircle the globe.

International sales, though, could stumble on overlong supply chains. Arden and Lewis built factories and warehouses, especially after it became clear that the factory Gladys rented in Paris and the London Coach and Horses factory worked well to keep French and British stores stocked. Haslam incorporated that idea into his European expansion blueprint. Local factories meant stores did not have to wait for the pink-and-gold boxes to ship from New York or London, and some products might be produced more inexpensively elsewhere. By 1923, the Arden line could be purchased in more than 650 retail spots globally.[29]

Closer to home, Arden and Lewis incorporated the laboratory at 665 Fifth Avenue to create the Arden Chemical Company.[30] From there, she and her chemist, A. Fabian Swanson, turned out even more Venetian products, including anti-wrinkle and healing creams, to add to her imports such as Savon Kenott toothpaste that she variously marketed as healthy for teeth and gums, good for fresh breath, and the best whitener for smokers' teeth.[31]

Product innovation was crucial in the intensely competitive cosmetics industry, where shrewd marketing was key to success. Arden correctly intuited the dramatic social changes around her. Americans in the 1920s sought "the good life" by turning purchasing into a pastime. They kept ahead of the Joneses with enthusiastic consumption of new gadgets, goods, and trends. No one wanted to look back at the carnage of war when neon lights beckoned.[32] Through the bold promises in her advertisements, the way her packaging connoted luxury, and her endless new product ideas, Elizabeth Arden read her era and became powerful, in modern terms, as an influencer—which led her to radio.

Little more than a "curiosity" at the start of the decade, radio rapidly proved itself indispensable.[33] It was another technology adapted for civilian use after World War I, although its exact application was initially uncertain. Questions about how and what would be transmitted, who would listen, and whether radio would catch on dogged the embryonic industry. Early listeners heard orchestras, comedy programs, educational lectures, and made-for-radio drama, but not advertising. Arden immediately saw radio's marketing potential. Over radio waves, she and her demonstrators could speak directly to women in their homes—hundreds or thousands at a time—dispensing tips and product advice as listeners ironed clothes, washed floors, or sipped coffee. One of the earliest shows, *Elizabeth Arden's Beauty Talk*, featured Esther K. Miller from the Arden counter at Pittsburgh's Joseph Horne department store. It played Thursday mornings after its spring 1922 debut.[34] Arden herself also took to the microphone to give beauty talks throughout the decade on topics such as "How to Care for Sunburn and Freckles" and "the care of the skin in hot weather."[35] Her titles sometimes broadened to catchalls such as "Health and Beauty" and "The Care of the Skin," or narrowed to a single beauty problem such as wrinkles or poor posture.[36]

The response was phenomenal. Arden replied generously to the mountain of letters she received, communicating empathy ("I know that where one is a busy housewife . . . it is hard to get . . . relaxation"), and handing out advice that nearly anyone could follow ("try to get a little rest period at least once a day," "drink plenty of milk," consider "a soothing, warm bath") before addressing the specific problem. "I am glad to tell you about some preparations for your hands," Arden wrote a listener, suggesting one nighttime and one daytime Venetian remedy. She sent along *The Quest of the Beautiful*, noting curative products. Arden always concluded on a positive note, stressing the "good result" that would accrue from adherence to her "right method."[37]

The success of her voice on radio led her to record instructive phonograph albums connected to another Arden first: an in-salon Department of Exercise. Arden was the earliest beauty culturalist to add a dedicated exercise room to her salons. Beginning in London in 1922, she introduced a gym space where women could find "tingling good health." She chose or developed exercises for their "*corrective* value" and told clients that fifteen efficient minutes a day at her salon would have the same positive effect "as hours of athletic sports." She hired and trained women as Department of Exercise managers, many of whom had college degrees in physical fitness, to lead classes developed "especially for women."[38] The sunny exercise rooms were equipped with satin mats, stretching bars, massage tables, and eventually record players. Over time, Arden introduced a number of machines and tools, such as the Frances Jordan Reducer, a two-foot-long, furrowed wooden rolling pin with handles. Her technicians used it at the beginning of exercise sessions to "stimulate the circulation" and "knead the flesh like the skilled hands of a masseuse."[39] The Reducycle was an early stationary bike. Paraffin wax baths helped women sweat off weight as they softened the skin. A vapor cabinet worked not unlike today's sauna suits, except the client sat passively in it. Bending, stretching, gentle calisthenics, cycling, rollers, rolling machines, and sweating, followed by massage, skin care, and makeup (and later hair) constituted the Arden Department of Exercise experience in the 1920s.[40]

In 1923, for those making good progress at her salons, she introduced a three-album set titled *Elizabeth Arden's Exercises for Health and Beauty*, with her voice on a soundtrack issuing directions.[41] Accompanying the 78 rpm records were her *Exercises for Health and Beauty* booklet, a diet form, a measurement chart, and stationery clients used to write to Arden for "personal advice and instructions."[42] She also sold her salon mat, "soft enough to protect the spine and light enough to take with you when you travel." Because this mattered, of course, the mat could be had in "several colors to blend with your bedroom" and at two different price points.[43]

While Arden did not invent exercising to music on records, she was among the very earliest entrepreneurs to do so, alongside pioneering Yale football coach Walter Camp and exercise authority Wallace M. Rogerson.[44] Camp's exercises resembled basic calisthenics. He taught his famous "Daily Dozen" before and during World War I to many men including, he proudly related, Franklin D. Roosevelt. Camp promised that any "man, woman, or child" could benefit from his exercises, but his ads were mostly targeted at men.[45]

Wallace Rogerson (always known by his first name) promoted his 1920 "Reducing Records."[46] He insisted that "food does not cause fat." Inactivity did. He urged the interested to "get thin to music and Nature will make your bodily proportions normal." He made an astonishing promise: "I'LL REDUCE YOU 5 LBS. FREE to convince you and I'll do it in FIVE DAYS' TIME." Wallace's ads featured an early use of before-and-after photographs as evidence that "in five thousand cases *I have not had one single failure.*"[47]

Arden made no such extravagant claims. Instead, she modestly pledged that her "Exercises for Health and Beauty" would "improve the vigor and tone of the whole body, correct specific faults of posture," and ameliorate "unlovely developments of different parts of the body." "Exercise," she stressed in her distinctive tone, "and you keep the blood tumbling along in a busy revitalizing cleansing stream." Better health resulted in naturally better skin. Arden calibrated a second assurance to the audience she knew so well: "With Elizabeth Arden's records you are exercising with another woman! . . . She is going through the movements with you. She is an expert—and in sympathy with your needs and longings." Empathy worked best, she believed.

But empathy had to rest on trust, so she described how she had "made exercise a profound study" by working "for months in her private gymnasium and in the laboratories." A perfectionist, she employed experts to hone her own fitness ideas. She could honestly claim that when women exercised to her records they were "working under the direction and the personal inspiration of a specialist." There were only half a dozen exercises, but they aimed at a multiplicity of targets. For example, the "Doughboy" would improve arms, neck, bust, intestinal system, complexion, blood circulation, and "the nerves of the back." The

"Scissors" assisted legs, hips, the back, and even the pelvic floor, "the uterus [and] ovaries."[48]

None of Arden's exercises were overtly for slimming, as were Wallace's and, to a lesser degree, Camp's. Yet the topic of weight loss permeated the 1920s because of the flapper silhouette and the decreasing number of women choosing to wear corsets. Arden's exercises would help, but she saved full-on weight reduction claims for her advertisements and two of her products. The booklet ended with an educational section on how exercise assisted the digestive and lymph systems, for, unlike Wallace, Arden insisted that "food is the fuel" for the "exquisitely tuned motor" of the human body.[49]

Not all food should be used as fuel, however. When *The Baltimore Sun* interviewed Arden, the headline was unambiguous: "'Slim Princess[,] Don't Dare Be a Sugar-Baby!'" Arden minced no words: "A sweet tooth is a menace to feminine happiness." Instead a sensible diet gave a woman beauty *and* health, plus the sought-after slimness. Women ignored her warning at their peril:

> There's the wicked chocolate cream, the insidious bonbon, the unnecessary afternoon tiffin a couple of hours before dinner, and, above all, the chocolate soda—all enemies of feminine slenderness. And oh, how I hate—yes, hate!—chocolate ice cream [and] malted-milk shakes. I verily believe they've destroyed more domestic happiness than any vamp . . . in the world's history . . . ! Yes, undoubtedly, the American woman eats too much sugar. She weeps and wails and buys lotions to reduce, and then stops at her favorite sweet shop on her way home.

This, Arden pointed out, was nonsensical. Women should substitute "fish, a little chicken, perhaps; green, leafy vegetables, simple salads, plenty of fresh fruit and vegetables . . . [and] eggs." She stated forcefully that "Beauty is more than 'skin deep.' . . . It may be summed up in two words, blood circulation. Generations past looked upon beauty as a gift of the gods, or . . . a sort of conjurer's trick." Her program proved that the right diet and exercise resulted in good health, and "health," she emphasized, "is beauty." She cautioned against "extreme" diets of any sort (the milk-and-boiled-potatoes weight loss regime was a popular, if unhealthy, contemporary example) and reiterated that exercise should accompany any sensible plan.[50] *The Baltimore Sun* provided an authoritative witness in Dr. Harvey W. Wiley, whose "ideas of simple eating habits agree largely with those of Miss Arden."[51] Wiley spent his long and prestigious career crusading on behalf of pure foods.

In her insistence on a "simple" and pure diet, Arden was also ahead of her time. While certainly there had been nutritional reformers, such as Sylvester Graham and Dr. John H. Kellogg, Arden made many more Americans aware of the connections among health, diet, youthfulness, and beauty. Her own research led her to these conclusions. Unlike Graham and Kellogg, Arden was not considered a crackpot; she was accepted widely as a sensible health adviser. And unlike Helena Rubinstein, Arden never sold a "vita-wafer" with a dubious promise of weight loss. In contrast to those who suggested that women should avoid strenuous exercise, Arden celebrated it. "Play hard, grow strong—and be lovely!" she enjoined. Acutely attuned to prevailing trends, she catered to the sporting New Woman of the 1920s, calling for "vigorous, rollicking, breathless play" to make "the figure lithe and graceful . . . the muscles firm and supple, [and] the blood race pink and witching through the cheeks." She waxed rhapsodic on the virtues of swimming, a "wonderful 'beauty-exercise.'"[52]

Women's athleticism was a relatively novel idea. Preceded by a few theories of movement, such as the Delsarte system, and by calls for sports among college women, exercise became a 1920s fad, peaking toward the end of the era. Urbanization had made Americans more sedentary, but World War I had highlighted the need for a populace of sound body. By mid-decade, exercising had taken off, especially among middle- and upper-class white men who had the most time and money. Blacks, rural Americans, the poor, and women often did hard, physical labor and frequently lacked access to playgrounds, parks, and recreation centers. Well-known workout guru Artie McGovern warned that a woman must use "discretion" when she exercised, "if she values her health," otherwise, "irreparable harm" would result. Physicians, sports authorities, and other experts cautioned that strenuous activity would cause masculine-looking muscles, an overly nervous disposition, and an inability to bear children. Exercise for women, according to contemporary thinking, was acceptable for only three reasons: beauty, weight loss, and to attract men. Elizabeth Arden's message conformed to this societal dictum, although she seldom mentioned looking attractive for men. Her insistence that beauty came from good health—which included physical exercise—put her ahead of the crowd. It took five years before any of her competitors and many health experts caught up.[53]

It took even longer before Americans shared Arden's devotion to the physical practice of yoga. She became a believer in the many benefits of yoga sometime around 1915. Seeking to avoid surgery for a hip injured in her teens, Arden found, she told a *New Yorker* journalist, "certain yogis who were grouped in meditation somewhere on Forty-Seventh Street." Marveling at their muscle strength and their flexibility, she willingly learned from them.

It is more likely that she came upon one of Blanche DeVries's all-women yoga schools that opened in 1914, a block away from Arden's Fifth Avenue salon. DeVries and her husband, Pierre Bernard, lived complicated and controversial lives, but by 1919, they had convinced Anne Vanderbilt to become their financial backer in what became "a haven for American yoga and a retreat for wealthy aristocrats."[54]

Yoga saved Arden from surgery. She made sure that yoga was taught in all her exercise departments, even though she did not refer to it as yoga because of the reputation it had among a generally xenophobic public. Several yoga teachings became central to the salon exercises she developed and to her own personal workout—she often demonstrated headstands, even into her eighties. Elizabeth Arden was one of America's earliest mainstream yoga practitioners.

THE PUBLIC ALWAYS wondered whether Elizabeth Arden was a real person. Like Betty Crocker, who was "born" in 1921, Arden personified a brand. Crocker, who was not real, nevertheless had a much more recognizable face that General Mills used early and often on packaging and recipe booklets. Arden almost never used her own visage in her advertising. To combat rumors that Elizabeth Arden was nothing more than a made-up name on a corporation run by men, Arden wrote the "I've Met Her" ad, wherein an unnamed woman confirmed that:

> she talked of her work, and her enthusiasm bubbled over. For years, she has spent every hour of her day in her Salons, giving advice to her clients on their individual needs; in the laboratory, supervising the making of her wonderful Venetian Preparations, modifying formulae, testing ingredients, experimenting, working; in the office, directing the work of her Home Course, answering the letters of women all over the country who look to her for advice on their problems of personal loveliness.[55]

It worked, as did her personal appearances on radio and the speakers' platform. The 1920s was a very good decade for Elizabeth Arden. Her wholesale business grew from about $30,000 in annual gross sales to $2 million in 1925 and $4 million in 1929. More astonishing were her earnings. In 1929, she made $400,000 in profits, and her salons and international business added a further $600,000 to that total.[56] Even in 1929 dollars, it had been a very good decade, indeed.

This phenomenal success was a long, long way from young Florence helping her father peddle vegetables. But since 1910 her goal had remained unchanged. "I love my work," she said. "It's the breath of life to me. The thought of beautiful women, all over the world, walking in and out of my salons, gives me a deep and satisfying happiness."[57] She had grown Elizabeth Arden, made it a global concern, and trained competent people to help her run it smoothly. Finally, Elizabeth Arden had time for something really new in her life: friends.

Seven

The Beauty of Friendship

Elizabeth Arden's life was her business. True, she had a husband. They owned a Park Avenue penthouse where two maids and a Swedish cook assisted with housekeeping and entertaining.[1] Beyond the couple's labor on behalf of the company, though, there was scant time for relaxation together and no hobbies united them. Even their travel centered on work. Elizabeth Arden was a job for Tom, but it was Elizabeth's whole existence. Friends had to grow from industry connections. There was no other way.

Sometime in the early 1920s, the Lewises encountered advertising executive Henry Sell. He mixed easily with Tom and he understood Elizabeth. He respected the totality of her—the visionary and the hard-headed businesswoman, the artist and the perfectionist. He had the gift of imagining, right along with her, every pink-and-gold product advance, and he could speak her flowery prose. Sell also appreciated the tough-minded CEO. He was an integral part of the company and of Arden's life for almost fifty years.[2]

Distinguished yet affable, Henry Sell knew everyone. Born in Wisconsin in 1889, he rose rapidly through a variety of jobs. He was a traveling salesman, a Marshall Field's salesclerk, a reporter for three midwestern newspapers, a jack-of-all-trades in the theater, an essayist on the topic of interior decorating that he parlayed into a volume called *Good Taste in Home Furnishing*, and a student at the Art Institute of Chicago before becoming book editor for *The Chicago Daily News*. By that time, a long list of personages had crossed Sell's path, including Carl Sandburg, Will Rogers, Clarence Darrow, W. C. Fields, Alfred Knopf, Charlie Chaplin, and Gloria Swanson. Because he served as an ersatz press agent for visiting members of the Irish Players, he met William Butler Yeats, John M. Synge, and Lady Gregory. In 1920, Sell accepted the editorship of one of *Vogue*'s close competitors, *Harper's Bazaar*. His circle broadened to include Europe's greatest living couturiers—Chanel, Lanvin, Lelong, Molyneux, Patou, and Vionnet—and he learned a great deal about French fashion. He became Jean Patou's "unpaid public relations representative" when the designer toured the United States. *Harper's Bazaar*, a Hearst-owned magazine, also brought Sell into contact with fashion photographer Adolph de Meyer and a slew of Hollywood celebrities, starting with America's sweetheart Mary Pickford and her husband Douglas Fairbanks.[3] Sell mingled with so many amazing individuals that his obituary tried to account for it by stating he had "something of a flair for attracting what nowadays are called 'the beautiful people.'"[4]

Harper's Bazaar publisher Chester Van Tassell introduced Sell to Elizabeth and Tom. At the time they met, she was "disturbed by the wild claims other cosmetics manufacturers were making for their products . . . [and] did not want to follow them." Arden's advertising copy promised many remarkable results but seldom veered off into full-blown fabrication. She worried that her competitors' unrestrained assertions would steal her customers. After World War I, advertising changed. As an industry trade journal noted pointedly, "satisfied customers are not as profitable as discontented ones." Businesses shamed and scared consumers with maladies real and imagined. Advertisements "encouraged self-criticism and distrust: 'sneaker smell', 'paralysed pores', 'vacation knees', 'office hips', 'underarm offence' and 'ashtray breath' had Americans running to the nearest store for the latest preventative or cure." Ads persuaded Americans to "consume their way out of any trouble."[5]

Arden was not above selling to women's fears. And her ads certainly encouraged women to look critically in the mirror or compare themselves against their friends. Still, she did not create fictitious problems just to propose an Arden product as a cure, nor did she promise that her lotions or makeup would impart film star looks or stop aging altogether, as Lux soap testimonials did.[6] And she truly believed that her muscle strapping, tapping, and consistent use of her Venetian line would lead to good health and improved appearance. She was uncertain, however, how to keep up with the competition's falsehoods without stooping to lies herself. Arden asked Sell. He suggested attacking from an unusual angle. State baldly what she'd been saying all along, he told her, because it was what she truly believed. His recommendation was a frontal assault along the lines of "NO COLD CREAM CAN MAKE YOU BEAUTIFUL."[7] His inspired and sensible suggestion—which she followed—was the beginning of their lifelong working relationship.

Her first volley along Sell's advice was the rather shocking "A Painted Face Is Disgusting." The ad played on lingering fears that "the lavish use of makeup implies the need of covering up some imperfection." Arden products could amend those imperfections by creating healthy skin. Cleanse, tone, nourish—then makeup would complement, not disguise. One of her greatest accomplishments was to shift American women from their moral avoidance of cosmetics to embracing them. But she did so while maintaining her fundamental belief that "if you just keep your skin healthy, it will be beautiful."[8] Wrongly applied or on unhealthy skin, "make-up is a cheap make-shift," Arden taught.[9]

Perhaps she was hedging her bets. Some observers surmised in the late 1920s that makeup was a fad: just as the flapper's hair bob was growing out and her skirts lengthening, so makeup might fade away. "It may seem absurd," *The Boston Globe* warned, "but it is well within the range of possibility that the lipstick will disappear from the use of millions of girls and women."[10] Or as journalist Nixon Waterman suggested in "The Vagaries of Fashion," the "present fashion for facial enhancement" is probably only a fad and "the clock will doubtless tick it away."[11]

The naysayers were wrong. Makeup had become normal. *The New York Times* admitted that men had come around, too: "Every woman now carries at least three male votes in her vanity case, rammed between the powder puff and the lip stick."[12] From shopgirls to the beautiful, brave aviator Ruth Elder, women depended on makeup. Elder flew for thirty-six hours, setting a record for the longest overwater flight (close to three thousand miles). She battled headwinds, fog, storms, a broken oil-feed line, and exhaustion, but the first thing she did when she climbed out of her plane was reapply her lipstick.[13]

Neither Sell nor Arden loved every aspect of the 1920s. Immoderate advertisements were only part of it. Overall Sell found the decade "smug," "carnal and . . . unattractive," and distressingly lacking in self-discipline. He agreed with British actress Sybil Harris's description of the postwar years as a time "in which glitter and show had replaced decency and beauty."[14] Arden found Sell's courtly demeanor an attractive antidote. They both believed in frank dealing, hard work, and understatement. Sell carried on a sideline, just as Arden had done in her early days. His was in public relations because it helped his magazine to have Jacques Worth, head of the eponymous haute couturier firm, and jeweler Pierre Cartier among his clients. At his suggestion, they advertised in the women's magazine *The Delineator*, as did Arden.[15] Seeking other notables, Sell turned to famous theatrical agent Elisabeth "Bessie" Marbury. She brokered celebrities, most but not all of stage and screen, who hoped to sell themselves to the highest bidder as an endorser or to gain publicity as magazine article subjects. Marbury was an exceptionally successful woman in the man's world of commerce, working in a field—theater—still considered immoral and inappropriate for "nice people." She took risks to create new pathways of doing business that treated the artists more fairly. She purposefully hired women, and she rested her decisions on cold calculations even as she valued relationships above all. It's no wonder that she saw Elizabeth Arden as a kindred spirit.

The two women met sometime in the early 1920s when Henry Sell presented Elizabeth Arden to Elisabeth Marbury—as a problem. His client Arden was high-maintenance. She took too much time, Sell grumbled, and she wanted too much "personal attention." Marbury advised him to distract Arden by introducing her to some of the famous people in his circle. Sell threw down the gauntlet. Arden already knew them all, Sell said—except her. Marbury took the challenge. In no time, she became the most important person in Arden's life.[16]

Elisabeth Marbury was descended from established New England families with unimpeachable social credentials. Bessie grew up the youngest of five, lacking nothing, including parental love. Her youthful idealization of the stage turned into a management career. She ran theaters, produced plays, negotiated contracts, and was above all an agent of the highest caliber. Her clients included global sensations such as Oscar Wilde and George Bernard Shaw, composers Jerome Kern and Cole Porter, and Black composer and conductor James Reese Europe. She redefined the relationship between artists and theaters, and between artists and agents. Marbury founded and ran two agencies, the American Play Company Inc. and the Elisabeth Marbury Company. She was as successful as she was unique. Unafraid to try new ways of doing things, Marbury "invented the maternal relation to the theater, and became the original incubator and breeder of dramatists." Her biographer called her "the most powerful woman in the American theater."[17]

Marbury's background gave her access to old money and high society even as her career introduced her to new money and popular entertainers. Her best friends were two enormously competent social activists: heiress Anne Harriman Vanderbilt and J. P. Morgan's daughter Anne (who had "a grip like a cowboy," socialite Rosamond Pinchot marveled after shaking hands with her).[18] Marbury's lover was pioneering interior decorator Elsie de Wolfe. For three decades, the pair lived and worked together on two continents. Internationally famous writers, artists, musicians, and anyone else who took their fancy gathered at their homes in New York and France. The couple, along with Morgan and Vanderbilt, were active philanthropists and reformers who moved in a worldwide circle of elites. They helped organize New York's Colony Club—an all-woman version of a posh men's club and a center of networking.

World War I shifted their relationship. While Vanderbilt, Morgan, and Marbury threw themselves into significant and conscientious volunteering, de Wolfe chose to spend her time with socialites, moving politically rightward, and pulling away from the others, including Marbury. By war's end, the couple no longer shared a home.

Marbury had a flair for persuasion and what would later be called "the art of the deal." Convincing New Yorkers to purchase Liberty Bonds brought her into contact with city politicians, who found her charming. While generally uninterested in woman suffrage up to that point, Marbury became fascinated with party politics and supported a trio of powerful New York politicians: Democrats Al Smith and Jimmy Walker, and Republican John P. Mitchel. Meeting with well-known female reformers, Marbury worked on Mitchel's 1917 mayoral reelection campaign. She joined the Democratic Party—alone among her friends—during Smith's successful governor's race in 1918.[19] Marbury served in official party capacities, as a 1920 convention delegate, for example. That was when she became entranced with Franklin and Eleanor Roosevelt.

As de Wolfe lingered in France, Marbury purchased a home at 13

Sutton Place in Manhattan. She hired up-and-coming architect Mott Schmidt to renovate it and reconstruct the exterior.[20] While she never lived there, Elsie de Wolfe's decorating genius was evident throughout. Together, the women transformed what had been a disreputable location overlooking the East River into a gentrified hot spot for the broadminded. At Sutton Place, Bessie Marbury, so morbidly overweight she walked with crutches, "had become the social lioness of New York." Instead of gathering to meet intellectual and artistic swells or the city's scions and socialites she'd invited, "they came to see Bessie holding court in a capacious antique chair set beside the fireplace in her library, smoking endless cigarettes, issuing edicts making or breaking reputations . . . and enjoying every minute of it."[21] Lacking vanity, one friend wrote, Marbury "wore her hair tossed carelessly on the top, and appeared in nondescript black dresses. But so pertinent and pungent was her wit that people crowded to be with her."[22]

This is the Elisabeth Marbury who took up Elizabeth Arden. Although a quarter of a century separated them in age, by 1930 their friendship was so obvious as to be mentioned in the press.[23] Some acquaintances were surprised, knowing that Bessie had no patience for "credulous" women addicted to "rejuvenating creams" whom she thought should instead "study the art of growing old gracefully."[24] Nevertheless, the two admired each other's unusual business expertise. While women have always been involved in commerce, there were very, very few female CEOs equivalent to Arden—not de Wolfe, not even Marbury.

Women in the first three decades of the twentieth century owned film companies, candy stores, boardinghouses, bus companies, dress and millinery shops, brothels, and several other kinds of businesses, but most were small, local, short-lived, or all three. Exceptions were few. After her husband's death in 1889, Anna Bissell took over the carpet sweeper company. Annie Turnbo Malone and Madam C. J. Walker made fortunes selling preparations to strengthen and grow the hair of Black women. Maggie Lena Walker became the first American woman to serve as president of a bank when she founded the St. Luke Penny Savings Bank for African Americans in 1903. In 1904, Lena Himmelstein Bryant created what would become known as the Lane Bryant Company, but she ran it for only five years, until her new husband grasped the reins in 1909. Actresses Mae West and Mary Pickford wrested charge of their own careers from movie moguls, and Pickford was an executive producer for and the sole woman among the quartet of entrepreneurs who created United Artists. In Arden's field, only Helena Rubinstein approached her achievements.[25]

Arden and Marbury were part of this rare group of early independent businesswomen, but Marbury occupied a status in society that Arden coveted. She became Arden's guide to and sponsor in an entirely new realm of wealth, the "liaison officer between commerce and society," as *Fortune* put it.[26]

"I have always maintained," Elisabeth Marbury declared sympathetically, "that to climb socially is legitimate, provided that in the struggle the machinery does not creak too loudly." She recalled how gatherings in her Gilded Age youth entailed "the careful combing of lists and the rejection of names on the plea of exclusiveness." But by the 1920s, society columns began to fill with people like Arden who would have been "cruelly snubbed and ignored" in that earlier time. Arden could never be "old money" like Marbury, but becoming part of the postwar "smart set" was possible. Arden strove to follow Marbury's advice:

> Take a house that is not too large. Have a faultless cook and an imaginative and experienced butler. Give generously to charities, but not so lavishly as to become conspicuous. Do not begin with more than one motor-car. Invite only the few already well selected, and allow your visiting list to expand normally. Do not rent an opera box at first. . . . Do not let any other woman discover that you are intelligent. . . . Be well

dressed, but never too well dressed. . . . Be deferential when
advisable, while preserving always a dignified independence.[27]

Arden longed to socialize with her best clients. Her problems were
threefold. First, being "in trade" with no desire to quit or sell her company. Second, high society had no pigeonhole in which to place a female
owner and executive. Third, she was unwelcome in the men's club of
successful industrialists but had little in common with most businessmen's wives.

With Marbury's help, and that of others, too, Arden moved on to the
periphery of high society in the postwar years. As Lady Troubridge described, the innermost circles remained firmly closed: "The old aristocracy [was] as aloof, as critical, and as oblivious of the rest of the world as
they ever were. They meet these '[fashionable] people' often, particularly at charity balls and bazaars, and they are exceedingly civil, but
there it ends. They never *mix*. . . . If any outsider tries to get in, they
close the ranks."[28]

Tom Lewis did not help. His tastes were rather more lowbrow, running to the entertainers who frequented Arden salons to preserve their
careers against advancing age, including Fanny Brice, Fannie Ward,
Billie Burke, and Burke's husband, theater producer Florenz Ziegfeld.
Arden lunched instead with Ethel Barrymore and Helen Hayes, who
were considered serious actors.[29]

Following Marbury's lead, Arden supported the Democratic Party,
attending fundraisers with the Broadway and Hollywood sets.[30] Arden
found these events useful for talent scouting. More than once she hired
actors whose celebrity status drew customers. Genevieve Daily signed on,
despite objecting that she knew nothing about cosmetics. "God gave
you good hands and a head. I'll give you the rest," Arden assured her,
and sent her off for training. Daily managed Red Door salons in Boston and San Francisco, working for Arden until retiring on her seventy-
fifth birthday.[31]

Another big find was professional dancer Wellington "Duke" Cross. Arden met him backstage after his Broadway performance in *No, No, Nanette*. Arden set Cross to work in the New York factory, then moved him to the head office to learn merchandising. He next became an overseas sales rep and, in 1931, the company's general manager.[32] Eventually he ascended to "vice-president international." Like Daily, Cross remained at Arden until his retirement, thirty years later. His wife, Katie Cross, also abandoned her stage career to become Arden's floral assistant. While she worked for Irene Hayes's Park Avenue floral shop, it was Katie's job to guarantee that the thousands of flowers sent by and to Elizabeth Arden were flawless. A lifelong friendship developed with both Crosses.[33]

By mid-decade, Marbury's advice was paying off. Having secured the penthouse and the servants, Arden—the woman and the business— began to donate and lend her name to charities, including the Metropolitan Opera, the New York Philharmonic, and the Henry Street Settlement.[34] She started to appear in the social columns while she simultaneously turned herself into an industry spokesperson. At the New York City Fortnightly Forum, a well-known debate platform for issues of the day, Arden was the only female speaker among four other prominent New Yorkers. The question they debated that night was "Do Our Morals Affect Our Styles, or Our Styles Our Morals?"[35]

European connections added luster to one's social credentials, so Arden made sure to advertise, cultivate, and donate beyond American borders. For example, patrons of London's "musically and socially exclusive" Lieder Club could lay aside their furs and study the Elizabeth Arden advertisement in their programs.[36] She took out notices aimed at *Country Life*, *The Times*, and *Tatler* readers for products and services available at her Old Bond Street salon or through mail order. Her donation to the Middlesex Hospital Reconstruction Fund put her name in the newspapers as a member of the Ladies' Committee.[37]

Portraits also signaled a certain rung in society. Marbury introduced

Arden to well-known Welsh painter Augustus John. A darling of the smart set, he painted legends like Tallulah Bankhead, George Bernard Shaw, Dylan Thomas, William Butler Yeats, among other literary and theatrical lights whom Marbury knew. Despite his credentials, Arden was not pleased with her portrait. In a formal, off-the-shoulder black gown designed by Charles James, capped by a pert black hat, she was swathed about with a pale, Arden Pink feather boa. She resembled a wide-eyed Eliza Doolittle in an unmatched, down-market topper. Her taut mouth suggested a censorious worldview—but Arden felt John had made her look too soft. His next attempt showed her steelier side, more business magnate than society dame. A sassy hat perched atop kicky curls. A black day coat replaced the gown, and a no-nonsense ascot gave an entirely different feel than the boa. This portrait "caught that radiant quality so appealing in Botticelli's 'Birth of Venus,'" according to one viewer. She sent the Doolittle-like painting to Teddy Haslam to hang in the London corporate office and happily displayed her favorite in her New York City home.[38]

Through Marbury, Arden also met the immensely talented Cecil Beaton—photographer, costume designer, interior designer, painter, and recorder of the life and ways of London's "Bright Young Things." Arden sat for Beaton around the time he became a *Vogue* photographer, the first step in what would become a long and distinguished career among society figures and royals. No matter. Arden loathed the photographs he took of her. Impetuously, arrogantly, she tore the proofs into confetti and dropped them at his feet. The story, and her reputation as difficult to please, made the rounds.[39] A different photographer in Marbury's circle, much further along in his career and vastly more famous than Beaton at that time—in fact, one who influenced Beaton—made a better impression on her. Baron Adolph de Meyer changed Arden's entire look without ever taking a single picture of her.

The baron was a celebrity photographer whom Beaton acknowledged as "the Debussy of the camera."[40] Today de Meyer's stunning works can be found in museum collections around the world. When Marbury introduced him to Arden, he was at the apex of his career. "*Chic*," according to one observer, "was the religion of the Baron de Meyer. Its every nuance was familiar to him."[41] From his beginnings in Europe as the Ballets Russes photographer when the dazzling dancer Vaslav Nijinsky starred, de Meyer created the field of fashion photography and then made it an art form.[42] Just as World War I commenced, *Vogue* hired him full-time. His photographs replaced the drawings that had been the magazine's stock-in-trade and thereby brought about a wholesale rethinking of fashion sales, high-class merchandising, and the very definition of glamour.

Fellow photographer and modern art promoter Alfred Stieglitz invited de Meyer to exhibit his photographs in his Fifth Avenue gallery and featured him in *Camera Work*, the magazine Stieglitz edited. The two men became friends as de Meyer's fame spread and women such as Josephine Baker, Greta Garbo, and Britain's Queen Mary posed for de Meyer portraits. Arden loved his artistic eye and hired him—to photograph not her, but her Venetian line.

De Meyer perfectly captured Arden's vision. The centerpiece was a lovely woman, hair held off her face by a white wrap from chin to crown. Equal parts glamorous and mysterious, she exuded no sex appeal, but rather an almost antiseptic, vaguely scientific air. Arden wanted women to see in the photograph the results of her skin care program. In nearly every shot, the model's hair was completely covered, as hair was not important to Arden. There were no Arden hairstylists at that time (the Ogilvies had moved into their own quarters by mid-decade), and she wanted potential customers to focus on the face as a canvas for Arden products. Seldom were hands shown in the photographs, and when they were, they did not belong to the model. The subtle message was that at an Arden salon, one could simply relax into the ministrations of the skilled practitioners, and all would be well, certified by science and defined by classical beauty. De Meyer's image, repeated with variations, debuted in late 1924 and would remain Arden's trademark look for the better part of twenty years.[43]

Early iterations credited the photographer, but never the model. She was almost certainly Miss France, Roberta Cusey. Known as one of the most beautiful women in the world, in 1927 Cusey competed in the Second International Pageant of Pulchritude and Eighth Annual Bathing Girl Revue but lost to Miss United States. Cusey later briefly became the spokeswoman for a soap made by James S. Kirk & Company.[44] Over time, her head morphed, in Arden's ads, into a "wax mannequin." Professional photographer Willis Hartshorn saw in this "a disturbing quality of constructed femininity . . . [whose] models become increasingly unnatural and stylized."[45] For Arden's purposes, however, "constructed femininity" was fine, as she was selling its building blocks. The de Meyer model was an "everywoman" onto whose increasingly blank face one could project one's own features—if one were white and ideally wealthy. Arden thought it "a masterpiece of understated elegance."[46] In every iteration, it was always and instantly identifiable with Arden.

Luckily, Henry Sell approved of the model. To Arden he continued to provide advice and solace, even though as an employee he was never her equal. He often bore the brunt of what he saw as her temperamental outbursts. At one point, Sell quit. "When our services are such as to be characterized by a burst of profanity and a slammed telephone before an office full of your staff, many of whom are also personal friends," he wrote, "it must be obvious that such services are either useless to you or that there is need for a new and clear understanding."[47] Five years passed. They preserved their friendship, and then Sell returned to work for Arden. He was not the only associate to find her occasionally unpredictable and difficult, as well as charming and generous.

Bessie was different. Marbury possessed patience, tolerance, the wisdom of age, and Arden's admiration. Always keen to learn from the older woman, Elizabeth understood that what Bessie taught she could learn nowhere else. She loved her and was grateful to her. Their rapport lacked the tempestuousness that characterized her relationship with Sell and with newer friends such as Rosamond Pinchot and Fannie Hurst. With the possible exception of Bessie, what everyone had to accept was that friends were wonderful, but business always came first.

Eight

Fashioning the
American Woman

O urs is the epoch of prosperity," Elisabeth Marbury wrote confidently in words that were undeniably accurate for Arden. When Henry Sell left *Harper's Bazaar* for *The Delineator* in 1926, he invited his friend Marbury to become a columnist. Her monthly offering, "Sayings of a Wise Woman," featured pithy paragraphs on idiosyncratic topics that included business, beauty, and advice. What people wanted was not despair, Marbury wrote, but rather "to be stimulated and inspired."[1] Believing this too, Arden poured forth innovations and continued her international expansion, solidifying the leadership of her empire. Competitors nipped at her heels, but none could catch her. None did exactly what she did. Other skin care experts sold their products, many copycat-similar to hers. Cosmetics firms advertised makeup, and most used class-based appeals. A few hopefuls tried without success to imitate Red Door salons. But only Elizabeth Arden so defined sophisticated feminine beauty that her name had literally become a synonym for indulgence in novels, plays, and essays. As the wild 1920s continued, Arden's business sailed on unperturbed.

She returned from her style-spotting transatlantic trips with trunks full of the latest trends—and not just in skin care. For example, when expensive silk fabrics became the rage in Europe in the 1920s, Arden's was the first salon to feature a line of French lingerie and lounging pajamas. This was smart, as *Women's Wear Daily* explained, because the personal nature of lingerie made women unwilling to purchase it in more public department stores. Arden tempted discerning clients on the lookout for the newest fashions and colors. Her piquant "apple green," "shrimp pink," or black nightgowns, matching robes, and "vest and step-in sets" featured "hand tucking, pleating, painting, or embroidery, or buttonhole edging, or lace of real Binche or Valenciennes." The distinction between lace made in Binche, Belgium, or Valenciennes, France, would be clear only to her most discriminating customers, but all women appreciated the breadth of choice.[2]

Arden's new finds transformed her clients' experience and definition of undergarments. Haute couture lingerie, before Arden, required fittings with a seamstress. Wealthy globe-trotter Diana Vreeland looked back on the phenomenon with astonishment: "I used to spend my day at fittings. I used to fit my nightgowns. I had three fittings on a nightgown. Can you imagine?"[3] Nineteenth-century underwear was "utilitarian and voluminous." Beneath floor-length gowns, Gilded Age women wore knee-length knickers, underskirts, and corsets, at a minimum. It was with the dawn of the twentieth century that underwear came to be made of something softer and lighter weight than linen or cotton batiste.[4] For those who could afford them, silk camisoles, petticoats, and nightgowns slowly became available, and European fashion designers added color, embroidery, and lace to the more form-fitting lingerie. In 1915, a brassiere covered a woman from the waist to the shoulders. Within a decade, it had shrunk. Made of cotton, often highly decorated but without elastic, it did not fit tightly, thus allowing more freedom of movement.[5]

After World War I, mass production began and prices dropped. Flappers, and even their more staid sisters, could purchase off-the-rack

tap pants, camisoles, thigh-length slips, and brassieres. Soon, rayon un-
derclothes could be had at significantly lower prices. But Arden only sold
"lingerie so cobwebby you could draw it through a wedding ring," and
she advertised it as a perfect Christmas present for a gentleman to buy
for a lady. Certainly, she insisted, women should also treat one another
and themselves with "cami-knickers," nightgowns, and other irresistible feminine underthings "in delicate pastel shades with hand painted
shoulder straps."[6] The outrageous cost was apparently worth it.

Arden salons offered more gift ideas to tempt customers—hand-knit
sweaters, extravagant three-tiered beauty boxes of her own design,
lamps made of curtseying Royal Doulton china figurines, "Spanish
shawl scarves," and even some truly one-of-a-kind items, such as a purse
"made from a magnificently embroidered Chinese Mandarin's coat—
two centuries old."[7] Such boutique items kept regular customers' attention while drawing in new shoppers who might then try a treatment.

Perfume was the most significant Parisian import to grace her salon
shelves in the 1920s. Customers loved it, and it added to her cachet.
Gladys connected her sister to Maurice Babani, a newcomer in the ancient trade of scent making whose line Arden introduced to America.
She called his "the only perfumes worthy of being sold with her famous
Venetian Toilet Preparations."[8] Babani's came gorgeously packaged in a
wonderfully shaped glass bottle with an art deco label. The names he
gave them suggested an exoticism that appealed to postwar Americans
newly cognizant of other parts of the world: Fleurs D'Annam, Yasmak,
Ming, Afghani, Daïmo. Babani contributed to Arden's sprightly ads,
telling her customers he hoped they would be "as happy in using them
as I have been in making them!"[9]

A revolutionary sales idea that she called "layering" occurred to
Arden. "Blending two or more Babani Perfumes to make new perfume"
guaranteed every woman a unique scent. It also guaranteed to double or
triple sales. Arden and Babani coordinated this effort, suggesting mix-
tures and results: "If you are conventional, dignified, stately—fond of

society and of beauty—you will find a most suitable perfume by blending Babani's Ambre de Delhi and Liegia." Or, "If you love freedom and
novelty, you can express this phase of your personality by a perfume
blended of Chypre and Saigon."[10] She flirted with the idea of allowing women to blend their own fragrance at the salon using a dropper.
"Every woman is a rainbow of moods," one Arden demonstrator told
her Des Moines audience as she showed how best to concoct an exclusive scent.[11] That method—mixing small amounts of different perfumes
in a store—turned out to be less profitable than selling two or more
bottles to each customer for layering at home, so she quietly dropped it.
No other retailer in the United States was suggesting layering fragrances then—only Arden.

Sales were so gratifying that, in appreciation for making him famous, Maurice Babani formulated a "personal tribute" to his friend
Elizabeth Arden in 1925. He called the perfume Mon Amie Elizabeth.
The scent was packaged in a classic square jar topped by a large, round,
faceted stopper. The gesture was flattering.[12] Even though Americans
held entrepreneurs in high regard into the early 1920s, Arden seldom
put her own face in her advertising. But her name became increasingly
a part of her product line. By December 1927, Arden had ceased to be
Babani's sole distributor, and within a year she had launched her own
perfume offerings with three more signature scents: L'Amour d'Elizabeth,
Le Rêve d'Elizabeth, and La Joie d'Elizabeth. What made hers distinctive, she said, was that they were "charmingly dedicated to human relationships and emotions instead of the usual flowers."[13]

Perfumes sold well, but only to a small slice of her customers. Most
American women considered scent a luxury saved for special evenings
out. Arden recommended to her patrons that they purchase several different fragrances, and to change their perfume with their outfits.[14] She
soon applied this idea to cosmetics, suggesting layering nearly every
makeup she sold. Women learned about her idea as she became more
invested in haute couture. That occurred through fashion shows, which

were, like layering, among the most popular and longest lasting of her
sales techniques.

ACCORDING TO DESIGNER LUCILE, Lady Duff Gordon, fashion shows
"turned the serious business of buying clothes into a social occasion"
and so they became all the rage.[15] Equal parts entertainment and serious marketing opportunities, fashion shows were the ideal afternoon
out. Women dressed to the nines, exchanged happy chitchat, and urged
one another to try new styles. Retailers found that fashion shows could
profitably draw in hundreds of women at a time. Arden did not yet consistently sell clothing, but she nevertheless spotted a huge sales opportunity. She could adorn every model with Arden makeup so that her
cosmetics became part of the complete look.

Staying current was overwhelmingly important. Everything—fabrics,
colors, silhouettes, hemlines—changed with the seasons. Magazines
and shows helped women follow fashion's dictates. The most well-off
purchased directly from haute couturiers in Paris or London. Other
women copied designs from magazines on their home sewing machines
or paid seamstresses to replicate the look. More and more, department
stores made ready-to-wear knockoffs available. "It was a wonderful thing
to be a young woman in society at that time," Nancy Astor's maid, Rose
Harrison, recalled. "You could afford to dress, indeed you were expected
to dress, elegantly, expensively and in the fashion." Lady Astor usually
donned a full "five sets of clothes in a day."[16] Such women wore morning gowns, tea gowns, evening gowns, and dressing gowns, but there
were also dresses for paying calls and attending church, lightweight
frocks for summer holidays, and special mourning costumes. Yacht-
ing, horseback riding, tennis, skiing, swimming—even archery and
hiking—necessitated distinctive garb. Millinery and shoe designers
also changed styles, as modes decreed larger or smaller hat brims and
taller or shorter heel heights. American housewives seldom needed as

many changes of clothes as Lady Astor, yet they still followed the trends or risked being "out of fashion."

The first major fashion show in the United States was held in 1895 in Madison Square Garden. After World War I, the events became so popular that *The New York Times* called them "a wild epidemic."[17] In the 1920s and 1930s, fashion shows tended to center around a theme, and often included a parade of historical costumes.[18] Fashion shows did more than put women in the know. By providing up-to-date style information, they gave women who experienced society as competitive an advantage. They publicized the work of the designers and employed seamstresses. And they created dreams. Lucile knew this: "There is not a woman in the audience, though she may be fat and middle-aged, who is not seeing herself looking as those slim, beautiful girls look in the clothes they are offering her."[19]

Fashion shows also brought together women and united communities, which is why they were frequently used as fundraisers, or to promote local businesses. A 1914 Chicago fashion show held at the Medinah Temple by and for Black women, for instance, included 250 outfits. It featured exclusively Chicago-designed and -crafted creations, and "ninety per cent of the goods used in making the costumes was manufactured in the U.S.," according to the front page of *The Chicago Defender.*[20]

Living mannequins were an essential part of the designer's vision at a fashion show. The great twentieth-century couturier Paul Poiret depended on his model to make the dress live "by her gestures and pose, by the entire expression of her body."[21] All eyes followed the beautiful creatures whom Arden determined would showcase her products with their every runway step. The message was that no woman was fully dressed without Elizabeth Arden.

In addition to her cosmetics counter staff and her traveling demonstrators, fashion shows became a regular and vital part of Arden's sales arsenal in the early 1920s. She oversaw the continual training that took place locally, regionally, and at the Manhattan headquarters. Whenever possible, she turned the schooling into useful publicity by sending saleswomen like Grace Doole back to her counter in Austin, Texas, with a framed Arden diploma.[22] Arden directed traveling demonstrators to remain for days at a time when she learned that lengthier stays allowed women to replicate their makeover at home, then return with questions—and even better, with friends. Demonstrators also began to give public lectures, usually in a department store auditorium, on topics such as "Health, Diet, and the Care of the Skin" and "Personal Charm, Diet, and Health."[23] The usefulness of Arden demonstrators was undeniable. Receipts during a one-week, on-site visit were "usually equal to a normal two to six weeks' business."[24] Some demonstrators, such as Lois Sue Gordon, Helen Martin, and Edyth Thornton McLeod, worked years for the company. McLeod eventually became an important public face for Arden, overseeing the expansion of fashion shows.[25]

Tom Lewis, as head of the wholesale division, and publicist Henry Sell occasionally traveled with the Arden demonstrators. Brother Bill Graham went along, too, apparently applying his business experience in glassware to cosmetics distribution. The trio made sure every step of the trip ran smoothly. They addressed product glitches while evaluating the demonstrators' work and relationships with department store sales staff. Sell analyzed the effectiveness of publicity on the ground.[26] Elizabeth Arden traveled, too, but she preferred to focus on her salons, leaving the beautiful demonstrators to her husband.

Arden's high salaries and personal training turned her hires into a contented, competent workforce whose members felt themselves part of a special sorority. Such women, she knew, were likely to provide the best service to the customers whose loyalty she prized. Arden's cosmetologists had to understand the science of skin care and appreciate beauty. She wanted smart, personable women whose outward appearance would do credit to the Arden name, who would take pride in their work, and who would cherish being an Arden employee.[27]

The burgeoning beauty industry provided a plethora of opportunities for women. Helena Rubinstein, who, unlike Arden, published her thoughts, listed the careers for women in the cosmetics field: "department managing, buying, financing, business managing, selling, operating, demonstrating, instructing, physical education, advertising, editorial work, art, decorating and display, bookkeeping, merchandising, direct mail, and clerical work." She insisted that women who interacted with the public "must be well educated and well mannered" and "must know something about psychology." Salaries in the beauty field could vary in the late 1920s, depending on one's job, from "$15 up to $500 a week."[28]

The value of cosmetics sold in America increased sixfold in a decade, topping $141 million in 1927.[29] "Beauty Trade Ranks as Big Business Now," *New York Times* journalist Virginia Pope headlined that year. Throwing in hair and skin care, the annual cost of "beautifying the American woman" came to $2 billion. *Cosmeticians* was a word just entering common usage then, referring to someone who worked with "the 'contouration' of the cheeks," or a "'beautician,' whose profession is 'beautistics.'" Pope reported that regardless of what she called herself, a woman could easily make a minimum of $60 a week plus tips, and many earned as much as $400 weekly. This was far above the average woman's weekly salary of $17.37, and nearly twice as much as the $31.48 weekly that a skilled man then earned in New York City.[30]

The sheer number of positions at Arden salons, factories, and warehouses in the United States and abroad, coupled with her commitment to hiring women, put her at the forefront of this twentieth-century trend. Her salon and sales staff, including managers, were overwhelmingly female. She routinely hired and promoted women in administration as well. While she could react with scorn to employees who fell short of her expectations, and anecdotes exist about her hiring and immediately firing people for failing to meet her standards, Arden could never be faulted for not hiring women at all levels. She saw thorough training and high wages as an investment in her people and her company.

Working for Elizabeth Arden was a golden ticket to careers in adjacent fields. Her New York advertising manager for most of the 1920s was Dorothy Cocks. After a successful tenure with Arden, Cocks moved to the beauty firm Lehn & Fink before opening her own agency and writing two books filled with Ardenesque insights and advice.[31] Those who stayed with Arden, however, were well rewarded. She sent lavish gifts to long-standing employees, invited them to travel with her, remembered their anniversaries, and handed out bonuses.

Arden cultivated and communicated with her sales force through regular circulars. Part training manual and part cheerleading, these letters made the saleswomen feel that they knew Arden and that she cared about them. Lessons about product purity, the efficacy of face patting, and introductions to new items made their jobs easier, too. Mary Weirick, a salesclerk at Boston's C. F. Hovey's department store, appreciated Arden's circulars. "It is so much easier to sell the products," she wrote her boss, "when they have been so thoroughly explained."[32] Women also loved the free samples often accompanying Arden's "nice encouraging letters."[33]

On November 2, 1926, Arden launched a "Salesgirls' Contest." She sent every one of them a note asking them to tell her which Venetian Preparation was their favorite, and why. So many excellent letters flooded in that Arden awarded two first-place prizes of her costly Beauty Box brimming over with Arden creams and lotions. She reprinted the best letters in full in a Salesgirls' Contest booklet sent to each saleswoman. The authors must have been thrilled to see their names in print, and it was a canny way for Arden to share dozens of useful sales techniques. She encouraged, "Keep this book about you for a long time. Pick it up and read one or two of the letters every day or so." She hoped it would help them "increase [their] sales."[34]

The saleswomen's letters spilled over with lavish compliments about the products and positive tips for selling. Most made clear they had internalized Arden's essential messages. "To preserve Youth and Beauty . . . we must have a clean, healthy skin," Irene Godsil of Galesburg, Illinois, enthused.[35] Sometimes surprise sales advice appeared: at least two saleswomen wrote of how they successfully sold Venetian Preparations to men for their own use.[36] Arden's sermons about selling multiple products were echoed back to her. Overall, though, customer satisfaction was their biggest motivator. Recommending Arden toiletries, "all unique in their perfection," made Jean Thompson of Long Beach, California, feel she was "rendering [her] customers a sincere service."[37]

The Salesgirls' Contest booklet functioned much like social media today. Saleswomen read one another's good ideas and then tailored them to their own customers. The contest and booklet epitomized Elizabeth Arden's leadership style. She was positive and invested in her employees. Pooling success stories meant more good ideas for all. Arden was self-possessed—confident in her products, sure of her hiring and training procedures, and certain of her sales force. Seeking and validating their ideas gave them a sense of ownership and agency while molding them into the larger Arden corporate family.

She was also a hands-on leader. Her lifelong habit of dropping in to meet them, to check their supplies and counter displays, and to inquire of their customers kept saleswomen on their toes.[38] Arden let clients know that she systematically visited her salons to "establish that intimate personal contact which makes for perfection in her work."[39] Her stops garnered publicity and helped her company maintain its reputation for being up-to-date with new products, techniques, and beauty concepts. Early April 1927, for instance, found her holding court in her Washington salon, dispensing advice on "the scientific care of the skin and figure."[40] The new watchword that spring was *soigné*—French, of course, because France was still the recognized measure of class and culture. Soigné, Arden explained, "expresses the sort of beauty the sophisticated woman desires: a cultivated, cared-for beauty which exceeds in delicacy the untrained beauty nature bestows." Soigné, thanks to her methods, could be had by all women, and she made sure her demonstrators communicated this message.[41]

The personal connection to consumers Arden encouraged allowed the company to weather rough waters when product purity concerns suddenly surfaced in 1927. The American Medical Association (AMA) called for the otherwise unregulated cosmetics industry to be covered by an expansion of the federal Pure Food and Drug Act. AMA physicians were responding to cases of cancer from the use of X-rays for hair removal and lead poisoning from "hair restorers," among other ailments they traced back to face creams and makeup.[42]

For information about their cosmetics, American women could look to two different places: the AMA and the Good Housekeeping Institute (GHI). Behind the regulation was a study coordinated by Dr. Arthur J. Cramp, director of the AMA's Bureau of Investigation. The nongovernmental Bureau of Investigation existed to analyze and report on potentially dangerous consumer products, from Crisco to cosmetics. Cramp explained that his office was "a clearing house for information on the nostrum evil, quackery and allied subjects."[43] He worried that "a number of scamps have crept into the [cosmetics] business" which otherwise "has been . . . perfectly reputable." He took aim particularly at hair dyes containing poisons, face creams made with mercury, and cosmetics that were nothing more than "clay and water."[44]

Cramp began as a high school teacher, but when a quack doctor's treatment killed his young daughter, Torrey, he vowed to fight medical fraud. He earned his M.D. in 1906 and joined the newly formed Bureau of Investigation the same year. He served that organization until his retirement in 1936. He gained a reputation for zealously rooting out substances and physicians harmful to the public despite limited resources and an insuperable and unceasing number of queries. When a doctor requested information about a drug, or an editor wanted assurance that an advertisement would not mislead the public, or a woman feared that a certain mascara might cause blindness, Cramp's team swung into action.[45] In 1927, Elizabeth Arden's Venetian Velva Cream came under the microscope when Dr. Harry V. Spaulding of New York City wrote the bureau about the product's safety.

Tom Lewis responded. Tactfully. Politely. Establishing a good working relationship was his primary goal.[46] Lewis was quick to answer Cramp's telephone call and request for samples. And he was thorough. Lewis made sure that Arden chemist Dr. A. Fabian Swanson sent the ingredients list not just for the Velva Cream but also for fifteen other Arden products.[47] Lewis told Cramp that their phone conversation had caused the Arden labs to look "very thoroughly into the perfume" in Venetian Velva Cream. They "found an odor which has a slight astringent effect and which might affect a few skins, bringing out a slight rash. This we have eliminated and hope by doing so have now made this preparation one which can be universally used without any trouble of even a slight kind resulting." Arden was willing, Lewis conveyed, to amend any problem on any product.

"There is one request I have to make," Lewis smoothly asked of Cramp, "and that is—after you have gone over this matter thoroughly I should welcome criticism from you. If you find there is anything we are doing wrong, which can be corrected, we shall be only too happy to do it and suggestions coming from you will be doubly appreciated."[48] Lewis was sincere, but he was clever, too. Arden had much to lose and sweet-talking the man in charge could not hurt. The tactic proved unnecessary, however. The AMA found that Venetian Velva Cream "contains nothing of a harmful nature . . . [no] heavy metals, halides, sulphates [or] boron compounds."[49] This satisfied Dr. Cramp. Thereafter, bureau responses to individual queries about Arden preparations repeatedly contained this sentence: "The Elizabeth Arden concern is, we believe, one of the high-grade companies employed in the manufacturing of cosmetics. Their preparations, to the best of our knowledge, are harmless."[50] Lewis's diplomacy paid off.

The Good Housekeeping Institute, an arm of *Good Housekeeping* magazine, began in 1909 to test products for consumer safety. The GHI granted its "seal of approval" to products passing its stringent laboratory tests. The high-circulation magazine had earned tremendous trust from its readers, who extended that confidence to items awarded the Good Housekeeping Seal of Approval. Once earned, the GHI Seal could be displayed on packaging and in advertising. One more important benefit accrued: only those products with the Good Housekeeping Seal were permitted to advertise in *Good Housekeeping* magazine. Twelve Arden toiletries had been so honored, including Venetian Velva Cream. Manufacturers like Arden had to request that the GHI test their items. The fact that she did so was an indication that, although Arden's was a luxury brand, her fervent belief in the Arden look and the quality of her merchandise meant she was happy to sell to anyone who could afford to buy her products. And as a capitalist, she was never averse to adding to her bottom line.[51]

The GHI Seal of Approval was a fine selling point, but Arden was never shy about proclaiming the science behind her products and their unsurpassed purity. "Miss Arden herself often tastes her Orange Skin Food to test its perfect consistency and smoothness," one ad read. This was possible because "a watchful regime like that of a food laboratory safeguards the making of every Elizabeth Arden Preparation. The creams are made of fine oils such as are specified for medicinal purposes or for table use. The colors which tint the powders are vegetable colors, approved by the government for use in foods." Eggs and lemon juice, for example, were the basis of several of her products. "You can *eat* the skin foods, if you wish," she swore.[52] Her staff eagerly told reporters about actress Josephine Whittell Warwick, who, while receiving salon treatments, always requested extra Velva Cream to feed to her dog. Or about the two women who survived a plane crash in the desert because, after running out of water, they safely drank Ardena Skin Tonic. Or about the cook who mistakenly used Arden's Orange Skin Cream instead of shortening in a cake. The woman of the house cheerily reported to Elizabeth Arden that "the cake had been served to the entire family, it had been considered delicious, and there had not been the slightest sign of any ill effect."[53]

Increasing scrutiny by men of an industry led by women providing goods and services to women may have helped spur the 1928 creation of a trade organization. Elizabeth Arden was one of the founding members of what became, in 1930, the Fashion Group. The fourteen powerful leaders who joined Arden came together to consider how best to assist one another while promoting their fields. They met at Mary Elizabeth's on Thirty-Sixth Street and Fifth Avenue, a popular tearoom surely chosen on purpose, as it was owned by a woman every bit as successful—or more so—than they were: candy entrepreneur Mary Elizabeth Evans.[54] Around the table sat fashion designers Lilly Daché, Claire McCardell, and Adele Simpson, with costume designer Edith Head and interior designer Eleanor Le Maire. *Vogue*'s editor in chief, Edna Woolman Chase, and its fashion editor, Carmel Snow, were present, as were *New York Times* fashion editor Virginia Pope; King Features' Alice Hughes; Tobé Coller Davis, columnist for the *New York Herald Tribune*; and Julia Coburn, fashion editor for *Ladies' Home Journal*. The forward-looking director of Lord & Taylor's Fashion and Decoration Department, Dorothy Shaver, attended, as did New York's First Lady, Eleanor Roosevelt, who had a long-standing interest in women's work and welfare. Also at the table was Helena Rubinstein. This was likely the first meeting of the two cosmetics titans. They were integral to the Fashion Group's founding and remained lifelong members.[55]

This gathering marked the start of what would become an extremely influential organization for women's networking and the advancement of the American fashion industry—including cosmetics and perfumes. The Fashion Group existed in part so that career women could support one another and counter stereotypes. The need for the former was palpable. Women in business were a minority, especially at the upper echelons, and men were moving into the cosmetics field. Many were graduates of business colleges where, nationwide, admissions were rising and curriculums standardizing. They applied an orthodox set of rules to every aspect of commerce, and their quantifiable, bottom-line thinking was often at odds with that of those taught by experience rather than professors.[56]

From their male competitors, businesswomen usually faced a relentless onslaught of negative assumptions about their abilities, second-guessing of their decisions, and dismissal of their ideas. Additionally, legal constraints and social conventions barred them from masculine spaces where deals were made. Most men believed women incapable of possessing the necessary qualities for business. Even advocates of women in industry, such as advertising professional George French, had conflicting views. He wrote in 1926 how "women are . . . more inclined to follow their emotions," and instead of leadership, "they exercise over their immediate superiors a sort of motherly care."[57] Meanwhile, other women looked askance at them for stepping out of their gendered sphere. Elizabeth Arden was protected to an extent by her marriage, and her sole ownership and control of her company allowed her to run it as she wished. But even she was only just being noticed by business journals.

ARDEN POURED HER PROFITS into global expansion. Frank G. McMann was the first Arden staff member to travel internationally in search of new markets since Gladys had gone to France six years earlier. McMann sailed to South America in 1926 and continued around the world to open some of Arden's seventy "new accounts" in "Germany, Austria, Italy, Egypt, India, Java [Indonesia], and the Federated Malay States [Malaysia], China and Hongkong . . . Japan, Hawaii . . . and the Philippine Islands." McMann granted an exclusive contract to one store per city, unless it did "not fulfill expectations." In that case, he had instructions to place the Arden line in a second store. McMann, one of those men with a business degree, logged nearly a quarter of a century in Arden's sales department.[58]

Promotion accompanied growth. She advertised in several languages, such as in the Spanish-language magazine *Cine-Mundial*. Thanks to McMann's initial efforts and the Arden sales force, Arden cosmetics were available in eleven Mexican cities stretching from Chihuahua to Veracruz, plus four cities in Puerto Rico, four more in Cuba, and across the Bahamas, the Dominican Republic, the Netherlands Antilles, Venezuela, Brazil, Uruguay, Argentina, Chile, Colombia, Peru, Bolivia, and Panama.[59] In Europe, three new salons opened, and advertising promptly started in newspapers and magazines aimed at readers in Madrid, Rome, and Berlin.[60] *Women's Wear Daily* reported that the Berlin salon, on the "fashionable Lennéstrasse . . . is already doing a hip, hip, hurrah business," and any German woman reading *Die Dame* could schedule a muscle-strapping appointment or a massage.[61] The Rome and Berlin salons built on the work done by Leo V. Talamini, an old army buddy of Tom Lewis's. Arden sent Talamini to Germany and Italy to establish retail branches and provide for manufacturing and product distribution.[62] She also made sure to advertise in periodicals such as *Asia*, the journal of the American Asiatic Association, so she could alert readers that her products were for sale globally at Arden shops that they could discover wherever they traveled.[63]

In Paris, readers of magazines like *Femina* learned that the Elizabeth Arden Red Door Salon had relocated in 1924 to 2 rue de la Paix.[64] *Vogue* called that street the "place of dreams-come-true, where every woman may gratify every wish," the "most luxurious, the most complete shopping street in all the world." Arden joined Worth, Cartier, Paquin, Dunhill, Ogilvie Sisters, and other stores whose very names bespoke elegance, between the Place Vendôme and the Palais Garnier. Arden's salon was a boon to Americans abroad. "One may overlook a few defects at home, but here," *Vogue* knew, "where one is surrounded by slender, chic Parisiennes . . . one longs as never before for a perfect figure and a perfect skin," both of which were within grasp at Elizabeth Arden.[65]

The reach of Arden's empire, *Fortune* magazine noted, made her both "internationally known" and splendidly rich.[66] Sales for 1925 increased 50 percent over 1924 and, Tom Lewis reported gleefully, "the outlook for 1926 is most encouraging; in fact, we expect a large increase in business during the coming year."[67] Arden's explanation for her success? "It is because I honestly believe all women are attractive. . . . When they come to me, half hopeful of beauty, half afraid that it may not be theirs, I cannot share their misgivings. I see them, not as they are, but as they CAN be."[68]

Nine

Exercising Modern Perfection

The 1920s were the making of Elizabeth Arden and of her company. There were, she delighted in saying, "only three American names that are known in every corner of the globe: Singer sewing machines, Coca-Cola, and Elizabeth Arden."[1] No one could disagree. Smart decisions, educated risk-taking, and perfect timing combined to make her enormously rich. But it was more than that. She was the sole proprietor of an international business targeting the luxury market yet selling to women of every economic background. Her products commanded respect for their purity. Her brand was instantly recognizable. Arden's innovations proliferated and her own creations took shape and then shelf space. Elizabeth Arden designed and supplied the exterior to match the New Woman. And when youth became the measuring stick for relevance in the 1920s, Arden was ready with a panoply of age-defying solutions.

The exciting pace of life, the new inventions, the exodus from farm to city, the marvelous modern movements sweeping through music and art, not to mention the financial success accompanying the lucrative stock market game and Florida land sales, all added up to a goodly number of women desiring Arden's ministrations, from the end of the war to the crash. Everyone who was anyone wanted to reap the rewards of a visit to an Arden salon—the pampering, the fresh appearance, the rare finds—or feel the social envy when breezily pulling a tube of Arden lipstick out of a purse. Having expanded abroad, it was time to upgrade at home. Disinclined to do things by halves, Arden enhanced her Chicago, New York, and Washington salons, turning them into latter-day fountains of youth and incomparably luxurious havens.

Chicagoans responded so enthusiastically to her toiletries that Arden spent $69,000 to purchase Gold Coast property at 68–72 East Walton Place. She tore down the extant residences and constructed a salon with a retail shop plus a manufacturing space. While the new edifices rose up out of pale Indiana limestone, Arden made sure her Windy City customers could still acquire her products at four other shops.[2] It would all be worth the wait, Arden promised, because everything available in Paris, "every firming pat and deft stroke," would soon be theirs, including "delectable negligees andsoforths," as a local magazine hinted archly, in her beautiful new boutique. She chose Joseph B. Platt as her designer, demonstrating a lifelong knack for identifying young artists and giving them the big chance that launched their careers.[3]

On Monday, October 25, 1926, Elizabeth Arden appeared in person at the opening to welcome her first customers to 70 East Walton Place. Through the Red Door, women *ooh*ed and *aah*ed over "all sorts of whimsies to flatter our frivolous feminine moments," as she put it. The beauty salon took up the second floor, and the third housed exercise and treatment rooms.[4] As her advertisements proclaimed, "Elizabeth Arden longs to put colour into the life of human beings; to give the results of her arduous studies to the women of Chicago."[5] Arden visited frequently, making herself available for a one-on-one "penetrating diagnosis," leading clients to "that delicious freedom of body that makes for a sense of well-being and is the true foundation of loveliness."[6]

New Yorkers watched as Arden converted the gorgeous Aeolian Building at 689–691 Fifth Avenue. Beautiful musical designs and symbols ornamented its corner facade. Nearby was Carnegie Hall, the American Fine Arts Building, and Steinway Hall, anchoring the music business to that segment of Manhattan. Arden hired architect Mott Schmidt to reconfigure the organ showroom into a beauty emporium. Schmidt had transformed Sutton Place for Elisabeth Marbury, Anne Morgan, and Anne Vanderbilt. He created a striking, and very modern, black marble signature entrance that stood out starkly from the Aeolian's neoclassical architecture. Hoots of derision and paeans of praise followed in equal measure, but the highly polished stone made the statement Red Doors distinct from the rest of the street-level space, which was occupied by famous shoemaker I. Miller & Sons. Two liveried doormen gilded Arden's entrance.[7]

For the interior design work, Arden engaged Chicago painter and designer Rue Winterbotham Carpenter. Born into wealth, Carpenter presided over the Arts Club of Chicago, sat on hospital boards, and donated her time to decorating for charity events. She was already known for her many noteworthy interiors, such as the Casino Club and Louis Sullivan's Auditorium Theatre. Assisting Carpenter was Russian expat artist and set designer Nicolai Remisoff, famous for the internationally popular but now all-but-forgotten review *La Chauvre-Souris*. His contemporary vision began a lifelong collaboration, and Remisoff became one of Arden's favorite designers.[8]

With their help, Arden rejected the rococo of the previous thirty years in favor of sleek modernism. No more overly coordinated suites of furniture, which were, Carpenter sneered, "about as interesting as a dinner-party of a dozen intimate friends, each one of whom is entirely familiar with all the normal thoughts of the other *invités*."[9] The old domestic salon feel was out. Instead, a cool, streamlined but sumptuous business space reflected the ethos of its successful owner. Everything about it earned plaudits from the press. "Glass walls painted in misty treatments" and soothing colors added to the smart feel of the New

York salon makeover, according to *Women's Wear Daily*.[10] *The New York Times* also approved: "A note of classic severity and yet modernistic feeling is presented by the walls of glass in jade green with cut glass feathers hiding the lights."[11] Green, silver, and black appeared throughout the shop, which was dotted with white satin couches. On an upper floor, "white-and-gold barred wall-paper, white furniture, and a jade-green carpet" provided a perfect backdrop for a *Vogue* photo shoot of evening gowns by Chanel, Vionnet, and Bendel.[12] Arden found her involvement in the remodeling enthralling.

On January 21, 1930, to great fanfare, crowds of women dressed to the teeth in designer clothing waited expectantly. Elizabeth Arden and Bessie Marbury stood shoulder to shoulder to receive customers and members of the press. Royalty attended, *The American Perfumer* breathlessly recounted.[13] Marbury's theater friends mixed with important society leaders, and two of her clients, classically trained dancers Harald Kreutzberg and Yvonne Georgi, provided "modern German expressionistic" dancing for entertainment described as "fantastic, bizarre, exotic."[14] Women clamored for appointment spots—for makeup tutorials, salon treatments, exercise classes under Ann Delafield—but also just for the chance to see inside the trendsetting salon that instantly became the model for all others.[15]

Less than a month later, in February 1930, Arden cut the ribbon on her new building in Washington, D.C. Mott Schmidt created another piece of statement architecture for her—six gorgeous stories faced with pale beige limestone built on the same site as the old. Copying New York, whole floors were set aside for office space, while treatment and exercise rooms took the middle floors. The salon had pride of place on the more private second floor, and—in a solid business decision— ground floor retail space welcomed all shoppers, not just those seeking treatments. Schmidt's Ardenesque "pink marble front" on the Georgian Revival–style building drew glowing reviews as part of the city's attempt to turn Connecticut Avenue into Washington's best shopping district.[16]

Arden was in her element, gracious to guests and gawkers alike. Beside her stood Jeanne Marie Adélaïde Doynel de Saint-Quentin, known as the Comtesse de Saint-Quentin. Widow of a French politician, mother of a diplomat, the comtesse belonged to a prestigious family that claimed noble blood. Arden, who had a soft spot for royalty, hired her for her international star power and her impeccable taste. Her job was to select the perfect items to sell in Arden boutiques.[17]

A somewhat different but similarly important employee was also present. Mildred Wedekind directed the Arden exercise programs and busied herself that first day giving demonstrations. She showed off mat routines and equipment ("rollers, electric cabinets, paraffine pack equipment, and all").[18] As a later Arden exercise devotee put it, there was "an almost Greek attitude about making the cultivation of the body uplifting and pleasurable, as well as ritualistic. There's a subtle flow of balm in the atmosphere that makes you begin to feel you're a really rather remarkable you."[19] Wedekind set the tone for Arden athleticism, and she was very persuasive. In under a fortnight, the Washington Department of Exercise had become "one of the busiest places in town."[20]

Vogue sent a reporter to experience "modern and feminine counterparts of the Roman baths." Rather than men meeting to "wrestle and bathe and to be rubbed with fine oils," women came together to disport themselves in an "atmosphere . . . of a gay and sophisticated country club." Every woman first had to present the treatment specialist with a doctor's note clearing her to participate. Then Arden staff gathered statistics using the fearful Shado-Graph machine that projected a life-size silhouette on the wall, laying bare every slouch and bulge. Treatment experts inquired about a client's digestion and "the position of [her] bones." Women, overstressed then as now, could next relax under a sunlamp, have a Swedish massage, and take a hot-and-cold shower.[21] "Soon," the journalist wrote, "you are fired with ambition to get down on one of the yellow or violet satin mats in one of the sun-swept exercise rooms and get to work." She was not being facetious. The exercise was "real work" and teaching by the Arden experts detailed and specific. To aid weight loss, the Ardena Paraffin Bath and the Ardena Roller gave "amazingly quick and efficient results."[22] Hollywood stars attested that one paraffin bath could take off up to six pounds.[23] The Ardena Giant Roller was likened to being "in the midst of a perpetual subway turnstile—though far more comfortable. . . ." This part of the treatment required blissfully little exertion. "You rest your arms on the supports and read Aldous Huxley's new book, while the rollers go round and round your hips and your waist," the reporter wrote in amazement. They supposedly "[broke] up the fat cells," which were then "carried from the system by means of diet, exercise, or massage." Exercise, tap, and rhythmic dancing to the hippest jazz tunes attracted women "merely for the fun of it, for the grace of it, and to keep in good shape."[24] *Vogue* conceded that Arden turned out "a new and healthier woman in the end."[25]

The Department of Exercise served more than socialites. Pregnant women learned the healthy "Indian way" of carrying the baby unobtrusively. Children were brought in to master proper posture. Workingwomen in search of rejuvenation spent their vacation hours there. And sometimes "a trio of grandmother, daughter, and granddaughter has been known to enrol and, after pursuing health and beauty along different routes, [end] up together in the tap-dancing room."[26] The goal was always to create "suave, graceful bodies and not the sturdy athletic type," Marcia Vaughn reported for *The Chicagoan*.[27]

Parisian fashion required exercise. By the end of the decade French designers dictated lower hemlines and the return of the waistline. The straight up-and-down flapper look gave way to a more old-fashioned, hourglass silhouette. Even Montana's *Great Falls Tribune* observed that the "masculine type of dress seems definitely discarded."[28] Women found this terrifying. Waists! Back in fashion! *Collier's* Betty Thornley investigated what this meant for the average woman. Her conclusion? Despair. "Waistlines were a secret, sacred sort of thing. Everybody was supposed to have one. . . . But most of us over thirty and practically all of us over forty simply hadn't a presentable waistline on the premises. Nice slim hips—oh, yes. But above them, something that only the angels saw, and perhaps the masseuse—a little insidious roll that coiled round like the snake in Eden—or a great big 'spare tire' roll that worried us seriously when we stood sidewise to the bathroom mirror." The clothes making their way across the Atlantic threatened to reveal what had been hitherto and happily hidden.

"Exercise it off," Thornley recommended, at the Arden salon. Follow the teachings of the "lovely slim creatures who sway about like white birches dipping to a breeze, instructors who show us what we once were and may be again." Learn to stand up straight, do the "Rope Pull," and the "Crash and Lift." Get out the mats, the ropes, and the rollers and do it on your own with Arden's records or take yourself off to the salon for some passive exercise with her "huge multiple roller [machine] that can do everything but talk" while it "works on whatever part of you needs reduction." "Miss Arden is no extremist," Thornley promised, "a pound and a half or two pounds" a week in weight loss was all she said one could sensibly achieve. Together, these "magic movements" guaranteed that the "most revealing French fashions" would fit. But Thornley was a realist and knew her readers. She concluded her article with a last-ditch notion: you could always pull out your old corset.[29]

Ah, but Arden would never resurrect the corset. That was going backward. Alas, exercise was difficult and boring. She may not have attended business college, but Arden knew well that bored customers would shop elsewhere, so she invented Plastic Exercises, available only at her salons. Plastic, in this sense, meant malleable, or, as she phrased it, "subtly model[ing] your figure as it develops grace."[30] The dance-like movements produced "slim hips, smooth shoulders, proudly lifted necks and slender willowy bodies" with "a graceful throat, [and] well-modelled ankles." She called the whole-body workout "a modern miracle."[31]

Modernism was a core selling point of Plastic Exercises. Although plastic, in the form of celluloid, had been around since the 1860s, its popularity leaped forward when inventor Leo Baekeland created the hard, colorful substance he called Bakelite in 1907. Used for jewelry, radio casings, high heels, chess sets, and many other sleek consumer products, it was ubiquitous by the 1920s. Plastic meant modern.[32] Arden's choice of name for her exercise was brilliant marketing. Plastic Exercises "are as definite, as crisply simple, as rhythmic," she stressed, "as all modern expression." Driving the point home, she emphasized that "affectations in exercise are as out of date as stilted manners."[33] She specifically targeted women who identified as "very modern, very fascinating."[34] She spoke to the gains in women's independence obvious all around them, calling Plastic Exercises "the most modern means of self-expression in its most perfect form!"[35]

A series of Arden ads featured photographs of women alone and in groups paused, mid-exercise, wearing one-piece, low-backed, short leotards. The women resembled lissome but grounded Martha Graham dancers. Among New Yorkers in the know, Graham's pathbreaking choreography was all the rage, and Graham's circle of acquaintances overlapped with Marbury's through their work at the Neighborhood Playhouse. Arden had almost certainly observed a dance performance at Graham's nearby Manhattan studio. Borrowing seems likely, especially as a curious *Vogue* reporter noted that Arden's Plastic Exercises "must be instilled into one, step by step, gesture by gesture, like teaching a dance sequence."[36] Banishing boredom by demanding close concentration to exacting movement was Arden's objective.

Arden created and taught other exercises. Some were available for purchase on her record albums, but in the salon there were added perks, always for a price. Well-trained instructors from around the globe provided personal attention to help women learn complicated moves. Celebrating with a "glowing . . . sense of triumph," clients could then opt for a massage, or spend meditative time in "quiet rooms that are truly quiet," or gain an artificial tan in "amusing little dressing-rooms."[37] In Washington, customers could access an early-version muscle warmer. The long, rectangular "sleeping box" (like "a doghouse with an arched entrance," as one journalist wrote) encased the body, with room to spare above and to the sides. The head remained on the outside. Inside, a fan diffused air at a constant eighty-six degrees. Its inventor, Milton Fairchild, believed that resting under what he called his "electric blanket" would improve sleep and overall health. Arden, always open to new inventions, thought it just the thing for women fatigued after Plastic Exercises.[38]

Exercise provided the slim, supple body that fashion demanded, but once achieved, an aging face would give one away. Arden had the solution for that, too. Her novel idea was the Vienna Youth Mask. No exercise involved. She claimed it was the best "natural method" for facial rejuvenation, especially for women over age forty.[39] Known as "medical diathermy," this treatment differed greatly from facials because it utilized electricity. The doctors who applied it called themselves "electro-therapeutists." They prescribed it for a range of illnesses, including high blood pressure, gonorrhea, pelvic inflammatory disease, hemorrhoids, and tuberculosis. Medical diathermy was on the rise in the postwar years as physicians sought the best ways to apply healing heat onto and into the body.[40] Heat has been a long-standing treatment for a range of disorders and can play an especially important role in relieving suffering from muscle injuries and arthritis. It is still administered today to combat aging. Arden learned about it from Dr. Eugen Steinach in Vienna (hence she called it Vienna rather than Venetian) where he had been using it with success on veterans' injuries.

Steinach was a well-known endocrinologist who experimented with injecting an extraction of the "sex glands" from "lower animals" into humans and deriving from it a "glandular treatment." Working with him was Dr. Erwin Last.[41] Last had a reputation for employing an anti-aging technique beloved by aristocratic Europeans who treasured his confidential assistance. He is remembered in the field of diathermy for his invention of "special appliances for its use in rejuvenation, and the removal of evidences of age from the face." Last combined diathermy with Steinach's glandular remedy. Arden knew about the "startling gland operation," but nothing like that was ever offered in her salons.[42] Repairing damaged glands had been part of her approach to beauty as early as 1917, when she first advertised her muscle-strapping treatment to promote "proper circulation and gland action" for improved skin.[43] A decade later, she declared that it made "every organ and gland . . . function effectively."[44]

Not until 1934, however, did she create and sell "Elizabeth Arden's Gland Cream." It was an anti-aging, hormone-based throat cream that she sold as lower necklines came back into style.[45] Estrogen, synthetic human growth hormones (HGH), and hyaluronic acid (often derived from cocks' combs) are still commonly used. Arden's insistence that exercise and a good diet were also necessary to say "Farewell to Age" is why she never promoted hormone creams quite as emphatically as other cosmetologists.[46] She was sympathetic to those who failed to see miraculous transformations. After one disappointed customer complained, the American Medical Association responded: "Even if 'living tissues' were put into the cream, we know of no evidence . . . that they would have any rejuvenating effect on the skin whatever." These qualms did not stop Arden from selling her Gland Cream—which she did until 1951—nor thousands of women from purchasing it. Regardless, Arden never promised miracles; only that it would "wage war on wrinkles," and though it was expensive (selling for what would be $230 to $460 today), she marketed it as a companion to the real star, the Vienna Youth Mask.[47]

For the next decade, the Vienna Youth Mask held pride of place in Arden's treatment rooms. She pioneered "high-frequency electrical currents to warm facial tissues in beauty treatments."[48] Medical historian James F. Stark credited her with employing "the most high-profile diathermy device of the period."[49] It was the talk of every city where women could access a Red Door salon. A nurse trained in diathermy and "a skilled electrician" began by applying "a radioactive cream" to the face and neck. Radioactive pills, creams, and other treatments were popular, especially in Europe, and considered rejuvenating.[50] The heat was added using a plaster of Paris (later papier-mâché) and tinfoil mask that—and this was an important selling point—had been created uniquely for each individual client by "an artist-sculptor." The same mask would be used throughout the full, thirty-treatment course. Arden's Vienna Youth Mask, one woman exclaimed, "pours new life into the skin and new strength to the structures beneath." And the experience was pleasurable. She declared that she napped while resting on "a small divan in one of the charming little rooms of the Arden salon . . . lulled and soothed by the gentle reverberations. . . ."[51] The heat increased blood circulation, diminishing the signs of aging as it did so, because, as Arden explained, "the blood [would] flow in a rich purifying stream to underlying tissues and muscles . . . charging them with new youth and vigor." It felt as if "electric energy were poured into your very veins."[52]

The best advertisement for the Vienna Youth Mask was Arden herself. "I had the privilege once," a journalist wrote, "of seeing [modern dancer] Isadora Duncan and Elizabeth Arden together. The latter claims to be nearly twice the age of the former. Yet in appearances this was exactly the reverse. The marvelous Isadora lived strongly and met Time as a humorous opponent. The interesting Elizabeth refuses to meet Time at all, but keeps her at a distance with a gentle firmness that she has gone so far to make a profession of and try to teach other women to do so."[53]

The Arden youth methods were dearly bought. A diathermy treatment consisted of thirty or thirty-two sessions and cost $200—or $3,600 today.[54] The exercise classes were less expensive, but the price was not negligible. The record albums were in line with others sold for the same purpose; still, it was clear that Arden's target client remained the wealthy white woman. For everyone else, Arden purchases were aspirational, occasional, or possible only in the small container size.

ELIZABETH ARDEN'S CREATIVITY had been evident from early on. She began by crafting a new name for herself, with a new persona to match. She launched her business with her own homemade concoctions, or at least her own labels. From the early whipped facial creams and the perfect shades of pink, her ingenuity encompassed what would ultimately become an astonishing ninety-seven patents. She invented products from perfume bottles to beauty boxes to face-patting tools. Many of Arden's designs became reality, and every single purse or cake of soap she fashioned augmented her bottom line.

She filed her first patent in 1923 and her last in 1949. Not surprisingly, Arden's initial devices were new and better equipment for her muscle-strapping system—a "Puffy Eye Strap" and a "Forehead Strap," both meant to tie around the face to hold astringent in place. Next came a complicated, multilayered, leather "Lady's Dressing Case." Its seven compartments, three of which were hinged to swing out sideways, were carefully conceived to restrain "powder and rouge boxes, salves, perfume bottles and sprayers, dressing gowns, hairbrushes and combs, toothbrushes, and electric lamp, etc." during travel. Its ornamented exterior complemented a silk-covered interior that looked beautiful closed for travel or open on a dressing table. Every case she designed had a mirror for ease of applying Arden toiletries.[55]

Ideas simply poured forth. The perfectionism and early parsimony underlying her business success hint that she may have felt she could do nearly everything better than anyone else, including product creation. It was her business, and no one knew it as well as she did. Besides, why pay someone when she could design it herself?

Improvements, pivots, responses to emerging trends—she was the industry expert. Every preparation that came from the Arden labs she tried first on herself. Then, to understand its effectiveness on different types of skin, she drafted (sometimes reluctant) relatives, friends, and employees. A 1935 *New Yorker* profile of Arden revealed how "secretaries, stenographers, and file clerks frequently work with one eye made up in gray-brown mascara and the other in straight brown, with each hand colored with a different nail lacquer" so that Arden could analyze colors. She corrected product flaws without hesitation. "If the chin strap is not right, she will take a pair of scissors and slash it, then and there, to the proper pattern," an employee testified. Another, quite used to her face being used as a testing ground, finally protested when her skin broke out and then sunburned despite using a prototype suntan lotion. Arden returned to the lab for a rethink. She soon emerged triumphantly "with a brand-new, and profitable, group of preparations" aimed at sensitive skin.[56] No one knew her toiletries or her customers as she did, and it was for her a short step from testing to tinkering, and from tinkering to inventing.

Arden almost never took public credit for her patented inventions. Inventing was considered a masculine field. Female inventors were frequently belittled because most of their inventions were for the home. Arden already trod a fine line as a woman business owner.[57] One of the rare occasions on which she allowed her name to be linked to one of her inventions was the 1930 wedding of Princess Marie-José of Belgium. After Arden presented the princess with an elaborate traveling box, *WWD* reported that it was "designed by Elizabeth Arden herself after the manner of the old dressing case of a Chinese empress."[58] In 1934, stores gave out a headband to keep the hair away from the face for ease of cleaning.[59] It was likewise described as having been "designed by Elizabeth Arden." Her bandeau became so popular that Arden renamed it "the Hair Protecta" and included it as a Beauty Box essential.[60]

Packaging offered new creative opportunities. There were iconic perfume bottles—one resembling a hand grenade, another with a glass hand wrapped around the container. The latter took shape in Baccarat crystal and held Arden's It's You and later Blue Grass perfumes.[61] A pale-green horse of her own design came inside another miniature blown-glass perfume bottle.[62] She created unforgettable compact designs, including one in the shape of a harlequin mask; another was a square with a graceful leaf etched on the lid.[63] Her "Looking Glass Lipstick" case flipped open to display a handy mirror.[64]

She invented boxes to market perfume, and cases of all sorts—day and evening cases, cigarette cases, manicure chests, large and small travel cases that held any number of bottles and jars, brushes, and cosmetics. There were talcum powder boxes and cold cream jars. For the salons, she drew up plans for "suction patters," an "electrode applicator for use in short wave radio therapy," display boxes, a "lipstick advertising device," a face massager, a shaving bowl, and a privacy screen. Other items she invented to sell in her salons included purses, handbags, pocketbooks, dresses, a girdle, jewelry, a "soap doll," holiday-themed perfume containers, presentation boxes, a "waterproof beach kit," a "ski kit," a "sport belt," a "cosmetic crayon container," a "combined lipstick holder and eye shadow case," and a "combination compact and cigarette case."[65] Her ideas were frequently pirated, and she was quick to sue competitors who infringed her patents.[66]

ARDEN'S GREAT FRIEND and mentor Elisabeth Marbury was in declining health. Once overseas travel became impossible in the early 1920s, Marbury bought rustic Lakeside Farm, located in Maine's Belgrade Lakes region. The interior, all wood paneling and leather furniture, was decidedly not designed by Elsie de Wolfe, now Mendl after her 1926 *mariage blanc* to Sir Charles Mendl. At Lakeside, Marbury fished, read, gardened, and tended her cattle. Arden joined her as often as she could, occasionally with Tom Lewis.

When the neighboring property went on the market, Arden followed Marbury's advice, "took a chance," and purchased it.[67] Working together in 1929, the pair supervised the building of Arden's new house and Rue Carpenter's interior designs. The activity caught the attention of *The Boston Globe*, which wrote approvingly that the "most notable" of the cottages being built just then around Belgrade, Maine, was Elizabeth Arden's "summer home."[68] It sat majestically above 750 acres of land sweeping down to Long Pond. Redolent with flowers and herbs, the property had a vegetable garden and stables, which she would soon enlarge. She renamed it Maine Chance (she appreciated a good pun). Arden's country home brought Elisabeth and Elizabeth closer. Their friends intermingled, wandering across the shared lawns for drinks and socializing.[69] Every possible weekend, Arden escaped New York City to rusticate.

Like newcomers everywhere, Arden met her neighbors. Two other cottages sat on the shore of Long Pond, one owned by New York financier Russell Gage Harper.[70] Harper and his wife, Anna, were golfers, fishers, and longtime, engaged summer residents of the Belgrade area.[71] He and former banker Tom Lewis likely enjoyed hashing over the day's financial news. Until, that is, one afternoon in late 1929. Even as movers carried costly antiques into Maine Chance, Harper was forced to resign as director of the Dayton Airplane Engine Company. The firm's stock value had halved that one fall day, and the business lost $250,000 in an instant.[72] The frenzied and unpredictable stock market could not go up forever, and when it crashed, it took the global economy with it. But not, it turned out, cosmetics.

Ten

Inventing Color Harmony

On October 18, 1929, Arden's entire New York payroll vanished—not on Wall Street, but when a desperate Brink's truck driver sped away with it. Raymond H. Gallagher, age twenty-seven, made his usual rounds, but this time he methodically plundered ten different Manhattan companies and absconded with $64,927. The pile of cash contained so many heavy silver coins that the police believed he had to have had accomplices. Neither he, nor they, was ever brought to justice. Arden lost the week's payroll. Eleven days later, the stock market crashed.[1]

The nation's economy had been shaky for many months. Throughout the autumn, Americans had grown accustomed to dire economic warnings, but at the end of October, the crisis well and truly hit. From New York to California, citizens were jolted awake by front-page headlines declaring "2nd Big Slump; Day's Loss Set at 14 Billions" and "New York Banker Sees Own Stock Fall $18,000,000 in Less Than [a] Week."[2] Global economies weakened. In the United States, Republican president Herbert Hoover seemed powerless. By 1933, the unemployment rate peaked at nearly 25 percent. The loss of jobs, homes, and farms was just the tip of the calamity. Soon, all but the very wealthiest felt the pinch. The Great Depression had arrived, and with it, deep gloom.

Except at Elizabeth Arden. Her sales and her spirits remained high because the economic downturn didn't seem to hurt her business.[3] The circumspect CEO was guardedly delighted to see her beauty preparations still flying off the shelves and her salons fully booked. Women, it turned out, would spend money on affordable luxuries like cosmetics despite financial fears. Keeping up appearances signified one's fortitude—or luck—in holding "Old Man Depression" at arm's length. Analyses by business historians suggested a slim silver lining: "Upper-middle-class citizens had relatively greater buying power than they had ever had [and] ordinary consumers who were not utterly destitute continued to buy for the rest of the decade."[4] This worked in Arden's favor. As the crisis deepened, her friend Rosamond Pinchot—who lost everything in the Depression—recalled rolling her eyes at Arden's feigned concern while "sitting in one of the exquisite and expensive chairs dressed in velvet and pearls. She started talking about the depression and said 'I don't know what's going to happen to us. I expect we'll all have to go down the drain together.'"[5] That did not occur. Arden's personal and professional fortunes protected her, as did carefully calculated risks and sensible business decisions.

The beauty industry proved largely impervious to the Depression because, as advice columnist Antoinette Donnelly asked rhetorically, "Lives there a woman who is happy without lipstick?" They would rather go without food, she declared.[6] The vice president of Charles of the Ritz, a competing luxury brand, agreed: "Women do not count the cost of beauty. They instinctively recognize that it is priceless and anything that aids them in preserving or increasing it, is entirely outside of price consideration."[7] Arden learned early that the public equated high quality with high cost, and so did not drop her prices. This guaranteed continued profit, while providing her customers the pampered feeling they craved when opening her pink-and-gold boxes. She did make sure to offer her toiletries in an array of sizes and prices for all pocketbooks. For instance, the smallest bottle of Ardena Skin Tonic sold for 85 cents ($15 today), and the gallon size cost $15 ($270). Venetian Orange Skin Food came in sizes retailing for $1.75, $2.75, $4.25, or $8.00. Most Babani perfumes ranged in price from $2 to $12.[8] And for those lucky few with still-full purses, Arden never stopped enlarging her salon treatment menu, her skin care line, or the gorgeous array of imported goods available in her shops. She had the funds to do it. Her wholesale business had doubled from 1922 to 1923, doubled again in 1925 to $4 million, and once more in 1929. By the time the stock market tumbled, her profits amounted to more than $1 million annually, or over $18 million today.[9]

Henry Sell, by 1930 president and owner of the Blaker Advertising Agency, advised his client Elsie de Wolfe Mendl not to bother marketing her interior design business at all until the financial nosedive had ended.[10] Arden disagreed with her friend's counsel. She predicted that advertising would be of greater importance than ever. She felt, as *Vanity Fair* editor Frank Crowninshield phrased it, that magazine advertisements were "magic carpets on which [American women] ride out to love, the secret gardens into which they wander in order to escape their workday world and their well-meaning husbands."[11] Arden spent $337,470 on magazine advertising in 1929 alone, a 10 percent increase over 1928.[12] She would never stop fueling her customers' dreams. That was one reason why Arden—initially at least—ignored the economic crisis. "If you should take a boat and sail around the world" began her ad in January 1930, a time when almost no one was contemplating a cruise. The impassive de Meyer model, arms resting on a crystal tabletop, gazed out at readers that month, surrounded by no fewer than fourteen expensive Arden potions.[13]

Ignoring Sell's advice entirely, Arden rolled out a series of bold ads for the d'Elizabeth perfume line that spring, featuring dramatic, modernistic photographs of the bottle and box she designed. The names of

her scents—joy, dreams, love, friendship (*en français, naturellement*)—
transcended grubby economic realities. The advertising language was
baroque, lyrical, over-the-top: La Joie d'Elizabeth perfume captured
that "spiral, bubbling thing which made you leap and run in the wind
and laugh without reason."[14] Le Rêve d'Elizabeth reminded readers that
"when one no longer dreams of the beauty that could be, he has begun
to die."[15]

She saved her most sentimental expression for the experience L'Amour
d'Elizabeth: "To love is to light a lamp within, which not only warms
and comforts you, yourself, but sends out from you a glow which cheers
and comforts others. It is better to cast your pearls of love before anyone, anything, than to keep them. You are thoroughly natural, thoroughly alive only when you are filled with love. . . . With love, nothing
in life is beyond bearing."[16] Dealing in such ethereal concepts was a
gamble. One can imagine a harried, worried housewife savoring such
advertisements as she might a novel, to be lifted out of the day's troubles. Indignantly tossing the ad aside seems a similarly logical response.
Look beyond financial cares, Arden seemed to say, but women forced
into more frugal living may have heard something quite the opposite.

The final advertisement in this series featured a photograph of Elizabeth Arden. It was the first time she ever authorized her own likeness
in an ad. Standing two thirds of the way up a curved staircase, the visual
reference is to *The Golden Stairs*, Edward Burne-Jones's 1880 painting.
Where his canvas shows women crowded on every step, Arden stands
alone, hand on hip, head tossed back, looking glamorous, young, and
carefree, nothing like an extremely busy forty-eight-year-old owner of
an international corporation. Characteristically, this full-page ad spoke
directly to the reader: "My . . . Salon, like my many others throughout
the world, is for one purpose—to help you find the beauty you are seeking. Each floor of my establishment is dedicated to beauty and health.
Each floor has something for you personally. It may all seem strange for
a moment and beyond your reach, but trust me enough to visit me, to

meet me, to let me show you every nook and corner, to take you into my secrets, to make you understand—for then I am sure that you will believe in me, in what I want to do for you and in what I can do."[17] Her special knowledge promised a better life, where mundane cares gave way to beauty, worries to joy. Her message appealed not merely to women in the abstract but to "you," the unique reader of her carefully crafted prose.

Eventually, though, even Elizabeth Arden had to pay attention to the suffering around her. In early 1931, she donated $100 to the Red Cross fund to assist midwestern drought victims. Later that year she "contribute[d] 5% of her December sales to the local unemployment fund." From Connecticut to Oklahoma to California, Arden shops and salons participated. An industry leader, she added to the relief efforts in cities where her stores were situated, setting an example others followed. Oklahoma City's Kerr's Department Store gave another 1 percent on top of Arden's 5 percent to the Community Fund. In New York, where the jobless rate was higher than the national average, Arden employees raised a significant $2,207.20 for the Emergency Unemployment Relief Committee.[18]

Even this seemed small in the face of such suffering, so Elizabeth and Tom Lewis proposed a coordinated industry-based fund drive to assist the needy. They assembled their colleagues in November 1932 at the Waldorf-Astoria. Representatives from the press and twelve cosmetics and perfume companies attended, including Houbigant, Coty, Harriet Hubbard Ayer, Yardley, and Pond's. A Salvation Army representative drove home the dire situation of those hardest hit. Philanthropist Marjorie Merriweather Post, head of the women's division of the New York City fundraising committee for which the Lewises hoped to build the industrial coalition, also spoke.[19] Ameliorative efforts increased as the Depression continued, and the couple's leadership did not go unnoticed.

Ladies' Home Journal asked Arden to write for the magazine's campaign to get women shopping again. "It's up to the Women" was designed to "restore prosperity, through wise spending and the release of hoarded money." Arden joined First Lady Eleanor Roosevelt, peace activist Carrie Chapman Catt, Richard S. Meriam of the Harvard Business School, as well as leaders of prominent women's groups such as the General Federation of Women's Clubs, the National Council of Jewish Women, and the League of Women Voters. Each of them urged women to spend to spur the economy. Arden was typically positive: "This is the moment to buy. A wise woman should take advantage of the opportunity to replenish her home and her wardrobe at unhoped-for prices."[20] *Ladies' Home Journal* insisted that every woman had it in her "power to keep factories running, to keep labor employed, to keep money in circulation. To trample depression underfoot right now."[21] Arden believed that "beauty and optimism go hand in hand. There never has been a time," she encouraged, "when by making the most of themselves women could do so much to cheer the world, chase despondency [away] and help bring back prosperity. Wake up," she cried, "and help the world right itself."[22]

Two decades of successful corporate leadership and international name recognition made her comfortable moving beyond beauty in her guest column. She condemned injuriously high rents and insisted landlords lower them. She lectured her fellow business owners to hire one more worker than strictly necessary to decrease the unemployment rate. She traversed well-trod ground when she suggested self-care: eat more "fruit, vegetables and salads." Give parties, "particularly for those who cannot afford them themselves." Stay active because "the really busy person has no time for depression." Don't procrastinate and don't be a pessimist, she counseled, doling out Elisabeth Marbury–like advice. "Spend for others, as that is the true secret of inner joy." Buy new clothes and give away the old. "Make yourself and others attractive," she enjoined. "So give—spend—and above all, smile." A lovely appearance and a positive outlook would make a difference, she promised:

"Come on, women of America, let us smile. Let us work. Let us be cheerful—beautiful! Let us spend well and wisely."[23] Taking her own advice, Arden spent money on large ads in *Ladies' Home Journal* throughout the rest of 1932.[24]

Vogue next solicited Arden's opinion. How should women think about makeup in the deep Depression summer of 1932? Maintaining one's highest peak of beauty was paramount, Arden answered. A properly made-up face gave the wearer a less "drab" and more animated visage and was the difference, *Vogue* agreed, between a woman's husband remaining optimistic and landing a job or not. But how to afford it? Arden's solution was to keep purchasing high-quality products, but to use less of them.[25]

Optimism was her consistent public tone, but as head of Elizabeth Arden, she knew to prepare for the worst. Losing her company was unlikely. According to *Women's Wear Daily*, not long before the Depression began, Arden led the field in sales, and her profits held steady in the months following the stock market crash.[26] Nevertheless, caution propelled her to consolidate mortgages on a factory she owned at 208 East Fifty-Second Street and to pay off debts.[27] Since property was always a safe investment, she purchased three nearby buildings, one of which she renovated into "rooming houses for Arden representatives in from the road, giving them food and lodging at reasonable rates."[28] Arden outgrew and sold a Brooklyn factory.[29] In 1934, she rented out the two-story penthouse atop her Chicago salon.[30]

Arden's New York City real estate investments included a long-term lease, with purchase option, on a site at 219 East Fifty-First Street and a three-story building at 212 East Fifty-Second Street. The former she meant to turn into a garage, and the latter she planned to remodel.[31] By mid-decade, her enormous wholesale division had shifted to 681 Fifth Avenue, where it sprawled across three floors. From there, products shipped to some five thousand retail outlets across the United States. Factories and warehouses in Toronto, Mexico, London, Paris, and Berlin replenished stores in other parts of the world.[32] At such a time of economic uncertainty, Tom Lewis said, "everyone will have to work exceedingly hard in order to build up and increase his business—it is not going to be easy."[33]

While Elizabeth Arden was managing all right, the same could not be said for her retailers. When the Depression cut into their overall profits, some of them decided to create their own store-brand cosmetics and skin care and thus undercut products they already stocked. Neither Arden nor Lewis was happy about it, but they believed their customer loyalty was strong enough to withstand the challenge.

Other retailers tried to increase sales by discounting Arden's cosmetics. This contravened Arden's entire rationale. It threatened the integrity of her brand, based as it was on its image as a luxury item whose value derived in part from the perception created by high prices. To stop this "underselling," in 1930 Arden required her retail stores to sign consignment contracts. These mandated that merchandise shipped to the stores remained the property of Arden until the consumer purchased it. Furthermore, they stipulated that retail stores would supply a cabinet or display case devoted exclusively to Arden products and place it in a prominent position. They also had to insure Arden products against theft or damage. Most important for Arden was the clause stating that retailers must sell only at the price she set. Stores had to dispatch monthly sales and stock reports to Arden to help her determine future supplies. A final clause guaranteed that Arden would receive all unsold product and monies due should a store go out of business, an important provision—for her, not her retailers—at that volatile time.[34]

In this also she was an industry trailblazer. It took two years before other "leading drug and cosmetic manufacturers," as *The New York Times* reported, began "adopting a plan of selling goods on consignment." Just as Arden had done, "manufacturers appoint[ed] retailers their agencies and ship[ped] them goods on consignment," starting in 1932. Following her precedent, the manufacturer retained ownership of the merchandise.

The retailer earned a commission equal to the difference between the wholesale and retail prices, both of which the manufacturer set. "This form of distribution," the *Times* determined, "is expected to become more popular during the rest of [the] year."[35] Industry insiders saw the wisdom of Arden's plan. *The American Perfumer* noted approvingly that "Elizabeth Arden always maintained this policy" to strangle "predatory price cutters" and concluded that she, alone among her peers, had made the smart business choice.[36]

Wary of losing sales while the Depression ground on, Arden purposefully tried to expand her customer base. To cultivate younger clients, Arden, working with local stores, advertised in the newspapers of elite East Coast colleges and sent representatives to conduct makeup demonstrations on campuses.[37] Looking to strengthen ties to the solidly middle-class, Arden partnered with the New York State Federation of Women's Clubs at their Home Making Centre during National Sewing Week. They asked her to explain "Cosmetics for Types" to enhance lessons about pattern sewing for "types." In this case, "types" referred to white women with different hair, eyes, complexions, and physical shapes and sizes.[38] Arden never truly warmed to selling makeup by type as Max Factor and others were beginning to do.[39] More important was the connection to middle-class women. Enlarging on that, Arden sent Edyth Thornton McLeod on a lecture blitz to women's clubs.[40] At the Filene's Clothes Institute, she and other Arden representatives taught businesswomen and clubwomen how to achieve the Arden look.[41] In the Bay State, McLeod also gave a talk titled "The Place of Make-Up in Fashion" to salespeople enrolled in a Retail Trade Board–sponsored continuing education class about ready-to-wear clothing. Good grooming depended on "the proper choice of cosmetics," she said, repeating Arden's mantra that "it was better to use no make-up at all than to use a make-up that was obvious."[42]

In the depths of the Depression, Arden next conceived an innovation so important that expanding her customer base was the least of its benefits. It increased her profits, enlarged her workforce, kept her name at the forefront of the industry, and changed the beauty field forever. It even altered the fashion industry. It gave women a wonderful excuse to buy countless shades of foundation, lipstick, rouge, eye shadow, and eyeliner. Elizabeth Arden debuted her million-dollar idea in the winter of 1931, and she called it color harmony.[43]

SHE SAID SHE CAME UP with the strategy the very second she turned a "faded, dimmed" client "in a brilliant red mandarine coat" into a ravishing beauty by applying lipstick to match. "She literally came to life," Arden enthused. The color harmony system decreed that makeup must complement clothing.[44] Before her "color science of make-up," women had been told—by Arden and others—that their cosmetics should go well with their eye color or complexion (which never changed) or hair color (which seldom changed).[45] Or that they should switch to different makeup according to the time of day (morning and evening) and with the seasons (there were only four). But the lives of the sophisticates who purchased Arden cosmetics required many clothing changes per day. Even more than that, new shades of blues, reds, greens, yellows, browns, grays, and blacks abounded, going in and out of fashion as designers directed. Arden's color harmony plan required matching makeup to a limitless number of perpetually changing clothing colors. Extremely profitable, yes, but she also saw it as the way to help women wear anything they fancied and still look beautiful. "You don't expect to wear your green beads with every sports frock or carry your pink chiffon hankie with every evening gown," Arden asserted, stating the self-evident. "Why, then, expect one make-up to do justice to every costume? Without being artificial (horrid thought) it is perfectly possible to vary your make-up so that you look surprisingly well in colors you never dreamed of wearing before." Arden's "revelation," as she called it, would overcome a woman's "distrust" of new colors and make her into "a harmonious whole."[46] Color harmony opened the entire world of color to womankind. Besides, it was fun! "Learn the joy and interest of matching your face to your gowns. Ask Elizabeth Arden. . . . She knows."[47] Color harmony instantly became the talk of the fashion world.

Like most revolutionary ideas, Arden's was triggered by important events swirling around her. In the mid-1920s, two noteworthy fashion considerations emerged: the ensemble and a greater emphasis on color. Neither was a strikingly original concept, but the matching outfit suddenly became a hot trend. Thanks to fashion magazines, women everywhere sought to pair the precise shade of their navy shoes with navy stockings and the same navy hat trim. Ensembles could be created by the designer as well as assembled by the customer. In 1925, *The New York Times* pointed out that "Now much thought, taste and discrimination are given to hat, shoes, hosiery, scarf, gloves, neckwear, even to such minor detail as the necklace . . . there is no longer any hit-or-miss in the designing of a costume: it is a matter of harmony."[48] Arden saw the missing piece. Cosmetics, of course.

Color came into its own in the prosperous 1920s. World War I broke the monopoly of the German dye producers and interrupted the export of French color swatches. American chemists stepped into the breach, creating brighter and longer-lasting synthetic hues. Wartime nationalism assisted the process, as did a belief that Americans deserved a uniquely American palette. New professions—color stylists, color engineers, color forecasters—grew up around the planned use of color. They created the Textile Color Card Association to decide on and publicize colors, which eventually became standardized. Marketers and advertisers applied psychological and scientific research from the 1880s to mass-produced items. Attempting to sell more cars, ovens, dinnerware, and nearly every other consumer good, manufacturers employed color. Standardized colors made it much easier not only for accessory makers to match textiles but also for the nation to adopt the same red for all stop signs, for example. Unusual color combinations appeared, sometimes in homage to the ethnic diversity of the United States and sometimes as a sales gimmick. Certain hues were assigned emotional values and applied to create peaceful domestic havens and safer working environments. More and more color crept into magazines and advertisements. Fittingly, Arden's first full-color advert in *Vogue*, in May 1931, was for her color harmony system.[49]

In the fashion industry, the 1920s also saw an enormous increase in ready-to-wear fashions, which were much more affordable than the designer garments on which they were modeled. A greater array of clothing, in a broader range of shades, easily purchased off the rack at department stores, brought fashion within reach of more Americans. Many people could not tell whether an outfit cost $10 or $100. Well-constructed ready-made clothing confused people who were used to sorting new acquaintances into social strata based on their outfits. The great democratization of clothing was assisted by the "long color spree" that began that decade.[50]

Arden was perhaps not the first to suggest that makeup should match clothing, but she was the most successful.[51] And her industry colleagues gave her credit for inventing it. Color harmony also became associated with her because of her emphasis on understatement, her position at the top of the beauty world, and her marketing virtuosity. "It was Elizabeth Arden," journalist Marcia Vaughn swore, "who originated the color chart for changing clothes and showed women how they could wear even the most 'impossible' colors and be flattered thereby."[52]

Because it was Elizabeth Arden who said that cosmetics must match costume, women complied. She established herself as the only expert who could unlock what she admitted was a complex system. To achieve true color harmony required an appointment with an Arden specialist and the use of her newly created Arden color chart, a paper wheel that lined up one of eight dress colors with the perfectly matched makeup shades. One industry insider called it "darn clever and it helps sell a lot of make-up preparations."[53] This color wheel justified the customer's purchase of cosmetics in several new color lines. Arden quickly and shrewdly packaged makeup sets in endlessly matching shades and marketed them as color harmony boxes.[54]

Color harmony rules were indeed convoluted. When pairing white with another color, if the white was closest to the face, dark powder and rouge in a warm tone were appropriate. If one donned one of the "tricolors" of red, white, and blue, then a darker foundation, powder, and rouge "to contrast with the white of your costume" was necessary, as was wearing matching red lipstick and blue eye shadow with black mascara. Arden suggested that blue-eyed women wearing a predominantly blue, two-toned outfit should use blue mascara overlaid with black mascara on the eyelash tips. Blue clothing called for lighter foundation and rouge, a pink-tinted powder, and a brightly colored lipstick. Brunettes wearing black clothes should put "light brown Eye-Shado over the entire eyelid, green Eye-Shado over the iris of the eye, and black Cosmetique [mascara] on the lashes." Layering colors was essential to the process and assured even more makeup sales. The rules were precise and always shifting as every fashion season brought in new colors. None but Arden cosmeticians could unlock the mysteries of how to wear "anything and always look beautiful."[55] Women were encouraged to bring or wear their ensemble for perfect harmonizing at the Arden counter.[56]

Arden then went one better. She enlarged her idea to partner with celebrated clothing designers, "cooperating in blends and shades on gowns and makeups" with master couturier Worth, for instance. She maneuvered a tie-in with Rodier, an old French textile manufacturing house known for its intricate weaves, and through Rodier, French designer Jean Patou, who featured Rodier's newest fabrics.[57] Arden's ad campaign used an imaginary three-way conversation to convert the timid: "Rodier says: 'My new Green is a change from the eternal obvious shades.' Woman says: 'I wouldn't dare wear it. It would make me look ghastly.' Elizabeth Arden says: 'No flower ever looks ghastly set against that green. And if you have reddish hair you will look ravishing in it. Use Blush Rose Rouge and Mat Foncé Powder. Then with your lips touched with Chariot Lipstick, with a shadow of Vert Mousse around your eyes, and with Green . . . yes Green! . . . Mascara on your lashes, you will look like a human flower."[58] When fashion designer Elsa Schiaparelli dictated the color combination of "Armadillo" and "Tunis Gold," Arden gamely followed with the advice to wear both her "Chinese Amber" and "Cameo Ocré" powder simultaneously.[59] As long as "Woman" followed Arden's makeup instructions—and purchased her color harmony boxes—the latest dress colors would be hers.

Vogue was converted. "Facing the New Colours" trumpeted the beauty queen's vision: "With the help of the perfect make-up, a colour that you have secretly coveted all your life, but sternly denied yourself as unbecoming, can become yours forever." *Vogue* helpfully explained how it worked:

> In making up for yellow, the fundamental idea is to deny all yellow tones in the skin itself. Elizabeth Arden created the evening make-up to complement the gown in Patou-yellow. . . . The powder is lavender and gives a luminous finish to the skin, receding all yellow. The cheek rouge is light and rosy in cast, and the lipstick is vivid, minus any orange note, which would be fatal with yellow. The double use of eye shadow is a special Elizabeth Arden trick that is remarkably effective. A very light brown shadow is shaded over the entire lid and then, directly over the iris, is placed a soft point of second shadow, lavender in this instance, or it might be green shadow for brownish eyes or blue for blue eyes. The lavender powder is primarily for evening, but so important is it in counteracting the yellow of the skin that, when yellow is worn in the daytime, a faint dusting of the lavender powder can well be applied over regular daytime powder.[60]

Confusing the rules for different shades could be avoided, *Vogue* advocated, by consulting Arden's "army of young women in shops throughout the country who have been trained to bring complexions, cosmetics, and costumes into one harmonious whole."[61]

With her creation of color harmony, Arden inextricably linked herself and her cosmetics industry to fashion. No woman could henceforth wear an outfit without considering matching makeup. Since fashion was a legitimate business with centuries-old roots, her field grew in respectability when she decreed that clothing must have matching makeup. And no one questioned her.

Two additional changes developed from Arden's color harmony system: the necessary expansion of her makeup line and the beginning of creative names for her hues. Emerging fabric colors required novel cosmetics colors. With a flourish in 1931, Arden introduced six fresh lipstick shades in unique tubes as dramatic as their names: Carmenita, Viola, Chariot, Printemps, Victoire, and Coquette.[62] Roaring past the old light red, medium red, and dark red, color harmony gave her a way to sell every woman a dozen different colors of every makeup.

Color harmony did not eliminate all the old rules. Cosmetics had to match clothing while simultaneously harmonizing with personality. This hearkened back to her Babani perfume sales tactics. "Obviously," she pointed out, "the same rouge and powder, the same lipstick shade that were so fascinating with your dark winter clothes, will look lifeless when contrasted with the brilliant shades of spring clothes."[63] The idea was that one could "be gay, or demure. Be dashing, or subdued. Be sophisticated, or naïve." Arden "endow[ed]" women "with the power to change your personality to suit your mood—or your gown."[64] In a single ad, customers learned that Viola lipstick was to be worn with blue; Printemps was best for pastel shades for those with "pink and white complexions"; Carmenita was designed "for brunettes to wear with dark colors"; and Coquette was "for the woman who likes a definite make-up."[65] This further confused the purchase and wearing of cosmetics. Arden in essence told women that their makeup should harmonize not only with every different outfit but also with the time of day, the season, their skin, their eyes, their hair, *and* their mood. This solidified the not-so-subtle message that a woman needed both a vast array of makeup and Arden's unique wisdom about how to choose and wear it.

Arden had solutions for problems which, if she didn't create, she certainly complicated. But to find answers, she promised, women need look no further than their local cosmetics counter. Stores selling the Arden line happily profited from women's pardonable bewilderment and began including makeup suggestions from Arden. Jelleff's invited women to imitate their model: "She's wearing red, and her Elizabeth Arden Make-Up is part of her costume." Her $25 suit would go best with Rosetta rouge, Rachel foundation cream and face powder, and Victoire red lipstick—with a blue or a green eye shadow.[66]

For her part, Arden retrained her demonstrators. Free consultations continued, but for lengthy lessons, Arden began to charge. Two thirty-minute tutorials at Filene's cost $5, for example, not an insignificant sum. J. W. Robinson advertised a special on a "course of six treatments—the famous Elizabeth Arden methods and preparations—for $15.00."[67]

Capitalizing on both the buzz and the perplexity, Arden created a fashion show with a color harmony centerpiece. Edyth Thornton McLeod wrote and directed it, and it became a department store blockbuster nationwide. In New York, more than a thousand women battled a blizzard to claim six hundred seats.[68] Arden's "Fashion and Cosmetics Show" included an explanation of her color-matching vision, French beauty secrets, an exhibition of posture and exercises, and a demonstration of skin care and makeup application. The grand finale was "a Mannequin Fashion showing by the Lipstick Ensemble Girls!" to prove that "any woman can wear any color."[69]

Tailoring her shows to her audience, Denver's A. T. Lewis & Son Dry Goods Company sponsored an Arden event held in the mirrored "Casanova dining room of the Brown Palace Hotel." Instead of French designers, the department store showcased "three generations of women with apparel for the large women who typified the grandmother, smaller sizes for the young mother and kiddies' clothing worn by a tot of five years."[70] In Kansas City, mannequins paraded among the cars at a big automobile show.[71]

Arden was on a mission. Professional women, western women, DAR matrons, debutantes—she wanted them all to learn the Arden color harmony method. Worth and Patou were just as important as more prosaic industry partners such as the Atlas Underwear Corporation. Atlas was famous for men's BVDs, but had recently begun swimsuit production. At a marine-centered fashion show in a New York Bloomingdale's, McLeod presented proper Arden skin care for beach and poolside, whether one wanted to achieve or avoid a tan. McLeod also tutored women in color harmony makeup for BVD swimsuits made in Arden shades, such as "Exotic" blue.[72] Color harmony applied even to one's underwear. The DeGarcey Company manufactured lingerie in three matching "Powder Shades" that sold well at Lord & Taylor.[73] Chicago's Mandel Brothers crowed, "It's all a grand new idea in lingerie that fastidious women will love."[74]

Throughout the 1930s, women clamored to learn how to match everything from their silk slips to their feathered hats using Arden's color harmony theory. They knew it was confusing. "What has happened is that women have had to go over their cosmetic articles, discard shades of lipstick and rouge, and replace them with what might be called 'better supporting' colors," Antoinette Donnelly harrumphed.[75] That's why Arden's color harmony boxes sold so well. They took some of the guesswork out of her system. She initially sold eight, keyed to colors like "Chinese Rust, Navy Blue, Perfume Green, [and] Starlight Blue."[76] Those were only the first of hundreds of Arden color harmony boxes.

Despite its complexity, color harmony proved so popular that other beauty companies had no choice but to get on board. Dorothy Gray, Arden's former treatment girl turned cosmetics executive, and Hollywood-based Max Factor paid attention. Factor hired film star Bette Davis to advertise his products, and in 1933 she swore that his Rachelle Powder "color harmony tone is perfect for me."[77] Neither Factor nor Davis explained the term. They didn't need to. By then Arden's phrase was ubiquitous. Although she trademarked Ardena and the names of some products, she did not trademark color harmony. Rubinstein avoided the exact words but admitted that "autumn colors and costumes call for new notes in make-up."[78]

In 1935, Cutex's "perfect harmony" campaign mandated matching lips and nails. By 1940, "Revlon's advertising campaign carr[ied] the same message."[79] The enthusiasm for color coordinating eventually reached ridiculous heights. Imitation may be the best form of flattery, but Arden could not support a competitor's absurd idea of "dinner mints of different shades of red which, when consumed, color the tongue the exact shade of the lipstick."[80]

Extremes aside, color harmony had become the norm both in and beyond her industry. Elizabeth Arden profited because she did it first. Liberating women to wear any color, deploying her army of demonstrators to new and continuing customers, writing her own fashion shows, partnering with the highbrow and the middlebrow, and broadening her product range even further helped her thrive during the first years of the Great Depression. She capitalized on trends—the ensemble, the availability of new colors—but she applied them through color harmony in a way that aided women, even as she first complicated and then simplified their lives. Hers, meanwhile, grew more secure. In 1931, Elizabeth Arden's personal income was "in excess of $700,000 a year." Today, that would be 15 million earned dollars. Annually. Journalist John Sinclair claimed in the *Los Angeles Times* that Arden's visible success was proof that cosmetics had "entered the field of big business." She was, since Helena Rubinstein had sold her company in 1928, the "only woman in this field who owns her own business."[81]

And Arden defined luxury. Every luxury brand sought a partnership

with her. The most sumptuous car in America—the $16,500 1932 Due-
senberg Special—contained a gold-plated movie camera and a built-in,
top-of-the-line Arden vanity case.[82] Only Arden was good enough for
American heroes like Amelia Earhart, the world's foremost female aviator. Boston's gift to this global celebrity was an opulent, fully stocked
Elizabeth Arden travel case. Arden retailer E. T. Slattery displayed the
case for curious Bostonians—and for those few highfliers with the
means to purchase an identical one.[83]

Elizabeth Arden transformed American consumer culture first by
making cosmetics mandatory—if one wanted to be fashionable—through
an astute courtship of upper-class women. Color harmony, another revolutionary and endlessly lucrative idea, spread far beyond her own field
into fashion and design. Her creative genius still influences those industries today.

Eleven

More Beginnings, and Endings

lizabeth Arden had a decision to make. Should she sell her company for $25 million? With that sum she would join the minuscule club of American multimillionaires and be one of perhaps three women who had earned, rather than inherited, their fortunes. She could buy a Manhattan mansion, a yacht, fabulous jewels, artwork by the old masters, and entrée to an even higher stratum of society. Arden spent little time debating with herself. She was flattered, but the answer was no. She remained as passionate as ever about making women beautiful, and excited about what she could accomplish next. She was already mingling with establishment types and minor royalty and by that measure had broken into high society. She spent real money on personal extravagances that no one in Woodbridge, Ontario, could ever have imagined. For years, she had been telling her employees, whom she thought of as family, "Beauty is power."[1]

It was nearly impossible to separate Elizabeth Arden the woman from Elizabeth Arden the company. Her work defined her life. Though she hired managers and publicists, she still oversaw every aspect of the business, including personnel, product design and development, and marketing. No ad copy ever reached the public without her scrutiny. She felt at the top of her game. She remained so extraordinarily young looking that no one ever guessed she was in her fifties. *Fortune* reported that "she has the figure and carriage of a girl of twenty."[2] Opera singer turned gossip columnist Cobina Wright described Arden as "small," "vivacious," and "an exceptional companion." To spend time with her "seemed like heaven." Wright gave her friend her due, writing that Arden had "made history," and that "probably no single woman of our times has so intimately touched and influenced feminine lives both at home and abroad as this imaginative, clever Canadian girl."[3]

Work energized Arden. Her clients inspired her. She loved every special event, every visit to her nearly thirty salons around the world. One interviewer explained how Arden's "hands are continually in motion" when she talks, "curving in consciously graceful gestures, or fluttering toward her own diaphragm to emphasize some point . . . about breathing or posture." Her "genuine passion for improving women's looks" made her "impatient with any woman who is not as beautiful as she might be," and when Arden encountered such a woman, as hard as she tried to stay mum, she was "impelled in the end to bawl her out affectionately," giving her exercise tips or steering her to a chair to reapply her makeup more becomingly.[4]

Across the Atlantic, Teddy Haslam remained Arden's highly effective manager for the British Empire, except Canada. Her regular trips to England and his annual visit to the United States kept their friendship current. Haslam was a gem among her executives, for he maintained the very profitable line to Harrods, the crème de la crème of British department stores where he had entered the retail business. Harrods branches in South Africa, Australia, and South America all sold Arden toiletries. *Harrods News* showcased the line and printed tributes.[5] Recently a very important personage, Lady Nancy Astor, had become an Arden convert when a bruise required cosmetic assistance before an evening out. An Arden beautician arrived and worked her magic. Astor seldom wore makeup, but the episode changed her mind, and every grand occasion thereafter called for the same Arden makeup artist.[6] This priceless endorsement made Teddy Haslam very happy.

When Elizabeth Arden visited England in 1932, Harrods made her the centerpiece of its "unique Beauty & Fashion Exposition."[7] After expounding on color harmony, Arden joined Lady Irene Mountbatten, film star Adolphe Menjou, British clothing designer Edward Moly-neux, and British actress Gladys Cooper to judge a beauty contest for charity. London society women competed by sticking their arms, legs, and ankles through a gold curtain to be assessed by the adjudicators, who had no idea to whom the limb belonged.[8] It was a fun event to raise money for Londoners hurt by the global economic depression. While there, Arden inspected her Old Bond Street salon and greeted long-standing customers who called for weekly treatments and first-timers wishing to meet the face behind the name.

Once she was back in the States, other new products and their pro-motion occupied Arden. Chief among them was her Ardena Bath, in which the client relaxed under almost ten pounds of warm, melted par-affin wax. Customers raved about how their skin felt afterward. The promise of significant weight loss and overall better health made Ar-dena Bath a salon favorite for more than three decades.[9]

An on-staff physician first certified a client's fitness, because "the Arden salons have never had an accident," *The New Yorker* pointed out in 1935, "and don't want one."[10] Paraffin immersion had been used for centuries. Arden adapted the idea from a World War I burn treatment found helpful for arthritis.[11] The paraffin hardened as it cooled. When peeled off, it released impurities and hydrated the skin. Other salons copied Arden's lead until paraffin baths became commonplace in the 1930s. A course of ten treatments cost $75.[12] Despite the high price, its popularity required that she offer it at all her salons. To the uninitiated, it seemed very odd. Ogden Nash, one of America's best-loved humor-ists, poked gentle fun: "In New York beautiful girls can become more beautiful by going to Elizabeth Arden / And getting stuff put on their faces and waiting for it to harden."[13] Poets might laugh, but women appreciated the blissful peace of thirty minutes of enforced immobility, and stepping out with softer skin and fewer pounds (even if it was due to temporary water loss).

The Ardena Bath worked one other miracle. Rosamond Pinchot, a young friend of both Arden and Marbury, was a member of the well-known family of political progressives. In the early 1930s, Pinchot was an actress and an aspiring writer with an active social life. She used Arden's paraffin baths to make sure, as she confessed to her diary, that "all the champagne I'd drunk the night before oozed out."[14] She was definitely not the only woman to use the Ardena Bath as an expensive detox method.

Less passive weight loss occurred under the eagle eye of Doris Craven, an exercise expert and long-term Arden employee. Craven, who often traveled with Edyth Thornton McLeod, helped women lessen the "'dowager's hunch,' the sway back and such common ills as round shoulders and stiff joints."[15] Excellent posture resulted from good health and a special Arden exercise program. The right posture could replace a corset entirely, but without Craven's oversight, kyphosis or lordosis might result. Elizabeth Arden explained to a reporter that the "debutante slouch" (kyphosis) was just as bad as the "sway-back carriage" (lordosis) because both harmed the spine and kept women from engaging in a fully vigorous life. Curing lordosis entailed lying on one's back on the gymnasium floor, and walking the feet up the wall, until "you are standing on your shoulders."[16]

The goal was to carry oneself as a queen, and Arden was renowned for emphasizing posture. Headstands helped. Arden learned to do a headstand through her first encounters with yoga. In middle age, she could still "flip her own toes in the air with Grade A skill," according to a bemused interviewer who witnessed it. Arden believed anyone could learn after one lesson and three days of practice.[17] Several sophisticates

were known for standing on their heads. Eleanor Roosevelt once impressed a White House visitor with a demonstration of her "yoga exercises," including standing on her head, "straight as a column."[18] Lady
Elsie Mendl learned to stand on her head at age fifty. She, like Arden,
was determined not to "go gentle into that good night," and both women
fought against age with physical fitness, creams, spa treatments, and
everything else at their disposal.

Arden watched in dismay as Bessie's strength ebbed. Marbury intended to land Maine for Franklin Roosevelt, the 1932 presidential candidate on whom the hopes of so many rested. She invited the Roosevelts
to campaign at Lakeside Farm. Franklin's schedule precluded the visit,
but Eleanor arrived with two powerful women: Marguerite "Missy" Le-
Hand, FDR's secretary and close confidante, and Mary "Molly" Dewson,
head of the women's division of the Democratic Party. They stayed the
weekend, adding celebrity allure to the luncheon Marbury hosted yearly
for a hundred or so of Maine's party bigwigs.[19] *The Boston Globe* observed that Arden "frequently assisted Miss Marbury as hostess."[20]
Speechmaking, cajoling, glad-handing, and spreading a sense of shared
purpose, Marbury and Arden labored long. They believed—wrongly—
that they had successfully convinced fifty of their neighbors to cross
party lines and vote for Roosevelt in 1932.[21] Instead, Republicans held
the state that November, one of only six to cling to Herbert Hoover.
The other forty-two joined the Roosevelt landslide.

Alas, Bessie did not live to see FDR inaugurated. Rosamond Pinchot
wept to her diary on January 22, the day Marbury died, "She was so
alive, full of enthusiasm and humor. . . . She was over 75 and must have
weighed 200 pounds anyway. Her face wasn't a bit good looking. It was
big and fat like the rest of her. Her eyes were tiny almost hidden and yet
when she spoke—or looked at you—you felt her great force, her intelligence, her life."[22]

Twenty thousand New Yorkers silently watched the twenty-limousine
cortege make its way to St. Patrick's Cathedral for the requiem mass.

Anne Morgan, Anne Vanderbilt, Eleanor Roosevelt, Rosamond Pinchot, and Fannie Hurst joined Arden in mourning. Democratic Party activist Emily Newell Blair noted that Marbury "knew everybody on two continents who was worth knowing," and most of them appeared for her funeral.[23]

Elizabeth Arden could not hide her heartache. She broke down in front of the open coffin at a private Sutton Place service for Marbury's closest friends. Arden said a final goodbye as she placed a rose on the casket just as it was lowered into the ground at Woodlawn Cemetery.[24] She took what comfort she could from the diamond name bracelet Bessie left her that spelled out *Elisabeth*.

Elsie de Wolf Mendl hastily departed Europe for America, arriving too late for the funeral but in time for the reading of the will. In recognition of their decades together, Marbury left her the bulk of her estate, including Lakeside Farm. Marbury hoped her friends would turn it into a vacation site for the American Woman's Association (AWA), an organization Morgan and Vanderbilt had created in 1913 for working-women. The AWA members hoped to improve the lives of laborers, taking them out of the insalubrious cities for a healthy, rural vacation.[25] Mendl, less a social activist than Marbury, found her former partner's idea impractical. Her preference was to sell Lakeside and pocket the money, but she consented to discuss terms with the AWA. Gathering at Arden's penthouse in June were Mendl, both Annes, Eleanor Roosevelt, and other members of the AWA board. They elected Cobina Wright as chair of a new committee to raise the $50,000 required to purchase and remodel the property and to create an endowment to continue Marbury's vision.[26] United in purpose, Arden, Roosevelt, Pinchot, Morgan, and Vanderbilt, with a less than fully committed Mendl, made the first donations.[27]

Impatient to rid herself of her old life, Mendl could barely wait for the fundraising campaign to bear fruit. She had already sold 13 Sutton Place; off-loading Lakeside Farm would sever her last connection with

Marbury. Elizabeth Arden interceded. She was more than happy to push out the woman whose marriage of convenience broke the heart of her friend—so she bought Lakeside Farm herself. Better for Arden, who loved Marbury, to hold the property while friends raised the money. It eliminated the threat of Mendl capriciously disposing of it.[28]

Further, Arden was already Lakeside's neighbor, and she found herself spending more and more time there. When *Vogue* asked society leaders in 1933 where they went to escape modern life, Arden rhapsodized about Maine.[29] She nostalgically landscaped Lakeside Farm with the same flowers Marbury had always planted, and continued to host gatherings for Hollywood friends and Democrats, some of whom she talked into donating to and even fundraising for what was morphing in the committee members' minds into a Marbury memorial.[30]

Marbury's death marked a new phase in Elizabeth Arden's life. Bessie had taught her a great deal and brought her into a group of strong, independent, activist women, including other successful businesswomen. Arden paid close attention to how they operated in the world—what they tolerated and what they did not, what they discussed, where they placed their energies, how they supported one another, and how they dealt with betrayal from friends and partners. She was a confident decision-maker with vast business experience. Her "passionate impatience with imperfection" was the stuff of legend, fueled by stories of her destroying thousands of dollars' worth of product because the shade of pink was not quite perfect.[31] She had captained another decade of phenomenal global growth in her company. She had made some excellent hires and learned bitter lessons from less well-thought-out personnel choices. In so doing, she had transformed the faces of American women. And she had built her beauty empire without benefit of high school, beauty school, or business college.

By this time in her life, at age fifty-one, having run her company for twenty-three years, Arden had also become set in her ways. Thanks to grueling work, long hours, unwavering focus, and a deep ambition rooted in the rocky soil of childhood poverty, Arden was a success by any measure. Grit and vision—her *own* vision—carried her to the top of her profession. Naysayers—largely male—abounded. Archibald MacLeish, the modernist poet and social commentator, wrote waspishly and with more than a little misogyny: "Elizabeth Arden is not a potential Henry Ford. She is Elizabeth Arden. It is a career in itself but it is not a career in industry."[32] Challenges from those who thought they knew better than she did, including and especially those whom she hired, wearied her.

Like all gifted leaders, Arden filled her corporate offices with the most talented people she could find using what *Time* magazine called "a native shrewdness at hiring smart people to work for her." Intuition often guided her, but it was not flawless, nor was she an angel. Her competitors claimed her business had a reputation for a "revolving door" as employees found themselves fired by a boss impatient with whatever they lacked—facility with salon treatments, commitment to the company, a sunny outlook—or angered at any sign of condescension toward her.[33] Sensational hires and fires made better newspaper copy than the women and men who stayed with her for decades—and there were many of those.[34] Arden's outlook echoed that of designer Elsa Schiaparelli, who, "Having once been poor herself . . . patiently pays her people more than she has to, and impatiently expects them to think as fast as she does."[35] Eventually intuition tempered by experience proved Arden's best personnel guide. Her corporate hires increasingly had Ivy League degrees or business-college diplomas. They had all been taught similar approaches to industry. Suggesting without sufficient tact that the founder was wrong in the manner she proceeded was not a recommended strategy for longevity at Elizabeth Arden. Not even Tom Lewis was safe doing that.

Challenging Arden could elicit an irate response. "Grudging acceptance" was high praise. She had a terrible memory for names, which offended employees. Frequently, her temper had a hair trigger, worsened by what Henry Sell thought was Arden's "slightly suspicious nature." This could cause apprehension in those who had to approach her. One Blaker account executive regularly took a sedative to calm her nerves before seeking Arden's approval of their advertising copy.[36] Adolph de Meyer found Arden to be changeable and arbitrary. "Her mind is active," he told Sell after a frustrating exchange, "and she rarely remembers, the week after, whatever it was she meant to say." He charged her with being irrational after she rejected photographs she had earlier accepted.[37] A 1930 *Fortune* magazine article called her "extremely domineering and erratic . . . often brusque, often tactless."[38]

She admitted her responsibility. She realized she occasionally forgot or double-booked herself, upsetting schedules. "I know I hurt people's feelings when they don't use their brains," she said, in a half apology. "One attitude I cannot abide is that 'the world owes me a living.' What nonsense. You have to work to become something and if you are not trained but eager to learn, that is all I ask."[39]

Janet Leckie, who worked for Sell, recognized that Arden treated "all those who served her" with respect, including her household staff, "store clerks, elevator boys . . . chauffeurs, doormen." Leckie acknowledged that Arden was "warm, gracious, thoughtful . . . with sudden bursts of generosity that could be overwhelming." She described the cosmetics magnate as a "brilliant marketing genius, a business wizard. Shrewd, determined, hard-driving, exacting, she had the faculty of charming back-breaking work out of her subordinates. . . . An early riser, she was willing to put in long, hard days in an austere, small office and expected as much from others."[40]

There were two women inside Arden, Leckie believed: the hard-driving business leader Florence Graham and the beautiful Elizabeth Arden, who felt she deserved to be "loved, admired, and cradled in luxury." Other people noticed this duality. Rosamond Pinchot charged that Arden "sees herself as a little 'itsy bitsy girly' half the time and a sort of female Napoleon the rest."[41] But there was only one Elizabeth

Arden. She may have climbed up from rural penury to a Fifth Avenue penthouse, but she did it herself and she made her own rules. She learned as she grew, and she decided early on not to prostrate herself at the feet of businessmen. She clothed herself with a femininity meant to disarm critics of her career and her wealth. "Kittenish," one friend called her.[42] Her voice was breathy, but her spine was steel. No male mentor stepped forward, nor did Arden seek one. If her ways seemed impulsive to men, it might simply have been that she lacked the business-school training that taught them the rules and the lingo. She may have used anger to respond to a lifetime of being dismissed or underestimated— by men and women in the beauty industry, as well as by reporters. Her "suspicious" nature may have accounted for her small circle of friends, or that could have been a result of a type A personality. Who could possibly care about the Elizabeth Arden company as much as she did? No one. Thus everyone fell short. Even Tom. Especially Tom.

The couple had been drifting apart for several years. Increasingly public rumors of his infidelity grew more frequent and believable. The trips with the beautiful demonstrators seem to have resulted in a certain slippage in his marriage vows, despite the frequent presence of his brother-in-law Bill Graham and Henry Sell. Being cheated on with younger women is never more humiliating than when one is the nation's expert on beauty and aging well.

But that was not what did it. In early 1933, Tom tried to wrest control of the company from her. He ordered "all the salespeople, buyers, and salons" to "direct all correspondence dealing with the firm to him at another address." That was the final straw. His attempt to take her place as CEO instantly backfired. Arden learned about his machinations and countermanded Tom's directive less than twenty-four hours later. Before another day ended, she had moved all his belongings out of their home.[43]

The separation surprised few. A working wife was bad enough, but to be her husband's boss? People could only shake their heads and shrug.

Anyway, as *Fortune* intimated, "she received little assistance" from him "when she was first launching the venture."[44] Arden had few complaints with the way Lewis ran the wholesale division. He had achieved modest recognition when the American Manufacturers of Toilet Articles chose him to chair its membership committee.[45] But when Lewis proffered his opinion and refused to back down when they differed, it rankled. He had advised her to accept the earlier purchase offer. She wouldn't hear of it. And she was right; he was wrong.[46] Lewis dismissed her famous color harmony idea as impractical. He could see neither the revolutionary freedom for women now able to wear any color nor the limitless sales potential.[47] At one point, she allegedly leveled her finger at her husband, reminding him crisply, "This is my business. You don't own a share. Nobody does except me."[48] She confirmed both her commitment to her business and her sense of betrayal when she confessed to an industry magazine: "My pride in the business, my idealism, caused the trouble between us. . . . I found I was out on a limb, so I had to cut the limb off, do you see?"[49]

Their lives had been moving in different directions for some time, held together only by the business. While Lewis had enjoyed the diversions of the demonstrators and the vivacity of attractive actresses, she had been spending time with Elisabeth Marbury in a circle of strong, independent women. They schooled Arden about how to live on her own terms, which for her meant concentrating on her corporation. She learned to live with her husband's adultery, but she would not ignore his takeover attempt.

So she sent Tom Lewis packing, first from her life, and then from her company. On January 29, 1934, *Women's Wear Daily* announced, "T. J. Lewis, for the past several years general manager of the wholesale division of Elizabeth Arden, has resigned."[50] *The Drug and Cosmetic Industry* added that Arden remained "president and owner, in complete charge of all divisions of the business."[51] With two friends, Lewis went off to establish Henrotin, Moss & Lewis Inc., an international bond sales firm.[52] In October 1934, a Maine superior court granted the un-contested divorce.[53]

Elizabeth Arden no longer had a husband with whom to talk busi-ness or accompany her on European inspection tours. Even though she and Tom Lewis had been collaborating less of late, she was equal parts furious and unhappy. Arden loved the beauty business, the adrenaline rush of profit, the creative joy of innovation, and the excitement of meet-ing interesting people on the world stage. The death of her dear friend Elisabeth was sad and unsettling. It was also the impetus she needed to throw off the social protection of a husband who cheated on, undercut, and second-guessed her. Such was the extent of her business success that the failure of her marriage seemed less to shake than to inspire her. Confident—even imperious—Arden retained the helm.

Twelve

Maine Chances

W ithout Tom, Elizabeth Arden poured her energies into two new, sweetly sentimental endeavors. The first, Maine Chance Spa, maintained her tie to Bessie. The second, Maine Chance Farm, reconnected her to her childhood. Being Arden undertakings, both had the potential for profit. She merged her property with Marbury's in New England to create the world's first luxury destination health spa. She loved the feminine domain she crafted at Maine Chance Spa, the camaraderie of the women who returned again and again, and the visible difference the Arden experience made in their lives. She built a second empire in Kentucky, carving out fame and fortune in the high-stakes world of thoroughbred racing. She found her Maine Chance Farm horses every bit as absorbing and comforting as those she remembered from her youth. Constructing two more successful ventures invigorated her. Maine Chance Spa birthed an entirely new industry, and Maine Chance Farm transformed her life.

IN JULY 1933, when Arden purchased Marbury's home in Mount Vernon, Maine, from Elsie de Wolfe Mendl, she hoped to expedite fundraising for the workingwomen's vacation site Marbury stipulated. There turned out to be scant enthusiasm on the part of Marbury's circle for that and the idea quietly vanished, as did a plan to turn the home into "a shrine for the Democratic party" or for Bessie.[1] Ultimately, Arden bought out the group's investment and took over the running of Bessie's house. She continued the Democratic Party soirees, remained close to political friends she had made through Bessie, and stayed intermittently active, backing Joseph V. McKee (who lost the New York mayoral race to Fiorello La Guardia), celebrating Maine governor Louis J. Brann, and hosting a picnic for FDR supporters.[2] Then Arden had a brilliant new idea. A bold and utterly unique idea. She would build one vast, gorgeous lavish spa to expand on her theories of holistic well-being.

Spas were not new. Ancient Greeks and Romans soaked away aches and pains in thermal waters, and spa-going for improved health was a craze across Europe and America in the nineteenth century.[3] But there was no hot spring at Maine Chance and her spa could never promise to cure gout or neurasthenia. Instead, Arden would promote her bedrock belief that "beauty comes from within." She would put every facet of her proven regimes into practice with women who would pay handsomely. She would turn rural Maine into a global destination for outer and inner beauty.

Within months, she had created what she termed "America's first, de luxe summer beauty-and-health establishment."[4] *Vogue* styled it "a woman's paradise." "You remember, in day-dreams," the lucky journalist sighed, "when everything you love most in life manages in some miraculous and incredible fashion to be all in one place at the same time? Well, that's the way it is at Elizabeth Arden's in Maine." For clients with disposable income despite the Depression, Arden offered bridge, tennis, horseback riding, swimming, and every Arden treatment. She provided a masseuse, a hair salon, well-appointed rooms stocked with Arden preparations, "perfect servants, and the most superb bed you ever slept on, and more—all wrapped round with a sense of being a favourite guest at a luxurious, flawlessly run country place." The long article was a tribute to Maine Chance Spa and Arden's commitment to quality. The only blemish was the nonalcoholic vegetable cocktails, which could never replace a good dry martini. On the other hand, they did have many fewer calories.[5]

A sprawling, two-story building stood at the center of Maine Chance Spa. Cheerful red-and-white-striped awnings flanked the front entrance. Beautifully manicured grounds, banks of flowers, and sweeping vistas out toward Long Lake drew up to forty women who came from across the country for stays lasting between a week and a month. The all-inclusive price was eye-wateringly high. Most guests were wives of successful men; others were famous in their own right. Judy Garland, Myrna Loy, Rosalind Russell, and Ava Gardner were among those who sought pampering at Arden's secluded spa. Tourists tried to get a peek at the movie stars, but staff protected guest privacy at all costs.[6]

The spa opened in mid-June and closed at the end of August. Eventually, Arden had the inspired idea of inviting students from New England women's colleges for the first two weeks, while the weather was uncertain, at a reduced rate. This allowed staff members to learn their duties faultlessly before the wealthier guests arrived; the practice also cultivated a younger generation of spa-goers.[7] By the time the students left, the large gardens had begun producing flowers for guest and dining rooms, and fresh vegetables and fruits for the table. The gourmet meals had been meticulously planned. Each worker felt comfortable in the job. Every detail had been perfected.[8]

Maine Chance catered to those who needed rest and those who wanted to be active. For the former there were facials, Ardena baths, manicures, pedicures, and enforced inactivity in the steam cabinet. Introducing novel treatments made clients want to return. In 1936, for example, Arden caught their attention with her early version of the Jacuzzi. The new Arden Foam Bath created a thick bank of bubbles that rose up to cover the tub thanks to the oxygen she pumped into the soap-filled water. It was like lying under a frothy, aerated blanket.

Such sybaritic occupations alternated with yoga, tennis, bowling, walking, boating, fishing, and horseback riding. No one went swimming or aquaplaning until her face was first evaluated to see which lotion was required. There were adepts galore to help improve nearly every aspect of a life: a "biochemist" for the perfect diet, doctors, a dentist, nurses, physiotherapists, a tennis pro, a golf pro, a swimming instructor, a tango teacher, an "Irish riding-master," a gourmet chef, plus an army of salon professionals. At various times, Arden offered classes in Hula-Hoop, gardening, archery, "vitamin cooking," and ballroom dancing.[9] Whenever possible, Arden hired experts of their craft as instructors. She lured Italy's best fencer, Olympic gold medalist Aldo Nadi, to teach for her in Maine and New York as he tried to establish himself in the United States.[10]

Nadi was haughty, arrogant, supremely conceited—and bored. "Where," he asked himself melodramatically looking around at all the women, "had I fallen to?" At her New York salon, he gave exhibitions and created the Elizabeth Arden Fencing Club. At rustic Maine Chance, "the boredom," he recorded, "did not lessen." He admitted to appreciating only the exquisite actress Lillian Gish, "who, as an artist, fell in love with fencing at first sight," and became good at it. What the other "pretentious" women under his tutelage thought of him is unclear.[11] Nevertheless, Arden's promotion of fencing by tapping such an internationally famous athlete helped kick off a nationwide fencing fad.[12]

At Maine Chance Spa, most women planned to lose a few pounds, but some simply sought peace and quiet. Playwright and novelist Edna Ferber, a rare "gainer" in the staff's parlance because she hoped to increase her weight, came "just to focus on one thing," according to Dan Hillard, a three-summer employee: "Getting that script down."[13] There were always rumors that some women came to "dry out" and ease their dependency on alcohol. That was no secret to those who worked there.[14]

The spa was a significant boon to the state. Locals found employment as cooks, chauffeurs, dining room servers, lifeguards, maids, gardeners, and animal tenders. Some lodged on-site while others lived at home. They did not do the jobs requiring beauty expertise, such as massage, hairdressing, or skin therapy.[15] For those positions, Arden brought Red Door specialists, like exercise manager Ann Delafield, north for the duration. Though the hours were long and the work seasonal, Arden paid excellent wages; some employees also received generous tips. As she bought up more and more land, the luxury spa became a major regional economic driver.[16] It "brought the world to Maine" with Swedish masseuses, French and Danish chefs, Italian hairdressers, and English managers. Such international experience among her experts was always a point of pride for Arden.

More than any other beauty specialist, Arden emphasized the connection between healthy living and external beauty. Hence the thought given to every minute and every calorie. Mornings began at 7:00 a.m. with breakfast in bed. It was very little food, but it was served on the finest china. On the tray next to the fresh flower lay a card detailing the day's activities in hourly increments. The extent of the exercises, some passive but mostly active, reflected the judgment of the physician who checked in every new guest. Homemade melba toast and vegetable juice was the midmorning dockside snack. Pampering might include facials, pedicures, the Ardena paraffin bath, and any other of a number of beauty and relaxation treatments. Lunch and dinner were communal for the dieters, who were encouraged to pick what they liked from the gardens for the European chef to transform for their meals. "Gainers" usually ate in their rooms, so as not to cause jealous cries around the table. Menus changed frequently, but they always featured the chickens, pigs, and beef and milk cows Arden owned. What she did not grow, she sourced locally.[17] After activities but before the "cocktail" hour came facials, manicures, and hairstyling. Guests dressed formally for dinner, glad to shuck their regulation one-piece, cotton exercise outfits that flattered no one. After the meal, they sipped tea from cups that staff aesthetically matched to their gowns. Before turning in early for their beauty sleep, women could play bridge or board games, and read or chat while listening to the loons on Long Lake.[18]

Like the snake in the garden, temptation sometimes appeared. Journalist Hedda Hopper loved to tell the story of how once, in the early years of the spa when there was still some overlap with Arden's political gatherings, she was a guest at a Democratic Party "whoop-de-do" at Maine Chance. The outdoor lunch was accompanied by plenty of spiritous libations for the politicians and a table groaning with baked hams, roasted turkeys, and platters of pastries prepared the night before by a large staff. Just settling in, drink in hand, Hopper was startled to hear herself hailed from an upstairs window. Film superstars Constance and Norma Talmadge, and their friend Constance Carver, beckoned conspiratorially. All three women had been at the spa for over a week, existing on "birdseed . . . greens, and non-fattening juices." The enticing smells from below, they confided to Hopper, had made them go "berserk." As soon as night had fallen, they crept unseen down to the kitchen, pilfered an entire turkey, and dashed back up to their rooms. In short order, they gobbled the entire bird. Their elation dampened a bit when they realized they'd have to dispose of the evidence. But how? They determined to bury it. Giggling, they snuck out with the turkey carcass and dug a hole across the road, with the moon as their only witness. The three miscreants confessed that their full stomachs quieted their guilt, and they slept like babies that night![19]

Maine Chance predated by decades today's destination spa. Arden's customer-first policy governed all aspects of life there. An impeccably trained staff saw to guests' needs and whims, as long as they did not conflict with their personalized, holistic training, rest, and diet regime. She brought together classic-but-comfortable interiors with magazine-cover landscaping for an escape guaranteed to refresh body and soul. Maine Chance Spa made Arden the unrivaled queen of luxury while simultaneously demonstrating that she was, as *The New York Times* ultimately admitted, "a woman of uncommon business talents."[20]

WHILE ELIZABETH ARDEN was busily opening her spa, "Elizabeth N. Graham" was renewing her childhood affection for horses. Cautiously at first, then, as she did with everything, all in. Thoroughbred racing was the avocation that rounded out her life. Elizabeth N. Graham, as she was usually known in racing circles, was neither the first nor the only woman to reach the winner's circle, but she is still remembered as among the most unusual. For Arden, horse racing was a monetized hobby—she was a capitalist through and through—but her horses were her babies, and her insistence on treating them well, including nursing them with her Arden skin care products, became the stuff of legend.[21]

This rediscovered love began as a lark. Sometime in late 1931 or early 1932, just as Lewis's repeated infidelities were becoming clear to her, Arden purchased the first of what would be, over the course of the rest of her life, hundreds of horses.[22] She may have been encouraged by acquaintance Sam Riddle, owner of the legendary Man o' War, or by any number of her wealthy contacts who raced thoroughbreds.[23] As "Mrs. T. J. Lewis," which, indeed, she still was then, she began to appear uncharacteristically in the sports pages. One of her two-year-olds, How High, racked up victories at New York's Belmont and Aqueduct racecourses.[24] A year later, How High was winning at Saratoga.[25] Alongside How High, Arden ran horses she quixotically named after friends. R. Pinchot, for example, took first place at the Jamaica Race Course in Queens.[26] Teddy Haslam didn't bring home the victories like R. Pinchot did, but his namesake enjoyed outings at the racetrack with his boss while in the States.[27]

A whole new world opened as she learned from equine experts such as Sam Riddle and Leslie Combs II, and studied rich owners and breeders whose pedigrees were as unimpeachable as their horses'. While anyone with enough money could buy and race horses, Arden found the old aristocracy did not initially warm to her. But unlike blue-blooded society, the thoroughbred world did admit industrialists.[28] Money talked in horse racing, even Arden's. Whitneys, Wideners, and Vanderbilts were box holders at Belmont, and eventually, so was Arden. By 1935, she was an associate member of the Santa Anita Turf Club, inducted in a year that included Liz and John Hay "Jock" Whitney, who, in addition to their thoroughbreds, owned a fabulous art collection; William J. Ziegler Jr., the heir to the Royal Baking Powder fortune; and Alfred Gwynne Vanderbilt Jr., thoroughbred breeder, racer, and racing promoter.[29]

The "sport of kings" included many notable queens. When Arden entered their ranks in the early 1930s, she was one of several women owners, but the only one who had made her money herself. There were few to no female trainers, groomers, or jockeys on the professional racing circuit. Mary Hirsch, daughter of trainer Max Hirsch, was the first woman to earn a trainer's license, in 1934, but in her short career she never worked for a major stable. She did, however, recognize that "you've not only got to be as good as a man—you've got to be better than a man."[30] The first female jockey, Diane Crump, wasn't even born until 1948. With her first thoroughbred purchases, Arden joined redoubtable female owners such as Helen Hay Whitney (Jock's mother), Lucille Wright Markey of Calumet Farm, and Ethel V. Mars of Milky Way Farm.[31]

Their presence did not mean perfect equality. Horse racing clubs discriminated. Gendered definitions of "women's work" consigned women to hostesses at trackside gatherings while men made the racing rules. Diane Crump's first pari-mutuel ride occurred in 1969. Women were not admitted to the Jockey Club until the 1980s. In that decade, *The New York Times* explained how "the cowboy mentality that dominates racetrack stable areas had until the last decade virtually excluded women from riding, training or even sweeping up, but women have not been barred from paying the bills if they wanted to undertake the risk of buying and racing a horse."[32] "It was a man's world—and it still is today,"

Kim Ryan, a former thoroughbred owner, breeder, trainer, and racer, seconded. In her experience, "female trainers and jockeys still have a terribly hard time of it" in the twenty-first century. Masculine track culture is ancient, omnipresent, and even if diminishing, Ryan believes, certainly enduring.[33] As a woman and an outsider, Arden moved with caution until time, seriousness of purpose, victories, and well-spent wealth eventually brought her into sportswriter Bert Sugar's "Millionaire Club" of racing farms. Even today, "admission" does not guarantee "acceptance" among the old guard. Arden worked hard and ultimately won both.[34]

She also faced a unique handicap connected to her business. Horse racing went hand in glove with gambling and other examples of what many people then considered gross immorality. Women led national efforts to eradicate racing. These were some of the same women who purchased, or might purchase, Arden cosmetics. This is why she did not race under the name Elizabeth Arden and knew that, if discovered and "the protests become too numerous[,] I'll have to withdraw from racing."[35] Women worked together with legislators like the Texas representative who railed against racetracks because he believed their very presence attracted a plague of "wild women" and corrupted youth. "I have seen the saloons, the brothels, 'Hell's Half Acre' in Fort Worth, the gambling joints, gambling on the race tracks," he frothed.[36] Women's clubs and PTAs across America lobbied to keep such wickedness out of their states, and to eliminate betting where racing occurred.[37] Arden, who was not herself a gambler, felt she had to erect a division between her worlds. Her stable began as "Mr. Nightingale" or "Nightingale Farms," and she asked to be known trackside as Elizabeth N. Graham.[38] Eventually, and long before she moved her horses out of rented stables and onto her own land in Kentucky's bluegrass region, she settled on Maine Chance Farm as the name for her racing empire.

The racing world today remembers Arden as a "lovable eccentric" for her great devotion to her horses.[39] "I always think of my fillies," she

said, "as very smart young ladies."[40] According to her friend Marylou
Whitney, Arden proudly "carried pictures of them in her billfold" because her horses "were like her children."[41] "She really loved animals,"
trainer George Poole seconded. "That was no put-on. She had a tremendous soft spot in her heart for animals."[42] All the rest—the teasing
and the calumny—grew from that fact. She sought trainers, grooms,
and jockeys who took seriously her dictum to treat her horses well. She
never condoned the use of whips on her horses, for example. She didn't
want anyone shouting at them. Arden's penchant for quick dismissals in
the salon carried over to the track. She is renowned for the great numbers of head trainers she hired and fired; sixty, by most estimates. Some
men were with her for less than a week and, when fired, had nothing
good to say about her. She told a reporter that it was not just rough
treatment of her horses that caused her to discharge trainers. "They go
by obsolete and unemotional rules. I know as much as any, and more
than most, about horses. They won't show or feel affection for a thoroughbred, and that's why most of them are dreadful trainers." The men
were happy to take the high salaries she paid. While "extremely difficult to please," the *Daily Racing Form* suggested, she "was also very generous to the horsemen she discarded like used cold-cream bottles: as a
result, there was always another one ready to step up to the firing line."[43]
Those who passed muster were highly complimentary.

It was odd enough to force winning trainers and jockeys to forgo the
whip, but Arden's reputation for unconventionality was even more fixed
in her belief that her horses should be treated like the "sensitive, proud
and spirited creatures" she insisted they were.[44] She required that her
stables be painted pink whenever possible, screened to keep out annoy-
ing flies, filled with soothing music, and scented with Arden perfumes.
Her horse blankets were made of cashmere. The horses' diets included
clover specially grown on the grounds of Maine Chance Spa and one
cup of olive oil a day to encourage shiny coats. And—this is what really
set all short-lived trainers to guffawing—her special, medicinal Ardena

Eight Hour Cream had to be used to massage the legs of tired horses and for cuts or bruises. She also used her "removing cream" to treat their hooves and ankle joints, and a special unguent for their bloodshot eyes. "Horses are just as sensitive as people," she reasoned. She made sure her stables were stocked with her products, especially Eight Hour Cream. She swore by it. As did some, but not most, of her trainers, all of whom she personally taught how to massage her horses' muscles. And when they wouldn't, she sent the physical therapists from her salons to do it.[45] Sometimes in exasperation, sometimes with affection, her trainers called her "Mrs. Mudpack," or "Lady Lipstick." Yet more than one journalist had to point out that, given her record, she was surely doing something right. "The success of her stable attests to the wisdom of her precepts," as one put it.[46] Whether her horses were happier with baskets of pink flowers hanging on the barn doors or not, such "eccentricity" had the further benefit of advertising Elizabeth Arden and her wealth to all who strolled by her stables.

Arden worked as hard on her horses as she did her business. She was not a detached owner. She watched their training every possible day, rubbed their sore muscles with her own expert hands, and conferred regularly with her staff. Famous thoroughbred breeder Leslie Combs II, who worked with her for decades, recalled Arden's ambition "to win and keep on winning." Marylou Whitney marveled at Arden's "incredible amount of drive." She thought it originated in Arden's childhood, when she "had to fight very hard and [had] been hungry." Whitney characterized Arden as "the most practical woman in the world when it came to her cosmetics business—[but] when it came to horses, she was a sentimentalist all the way through." Nearly everyone agreed with Whitney, but no one could deny how Arden loved her horses, and the much remarked upon cosseting was the result.[47]

In her first two years of racing, she had a solid fourteen victories to her credit. Her horses raced on the East Coast, in the South, and in California. By 1934, one of her horses was labeled a Kentucky Derby prospect.[48] In 1935, Arden established a stable at Santa Anita, under general manager Charles H. Strub and trainer "Pinky" Grimes. Twenty of her thoroughbreds, including one she named Maine Chance, would be trying their luck on the West Coast circuit that year wearing her red, white, and blue racing silks (it would not be long until she changed the red to a deep Arden Pink).[49]

IN THE 1930s, Arden relaxed into her wealth and moved beyond Elisabeth Marbury's warning to begin only with one "motor-car." To her Rolls-Royce and her 1934 Duesenberg, she added a gold 1935 Cadillac Town Cabriolet with backseat floor coverings of white fur, to sink her bare toes in while her chauffeur drove and she worked.[50] She redecorated her Fifth Avenue penthouse in silvery grays that even Rosamond Pinchot approved of, calling it "vast and lovely . . . such luxury—cool and modern."[51] A long glass solarium wall afforded a perfect Central Park panorama, while indoors, Nicolai Remisoff's enormous, painted double-sided plumes reappeared throughout, like a theme. He decorated the bar with stylized Napoleonic era soldiers in all their martial glory. Pinchot described how "the walls are glass and on them are painted the most delightful and extravagant cavalry officers mounted on equally mad horses. The horses have pink and green tails and manes. They rear and prance. The bar is black. The furniture is black and chromium. It's all terribly grand and rich."[52]

"Grand and rich" helped impress the hundreds of people Arden entertained there, including the roster of "journalists and publicity women" she invited to her penthouse like clockwork every Wednesday. She used the time to hint about her newest creations, sniff out details of competitors' ideas, and angle for positive press. She plied the reporters with "magnificent" food, according to Pinchot, who dropped in on one such luncheon. "I like the women," Pinchot wrote in her diary, "but the best feature was the giving of a lovely evening bag worth at least $50 to each

The Quest of the Beautiful

In 1911, less than a year after she opened her own salon,
Elizabeth Arden published *The Quest of the Beautiful*
to publicize her beauty philosophy, services, and
products. It stayed in print for two decades.

Arden, seen here in her late
thirties, loved all animals,
especially dogs and horses.

Arden in her forties,
taken in the late 1920s.

Taking Elisabeth Marbury's advice, Arden had her portrait painted. This one, by Augustus John, was unsatisfactory and she consigned it to the London office. John's second attempt met with her approval.

Fashion shows provided women with camaraderie, excitement, entertainment, and examples of the latest styles. They were among Arden's best sales venues for cosmetics, fashion, and her color harmony idea.

Elizabeth Arden converted the highly decorated, neoclassical Aeolian Building into her flagship Fifth Avenue salon in 1930. Architect Mott Schmidt's modern facade included Arden's Red Door. Rue Carpenter and Nicolai Remisoff collaborated on the interior designs.

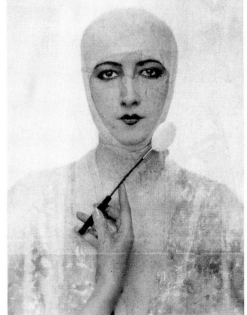

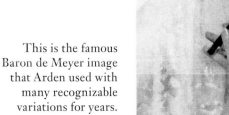

This is the famous Baron de Meyer image that Arden used with many recognizable variations for years.

Ardena Muscle Oil, with an Arden pink label and ribbon, circa 1930s.

Elizabeth Arden designed, patented, and sold many types of travel and vanity cases like this one throughout her career, most with a mirror and all of them stocked with her products.

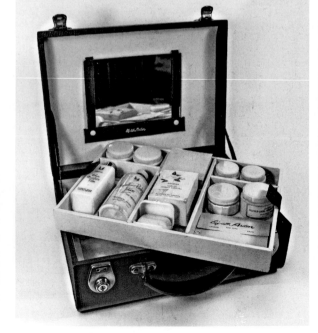

The businesswoman and her staff in 1935.

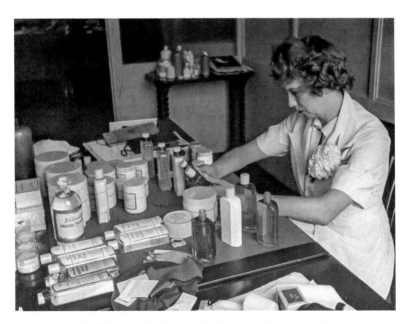

Well-known for her perfectionism, Arden closely
examined samples before authorizing their production.

Maine Chance Spa, in Mount Vernon, Maine,
where Arden created the luxury spa experience.

Despite their significant differences, Elisabeth Marbury became Elizabeth Arden's guide to the mores of America's East Coast establishment elites, and one of her dearest friends.

Elizabeth Arden's 1933 Christmas card—a Maine Chance mélange: animals, gardens, relaxing, and aquaplaning in a women-only space.

The busy cosmetics executive at her dressing table, spraying perfume from the bottle of her own design.

As America's beauty expert, Arden was always elegantly made up and attired, ready with the perfect outfit for every event, as this publicity photo suggested.

Professional ballet dancer turned Elizabeth Arden exercise instructor Dyta Morena readies two debutantes for their roles as living mannequins in a New York charity fashion show.

(Left to right: Carolyn Widman, Dyta Morena, Joan Macomber.)

Arden entertaining a friend at her New York City penthouse. The Nicolai Remisoff wall painting proved her modernist sensibilities.

A smiling Elizabeth Graham, as she was known at the racetrack, watching her thoroughbreds in 1939.

As this British woman relishes her Arden beauty case, the ad highlights two famous Arden ideas: "cleanse—tone—nourish" and color harmony.

Arden's Blue Grass–perfumed booth in the 1939 New York World's Fair Cosmetics Building offered makeup and color harmony classes, salon services, demonstrations, and product sales to fairgoers from around the world.

Elizabeth Arden helped to pioneer descriptive colors for her products, sometimes with backstories, to pique the attention of clients. This *New Yorker* cartoon from 1940 shows one such enthralled customer.

"It happened like this. One day Miss Arden was looking at a beautiful sunset ..."

Depending upon one's point of view, the charismatic Bengamin
Gayelord Hauser, Arden's short-term nutritional adviser,
was either a genius or a charlatan.

Alfred Stieglitz and Georgia O'Keeffe seated before
a painting by John Marin, circa 1942.

Vigilant

FOR THE

Navy Nurse

The Navy Nurse needs a coiffure that will be as smart and becoming under her white coif on hospital duty as it is under her officer's cap on parade. Its versatility will determine serviceability. Vigilant is extremely right for the arduous requirements of a service woman in the field or on post. A short cut parted in the middle and drawn back smoothly on top into a half-halo that forms a frame for the lower half of the face, it has dignity as well as charm and is easy to keep trim and smooth-looking.

Brave color for the lipstick of the Navy Nurse is Victory Red—When on leave she may enjoy the rosy crimson of Radiant Peony lipstick and nail polish. The loveliest shade of powder for those wearing dark blue is Lysetta.

Arden's *On-the-Double* pamphlet demonstrated how the most becoming hairstyles worked with every service cap.

guest. We chose materials and gave our addresses for the finished bags."[53] This was the shrewdest sort of marketing mixology: an exclusive setting, powerful colleagues, excellent food, and a free, top-end, custom-made, wholly unique Arden purse. It guaranteed complimentary coverage in copy and conversation. She continued this tradition for decades.

In addition to business and racing associates, Arden nurtured old and new acquaintances. She joined friends of Ralph Pulitzer for dinner on the Italian ocean liner *Count of Savoy*, well-known for its modernist interior decoration. Pinchot found Arden nosing around the ship, admiring the decor, and "ecstatic as usual. She scuttled along the corridors gasping with delight to Pulitzer." At Arden's insistence, everyone trooped to the Met to see *The Emperor Jones*, the controversial Louis Gruenberg opera that had made its world debut a week earlier. It featured bass Hemsley Winfield of the New Negro Art Theater Dance Group. The focus on African American characters (even though Lawrence Tibbett played the starring role in blackface), and the fact that Gruenberg incorporated both jazz and spirituals in his score, made *The Emperor Jones* highly innovative for the time—an opera for the bold.[54]

Another friend, Fannie Hurst, known for the unvarnished realism of her novels, became famous thanks in part to a work ethic every bit as fierce as Arden's. The daughter of impecunious German-Jewish immigrants, Hurst grew up in Missouri. After graduating from Washington University in St. Louis, she tried to establish herself as a writer in New York City. Her magazine articles and short stories explained the difficulties of the working poor, and she spoke on behalf of other marginalized groups, including Blacks, women's rights activists, and Jewish refugees.[55] A Red Door salon regular, she developed a friendship with Arden at luncheons and parties. Arden sent Hurst gifts of flowers and perfumes, and the novelist appreciated her "sweetness and thoughtfulness" that "seem to know no limits."[56] She listened to Arden's radio shows and helpfully forwarded the name of a possible exercise director who seemed to be brimming with "subtle, modern and highly efficient" methods.[57]

Hurst wrote Arden into her highly successful 1933 novel *Imitation of Life*, basing the barely disguised character of Virginia Eden on Elizabeth Arden. Eden, Hurst penned, was "author of one of the most alluring and remunerative phrases of modern industry, 'Beauty culture.'" The lovely Eden unnerved people with her perceptive command of business. Her "teeth were as pointed and polished and incisive as a terrier's, and with them, when she sank, she drew blood," Hurst wrote. Yet she gave beneficently, "with even a higher and freer hand than the one with which she commanded. Her servants quailed before her tantrums and reaped the harvest of her quick spasms of self-reproach which she expressed in the form of showered affection and gifts." But "they adored her, and [while they] left in frequent huffs," they always returned, "on a more intimate and more firmly intrenched basis."[58] Eden was not a main character in the book, nor in the 1934 film version, and Elizabeth Arden never put to paper her thoughts as to the verisimilitude of the pen portrait, but her friendship with Fannie Hurst continued long past *Imitation of Life*.

More dangerous than an insightful novelist friend was a gossip columnist pal. Hedda Hopper, born Elda Furry, was smitten with the stage when young. Like Arden, Elda grew up poor and worked hard, eventually getting cast in a show that solidified her desire to act. Moving from Pennsylvania to New York, she married impresario and bounder De-Wolf Hopper. A son and a divorce followed. Again, like Arden, Elda changed her name, in what one journalist called "a commendable but futile effort to disassociate herself from Hopper's four previous wives, who were confusingly named Ella, Ida, Edna and Nella."[59] When she met Arden, Hedda Hopper had abandoned acting but not quite begun her newspaper career, and so agreed to Arden's suggestion to take the two-week Arden beauty culturalist training.[60] The women became friends, although Arden was smart enough to push Hopper to arm's length once the latter's columns grew barbs. Before then, however, Hopper enjoyed Arden's "devastating sense of humor." They *ooh*ed and *aah*ed over Arden's beautiful thoroughbreds at Saratoga. Hopper, who gave treatments and dazzled salon clients as a former actress, learned the industry from the inside. "The profits," she marveled, "would stagger a maharajah."

She also marveled at what she thought was the millionaire's mean streak. Hopper's ears burned overhearing Arden annihilate Saks Fifth Avenue president Adam Gimbel after one of his saleswomen called a $5.95 purse "just as good" as the $20 Arden evening bag on which (adding insult to injury) Gimbel had modeled it. Worse was a case of miserliness Hopper observed. Salon employees had to wrap the hundreds of Christmas gifts Arden handed out—in addition to their own jobs during the seasonal rush. Hopper hated that Arden would not hire extra help and didn't care that the rest of them worked their fingers to the bone. Following the employee party, Hopper quit. She nevertheless maintained a grudging awe for the cosmetics magnate. "A brilliant executive," Hopper summarized in her memoir, "Elizabeth Arden has succeeded in everything she's undertaken. She understands the foibles of women. Her exercise rooms are things of beauty." But, Hopper concluded nastily, "there are showmen in other businesses besides motion pictures."[61]

As it turned out, Hedda Hopper became her own showman a few years later in a film starring the Elizabeth Arden Salon. She played herself, a dirt-digging gossip columnist in the famous Clare Boothe Luce play turned movie *The Women*. Luce's own misogyny ran through the show, according to actress Ilka Chase, who knew the author and described Luce as "the bland and lethal lady who in that little effort limned her sex in vitriol." Chase read the filmscript, at Luce's insistence, to consider the part of Sylvia Fowler, which she had played onstage. "My first impression," Chase wrote later, "was twofold: one, that it had the fetid atmosphere of a badly ventilated women's washroom and ... two, that it would be a hit."[62]

This unusual Hollywood picture, adapted for the screen by Anita Loos, featured several scenes set in a salon modeled specifically on Arden's.[63] Those who had never been could see a replica of the flower-bedecked foyer, the expansive dressing rooms, and the sylphlike models floating around displaying undergarments for sale. They could watch spa treatments, exercises, and a manicure in progress. Perhaps best of all was the lengthy fashion show, a six-minute Technicolor extravaganza cut into the middle of the otherwise black-and-white film. *The Women* provided a glimpse of the pampering possible at a salon like Arden's.

It also showed cattiness, betrayal, heartache, pettiness, and a stupefying level of self-absorption. As the posters boasted, the film had "a manless cast," not even male animals or portraits, but was nevertheless "All About Men!" Like Chase, some thought *The Women* horribly belittling. Others, though, saw more empowering aspects. Historian Jennifer Scanlon wrote that "women's ongoing conversations about men in the film, including those in the beauty parlor scenes, reveal a discourse crafted not to please or seduce men, but rather to analyze them and put them, figuratively, in their place."[64] Regardless of one's interpretation, *The Women* was among the most profitable films of 1939. Its worth to Arden lay in the lush salon scenes and the desire it created in filmgoers to seek out their own Red Door experience.

Between the play and the film, *The Women* reached a vast audience. Arden always loved the movies, but more and more high culture interested her and became the source of another influential friendship. Moving among art collectors such as horseman Jock Whitney, gaining her own living space, and staying abreast of cultural trends spurred her to investigate modernist art. She had begun collecting with Marbury's guidance, acquiring works by Marc Chagall and female painters including Mary Cassatt and Marie Laurencin.[65] Then Anne Morgan brought Alfred Stieglitz and his wife, modernist artist Georgia O'Keeffe, into Arden's life.

Stieglitz was two decades older than O'Keeffe. Despite O'Keeffe's avowed commitment to feminism, Stieglitz dominated both the relationship and his wife's career, a thing Arden never allowed in her own marriage.[66] Nevertheless, Arden admired O'Keeffe's work. She purchased her first painting from her in 1932. Four years later, Arden sought a commission. O'Keeffe was pleased. She wrote proudly to a friend that Arden had given her an "order for a big flower painting" and that she had landed the assignment on her own, without the help of Stieglitz. One scholar called Arden's support "an important step toward O'Keeffe becoming more independent as an artist."[67]

Arden wanted to hang the painting in the exercise room of her recently remodeled flagship salon where every socialite would see it. Trusting O'Keeffe's vision absolutely, Arden promised her $12,000.[68] It was an outrageous sum of money at the time, just over $265,000 today. An art patron that generous had to be cultivated. O'Keeffe may have secured the commission, but it was her husband who carefully fostered Arden's friendship, and in the most flattering terms.

Stieglitz wrote Arden fond letters, praising her fabled energy and cautioning her considerately against "spending [her]self to the limit." You are, he told her, "a lovely person," and "certainly a miracle."[69] Knowing how she felt about her "babies," he complimented her horses and followed their victories. "I do love a real racehorse, and everything that is thoroughbred in whatever form it may walk the earth," he fawned, in a not-so-subtle comparison to the cosmetics queen.[70] The acerbic Rosamond Pinchot found Stieglitz unappealing. She happened to be present one day in 1933, not long after Arden had tossed Lewis out of her life. "Eliz. and the great photographer Stieglitz were choosing a Georgia O'Keeffe painting for the main room," she recalled to her diary. "Stieglitz a querulous, opinionated old man with tufts of gray hair growing out of his ears. He talked much about how he hated commercialism. Yet I bet he struck a hard bargain with Elizabeth."[71]

Stieglitz trod carefully with Arden, adroitly stressing the doyenne's proprietorship of the artwork under way. He told her how "enthusiastically" O'Keeffe was "working on the painting for you," how much she "continues to enjoy hugely working on the canvas which is to be yours when finished." He emphasized the exclusivity of her commission. Neither of them had seen a prior sketch of the painting as O'Keeffe allowed no previews.[72] No matter. It was a masterpiece. O'Keeffe titled it *Jimson Weed*, but Arden called it "The Miracle Flower." Four colossal white jimsonweed—or *Datura*—flowers filled the nearly six-by-seven-foot canvas. They suggested suppleness, movement, grace, and a tough delicacy. It was perfectly placed in Arden's "Gymnasium Moderne," reflecting, or perhaps spurring, the clients' own lithe stretching and bending while reinforcing the salon's cool modernism.[73]

Arden and O'Keeffe could hardly have been more different in appearance, yet they shared a commitment to their careers, a unique vision for themselves, and a visceral pursuit of beauty.[74] Arden eventually purchased two more paintings and publicly promoted O'Keeffe.[75] "I am telling everyone and simply raving about my divine picture. . . . I met millions of grand people in Phila.," she wrote Stieglitz, "and also told them of the exhibition. I do hope to raise Georgia O'Keeffe's work to the highest place in this kingdom of ours—for she is a very glorious person."[76]

The timing of Arden's support of O'Keeffe may or may not have had something to do with Helena Rubinstein. Madame sold the American arm of her company to Lehman Brothers in 1928, yet the brand remained a potent competitor. Both companies continued to cater to "fashionable femininity," even though the look of their makeup, their packaging, and their salons remained as dissimilar as their patrons. Arden buttressed the conservative WASP status quo, with Arden Pink set amid the pastels she preferred, accented with the greens and golds introduced in Rue Carpenter's remodeling. Arden's look was classic, detached, elegant, and refined, with a modernist overlay. Rubinstein pre-

ferred her modernism in a riot of warm colors. The royal blue, dark
rose, and saturated reds and greens of her first salon stood in stark contrast to Arden's. Rubinstein's "displayed an orientalist theme and was
outfitted with 'exotic' gold sofas, Chinese wallpaper, embroidered pil-
lows, and black tables." Sculpture, hand-painted furniture, and modern
art completed the look. She played up her European birth and connections, which resonated with the avant-garde. As tastes changed, both
businesswomen updated their salons, because, as a reader of *Modern
Beauty Shop* asserted, "the streamlined girl of today demands her beauty
services in a shop harmonious with her own modernity."[77]

One important interior feature for both women was art. Rubinstein
was a serious collector. Her eclectic personal assemblage spilled over into
her salons, making them a reflection of her own tastes. She owned works
by Picasso, Miró, Brancusi, and Matisse and through the 1930s and
1940s added paintings by Modigliani, Dalí, Laurencin, Kandinsky, and
other modernists whose art has stood the test of time.[78] She remains
best known for her historical African and Oceanic art. *L'art primitif*, as
it was called in the 1930s, was becoming chic among certain farsighted
American collectors, especially after the Metropolitan Museum of Art
held an exhibition that included some of Rubinstein's pieces in 1935.[79]

Modernism reigned. It had moved well beyond the cognoscenti who
first embraced it in the late 1890s. Mainstream modernism, including
art deco, had come to dictate clothing, package, industrial, interior, and
architectural design. Streamlined and aerodynamic, it could entail caprice,
asymmetry, and broad curvilinear shapes, but it lacked the excessive ornamentation of the past, as though the protracted Great Depression
had stripped everything down to its essence. Modernism affected classical music, theater, literature, and poetry, and to be au courant, beauty
influencers such as Elizabeth Arden had to lead—or at least reflect—
the changing times.

She knew this. In New York, her Easter window display of "St. Theresa with an Easter egg" could not have been more cutting-edge. She

made explicit reference to the sensational *Four Saints in Three Acts*, a modernist Broadway opera that was virtually incomprehensible to all but the most sophisticated culture mavens. Composer Virgil Thomson's neoclassical music was the most traditional part of the production. Gertrude Stein wrote the libretto, which contained nonsensical but catchy lines such as "Pigeons on the grass alas." It was the first U.S. opera with an all-Black cast that did not feature a specifically African American storyline. The set designs by Florine Stettheimer, a well-known modernist painter (and friend to Stieglitz, O'Keeffe, and Marcel Duchamp), employed feathers, coral, silver, and cellophane. It wasn't her first use of it, but the whimsical cellophane palm trees and the artistic cellophane covering the back wall began a national obsession for the stuff.[80]

Cellophane became the design centerpiece of Arden's vision for her niece's debutante ball at the Ritz-Carlton. Using the relatively new and *très chic* material was Arden's idea. "The ballroom should be decorated, I think, in different-colored cellophane. I want Prince of Wales feathers of cellophane twelve feet high in pale pink. That gold border at the top of the room must be covered over with cellophane ruffles," she told Kate Drain Lawson, a designer whom she had hired fresh from her work on *Four Saints*.[81] For debutantes Beatrice Graham and Beatrice's friend Jean MacKinnon, the columns were "festooned with white cellophane plumes. Pink cellophane shading to white draped the stairway leading to the ballroom" and the receiving line.[82]

At the head with Arden stood Jean's parents. Her mother, Mary MacKinnon, was a Florida art friend, involved in creating what would become the Society of the Four Arts in Palm Beach. Next was Beatrice's mother, Ada, but not her father. Bill Graham was battling unsuccessfully to save his glass company from bankruptcy, and Arden had not forgiven him for having assisted Tom Lewis's infidelities. Ada and Bill's other daughters, Patricia and Virginia, were there. Arden had taken the eldest, Pat, under her wing and would soon employ her long-term.[83]

Also present, after their recent honeymoon, were sister Gladys and her new husband, Henri, known publicly as the Vicomtesse and Vicomte de Maublanc de Boisboucher.[84] They were not the only titled guests among the hundreds at the debutante ball, as a trio of gossip columnists noted. Walter Winchell, chief among the journalists, quipped that Beatrice and Jean were "the cellophane celebutantes of the year."[85] Arden's hosting was a great hit, serving several purposes, including assisting her family and displaying her artistic sensibilities.

Cellophane also modernized her packaging and showed off her products beautifully. Her Bon Voyage Box contained two magazines and a dozen neatly packed bottles and jars "lost in billows of Cellophane" for maximum customer awe. Arden designed and patented an amusing holiday gift of two cellophane bells holding perfume bottles.[86] Cellophane for sales and decorations, prominence at *The Emperor Jones,* and promoting America's most famous female artist proved Arden's modernist credentials.[87] For *Vogue* she posed proudly alongside O'Keeffe's glorious painting at her salon's reopening, the simultaneous embodiment of tasteful modernism and timeless elegance.[88]

Thirteen

Business Savvy
During Hard Times

She had made it. "Queen Elizabeth," *Fortune* crowned her in 1930. She stood alone at the top. Helena Rubinstein bought her own company back in 1931, after the new owners insisted on volume sales to down-market retail outlets, but Madame was still, the business magazine *tsk-tsk*ed, stuck in that slump, and her "salons have passed their days of great chic."

Arden, on the other hand, had an "occult foreknowledge" of her field. *Fortune* called her a trendspotter and a trendsetter: "She always seems to know, months before her competitors, when it will be fashionable to look artificial, when it will be better to look natural." Although still purposefully cloaking her "extremely dominating" personality in the feminine exterior her era demanded, Arden had succeeded, in life and in business. It was a tremendous accomplishment, for everyone knew, as Rosamond Pinchot observed, "women in the professions can't attain national reputations except in very rare instances."[1]

Arden was that rare instance. She had mastered every aspect of her business. She had created a unique, global, and instantly recognizable brand from scratch, never compromised on quality, remained fixed on her ideal customer ("a refined and enthusiastic Junior League" sort, according to *Fortune*), taken calculated risks, fine-tuned worker training, valued employee loyalty, splashed out on publicity, mostly kept her tendency toward micromanaging in check, and made an enormous fortune in toiletries at a time when Americans had more cars than bathrooms.[2] One industry insider credited Arden's success to "her drive as an innovator, her endless quest for perfection, and her basic honesty toward her clients."[3] *Fortune* concurred: Elizabeth Arden was "the most illustrious firm engaged in the world's beauty and cosmetics business."[4] She declared that "the thought of failure never crossed my mind."[5]

To borrow twenty-first-century verbiage, Arden was nimble, an agile industrialist able to pivot quickly to take advantage of market changes. She kept current with a zealot's passion, gathering fresh concepts everywhere: film magazines, female journalists, Parisian cafés, Fashion Group newsletters, her competitors. A continual rollout of new products during the nation's worst economic downturn seemed a terrible notion to most business leaders, but not to Elizabeth Arden. Retail sales nationwide almost halved between 1929 and 1934. Sales of cosmetics dropped by only 16.7 percent in that period, and Arden saw opportunity.[6] "This depression," she calculated, "is going to make a lot of manufacturers pull in, economize, cut down—and that leaves us a clear field."[7] She took full advantage. By 1938, Arden offered products "in 595 separate shapes and sizes." This is an extraordinary number, but, as a trade journal noted sagely, "at a gross of from $3,500,000 to $4,000,000 a year, which supplies a $200,000 living for its proprietor and work for nearly 1,000 employees who are pretty handsomely paid, Miss Arden has what is called a sweet business."[8] Her creativity transcended marketing.[9] Aware of how more exciting products could lead to higher profits and happier customers, Arden secured sixty-eight of her ninety-seven patents in the 1930s. She developed some of her most iconic and longest-lasting sellers, items still in use today, during this decade of despair.

Fierce competition drove her. Soon in comeback mode, Helena Rubinstein could not be dismissed. Lehn & Fink bought Dorothy Gray in 1927. *Parfumeur* François Coty launched a range of popular face powders in the late 1920s, at about the time he purchased Marie Earle. Coty was almost as tough a rival as newcomer Charles Revson.[10] In 1932, Revson introduced his colorful Revlon nail polish (Arden had been selling liquid nail polish since 1920, Rubinstein since 1928), before charging into cosmetics. Of these, only Rubinstein and Gray truly marketed to the high-end customer.

Arden's tony salons separated her from the herd. To the dancing and fencing under the O'Keeffe in her Gymnasium Moderne, Arden added Ping-Pong, paddle tennis, badminton, and Exercycles.[11] Women sought out her Scotch Hose hydrotherapy treatment and the experience of wearing her disposable paper "color cape" in the season's sixteen new shades to facilitate color harmony.[12] To sell as gifts in her salon shops, she designed a Bicycle Kit, a Beach Bag, perfume pins, and a clever "automatic lipstick" that could be worked with one hand. For home use she devised an electric depilatory and a "Face Moulding Home Treatment." A popular new perfume called "Tuberose" flew off salon shelves, especially after she renamed it "Gardenia" upon discovering that no one could pronounce Tuberose.[13] Endlessly advocating multiproduct use, she invented compact cases to hold dry rouge in seven colors and others for five shades of powder.[14] Competing cosmetics firms quickly snapped up her ideas.

Her newest development was adding hair care to her total beauty concept. Arden "invented the modern beauty salon," according to Janet Leckie, who watched its birth.[15] Hairstyling had been part of the Maine Chance Spa experience, but in 1934, Arden built a stand-alone salon called Le Printemps.[16] There, male stylists reigned supreme. *Vogue* believed their presence resulted in "no noise or rushing about, or displays of temperament." Instead of drama, Jean and Alexandre—male stylists always seemed to go by a single name, usually French—colored, permed, shaped, and cut hair while supervising the other hairdressers with a cool efficiency.[17]

By the spring of 1936, she moved the men inside the Fifth Avenue salon, under the direction of "the sculptor Leonardi."[18] Cosmetics was a necessity for fashion-conscious women of nearly every class, race, and background by then, and professionally styled hair nearly matched makeup in importance for Arden. Wealthy women made weekly hair appointments. Charity events, parties, balls, and other celebrations required extra bookings. Like Maine Chance and treatment rooms, hair salons were another female space. By adding them, Arden deftly identified and took advantage of a social trend with enormous benefits to her customers, her employees, and her own bottom line.

Soon every Red Door salon contained a brand-consistent beauty parlor. She called them *salons de coiffure* to emphasize the connection to European high fashion. Her distinctive marketing persuaded the tentative. For example, Leonardi was not just any hairdresser. He had an artist's "knowledge of line with a flair for catching and emphasizing the keynote of a personality." Nor did he style hair in just any way. "First, Leonardi makes a mask of your face and head and then arranges various coiffures that idealize your features." Clients were to engage in a dialogue about their preferences. "This new technique" offered a chance to "study ourselves critically and try the effect of several arrangements before sitting for the actual coiffure!"[19] It was startlingly near to the twenty-first-century ability to upload one's headshot to envision a virtual hair or cosmetic makeover. Leonardi's mask would have been infinitely more time-consuming, but trying on potential styles was surely just as much fun then as now.

Male stylists were Arden's stock-in-trade. The only men seen in her salons, they hailed from Europe where the training was thorough, and she could boast of their awareness of the latest looks. The star of her empire in the 1930s was Guillaume of Paris, whose presence was almost certainly a result of sister Gladys's persuasive abilities. Once it became known that his clients included the Duchess of Windsor, women packed his lectures on hair and fashion. Arden shuttled him to salons coast to coast, flew him to openings, put him in front of reporters, and had him design a personalized "Guillaume look" for every woman who could afford it.[20] Classic French painters inspired him to create dainty, feminine, Arden-approved styles with names to match, like Versailles and L'Aiglon.[21] Guillaume's "life's ambition" was "to make beautiful women more beautiful" and his new boss emphasized that only his consummate artistry could complete the head-to-toe Arden look.[22] Guillaume became the model for other male stylists Arden hired and promoted as her *salons de coiffure* grew in importance.[23]

A unique part of the Arden salon experience was the live lingerie display, as featured in the film *The Women*. Thinking of both sales and customer comfort, Arden dressed beguiling models in couture lounge and intimate wear and sent them strolling among customers held captive by rollers, perm rods, and hair dryers. Arden's clients delighted in these diaphanous dreams, which she had been selling selectively since 1925. In the mid-1930s, Arden, always infatuated with titles, hired a widowed Russian princess and former *Ziegfeld Follies* girl, Ketevan "Ketto" Mikeladze, to design one-of-a-kind negligees.[24]

Expansion during the Great Depression helped keep Arden profitable. By the end of the 1930s she owned twenty-six salons across North America and Europe and had moved into the South American market. She had factories in New York, Paris, Berlin, Toronto, and Mexico City, while Teddy Haslam oversaw the move from the old London plant in Coach and Horses Yard to a larger, purpose-built one in North Acton.[25] A year after the stock market crash, she purchased a sizable San Francisco warehouse to supply retail outlets in Hawaii and the Philippines.[26] She set up a subsidiary in Canada, a place she occasionally but sentimentally visited.[27] As far away as Singapore, women purchased products from her trained saleswomen.[28] Since the 1920s, Arden goods had been available on every continent except Antarctica.[29] *The New Yorker* noted with some surprise that "she has continued to extend her wholesale trade with a zest which causes some conservatives to prophesy gloomily that she will ruin the business by overexpansion." But the magazine had to admit that she "can afford to be indifferent to such predictions. She is the sole stockholder and complete dictator of the business."[30]

She refused to discontinue colors, even if the number of women wanting a shade was very, very small. This was how Arden defined customer loyalty—it was about *her* being loyal to her customers. Her practice contradicted everything men learned in business school, but explains in part why her product list was so much longer than those of other firms. Where salons became so popular that women had trouble booking appointments, she built on or built more. The three Arden salons in Los Angeles were always full, so she opened a fourth, on Wilshire Boulevard.[31]

To check on progress there, Arden visited in March 1933. She arrived in California in the midst of a catastrophic earthquake that toppled buildings and killed more than one hundred people. Somehow she reached her salon, inside the J. W. Robinson department store, where she met with frightened employees.[32] Reporter Alma Whitaker found her there, looking like a queen in a flower-strewn bower, "weighing 114 pounds, all in the right place for a 16-year-old figure, and living up to her own best advertisements." Whitaker dubbed her the "High Priestess of Pulchritude," and sought her advice. "Out here," Arden waved her arms, "where you literally eat sunshine, where flowers and luscious fresh fruits abound on all sides, there is no excuse for any woman not to be beautiful!" And that was the most important thing. "Women know that health and beauty give them courage and confidence. That's how those wonderful English women licked the depression in Britain," Arden asserted. The reporter bit. "Tell us how to lick it here," she pleaded. Arden grew stern. "Every woman should take the juice of two lemons in cold water every morning. Half an hour later, a glass of orange juice or

some of your other fine fruits. That's all for breakfast. . . . All women
must walk a great deal. In this dry climate use olive oil generously, both
inside and out." Exercise was nonnegotiable. She shimmied to the floor
to demonstrate. No one did Arden like Arden.

Then followed a curious list of what not to do. Cut back on playing
bridge: it "broadens the hips, ruins the neck muscles, spoils the eyes,
mars the expression of the face." No plucking the eyebrows: it "denude[s]
the face of intelligence." No wearing slacks: "Why imitate the men?"
No facelifts: "Dreadful! They should have their brains lifted first. The
wrinkles that come with laughter are beautifying. One can pat them out
at night," she nodded, without noticing the contradiction. And it was
simple. No need to separate "antiwrinkle, velva and muscle oil creams."
Arden admitted that she slathered them all together, to the journalist's
relief. Finally, no soap and water. Whitaker gulped and "confessed to
having used it three times a day all my life." Arden's eyes narrowed.
"For which reason," the beauty queen leveled, "you have the complexion of a healthy man."[33]

Whitaker retreated to the safer topic of the Wilshire Boulevard
salon. Its manager, Eileen Scott-Williams, "moved in the most patrician English society and was presented at court."[34] Married to a career
British army officer, the multilingual Scott-Williams joined the London salon after World War I. Her previous stage training proved useful
as she traveled Europe demonstrating Arden's methods. Scott-Williams
had managed the Berlin Red Door Salon until Adolf Hitler came to
power and made her task of publicizing the latest cosmetic trends more
difficult. He insisted on a natural look for women, claiming that makeup
was not suitable for his ideal German frau.[35] That was when Elizabeth
Arden transferred Scott-Williams to the Wilshire salon, replacing her
in Berlin with a German manager.[36]

In June 1933, Arden appeared as usual for the grand opening.[37] Los
Angeles news outlets covered both her and the event prominently. The
facade of white marble, black trim, and striking Red Door replicated

New York's. The interior was the "decorative dream fulfilled [by] Adrian, the famous Metro-Goldwyn-Mayer stylist." Adrian Greenburg—always called simply Adrian—already had dozens of film-costume credits. He did not usually dabble in interior design, but he poured on the drama for Arden. He reproduced the exterior colors for the large, circular main salon, adding hues to enhance the spaces where the spa treatments, including diathermy and now Pulsotherm (for "exercising every muscle of the face"), occurred.[38] In the third-floor "Garden of Arden," the *Los Angeles Times* described how Adrian's "painted tin . . . awnings" complemented the "furniture of a soft blue-gray tint blending with the living plants and tropical vines and giving a charming outdoor atmosphere."[39]

To oversee the important Exercise Salon, Arden hired Francesca Braggiotti Lodge, a dancer and actor who had just finished shooting *Little Women* with Katharine Hepburn. Lodge's Hollywood contacts augmented Scott-Williams's, bringing additional celebrities through the Red Doors.[40] For Arden, California appeared more entrancing with every visit to salons, celebrities, and racetracks.[41]

Commercial air travel facilitated her West Coast infatuation. Arden quickly became a TWA Sky Chief regular, flying thousands of miles each year. Her experiences spurred her to create lightweight aluminum containers to manage baggage weight limits. Some she lined with rubber to keep glass jars from jostling. She also pioneered travel sizes for her products—she called them "gift petites."[42] Even though flying could be noisy, cold, and uncomfortable (international jet travel was not introduced until 1952), Arden loved it. Airplanes were glamorous. Only the brave allowed themselves to be borne aloft through the skies. She told *Life* magazine that flying was her "refuge from never ceasing telephones" and praised overnight flights as "a cradle in the skies." The practical executive appreciated "the time saved [which] enables me to do ever so much more work, and have more fun."[43] Not bad for someone who rarely did commercial endorsements. Should there be any lingering doubt, Arden so trusted air travel that she was among the first owners to move her precious thoroughbreds by plane.[44]

California's salubrious climate reinforced Arden's long-standing commitment to holistic health. She found there ample advocates of her belief in the importance of a good diet as the basis for healthy skin and optimal energy. Elizabeth Arden was far ahead of the nutritional vogue then sweeping the nation. For years, she had preached that total health was the prerequisite for true beauty. While many of her ideas might not pass muster in the twenty-first century, her advocacy of proper nutritional choices for better health was sound. To publicize her message more broadly, she partnered with a man who skyrocketed to fame thanks to her: the smooth-talking, attractive, and oh-so-flattering rapscallion Bengamin Gayelord Hauser.

Moderately successful by the start of the 1930s, Hauser called himself a "food scientist," despite having absolutely no formal training in nutrition or science. But he did have a gorgeous face, an earnest manner, marvelous oratorical skills, and a fantastic presentation style that filled venues with fans eager to hear his free advice and to purchase his books and products. Arden promoted Hauser not only because she already shared his philosophies, but also because she thought he would be the perfect complement to broadcast her beauty concepts. Arden took him up, introduced him around, and hosted parties in his honor.[45] Her willowy exercise team appeared onstage with Hauser, publicly conveying her endorsement.[46]

Hauser shared Arden's conviction that beauty and health were in one's own control. That smart food choices would result in looking and feeling better. That positive messaging was preferable to guilt or shaming. They concentrated particularly on elite white women of a certain age, the demographic driven by internal fears of senescence but with money to spend. Arden responded to Hauser's optimistic encouragement to "middle-aged and older women to branch out into new careers and to live for themselves instead of for family members"; indeed, that was her life.[47] Relentlessly upbeat, promising all manner of benefits, they made an impressive duo. Frequently traveling with them was Frey Brown, Hauser's long-term business and life partner, equally handsome and charismatic.[48]

Like Arden, Hauser was an immigrant. And like her, he had changed his name. Born twenty-six years after Arden, Eugene Helmuth Hauser left his native Germany for Chicago at sixteen. In the autobiographical *Diet Does It*, he wrote of being on death's doorstep because of a "tuberculous hip" that resisted healing. Physicians gave up, so his family sent him "to die in the serenity of the Swiss mountains." But there, to his everlasting joy, he met an old mountaineer who divulged that "only living foods can make a living body." Hauser thereafter eschewed "dead foods" and ate only "fresh young growing things, especially the green and yellow vegetables saturated with the earthy elements; lemons, oranges and other tree fruits, full of sunshine and living waters."[49] Cured and converted, Hauser found his calling.

Diet Does It recounted his studies with European dietetics experts and his arrival in the United States in 1923 to impart his "intelligent system of eating." Hauser's New School of Health could not accommodate all who yearned for his wisdom, so he took to the lecture circuit.[50] With immoderate overstatement, he called himself "the 'Internationally Famous Young Viennese Scientist: Bengamin Gayelord Hauser.'" He emphasized his (fictive) scientific credentials by teaching in a white lab coat beside "Chemical Man," a "larger than life model of the human digestive system" of his own creation that allowed him to conduct ersatz but compelling scientific experiments onstage.[51] In 1927, he relocated to California, plugging his "wonderful new science of Chemicanalysis" and his "famous Eliminative Feeding System."[52] Within five years, the latter had morphed into his "Harmonized Food Selection," borrowing, intentionally or not, from Arden's color harmony wording.[53] By the summer of 1933, he was signing books for legions of disciples.[54]

Hauser focused exclusively on diet until he met Arden and learned about beauty. He observed her expertise and her salon operations. He absorbed, copied, repackaged, and plagiarized her ideas. Three days after a 1934 luncheon in his honor at her home, for example, newspapers announced his "beauty cocktails." Any woman drinking them would "quickly become beautiful," he proclaimed, as the "spinach, carrot and orange juices" were "a means of gaining a beautiful complexion." That's when he shamelessly started to refer to himself as a "beauty psychologist."[55]

In *Diet Does It*, Hauser brazenly took credit for teaching Arden the beauty laws she herself had promulgated for two decades. "My far-sighted associate [Arden] who had gained fame and a fortune by devising the ultimate in external aids to beauty now realized," he dissembled, "that true beauty came from within and was a reflection of inward health which no amount of creams, rouge, or lipstick alone could duplicate." He urged women to try what he called his unique "Eat and Grow Beautiful" plan.[56]

Two years into their working relationship, Hauser poured his—or Arden's—theories into a book. As Hauser's biographer detected, *Eat and Grow Beautiful* "marked a departure for Hauser: there was no mention of food . . . and there was less advice on eating and more on beauty, lifestyle and health."[57] And the nutritional advice he did include was reborn as the "Cosmetic Diet." Look to your mirror, he advised women. You can make positive changes in your health and your appearance through your diet and posture.[58] This was vintage Elizabeth Arden. Her influence on him was lasting. Two decades later, Hauser published a hugely successful book with a title straight from Arden: *Look Younger, Live Longer*.[59]

Hauser was not without critics. Physicians lambasted his lack of credentials. He was neither a doctor, a "beauty psychologist," nor a "food scientist" as he claimed. Audience members expressed concern about some of his ideas. "Lack of calcium produces fear of the dark, nail biting, gossiping," he offered, while telling his listeners—in another origin-story version—that he cured his own "tuberculosis of the hip by eating '36 lemons a day,' for one or two weeks." In fact, as early as 1926, letters about Hauser swamped the American Medical Association's Bureau of Investigation. Doctors, professors, and everyday people worried about his advice and the number of "graduates" he was unleashing, "entitling them to practice his nefarious and doubtful methods on innocent fellow human beings to the detriment of their health, sanity and well-being."[60]

Medical researchers recognized that Hauser's claim to have earned the right to call himself "Dr." was false. They blasted him as a member of a "drugless, healing cult," a "food faddist" guilty of "quackery."[61] They derided Hauser's courses, such as "How to Spiritualize Your Bloodstream by Eating, Breathing, Bathing and Thinking Correctly" and "The One Fundamental Cause of All Disease and How to Obliterate It."[62] By 1929, AMA investigators learned that Hauser had been arrested so many times in Florida for lacking the proper licensing that officials had banned him from the state for life.[63] The Food and Drug Administration compelled him to stop selling "'Slim' (containing the harmful drugs senna, bladder-wrack, buckthorn bark), 'Correcol' (consisting of weeds and gum), and Hauser Potassium Broth (a mixture of alfalfa, okra, beet tops, etc.)" because he "sold [them] under false and fraudulent claims."[64]

Arden likely knew none of this when she made Hauser the Maine Chance "nutritional director" in 1935. He had been on the lecture circuit with "Eat and Grow Beautiful" and "Youth and Beauty through Food," promoting a weight loss diet of "grilled grapefruit, mushroom burgers," and blackstrap molasses.[65] Like today's celebrity chefs, Hauser personally supervised the spa's kitchen and worked one-on-one with enthusiastic Arden clients. He instructed women to follow his "elimination diet" for the week before arrival, to make their spa weight loss more effective. Those who put their "dietary destinies" in Hauser's hands in this way were almost guaranteed to lose weight since the "elimination diet" consisted entirely of fruit juices, vegetable broths, lettuce salads, fresh fruit, and shredded vegetables sautéed in butter. A week's faithful adherence was certain to drop a dress size—or two.[66] He began advertising himself as "diet advisor to the world's most beautiful women."[67] He and Arden were often together through the mid-1930s, frequently seen in the company of important political, business, and social leaders.

By 1938, however, Arden terminated Hauser's association with Maine Chance.[68] It could have been because she discovered the same hypocrisy in "Dr." Hauser as columnist Alice Hughes did after watching him "tear into a lot of grub" at a party in 1939.[69] Hedda Hopper called him the man "who made spinach fashionable on three continents," but suggested roguishly that she "got a giggle" when she learned about the study of malnutrition he was making in Europe. It was definitely not a "first hand" study, she laughed, because Hauser was the guest of Lady Mendl, famous for having "the best chef in Paris."[70] More than likely, however, Arden jettisoned Hauser when the AMA published "Modern Medical Charlatans." This short, devastating article demolished Hauser's claims and concluded pithily, "It is remarkable how much utter nonsense is promoted in the name of scientific dietetics."[71]

Elizabeth Arden's reputation escaped unscathed from her flirtation with Hauser. While their paths converged, she benefited from the publicity, but when his claims endangered her customers' health and her brand, she purged him comprehensively. He eventually resurfaced, and it must be said that he was not wrong about everything. In the 1950s, Gayelord Hauser popularized a barely known food that he claimed aided longevity. With his renewed superstar backing, yogurt took off in the public imagination, becoming the billion-dollar seller it is today.

AT A TIME when the world seemed gray and gloomy, Arden embraced highly entertaining promotional tactics. She went big, with a six-foot-tall model of a female head. As she applied cosmetics to a human, an artist copied her actions, putting the same makeup on the jumbo head as a live audience watched.[72] And she went small, with a miniature sales force of dolls representing every country where she sold her products. Meticulously patterned on the exhibits in a Paris ethnographic museum, the figurines wore idealized folk costumes with harmonizing Arden makeup and nail polish. They toured the country accompanied by three human "Foreign Ambassadors" who lectured in six different languages to those who thronged department stores to see this "Beauty League of Nations."[73]

Perhaps Arden's most successful marketing coup was the bizarre but fabulously popular Gaba Girls. Arden was one of the first businesses to acquire these life-size mannequins ("beautiful, but dummies," as reporter Janet Mabie truthfully put it), stylish and natural-looking, and very different from the scary, unwieldy wax figures of the past. As early as the spring of 1934, Gaba Girls sporting designer fashions and matching Elizabeth Arden makeup mesmerized shoppers and drew large crowds to her salons and events.

Lester Gaba, from Hannibal, Missouri, initially created the mannequins at the behest of Mary Lewis, the vice president of New York's Best & Co. department store. They, and he, became an overnight sensation. Gaba intentionally modeled his Gaba Girls on "typical American gals." "There was nothing," he acknowledged, "oo-la-la about them. Not a lifted pinkie in the lot. They all had cute contemporary hair-dos, and tiptilted noses, and one even had a sprinkling of freckles, and was pigeon-toed!"[74] As a sales gimmick, Gaba and Mary Lewis hosted a cocktail party in honor of the Gaba Girls. The zaniness of it made it a smash hit. Besotted journalists raved about their immobile charms.

The Gaba Girls frenzy intensified and then centered on one in particular, Cynthia, based on Saks model Cynthia Wells. So lifelike was Cynthia that Gaba had a second one made just for him to squire around. Together they embarked on grand adventures. Internationally known hatmaker Lilly Daché invited Cynthia to the opening of her newest millinery salon. It was, Lester Gaba admitted, "probably the first time in history that a hunk of plaster got invited to a party." Cynthia followed this splendid success with a dizzying whirl of soirees thrown by all the best people, including Elizabeth Arden. Gaba and Cynthia "dashed from '21' to El Morocco, from the Stork Club to the Colony [Club]."[75] Haute couturiers vied to dress her. Tiffany and Cartier draped her in jewels. Lester and Cynthia were photographed at the symphony and the opera. Cynthia appeared in films, magazines, and shopwindows. In 1937, Cynthia visited England, Japan, and Australia. She and her newest sisters—whom Gaba fashioned on society women and Hollywood stars—set the bar for elegant sophistication. Elizabeth Arden saw the potential early and capitalized on it. The Gaba Girls' omnipresence was the mute but perfect vehicle for publicizing her color-matching makeup.[76] When a Gaba Girl hit the town, she was wearing Arden cosmetics.

Arden followed this success by turning her Fifth Avenue salon windows into a whimsical marionette show.[77] Captivated New Yorkers peered into a miniature pink exercise room complete with slant board, record player, and itsy-bitsy Arden records. A smartly uniformed Arden puppet helped a client puppet stretch her wooden muscles. A treatment room marionette gently placed a Velva mask on a puppet reclining gracefully in a chaise longue, feet up on a tiny footstool.[78] "No one would budge until it was all over," *Vogue* reported.[79] Human-size versions of the hats and gowns were available for sale in Arden's salon.[80] The Arden puppets were a sensation, playing twice daily and propelling profits upward. They were also more evidence of Elizabeth Arden's ability to identify, seize, and exploit cultural trends. Her puppets played to audiences from Boston to Los Angeles two years before the first-ever American Puppetry Conference and Festival was held.[81]

Involved since the early 1920s in radio promotions, Arden continued to be a familiar household brand through *The Women's Radio Review*, a broadcast begun in 1931 over the NBC-WEAF network.[82] She was in the vanguard. The *Radio Directory* editor claimed in 1938 that "daily programming . . . first became notable in 1932." In that year, 64 percent of homes with radios had them on at some point in the day. John Karol, research director for CBS Radio, reminded Fashion Group members that twenty-six million American homes had radios in 1938, while only eleven million had telephones. Daytime radio targeted housewives, who preferred a fifteen-minute show five days a week.[83] Arden tried out several different types of programs, like a thrice-weekly musical performance out of Salt Lake City in 1932—all of them ahead of the curve.[84]

Two years later, with the aid of Vassar graduate and theater producer Barbara Butler Tappan, Arden started her own national radio program from WABC studios in New York City.[85] "In her brisk, vital way," as her ads worded it, Elizabeth Arden spoke weekly on "the beauty-duty of every woman." Accompanying her was the famous high-society newspaper columnist Cholly Knickerbocker, aka Maury H. B. Paul, a man whose life a friend described as "a candid striving for effect, to which he is impelled by the honest desire to have people notice him."[86] While a very different man than Hauser—Paul was unquestionably identified with American blue bloods—this marketing partnership was also a triumph while it lasted.

Paul's stock in trade was dishing delectable gossipy tidbits about "Café Society," a term he coined.[87] Arden's talk was the ostensible point of the show, but what listeners really wanted to hear was Cholly Knickerbocker dissecting Kentucky Derby attendees or Windsor Castle guests. Widespread acclaim caused WABC to lengthen the show to thirty minutes and expand to forty stations nationwide.[88]

Knickerbocker aimed at exposing society's foibles. It was the perfect foil for Arden products.[89] After all, the more an everyday woman believed she knew about high society, the more she could see its members were only human, too, and the more she felt entitled to use the cosmetics by which they swore. Arden's spots—really more like infomercials—ranged from "Beauty Preparations for Summer Cruises" to "Bridal Gifts." She tied them to Knickerbocker's "patter of hot news and frivolous comment," and then featured the products in follow-on print ads.[90]

Even though Knickerbocker was a fan of Arden, or Ardenesque, products—he insisted his own mother retire nightly "in an elaborate arrangement of creams, hair net, and chin strap"—the program was short-lived, perhaps because of conflict between two titanic egos. Cholly Knickerbocker's assistant referred to Arden as "difficult," but the sybaritic, condescending, snobbish Knickerbocker had the same reputation.[91] Other problems surfaced. *Variety* thought the show had "considerable potential interest to womankind" but lambasted Paul's "thin, high and scratchy voice." The entertainment magazine also complained there was just not enough gossip: "His society people are unlabeled, his incidents unidentified as to date or family."[92] The tattling was too vague. Arden moved on.

Encouraging cash-strapped customers to part with their money for products that were never absolute necessities meant taking creative risks with production and marketing. Arden's sales figures remained buoyant in the 1930s because she was very good at that. From the mystique of her salons to the surrealism of marionettes and the novelty of radio, Arden had a knack for infiltrating the American psyche. While her "occult foreknowledge" of her field may have had a dash of instinctive magic, it was also the predictable harvest of wise decisions and hard work.

Fourteen

Marketing Value

Distinctive marketing took Arden far in the 1930s, but new products made the messages stick. Two stand out from the dozens she launched during the Great Depression: Eight Hour Cream (November 1930) and her signature Blue Grass perfume (September 1934).[1] Both are still being sold by the company that bears her name. A twenty-first-century journalist calculated that a tube of Eight Hour Cream is purchased every minute of every day.[2] Eight Hour Cream and Blue Grass led what was a massive outpouring of new items for a second decade in a row.

From the start, Arden advertised Eight Hour Cream as medicinal. An all-purpose ointment chiefly consisting of petroleum jelly, vitamin E, and salicylic acid, the salve has a startling orange color and an equally unforgettable aroma. Eight Hour Cream, she advised her customers, was a wonder. It cured cuts, burns, sunburned skin, and scars; vanquished pimples and cold sores; decreased the oiliness of skin; soothed ragged cuticles and chapped lips; smoothed unruly eyebrows and frizzy hair. The name came from her promise that healing would happen overnight, during eight hours of sleep—although a persistent tale tells how Arden restored to health a neighbor boy's scraped knees by treating them for eight hours with her cream.[3] The Arden company line held that while experimenting in the laboratory one morning, Elizabeth Arden noticed an employee with a cold sore. She dabbed on a bit of her new cream. By the end of the eight-hour workday, the sore had disappeared and the product had been named.[4]

Blue Grass became Arden's best-known scent, sprayed—by her command—throughout her salons at frequent intervals. It celebrated her equine passion. She boosted it as a fragrance "that comes from Paris, but makes you think of the blue skies of Kentucky."[5] It was, admittedly, a narrow band of women who could imagine anything at all about Kentucky, as most had never been there and few who lived in that persistently poor commonwealth could afford Arden's prices. But she adored the Blue Grass State where her darling thoroughbreds raced and where the pinnacle of her hopes—the Kentucky Derby—dangled tantalizingly before her.

The scent had, in fact, originated in France, almost certainly when Elizabeth and Gladys visited Grasse. Not far from Cannes, Grasse was the epicenter of the French perfume industry, known for centuries for its cultivation of plants and flowers used in perfume making. Arden had certainly heard of it, for just after World War I she had donated to a relief fund for the town's struggling widows and orphans when men in the perfume business failed to return from the trenches.[6] In 1926, Eugène Fuchs abandoned his law career, moved to Grasse, and began to create fragrances at his Maison Fragonard. His enthusiasm turned Grasse into an exciting stop for wealthy vacationers wanting to tour the perfume factories.

When the Graham sisters arrived, Fuchs's son Georges ran Fragonard and it was he who worked with Arden to produce and ship the scent, which she named Blue Grass, to New York. From there it was bottled, labeled, and distributed to her retail outlets around the world. Blue Grass was an instant hit and took on a life of its own, appearing in many different guises. Arden offered it in several sizes and tucked it in all manner of traveling cases, pocketbooks, and seasonal gift items. When customers snapped up Blue Grass–scented dusting powder, she developed an entire line—from shampoo to nail polish—infused with Blue Grass.[7]

Nicolai Remisoff designed the original Blue Grass advertisement. He created a white, Chagall-like horse floating in a blue field. Its tail and mane blew whimsically in opposite directions as a star, encircled by small clouds, hovered above. Arden rhapsodized that it "captivated our whole imagination" and professed herself "simply delighted with it."[8] Three years later, she replaced his art with hers. She drew a chunky, rearing horse wreathed in flowers. It became her long-lasting patented trademark, synonymous with the scent, indelibly linking it to the high-status world of thoroughbred racing. She designed and patented several horse-themed items connected to Blue Grass, including perfume bottles—one came with a little plastic rearing horse inside it—guest soaps, and jewelry. She even had it printed on fabric and made into dresses.[9]

As HARD TIMES PERSISTED, Elizabeth Arden finally had to rethink her advertising message. Dwelling too much on the Depression could scare clients. Ignoring it might make her seem callous. Her new campaign marketed value to solicit customer loyalty. Competitors' free samples, she preached, were not free and meant "you have been paying too much before." "Quality means *Economy* . . . Economy means *Wise Spending*," she stressed.[10] "By refusing to be deceived by offers of 'free' preparations . . . by considering the *contents*, not the camouflage of attractive wrappings . . . by insisting upon having the one group of preparations whose quality has remained unchanged—you have helped us to maintain the standards of Elizabeth Arden's Preparations." In case that was a step too far, she sought an honest middle ground: "When you buy

Elizabeth Arden Preparations, true enough, you pay for what you get. But . . . *you get what you pay for!*"[11] The very quality of her products made them economical.[12] "Buy bargains in haste and repent at leisure," she warned.[13]

Her products' worth became her talking point. Don't buy cheap cosmetics just to try them, since Arden toiletries were proven to work. Don't be taken in by a "fancy container" or a "paid endorsement" for, she cautioned, neither had "the slightest effect on quality."[14] Eventually, and uncharacteristically, she boasted that a ten-week supply of Arden's basic skin preparations (cleansing cream, astringent, and moisturizer) averaged only fifty cents a week, and the same was true for three months' worth of her foundation, rouge, powder, and lipstick.[15]

Arden suggested low-cost or long-lasting budget stretchers, such as "indelible" makeup.[16] Arden's was probably the first branded indelible lipstick advertised by a commercial beauty concern, back in 1922, and she was among the earliest to offer waterproof mascara as well.[17] While indelible lipstick could ruin fabrics and seemed unhygienic to some, indelible mascara had few detractors. No woman wanted black puddles under her eyes as she left the movie theater or the swimming pool.[18] Undeniably, though, indelible cosmetics saved money.

False eyelashes lasted even longer. Used for centuries by the demimonde, they were considered an extreme form of disguise and thus wholly disreputable. But in Europe, "women without long eyelashes" had already begun "to look a little funny."[19] In America, dramatic lashes on Hollywood close-ups were seductive. Respectable women gained permission to try them with Arden's unimpeachable recommendation.

She never stopped pushing color harmony consultations, but she began to recommend them as educational and economical because they taught how to avoid spoiling a new outfit with "injudicious make-up."[20] And because even millionaires were not immune to the Depression, Arden specialists could, she noted without a speck of irony, color-match makeup to mink coats.[21] Everyone who has ever had a beauty consultation knows what Arden understood: it's very difficult to keep the pocketbook closed when being lavished with personal attention by a flattering demonstrator.

Arden sought other ways to market value. A less expensive version of her full salon regimen that she called the "Debutante Treatment" guaranteed "Loveliness with Economy." In only thirty minutes, and for a mere $2.50, a woman would be "cleansed, refreshed, and treated to a delightful new make-up" and a free color harmony chart.[22] She began offering group discounts on exercise classes and dropped prices during the summer when more Americans went outdoors.[23] Elizabeth Arden introduced gift certificates in 1936—a year before Rubinstein, and before they became common among other merchants. Every salon treatment and toiletry item could then be economically gifted, in whole or in part.[24]

The most repugnant idea to reduce retail prices circled Arden like a hungry shark and she resisted until she was the very last in the business to adopt it: a nationwide sale. Loathing of sales united manufacturers and retailers. In 1938, wrote _The Drug and Cosmetic Industry_, sales "ran riot, the final straw being the entrance of Elizabeth Arden into this type of selling, with a 20-per-cent-off sale in June." Employees found sales difficult to manage. Retailers felt sales cut into steady purchases. Everyone in the business believed that "prestige and glamour [were] being sacrificed to bargains." A buyer for a Buffalo, New York, department store fretted that "half-price sales and free merchandise, or whatever you want to call it, have certainly done away with keeping customers interested in a complete treatment and large sizes are no longer in demand."[25]

Memorable marketing, Arden felt, was better than sales. In addition to Gaba Girls and puppets, she commissioned Paris-trained artist Clara Fargo Thomas to create a gargantuan, eleven-foot-tall mural, almost eighty feet long. In fourteen tempera-on-wood panels, _A Pageant of Beauty_ illustrated cosmetics history from Queen Nefertiti through China,

Greece, Rome, India, and the European Renaissance before concluding in the twentieth century. Arden's splashy English premiere raised
money for playgrounds through King George's Jubilee Trust. She then
shipped the mural across the Atlantic for a New York opening at Saks
Fifth Avenue. Artist and patron posed together for photos with the
mural as background. A fortnight later, the outsize artwork embarked
on a tour of major American cities, sometimes punctuated by Arden's
appearance.[26]

After a year's perambulation, the mural went to Mount Holyoke
College in Massachusetts, part of Arden's consistent outreach to the
younger generation through engagements with women's colleges.[27] *The
Mount Holyoke News* emphasized its considerable pedagogical use, especially for history and art classes. "It may be somewhat of a surprise,"
undergraduate journalist Mary Wick wrote, "that one thousand years
before Christ women were as much given to the use of lipstick and mascara as today." Mount Holyoke paid to transport the mural, which
Arden loaned for free. She sent along two thousand exhibit brochures at
no cost. Arden intended *A Pageant of Beauty* to rest permanently in one
of her homes.[28]

Her mural eventually settled down, but she continued traveling to
maintain ties with clients and friends overseas as political tensions increased across Europe. Far-right street demonstrations in Paris generated
anti-fascist responses as French parliamentary leaders looked nervously
eastward to Hitler's consolidation of power in 1933. Still, the salons remained open in Berlin and Rome and, under Gladys's careful management, across France.[29] Everyone appreciated the precious firsthand
updates when Europeans such as French couturier Jacques Heim visited
New York. He was welcomed warmly at a luncheon with Arden, Rubinstein, Condé Nast, Hattie Carnegie, Adam Gimbel, and Edna Woolman Chase, all eager for news.[30]

The planned coronation of Great Britain's newest king in May 1937
was a happy distraction. It was the perfect time, Arden felt, to introduce

"Coronation Red" lipstick, then an entire "Royal Make-Up" line, and Coronation color harmony boxes. Her "Royal Lipstick" came in a winsome case with a crown on top that was both decorative and useful because it contained Blue Grass perfume that "scented the lipstick itself." All her advertisements featured women in tiaras as the excitement intensified.[31]

King Edward VIII's unexpected abdication necessitated a seismic change of plans. He stepped down to marry American divorcée Wallis Simpson. They were known thereafter as the Duke and Duchess of Windsor. His brother ascended to the throne instead, becoming King George VI on the same day that had been planned for Edward. The world celebrated anyway. Arden was in London for the parties and parades, and possibly the coronation itself.[32] Luckily for her, none of her advertisements included the name of the king-to-be, nor of Simpson, so while the wearer of the crown changed, Arden ads remained relevant, unlike those of many less lucky royal souvenir sellers.

"I HAVE BEEN FRIGHTFULLY busy all summer," Elizabeth confessed to Alfred Stieglitz in 1936.[33] It was not just innovation, travel, sales, and marketing that crowded Arden's hours. As her fame increased, so did the demands on her time. Even the president called on her.

Elected in a landslide in 1932, Franklin Roosevelt personified the hopes of millions of Depression-blighted Americans. Elizabeth Arden was as far from destitute as her luxury creations were from drugstore cosmetics, but because she had loved Elisabeth Marbury, Arden was a Democratic Party fundraiser and a Roosevelt supporter. Although never close friends with the First Couple, as a global industrialist and an internationally known American brand, Elizabeth Arden was definitely on their radar. That may be why Roosevelt selected her to serve on the Women's Committee of the National Recovery Administration (NRA). Arden, Amelia Earhart, Fannie Hurst, Lilly Daché, and Barnard College dean Virginia Gildersleeve represented their fields as the National Industrial Recovery Act swung into effect. It required employers to follow the new NRA rules regarding child labor, minimum wages, and maximum hours. The women were to "marshal public opinion in the right direction by appeals to the employer and the consumer." Businesses that adhered to the act's requirements earned the right to display a patriotic blue-eagle symbol on their premises and in their advertising, which Arden promptly began to do.[34]

A similar NRA initiative brought Elizabeth Arden and Helena Rubinstein together. They met with beauty experts Clara Ogilvie and Kathleen Mary Quinlan and three women's magazine editors in New York City to encourage toiletries vendors "to sign up under the NRA." Given the sales experience represented, plus the women's highly competitive natures, it was no surprise that the committee met with "very satisfactory" results.[35]

Cosmetics concerns employed a large percentage of women, bucking the powerful prevailing social belief that wives should not hold jobs if their husbands worked. Most skilled salon labor was considered unsuitable for men, except hairdressing. Men sold cosmetics wholesale, but not retail; nor did they serve as demonstrators. Arden had long hired women at all levels. Her European division managers were mostly men, but women ran salons and departments in every country. Business expert Catharine Oglesby calculated that there were "half a million women" in cosmetics in the United States in the mid-1930s and that more women worked in and found jobs with better salaries there than in any other industry.[36]

Oglesby had been Arden's advertising manager and Rubinstein's promotion manager before starting her own ad agency.[37] She was just one of many female publicity agents Arden hired.[38] Arden's best employees lived a life unimaginable for most women of the time. Gwen Bett—who spoke five languages—began in Arden's London salon. She "traveled down the Rhine giving treatments," and spent sixteen months in Stock-

holm and two years in Rome opening new Red Door salons and training the managers. Willa Lynn journeyed to China and the Philippines
to teach Arden skin care methods.[39] Mignon Scantlebury, an Australian, circled the globe during her thirty-year career with Arden. Known
as Miss Sydney, she oversaw Red Door trainees before spending her last
decade managing the Washington, D.C., salon.[40]

Working for Arden helped many employees to independent beauty
careers of their own. Helen Cornelius was a dependable and game Arden
publicity head, popular with others in the industry. She went solo after
eighteen months, opening her own agency and becoming vice president
of the Fashion Group in 1939.[41] Arden's personal assistant, Margaret de
Mille, moved on after five years to a varied three-decade career in fashion.[42] At least two women capitalized on what they learned to write
books. Edyth Thornton McLeod appropriated her former boss's theories and methods for *How to Sell Cosmetics*.[43] Margaretta Byers stole Arden's color harmony ideas and folded them into her book, *Designing
Women*. In it, Byers classified the temperaments of women, including
Arden, whom she categorized as a "Coquette": a "feminine, frivolous
woman, gay, provocative, demure, fragile." Byers may have known Arden's theories, but she missed the measure of her former boss.[44] As one
admirer put it, Arden "was about as fragile as a football tackle."[45]

As Arden knew and FDR learned, providing jobs wasn't enough to
stem the nation's economic pain. She contributed money, time, and ingenuity to many different causes and charities throughout the Great
Depression and beyond. She cut her own salary by 33 percent.[46] As volunteer agencies formed at the city, state, and national level, Arden was
frequently tapped to lead donation drives in the cosmetics and fashion
industries. She was often the only female heading such corporate initiatives. Her leadership of the Family Welfare Committee's cosmetics
subcommittee in 1933, for example, raised $7,712.[47] For five years, Ar-
den chaired the Red Cross toilet preparations group where she effectively increased membership and fundraising.[48] These efforts brought

her once again into contact with Helena Rubinstein when both were invited to a tea for urban and suburban members of Anne Morgan's American Woman's Association.[49] Arden and Rubinstein were also among those gathered under the banner of the National Federation of Business and Professional Women (NFBPW) during a week devoted to encouraging women's work. They hosted separate events at which they told their success stories to encourage the NFBPW to carry on making, as its motto proclaimed, "Better Business Women for a Better Business World."[50]

Such leadership, plus Arden's support of President Roosevelt, resulted in an invitation to his first annual White House Birthday Ball in early 1934. It functioned as a fundraiser for his Warm Springs Foundation to aid infantile paralysis (or polio) sufferers.[51] She remained committed to the fight against that terrible disease, which struck Roosevelt when he was thirty-nine years old, immobilizing him from the waist down.[52]

Lending her name, giving her time and money, and appearing in the company of other well-known philanthropists and industrialists buttressed the caring image she cultivated in her advertisements, allowed people to feel that they knew her, and added to the overall sense that she and her cosmetics line could be trusted. When her employees contributed, as they did across the country, that reflected well on her, too.[53]

The point is that Elizabeth Arden did not simply pull out her checkbook, although she also did that. She participated actively in numerous causes yet concentrated her efforts on health care, classical music, education, and child welfare. She gave lectures, made radio broadcasts, chaired committees, donated Arden products, opened her home and her salons for benefits, sponsored fundraisers, and ran charity fashion shows for organizations ranging from the New York Philharmonic to the Girl Scouts. Seldom parsimonious, Elizabeth Arden gave because she wanted to, and her lengthy list of charitable giving went on long after the Depression ended.[54]

Fifteen

New Directions

F or those living through it, the Great Depression seemed end-less. Elizabeth Arden knew two things for sure. First, profits would keep rising only if she could creatively capitalize on the American hunger for distraction. Second, it was harder to do that than it should have been. Democrats in government, she came to believe, were to blame for the country's interminable economic woes, and at even greater fault for tying the hands of industrialists with unnecessary regulations. Frustrated herself, Arden understood why Americans vanished into the imaginary worlds created by radio and film.

In a move that shocked the industry, Arden "invade[d the Holly-wood] makeup biz" by purchasing the DeLong Makeup Products Company in 1935 and rechristening it Elizabeth Arden Theatrical Products.[1] She hired modernist artist Paul Frankl to design a suitable interior for the old DeLong building on Sunset Boulevard and maintained Robare DeLong as head of her laboratory.[2] She launched her film makeup line to the boisterous well wishes of celebrity friends such as David O. Selznick, Carole Lombard, and Gary Cooper.[3] Their unhappiness with the film makeup of the time no doubt suggested the idea to her. They joined in "an extensive round of" promotion for her makeup.[4] The entertainment magazine *Variety* claimed Arden was in it for the profit. She was "out for blood" and trying "every angle" to land film contracts in her competition with Max Factor and the Westmore brothers.[5]

Formerly collaborators, the Factor and Westmore companies were locked in a battle to control film makeup. Factor had been in the business since its inception, branched out to drugstore sales, and had just about every stunning Hollywood siren shilling for him. The Westmores' father, George, established the family name as a wigmaker and makeup artist in the 1910s. Just days after Arden started in New York, his four sons opened the House of Westmore on Sunset Boulevard. Big stars like Bette Davis and Claudette Colbert appeared in Westmore ads.[6] But Arden shunned endorsements, neither dropping names nor chasing celebrities for testimonials.

The Drug and Cosmetic Industry reported that "this unusual departure by Elizabeth Arden is being watched with great interest by the industry." The question was, Could a traditional makeup firm move successfully into film? She initially kept DeLong's "Nuchromatic" name and soon expanded upon his abbreviated product line, offering a panoply of Arden Nuchromatic Screen & Stage Make-up for sale in "burnt orange and brown" packaging with "[a] Hollywood address and [a] movie camera" instead of her "chaste and unchanging" pink-and-gold boxes.[7] Arden meant it for use on film sets, but she also offered it to her regular clientele. Her demonstrators taught that Nuchromatic was just the thing when a little drama was needed. Arden's trendspotting reputation made at least one industry insider certain that her movie makeup for film stars and filmgoers was a sure success.[8]

Why did she move into movie makeup? Practically, to profit from Hollywood's unstoppable rise. Personally, it was love. She grew up alongside black-and-white silent films and marveled as they blossomed into Technicolor "talkies." In 1910, the year Florence Graham opened her doors with such hope, the word *star* first appeared to describe a movie actress. Films about working girls like her soon gave way to stories showcasing high fashion and conspicuous consumption.[9] Arden's success was partially her lucky timing. Women wanted to look like screen actresses and though her target market was patrician, she gladly sold to anyone with stars in her eyes. Plus, both male and female actors wore film makeup; this was useful as she contemplated men as clients.

Arden did more than create movie makeup: she made and appeared in motion pictures. *The Film Daily* praised the 1933 newsreel *Broadway Gossip* "featuring a nice variety of slices from real life caught hot with the camera," including Arden lecturing about business success.[10] She liked what she saw and then produced *Steps to Loveliness*, a demonstration of how to use Arden products at home shown in store auditoriums. *Steps to Loveliness* was so popular that tickets were required to reserve a seat.[11] Scarbrough's in Austin ran the film eight times in one week and capitalized on the excitement by bringing in Arden demonstrator Edith Cravens for "a frank and helpful discussion of your own beauty problems." Stella Harding did the same at the much larger J. W. Robinson store in Los Angeles.[12] While not a film celebrity, Arden was famous enough that aspiring actress Eunice Quedens renamed herself Eve Arden to borrow a little of her star power, and Samuel Goldwyn considered making a film called *Beauty Parlor*, set on location at Maine Chance and starring the glamorous Merle Oberon as Arden.[13]

Fellow Santa Anita Turf Club member Jock Whitney may have nudged Arden into film makeup. Whitney founded Pioneer Pictures in 1933 because of his interest in the potential of color film. A member of one of America's eastern old money families, he invested thousands of dollars in Technicolor, an invention that thrilled audiences but made actors despair. Early Technicolor film distorted the traditional greasepaint look of actors—so much so that some refused to have anything to do with it. There is evidence that Arden's January 1933 *Steps to Loveliness* was filmed in early Technicolor.[14] Perhaps her cosmetics expertise and the chemists on her payroll found a way to diminish the distortion, for Elizabeth Arden Theatrical Products debuted two years later, just as Whitney teamed up with David O. Selznick to form Selznick International Pictures. Did Arden and Whitney put their heads together about the Technicolor makeup problem? It seems likely.

When Whitney took the helm of Selznick Pictures, he gained a powerful partner. Selznick's deep roots in filmmaking and his successes made him a dominant industry force. Whitney and Selznick shot blockbusters like *Gone With the Wind* and *The Prisoner of Zenda*. In 1936, they produced *The Garden of Allah*, based on a 1905 novel and starring Marlene Dietrich, Charles Boyer, and Basil Rathbone—all of whom wore Arden's Nuchromatic Screen & Stage Make-up. The next year, *A Star Is Born* showcased Janet Gaynor in Nuchromatic.[15] Longtime Paramount Pictures makeup head and Westmore brother Wally admitted to favoring Arden's film makeup for Technicolor's closest competitor, the Keller-Dorian color filmmaking system.[16] Encouraged, Arden considered opening a second factory in England just to produce film makeup.[17]

It was not to be. Though the makeup was used in other movies, Arden's Nuchromatic adventure was short-lived. Robare DeLong sued her for $250,000 that he claimed she owed him in royalties, and he sought to bring an injunction against her even as he set about trying to open a rival film makeup company.[18] Max Factor's pioneering Pan-Cake makeup fixed the distortion problem altogether in 1937, and that's when Arden ceded the field.[19] She wound down Nuchromatic Screen & Stage, but slowly, because she found she could repurpose it for portrait photography, then undergoing a renaissance thanks to affordable handheld cameras.[20]

The emerging medium of television presented a different conundrum. In June 1938, the Fashion Group invited Amelia Umnitz to speak about the puzzling problems TV lights caused for makeup. Umnitz was

NBC's style expert and fashion editor, plus the company's only female television announcer. She had been broadcasting fashion shows and even crocheting contests as executives sought the right formula for the new technology.[21] Television—which was only black and white then—began with actors in clown white and black makeup. Mechanical improvements required changes. Close-ups necessitated different makeup than long shots. Red turned a strange color under the lights. What to do with lips was perplexing. "Having been 'conditioned' by [black-and-white] movies," Unmitz said, "the public expects to see lips that are black and shiny." At that time, television producers were limping along with an unconvincing deep red lipstick overlaid with brown. Umnitz thought that if useful television colors could be created, they would be too dark for daytime wear.[22]

After a year and a half of laboratory trial and error—during which time Roosevelt became the first president to appear on television when he opened the World's Fair on April 30, 1939—Arden unveiled "Telecast Red" lipstick, a "very rich, deep, black tulip tone." She had the nascent TV industry in mind, but, like Nuchromatic, marketed it to her regular clients, too. It debuted just weeks after the Television Ball, perhaps the first televised fundraising event. Twelve NBC televisions set up in the Waldorf-Astoria foyer and one at the Goddard Neighborhood Center allowed those attending and those benefiting to watch the elaborate fashion show in real time.[23]

Arden explicitly linked her new shade to the event: "Remember the exotic mahogany-brown make-up the telecast models wore at the Television Ball? The debs liked it so much they wore it to lunch at the Stork Club next day," Arden's ad read. So she "quick as a flash, thought up Telecast Red," which was "a little daring, and definitely an exciting change." In keeping with color harmony, she sold one version of this makeup line for blondes and another for brunettes, followed shortly by matching nail polish and color harmony boxes.[24] It is unclear whether

Arden's Telecast line was used extensively, or at all, in television studios. She may just have been the first to jump on an evolving trend by creating everyday makeup based on the real, and still fairly odd, thing.

Or perhaps the second. In 1932, Max Factor was one of several sponsors of a television show that could be seen only in the Los Angeles May Company's department store window. In 1936, he advised all performers to learn how very different television makeup was, because TV was coming, ready or not. Factor thought purple would work for lips and contouring, and blue eye shadow might fool the treacherous television cameras, so he copyrighted "Television Blue" and experimented with "a whitish-gray base, black eyebrows and blue lipstick."[25] Factor did not live to see his faith in television fully rewarded.[26] After his 1938 death, his son, Max Factor Jr., carried on the company and the research, deciding that television broadcasts demanded "white highlighting around eyes and nostrils and heavy blue-black lips" to create a natural appearance.[27]

While she worked to solve the television makeup problem, Arden expanded her radio presence by sponsoring a nationwide sixty-minute music program known interchangeably as *The Hour of Romance* and *The Hour of Charm*. Both names captured perfectly Arden's gossamer pink world. By this time, Arden had fifteen years' experience with radio. She had done on-air interviews herself on both coasts, sponsored shows, and even, as a tie-in to *The Garden of Allah*, gave a "special preview broadcast" of the film on KMTR-Hollywood.[28]

But *The Hour of Romance* was big-league radio. It debuted before a live NBC audience on September 29, 1937, and played nationwide on at least seventy-five stations.[29] Arden sponsored Eddy Duchin, a popular orchestra leader she signed to a fifty-two-week contract.[30] He always opened with "The Loveliness of You" followed by dance numbers and well-liked tunes, such as "Hasta Mañana" and "Whispers in the Dark," sometimes with guest vocalists. Arden "personally select[ed] all the songs and [sat] in on rehearsals," according to *Variety*.[31] It was, *Motion Picture Daily* summarized, "a straightforward popular music show, with the Duchin orchestra offering melodies in a finished, beautifully orchestrated style."[32]

Between musical intervals, Arden gave uplifting mini-lectures with titles such as "What Every Woman Wants to Know." The melting voice of a skilled radio performer concluded by offering her latest booklet, *Professional Information*, free to listeners.[33] *Radio Daily* noted that Arden "faltered once or twice" in her delivery but gave her an otherwise positive review.[34]

She launched an on-air "Cinderella" contest in February 1938 for the best rejoinder to "What is your most personal beauty problem and why haven't you overcome it?"[35] She corralled her friends as judges: Lord & Taylor vice president Dorothy Shaver; Bonwit Teller president Hortense Odlum; and Mary Lewis, vice president of Best & Co. The winner received "a three-week stay in the big city at the 'very best hotel,' and a complete course of beauty treatments in Elizabeth Arden's Fifth Avenue Shop."[36] Popular acclaim caused her to repeat the contest.[37]

FRANKLIN ROOSEVELT ALSO UNDERSTOOD the power of radio. Early in his presidency, he signed the Communications Act, which created the Federal Communications Commission and gave the federal government oversight of the radio, telephone, and telegraph industries. It was another red flag to Arden. Never quite as committed to the Democratic Party as her late friend Bessie Marbury, Arden lost patience with Roosevelt's New Deal regulatory policies. Like many other moguls, she believed they tied her hands in unhelpful ways.[38]

The 1936 Robinson-Patman Act precipitated Arden's final break with the Democrats. Congress intended the legislation to end unfair price discrimination by making it illegal for manufacturers to charge retailers different prices for the same products, because this often favored large stores over small. The law hurt Arden because she linked her wholesale discounts to a retailer's sales volume. At the top end, those who sold more than $7,500 per year of Arden goods received 40 percent off list price. Retailers with annual sales of less than $200 only received a 25 percent discount. According to the complaint lodged against her by the Federal Trade Commission (FTC), Arden further discriminated by paying to transport products to some retailers but not others, and by augmenting the advertising budget of select customers.[39]

Arden was not alone. The FTC also targeted Charles of the Ritz, Coty, Richard Hudnut, Primrose House, and Bourjois. Nor were the accusations limited to cosmetics firms. Grocery wholesalers, pharmaceutical companies, and other types of businesses functioned similarly and so ran afoul of the new law, which had as many detractors as supporters. This was in part because of the widespread confusion regarding the nature and purposes of the Robinson-Patman Act. U.S. District Court judge Walter C. Lindley huffed, "I doubt if any judge would assert that he knows exactly what does or does not amount to violation of the Robinson-Patman Act in any and all instances."[40] The attorney for the Toilet Goods Association agreed. "I have not yet met a lawyer who said he knew what the Robinson-Patman Act meant. . . . No business man would have drawn up such a law. It has been called 'God's gift to Certified Public Accountants.'"[41] Arden felt the act removed one of her strongest incentives to encourage retailers to buy and sell more of her toiletries. It was nothing less than unwarranted federal interference in her business and a hindrance to her profitability.[42]

Adding insult to injury, a simultaneous FTC charge of false advertising forced Arden to stop making claims about some of her best-known and best-loved products. She could no longer state that Ardena Velva Cream Mask, Orange Skin Cream, or Eight Hour Cream prevented wrinkles, recontoured the face, or provided "nutrition" to the skin.[43] She could not assert that Venetian and Ardena Eyelash Growers actually made eyelashes grow.[44] She had already fought that battle years earlier against the American Medical Association, when Tom Lewis's diplomacy kept her claims intact. But a new Food, Drug, and Cosmetic Act in 1938 had the power of the federal government behind it. It was frustrating to be forced to retract promises made to her clients. Such a law "completely ignores the fact that for centuries women have bought face creams knowing full well that they do not come from a cow," one Yardley executive argued.[45] A provisional ruling that coal tar could no longer be used in mascara drove Arden to complain. She met with FDA bureaucrats and "accused them of interfering with her crusade to make American women more beautiful," *The Christian Science Monitor* noted dryly.[46]

Brushes with the feds convinced Arden to listen sympathetically to anti–New Dealers. She moved to the right toward the pro-business party of new friends such as Republican moderate Jock Whitney and Hollywood studio CEOs. She would never go as far as her libertarian, isolationist pal Hedda Hopper, but she empathized with businesses charged with breaking regulatory and antitrust laws.[47] She joined *Vogue* editor Edna Woolman Chase on the Women's Non-Partisan Committee to help put a Republican on the New York Supreme Court.[48] At the 1939 Advertising Federation of America's annual conference she spoke alongside George Sokolsky, a conservative *New York Herald Tribune* correspondent and New Deal critic.[49] Their topic was "Advertising Today Builds Tomorrow's Prosperity."[50] She sidestepped outright disparagement of Roosevelt, but her political transition was nearly complete when she perceived that Republican policies protected her company. Like most business owners of the era, she generally kept her politics private, at least while the other party was in power.

In October 1938, as she was nearing sixty (not that anyone knew her actual age), *Fortune* magazine ran a lengthy feature story on Elizabeth Arden. Such coverage was quite a coup, or it would have been had it not been so thoroughly condescending in tone. Arden baffled the *Fortune* journalists. The premier magazine for businessmen began with a description:

She is a small woman, standing no more than five-foot-one in
high heels. She has the figure and carriage of a girl of twenty.
She could not be more interested in bodies if she were a surgeon. Her naturally pretty face is carefully groomed, as it must
be, but she uses her cosmetics unobtrusively. Her hair is
reddish-brown with flecks of gray, and she wears it short. Her
eyes are wide and blue, and she smiles often, in a fixed, indefi-
nite sort of way. When not aroused, she speaks in a soft, light
voice. Her diction and manner of speech are the result of a
three-year grooming undergone while she was in her early
twenties.

Certainly she was physically attractive. Yet *Fortune* saw something
false about it, something learned, or faked. Underneath it all was a
flawed, unpredictable despot wielding entirely too much power for a
woman:

> She is the sole proprietor of the salons, the sole stockholder . . .
> of all the Arden companies save one, the autocratic boss of a
> thousand-odd employees. She is erratic, unpredictable, vague,
> and tempestuous. She is capable of rages at which strong
> men turn pale. As a businesswoman she is a cost accountant's
> headache. . . . She has probably *earned* more money than any
> other businesswoman in U.S. history, and she has done it by
> commanding the sun to stand still until she got the right shade
> of pink in a bottle, the right texture of cream in a jar, and a rib-
> bon tied *just* so around a hundred thousand soapboxes.

Her managerial skills were unprofessional and she had no head for
business. She left potential profits on the table, *Fortune* reported. Her
salons, it was rumored, didn't make money. Her earnings came from
the wholesale arm, but she micromanaged directors so they quit—or

she fired them arbitrarily. All sound businessmen knew the best way to run a company was to concentrate on a "few fast-moving, large-volume items" yet Arden manufactured too many products and sold them in far too many shapes and sizes. As a capitalist, *Fortune* scoffed, Arden had it all wrong.

Seeking some way to explain her achievements, they went low: "Perfectionism is one answer, but only a partial one, to the resounding Arden success. A flair for thinking up new products and packages and styles and services that women will want and buy, is another answer, likewise partial. The nearest approach to a total answer is that . . . she has consistently followed one of the shrewdest and most vital showman's instincts anybody ever possessed. Her salons, her stables, her perfectionism, her rages, her eccentricities are all part of the Great Show." Translation: she was the P. T. Barnum of cosmetics.

Like Barnum's, though, her customers were satisfied. While the editors hated her success, they had to give her a little credit. They halfheartedly noted her "courage, vitality, and passionate belief in herself, her ideas, and her products," and admitted that she was "tops—absolute, unqualified, unarguable tops—in the 'treatment' cosmetics business. In this chancy field of enterprise, ruled by high price, high style, and high tension, Arden was first to arrive, and she has been the Tiffany of her trade for all the years since then. Other lines, other salons, most notably those of Helena Rubinstein, may grow and prosper, but none have yet been able to achieve the size or, more important, the prestige of Elizabeth Arden." And that can be attributed only to Elizabeth Arden herself, for *Fortune* conceded that "she is the absolute dictator of [her company's] policies; its policies are her whims and . . . she has a whim of iron." While that may describe exactly how men like Andrew Carnegie and George Pullman made their fortunes, it was inappropriate in a woman: "Her success is a constant mystery and bewilderment to outsiders." It certainly seemed a puzzle to the men of *Fortune*.[51]

Others were less confounded and more laudatory. Neiman-Marcus vice president Stanley Marcus named Elizabeth Arden one of a "select group of world-famous designers" as he granted her a Neiman-Marcus Award for Distinguished Service in the Field of Fashion for 1939. A standing room only crowd of two thousand people applauded as Arden's name was announced. She was the first cosmetics creator to win.[52] Over the next six decades, this accolade was earned by more than one hundred people, but never, it might be noted, to Helena Rubinstein.

By the end of the decade, Arden was a sought-after industry leader who moved effortlessly among nobility, high achievers, and society elites. She had a box at the Met.[53] She judged the 1938 Advertising Awards, alongside William Paley of CBS.[54] With Paley, she, Jock Whitney, flying ace Eddie Rickenbacker, Laurance Rockefeller, and others made up a happy group at the gala *Gone With the Wind* opening in December 1939.[55] She was seen at Cape Cod regattas, the exclusive North Wales Club in Virginia, art openings, and every important horse race and social gathering from Saratoga to Santa Anita. When she helped organize a fundraiser for Denver's National Jewish Hospital in Stanley Marcus's honor, she was the lone woman joining him on the dais. She was one of twenty-three celebrities in the book-length anthology *Profiles from* The New Yorker.[56]

Arden justifiably received credit for color harmony. She had introduced it in 1931 and not long after it had taken on a life of its own. No company, no CEO, could do anything but fall in line with Arden's dictate to matching clothing with cosmetics. What today's critics might call "matchy-matchy" had become, thanks to Arden, de rigueur—and for nearly every part of the body. It was an extremely lucrative idea. She never disabused anyone of the belief that without her skill, sartorial disaster was inescapable.

Autumn evening gowns in 1937 required Arden's "Sequin Make-Up" while dress shades for winter 1938 needed her mascara in green, light blue, dark blue, violet, *and* copper.[57] The real star was "Cyclamen"—a prodigiously popular and lasting color, as it turned out—eclipsing both

her "Sky Blue Pink" and a pink she created specially to match French
designer Jeanne Paquin's "Fondant Pink."[58] In the spring of 1939, the
Cyclamen craze continued, as Arden added new reds and browns, still
harmonizing her shades with exclusive designers like Lelong, Molyneux, Chanel, and Schiaparelli.[59] Other product lines, including shoes,
hosiery, and girdles, jumped on board, creating and marketing their
products to go with Arden's colors. Such coordinated color harmony
promotions continued consistently for three decades.[60]

This was an important change. Instead of Arden creating colors to
coordinate with clothing, now designers—from veil makers to jewelers
to ball gown couturiers—followed her. "On the argument that knowledge of the correct makeup to wear with the colors used in their new
collection will help to promote sales," *Women's Wear Daily* reported in
June 1939, "Spectator Sports, Ltd., London garment manufacturers, are
tabbing their clothes with Elizabeth Arden makeup instructions." In
fact, the article continued, a Scottish sweater manufacturer "recently
asked one of the leading cosmetic producers to supply them with their
coming makeup colorings" rather than the reverse. The reason? "This
attention to cosmetics on the part of garment houses here seems to have
sprung mainly from the fact that the beauty people were ahead of most
on cyclamen."[61] Of course, it wasn't "the beauty people"; it was Elizabeth Arden. She invented Cyclamen.

Determining fashion's colors meant being out in front. To maintain
this preferred position, Elizabeth Arden teamed up with Color Affiliates, a small group of wholesalers that chose colors and harmonized
them across their accessory brands and seasonal ready-to-wear clothing. Color Affiliates included manufacturers of gloves, shoes, millinery,
and fabric. Together with Arden's complementary makeup, they coordinated, sold, and advertised matching and harmonizing colors for every
new season.[62]

Just as she partnered with couturiers, Arden premiered makeup and
perfumes with department stores nationwide. Many stores had their own

fashion departments. Lord & Taylor milliner Sally Victor designed "Lipstick Hats" to match six Arden lipstick colors.[63] Best & Co. chemists invented their own shades. Understanding they would sell better under the Elizabeth Arden brand than their own, they partnered, making Arden hues available on Best & Co. exclusive products. Bonwit Teller's milliners created hats to coordinate with Arden's scented Valentine's Day sachet.[64] Woodward & Lothrop teamed up with Arden's "White Orchid" perfume to urge 1940 brides to have an "orchid wedding."[65] That highly popular campaign began the country's long love affair with orchids.

LOOKING TOWARD THE FUTURE was an American pastime and in April 1939, all eyes turned to the New York World's Fair, where the theme was "The World of Tomorrow." Fair organizers consulted Elizabeth Arden and other fashion executives in a July 19, 1937, meeting at the Empire State Building. Called the Fashion Council, the leading members formed a Coordinating Council of twenty-four, including Arden, Dorothy Shaver, Mary Lewis, Carmel Snow, and Edna Woolman Chase. They brainstormed ideas for the Hall of Fashion, which was to include a section called "Vanity Fair" or "Cosmetic Building"—there was little enthusiasm for either name—for the toiletries display.[66] The director of concessions explained the fair would take at least 10 percent of the income from exhibitors. Originally contemplating erecting her own building, Arden pulled back because of cost concerns and instead rented space alongside other cosmetics sellers.

The "World of Tomorrow" theme suggested confidence, which included the expectation of a record-breaking domestic and international World's Fair attendance of sixty million visitors.[67] Organizers assembled a time capsule to mark the occasion. They chose three items "pertaining to the grooming and vanity of women": a hair clip, a Lilly Daché hat, and the Elizabeth Arden Daytime-Cyclamen Color Harmony Box.

What those who dig up the capsule in the year 6939—five thousand optimistic years in the future—will think of it can only be imagined, but Arden was delighted at her product's inclusion.[68]

She began her publicity by inviting new and old clients "from north, east, south and west and across the seas, to come to her New York salon during the World's Fair season."[69] Knowing that time would be short for the busy visitor, Arden stressed convenience. She opened early and added extra classes. Pink-jacketed associates taught eight eager students at a time how to get that Arden look in an abbreviated course. Out-of-towners joined local ladies of leisure, augmented by the city's workingwomen during lunch-hour classes. The mix made for chatty and inquisitive learners.[70] At the fair itself, Arden held makeup demonstrations, consultations, and color harmony fashion shows in her beautiful Blue Grass–scented temporary store. Occasionally, Arden employees made presentations to groups. For example, Helen Cornelius spoke about "Fun, Facts and Fashions in Cosmetic Displays and Promotions" to an audience of advertisers who gathered from around the country on "International Association of Display Men" Day.[71]

The 1939 New York World's Fair ran from April through October. Arden tinkered with her roster of classes. When the fair ended, she relabeled one variation as her "New School for Co-ordinated Beauty." It continued the eight-student, forty-five-minute format, but stretched into an eight-week series of thrice-weekly classes and cost a hefty $125. The topics were largely the same: care of the skin, hair, hands, and feet; makeup application and color harmony; nutrition and healthy diet; exercise and posture. They built upon the "Maine-Chance-in-Town" course she had debuted a year earlier. It provided the Maine Chance experience—exercise followed by pampering and rejuvenation—packed into a very full day.[72]

The class she marketed to workingwomen grew in importance as the number and percentage of women in the labor force rose. Women moved into an ever-broader array of jobs as the nation became what President

Roosevelt called "the arsenal of democracy." For the National Federation of Business and Professional Women's Clubs, Arden joined Judge Dorothy Kenyon and photojournalist Margaret Bourke-White to speak about the importance of meaningful careers.[73] For what she styled "Professional and Business Women," Arden created her "Quick Make-Up Kit," designed to be kept in "an important lady's desk," and classes that began after the workday concluded.[74] She aimed a set of daily home-treatment schedule cards at "hands ravaged by the typewriter."[75] Professional women eagerly signed up for her sessions, reassured "because Miss Arden herself is a career woman," and "career women are her special concern."[76]

Like all Americans, beauty insiders worried about the possibility of another world war. To strengthen ties across the Western Hemisphere, Bonwit Teller organized a goodwill Fashion Tour of South America, sending to Buenos Aires and other big cities representatives from the brands Bonwit Teller carried. Arden did the makeup for all the models. She and her publicity head, Helen Cornelius, attended a large luncheon presided over by Bonwit Teller's president, Hortense Odlum, where attendees hashed out the details. They decided the tour should be noncommercial, so no orders would be taken nor would any goods be brought to South America to sell.[77] Since Bonwit Teller carried Arden's entire line and she had several salons in South America, she was extremely interested in the endeavor.[78] All shrewd North American industrialists looked closer to home for business connections, raw materials, and markets in the late 1930s. It was only prudent. Westward, Imperial Japan was on the march. Eastward, the Atlantic Ocean was fast filling with Nazi submarines. War threatened once more.

Sixteen

War Begins in Europe

I t was a very different sort of April in Paris for Elizabeth and Gladys. The sisters' 1939 reunion was delightful, as always, and made sweeter by the celebratory unveiling of the luxurious new Red Door Salon. But they conducted their inspection tour of factories, warehouses, salons, and retail outlets with mounting concern about Hitler's intentions. Elizabeth repeatedly begged Gladys to return to New York with her, to escape before what was surely going to be another terrible war.

Gladys resisted her sister's entreaties. She had worked so hard. The initial months of happy dreaming had given way to tough-minded negotiations with French bureaucrats, and then alternately to pushing and praising temperamental artists. When the relocated salon opened in Paris's ultrafashionable Place Vendôme, everyone agreed it was *très magnifique.* An oversize "Sky Blue Pink" model of Elizabeth Arden's flower-draped horse welcomed guests. The salon's sparse, "delicately, aggressively modern" exterior hinted at innovative ideas inside. Interior designer Raymond Nasenta drew a vibrant green line of carpet up the stairway to complement the bold salon floor done in Arden's new violet makeup color "Prince's Feather." White walls "patterned in enormous bouquets" drew the eye upward. Gladys hired costume designer Marcel Vertès to etch impressionistic, golden outlines of cherubs and winged horses, a commission that propelled Vertès toward the apex of his career. Étienne Drian painted his characteristically stylized female silhouettes throughout the salon. Curtains made of sheer material stamped with Elizabeth Arden's signature rustled gently against tall windows. On the roof, a garden oasis with solarium beds beckoned.[1]

The crème de la crème of French society turned out for the formal opening of Arden's "Place of Beauty." The sisters reveled in the moment. Guests danced to Maxim's orchestra following La Mode et la Beauté fashion show. André de Fouquières, "the most exquisite of twentieth-century dandies," emceed.[2] The revue included the Shado-Graph, Arden exercises, mannequins circulating in costumes inspired by her Blue Grass, Cyclamen, and Day and Night perfumes, and a demonstration by a Hollywood makeup artist.[3]

The grand opening failed to diminish Elizabeth's anxiety regarding her sister. Henri de Maublanc's impatience with the chaos of French politics in the 1930s made him look favorably on right-wing politicians while Gladys opposed her husband's growing affinity for national socialism. Their marital troubles were worrisome, certainly, but the real fear was broader. In early April, with last-minute preparations for the Paris salon event under way, another democracy fell when Francisco Franco's pro-Nazi forces declared victory in the Spanish Civil War. Then Mussolini's Italian fascists entered Albania. The threat of conflict and its effect on commerce had become an ever-present concern. Elizabeth reluctantly signed a document transferring the French side of her business from Gladys to Henri in hopes that his political leanings would keep the company safe should the Nazis capture France. If the Nazis invaded and lost, then the business might be protected by de Maublanc's status as minor nobility.[4] With a sinking feeling, Arden boarded Cunard's newest luxury liner, the *Queen Mary*, and sailed home. All the passengers were anxious.[5]

Reading the future correctly, Arden began selling, in her London shops, a "gas mask bag" described as "a water-proofed fabric shoulder strap handbag to hold the mask" with a tray to keep cosmetics in order. She also sold a small, flat "'service kit' . . . for uniformed clients" filled with Arden makeup.[6] Gas masks had appeared in Vienna store windows in late 1938, and by the spring of 1939, Parisians were being instructed in their use. Gladys may have suggested some sort of clever gas mask/makeup bag to her sister, and the rollout happened quickly.[7] Arden was the first to dream up and market anything like this. It was August 1939.

She was just in time. Less than one month later, on September 1, 1939, Germany attacked Poland and World War II began in Europe. England and France led the Allied response to Nazi aggression. British author Lesley Blanch wrote of the grim and determined attitude to this second go-round of a global conflict. There was less of World War I's "champagne hysteria" and "jingo braggadocio." Instead, steely-eyed Brits just got down to "the unlovely, bloody business" again. Battling for more than Poland, for more than the British Empire, they were fighting "for the whole future of civilization." Sandbags and blackout curtains appeared. Civil defense drills and uniforms replaced theater performances and ball gowns. Cecil Beaton and Noël Coward took up war work. Even the beautiful *Queen Mary* was surrendered to the effort. Repainted and stripped of its gold fixtures and mahogany paneling, it became a swift British troop ship dubbed the "Grey Ghost." No one knew how long the war would last, but it had to be won, and life had to go on.[8]

Smart industrialists like Elizabeth Arden—especially those who had lived through World War I—saw the warning signs and prepared early for shortages, price increases, and other obstacles to business. Within a week of the Nazi takeover of Poland, luxury shops in France's capital closed. People fled to the countryside. The new Red Doors in Paris were shuttered, though women could still receive treatments, which suggests that Gladys and her salon manager, Solange de Luze, remained in place. European men enlisted or were conscripted, leaving jobs that women filled. Merchants in Allied countries asked for immediate cash payment from America because of the rapidly deteriorating economic situation. *Women's Wear Daily* reported on September 7 that French manufacturers and exporters were scrambling to locate ships from neutral countries while hoping to be paid expeditiously. Some industrialists used their own funds to support the families of employees who had left to fight. Thus it was essential that American firms paid European wholesalers and distributors promptly.[9]

Importing and exporting became complicated as the war drew in more countries and the seas filled with armed vessels. Governments took firm control of financial markets, industrial output, raw materials, price setting, and manpower. Fashion and shopping reflected the belt-tightening. Elizabeth Arden could not keep enough "long-sleeved woolen nightgowns" in stock in Paris.[10] In London she sold dresses that could be quickly shrugged on over pajamas during an air raid.[11] Henry Creed & Company made a "skirt-cape" to be worn as either an overskirt to ward off the chill in an air-raid shelter or a cape for protection against the elements. Trench coats received rabbit fur linings for warmth. Blackouts made white accessories popular. Sturdy shoes were crucial.[12] Some British department stores converted their "bargain basements" to "Safety Basements" as fear of air raids became part of urban life.[13]

By the end of September, other manufacturers had joined Arden in selling gas mask cases, and she created a new one in "waterproof cotton." Rumor had it that both Lady Nancy Astor and Rose Kennedy (wife of U.S. ambassador Joseph Kennedy) owned them.[14] Arden also introduced a government-approved "gauzy gas mask" lightweight enough to fit into its companion purse.[15] Hoods made a sudden comeback because, unlike hats, they could be worn over a gas mask. Discreet belts with hidden compartments kept valuables close when German bombs sent citizens running to air-raid shelters.[16]

Edna Woolman Chase felt the American design industry was much better equipped this second time around to carry fashion forward, whatever might befall European artists. Before a Fashion Group luncheon, she personally took credit for showcasing and encouraging the talents of U.S. designers during World War I and through the 1920s. If Paris—still the Western world's cultural capital—was hammered by fascism, Chase believed Americans would pick up the fashion flag. "Besides," she said, "there is always something about the psychology of war that seems immensely stimulating to love and to fashion. Men in uniform always stir the feminine emotions, and women in love always want to look their loveliest—so naturally, the beauty parlours flourish and the dress-makers prosper."[17] Her sentiments might be dated, but her larger point about the turn toward a greater appreciation for American fashion was correct. The Fashion Group led several undertakings to boost the nation's couturiers, milliners, accessory makers, and related fields in fabric, color, and wholesale and retail sales. Sportswear, sun wear, and separates came to be seen as particularly American specialties, mass-produced, ready to wear, and contributing to a signature "American Look." This shift was many years in the making, but the war in Europe hurried it along.[18]

Overseas, Arden teamed up with others to present fashion shows in the British hinterlands. As Londoners left the capital for cities such as Bristol and Manchester, Arden made sure to continue to pique women's interest with new cosmetic and fragrance lines.[19] After closing at the start of hostilities, European fashion houses vowed to remain open to provide employees with jobs and customers with pretty, morale-boosting distractions. Restaurants and concert halls reopened, too (although often away from city centers), so Arden modified her gas mask/makeup case design for evening wear. It was sensibly constructed of waterproof white velvet.[20] She engaged modernist textile designer Marion Dorn to create patriotic-themed silk fabrics for blouses and scarves to sell in her London salon. Dorn obliged with "Dig for Victory," "Happy Landings," "Anti-Gossip," and "Hearts of Oak."[21] Everything was useful, patriotic, or both.

Those who remained in large cities had to be prepared. Diana Wall, director of Arden's London salon, carried a purse filled with such an astonishing array of items that *Vogue* felt compelled to list them all:

> For air-raid precaution, it includes adhesive tape, electric [flashlight], string, pins, dark spectacles, and a scout knife. For comfort, there are fruit drops, chocolate, a small packet of biscuits, bicarbonate of soda, cigarettes, and matches. For entertainment, a good book and a pack of cards. For official or business use: passport, ration card, petrol ration card, blood transfusion card, identity card, cheque-book, address-book, note-paper, envelopes, stamps, fountain-pen, pencil, and blotter. For vanity: cleansing cream, tissues, eye lotion and cup, Velva cream, powder base, powder, lipstick, emery-board, orangestick, a clean pair of stockings, handkerchief, clothes-brush, and a small sewing kit.[22]

Like her dependable manager, Elizabeth Arden was also prepared. Remembering World War I, she "bought huge quantities of oils, essences, and other ingredients" to stockpile against the inevitable time when the conflict limited supplies. Learning from history would see her through with minimal disruptions.[23]

Patriotic themes and colors appeared in fashions stateside. Advertisers began waving the flag as early as the mid-1930s and Arden was no exception. Despite tremendous resistance on the part of most Americans to joining the fight, red, white, and blue were popular. Billing herself the "Arbiter of American Beauty," Arden introduced an entire line of American Beauty makeup, which included "Stop Red" ("the reddest make-up red of all," spring 1939), "Schoolhouse Red" ("named for an American tradition," spring 1939), and "Cinnabar" ("the red russet color that spells Autumn in America the Beautiful," fall 1940), among others.[24]

A Ritz-Carlton fashion show featured the new reds, with "The Elizabeth Arden Girls" demonstrating bending and stretching to achieve the hourglass figure. It was back for wartime, and exercise would help women gain the ideal waist size of twenty-three to twenty-five inches.[25] Since the summer of 1940 bared the midriff, Arden also suggested her new "slenderizing treatment" to decrease "those equatorial bulges," using "electrical impulse," in addition to exercise.[26] Mannequins in Arden negligees (silk, not wool) and matching American Beauty makeup concluded the revue.[27]

In March 1940, Gladys, viewing an ever-worsening situation, put a dozen clothing ensembles created by Molyneux, Paquin, Balenciaga, and other haute couturiers on a ship bound for New York. There her sister exhibited them nationally for donations to French war relief.[28] Three months later, as Americans looked on in horror, the unthinkable happened: Germany conquered France. The Nazis divided it into a German-occupied north (which included Paris) and a smaller geographic region in the south known as Vichy France, where they left the French in nominal control.

Elizabeth lost contact with her sister. Frantic, she asked Teddy Haslam to post an ad in *The Times* of London seeking information about Gladys or Henri de Maublanc.[29] Whether or not Haslam received a reply to his July 1, 1940, request, the couple did at some point return to Paris. Gladys and Solange de Luze soon found that proud and defiant Parisian women recommitted themselves to maintaining their beauty despite the deprivation and humiliation of Nazi occupation and regardless of the danger. Frenchwomen determined to dress "wisely and with dignity," according to designer Lucien Lelong, then president of the Chambre syndicale de la couture parisienne, which regulated French fashion. Lelong, Gladys, and all those who catered to wealthy patrons found themselves walking a fine line. Unlike most Frenchwomen, the wives and mistresses of Nazi officers had money to spend on tailor-made clothing and the leisure time to exercise, learn face patting, and laze on the sundeck at the Red Door solarium. Allowing them in was repugnant. But refusing them entrance could bring swift and terrible retribution.[30]

Having vanquished France, Hitler turned north. The Battle of Britain began on July 10 and continued for three long months. From September 1940 through May 1941, the Luftwaffe switched to a hellish bombing campaign known as the Blitz. The British suffered immeasurably but held firm. In the midst of it, Diana Wall organized the Fighter Fund to raise money from fellow owners and employees of Bond Street's luxury shops. Proceeds went to the Royal Air Force.[31]

The Fashion Group kept American industry insiders informed. Ten months into the war, Louise Macy provided an eyewitness account of the thousands of wounded, starving, desperate Belgian and Dutch refugees straggling into Paris, victims of Nazi bombing and strafing. "All business rivalries were forgotten," the fashion journalist noted, when Schiaparelli, Molyneux, Lelong, and Lanvin contemplated becoming roommates in Biarritz to "throw their talents together in one big pool for the good of the industry and of France." Elizabeth Penrose, editor of English *Vogue*, described the "horror that is Hitler's blitzkrieg." She called on Fashion Group members to buy British products to help the English economy. Penrose saw cooperation replace competition there, too, in the form of a British export pool. Remind customers, she urged, that "with each new English sweater she puts on her back, she also builds another stalwart stone into the dam that is holding back . . . the black waters of the Nazi flood from engulfing us all."[32] Schiaparelli, then on a fundraising tour of America, echoed the sentiment: "A dress bought in France was equivalent to an aeroplane engine built in America for France."[33]

"Cosmetics and perfumes are as vital to the morale of a people during a national emergency as guns and other war materials are to the defense of the nation," S. L. Mayham of the Toilet Goods Association told Fashion Group members in May 1941.[34] Or, as the widely copied Revlon ad put it, "Morale Is a Woman's Business."[35] Women who worried about compromising the war effort by buying toiletries found reassurance wrapped in patriotism. "Go Ahead!," *Cosmopolitan* instructed, "Look Your Best for His Sake" because "if Uncle Sam had needed the materials, you can be sure he would have asked for them."[36] Where raw materials were scarce, as in Nazi-controlled Grasse, for instance, American perfumers looked elsewhere or substituted synthetic miracles produced by American chemists. Mayham predicted no real shortages but was quickly proven wrong.

Speaking on "Morale of Women in England," a London decorator told the Fashion Group that British cosmetics production was down 75 percent because raw materials and labor were scarce. Containers were also in short supply, so customers returned their bottles and jars to be refilled. To buy makeup, women put their name on a list at their local store in hopes of being notified when a shipment came in. Those first to respond could make a purchase—but only one item. Still, the speaker swore that Englishwomen all felt that "[t]hey can't work smartly if they don't look smart," so they made every effort to wear makeup and bright colors, and to "make do and mend."[37] Fashion Group members pitched in to help their European industry colleagues by holding events such as the Grab Bag Party for the British War Relief Society, donating clothing for British servicemen, and auctioning designer dresses.[38]

Arden contributed to Bundles for Britain, the Committee to Defend America by Aiding the Allies, and the Allied Relief Fund, and held benefits for the Vichy French.[39] Never one to miss a rollout opportunity, she partnered with the British American Ambulance Corps Textiles Division to create forty patriotically themed fabrics to be made into nearly anything wearable. Arden was a "cooperating" partner, doing her color harmony magic and selling scarves made from their prints. "Stand Up for Liberty" and "Anchors A-Weigh" were self-explanatory. "Let's Go to the Country" was "vivid with vegetables," suggesting a return—long before the U.S. government recommended it—of the World War I Victory garden.[40]

Support for France ran high. Anne Morgan, who strove selflessly to relieve French suffering during World War I, sprang back into action. Her American Friends of France raised money for French evacuees. She cajoled an extraordinary group of people, many of them her friends, into submitting recipes for a cookbook. A partial list included Salvador Dalí, Eleanor Roosevelt, Charlie Chaplin, Helen Keller, Clare Boothe Luce, and Laurence Olivier. Many from the fashion industry contributed, such as Cecil Beaton, Ilka Chase, Christian Dior, and Schiaparelli. When published in 1940, *Spécialités de la Maison* contained Arden's slimming recipe for Pineapple Sherbet consisting of only one pineapple, half a cup of honey, and the juice of two lemons.[41] This seems perhaps a tiny effort in the face of what would turn out to be a war of unmitigated evil, but the universal shock at the fall of France catalyzed hundreds of relief efforts, large and small, all of them aimed at ameliorating a horrible situation only dimly glimpsed from afar.

For most Americans, the European war did not markedly alter daily life. Even for Arden, film and museum openings continued, as did non-war-related fundraising efforts and her pursuit of new products and markets.[42] In a news-obsessed time, Arden recycled something from her earliest days. She called it her Personal Analysis Service. Upon request, she mailed a questionnaire and makeup chart. When she received completed questionnaires, Arden replied with an individualized breakdown of her customer's beauty flaws and how to improve them, plus a personalized color harmony chart and a suggested product list.[43]

American industry leaders looked with simultaneous alarm and anticipation to one near-certain change: the inability of Paris to maintain its top fashion spot. The ongoing Nazi occupation of France opened a path for U.S. designers and wholesalers, and smart executives found ways to take advantage of the opportunity. Arden gradually moved beyond lingerie, sleepwear, and the occasional designer piece to selling a larger range of clothing in her salons. The greater her connection to fashion firms through her color harmony idea, and the more the focus on American design grew, the more she stocked "daytime dresses," "summer frocks," and "play clothes."[44] All of her American salons ran the same ad, so it is likely that she was not selling one-of-a-kind items but rather some version of ready-to-wear garments, a clothing category that had grown in importance and sales volume during the Depression.

When the industry leader spoke, journalists listened. Elizabeth Arden began announcing her seasonal colors by inviting fashion reporters to a party at her Manhattan salon. She plied them with drinks and nibbles as models in gowns with harmonizing makeup and the latest hairdos from Arden stylists paraded. In the fall of 1940, she introduced her "jewel tones" cosmetics, and gave journalists a glimpse of "modern baroque designed" jewelry and hats from her personal collection.[45] Jewel tones matched to one's jewelry truly signified an end to the Great Depression.

THIS NEW ERA brought a fundamental change for Elizabeth Arden. In the 1940s, she grew more public in her politics and completed her transition from Democrat to Republican—although that did not stop her from pitching an Arden salon ad explicitly to the women attending the 1940 Democratic National Convention![46]

Arden had attended Roosevelt's 1939 Birthday Ball. It raised more than $25,000 to battle infantile paralysis, in part from thousands of donated dimes in what was fast becoming known as the March of Dimes.[47] Despite sharing his commitment to worthwhile causes, she, like many

Americans, thought of a potential third presidential term with distaste. This added to her conviction that FDR's regulations unfairly curtailed her ways of doing business, and Arden switched her allegiance for good.

In 1940, she attended the Republican National Convention in Philadelphia as a Wendell Willkie supporter. She decided her presence was necessary. "This year is so pivotal," she told the press. "We don't want to be lost."[48] Her Willkie button and her seat next to the candidate's wife, Edith, made her position clear. Like Arden, utilities executive and corporate attorney Wendell Willkie had abandoned the Democratic Party in 1939. He was a political moderate. Willkie did not favor American isolationism, unlike more right-wing Republicans, such as Alice Roosevelt Longworth, daughter of former president Theodore Roosevelt, also much in evidence in Philadelphia.[49]

Arden's contributions appeared in print alongside those of other big GOP donors such as Rockefellers and Vanderbilts.[50] So did a photograph of Arden, Edna Woolman Chase, Hortense Odlum, Mary Lewis, and banker Mary Vail Andress, five businesswomen looking very pleased with the pro-Willkie speeches they had just given on national radio. "They say the moment breeds the man," Arden explained. "How thankful we Americans should be to have this great man, Wendell L. Willkie, appear at this crucial hour in our history." Lewis warned her fellow citizens that President Roosevelt had "gotten a 'swelled head,'" suggesting the third term was an important issue for her. The other three women accused FDR of poor business decisions, pointing to a larger dissatisfaction shared by many of the nation's industrialists.[51]

Meanwhile, GOP women were happy to have the beauty magnate on their side. To explain to their members how the nominating process worked, some Women's Republican Clubs held mock presidential conventions. At one of these, Elizabeth Arden earned the nod, because "she would be so pleasing to the eye of the voter and would undoubtedly conduct a beautiful campaign." In 1940, when Arden was again nominated, the mock convention goers dissolved in peals of laughter when

"Elizabeth Arden" hastily withdrew because she would not admit publicly to being the minimum age to run for president—which is thirty-five![52]

Not long after the actual Republican convention, the 1940 World's Fair opened. First Lady Eleanor Roosevelt cut the ribbon to inaugurate the World of Fashion Building before lunching with Arden, Rubinstein, and thirteen other fashion executives. The fair was held over because organizers did not make enough money in 1939.[53] The new theme, "For Peace and Freedom," switched "the fashion spot-light" to America, "now that Paris fashion is temporarily isolated."[54]

Inside the pink-and-blue World of Fashion Building fairgoers attended twice-daily fashion shows, lectures, and benefits like "Hats for Headliners," which raised money for refugees through the United Committee for French Relief.[55] Women walked through Arden's "huge shell-pink canopy," into her Blue Grass–scented "Isle of Beauty" exhibit to enjoy a salon treatment in an "air-conditioned miniature booth" or shop for souvenir beauty boxes.[56]

Classes for fairgoers and locals turned into a fad. Elizabeth Arden offered them to teens, college students, workingwomen, and society ladies. They were so sought after that Tobé Coller Davis—better known as Miss Tobé—required her students to attend. Former fashion reporters, Miss Tobé and Julia Coburn had founded the Tobé-Coburn School for Fashion Careers in 1937. They sent their students to Arden to learn how to look their best.[57] From these fair offerings, Arden spun off her "Beauty Career Classes," which promised "a complete head-to-toe do-over" in makeup, posture and exercise, and skin and hair care.[58] Arden was neither the first nor the only beauty professional to offer classes. She was simply recognized as expert by everyday women and by colleagues such as Miss Tobé and Miss Coburn.

The fall of 1940 saw the conclusion of the World's Fair and the election of Franklin Roosevelt to a third term. Arden's regret must have deepened when she learned that the federal government's attempt to meddle in her business—or, as Roosevelt might have put it, to create clear, plain, and honest labeling—continued. Professor Catherine Gosney of the Virginia State Teachers College wrote the AMA asking about eight of Arden's preparations. All were "harmless," the AMA responded, though two skin creams were not always "reasonably advertised." Several months later, the AMA gave Arden's Sleek Hair Remover its approval. But the Federal Trade Commission came back at Arden in 1941 and 1942 for misleading advertising regarding "Ardena Sensation Cream, Joie de Vivre, and Ardena Skin Lotion."[59] She vowed to reword her ads.

Helena Rubinstein did not get off so lightly. AMA investigators told Gosney that "on the whole," Rubinstein toiletries "are fairly harmless." But their dismissal of Madame's claims was scathing:

> We consider certain of [her products] silly or worse, particularly those that have been, if they are not still, represented as "youthifiers" and "rejuvenators," as there is no such thing. In fact, such representations are banned under the new Food, Drug and Cosmetic Act passed in 1938. Furthermore, we are of the opinion that the Rubinstein "Pasteurized Face Cream" is another piece of hokum. We might add that we also take exception to the Rubinstein "Reducing Jelly" and "Reducing Soap," as one cannot, of course, reduce weight by applying ordinary cosmetics to the body.

The AMA physicians listed *nine more* Rubinstein items by name and dissected her ingredients, her claims, or both.[60] Overall, Arden's commitment to pure ingredients and her discomfort with puffery meant that she avoided the worst condemnation from the AMA and the FTC—as well as the considerable expense of being forced to change packaging and advertising. Still, she didn't like it.

ARDEN SET OFF for Boston and the annual autumn Conference on Distribution. The war's interruption to business was the pressing topic. The times called for ingenuity, and as Arden spoke from the podium, she joined her experience and ideas with those of Chase, Schiaparelli, Sara Pennoyer of Bonwit Teller, and others as they focused on topics of immediate concern: "The Effect of War Conditions on Distribution," "War Emergencies and Trade Practices," and "The Retailer, Consumer and National Defense."[61] Their starting point was Paris's demise as the global fashion epicenter. Whether temporary or permanent, no one yet knew.[62]

Arden's message was striking, impassioned, and heartfelt. She provided a brief history of the industry she molded. "The cosmetics business" was, she said with pardonable exaggeration, "an American institution. It was here that it first took root. The quest for the beautiful spread to the four corners of the earth." She mentioned color harmony as one of the pillars of her success. But it was the clarification of why she did what she did that drove her to a fever pitch:

> It always irritates me to have people think of cosmetics as makeup. Makeup is only the fringe of it. It's the gay banner you unfurl just before you start off. If make-up were all there is to cosmetics I think I would be tempted to close my business. It's making people over, and as a result making their lives over that makes this business worth doing. Cosmetics are a whole crusade for a fuller life, a well-cared-for skin is beauty, exciting and inspiring, like a face with a lovely secret. And woman should have many faces. Why should she present the same one every day? A woman shouldn't wear the same kind of face any more than she should always wear the same kind of clothes. She should be many sided.

Cosmetics boosted a woman's confidence, and she tied this to the European war: "As long as women look to their lipstick before hurrying to a bomb-proof shelter their nation need not worry about morale." Intrepid British women were "laying in supplies of cosmetics" because the connection between looking one's best and keeping up a fighting spirit was self-evident.[63]

Then Arden's talk turned more serious. It was time for America to cease acting "like a busy little sister to Paris," content with "copying" and distributing French fashion "while we ignored our own superb artists." Ruefully, she admitted that some had "fled to Paris to live and work." Her conclusion was a ringing welcome home. We "offer our belated homage to the young designers who will make American fashions of tomorrow," and she invited all "the brilliant artists who come to us as refugees—we are glad and proud that America can offer them sanctuary."[64] Arden was by then experienced in transferring employees away from war zones and hiring those Europeans who fled the danger.

One employee who would not leave permanently was Gladys. Still keeping the French arm of Arden open, Gladys found a way to join her family in America for the holidays.[65] While in the States, she accompanied Elizabeth to California, where her big sister was honored at an Assistance League luncheon in Los Angeles. At a party at Cobina Wright's Hollywood home on January 9, 1941, Gladys and Elizabeth were dual guests of honor. Barbara Hutton sailed in on Cary Grant's arm. Mary Pickford sparkled, resplendent in sapphires. Edgar Bergen and his puppet sidekick, Charlie McCarthy, amused the other seventy-five guests. British actress Gracie Fields concluded an impromptu concert with "There'll Always Be an England." Everyone sang along, remembering the shocking photographs of "the second great fire of London" caused by the Blitz only twelve days earlier. American sympathy for those resisting the Nazis was running high, and the Vicomtesse de Maublanc provided eyewitness testimony about life under almost seven months of German occupation to engrossed partygoers.[66]

While the honors were lovely, the real purpose of Elizabeth Arden's time in California was the creation of a Technicolor film, alternately titled *The Belles Are Told* and *Orchids to Charlie*, whose proceeds would go to the British War Relief Society for needy children.[67] The cast was led by Jinx Falkenburg, Frieda Inescort, and Victoria Faust—all famous then, but largely forgotten today. Will Jason directed and Arden produced, after a work-around. The Technicolor Corporation, which made the celluloid film on which the movie would be shot, would not allow anyone other than "an experienced producer" to use its product. Thus, Arden "created a special company—Will Jason Productions, Ltd.—to make this film, and Jason's title was changed to that of producer," since he met Technicolor's requirements.[68]

The plot came from her 1930s fashion show "Farewell to Age." Falkenburg played the dowdy friend who visited the celebrity and learned how to make herself beautiful with proper attention to her skin, posture, and overall health.[69] It premiered in July 1941 at Wright's home before an all-star audience that included Gloria Vanderbilt, Basil Rathbone, and Nela and Arthur Rubinstein.[70] The film was meant for private gatherings and does not seem to have been shown in public theaters. Hedda Hopper suggested that it cost $75,000 to make—an astounding sum then, and unlikely to have been topped by donations.[71]

The war grew closer. No matter how urgently Americans hoped the conflict would not draw in the United States, the British obviously needed assistance. It was also becoming clearer by the day that the stakes were too high to remain aloof. The Nazis could not be allowed to win. Women's groups like the American Women's Voluntary Services (AWVS) continued to raise money and awareness. The AWVS bound together society women, civic reformers, and businesswomen who believed that preparing for American entrance into the war was sensible. Founded in 1940, and led in part by Republican May Ladenburg Davie, the women of the AWVS gathered in the fall of 1941 to hear Elizabeth Arden speak at their Training Institute. Most of the topics concerned civilian defense. Lecturing alongside famous settlement house workers, labor leaders, and politicians, Arden alone came from the beauty industry. Yet everyone understood that her subject was vitally important. Arden provided guidelines to getting in shape for the coming conflict. These "Rules for Fitness" were:

1. A burning desire to win.
2. Courage to carry through.
3. Desire to exercise.
4. Determination to diet.
5. Breathe deeply.
6. Maintain perfect posture.
7. Willingness to sacrifice comfort.

Working with the AWVS, Arden created a physical fitness course for their volunteers nationwide. She undoubtedly had input from Walter Saxer, the "Swiss physical culture expert" she had hired to teach at Maine Chance. Her backing launched him on a long and distinguished career as a Hollywood fitness guru. Saxer's exercise ideas leaned more toward calisthenics than Mildred Wedekind's, whom he had replaced. The Arden-Saxer program codified those offered by local AWVS headquarters as early as July 1940.[72] "Physical fitness" was a term suited for defense work, and it lacked any suggestion of a dilettantish debutante's pampered afternoon at a Red Door salon.[73] That was perfect for the AWVS, but not for Arden's usual customers. Just as she had done with her Beauty Career Class, Arden adapted. She quickly introduced what she renamed "Beauty for Defense—Physical Fitness for the Woman of Tomorrow" classes based on her AWVS course and intended for every interested woman. A good idea was a good idea, after all.[74]

AWVS preparedness required members to be in tip-top shape to meet all emergencies. Its members wore distinctive uniforms in a public declaration of their training and commitment. The initial call went out for anyone who could help the Allied war effort in any way possible—knitting, sewing, typing, cooking—and the racially integrated organization developed in size and authority as the months passed. Soon the AWVS mustered a corps of women trained by mechanics to maintain and drive cars and ambulances. They became experts at making, gathering, and sending relief items to England. Physicians taught them first aid and wound care; they also sewed hospital gowns and assembled surgical dressings. The AWVS schooled women in office skills, air-raid and urban evacuation procedures, map reading, and nutrition. Arden's program for getting in shape was an integral part of moving from a peacetime laziness to the disciplined mind and body required for war. Mightily impressed with the organization, she remained involved with the AWVS for the rest of her life.[75]

European battles continued while the Japanese conquest of its neighbors grew more worrisome. In response, American industry roared back to life. Men returned to work, and more and more women joined them. Not everyone believed that women should be employed outside the home, although volunteering was unproblematic. The National Federation of Business and Professional Women bravely waded into the dispute about women working by holding a debate at their national conference on the topic of "Do Women Belong in Business?" between Clarence Francis, the president of General Foods, and Elizabeth Arden. An audience of one thousand listened as Francis began well with "Women belong in business." But he quickly descended to stereotypes. Once in business, he lectured, women should not be "'barkers,' snapping at every one; 'wheedlers,' hinting continually; 'weepers,' 'apers,' refusing to be themselves, or 'blitskriegers' who want matters handled according to their ideas and at their convenience."[76]

Arden strode to the podium. She scoffed at "the all-too prevalent assumption that women are handicapped by sex and temperament to assume managerial and executive duties." Indeed, she responded coolly, "women invented management. . . . Government itself is simply a magnified copy of household law and order for which our great-grandmothers furnished the pattern. The very word 'economics' means home regulation."[77] What the presidents of the Baltimore & Ohio Railroad, Western Union Telegraph, and the Electrical Testing Laboratory thought about that was not recorded by journalists. But AWVS president Alice McLean was in the audience, too, and her approval of Arden's forceful rebuttal may be assumed.

Workingwomen wanted patriotic cosmetics and Arden obliged. "Victory Red" launched in September 1941 as "a color to brighten R.A.F. Blue and Army costumes," and it signaled that Arden was no isolationist. The "Victory Red" *Vogue* ad was memorable. Arden model Constance Ford brought a photograph of herself to her boss's attention from among many others taken by Philippe Halsman. Arden recognized the artist's originality and became interested in his story. Halsman was a Latvian Jew living in France doing well-regarded portrait photography. He escaped the Nazis by moving to the United States with the help of his acquaintance Albert Einstein. In New York, Halsman had been subsisting on the edge of poverty, barely able to support his family. Arden launched his American career. Today Halsman may be best remembered for his "Jump" series, but his photographs of Einstein, Marilyn Monroe, Louis Armstrong, Eleanor Roosevelt, and John F. Kennedy are iconic. After the Victory Red advertisement, *Life* magazine hired Halsman for the first of what would be 101 cover shots, and he became famous in his adopted country.[78] Pamphlets and other ads for Victory Red lipstick, rouge, nail polish, and color harmony boxes ran throughout the war and into the 1950s.[79]

The twin imperatives of defending the homeland and preparing for military engagement grew more urgent with each month of 1941—although isolationists remained voluble. On the federal level, President Roosevelt created the Office of Civilian Defense and put New York mayor Fiorello La Guardia in charge. "If we never need what we learn," La Guardia reassured doubters, "we lose nothing; if we never learn what we may need, we may lose everything." State agencies formed quickly. The Massachusetts Women's Defense Corps (WDC) under Colonel Natalie Hays Hammond mobilized eight thousand Bay State women. Elizabeth Arden threw open her Boston salon and invited Hammond and her staff to watch Arden trainers demonstrate the AWVS physical fitness program. The colonel urged WDC members to take the course that Arden promised to provide for free "so that they may be able to . . . work more efficiently." Hammond ceremoniously made Elizabeth Arden an honorary WDC member. Looking, *The Boston Globe* reported, "slim and as decorative as her ads in deft black, red roses and mink," Arden accepted.[80] Before leaving Boston, she paused to speak to the assembled students of the Vesper George School of Art on the topic of "'Health and Beauty' and the relation of beauty to keeping up the morale for defense."[81] Arden had made significant inroads into the civilian defense and preparedness communities. This was a good thing, because exactly two weeks after her talk to the art students, Imperial Japan bombed Pearl Harbor. The war that few Americans wanted, but for which so many Americans had prepared, arrived at last.

Seventeen

Beauty and Morale

The situation in Germany was very different in 1928 when Arden first staked a presence there. Hers was one of several American firms that took advantage of the nation's pre-war "low costs and more stable labor conditions, less burdensome taxes than in neighboring countries and [its] most-favored-nation treatment under treaties with almost all other countries."[1] Arden expanded quickly beyond her Berlin Red Door Salon, adding a well-functioning manufacturing plant and a national distribution system. She put American William T. Carlson, freshly graduated from college with a German major, in charge of her Arden Chemical Company Berlin branch. In 1931, Eileen Scott-Williams arrived to oversee the salon. Arden correctly read the increasingly troubling political situation, and transferred both employees out of the country just before Hitler's rise to power in 1933. She moved Carlson to Paris and sent Scott-Williams to California.[2] Evidence quickly mounted that fascist Germany was unpredictable at best, and probably something much more foul. It did not help that Hitler publicly opposed what he called the decadent look of American women. From afar, Scott-Williams saw this as a challenge. Once the Wilshire Boulevard salon was successfully up and running, and because it appeared at the time that she would be safe enough, Arden allowed Scott-Williams to return to Berlin. Rebuffing his attack on "artistic aids to female beauty" would be, the *Los Angeles Times* cheered, "a task worthy of her talents."[3]

Scott-Williams had her work cut out for her. Germany forbade women to practice law or serve in the government or military. Many Nazi leaders, including Joseph Goebbels, Rudolf Hess, and Hitler himself, were on record declaring that a woman's "most important role was motherhood."[4] A 1934 Fashion Group luncheon speaker growled: "I have recently returned from Germany where I have seen first-hand the incredible scuttling of women back . . . to the shadow of the kitchen stove."[5] Nevertheless, Scott-Williams tempted Berliners with luxurious skin care treatments and the vilified cosmetics.

The Third Reich did approve of Arden's emphasis on exercise. Her advertisements in German magazines such as *Die Dame* and *Die Neue Linie* emphasized the outdoor life and the athletic figure. "Slim, graceful, young and vivacious! You are thinking," her ad suggested, "it is not as easy as it sounds? It is as easy as a couple of gymnastic exercises in Elizabeth Arden's wonderful new salon. In an astonishingly short time your figure and vitality, even spirit and soul will be rejuvenated." Four slender women photographed doing graceful Arden exercises in the open air accompanied the ad.[6] Even though Scott-Williams made much more headway with exercise classes than with cosmetics, Arden appears to have recalled her again to the United States in 1936.[7]

By 1937, though, the Nazis changed course regarding female appearance. According to German journalist Otto Tolischus, they did so to try to display themselves as rational leaders of a modern country. Instead of a forced embrace of "*kueche, kinder, kirche*," a national equating of "dowdiness" with "respectability," and the belief that "hefty marching feet were proof of National Socialist devotion," a sophisticated look became acceptable. Makeup, haute couture, and "personal splendor appropriate to the proclaimed splendor of the Third Reich" were now in

line with Nazi goals, Tolischus reported. He cited the Reich Youth
Minister saying that "the more beautiful German girls become the
more proud and self-respecting they will be."[8] Minister of Propaganda
Goebbels then held that makeup could entice German women to embrace Nazism.

Once Nazi leaders came around to the thinking of other Western
nations by approving of cosmetics, Elizabeth Arden used fundamen-
tally the same ads in Germany as in the United States—but not to endorse Nazi values. Healthy skin, sufficient exercise, and understated
makeup created the Arden look, not a Nazi.[9]

When internationally known businesswoman Elizabeth Arden visited Germany in 1937, she naturally received and accepted invitations
from top government officials. That did not sit well with gossip columnist Leonard Lyons. In between fluff about a divorcee's weight loss and
scuttle about a former child star, he revealed that Arden had socialized
with Hermann Göring, Hitler's right-hand man. "'Oh, that Goering,'
the beautician stated, 'he's charming and darling' . . . 'You mean,' she
was told, 'from a beauty-cream standpoint, of course!'" Lyons's next
column suggested Arden's naivete: "'So Elizabeth Arden saw this decoration around Goering's neck,' one of her friends whispers. 'She asked
him what it was. Goering said: "This is the biggest Order in the
World!"'"[10] In 1937, Göring's medal was likely the prestigious Pour le
Mérite (known as the Blue Max), earned for gallantry in World War I.
Hitler did not bring back the Iron Cross until 1939. Lyons's insinuation
was thus smarmy and slanderous. Arden was used to being underestimated, but it turned out that she was a more committed patriot than
anyone knew.

Returning to the United States, Arden found herself confronting
two serious allegations. The fact that women attached to high-ranking
Nazis used Arden toiletries partly lay behind the charge that her salons
"throughout the American republics" were "clearing houses for Nazi
activities." The anonymous accusation was made to FBI Special Agent

Arthur M. Thurston in October 1941—two months before Pearl Harbor. This charge suggested that Arden opened salons and retail outlets in South and Central America to serve as sites of Nazi collaboration, rather than to logically expand her business throughout the Western Hemisphere at a time when war ravaged the Eastern Hemisphere. The FBI found "no info in files reflecting this [accusation] is true."[11]

The second allegation came in the form of a letter to the New York *Daily Mirror* in March 1941, written, bizarrely enough, by someone named Elizabeth Lewis. She declared that Arden had "nazi interests," and ticked off her evidence. First, *Die Dame*, which had become a Nazi propaganda magazine after 1937, had published a feature favorable to Arden.[12] Next, Arden had photographs in her office snapped at a Berlin racetrack showing her standing with "several nazi dignitaries." Further, Arden displayed in her home an inscribed photograph of an unnamed Nazi officer taken during her 1937 annual European business tour. When Lewis—who had seen the photo herself in Arden's penthouse— questioned Arden about it, the latter said that the officer had "been simply charming to her." And, finally, a recent "nazi controlled Paris magazine" contained only one advertisement from an American firm: Elizabeth Arden.[13] These charges also went nowhere because the FBI knew something Arden's accusers didn't. Elizabeth Arden was not a Nazi. She was an FBI informant.

Officially, she was a Special Service Contact (SSC). These were "prominent individuals who volunteered their services to the FBI during periods of National emergency." The program started three weeks after the Japanese bombing of Pearl Harbor, although the record is silent as to when Arden enlisted.[14] SSCs kept their ears open and their mouths shut, reporting to the FBI anything they heard that might jeopardize national or Allied security. They could come from all walks of life: government (Joseph P. Kennedy, who later found much to admire in fascism), entertainment (Elsa Maxwell), sports (Ty Cobb), and business.[15] Arden's international circles put her in touch with powerful people of all political persuasions. Her massage and manicure tables, exercise and dressing rooms were sites of conversation, gossip, and informal exchange among influential women, including wives and sweethearts of prominent politicians, industrialists, and bankers. Arden associates were perfectly situated to overhear information of use to the Allies. Her salons were unlikely to be hotbeds of Nazism—except in fascist-controlled countries.[16]

Arden was not a fascist, nor a sympathizer. She got several employees out of Europe ahead of the German advance, worked hard on and donated much to pro-Allied causes, and called on FBI director J. Edgar Hoover in 1943 for a personal favor. Beyond the Leonard Lyons gossip column and the Elizabeth Lewis accusation the FBI dismissed, there was no other suggestion of her consorting with Nazis or supporting fascism in any way.

If anything, Arden was held up as a model patriot. Her war work included keeping morale high on the home front. By May 1942, half a million women had taken jobs in defense industries (about 10 percent of the total), and that number increased to four million by year's end.[17] The link between morale and beauty never wavered. "Is Beauty Worth Half a Billion?" *The New York Times* asked incredulously. The answer was yes. American women spent more money on cosmetics than ever before, and 1942 bid fair to surpass that. Twenty million dollars' worth of lipstick, $60 million worth of cold cream, and another $60 million of powder was just the start. Interviews turned up a slew of positive responses to the newspaper's question. Physicians, scientists, and "morale experts" linked makeup with increased industrial efficiency and the avoidance of mental depression. "Lipstick is like laughter," one psychiatrist explained.[18] "Feminine Role in National Defense Starts at Beauty Shop, Says Expert," declared the *Los Angeles Times*.[19] "Beauty of the Nation's Women Most Important Wartime Factor," a *Boston Globe* headline proclaimed. The article emphasized that "American women have

a triple job to do of home work, defense work, [and] maintaining morale."[20] A confident, attractive, and well-groomed woman will be more
effective at home and on the job, and "will be a cheering sight to all who
work around her, and will provide for those who are fighting a symbol
of the beauty and sanity of the life they are fighting for."[21] This ubiquitous message was partly rooted in gendered fears of women becoming
too independent or masculine as they donned slacks and picked up
pneumatic drills.[22]

The cosmetics industry boomed as fashion and toiletries insiders reiterated, self-servingly, that beauty was critical in wartime. They also
made an economic point. *Vogue* stressed that fashion "pays taxes, pays
workers, maintains morale, and can flourish on materials the fighting
forces do not need." Patriotic American women would dress in sack-
cloth to help the war effort, the editors admitted, but such a "noble
sacrifice" would be misguided. Before Pearl Harbor, clothing was the
country's second-largest industry. Abandoning it now would only harm
the economy. *Vogue* urged readers to buy the very best they could afford
with an eye to "hard usage" and a classic style. Like cosmetics, any
wearable item for sale in stores was made "with full Government approval," so buyers could lay aside fears of causing a soldier to go without. The federal War Production Board had already rationed wool to
make sure there was enough for military uniforms. *Vogue* predicted that
rubber and silk would be next, but that neither would be a hardship, as
rubber was a recent addition to foundation garments and rayon and cotton could substitute for silk.[23]

Stanley Marcus, textile adviser to the War Production Board, urged
his colleagues to use the coming disruptions to spur their creativity.
When French designers ran out of matching thread, for example, they
made contrasting thread chic. He explained, in March 1942, to eight
hundred Fashion Group members, that supply chain impediments called
for resourcefulness from everyone: designers, buyers, manufacturers,

wholesalers, even fashion magazines. Arden publicity head Ruth Mills took up the refrain at the April luncheon. It would be neither "patriotic [n]or helpful to morale" for women to eschew cosmetics. Neither should they try to concoct their own at home. Instead, moderation in purchasing and use was key. The central messages were clear: the war came first, a woman's duty was to remain beautiful, and obstacles should be met with ingenious new designs and products.[24] Not everyone agreed. Calling himself a "'conscientious objector' to all wartime rationing," Senator "Cotton Ed" Smith of South Carolina fumed, "Why, they even tell me that now they're taking the ruffles off ladies' lingerie. . . . Who in hell expects to win a war that way?"[25]

Arden piled on the patriotic ads, products, promotions, and partnerships. Advertising copy became more urgent: "Walk—and like it!" she wrote in her Foot Kit ad, while her Hand Kit advertisement showed a woman using a power drill.[26] She saw her job as safeguarding "the beauty of women who face long hours in new defense duties."[27] She understood the changed reality: "You lead such a complicated life today . . . rushing from nurses' aiding to selling bonds, to working at the Red Cross center. And yet, evening hours must find you fresh, lovely and inspiring."[28]

The cause-and-effect linkage of beauty with morale was omnipresent: "Today, as never before, beauty is an essential, because it stands for courage, serenity and for a gallant heart. So make yourself a promise for 1942: That you will do the very most for your beauty." This copy launched her "Beauty Essentials" line. One handy box each for normal, dry, oily, and blemished skin aimed to simplify. Next came her "Elizabeth Arden Efficiency Plan," her name for classes teaching good health, beauty, and physical exercise habits. Customers received her free illustrated booklet containing instructions for "Systemized Skin Care" and a "Speed Routine for Lovely Hair."[29]

Soon she applied the Efficiency Plan idea to a new "Midsummer Isle" department at her Fifth Avenue salon. In this beauty assembly line

women passed from station to station and emerged completely re-
done. The Electro Wax removed leg hair in the Wax Works Room. A
ten-minute pedicure and the application of "cosmetic stockings" were
followed by a "Chilled Face" treatment, a "Menthol Cool Body Massage," and makeup reapplication. Patrons exited, newly glowing, through
the "Sun Shop," tempted by an array of goodies. Efficiency in one's
beauty treatment meant more time for war work—or the beach.[30]

When the Greater Boston United War Fund kicked off its Red
Feather campaign, Arden joined, creating matching "Red Feather"
makeup, lipstick, rouge, and nail polish. A version of the Red Feather
campaign had been used off and on in the United States since 1919.[31] A
bright reference to the feather Yankee Doodle stuck in his cap, the color
and the single-feather design were woven into or stamped onto fabric
for dresses, men's ties, slippers, and all manner of accessories. More
than fifty Boston store windows displayed Red Feather items. The idea
spread nationwide. Arden incorporated it into her sales and marketing
campaigns and tied it to lectures Mildred Wedekind—now millinery
expert—had been giving around the country.[32] The talks featured a
pre-war sales idea of Arden's involving living mannequins wearing
masks. They were used in fashion shows and living window displays,
and audiences thrilled when the Greek "statues" actually came to life.[33]

Arden filled the need for new hairstyles to accommodate uniform
caps. Setting her designers to work, her hair salons across the country
advertised cuts and permanents for short hair providing "downy, duck-
tail curls twinkling to a graceful upsweep [which would] soften the
lines of the uniform cap and make becoming, even flattering, the harsh-
est regulation headgear."[34] She gave each a name, such as "Clip Top," so
that women could ask for a specific look. "Sir Galahad" was "regulation
for volunteers because it clears the collar—is always in place—and
makes any hat becoming," including military covers and nurses' caps.[35]
The "Winged Psyche" hairstyle would dazzle the faraway sweetheart:
"It makes you look the way he dreams about you."[36] Arden focused on

beauty—and on sales, since the number of women wearing defense work and military caps was proliferating.

But the practicality of short hair was uppermost in the mind of at least one female physician. She begged British *Vogue* to decree short hair fashionable—because up to half of all female war plant workers in Great Britain could be absent at any one time because of lice. Medical appeals to "common-sense or war responsibility" did not convince women to cut their hair, but if *Vogue* sanctioned it, then war workers would shorten their locks.[37] This was not lost on Arden, who advertised these attractive new short looks as part of her Beauty Essentials line.

World War II–era advertising to women, Arden's and everyone else's, carried a consistent message: the patriotic American female was responsible for national morale and for preserving her femininity despite long days of volunteering or working on the assembly line. "The hand that rocks the cradle—washes the dishes—grinds the valve—sets the rivet," began one ad, "can still be . . . sweet to hold if it belongs to a woman wise enough to use Elizabeth Arden's Hand Lotion."[38] Beauty for Defense classes morphed into "The Miracle of Susan," Arden's defense-plant-worker ad. Susan was "a nice person, but overweight and terribly unhappy about the way she looks. She is absolutely unable to rise to these demanding days, because she is not physically fit." But Arden's multifaceted solutions, shown in a series of photographs, soon had Susan "breez[ing] through her defense work, interested, alert, and physically fit."[39] As an inducement to (white, affluent) nascent Rosie the Riveters, she offered her own "defense dividend" of 20 percent off on face and body treatments during the hour before the work shift began and the hour after it ended.[40] These courses could be taken in department stores and in Red Door salons. "Victory grooming," she called it, and sent her representatives to talk to women's clubs, part incentive and part patriotism. Other beauty experts, including Rubinstein and Gray, quickly copied aspects of Arden's programs, but they emphasized relaxation more than wartime physical fitness.[41]

Arden rolled every part of her victory grooming into one grand defense-themed revue. "It was all exciting and different," Virginia Pope wrote ecstatically in *The New York Times*. "Elizabeth Arden was putting on a show." And put on a show she did! Throwing the audience in the Ritz-Carlton's Oval Room into sudden darkness to simulate a wartime blackout, three models painted with phosphorescence exercised with oversize hoops in a stunning visual display. Arden showed that staying in shape was possible even under the worst circumstances. A mock air-raid siren startled viewers, but the models quickly tossed on "hooded overalls of crêpe. These were," Pope affirmed, "not only practical but attractive gowns that no woman would mind being seen in." The man-nequins showed off their short hair, clipped fingernails, and "liquid stockings." They stressed Miss Arden's color harmony "wartime credo" that one's "lips must be of the shade that goes with their defense blue or khaki." True to the Arden way, it concluded with models in "dainty negligees" of "Arden pink, violet-y blues, [and] rose-pink," because every hard day at the defense plant deserved an ultrafeminine ending. The finale featured a dancer modeling a "gray chiffon [dress] representing 'Blithe Spirit'" from the November 1941 Broadway premiere of Noël Coward's popular play about a ghost, for which Arden had created the makeup for the two female leads. Ever aware of the tie-in, Arden's "Blithe Spirit" cosmetics for everyday wear gave a pearlescent look to the skin. It was particularly "lovely with silvery hair, silver fox furs, [and] grey chiffon evening gowns."[42]

Cognizant of the connection between morale and entertainment, Arden joined with Broadway friends to help birth an extraordinary so-cial club for servicemembers when she donated "all food and cigarettes" to the Stage Door Canteen.[43] This was a labor of love by five women connected with the theater who had provided similar assistance during World War I. In 1942, they reconstituted themselves as the American Theatre Wing and opened an interracial gathering spot in the base-ment of the Shubert Theatre where members of the Allied military gathered nightly to eat, dance, relax, mingle with, and be entertained by stars of stage and screen. "Over the course of its brief history," historian Andrea Nouryeh recounted, "the canteen entertained more than 3.2 million servicemen from all of the Allied nations and served more than 720,000 sandwiches, 438,000 cups of milk, 5,000 pounds of candy, and 3.5 million cigarettes."[44]

Another program boosted morale by encouraging her employees' war efforts. Diana Wall had last been in the United States in February 1938 to share European style tips with Californians.[45] That was a very different place and time than London in 1942 where the resourceful Wall led salon coworkers into forming a Women's Home Defense (WHD) group. These were composed of volunteers who pledged to defend themselves and their communities in case of enemy invasion. They learned how to shoot, throw hand grenades, slip quietly through darkened streets, locate cover, sleep rough, and manage field cooking. The British Ministries of Agriculture, Health, and Information, plus the BBC, the Admiralty, and businesses like the Arden salon, had active WHD units. These brave women promised to stand up to fascist invaders in a practical way.[46] Diana Wall somehow kept the Red Doors open, despite volunteer duty and shortages of product and personnel.

Across the English Channel, conditions deteriorated in German-controlled France, where Gladys remained, resisting her sister's urgings to leave. As supplies dwindled, women substituted Arden's leg makeup for the silk the government commandeered for parachutes.[47] The few who could afford luxury goods kept some couturiers, including Nina Ricci, Jeanne Lanvin, and Lucien Lelong, open.[48] Most others shut down. Food became scarce; black markets sprang up. Nazis began rounding up Jews, enemy aliens, and suspected Resistance members in July 1942.[49] Gladys was the Canadian-born wife of a Frenchman with an American passport. Any way the Nazis viewed her, and despite the fact that officers' wives frequented her salon, the Vicomtesse de Maublanc was an enemy alien in their midst.[50]

As the reality of U.S. involvement in the war sank in, information and forecasts appeared to help businesses. Buyers became aware that purchasing power was shifting from the "white collar to the industrial worker" thanks to high-paying war jobs.[51] Lower-cost drugstore cosmetics sales jumped because so many women suddenly sought employment outside the home, choosing to wear makeup as they did so. A Macy's representative categorized female customers in November 1942: First, she charged that one third didn't "seem to realize that there is a war to be won." They hoard; they complain about quality; they demand what they cannot have. But defense plant workers required "abrasive soaps, protective creams, softening lotions for after work [and] quick facial cleansers." Those volunteering for military service needed "colorless nail polish, solid cologne (non-spillable for traveling) and perfume sticks," all in small sizes. Men in the military, however, spent as though "money is no object . . . the price tag for him being the mark of quality." Allied servicemen from abroad shopped both for what the women in their lives requested and for anything they could get in quantity, such as "lipsticks, cold creams, preferably in tins, compacts," and nail polish. To ameliorate the situation, stores like Macy's began an education campaign to teach customers to buy large sizes, refillable containers when possible, and only "tested, reputable products." Additionally, they must expect to help themselves, as "salespeople are getting scarcer."[52]

Be prepared for shortages and possible governmental price controls, other experts warned.[53] The cosmetics industry faced fewer scarcities, in part because of the availability of natural and synthetic substitutes.[54] But they did come. Among the first shortages was metal. Arden introduced refillable lipstick in every shade in the spring of 1942, training her retail staff to teach customers how to fit the refill properly. She had sold refillable products in the 1920s, including a sterling silver compact case and a perfume container, so this was a known concept.[55] She added refillable ceramic and then composition paper lipstick cases to her product line in the fall as metal prices shot up.[56] Neither was as durable as metal, but both were better than the cellophane wrapping that encased English lipstick.

Teddy Haslam managed to leave Great Britain for his regular U.S. visit about that time. He came with warnings about how government-mandated cosmetic production cutbacks led to bootlegging. Several women were hospitalized after using an unmarked mascara that turned out to be shoe polish. Finally understanding women's devotion to their cosmetics, Parliament allowed more makeup to be made and sold. Haslam thought the American government did a better job of industry oversight and believed a similar situation unlikely to arise in the States. Still, cosmetics in England were taxed at a steep 66 percent. Women struggled to buy what they could to buoy their own spirits and those around them.[57]

By the end of 1942, significant shortfalls were apparent in America, too. Plastic, elaborate glass bottles, beautiful boxes, imported French perfumes, and nail polish were disappearing. The latter required nitrocellulose, which was also necessary to make "smokeless powder" for ammunition. The federal government reduced the number of nail polish shades from unlimited to six. Chemists worked around the clock in pursuit of alternatives for nitrocellulose and other scarce raw materials, including natural scents.[58]

Shortages and work-arounds made Arden think differently about another aspect of her industry. While she adored Parisian fashion and knew French designers well, she was also a realistic businesswoman. Women's war duties required simplicity of dress and less formal entertaining. She had stripped skin care and makeup to their minimum with her popular Beauty Essentials line. It was time to apply the same idea to clothing. The moment called for a larger commitment to ready-to-wear, off-the-rack garments. She introduced swimming suits and beachwear to her Miami salon, for example, and sought American-made goods. She firmly believed, though, that women would never abandon the desire for exquisite garments, and she witnessed this firsthand when three thousand people at the ninth annual Fashion Congress in 1942 *oohed* over her delicate and expensive tea gowns.⁵⁹ She also believed that once the war ended, designer clothing would make a comeback. How could it not? Women of a certain class would always yearn for one-of-a-kind creations. But it was wartime. So she expanded her salon sales space to incorporate more ready-to-wear fashions while counting on the return of haute couture. These were important decisions with long-lasting repercussions. Arden kept a sharp lookout for new designers, as she tried to predict what sales potential would be in the postwar fashion landscape.

NINETEEN FORTY-TWO WAS THE YEAR that the Fashion Academy put Elizabeth Arden on its Best-Dressed List. The judges paid special attention to women who wore "clothes in keeping with their personal budgets." This was amusing, as there was little Arden could not afford. Still, it was an honor to be recognized for one's appearance.⁶⁰ Diminutive, trim, favoring understated, feminine fashions, she had flawless skin under her perfect makeup. Among friends, she smiled frequently, and could be coquettish with handsome men. "True beauty comes from within—an inner radiance of the soul shining through," she told a group of Catholic women in Boston. "Age has little to do with beauty except to bring more mellowness and charm."⁶¹ Cobina Wright wrote in her memoir that "if anyone is ever down, be it an old friend, employee, new acquaintance, Elizabeth Arden can be counted on to do more than the right thing. She does the kind thing."⁶²

Wealth, beauty, femininity, kindness—any one of these qualities could have attracted the attentions of an eligible and aristocratic Russian exile during that already tempestuous year. Prince Michael Evlanoff came from "a family dating back to the Tartar war lords of the twelfth century," and was himself a World War I veteran, *The New York Times* reported romantically. He left Russia following the revolution that eventually replaced the czar and his aristocrats with a theoretically more egalitarian communist state. Evlanoff lived in Paris before immigrating to the United States in 1941. Soon he appeared at all the best parties and in society columns everywhere.[63] Arden and Evlanoff became an item. They saw more and more of each other until, the day before her birthday, they married under the tall white steeple of All Souls Unitarian Church in Manhattan. Teddy Haslam gave the bride away. Best man Prince Nicholas Orloff signed as a witness.[64] The bride wore a navy blue confection created by her fashion designer friend Charles James. A small reception followed at Arden's Fifth Avenue penthouse before the newlyweds (James trousseau in tow) departed for a Tucson honeymoon.[65]

The marriage between the sixty-one-year-old Arden—who entered her age as fifty-five on the marriage certificate—and the forty-eight-year-old Evlanoff kicked up an instant spate of malicious, but possibly true, gossip. He married her for her money. She only married him for his title—or, she really married him because Helena Rubinstein had married a prince four years earlier and was lording it about as "Princess Gourielli."[66]

Other men had been linked with Arden. As her era's personification of the feminine, she was seldom seen in public without an escort. Leslie Combs accompanied her to thoroughbred events. Henry Sell squired her to industry gatherings. Tom White, Hearst executive and brother of Carmel Snow, became a special favorite. Like Combs and Sell, White was married. If Arden and White had an actual affair, it was never documented. Whether Elizabeth Arden truly fell in love with Evlanoff is also unclear.

She married him because she was lonely—or so she told an FBI investigator to whom she turned for help. Evlanoff claimed he wasn't marrying for money, that he had a substantial income of $1,000 a month. Such financial independence meant that he would not mooch from her and that money would never become a problem between them. "He was the type of man she thought would be entertaining to her," the FBI agent reported, "and so she married him."[67]

She regretted the marriage almost immediately. Not only was he actually penniless, he was "costing her a great deal of money." Arden sought J. Edgar Hoover's help to recoup funds that she had given Evlanoff to cover a $30,000 gambling debt he had failed to mention. She feared publicity, she told the agent, which is why she paid off his debt.[68] Adding insult to injury, Evlanoff was not even a real prince. Gossips suggested that Evlanoff's other misstep was to invite his boyfriend on their honeymoon. Apparently, his inclusive sexuality had not registered with Arden.

At one point in the midst of it, Arden spoke candidly to a friend who took word-for-word notes. "My husband is a spider," Arden seethed, "dropping brown balls of poison. . . . Of course he could be charming and we had some very amusing times but he is worthless, that man. He is not a prince at all. That was pure fake. . . . I have all the letters about his background in my safe. He trembles when I tell him about it." She divulged Evlanoff's promise to go if she gave him $200,000. "Not a penny," Arden vowed. "I pay my lawyer to get the divorce, but to him, nothing." He wanted to maintain the enviable lifestyle she provided for him, she said. But she wanted him gone.

Evlanoff's mendacity appalled her. He lied about "that man the Baron," who was supposedly a comrade in arms from fifteen years ago, when in fact, she said, they had met only twelve months earlier. "My husband would lie in bed in the morning," Arden recounted, "talking an hour over the telephone to the Baron. . . . When I would come in he would say 'Excuse me' and then go on talking." When her friend asked what they spoke about, Arden replied, "How could I tell? It was all in Russian. But his boy friend did not have a good reputation." The experience led Arden to admit, "I look at every man now suspiciously."[69]

Arden divorced Evlanoff on February 7, 1944, again in Maine, and again for "cruel and abusive treatment."[70] Their marriage had lasted just over one lonely, heartbreaking year. It was the last time she would be tempted by the hope of matrimonial bliss. Besides, she had other things to do. There was a war to win, and Elizabeth Arden was eager to play her part.

Eighteen

"For Beauty on Duty"

E lizabeth Arden did not join the military—no matter how she fudged her age, she was too old—but she could and did assist those who served. During World War II, she gave generously of her time and money in ways that linked the prevailing belief that looking good meant feeling good with her own strong support for Allied military objectives.[1]

Patriotism was at the heart of it. When war threatened, Arden sought public and private opportunities to aid American aims, allies, and armed forces. Like other CEOs who embraced patriotic advertising, she was not blind to potential profit. Linking her brand with the nation's struggle marked her as a good corporate citizen. As a bonus, increased sales and customer loyalty might follow.[2] The federal government's diversion of resources complicated wartime production and distribution. Personnel challenges emerged as her employees left civilian work for war jobs. As in the past, Elizabeth Arden juggled many projects simultaneously and mostly successfully, but during World War II, she also forged strong, lasting, meaningful ties with U.S. servicewomen.

To support the Allies, promote goodwill, increase her customer base, and maintain her primacy, Arden continued to give away pink-packaged products at war-related fundraisers such as the District of Columbia Navy Relief Society's fashion show.[3] Arden joined the Citizens Committee that selected and supervised thirty couturiers and an equal number of debutantes who modeled formal gowns for the Army and Navy fashion show. It was such a complicated affair that the production head of Radio City Music Hall was summoned to stage-manage.[4] Her Red Door salons furnished cosmetics and skin creams gratis to local talent contests, game nights, and every other sort of program benefiting the military. She gave freely to the Red Cross, the American Field Hospital Corps, the British War Relief Society, and New York City's Defense Recreation Committee, pleasantly aware that each perfectly wrapped bottle and every flawlessly choreographed photo opportunity garnered positive publicity.

Purchasing war bonds had a similar effect. Patriotic Americans loaned the federal government money to finance the war by buying bonds. Everyone from 4-H to Hollywood celebrities encouraged supporting the war through bond sales, including Arden. In Great Britain her ads had a different emphasis: "Think how much less you do—and can—spend nowadays on Elizabeth Arden preparations than you were accustomed to spend in days gone by. What's become of the difference? See that it goes straight into 3% Defence Bonds."[5]

In one case, Arden bought a whopping $32,000 worth of bonds (more than $575,000 today) to celebrate Florence Delaney's thirty-two years of loyal service and to support her in retirement. Delaney had long since moved past bookkeeper to head corporate accountant. Arden meant the bonds to provide a sizable—if delayed—nest egg for Delaney, who would not be able to access the money until war's end. The gift acquired unintended publicity when Arden discovered that attorney Maurice B. Gladstone, whom she charged with purchasing the instruments, purposefully bought a different type of war bond that cost less up front.

When he pocketed the difference, his illegal—and anti-American—actions shocked the nation.[6]

Women gained many opportunities in this war, as they had in World War I. Elizabeth Arden watched with pride as barriers to military enlistment began to fall in May 1941 after Representative Edith Nourse Rogers (R-MA) introduced a bill to allow women to serve in the U.S. Army. Supporters characterized a woman's auxiliary as another step toward full citizenship and an affirmation of women's ability to put their patriotism into practice by doing jobs that would free up—not supplant—men in the armed forces, while gaining military entitlements. American women could do no less than their British sisters, who were already in uniform. And it was not that far a step beyond volunteering in preparedness and defense organizations. Indeed, women had fought in every war, but had never been considered part of the military nor entitled to military benefits. Powerful women backed the idea, including Eleanor Roosevelt, Virginia Gildersleeve, and Oveta Culp Hobby of the federal War Department.

But detractors feared such a future. Women protecting men? Abandoning the family? Becoming mannish? It was not what God intended. It could never work. Women were weak, insufficiently disciplined. They were ditzy, gossipy, irrational, and utterly unsuited to military order. From within the armed forces and without, substantial resistance met the idea of women joining up. Nevertheless, the patriotic argument combined with memories of the army's very real need for women's secretarial and communications assistance in World War I won the day. President Franklin Roosevelt signed Rogers's bill into law on May 15, 1942.[7]

Women rushed to join. Soon they had choices. They could be members of the Women's Auxiliary Army Corps (known as WAACs until July 1943 when they "converted to full military status" as the Women's Army Corps, or WACs).[8] After July 1942, they could enter the U.S.

Naval Reserve as WAVES, Women Accepted for Volunteer Emergency Service. The U.S. Coast Guard Women's Reserve was created in November 1942. They were called SPARS, a contraction of the Coast Guard's motto, *Semper paratus*, or "Always Ready." Skilled female aviators remained civilians, but could become Women Airforce Service Pilots, or WASPs.

The same bill that created the WAVES opened the possibility of a female U.S. Marine Corps reserve unit. Not until late 1942 did Commandant of the Marine Corps Thomas Holcomb give his approval. Ideas for nicknames flooded in; happily, WAMS, Femarines, Glamarines, and Sub-Marines were all rejected. Holcomb told *Life* magazine in no uncertain terms: "They are *Marines*. They don't have a nickname and they don't need one. They get their basic training in a Marine atmosphere at a Marine post. They inherit the traditions of the Marines. They *are* Marines."[9] They were referred to most frequently as Women Reservists, or WRs. The remarkable Ruth Cheney Streeter became the first director of the WRs, charged with locating and preparing one thousand officers and eighteen thousand enlisted women. Training began in March 1943.[10]

As far as the military was concerned, the purpose of allowing women in was to "Free a Marine to Fight." This they did. Women drilled, got in shape, learned the jargon, undertook basic and specialty training, and assumed more than 225 jobs, including parachute rigging, weapons repair, computing, intelligence work, air traffic control, navigational training, meat cutting, toxic gas handling, and dozens of clerical tasks.[11] Women served in every theater of war and relished their overseas postings. And everything they did, they did in uniform. They were expected to maintain military standards in their appearance, as spelled out in the uniform regulations.

Uniforms were controversial. Even though Girl Scouts, the Salvation Army, Red Cross workers, and many defense groups regularly wore uniforms, and even though many women's groups—such as the U.S.

Army Signal Corps Telephone Unit and the U.S. Navy Nurse Corps—
had done so during World War I, there remained a general fear that
uniforms made women appear overly masculine. The military was sensitive to this charge. Newspapers, trying to help, reported earnestly
that the army required pink cotton underwear for WAACs.[12] For many
Americans, women who "wore the pants" threatened prevailing notions
of male power and authority, in and out of the armed forces. Regardless
of the safety of trouser-covered legs in bug-infested climes, or the efficacy that slacks provided while working around machinery, resistance
continued.

The uniforms of the U.S. Marine Corps Women's Reserve benefited
from having been created after the ill-fitting WAAC uniforms, which
had been designed by committee, overseen by the U.S. Army Quarter-
master Corps, and were—unsurprisingly—unattractive. They were also
created after World War I veteran and American couturier Mainbocher
designed the smashing uniforms of the WAVES.[13] General Holcomb
chose Anne Adams Lentz to do right by the Marines. Lentz had a background in school uniform sales and experience with the disastrous
WAAC design. When Holcomb insisted that the WR uniforms be as
indistinguishable from the men's as possible, Lentz knew the errors to
avoid. And because she had volunteered to become the first Marine Re-
servist, Captain Lentz would also have to wear the "tailored femininity" he tasked her with designing.[14]

She began by guaranteeing that male and female Marines donned
the same traditional forest green. Then, like all Marines, women wore
the Eagle, Globe, and Anchor. Lentz borrowed the traditional Marine
scarlet from the men's trouser stripe to use for the chevron on the wom-
en's sleeves, their cold-weather scarf, and the cord on their distinctive
winter service hat.[15] In general Lentz's work drew applause because the
WR uniforms closely resembled the men's and yet flattered the women.

One element of the women's overall look remained stubbornly impervious to the requirement of military standardization, however: makeup.

While the rule book governed how much and what kind of makeup a WR could apply, it required neither the wearing of cosmetics nor gave color guidelines. The lack of consistency discomfited the top brass, who felt that any satisfaction of gazing upon an unvarying sea of green was destroyed by clashing oranges, pinks, and reds. It was unprofessional. It was unmilitary. Elizabeth Arden had the solution.[16]

In the early spring of 1943, a group of uniformed WRs just past basic training traveled to New York City. One of them had recently left her job in Arden's lab to enlist. She wanted to show off her new uniform to her former coworkers. As they gathered around her, exclaiming, Elizabeth Arden's disembodied voice echoed down from above: "Your lipstick does not match your uniforms. I can fix that." As the women tried not to stare, Arden swept down the stairs to announce she would personally create the perfect shade of Marine scarlet. In a matter of weeks, she unveiled (and copyrighted) "Montezuma Red." She took the name straight out of "The Marines' Hymn," whose lyrics every Marine and millions of civilians knew by heart. With this new, rich (and patented) shade of red, each WR could match her nail polish to her lipstick to her rouge, and every WR would match every other WR. Arden sent "a few thousand" tubes of lipstick to the WR for free, a gesture that decisively convinced those in charge.[17] New uniform regulations stipulated that Arden's "Montezuma Red" lipstick, "neatly and thinly applied," was "the proper . . . hue." Nail polish was not required, "but if worn had to match the lipstick."[18] Arden had successfully restored military order with color harmony.

Major Ruth Cheney Streeter and Captain Anne Lentz invited Arden to Marine Corps Women's Reserve headquarters at Camp Lejeune in North Carolina to introduce Montezuma Red to the women and experience their response firsthand. It was an immediate hit. The Marines celebrated her gift by treating her to a very special day. Three thousand WRs paraded past in a formal drill in her honor. Arden found the spectacle electrifying. She called it an unforgettable "lesson in discipline symbolizing what seemed to be classic beauty and order." To a friend she confessed the excitement of that moment: "I stood up and looked at the lovely, expectant faces of the girl Marines. I told them that seeing them before me in their uniforms, so eagerly devoting themselves to our country, I, for the first time, felt envious of their youth. It would have made me even more thrilled to have been one of them."[19]

Sergeant Claire W. Cummings was the WR "assigned to escort the Commandant and Elizabeth Arden" at Camp Lejeune and to show her "the beauty salon for the WR's as her products were used throughout."[20] Perhaps she toured a barracks like WR Faye Shumway's that "reeked with" the "red, red nail polish" that "we all wore."[21] The Marines of the Women's Reserve were proud of their customized color. They displayed a tremendous loyalty to Elizabeth Arden and to her products, wearing them for decades past the war's end.[22]

Arden and the Marines gained much from this mutual appreciation society. Hers was an internationally famous, select cosmetics brand, sold in only the best stores from Rio de Janeiro to Montreal, from New York to Paris. An Arden imprimatur for the Marines would stamp them as the most exclusive and the most feminine of all servicewomen. This partnership was a recruiter's dream! And when, not long after, Arden skillfully wove together the fascination of the Marines and the allure of Montezuma Red in a stunning advertisement to civilians, the WRs were overjoyed.[23]

Arden paid homage to WRs in the art and the text: "Elizabeth Arden's newest lipstick color—Montezuma Red . . . inspired by the brave, true red of the hat cord, scarf and chevrons of the Women in the Marines." Wearing Montezuma Red with civilian "black, white, gray, beige, navy and tweeds" would, Arden claimed, be "a tribute to some of the bravest men and women in the world." But her ad was more than an ad. The glamorous model and her gorgeous red were their own recruiters. The copy read: "Free a Marine to Fight! Share the great traditions of the Marines! Join the U.S. Marine Corps Women's Reserve."[24] When women—WRs or civilians—purchased the entire Montezuma Red makeup line, it came with a specially designed "Marine Green" case made of felt, stamped with the "gold USMC emblem" and tied with a Montezuma Red cord. Patriotism, pride, and promotion all in one.[25] By 1944, according to Shumway, "we were issued two uniforms, two pairs of dungarees, four tee-shirts, one white towel, one cake of Lifebuoy soap, [and] one tube of lipstick called Montezuma Red" on their "first day in the Marines."[26] Montezuma Red was the only cosmetic color sold in the post exchange where WRs shopped and was available in on-base beauty parlors as well.[27]

Arden's support for the WRs didn't stop there. The two-year anniversary of the Women Marines called for an oversize congratulatory *New York Times* ad from Arden, replete with yet another enlistment call.[28] She drew up and paid for a colorful multipage recruiting pamphlet titled *Give the Marines a Boost; They Free a Marine to Fight*. It was generously illustrated with photos of Marine life taken when Arden had traveled to Marine Corps Base Quantico to meet with women. Pictures of WRs donating to the Red Cross, queuing for mail from home, repairing transport vehicles, posing with the buses they kept running, and modeling three different uniforms ("because we know that women are interested in what other women are wearing") made the Marine Corps look appealing. There was even a photograph of Sergeant Duffy, the very cute English cocker spaniel mascot whom Arden had given to the WRs.[29] The women appeared competent, professional, and as though their lives and their work had significant meaning. Sharply dressed Marines, beautifully coiffed and made-up—but having a little fun, too—must have been an effective recruitment tool. In no way could the WRs be accused of looking masculine, even in their overalls, even with axle grease–stained hands. Captain E. Louise Stewart, head of the WR Division of Public Affairs, conferred frequently with Arden, and approved of the positive light in which Arden always cast Stewart's sisters in service.[30]

While Arden may have had a soft spot for the WRs, she made sure to help all military women with the vexing conundrum of how to do their hair so that it met regulations and still looked good. She consulted with WAC leaders in the construction of the sixteen-page pamphlet entitled *On-the-Double* but included hairstyles specific to each branch's covers.[31] A helpful equipment list and detailed instructions on how to set, comb, groom, and keep each hairstyle neat appeared alongside harmonizing makeup color suggestions for summer and winter uniforms.[32] She dedicated the booklet "to the women in uniform."[33]

It must be noted that Arden's booklet contained no hairstyles aimed specifically at Black servicewomen. The army was segregated during World War II. It had a quota of 10 percent, and that is what WAAC director Oveta Culp Hobby said she would follow regarding female recruits. The small number of African American women allowed into the WAAC from the beginning was joined by a slightly larger number of army nurses. Black women eventually became WAVES and SPARS in minute numbers but not until the last months of the conflict; none served in the Marines until after World War II ended, and Arden paid little or no attention to their needs.[34]

ANOTHER HIGHLY SUCCESSFUL wartime endeavor entailed a partnership with one of the nation's leading sororities. On January 15, 1943, Arden introduced the first "Elizabeth Arden Lounge" inside a Service Women's Center. Kappa Kappa Gamma (KKG) sponsored these way stations open to women in the Allied armed services, and they became popular places for regrouping, meeting friends, dropping off luggage, recovering from travel, and finding entertainment such as Ping-Pong, lending libraries, picnics, and teas. In line with their philanthropic mission, Kappa Kappa Gamma alumnae volunteers welcomed servicewomen, stocked the centers with stationery, candy, needles, thread, and other essentials, and doled out local information such as the whereabouts

of affordable hotels and the nearest skating rink.[35] While Elizabeth
Arden had been donating to, working with, and cultivating college
women as customers for many years, the direct connection between
Arden and the Kappas was Arden's niece Virginia Graham Wobber.
She had been an active KKG while a student at Sarah Lawrence College, and in the 1940s worked in publicity for the Arden corporation.
The [Kappa] Key credited Wobber's assistance in "establish[ing] the
beautiful and luxurious Elizabeth Arden powder rooms in our service
women's centers."[36] Other Kappas in Arden's employ helped in various
ways, too.[37]

The main Service Women's Center was housed in the grand Biltmore Hotel on Madison Avenue, not far from Arden's headquarters.
Out-of-town servicewomen made a beeline for it when they could get to
New York City, as did those training nearby, such as the WAVES at
Hunter College.[38] If they were lucky, they arrived on a weekend when
the Kappas were hosting a dance, always appreciated by the women and
the military men who joined them. Eventually, fourteen Service Wom-
en's Centers opened in towns near military bases, including Honolulu
and Denver, and in important railroad junctions such as St. Louis and
Baltimore. Every one of them (except Des Moines) boasted a lounge full
of complimentary Arden toiletries to refresh weary servicewomen. According to The Army Nurse newsletter, they provided everything a visiting servicewoman needed, including "radio broadcast tickets," writing
desks, and makeup—naturally—in a gracious and "hospitable atmosphere."[39] Some KKG–Elizabeth Arden Powder Rooms assembled later
in the war had a manicure "bar" and a shampoo room for women to use
while their uniforms were laundered in an on-site electric washer and
dryer.[40]

Arden urged Kappas toward a standardized interior design with a
long, mirrored, centerpiece makeup table, Arden Pink on the walls, and
a signature pink, turquoise, brown, and chartreuse plaid for furniture
and drapes. This was only a guide. She acknowledged that "your deco-

rative scheme will depend on the size of the room, what you can assemble and your budget."[41] In Seattle, no Arden plaid could be found, so resourceful Kappas hand-painted the plaid on the walls.[42] El Paso KKG alumnae chose a "Mexican theme" featuring tin mirrors and folk art figurines.[43] Local dignitaries celebrated every new Service Women's Center's opening, and some were broadcast live on radio.[44]

In most centers, officers and enlisted women had separate powder rooms. In all of them, however, Arden made sure there were bottles and jars full of cleansers, toners, and moisturizers, as well as a full line of cosmetics, which the servicewomen especially prized. As one army nurse declared, "If ever I should stop using make-up there would be nothing left of my morale. A fresh application of lipstick, my helmet at a jaunty angle, and I was ready for anything."[45]

Arden doted on servicewomen. She put in personal appearances at center openings, anniversaries, and dances. She held a mixer for enlisted personnel at the Biltmore center, welcomed them herself, provided door and dance contest prizes, and handed out free lipstick for each of the women among the five hundred revelers. She "made possible" a party for female and male officers at the Princeton Club where she dropped in to socialize. These are just two examples among many gatherings she attended and for which she paid.[46] For the second birthday of the Women Marines, Arden ordered a cake specially "decorated with a large replica of the Marine insignia done in icing" and thirty-five tubes of Montezuma Red lipstick "placed like small red candles around the top layer." After the two tall birthday candles were extinguished, Arden happily handed round the lipstick.[47] They loved her for it.

It was important to her to circulate among the women in uniform, to express her gratitude and her pride, to talk with them and to listen as they spoke of their hopes and fears. Six decades later Faye Shumway still thought it "was awfully nice of Elizabeth Arden. And when," she told an interviewer in 2007, "I go into Nordstrom now or some of these highfaluting stores, and I tell the cosmetic girls that story, they all gather round me like I'm a celebrity of some kind. They want to know . . . about it. And they just can't believe that something like that went on."[48]

As Arden learned more about the needs of women in the military as well as women ordnance workers (known as WOWs before they were called Rosie the Riveters), she catered to them more precisely. She created a lockable "Barracks Box," also called a "Service Box," that she marketed to WACs, WAVES, SPARS, and Red Cross volunteers. Available in navy blue or khaki, they were meant to be beautiful as well as practical, and came richly stocked with "fluffy cleansing cream, skin lotion, hand lotion, face powder, lipstick, orange skin cream, eight hour cream, 'sunpruf' cream, foot powder, toothpaste, washcloth, water-repellent case for soap, 'filmofoam,' mirror and a removable tray for personal articles." It sold for $10 and could be purchased by the women themselves or by family or friends as gifts.[49] Filmofoam was meant to replace hand soap for travel or emergencies. It was a small, inexpensive, blue or pink wafer that lathered with a tiny amount of water. At least one journalist suggested filmofoam would be useful in Europe where soap was scarce.[50] Arden also repackaged her leg makeup and her foot care products to appeal to servicewomen and aimed her "Efficiency Line" at them.

During the war years, Arden recruited for military service or volunteer war work through advertisements and customer outreach programs. Mildred Wedekind toured department stores with a new skit about how to achieve Arden's "War Face."[51] Beauty's compatibility with efficiency, hard work, and physical fitness featured in ads: the "'right face' for today" belongs to the woman who "cares for her beauty with scant minutes [and] devotes long hours to serving others."[52] She took as a given that her customers were pitching in: "[We] serve you well while you serve others."[53]

Another widely distributed, purposely generic advertisement featured a woman in a uniform shadowed by a man. "Frankly," the header read, "he was Fascinated." The woman looked forward, into the distance: trim, beautiful, feminine. The man sat behind, in a civilian suit, eyes riveted on her: "She had a certain elusive charm that defied description— invariably *men* appreciate the sensitive understatement of Elizabeth Arden lipstick shades which make them aware of the woman, not the make-up." The copy spelled out Arden's color harmony for uniforms.[54] If a woman was not yet involved, this ad suggested, she could sign up for volunteer work or enlist and thereby gain that "elusive charm" that accompanied the use of Arden cosmetics.

VENERATING BEAUTY IN WARTIME is a tacit admission that war is inherently ugly. Physical battle scars are a reality of fighting. The terrible weapons of World War I, including poison gas and rapid-fire machine guns, caused disfigurement and distress. Dr. Harold Gillies, a New Zealand physician, devoted himself to the difficult task of reconstructing veterans' faces. He gathered around him a cadre of dedicated doctors seeking to learn what he knew. His innovative work earned him renown as the father of modern plastic surgery.[55]

Tough and flinty, Gillies also had a broad sympathetic streak. Between the wars, while in private practice in London, he once treated a woman with a devastating facial mutilation caused by lying, incapacitated, for several hours in the embers of a coal fire she fell into because of an epileptic seizure. The fire permanently blinded and disfigured her, and even Gillies's considerable skill could never return her to her former appearance. According to his biographer, Gillies "believed that the best possible tonic for Mrs Brown after her dreadful experience would be the heartfelt approval of her family and friends." So he sent her off to the Elizabeth Arden Salon. There, "she was given cosmetic treatments of the most expensive kind." Dr. Gillies was pleased to learn that "the gasps of astonishment and delight that greeted her homecoming 'boosted her morale no end.'"[56]

Several years later, in October 1941, Gillies was in Chicago with his daughter Margaret, who was then serving with the Women's Royal Naval Service (WRENS). By that time, the deadly damage done by World War II bombing in Europe recalled Gillies and other plastic surgeons to wartime service. Seeking to impress on the then-neutral Americans the appalling effect of Nazi weaponry on soldiers and civilians alike, Gillies presented a lecture to an audience of two thousand physicians and their wives with color slides of his surgeries following the London Blitz. The photographs were so gruesome that several of the women fainted. After the lecture, Arden sought out Margaret Gillies. How, she asked Margaret, could she further Dr. Gillies's work which she "admire[d] so much"? Arden offered him some of her skin products, which he gratefully accepted, in part because, as he told his daughter, Arden treatments "had changed her from a 'nice English girl into an American.'"[57] It was a compliment. He meant that Arden's facial care routine made Margaret's skin as clear, bright, and elastic as a Hollywood starlet's.

Arden worked with her chemists to devise a restorative salve and then visited hospitals to make people aware of its therapeutic properties.[58] Her scar cream was meant to hasten recovery after reconstructive surgery, and to heal rather than disguise injuries. Foundation makeup and specialized concealers could do that, but her goal was to assist the noble efforts of Dr. Gillies to ameliorate the sufferings of veterans and other burn victims more permanently.

Women in the military during World War II were alternately deplored, lauded, and forgotten. U.S. Marine Nancy Wilt affirmed that Arden took special care of vets, giving "jobs to returning women veterans and a number of male servicemen [who] held degrees in chemistry."[59] When decorated WAC Irene Brion disembarked in California after having served in the South Pacific, she remembered being met by only a small group of fellow WACs. It was "neither surprising nor disappointing. I would hardly have expected to be welcomed by a crowd of flag-waving, cheering civilians," Brion recalled stoically. "Unlike the men, we service women weren't regarded as heroines."[60] The difficulty female veterans faced gaining access to health care, education, loans, and other benefits would prove her right. But to Elizabeth Arden, each and every woman who donned a uniform was a hero, and she proved that by her service to them.

Nineteen

The End of World War II

In February 1944, Elizabeth Arden received terrifying news: her sister was in a concentration camp. Gladys had been courageously helping downed Allied airmen avoid capture, which the Germans labeled "espionage and communicating with the enemy." According to London's *Daily Express*, Gladys was among the "aristocrats belonging to the French Red Cross" caught in a Nazi "round-up" of six hundred people, including Paris salon manager Solange de Luze. Gladys was put into "a German cattle train," and her destination was Ravensbrück, outside Berlin, the only concentration camp built specifically for women.[1] It held those whom the Nazis considered political enemies, or inferiors— but not specifically Jews. Most sent there were non-Jewish Europeans; few were British. Even fewer were American.

Ravensbrück was horrific. The approximately "130,000 women [who] passed through its gates [were] beaten, starved, worked to death, poisoned, executed and gassed." They were also used in medical experiments.[2] "As we went into Ravensbrück it was as if God had remained outside," survivor Geneviève de Gaulle later wrote. "The women already there . . . were living zombies drained of expression." Another survivor, Jacqueline d'Alincourt, recalled her arrival at Ravensbrück: "Naked, penned up, pressed one against the other, all ages thrown together, we went to the showers. We avoided looking at each other before being handed the striped bathrobe, before learning by heart in German the number assigned to each of us, sewed on the sleeve."[3]

Gladys de Maublanc and Solange de Luze were part of the French Resistance.[4] They likely volunteered on the Comet Line, an organized underground movement to assist Allied airmen trapped behind enemy lines escape to Great Britain. Several Comet Line workers were betrayed at the time Gladys and Solange were captured. Gladys later admitted to having taken "many risks to aid Allied aviators shot down over France." Her actions were guided in part by "the hope that some mother somewhere would also help her American aviator son [Lieutenant John Baraba] if he should ever need aid."[5] Military scholar Peter Hore pinpointed Gladys as one of 959 women picked up by the Nazis on January 31, 1944.

Almost nothing is known about her time at Ravensbrück. Hore found that "friends who had worked together in the Resistance formed little groups whose camaraderie in the coming weeks and months would make an essential difference to their prospects for survival."[6] Gladys endured the unimaginable for more than half a year at Ravensbrück, where "her spirit and her encouragement kept the strength and morale of other prisoners high."[7] Elizabeth knew nothing about how her sister was faring, only that she was in this hell.

Frantic about Gladys and depressed over the debacle of her second marriage, Arden went to ground. "Now that Elizabeth Arden has shed her title," Hedda Hopper wrote with considerable snark, "she's taken a ranch at Phoenix, Ariz., for six weeks of meditation."[8] The quiet of the desert calmed and captivated Arden, and she made an interesting new friend there, Ada Peirce McCormick. A Maine native, McCormick moved with her husband to Tucson in 1931 for her health. She was active in civil rights and social justice movements, and edited a magazine titled *Letter* devoted to improving national and international relations. The two women found much to discuss, including Maine Chance in McCormick's home state.

After Phoenix, Arden sought sororal solace among her Kappa friends at their alumnae house, the two-story Boyd Hearthstone mansion in Winter Park, Florida. She spent a fortnight there, "truly appreciative" to have been spoiled by the women of KKG.[9] Recovering from the sting of her second divorce, frustrated and stymied in her attempts to free Gladys, Arden turned her focus back to business.[10]

ARDEN HAD LONG considered establishing her own in-house couturier, and now set about implementing it. A June 1944 page-one *Women's Wear Daily* story verified rumors of Arden's fashion design studio by announcing Viola Herspberger as its director.[11] Herspberger's job was to staff the cutting and sewing rooms with an expert workforce that would be ready and waiting once a designer appeared.[12] This was a brilliant idea at a brilliant time. The war had interrupted European fashion design and cycles, and Arden aimed to step into the breach to entice clients who had been buying one-of-a-kind lingerie and other items of clothing from her for decades. If high fashion is "dress in which the key feature is rapid and continual changing of styles," then it was also high profit.[13]

Seeking the nation's most gifted designer to guarantee the success of her newest risky venture, she found Charles James. They had met in New York in 1929—thanks to the queen of connections, Elisabeth Marbury—when James was a uniquely talented but unknown milliner. They got on well. Soon after, James left for England and gained public acclaim for the wedding gown he created for the sister of his friend Cecil Beaton. As World War II began, James returned to America. He designed the dress and trousseau for Arden's second wedding. Arden and James had a decades-long incendiary friendship marked by fits of pique, bouts of betrayal, and mutual frustration—as well as lucrative business dealings and an enduring appreciation of each other's abilities.

It would be easy to fault the domineering and ambitious Arden for the periods of meltdown. But James's own biographer blames James. He was "snobby and sardonic," Michèle Gerber Klein wrote, addicted to gossip, prone to pranks, "supremely individualist and self-promoting," "unyielding, belligerent," and an "unreasonable dreamer." One friend lamented that James "immediately bit the hand that fed him and insulted his most important customers." Another admitted that he was "self-destructive," and that "perceived betrayals could spark from him cruel and acerbic critiques, litigation, and a sustained and consuming rage." Klein summed up the relationship between James and Arden as "profitable, histrionic, and highly complicated."[14]

Why, then, work with him? Because Virginia Woolf proclaimed him "a genius." Because Cristóbal Balenciaga pronounced him "not only the greatest American couturier, but the world's best." Because other fashion designers—Coco Chanel and Elsa Schiaparelli among them—wore his creations. Christian Dior said he was "the greatest talent of my generation," and admitted that James's work inspired his own famous 1947 "New Look."[15] The designer's brilliance was never in question. Mentored by Paul Poiret, James had "a ferocious talent for creating unexpected beauty," a network that included the crème de la crème of Anglo-American society, and the ability to be charming and generous.[16] For a time, James was Arden's preferred escort as they sailed out together to mix with luminaries from stage, screen, and society. In 1943, Arden signed James to a business "partnership for life," which made him "wild with enthusiasm" because he knew how her sponsorship would benefit him.[17]

Elizabeth Arden launched James's American career. She gave him carte blanche (and a budget) to update the second floor of her Fifth Avenue showroom. His designs would sell in her salons exclusively, bearing a Charles James label. She expected him to work with her on publicity.

"Dear," she told him, "if you want to get into the papers, take the pictures and stories to the newspapers, yourself, and sit there, until they see you if only to get rid of you. It works. I know. I've done it myself."[18]

Arden's hunch about James's talent was correct: he soon became a force in haute couture. Women thronged Arden's salon to see his architectural dress designs, draped and sculpted and anything but traditional. "Mathematical tailoring combined with the flow of drapery is his forte," *Vogue* wrote in 1944. "His continuity of line is never accident, but planned. His asymmetry is born of a mastery of symmetry." James swore that he was "dead against deadly symmetry," so dresses often covered only one shoulder, and coats had two layers of different lengths.[19] He put the international film star Marlene Dietrich in a "satin dinner sheath, asymmetrically slit to the skin from shoulder to hip, and tied with bows."[20] His exhilarating vision of gowns created and held up by architectural and engineering principles attracted prominent new clients.

The business partners decided to introduce James's designs to the maximum number of discerning eyes, so they chose the centerpiece fashion show during a Red Cross benefit at the Ritz-Carlton. For "One Touch of Genius: New Posture in Fashion," Charles James dreamed up "dresses, suits, coats and negligees" with what *WWD* called (pre-Dior) "a new look." These "arrestingly new and important" skirt silhouettes with "asymmetrical cuts and draping" presaged smaller shoulders, greater femininity, and a look of simplicity achieved through intricate draping, gathers, and hidden seams. "Interesting," *WWD* mused, "that they were presented under the aegis of Elizabeth Arden who plans these clothes as an exclusive feature of the couture salon." *Vogue* editor Babs Simpson sighed. "Charles James brought America a level of luxury we'd just never seen before." And in more than one way, the designs and the show purposefully linked Arden's beauty ideas with fashion. *The New York Times* described the costumes as "especially designed to bring out the beauty of the figure which is based on correct posture," and noted that Arden's "exercises to correct posture faults and to increase flexibility were demonstrated."[21] *Vogue* gave an insouciant shrug: "For these custom-made figures, custom-made clothes are a logical sequence."[22] By establishing James in her showroom, Arden made real her belief that women would clamor for high fashion after the war.

Fashion rules for dress, hair, and makeup remained vitally important. They separated those who had the time, knowledge, and financial wherewithal to concern themselves with such things from those who did not. Fashion rules followed class lines. Upper-class women who saw themselves as protectors of gracious living, or who simply enjoyed following trends and looking good as a sort of hobby, sought the expertise of figures such as Elizabeth Arden and Charles James—and did not see a global war as an excuse to lower their standards.

By MID-1944, fighting had been going on in Europe for nearly five years. Americans looked ever more optimistically to the war's end as hard-won Allied naval and land victories in the Pacific provided fresh hope that the Imperial Japanese forces were ultimately doomed. In Normandy, Operation Overlord began on D-Day, June 6, 1944. Once the Allied forces secured a toehold, they moved inexorably toward Nazi Germany. Victory was not instant. The Nazis razed Warsaw, condemning people to concentration and death camps. In retaliation for D-Day, they unleashed their V-1 "doodlebug" rocket bombs on London.

Elizabeth Arden mourned when Diana Wall died in a V-1 attack during a church service at the Guards' Chapel, near Buckingham Palace, on June 18. The Nazis made a direct hit, killing 121 people. Diana, who had managed the Bond Street salon since January 1926, had been a member of the Westminster Women's Voluntary Service mobile canteen team. She and her husband, Gordon, a Grenadier Guard, died together in their uniforms.[23]

Some good news may have reached Arden not long after. An eyewitness account by Odette Fabius, a French Resistance member and

Ravensbrück internee, provided greater detail about Gladys. Fabius's memoir suggested that in addition to working on behalf of the Resistance, Gladys also underwrote the efforts of Philip Jones, another Resistance fighter and a member of the Secret Intelligence arm of the American Office of Strategic Services. Gladys and Jones thought that their proximity to Henri de Maublanc, considered a Nazi sympathizer, would protect them from German suspicion. Fabius attested that Jones "had for cover an important position with Elizabeth Arden" and that "Gladys de Maublanc paid him money for his activities. This was unfortunately found in Philip Jones's notebook," which is why, she continued, the Nazis arrested them. Fabius found Gladys "a very charming companion" for the time they were together at Ravensbrück. But Gladys was moved away from the internment camp once "her sister paid a very high deposit from New York, after [Gladys's] husband, the count de Maublanc, a Pétainiste, intervened." A "Pétainiste" was someone who supported Philippe Pétain, the collaborationist leader of Vichy France. Fabius suggested that de Maublanc's Gestapo contacts, greased with his sister-in-law's money, released Gladys from Ravensbrück. No one could tell Arden where she had been taken.[24]

By August 1944, Allied forces liberated Paris, a celebratory turning point, but not yet the end. War work continued. Arden helped organize the Citizens Committee for the Army and Navy benefit fashion show to support recreational activities for military personnel. She spoke to girls of the Washington-Lee Cadet Corps in Arlington, Virginia, about correct posture and good grooming. The women's division of the New York War Fund, on whose executive committee Arden sat, determined to raise more than $17 million to assist "civilian war aid groups." A goodly number of strong-willed women served alongside her, including Virginia Gildersleeve, Helen Hayes, Dorothy Hearst Paley, and philanthropist and fundraiser Adele Rosenwald Levy.[25] Concerns about refugees increased, and American women experienced with the issue were looking ahead to the postwar world.

Then, finally, Arden received the news she had been desperate to hear: Gladys was free! In August 1944, she learned her sister had been transferred to Vittel internment camp, built by the Nazis for American and British prisoners. Vittel bore little resemblance to Ravensbrück. Vittel was a "model camp" used by Germans as propaganda to prove to the world how well they treated their internees. The Free French reached Vittel on September 12, 1944, one month after Allied forces freed Paris.[26] Gladys celebrated her release by hosting a Red Cross Christmas party at the Paris Red Door Salon for fifty-two French war orphans in December 1944, no doubt a bittersweet gathering amid the dawning recognition of the extent of continuing wartime suffering.[27]

How many heroic risks Gladys Graham de Maublanc took on behalf of the Allied war effort—and how much her sister intuited about her work—have not been recorded. Gladys confirmed to *The New York Times* that "women in France had dared grave personal danger to feed, clothe, hide and buy railway tickets for airmen." Assuming Gladys did support the Resistance work of Philip Jones, neither she nor Elizabeth (if she knew) would ever have made that public. Her efforts on behalf of the Allies were enough for the Nazis to send Gladys to a concentration camp and for the postwar French government to award her the Legion of Honor, the nation's highest decoration, "for her military services."[28] Plans were soon under way to reunite Gladys with her American family members.[29]

FREED FROM THE OPPRESSIVE worry about her sister, Elizabeth Arden burst forth with renewed creativity. It centered first on television. She was the only cosmetics leader who took part as General Electric (GE) and the Associated Merchandising Corp.—a firm that bought clothing in bulk for American department stores—crafted a test television show in 1944 that included an Arden makeup demonstration. GE boasted that television would soon be "a billion dollar industry" and wanted to make sure that retailers got "their share of it."[30] Arden was game. She had been an early adopter of radio for product promotion and had witnessed the boost in sales of makeup thanks to the movies. War had slowed television's development, but peace on the horizon revived research and testing, especially regarding the possibility of color transmissions. Color TV would make all the difference for cosmetics and clothing. Even though in 1945 there were only 7,000 home television sets nationwide, of which 5,100 were in the greater New York City area, Arden saw the future.[31] "There will be *nothing* but television after the war, I feel sure, and it's good to get in on the beginning," she enthused.[32]

In October 1944, her Elizabeth Arden "Fashion Floor" showroom finally opened to tremendous acclaim. She enticed her friend, the eccentric Maria Ruspoli, the Duchesse de Gramont, to be a sort of saleswoman—really more of a titled draw to entice customers to shop what *WWD* opined was "a collection . . . thoroughly modern" and "strictly for sophisticated tastes." Dresses in "unusual combinations of color," featuring an abundance of material draped in several types of folds, suggested that wartime privations were over.[33] This may have been when Charles James debuted the soon-famous infinity scarf that he "invented . . . for Elizabeth Arden."[34] *The New York Times* lauded the "imaginative collection of dresses, suits and coats," including a "floor-length satin coat" made "of brilliant green with a huge black velvet bow at the neck," as well as negligees, lingerie, and hostess gowns.[35] Barbara E. Scott Fisher, *The Christian Science Monitor*'s fashion editor, rhapsodized over the "startling and exquisite beauty" of the clothing, which she found "as young, proud, and victorious as the American figure itself."[36]

"To Elizabeth Arden," Fisher acknowledged, "there has always been a close relation between a perfectly-proportioned, well-poised figure and a beautiful dress." Arden's brilliance, she thought, was to sort women into five body types—"the square, the pear-shaped, the triangle, the string bean, and the round"—and to use these categories to create clothing to improve the imperfect body, just exactly as Arden's makeup corrected a slightly flawed face.[37] These categories were short-lived and influenced by work Charles James had under way with curator Michelle Murphy at the Brooklyn Museum, compiling standard patterns based on women's physical measurements.[38]

The application of science to aesthetics was nothing new to Arden. Long stressing posture as the first way to overcome flaws, she reminded women to "guard your proportions and walk like a queen." James's clothes were stunning, the colors sublime, the cuts flattering, and the details flawless. They were "designed [to] either disguise [the body's] deficiencies or be so becoming as to achieve the effect of a more beautifully proportioned figure." For Arden, this line of corrective clothing—although she never called it that—was "merely approaching her favorite theme in a practical manner."[39] Glad to have data points, Arden released to the press her ideal proportions for women of all heights. For example, women between five feet three and five feet five should have a waist "9.5 inches smaller than the bust, and the hips one-half inch larger than the bust." The bust for five-feet-tall women should be 31.5 inches and increase one-half inch for every inch in height. It was all about proportion.[40] Those women who failed to measure up could find fixes at Maine Chance, or any Arden salon or beauty counter.

James and Arden participated in the first annual March of Dimes Fashion Show. The New York Dress Institute (NYDI)—formed in 1941 to promote American fashions—sponsored the revue, designed and produced by Lester Gaba. Since NYDI publicist Eleanor Lambert had invited Coty to provide makeup for the fashion models, Elizabeth Arden hoped to make an especially big publicity splash for her design studio with James's frock.[41] The selection committee had accepted his closely fitted, deep green décolletage gown, worn by internationally famous burlesque star Gypsy Rose Lee. Her appearance caused a stir, but James was not there to see it. An assortment of troubles between Arden and the designer resulted in her firing him before the event and warning him to stay away. Instead, he appeared—an interloper—at her post-show party, waving a court order mandating back pay.[42]

Thus the "permanent partnership" between James and Arden proved anything but. Cracks emerged early. He believed she owed him money. She thought he overspent wildly—especially in redecorating the Fashion Floor. She tired of his pranks—one of which involved putting an oversize red vase in her salon window and then backlighting it so that, as one of her horse racing friends snickered, it gave off a brothel-like glow. Another antic involved James lighting a real fire in a fake fireplace and "smok[ing] out several floors of the Arden establishment." The building manager failed "to strangle him to death." "Too bad he didn't try again," Arden fumed.[43]

Both could be single-minded, but the bulk of the responsibility for their disagreements must fall to James. "In an industry where complex personalities are very much the norm," one insider wrote, "Charles James stands out as one of the most complicated, contradictory and difficult. . . . He unerringly destroyed almost every working and social relationship with his erratic habits, eccentric attitudes and fluorescent temper."[44] To her credit, Arden hung on longer than most of James's friends. His biographer calculated that James's "association with Elizabeth Arden had proved priceless. It had given him weight in the American fashion community. Even more, it had yielded him a treasure trove of supporters and patrons, and a mission that would define his life and the legacy he would work so hard to memorialize."[45]

James enjoyed lasting fame. Celebrated women sought his designs. Museums snapped up his gowns, even while he was alive. He is recognized today for creating the first sports bra, the first puffer coat, and the infinity scarf. His designs—for gowns known as the Clover Leaf, the Butterfly, the Tree, the Swan, the Ribbon, the Diamond—are iconic. Arden had early recognized his brilliance. Launching her haute couture line with James was masterful. But, as with everyone else in his life, James could not work closely with Arden, even though he professed to an interviewer, "I've always adored Miss Arden, in spite of everything."[46] Her "role in [his] life," he wrote her decades later, "was that of one who inspired my best work."[47] Charles James remained a sort of friend until Arden's death, but he was most notable as the first of several legendary couturiers with whom she would redefine her salon as the go-to destination for high-quality, unique fashions, a place where social elites and First Ladies would shop.

IN THE FALL OF 1944, Franklin Roosevelt ran for an unprecedented fourth term against Republican Thomas Dewey. Like most other large industrialists, and nearly everyone in the cosmetics industry, Arden supported Dewey. She donated determinedly to the GOP that year, just as her firm had been slapped—again—by the Federal Trade Commission for favoring her larger retailers by offering demonstrators to them but not to her smaller retailers.[48] Big business agreed that Roosevelt, in his attempts to fight the Great Depression and then World War II, had overstepped what was sensible for industry. It was time to elect a Republican who would abolish regulatory laws and agencies that cut into corporate profits. She was destined for disappointment when Roosevelt won and was duly inaugurated in January 1945. He served only eighty-three days of his fourth term before he died on April 12. A fortnight later, Hitler committed suicide. Victory in Europe Day—VE Day— occurred on May 8, 1945, the celebrations tempered by the deepening awareness of the Holocaust. President Harry S Truman brought the war in Asia to a formal end on September 2, 1945.

The close of the war concluded the able partnership between Elizabeth Arden and Kappa Kappa Gamma. WAVES, WACs, SPARS, and Women Marines traded their uniforms for civilian clothes, and Service Women's Centers began to close or convert to Veterans Centers.[49] Kappas in Portland, Oregon, reported in October 1945 that their "Arden powder room" had morphed into "an important part of the General

George A. White Veterans' club." In addition to the Arden makeup bar, there was ample space to rest, shower, launder uniforms, and utilize the Arden manicure cart and the Arden shampoo room. "The walls [were] Arden pink," the curtains lovingly sewn by KKG alumnae, and "Kappa husbands" crafted shelving units to hold Arden toiletries. Kappas donated flowers, artwork, and money to help the conversion, in Portland and elsewhere.[50]

The centers made an enormous impact on servicewomen and on Kappas, and praise showered down on Elizabeth Arden from the national organization and from individual women. One navy nurse penned in Honolulu's guest book, "This place is a life-saver." Another called it "heavenly," while a third believed it "the nicest place" in town. The KKG hostess wished that Arden had "heard three sun burned Navy nurses giving thanks and testimonials for the skin lotion."[51]

With the war over, advertising reflected the increased optimism of peace. Arden's "Winged Victory" inspired a partnership with milliner Jeanne Tete who created hats to complement the new "rosy red" makeup.[52] In September, Marshall Field & Company led manufacturers in the creation of "American Claret," billed as "the color you'll love to wear this glorious autumn when your Johnny comes marching home!" It was the "first coordinated color promotion the store has developed since wartime restrictions precluded such efforts."[53] Arden's wine-themed tie-in was "Red Grape" lipstick, rouge, and nail polish—sold separately or in a color harmony box.[54]

Many Americans feared another postwar economic downturn as the federal government lifted wartime price controls and spent less on armaments. Only real doomsayers thought toiletries would suffer. Women had purchased steadily through nearly seventeen years of Depression and war, and as 1945 year-end tallies showed, in the cosmetics sector, profits rose another 5.2 percent.[55]

Other concerns accompanied war's end. How much would business be affected by the division of Europe and the gulf between the United

States and the communist Soviet Union that would soon become the long Cold War? Would Paris regain its central cultural role? Leon Stein of the International Ladies' Garment Workers' Union emphasized that there must be no more bowing to Paris, and most U.S. fashion insiders agreed. Stein prophesied that "American designers 'have little need for [Paris's] antiquated inspirations, resorts, race tracks, fashion magazine vignettes, salons and the chit-chat of the 100 leading families.'"[56] The war did decenter Paris but failed to doom the classist, racist, aristocratic world in which Arden's client base operated. Elizabeth Arden embraced change while maintaining her classic look and her commitment to healthy beauty practices. Two tough decades were over. She set about patching up her global business empire, determined to sustain her success—but to enjoy it, too.

Twenty

The Horsewoman

The United States of America was the wealthiest and most powerful nation in the world as the postwar era dawned. Its territory had largely avoided conflict, unlike much of Europe and Asia. No other country possessed atomic weaponry. The economy was strong and growing stronger thanks to technological breakthroughs in physics, chemistry, medicine, and electronics. Wages were rising and American industry was the envy of the planet. While America was not without problems—racism and sexism, for example, had not disappeared— the overall mood was buoyant. The American fashion and cosmetics industries had staked out a fresh and desirable look different from that of Western Europe, a thing to celebrate, according to titans like Elizabeth Arden.

Fashion and toiletries had always had transatlantic connections, but the largest cosmetics firms, beneficiaries of women's splurges during the Great Depression and of the patriotic imperative to look good in wartime, embarked on "full-fledged market expansion." In 1950, North American women bought 66 percent of the world's cosmetics. U.S. firms recognized that vast untapped markets existed elsewhere, but there were obstacles to growth.[1] Not all women preferred the same beauty products, few could afford them, some countries disallowed American-style advertising, and governments differed as to acceptable ingredients. Potential customers required reformulating products because of "differences in skin tone, hair texture, diet, and climate."[2] Many women in these new regions needed training in how to choose and use cosmetics—exactly the sort of education that Arden had supplied since the 1910s. Companies with a product list that went beyond makeup to soaps, toothpastes, deodorants, and shampoos fared the best.

Business expansion in the prosperous postwar decades brought seismic shifts. In 1947, Unilever purchased Harriet Hubbard Ayer. Two years later, Gillette incorporated the Toni Company, best known for its home permanents. In the 1950s, Chesebrough scooped up Pond's, Prince Matchabelli, and Cutex. Bristol-Myers bought Clairol. Two new rivals emerged. Estée Lauder, born Josephine Esther Mentzer, created her cosmetics firm in 1946 and patterned it on Arden's, down to her use of pink packaging and her goal of cornering the prestige market. Barnard College chemistry graduate Hazel Bishop launched her firm in 1949 with a highly advertised "No-Smear Lipstick."

Helena Rubinstein continued to roll out cosmetic and treatment innovations, but with difficulty. Before World War II, Rubinstein's salons stretched across North America and Europe, into South Africa, South America, and Australia. While the war raged across Europe, Arden's Paris, Berlin, Madrid, and Milan salons remained open. Rubinstein, though, was harder hit by the war—her London salon was bombed while Arden's was not, for example—and under cover of vicious antisemitic legislation, Nazis commandeered some of Rubinstein's property. She had trouble recovering quickly.[3] Like Arden, Rubinstein still ran her business personally, but it was by then publicly traded, making Madame responsible to shareholders. Arden remained her own boss.

No other cosmetics firm was like Elizabeth Arden. There was, after all, an established Arden look, but no comparable Rubinstein look.

Arden held her reins firmly, confident she was providing well for her long-term customer base. After the war, wealthy women grew wealthier and the middle class expanded. Unaffected by industry changes, Arden remained a one-woman business with a clear brand and image. She was ready to extend further her thirty-year lock on the global prestige market.

Arden did not stand still at the top. The Nazi occupation of France hampered Parisian dress design and production—the competition, in other words, was in disarray. Brilliantly launched in the public eye with the innovative Charles James, Arden's haute couture initiative gained positive and wide press coverage, as well as immediate customer loyalty. After James's departure, she could have closed the Fashion Floor, but as a public figure of discernment with legions who thought of her as "less a person than a school of thought," she wanted to carry on.[4] Arden also continued her Fashion Floor because she disliked World War II–era clothing. She found it unbecoming and masculine and looked forward to creating her own designs and working with talented artists to re-shape the look of the American woman.[5]

Her next couturier was Don Antonio Cánovas del Castillo de Rey. The Spanish Civil War pushed Castillo from the country of his birth to France, where he worked with top fashion designers including Robert Piguet (who would later instruct Christian Dior and Givenchy). Castillo remained in France for the duration of World War II and when powerful *Harper's Bazaar* editor Carmel Snow visited in the spring of 1945, she noticed that Castillo was "really making charming clothes and some of the best hats in Paris."[6] Not long after, and possibly at the urging of Gladys, Arden whisked Castillo across the Atlantic.

He debuted with a few gowns before an audience of three thousand at the second annual March of Dimes Fashion Show in January 1946, but the first public glimpse of his broader collection occurred on her Fashion Floor the following month. It heralded a new dawn. Castillo turned Arden's vision, a contrast to the popular and practical workaday dresses then shown by Claire McCardell, into reality. Castillo necklines dipped flirtatiously low. He softened hips and sleeves with pleats. Shoulder pads disappeared in his delicate "bird-wing" silhouette, which he explained as "having the look of a bird poised for flight." He loved embroidered "capelets" and finished each outfit with unusual hats and accessories.[7] In his third show—his "Picasso Collection"—Castillo introduced "side-saddle drapes" for skirts, a way of wrapping the fabric around to the back to resemble a silken waterfall. He continued his emphasis on décolletage, "lowered waistlines," and slim silhouettes. He lengthened his capelets into "dominos" and shortened his ball gowns so ankles peeked out underneath layers of chiffon and taffeta. Virginia Pope led the cavalcade of enamored fashion editors.[8]

Frequent front-page articles kept Castillo's seasonal fashions and Arden's carefully chosen colors before the public. Many of his fabrics contained shades matching and named after her makeup. Soon her cosmetics ads featured models wearing Castillo's color-harmonized frocks, giving Arden the ability to sell makeup and clothing concurrently. Her Fashion Floor seated 250, and every show tempted consumers with product tie-ins.[9] Audiences consisted of cosmetics buyers, fashion journalists, society women, and Broadway costumers and the stars they dressed, like Ginger Rogers.[10] Soon the pair broadened their reach so that made-to-order Castillo creations became available through Neiman-Marcus and similar upmarket department stores. For five mostly good years, Castillo's designs were synonymous with Elizabeth Arden, adding considerably to the luster of her brand and establishing him as one of America's most important couturiers.[11]

HORSES STILL BROUGHT PROFOUND joy to Arden. She talked about them to anyone who would listen. She put their pictures on her Christmas cards. She lavished them with time and Arden products, and spent hours massaging their knotted muscles. Her racing friends had come to overlap with her social circle, even more when Hollywood stars such as Bing Crosby and Betty Grable began to purchase racehorses.

During World War II, federal rationing of rubber and gasoline had curtailed the thoroughbred horse racing season. Some courses nixed pre- and post-race festivities. Regardless, horse racing attendance soared as other sports cut back, and Americans remembered fondly the past equine magic created by legends Man o' War and Seabiscuit. Elizabeth Arden's horses had been winning some and losing some, competitive but not to the degree of her ambitions. As she had prepared her company and her clientele for the war, so she set about strengthening her thoroughbred empire. She applied the same genius to horses as she did to cosmetics, believing that "a beautiful horse is like a beautiful woman."[12]

First she had to survive every owner's worst nightmare. In March 1937, a fire coursed through her Belmont Park stable, killing three of her prizewinning horses. She told a reporter that the monetary loss was inconsequential compared to the fact that all three were "her favorites." The wife of Percy Jarrett, Arden's trainer, heroically attempted to save the animals by sprinting into the burning building to release them, but she could not shoo them outside. Luckily, most of Arden's horses were wintering in Columbia, South Carolina. The financial hit was approximately $15,000 (more than $320,000 today). No cause of the fire was ever found.[13] Arden was so upset by the recurring vision of the creatures suffering in the flames that she could not stop crying during a sad aria from *Madame Butterfly* at the Met. "It reminds me so much of my little horses," she sobbed.[14]

She determined to rebuild. Since she had purchased her first horse in the early 1930s, Arden had grown more sure-footed in the business. Cobina Wright spent a great deal of time with her friend at the races and elsewhere, and testified that Arden knew what she was doing. Her horses, Wright insisted, "thrived on baby talk, were completely comfortable in stables that knew the touch of an interior decorator, [and] ran magnificent races after the 'little darlings' had been rubbed down with Ardena skin tonic when they had colds because their owner thought it 'smelled much nicer than that horrible horse liniment.'"[15] Arden stood out as an oddball owner for her insistence that her horses be treated kindly, but in April 1940 she found someone who shared her training philosophy.

When Arden hired her, Elizabeth Cromwell Bosley "hit the big time among turf trainers," the *Chicago Tribune* reported. Bosley replaced Louis Feustel, famous for having trained Sam Riddle's great Man o' War. Described at her signing by most papers as a "Maryland society matron," journalists admitted that by "taking over one of the major racing stables in the turf world, [Bosley] advances to a spot higher than any woman trainer has ever reached before." Bosley had experience raising and training racehorses. She had won $24,337 in 1939, and even more than that a year or so earlier with a horse who began as her children's pet and with whom she scored six victories in a row.[16] Arden liked winners.

She hired Bosley because she trusted women, but even more because Bosley believed that "the secret" to training horses "was tenderness, an absolute absence of old-fashioned methods of the rigid discipline that often led to brutality, and above all the inculcation of confidence." The racing world reacted positively to this feminist act of putting a woman at the helm of the powerful Maine Chance Farm, and Bosley began well. Alas, the association ended too soon. Just nine months later, Elizabeth Bosley died in a car crash. By then, though, her obituaries substituted "society matron" with "Ranking Woman Horse Trainer" and "Noted Turfwoman."[17]

To follow Bosley, Arden chose one of the racing world's greatest. "Silent Tom" Smith had trained Seabiscuit, 1938 Horse of the Year. Seabiscuit won races. A lot of them. And money. A lot of it. Seabiscuit earned more than any horse in the world at the time, thanks to Smith. Silent Tom also shared his new boss's feelings about horses. "'It's easy to talk to horses if you understand their language,' he once said. 'Horses stay the same from the day they are born until the day they die; they are only changed by the way people treat them.'"[18]

Everyone recognized that Smith's way was different. "More harm can be done by overworking a horse than by going easy with him," the trainer believed.[19] One of Smith's protégés at Maine Chance Farm affirmed that "no trainer devoted his time more completely to his horses than did Smith. . . . He lived near his horses, either in a cottage beside the track or in a quiet section nearby. . . . If he had a sick horse, he'd drag out an old cot and sleep at the barn." Instead of daybreak workouts, Smith waited until the horses had digested their breakfasts. He made sure of their comfort in ways Arden found reassuring.[20]

Without good horses, though, a trainer has nothing. That's where Leslie Combs II came in. By the time Arden met him, Combs had almost finished purchasing the more than one thousand acres of his Spendthrift Farm outside Lexington, most of which had once belonged to his grandfather. The shrewd, determined, charismatic fifth-generation Kentuckian slowly but surely built a stable of horses and a reputation as the region's best consignor. Arden sought Combs's advice before she acquired her thoroughbreds, and for more than two decades reaped the benefit of his expertise. For three years in a row—1943, 1944, and 1945—with his guidance, Arden outspent every other buyer, intent on the fastest racers. Among the thoroughbreds Combs suggested were Star Pilot, Beaugay, Knockdown, and They Say, all of whom recouped her outlay. That winning quartet represented a fraction of the many successful horses Combs recommended in their long time together.

Combs once told a journalist that Arden "wouldn't buy a horse without us passing on it. . . . Each year, she'd say, 'I want you to pick out the 15 best yearlings you see.' So, we'd pick out the best 15 and of them, she'd pick out ten herself. Elizabeth didn't know a thing about the pedigree, soundness or conformation of a horse—the trainer and I handled that for her. She just liked what she liked, the way they looked at her.

She'd say the horses smiled at her when she went by.'" Tom Smith had a different take, telling *Time* magazine that "she picks horses for their long beautiful tails."[21]

Well, maybe. She admitted to preferring beautiful horses, but this is almost certainly not how Arden would have characterized the purchases. She firmly believed that she knew more about horses than any trainer except Smith.[22] That, naturally, never sat well with the trainers. She was with her horses hours on end, unlike most owners, and could be found around the barns or tracks several mornings a week. "She seemed oblivious of wind and weather while watching her horses, even when suffering from colds," one reporter marveled.[23] Arden made the final call as to which horse would enter which race, and which jockey would ride. She kept the same close control over her thoroughbreds that she did over her cosmetics. Intimately involved in both businesses, she trusted her own judgment.

Was Combs exaggerating for storytelling purposes? Did his southern male chivalry blind him to her authority? Was she so experienced at playing the breathy blonde stereotype that she fooled him? Arden's reputation as a track eccentric grew story by hilarious story until it became impossible to tell truth from fiction, and perhaps there came a point where one could say nearly anything about Lady Lipstick and it would be believed. These things were all and simultaneously true: Combs worked for Arden for twenty years, they enjoyed each other's company, she appreciated his know-how, he was glad to make money with her as a client, many of her horses—some he had selected and others he had not—won many races, and very few big owners ever bought horses without input from someone like Combs. Especially not one concurrently running a global business. Everyone knew where the buck stopped. As one trackside reporter wrote, Combs and Smith "help in her decisions. But she has final say in operating her Maine Chance Farm stable."[24]

The team of Arden, Combs, and Smith paid off handsomely. In the 1940s, Combs explained how Arden had "30 or 40 broodmares a year,

[plus] the foals, and, I'd say, 75 to 100 horses in training." In 1945, Maine
Chance made *The American Racing Manual*'s list of top ten stables and
remained there for eleven consecutive years. Also in 1945, Arden earned
$589,170, "a record sum for any woman owner the world over," accord-
ing to *Turf and Sport Digest*.[25]

. In 1945, hopes were high and the praise fulsome. Arden had a slew
of champion two- and three-year-olds: Beaugay, Star Pilot, Lord Boswell, Magnific Duel, War Jeep, and Knockdown, among others. Maine
Chance Farm was the talk of the racing world. But then in November
came a crushing revelation: the powerful Jockey Club accused Silent
Tom Smith of doping. Arden was shocked. "This is a terrible thing to
have happen just at a time when we were so proud of our victories," she
said. "My horses don't need stimulants to win races." Smith's record,
she emphasized, "has been spotless and I made sure that he was not a
betting man before I employed him," and, she added for good measure,
"I do not bet." Arden stood by her trainer, earning high marks in the
racing world for her loyalty.[26]

Arden's repeated appearances in the winner's circle may have prompted
officials to scrutinize Smith's training methods. People grew suspicious.
How could a woman—a woman in trade, not one who was born to the
thoroughbred world or who was spending her husband's money like other
female owners—win so consistently? Surely this was impossible without some sort of wile.

The Jockey Club, created in 1894 by eight East Coast social elites,
launched the investigation. Its mission was to police thoroughbred breeding and racing. Even today, the Jockey Club keeps the official *American Stud Book* listing all the thoroughbreds born in the United States
and Canada, guaranteeing the lineage of racehorses. Through the years,
the men of the Jockey Club—and they were all men until the 1980s—
enlarged their mission to oversee labor relations, animal welfare, and
abuses that might taint racing's good name.[27]

As Arden's earnings mounted, Jockey Club stewards, with the aid of

Belmont authorities, began keeping an ever-closer eye on her stable until they finally undertook what thoroughbred race expert Milton C. Toby called "a clandestine investigation of Smith and the Maine Chance operation." After a "stakeout," they found three instances of an atomizer being used on Arden's horses.[28] Atomizers, of course, chiefly dispensed perfume. Arden herself had invented and patented new atomizers. The charge that stuck occurred just before the bell at Jamaica Race Course in Queens, New York, on November 1, 1945, when one of Smith's assistants sprayed Magnific Duel with a 2.6 percent solution of ephedrine. Challenged four days later, Smith was stunned. He customarily sprayed horses with stuffy or runny noses with a mixture of vinegar and salt water to make them sneeze to clear their noses and breathe better. Occasionally he sprayed ephedrine on a horse with a bleeding nose—but never before a race.[29] It didn't matter. The Jockey Club stewards unanimously revoked Smith's license and retracted Arden's winnings from Magnific Duel's race. Owner and trainer instantly appealed.

On November 8, Smith stood before the Jockey Club and a Joint Board of Commissioners from the New York State Racing Authority. Elizabeth Arden made sure that the best team of New York City attorneys she could hire was there to defend him. She also employed doctors, pharmacists, and chemists at three different universities to conduct tests on the effects of ephedrine on horses. The hearing began poorly for the Jockey Club. Their inspectors failed to question Smith as to the atomizer's contents on October 20, found no ephedrine in a sample they had taken after searching the barn on October 25—nor any drug in any Maine Chance horse ever—and weren't sure which horses they said they saw him spraying on November 1.[30]

The defense lawyers called on Dr. Harry Gold, whose credentials provide an indication of the seriousness with which Arden took the case. After all, she had spent her career guaranteeing the purity of her cosmetics to customers worldwide. A suggestion of cheating or impropriety at Maine Chance Farm might easily affix itself to Maine Chance Spa and her toiletries. *The Blood-Horse* described Gold as "one of New York's outstanding pharmacologists and cardiologists . . . an associate professor of pharmacology at the Cornell University Medical School, and . . . a consultant to half a dozen New York hospitals, . . . to the council on pharmacology of the American Medical Association and consultant to the government's Office of Scientific Research and Development." Upon learning that the trainer sprayed four times in each nostril of the horse, Gold experimented with the atomizer and found that "the amount which entered [Magnific Duel's] system would be 0.003 milligrams." This tiny amount would have no effect on a horse. "I doubt," Gold sniggered, "if it would even have any effect on a flea." In a further experiment, he injected "into the horse's muscles . . . more than 100 times as much [ephedrine] as could be administered by eight squirts of the bulb." Dr. Gold's conclusion was that Magnific Duel "was not at all affected" by the spraying.[31]

Dr. David Buckingham, veterinarian to U.S. presidents, concurred with Gold and stated that even twice as much ephedrine would be useless for making a horse run faster. "You might just as well pour water on his tail," the vet scoffed. The Jockey Club's own experts had to admit that delivering any sort of medicine by the nose was "the least effective" way to do it.[32]

When Tom Smith took the stand, he explained that he had never directed his assistants to use any nasal spray—neither the ephedrine nor the vinegar-and-saltwater mixture. He swore that he never gave a horse any sort of drug to make it go faster. He had consulted a vet about the use of vinegar and salt water, and he carefully explained that he first used the ephedrine on himself when a pharmacist suggested it as a nasal spray after Smith had broken his nose in the spring of 1945. This was not unusual. Ephedrine did not require a prescription. Even Elizabeth Arden attested to being a longtime user of that remedy.[33] Smith told the panel that the druggist "assured [him] that there were no narcotics or stimulants in it," and with that expert warrant he tried it on the thoroughbreds, but never before a race.[34] If the assistant had sprayed Magnific Duel with ephedrine, he had done so without Smith's knowledge or direction. The assistant had taken it upon himself, but had also confused the atomizers—using the one with ephedrine instead of the vinegar and salt water. Smith, sixty-seven years old at the time, impatiently growled that if he was going to dope a horse—and never in his long career had he ever been accused of that—he sure wouldn't drug Magnific Duel because that horse was already expected to win.

"I hope the board will give Mr. Smith a complete vindication," Arden vice president Charles Mooney told the press. "Mrs. Graham has sincerely tried to keep her racing on a very high plane and has spared no expense." Mrs. Graham (i.e., Elizabeth Arden) did not attend the hearing—Leslie Combs went in her place—and no one asked for her testimony.[35]

On February 15, 1946, the judgment came down. The earlier decision stood: Smith lost his trainer's license for a year. The racing world responded that the punishment was too harsh. No one could prove Smith had doped any horse. True, the law stated that the trainer was responsible for the actions of his assistants, but no one could prove that the assistant's administering a few squirts of ephedrine had been anything but an honest mix-up of atomizers. At the very highest point thus far of Arden's racing success, she lost her best trainer to what seemed like unjustified charges leveled during a witch hunt caused by her unusual achievements as an independent businesswoman.

And it was supposed to be her year at the Kentucky Derby. Maine Chance had "the winningest ways in U.S. turfdom" then, according to *Time* magazine. Rumors flew that Arden would enter an astonishing four horses, which she could do because she had such stable depth. The winner—surely one of hers—would earn the largest Kentucky Derby purse to that point: $100,000. But how was she to do that without her best, most sympathetic trainer?[36] Unable to look back, Arden moved ahead. She hired Roy Waldron, who promptly won the Pimlico

Futurity with Jet Pilot. Nevertheless, his methods were incompatible
with her philosophy, so she turned instead to Tom Smith's son James in
hopes he would also prove a successful horse whisperer. She knew—
everyone knew—that Silent Tom would still be omnipresent, as indeed
he was. Jimmy made a promising start. Knockdown took first and Star
Pilot took second in the Santa Anita Derby—a $94,680 good-day-at-the-
track purse for his new boss. Jimmy then confidently readied Lord Boswell, Perfect Bahram, and Knockdown for America's celebrated Run for
the Roses.[37]

Suddenly, two days before the Kentucky Derby, a tragedy of epic
proportions occurred. A fire began early Thursday morning, May 2,
at Arden's rented stables at Arlington Park racetrack in Illinois. In the
initial reports, the fire was discovered when groom William Bayton
smelled smoke. He raised a cry, threw a bucket of water on the flames,
and tried to rouse the other grooms and trainers from their sleep. Amid
the ghastly squealing and trumpeting of terrified horses, they managed
to rescue twelve but could not stop five others from rushing back into
the burning stable. Nor could they save the rest. Night watchman Gilbert Jones told reporters that he saw flames and ran in to rescue his
"favorite," Beaugay. Beaugay was one of only seven horses saved from
what was "the costliest fire in turf history," and she was one of Arden's
favorites, too.[38]

Twenty-three thoroughbreds valued at an unimaginable $500,000
died. Investigations began immediately. The state fire marshal, the
Cook County Highway Police, and Illinois Racing Commission (IRC)
members picked their way gingerly through "the smoldering ruins of
the razed barn [and] the scorched carcasses of many of the best 2-year-
olds money could buy."[39] The IRC's Ednyfed Williams, a prominent
attorney who had chaired the commission since June 1941, immediately
ruled out both arson and faulty wiring. His initial conclusion was "spon-
taneous combustion . . . or 'carelessness,'" which he laid squarely in
the laps of the African American grooms.[40] Two of them, Williams

insinuated, should have been on duty, but neither was there. John D. Jackson, general manager of the Arlington Park Jockey Club, speedily agreed with Williams.

Although this disaster came, "on the eve," as *The Boston Globe* put it, "of [Arden's] bid for almost certain glory in Saturday's Kentucky Derby," she persevered.[41] She finalized the decision to enter three horses in the race and chose three exceptional jockeys: Eddie Arcaro, Bobby Permane, and Ted Atkinson. Turf writers were kind to her.[42] Noting that she was grief-stricken, "shocked," and "obviously upset," they left her alone.[43] The IRC expressed its condolences, calling her "a fine sportswoman" and "a great credit to American racing."[44] She told *The Blood-Horse* that the fire would not deter her.[45] Accordingly, she followed her Derby contenders south to Louisville but sent her own investigator to Arlington.

Five days after the fire, the police announced they had a confession. African American watchman Gilbert Jones admitted to leaving an electric heater running in Tack Room 38 while he and groom Joe Carter drank themselves into whiskey-enhanced oblivion. "I was asleep about three and one-half hours and was awakened by the screaming and kicking of the horses and the smell of smoke," Jones admitted. "Before I went to sleep I believe I was 'intoxicated' . . . and when I awoke I was in a dazed condition. After opening the tack room door I then ran to the other side of the stable and started to open the stall doors to let the horses out. The fire seemed to start burning the entire stable at the same time and there was nothing more I could do."[46] Carter and groom William Bayton verified Jones's version of that horrible night. Even though he claimed he had helped lead six horses to safety after the smoke woke him, the Cook County Highway Police said Jones would be charged with "criminal negligence."[47] The IRC was satisfied with Jones's "drinking orgy" confession and closed the case on May 7.[48] Arden was not so sure. Having seen her trainer suspended for no good reason and now experiencing a second devastating fire, she wondered whether the racing establishment was trying to damage her chance of winning the Derby. The businesswoman trusted those she hired to work closely with her horses. Loyal to her employees and suspicious of the police findings, a sliver of doubt entered in.

This prompted her to hire noted detective Sheridan Bruseaux, owner of the Keystone National Detective Agency in Chicago (later special prosecutor for the state's attorney of Cook County and member of the Chicago Crime Commission).[49] Did Arden hire Bruseaux because of his social prominence and his fame as a gumshoe or because she thought an African American investigator might secure an uncensored story from three Black laborers? Either way, it took Bruseaux only two days to report that Jones had given his statement "under duress." Jones then publicly recanted. Thanks to Bruseaux, the charges were reduced to "disorderly conduct" for Jones and drunkenness for Carter.[50]

The Chicago police and the IRC found no definitive cause for the fire. They discounted faulty wiring, electrical trouble, and arson. The racetrack was cleared of wrongdoing. Journalists took to calling it a "flash fire," with no attributing cause.[51] It was not the first time Detective Bruseaux had discovered police "negligence." This, too, Arden must have known.[52]

The only thing remotely positive in this heartbreaking tragedy was that her horses were fully insured.[53] Arden, a shrewd businesswoman and not a gambler, operated unlike most other stable owners of her size who bet that they would never lose more than one horse per year.[54] The magnitude of her loss, however, caused racetrack owners across the nation to upgrade their facilities. Wooden barns were rebuilt of fire-resistant brick. Electrical systems were modernized. Fire hydrants and hoses were installed closer to the stables.[55]

THE 1946 KENTUCKY DERBY brought no cheering news. The strongly favored Knockdown took fifth, and Perfect Bahram eked out a disappointing ninth. Lord Boswell finished fourth, not much better than the fifth spot he ran in the Belmont Stakes at the end of the month. Arden made the cover of *Time* magazine, which was important and gratifying, but cold comfort compared with the Derby loss. Hedda Hopper saw that Arden was "in a bit of a daze, understandably so."[56] But she did not give up, as some predicted she would. Numb as she was, Arden forced herself to bid on the next crop of potential winners at the Keeneland and Saratoga sales, and kept an eye on the horses that might make good on the promises of 1946—especially Jet Pilot. He already had a bit of luck attached to him. Jet Pilot was the smallish red thoroughbred who had escaped the fire when Arden sent him to Kentucky to train along-side her three Derby hopefuls. He ran and won the first race at Churchill Downs. Watching Jet Pilot fly by the post, Arden and Combs glanced at each other. "He is the 1947 Derby winner," they told sports reporter Grantland Rice. "He can't miss. Don't forget him."[57]

Louisville on Derby Day 1947 dawned chilly and cloudy, but the weather cleared for the afternoon's main race. The Kentucky Derby was a national event and celebrities from politics, sports, and entertain-ment appeared dressed in their Derby best. Parties had been going on for days. Luminaries consumed mint juleps and honey-bourbon glazed hams before gathering to watch "the fastest two minutes in sports." Arden and Tom Smith—now reinstated and rehired—had decided to train Jet Pilot "very lightly." They concluded that he was "fit" and ready, even for the muddy track. They underlined to the skilled jockey Arden selected, twenty-three-year-old Eric Guerin, that he must not use the whip—Arden never allowed the whip—but instead to "nurse him."[58]

The advice Arden always gave every one of her jockeys was to "get out in front and go, go, go!" That is exactly what Guerin did. Jet Pilot was first out of the gate and he never fell behind. "I could tell when he passed the stands the first time," Smith enthused, "that he was going to win the race." Arden was sure, too. "Last year I nearly died during the race," she exclaimed, but this time, "I just wasn't the least bit ner-vous."[59] The depth of her exultation is clear from one of the post-race photographs of her next to Jet Pilot, bedecked in his blanket of roses. Trim, and looking every inch the owner in a dark suit, high heels, and a brimless hat, Arden appears to be letting out a whistle of relief. Next to her Silent Tom Smith is fixated on Jet Pilot, while Guerin's grin is as big as the bouquet of roses he's holding.[60] In the winner's circle, the normally unflappable Arden "tugged at her jacket to straighten it" and "was almost too excited to talk." Luckily, for this greatest of victories, she had only to smile, accept the famous gold trophy, and pocket the prize money.[61]

Twenty-One

"Beauty Is Power"

lizabeth Arden was always her own best advertisement. Still slender and fit in her mid-sixties, her peaches-and-cream skin and stylish clothing made her look years younger. "If lines there are in the Arden face, you have to look to find them," fashion journalist Peggy Preston marveled. "And her waistline is as trim as a young athlete's." Endlessly ebullient, "little Miss Arden hardly looks the part of a woman who has headed a famous business concern for more than 30 years." The habit of leadership made her "a human dynamo," according to reporter Genina Gavin. "Dainty . . . with gray blue eyes and ash blonde hair. She is so tiny, and so completely feminine, that it is hard to imagine her as one of the most famous business women in the world today."[1]

And yet she was. Her personal worth was rumored to be in the $20 million range. She lavished money on Maine Chance Farm thoroughbreds but also invested continually in her business. Global expansion, movement into new technologies, and product development kept her busy. Arden remained at or near the top in the Fairchild Retail Advertising Index tabulating the amount of money stores spent to promote toiletries, a sign of strong consumer demand.[2] She reportedly declined another multimillion-dollar takeover offer in 1947.[3] She would never sell. Her rule in life was "work and keep happy."[4] "There's so much to be done," she said, with a contented smile. "I do not have a minute to myself."[5]

With every year her power increased. Both *Coronet* magazine and the Federation of Jewish Women's Organizations chose her as a Woman of Achievement. New York governor Thomas Dewey gave a civic award to fifty-seven people, all of whom were listed in *The New York Times*. The only one not requiring an identifier was Elizabeth Arden. From Windsor Palace to Wichita, women wanted her opinion on health and beauty. Business leaders sought her secrets and copied her successes. Philanthropists begged for her patronage. Arden's cultural influence was broad. She was called "prophetic in her exquisite taste." When she, the "high priestess of the cosmetics industry," decreed that "we've had enough of those darkened, artificial complexions" and it was time to emphasize pink and pretty, the entire fashion world followed.[6]

She could be charming, warm, and generous. The *Washington Post* columnist Mary Van Rensselaer Thayer lost her journalistic objectivity entirely upon meeting Arden at the Women's National Press Club Jamboree for Prominent Women. Arden welcomed Thayer to her Mayflower Hotel room early one morning, where she had already exercised, breakfasted on hot water with lemon, and "polished off more business than you or I do in a year," Thayer marveled. She complied rapturously when Arden offered to demonstrate her newest toiletries on Thayer—including a sneak preview of a product as yet unreleased.

Pulling from an overflowing closet, Arden punctuated her life story with a personal fashion show of extraordinary clothing, some of her own design. This last stunned Thayer, who was "almost too distracted to gather that when dressmakers began going into the cosmetics business, Miss A. reversed the process, plunging into dressmaking herself." Fashion designer Coco Chanel was the famous "dressmaker" who entered Arden's field with Chanel No. 5 perfume, which had already been a top seller for more than two decades. Arden told Thayer that she moved into fashion because she adored her color harmony idea, but to coordinate her makeup with clothing perfectly, she had to do it herself.

As she modeled one outfit after another for her enchanted guest, Arden's running commentary accelerated. "To feel right, you've got to look right." Women "should relax more, pay more attention to food, less to drink." Stretch, take vitamins, substitute water for fruit juice. "The most unhealthy women . . . are chain smokers." Do the new Arden waist exercises—they really work! Thayer, agog, kept scribbling. Arden was "a dynamo of energy, often physically sustained . . . by her belief that life is a continual challenge to be met and overcome." Then, ready to go—early—Arden blew past the star-struck journalist with "Remember, never be a tortoise!"[7] Hours later, during the jamboree, someone fainted. "Suddenly," Thayer recorded, "a small woman pushed through the agitated crowd, said firmly, 'I'm Elizabeth Arden. I know exactly what to do.'" Fingers long practiced in the art of massage capably brought the woman around.[8] Thayer was not at all surprised.

FROM HER SOCIAL and financial vantage point, Arden remembered Bessie Marbury's advice from long ago: "Give generously to charities, but not so lavishly as to become conspicuous."[9] By this point, giving was second nature, but Arden's fame made remaining inconspicuous difficult. Her charities ranged widely—from religious-based entities such as the National Council of Jewish Women and Manhattan's St. James' Episcopal Church to veterans' organizations.[10] Frequently she served as a society's patron, donating her time, money, or name. Her decades-long habits of providing auction items and making outright financial gifts continued unabated.

Because good health was fundamental to her understanding of beauty, supporting health-care agencies, including the Red Cross, the March of Dimes, the American Heart Association, Denver's National Jewish

Hospital, and St. Barnabas Hospital in the Bronx, was central. She donated to the battles against multiple sclerosis, muscular dystrophy, and cancer. She contributed time and money to Chicago's St. Luke's Benefit Fashion Show for more than thirty years, and supported children's health-care initiatives, including a proposed plastic surgery unit for what would later become Children's Hospital Boston.

One of her most important commitments was to the Cradle Society, an adoption home in Chicago often used by celebrity couples, such as Dolores and Bob Hope. From 1949 until her death, Arden sponsored the Cradle's main fundraiser, a fashion show eventually named after her and attended by thousands of people. Year after year, Elizabeth Arden poured out her time, ideas, money, and energy on behalf of the charity.

Classical music was another beneficiary of Arden's generosity. She underwrote symphonies, operas, music scholarships, and musicians' pension funds for years, sponsoring, among others, the New York Philharmonic, the National Symphony Orchestra in Washington, D.C., the San Francisco Opera, the Tulsa Philharmonic, and the New England Opera Theater.[11] For two decades, Arden supported the Musicians Emergency Fund, which subsidized the Hospitalized Veterans Service's transatlantic Music in Hospitals program that originally sent classical musicians to New York City's hospitals to give military veterans music lessons. It eventually grew to provide "recreational music and therapy" in twenty-seven different hospitals by 1955.[12]

Education was a third major charitable area, particularly women's colleges, whose alumnae were a source of employees and customers. She gave to Wellesley, Finch, Barnard, and Mount Holyoke, among others.[13] To Smith College in Northampton, Massachusetts, Arden contributed $20,000 in 1947—approximately $275,000 in today's money—to create an annual scholarship for a senior with "good scholastic standing, a position of leadership, a high standard of health and an attractive personality and appearance." In these and other ways, Arden became "one of society's pre-eminent Lady Bountifuls."[14]

Public generosity added to the luster of her brand, which was already a cultural shorthand for empyrean luxury. *The New York Times* labeled Lou Stillman, owner of a gym where the greatest boxers trained, "the Elizabeth Arden of the jab and jolt set."[15] Art critic Charles Poore referred to restoration work done on damaged canvases as "one of those Elizabeth Arden beauty treatments."[16] At the 1950 Soviet-led World Peace Congress organization meeting in Warsaw, the East German representative called the Soviet Union the "Elizabeth Arden of the World" because the USSR hoped to use atomic power to "transform the face of deserts." Reporters rushed to see what Arden had to say about this. She was diplomatic: "If my name is linked with changing faces, let me say that faith in Beauty itself is the first requisite. Beauty cannot belong alone to either East or West—it is universal. . . . It does not need an Iron Curtain nor has it use for masks of any kind since its very existence depends upon friendship, sincerity and truth!"[17]

Entertainer Billy Rose called his habitual lateness "all Elizabeth Arden's fault" because of his wife's insistence on a time-consuming ritual involving "oils, unguents, creams, lotions, pigments, perfumes, pads and brushes."[18] Rose was joking but British mystic Aleister Crowley placed the entire burden of women's vanity at Arden's Red Doorstep in his poem entitled "The Jungle of Elizabeth Arden."[19] Ilka Chase, daughter of Edna Woolman Chase, found Arden "a lady of stamina and achievement . . . who hides her brains behind a bland baby face," a woman who "built an industry independent of masculine aid and has held it against the encroachments of banks and syndicates who wished to help lap up the gravy." Arden mystified Chase: "To meet her is to wonder whether she knows about coming in out of the rain . . . and while you are thinking it, she is whipping up another million dollars."[20]

Stories developed about Arden, some more believable than others, but all attesting how, in her sixties, she was comfortable in command. Sitting beside First Lady Bess Truman at a table of cabinet wives during a Washington fashion show, the beauty expert frowned darkly at the cream soup. According to the reporter, "As gay, plump Mrs. Fred Vinson started to dive in, she heard the icy voice of authority. 'Fattening and also constipating,' said Miss Arden as she pushed her plate away. Mrs. Vinson sighed but obediently followed suit. The entree was creamed chicken. Even more majestically Miss Arden pronounced the death sentence and the ladies meekly nibbled at it." Dessert was, of course, ice cream. "Mrs. Vinson by that time was hungry and defiant. She ate it." The punchline? "Miss Arden was true to her waistline. She spurned it."[21]

Still, as she possessed the magic trio of money, fame, and power, no one who wanted an event to be successful failed to invite Arden. She spoke on the *Betty Crocker* radio show.[22] She attended the American Fashions competition as a guest of *Chicago Tribune* owner Robert McCormick. There she encountered the talented twenty-six-year-old winner of four design prizes, William R. Blass of Fort Wayne, Indiana—soon to rocket to success as Bill Blass.[23] At Mayor William O'Dwyer's request, she joined his planning meeting for New York City's Golden Jubilee.[24] She was frequently a guest of honor at benefits large and small, such as for New York's School Settlement Association and the Boys' Athletic League.[25] From banquets to balls to industry-sponsored trips, Arden attended an increasing number of events, many of which introduced her to rising fashion stars like Pauline Trigère and Vera Maxwell.[26]

A heartening laurel came Arden's way when Syracuse University awarded her an honorary degree. The chancellor called Arden a "pioneer in [her] field, woman of sophistication and culture, administrator, sportswoman and business leader whose example is an inspiration to all ambitious young women."[27] Her fellow awardees included composer Virgil Thomson, diplomat Dr. Ralph Bunche, and a former Canadian prime minister. Arden later repaid Syracuse University with a fashion show to benefit their development fund. Afterward, the Syracuse Kappas, warmly remembering her help during World War II, threw a party for her.[28]

The woman who should have been celebrating with her, Florence Delaney, her dearest and longest employee, died in 1949. Delaney had labored side by side with Arden since the very beginning, as book-keeper, accountant, director, and manager of the flagship Manhattan salon. From their earliest days together Delaney had taken devoted care of Elizabeth and fussed over her welfare. Arden reminisced to a friend: "When we first started . . . I hired a charming little girl to do my books for me. . . . She didn't know much about it, but she was so willing, so kind—we all loved her. And then as we began to grow, I hired a regular accountant, and after the first day on the job, he came to me and said I would have to fire our little girl—she wasn't efficient enough! Of course, I fired HIM—on the spot!" Laney was, Arden acknowledged, "mainly responsible for the success of our 5th [Avenue] salon." Arden closed the salon on the day of Delaney's funeral as a mark of respect.[29]

Staying busy helped her manage her grief. Arden had become a sought-after lecturer with a strong and positive message. She was good at it. She especially enjoyed speaking to audiences of women, like the Mu Phi Epsilon music sorority and the Business and Professional Women's Club. "Health and beauty are the main ingredients of happiness," she said, and every woman had it in her power to change her future. Arden had long preached the idea that beautiful women were likely to go fur-ther in their careers because looking and feeling good contributed to vitality and a self-assuredness that motivated one to try new things and to succeed.[30]

Republican Party leaders took advantage of her influence. New York governor Thomas Dewey appointed her to the state-level Women's Council, which was charged with proposing solutions to problems women confronted in education and the professions. Arden sat on the thirty-four-member Advisory Council where, for several years, she helped promote fashion, design, cosmetics, and health careers. Arden authored a booklet titled *Why Do You Look So Nice?* to provide profes-sional grooming tips for women entering or reentering the workforce.[31]

An updated, retitled version received a strong recommendation from the beauty columnist of the historically Black *Pittsburgh Courier*.[32] Women's Council members offered one-on-one mentoring advice to and headed clinics for women seeking employment. The object was for New York's businesswomen to share their experiences and give a hand up to other women.[33]

As the 1948 Republican Party convention neared, Arden rented an apartment in Philadelphia to be close to the action when Dewey won the presidential nomination.[34] Alas for Republicans, they failed to consult the woman who knew the most about television makeup before they put on the first (partly) televised convention. Clare Boothe Luce, *The Washington Post* reported, "wore the wrong kind of outfit and warpaint and showed up on the screens looking like a stand-in for the ghostly Leonora Corbett in 'Blythe Spirit.'" Luce looked pale on-screen because she chose to play to the live audience, forgoing the dark purple lipstick that showed best on television. Meanwhile, Dewey's five-o'clock shadow made him look thuggish. Arden could have helped them both.[35]

The GOP platform called for shrinking federal regulatory agencies. Arden was entirely in favor of this. She deeply resented federal regulators. The 1936 Robinson-Patman Act had outlawed differential pricing, and the FTC recently issued a cease and desist order to ban certain types of discrimination at the point of sale, claiming that these practices gave large stores, some 10 percent of Arden's customers, an unfair competitive advantage and dented the sales of smaller outlets by denying them market share.[36] More punitively, the government redoubled earlier charges from 1936 that Arden used her demonstrators selectively (only at large retail outlets) and deceptively. She trained and paid the demonstrators, but the FTC alleged that the average customer believed they were store employees recommending freely from all cosmetics brands rather than Arden reps pushing Arden products. She maintained firmly that the job of her demonstrators was educational. Her counter clerks always rang up the sales.[37]

At the time, Arden products were sold in 25 specialty shops, 725 department stores, and 2,250 fine drugstores across the country.[38] Sending demonstrators to all of them would have been prohibitively expensive and ultimately unprofitable. Demonstrators traveled primarily to big, urban department stores with high-volume sales. Their arrival was well heralded, and customers came in droves to learn how to apply and harmonize products. Successful demonstrators supercharged fashion, illustrated the need to discard old styles and adopt new ones, and schooled women in the Arden look. She was not alone in employing demonstrators, but Arden's company was the first, although definitely not the last, to run up against this aspect of Robinson-Patman.[39]

Six other major firms faced a similar charge. The cosmetics industry as a whole and the Toilet Goods Association rallied around Arden, pointing out that demonstrators helped both wholesalers and retailers, and demanding that "the right of private enterprise to employ and distribute sales help at its discretion should not be destroyed."[40] *Women's Wear Daily*'s national survey found far greater resistance to the idea of offering incentives and commissions to salespeople than to the use of demonstrators.[41]

Arden requested a judicial review of the FTC decree, and then petitioned the U.S. Supreme Court.[42] The court refused to hear the appeal. Arden had to comply, either by ending the use of demonstrators or supplying them to all retail outlets.[43] Meanwhile, as the other six cases resumed, Coty president Philip Cortney proved a particularly outspoken opponent of the FTC interpretation of Robinson-Patman.[44] Bringing his company's demonstrators before the commissioners to show what they actually did, he accused the FTC of "digging up scarecrows" in their rush to "distort" the language of the act. Claiming that Coty did not use demonstrators in the way Arden did, he asserted that the act nevertheless "undermine[s] competition, incentive and the spirit of enterprise which are the backbone of democracy."[45]

The onslaught caused the FTC to drop its complaint against all seven cosmetics firms.[46] The Toilet Goods Association publicized comments from satisfied retailers. "We are supplied with excellent demonstrators, live promotion stunts, cooperative advertising offers, booklets, samples, and everything we can possibly need," one affirmed.[47]

Some stores did, however, end the practice. Neiman-Marcus switched to its own salespeople, training them to sell all products in the toilet goods department, reflecting storewide practices.[48] Others, in contrast, clearly preferred having any kind of on-site experts. Their benefits were obvious. One male makeup artist Arden brought over briefly from her Paris salon "more than doubled" the week's sales at Carson Pirie Scott and Lord & Taylor. The Dallas cosmetics department head said fervently: "We wish we could keep him for a month!"[49]

To assist with the legal headaches and her company's continuing growth, Arden tapped dapper American Carl Gardiner in 1948. It turned out to be another excellent hire. Gardiner brought two decades of experience from La Cross–Schnefel Bros., makers of implements for fingernail and toenail care. "Mr. Gardiner is a treasure," Arden wrote, and he served thereafter as her trusted and loyal executive vice president.[50]

Flying in the face of the FTC, Arden launched another hugely successful endeavor involving a variation on demonstrators. She took her salon makeup classes to department stores, reaching hundreds of students at a time. In September 1949, for example, twelve Elizabeth Arden demonstrators provided complimentary "Elizabeth Arden Beauty Classes at Woodward & Lothrop," in Washington, D.C.[51] The personal touch continued, it seemed, on the Federal Trade Commission's own doorstep. For three decades, Arden had provided makeup as a complement to fashion shows featuring other designers' works. Once her Fashion Floor launched, she paired her cosmetics with her own clothing line. But as the popularity of fashion shows began to wane, Arden transformed her beauty classes to focus entirely on Arden skin care products, cosmetics, health routines, and hairstyles. They offered tremendous sales potential.

Partnering with Brooklyn's Abraham & Straus store, Arden mounted what the press release termed "the most fabulous beauty class in history!" For the grand launch, she brought together not "demonstrators" but rather some of her most impressive experts. Medea Ball was vice president of Arden's South American division. Eileen Scott-Williams had managed Arden salons around the world. Like Teddy Haslam and Wellington Cross, who were also present, Ball and Scott-Williams were decades-long employees. From her Fifth Avenue salon came makeup director Peter J. Vest, as well as the head of the dance and exercise department, Morena. Five thousand women signed up in only one week in June!

The free, two-hour class taught earnest clients the Arden look basics. Wearing plastic capes, seated on both sides of long tables, and peering into individual mirrors, the women had in front of them all the products necessary to try every technique. Scott-Williams gave lessons in Firmo-Lift patting and tapping. Ball demonstrated makeup color harmony and corrective skin care treatments. Vest shared makeup application secrets. The store provided space for women to practice posture and firming exercises under the guidance of Antoinette and Morena (both women were mononymous). The class was offered twice a day for a week, with a special one-hour, evening "business girls' section." It was, *WWD* attested, the first time such a thing had ever been done in a store.[52]

Elizabeth Arden was present to oversee and lend a hand. She invited journalists to hear the backstory over lunch with the Abraham & Straus and Arden teams. It had been a sensational week, "worthy of every effort put into it" and "a definite asset to the store." The pupils loved the one-on-one beauty consultations available after class.[53] The event so increased Arden sales, publicity, and goodwill that she next sent her staff to Woodward & Lothrop, where more than three hundred women enrolled.[54] In Dallas, five hundred enthusiastic attendees appeared; another two hundred had to be turned away.[55] Medea Ball returned to

South America in 1950 to begin similar courses in the Buenos Aires Harrods.[56] These department store classes grew in importance and spread across the nation, sometimes aimed at teens, sometimes at workingwomen, mostly geared to a general audience. They were hands-on and fun, a short-term investment for the women but long enough for Arden to teach the rudiments of her system, and they concluded with individual consultations and free products that clients adored. Over time, Arden beauty classes replaced the fashion show as a female space, simultaneously public and intimate, and they continued to be highly subscribed for a quarter century.

With and without demonstrators, from Boston to Boise, Arden cosmetics, lotions, and perfumes sold well. New stores provided counter space, and special retail promotions, such as "Beauty Fair Week," kept Arden's line front and center.[57] Her latest inventions included an electric version of her long-selling face patter and the Eye-Stopper pencil with a built-in sharpener to keep a pointed tip on the eyeliner. It came in black, brown, dark brown, and blue, and could be used for eyebrows as well.[58] Another new product was a pink "Top to Toe" box of items for face, fingers, legs, and feet.[59] She modernized and rereleased her weight loss and toning record albums.[60] Since 1917 she had been advertising her ability to help young women with blackheads, and in 1949 she offered ameliorative salon treatments, either one session or a series.[61] This focus on youth continued from the early part of the 1940s when she doubled down on sales to younger women and maintained "rhythmic exercise and grace" classes for children.[62] The "Teen Age Class," begun in 1944, was still being given at department stores and in salons well into the postwar years.[63]

The salons she loved continued to thrive with updating and expansion. In 1949, for instance, San Francisco required a larger, more modern space near Nob Hill, so she called on her old friend Nicolai Remisoff to design both the interior and exterior.[64] He created a spectacular garden entry to the retail space, but the real draw was the glamorous second-story swimming pool for resistance exercises. It was the first time a salon boasted this facility. The third floor featured pastel treatment rooms plus a mirrored staging area to show Castillo's line to perfection. Above that was the hair salon and a popular flower-bedecked rooftop lunchroom.

Success also crowned her Fashion Floor. Soon women such as Pamela Churchill and a young Jacqueline Bouvier (about to become Mrs. John F. Kennedy) appeared in the pages of magazines wearing Castillo from Arden.[65] Made-to-order clothing entailed exceptional fabric, design, and the satisfaction of knowing that one's frock was nearly unique. "Nearly" because made-to-order gowns were produced for up to three dozen women.[66] Such costumes necessitated fittings and close work with the designer and the dressmakers. Made-to-order clothing, as opposed to ready-to-wear or off-the-rack, was, as *Vogue* put it, for "women who vote straight tickets in non-banal taste; whose lives, from their collections of bone china through their grocery lists, reflect a taste for the rare and special." This was what Castillo provided at Arden's Fashion Floor: "fashionable, but timeless, not controlled by any trends."[67]

It was big news, then, in 1949, when Arden and Castillo entered the wholesale ready-to-wear market. He created an entirely separate collection of thirty-five pieces to sell "on a franchise basis."[68] They were late to this game, as women could already purchase off-the-rack Hattie Carnegie, Adrian, Mainbocher, and Henri Bendel ensembles at those designers' stand-alone stores, as well as an array of fine designers in Bergdorf Goodman, I. Magnin, or Jay Thorpe. The dresses sold for around $40, still well outside most women's budgets.[69] How women wore them was also beyond Castillo's sartorial dictates. "I have one ambition," he remarked with frustration, "to have a special label for my cocktail dresses. It will say, 'Designed by Castillo. Poison before 6 o'clock!'"[70]

For two decades, Arden had been selling items by an array of designers. At her Fashion Floor, she occasionally offered scarves by Jean

Hugo, bathing suits by Charles Nudelman, and dresses of her own creation and by some whose names did not always make the label, such as Mark Mooring.[71] Castillo also branched out on his own, not just creating for the ballet and theater but also designing housecoats fabricated by the Schildu company, which were marketed to "the average American woman's pocketbook."[72]

Virginia Pope thought Castillo's award-winning vision improved every year.[73] His fourth made-to-order collection was "sumptuous," his fabrics "magnificent." Pope loved his suits, coats, and daytime dresses, but she raved about his gowns: "The most glamorous, and we mean glamorous, was a gold taffeta with its immensely wide skirt cut in petal points that were lifted from the floor at the front and barely touched it at the back. A cloud of net swathed the bare shoulders" of the model. The whole collection left the usually hard-boiled and difficult-to-impress editor breathless.[74]

But the Arden-Castillo partnership was short-lived. The first rumor that Castillo was leaving appeared in June 1950.[75] As he conjured gorgeous high-society wedding gowns and dramatic Broadway costumes, Castillo decided that the autumn collection would be his last for the woman who had made his reputation.[76] He was off to Europe, under the eventual sponsorship of Lanvin—*la maison de couture*, not the woman, as Jeanne Lanvin had died in 1946.[77] In his wake, Arden cleared house, tossing all Castillo garments into an August sale.[78] If it was pique, it was fleeting. The two maintained a cordial working relationship into the next decade, with Arden serving as "commander-in-chief of the make-up for Castillo" and conducting his shows when he opened his own fashion house.[79]

Even without him, Arden's July 1951 Fashion Floor designs received overwhelmingly positive reviews. "Hers were the most beautiful clothes of the presentations," the *Chicago Tribune* reporter wrote of the New York Dress Institute's Couture group show. Arden's unnamed designers created suits of "flawless perfection." A "hauntingly beautiful white satin ball gown . . . might have stepped out of a portrait by [John Singer] Sargent." The entire collection was "superb." "No woman," the *Tribune* insisted, "should miss it."[80] With the salon already known far and wide as the place to go for designer clothing and bridal gowns, in 1951 Arden debuted a full ready-to-wear line of resort wear.[81] The reputation she built carried her. It was enough to know that the clothing had been purchased at Elizabeth Arden.

Whether made-to-order or ready-made, fashions of the early Cold War years required a "pipestem thin" figure and a wasp waist.[82] This silhouette had crystallized around Christian Dior's famous New Look in early 1947. The tailored World War II–era dresses made without extra fabric (because it was rationed or difficult to procure) gave way to Dior's exuberant full skirt below a tiny, cinched waist. Above was a jacket with a fitted bodice and a peplum. A wide, circular hat topped the outfit. A version of it, called "Bar," appeared on the front page of *WWD* a month after its Paris unveiling.[83] The dress was either enchanting (so feminine after the mannish war years) or awful (squeezing women back into corsets). Either way, designers both foreshadowed Dior—he gave credit to Charles James, and Castillo had already been showing tiny waists and full skirts—and quickly followed his lead.[84]

The New Look required svelte figures. By 1947, Gladys Graham de Maublanc was firmly back in charge of the Paris salon. She immediately introduced an exercise plan to shrink women's waistlines. She called it "the Guêpìere Treatment." A guêpìere (also known as a basque) is a corset that uses hooks and eyes in the front instead of lacing in the back. Ideally, the Guêpìere Treatment whittled the waist so that no minimizer was necessary, but in the meantime, as women dieted, exercised, and used Arden's prescribed electric treatments, staff taught them how to move and sit in the tight foundation garment. Parisian designer Jacques Heim promoted a strict diet he billed as easier for American women than wearing a basque, and he required his own models to follow it.

In the United States, Arden also advanced an updated diet plan. Her exercise director went on record: "Overweight is a psychological problem today." Weight loss should be thought of as "a medicine. It gives a moral uplift. You look better, feel ten times better when you're the correct weight, and of course, your clothes fit as they should." She emphasized that "nine-tenths of reducing is all in the mind." Once it was disciplined, the rest is "easy." Five minutes a day to stretch, and attention to the correct posture that Arden had always stressed made a real difference in both temperament and waist size. Arden's booklet *Diet Charts* laid out weekly menus according to three options: reducing, maintaining, and gaining.[85] Arden, de Maublanc, and Heim were out in front of an ever-larger number of fashion and health specialists finding ways for women to squeeze themselves into Dior's New Look.[86]

Overseas, Gladys—now widowed after Henri de Maublanc de Boisboucher's death in 1948—established a new factory and grew the six beauty salons to eight. She introduced on-site hairdressers to the Place Vendôme salon.[87] Elizabeth sent the head of her New York coiffure department to train the Paris stylists. Short hair was still in, as was the conceit that beauty culturalists everywhere must "understand the 'psychology' of a face."[88] This message made its way to Hong Kong via the opening of an Arden salon in the luxurious Lane Crawford department store there.[89]

Reports came in from around the globe. Arden was "one of the favorite American brands" in Mexico because her cosmetics were available in colors for a wide range of complexion shades. Arden toiletries were bestsellers in Baghdad. A traveler in Tibet attested to the "keen demand" for Arden goods found high up in Lhasa. In Brazil in 1948, Lester Gaba wrote that São Paulo's largest department store filled an entire shop window with a Blue Grass perfume display. Arden opened a salon in Zurich with hairstylists and "a school for home treatment and the first beauty school in Johannesburg since the war's end." Forty saleswomen traveled to the city from across South Africa to learn from an experienced Arden trainer.[90] Because the country imported 80 percent of its toiletries from the United States and England, there was deep concern at the time among cosmetic manufacturers that South Africa would cut imports by half.[91] That threat did not cause Arden to pull back, nor to scrimp on her salesforce training. In Australia, Arden general manager Philip Keen built networks across the nation.[92] With two dozen other firms, Keen participated in an enormous show, held in three different Australian cities, to promote American fashion. American culture spread purposefully around the globe in the Cold War years, as industrialists crowed that every U.S. design was a testament to the superiority of democratic values over communism.

Airline travel made global business easier. The British Overseas Airways Corporation (BOAC) was advertising "a thousand routes around the world" by 1949. Seeking to add greater luxury to its experience and induce more people to fly, BOAC joined with flight fanatic Elizabeth Arden. First, BOAC painted the bathroom on their "City of London" "flying boat" Arden Pink. Then they created a lavish toiletries kit.[93] It was a logical collaboration. Since 1939 she had been selling her own flight bags full of toiletries in lightweight, unbreakable bottles. By war's end, the entire cosmetics industry had experience with cardboard containers and had begun experimenting with the evolving plastics field as well. Arden soon made her two Speedbird Kits available for sale at select stores.[94] The Arden-BOAC partnership lasted until the 1960s and included Arden training for BOAC flight attendants.[95]

Putting her products and services before women able to take advantage of the wonders of international flight made good business sense, as the world was recovering slowly but surely from World War II. She had foreseen a greater interconnectedness and maintained close ties with her managers abroad while actively seeking new retail outlets as she had always done. Her next big ideas, though, were closer to home.

Twenty-Two

Maine Chance Phoenix

Arizona had been a haven after Arden's divorce. She never stopped thinking of it that way. The vibrant desert Southwest that aided her emotional recovery also returned her Phoenix friend Ada McCormick to physical health. So why not for her valued clients as well? The region's population and opportunities were expanding exponentially after World War II, abetted by modern air-conditioning since 1947. That's when Arden announced she had purchased "the most beautiful place . . . built right into the Camelback Mountains."[1] Against that stunning backdrop, on one hundred acres abloom with roses, jasmine, and bougainvillea, she opened her second Maine Chance Spa. Arden built "a golden cocoon, from which a butterfly emerges," a place women went "for peace, rest and the building of beauty reserves!"[2]

Maine Chance Phoenix replicated her New England success and earned a similarly gratifying *Vogue* review: "You are soothed, ministered unto, fed a prescribed diet, enveloped by everyone's interest in you." The food was "delectable," the "service a joy," the beds heavenly. Every room was "stamped, recognizably, with the hostess' taste." Modern art adorned the walls. Pink bottles crowded the dressing tabletops.

Fresh flowers scented every room. On the breakfast tray beside the grapefruit and black coffee perched a personalized schedule on a cute little red, white, and blue card. Hourly activities were chosen to meet specific needs: facials, massages, hairstylings, manicures, pedicures, and several sorts of passive and active exercise.

Most of all, there was the pool. It was the center of the western spa in the way the lake was the focal point in New England. "Beauty hydrotherapy," Arden's name for aquarobics, was a novel feature, and she would add pools and water exercises to future salons.[3] In Phoenix, nearly every treatment took place in spaces open to the warm desert air and near the gorgeous blue water. Women exercised in sight of it, eager to hop in after the last stretch. Poolside relaxation encouraged a deeper unwinding.

As in Maine, snacks were forbidden and low-calorie herbal mocktails substituted for alcoholic drinks. Vegetables from the on-site garden and fruits from her citrus grove starred in meals. Usually guests dressed for a formal dinner, but occasionally the master chef indulged them with steaks cooked over an open flame and served al fresco. Those who took advantage of Arden's chauffeured car might recount their visits to Superstition Mountain, the Apache Trail, or Frank Lloyd Wright's Taliesin West.[4] Friendships developed beside the pool, under the stars, and over the canasta table.

Old and new clients hurried to Phoenix to try it out. Hollywood celebrities found their way there easily. Snowbirds gladly escaped northern winters. Even Eleanor Roosevelt, who, despite having known Arden for two decades, never evinced a real interest in beauty or health, stopped by Maine Chance when work brought her to Arizona. In her "My Day" column she recorded: "Elizabeth Arden has bought one of the most beautifully landscaped places around here, with an expanse of lawn that takes your breath away in this desert region. . . . As we walked out past the house to the swimming pool, the air was sweet with the smell of orange blossoms."[5]

A Maine Chance sojourn was expensive, but *Vogue* pish-poshed the cost entirely. Lessons learned far outlasted the stay: "how to care for your complexion, and what lotions and potions make it bloom; a routine of exercises which you can run through daily to keep your figure flexible; a list of foods which are best for you, because of health, or weight—and menus which you can follow at home . . . ; an idea of how to keep your hair glowing, your scalp toned; and best of all, the benefits of relaxation." The magazine staff believed that a stay at Arden's even caused women to behave better: "The whole place and its atmosphere are so nerve-straightening that brittle manners, sharp voices, and endless conversational git-gat-gittle are left behind."[6] That surely was priceless. The actual cost was $400 per week, or $450 en suite, approximately $6,000 today.

Arden priced both spas similarly. Neither one ever made much—if any—profit. She ran them for the pure love of it and because she knew her health and beauty program was more effective when practiced for a full fortnight under her supervision. Economist Sylvia Porter spent the recommended two weeks in Phoenix totaling the costs and benefits. Every day, she mused, well over a dozen experts waited on her, styling her hair, providing massages, manicures, pedicures, facials, physical workouts, and "a half-dozen other luxurious health services," plus there were "superb meals prepared by a French chef." Each treatment or repast, if individually priced and tallied, would exceed by a vast sum what Arden charged for a week. It was glorious! Totally worth it! But Porter warned entrepreneurs against copying Arden's model: "Probably only a woman with an earned fortune in the bank plus romance in her soul would so persistently lose money on so grand a scale in pursuit of beauty for others."[7] For three decades Arden's luxury spas reigned unchallenged. Not until the 1960s, when California's La Costa opened and when Neiman-Marcus paired with Charles of the Ritz to create the Greenhouse spa in Texas, did Arden have significant competition.[8]

With the debut of Maine Chance Phoenix, Arden launched makeup colors cleverly named to keep Arizona uppermost in her clients' minds. Desert Sun, Sun Gold, Sun Drama, and Cactus Red complemented the yellow-hued fabrics on her Fashion Floor. Full-color magazine ads had a distinctly southwestern look.[9] Arden said she drew the palette to beautify her customers' faces straight from an inspiring Phoenix sunrise. When she had settled on "just the right color for my Desert Pink lipstick, a friend came from Paris with a new hat." She laughed happily at her divination: "It was exactly my Desert Pink." The appreciative interviewer also saw more evidence of Arden's "sixth sense for colors about to come into fashion."[10]

By far the most famous woman seeking relaxation at the Arizona Maine Chance was First Lady Mamie Eisenhower. She had been an Arden client for some time before she visited the Phoenix spa. Elizabeth and Mamie had known each other since the late 1940s when their social circles overlapped. Mamie patronized the Paris Red Door Salon and so also knew Gladys.[11] As a Republican, Arden publicly backed Dwight Eisenhower's attempt to secure the 1952 presidential nomination.[12] During the party's national convention in Chicago, Arden sent a handwritten note down the hall of the Drake Hotel to Mrs. Eisenhower, offering to put an Arden "hair dresser and face treatment girl at your convenience."[13] As the weather was stiflingly hot and the convention filmed live for television, it was a thoughtful gesture.[14]

Everyone who "liked Ike" congregated at Arden's convention parties. She became a leading Republican socializer, a counterpart to the Democrats' "hostess with the mostest," Perle Mesta. Arden's gatherings drew the powerful Alsop brothers (Joseph and Stewart were both influential journalists), Pulitzer Prize–winning reporter Anne O'Hare McCormick, and Clare Boothe Luce, then awaiting the results of a vice presidential draft that never materialized. Not attending, presumably, were Hedda Hopper and Alice Roosevelt Longworth, as they were on record for Robert Taft.[15] When the votes were tallied, Dwight D. Eisenhower won the Republican nomination, and across America, people watched from their own living rooms as he kicked off his presidential campaign.

Television was becoming increasingly influential. The Eisenhower-Nixon team made good use of it with political ads, helped in part by Arden's racecourse friend Jock Whitney, a GOP consultant.[16] Convinced from the beginning of television's potential, Arden had considered purchasing a TV studio. Perhaps she should have, because television grew steadily by every conceivable measure.[17] A Fashion Group luncheon speaker explained that in July 1948 there were 240,000 televisions in New York and 420,000 nationwide, 80 percent of which were in people's homes. Only 42 companies advertised on TV in 1947. One year later—the year Arden almost bought that studio—374 did. Her instinct to create her own filming space was on target.[18]

The beauty industry took longer to catch up. Not until 1950—when closer to four million homes had TV—did the New York Dress Institute start beaming five-minute fashion shows to stations across the country. They were black and white, and silent, necessitating a live announcer to read over the film.[19] That year, the Atlanta department store J. P. Allen broadcast a show about fashion that was surprisingly effective for sales—especially among men! Husbands phoned the store to order outfits they'd seen as a Christmas gift for their wives. Bosses sent their secretaries to Allen's to purchase dresses they liked for their spouses. And women appeared, cash in hand, to buy "whatever my husband saw on your television show last night."[20]

Color television was in its infancy, but everyone who depended on customers falling in love with particular shades and hues craved the technology. One big technical question was how to show programs produced in color on black-and-white TV sets. Only a small number of owners wanted to shell out the extra $65 to $100 for the plug-in converter that allowed their black-and-white TV to receive color transmissions. Nevertheless, Elizabeth Arden was in the forefront here, too: she sponsored the "first regular commercial broadcasts of color television" on CBS.[21] The innovation would become synonymous with the 1950s, a decade known for staggering economic growth and exciting inventions such as the credit card, Teflon, Barbie dolls, microwave ovens, and computers.

In the 1952 presidential election year, fifteen million homes had television sets.[22] Soon Americans were watching many hours of programming a day.[23] They could have seen Arden making several guest appearances, displaying current fashions, or chatting about cosmetics as she did on *The Kate Smith Hour*.[24] Viewers would have noticed Arden's name and her featured product when she sponsored episodes of *Home*, hosted by Arlene Francis, on NBC.[25] Locally, TV watchers might catch programs created by stores selling Arden products. Woodward & Lothrop, for instance, filmed *Inga's Angle* wherein "Inga will tell you how many ways Elizabeth Arden helps to make your hair more beautiful."[26] Industry research proved TV advertisements to be effective. Arden learned this firsthand when the Joseph Horne store suddenly sold out of her Eight Hour Cream because well-known TV personality Arthur Godfrey extemporaneously attested on air to its effectiveness.[27]

Even in black and white, Eisenhower's political TV ads helped him win in a landslide, making him the first Republican president in twenty years. With undisguised fervor, Elizabeth congratulated Mamie: "I feel that God must love the American people very much to have granted us such a glorious leader, so deeply needed at this time."[28] She was engrossed in the run-up to the inauguration, especially as the future First Lady was already her client.

The Eisenhower presidency ushered in a time often remembered as the calm before the 1960s storm. The baby boom, the rise of suburbs and the two-car family, television's increasing popularity, the high percentage of Americans who declared a belief in God, the broad conviction that the family was the cornerstone of American life, and the twinned rejection of communism and commitment to and pride in the American system of government gave a sense of unity and common purpose to many people.

The Eisenhower era was full of changes for women. Rosie was told to put away her rivet gun and return home. The median age of marriage for women dropped to twenty. More than two thirds of all Americans over age fourteen were wed. Famous columnist Dorothy Dix had mourned the disappearance of spinsters—which she blamed partly on makeup![29] The social arc bent toward matrimony and children. Maternity departments sprang up in stores. Advertising focused on family life. The wife's role was widely seen as supporter of her husband's career. Reality often clashed with the societal ideal, and in fact, women continued to work outside the home (children are expensive!) and to pursue higher education. Non-white Americans still faced obstacles to full participation in most of the benefits of postwar America.

As the inauguration neared, Arden learned that Mamie was "having difficulty finding the right hairdresser for your precious, 'much-discussed' bangs." Thus, at an agreed-upon time, Arden's hairstylist and manicurist appeared to prepare Mrs. Eisenhower. Their ministrations, Mamie confided, "were blessings indeed and helped me look my best and feel my most confident." Mamie planned to contact Arden's salon for "someone there on whom I might call" when settled in the White House.[30]

Mamie Eisenhower's bangs were her trademark. Because she both reflects and drives fashions, the First Lady is always imitated. News headlines such as "Mrs. Eisenhower Brings Bangs into High Fashion" and "U.S. Women Copy Hairdo of Mrs. Eisenhower" were common.[31] Even Second Lady Patricia Nixon wore bangs.

But not everyone liked them. Most adult women found them difficult to wear. During National Beauty Salon Week, several hairdressers insisted that "bangs are not stylish!" Ditch them, they urged Mrs. Eisenhower.[32] A British journalist sniffed that bangs were "more fit for the college girl on campus than the President's wife."[33] Elizabeth Arden

Arden recommended an interior design in turquoise, chartreuse, brown, and pink for the Elizabeth Arden Lounge inside the Kappa Kappa Gamma Service Women's Centers used by grateful women in uniform during World War II.

Arden demonstrates her skin care line to a group of rapt SPARS (U.S. Coast Guard Women's Reserve) at the Arden makeup bar in the Kappa Kappa Gamma New York Service Women's Center.

Arden cutting the cake to celebrate the two-year anniversary of the Kappa Kappa Gamma Women's Service Center as WAVES Anne A. Lenty and Marine Elizabeth Crandall look on.

Looking every bit the regal cosmetic queen, 1947.

Arden's Pure Red advertisement from 1955, suggesting the continuing connection with scientific skin care and obligatory color harmony recommendations.

PURE   RED

Imagine the vibrant heart of a red rose,
distilled through purest light rays and you have
Elizabeth Arden's pristine Pure Red—a colour
of radiant brightness for every woman's lips.
For this, remember, is that rarest of reds, Pure Red
—wonderful with the leafy greens of Spring,
brilliant forecast for fashion's choice. Wear Pure
Red creamy Lipstick with pure Red Cream
Rouge and exquisite Elizabeth Arden
Powder harmonised to your complexion

Elizabeth Arden

An iconic Charles James design, the Butterfly gown weighed nearly twenty pounds. Constructed with golden tulle wings, this version has a beautifully formfitting ruched sheath of pale silk.

Elizabeth Arden with her
niece, Patricia Graham Young,
at Arden's home in Kentucky.

Opera star Martha Lipton
sweats off the weight in a
heat box at Arden's Maine
Chance Spa in Phoenix.

While an instructor oversees aqua exercises, other Maine Chance
Phoenix clients enjoy spa treatments in the shade.

The rooftop Arden salon in San Francisco, where women have their hair and nails done while sipping slenderizing vegetable drinks.

The Eisenhowers and the Nixons in 1956, when both the First and Second Ladies were good customers of Arden's.

Arden with jockey Edward Decker at Miami's Hialeah Park Racetrack in 1957.

Only the best for this Kentucky Derby winner! Racing cartoonist Pierre "Peb" Bellocq captured Elizabeth Arden's luxury status while subtly nodding to her important role in the thoroughbred racing world.

"Elizabeth Arden, I hope?"

Handbags, clothing, cosmetics, skin care products, and gifts tempt
1950s shoppers in the Palm Beach Elizabeth Arden Salon.

Arden and her sister
Gladys, the Viscountess
de Maublanc, alight
from a British Overseas
Airways Corporation
(BOAC) flight in 1959.

On behalf of the French government, Ambassador Hervé Alphand awards the order of Chevalier de la Légion d'honneur to Arden in 1961, in recognition of her contribution to the cosmetics industry. It was one of the greatest honors of her life.

Cosmetics pioneer and powerful competitor Helena Rubinstein at her desk in 1962. Rubinstein and Arden worked together on several projects in their shared field, and were complicit in publicly cultivating a lifelong feud.

In 1962, Arden purchased Barretstown Castle in County Kildare, Ireland, where she hoped to entertain friends and to breed and stable her thoroughbreds.

The elegant facade of
the Arden Salon on
Bond Street in London.

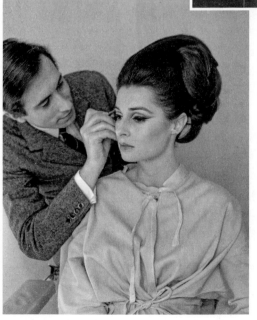

Artistic genius Count
Pablo Manzoni helped
Arden stay up-to-date
in the 1960s with his
innovative eye designs.
Celebrities and royalty,
like Princess Elizabeth
of Yugoslavia, flocked to
Arden salons to have their
makeup done by Pablo.

Arden accepting the Ladies' Annual Sportsmanship Award given by the Kentucky Thoroughbred Breeders' Association. Arden's tenacity, generosity, and commitment—plus her victories—eventually earned her acceptance in the "sport of kings."

Oscar de la Renta stands behind his boss and her guests at the 1964 Elizabeth Arden International Ball in Newport, Rhode Island.

In 1963, Arden hired Oscar de la Renta, the last
in a stellar list of fashion designers she turned into
legends. This off-the-shoulder asymmetrical silk
cocktail dress is one of his creations made
for Arden's label in 1965.

Elizabeth Arden's marketing genius included regular meetings
with journalists at her New York City penthouse. She shared
new products with them and learned about competitors'
ideas, while garnering good publicity for her company.

A publicity photo of Arden instructing her chemists in the lab, demonstrating
her hands-on leadership, her deep understanding of her products, and the
scientific—hence safe and effective—basis of her skin care and makeup.

Publicity photo of a radiant Elizabeth Arden.

never criticized. She consistently helped Eisenhower maintain her look, sending hairdressers to her in D.C. and elsewhere, and creating diagrams for other stylists to follow when hers could not be present.[34]

For her part, two months after the inaugural, the First Lady invited Arden to a tea party, the first of several White House events in her future. She had not been inside the presidential mansion, Arden told the Eisenhowers, for two decades.[35] One of the most exciting invitations came in 1954 when she had the welcome chance to renew her acquaintance with Queen Elizabeth The Queen Mother.[36]

They had met one year earlier when Arden and Gladys were in London for the coronation of young Queen Elizabeth II. During that festive visit, Arden dined with Australia's prime minister, Robert Menzies, and his wife, Pattie; watched Britain's greatest jockey, Gordon Richards, win his first Derby at Epsom; and attended a coronation party given by Perle Mesta, who was evolving into a friend. As a guest on BBC radio, Arden recounted to millions worldwide the story of how "beauty became [her] life study." "Beauty is more than skin deep," she emphasized. "It depends on health and diet, of course." She signed off graciously, describing the "deep impression of the feminine beauty I've seen in the Coronation—and the shining example of the Queen—there for every girl to follow."

The coronation was good for business. First stop: the Bond Street salon to greet customers old and new enjoying beautifying treatments preparing for parties and balls. Arden took her office staff to lunch at Claridge's. She checked in with factory workers who were in a tizzy because the Lord Chamberlain ordered that "the Peeress's retiring rooms in the House of Lords on Coronation Day" must be stocked with Elizabeth Arden toiletries, especially her "Coronation Pink" lipstick and rouge because "most peeresses are Miss Arden's clients" and "on such an occasion nothing but the best could be good enough." That factory also produced the "Pink Perfection" lipstick that the *Scottish Daily Mail* handed out when the new queen made her state visit to Edinburgh.

Twenty-seven lucky women named Elizabeth sharing the same birthday as the young monarch received this clever "gift from Miss Arden." As part of the celebration, all Elizabeths everywhere were encouraged to give to the queen's charity (the National Society for the Prevention of Cruelty to Children) and then have their names inscribed in a donor book. Elizabeth Arden made a point to be among them.[37]

Arden never boasted publicly of her most famous clients. Although she gave the First Lady a 10 percent discount and sent her gifts, she never mentioned Mrs. Eisenhower in advertisements or speeches. The same was true for the queen and the other British nobility who used her toiletries. While it was common knowledge that the Duchess of Windsor had weekly salon treatments—gratis—no one learned that from Arden. It was journalists who divulged that Princess Margaret's bridal trousseau contained silk lingerie from an Arden boutique.[38] Eventually Arden's discretion, and the fact that the queen mother and the queen truly did like and use her products, resulted in two royal warrants. This mark of favor allowed Elizabeth Arden to display the royal coat of arms on her packages, products, and stationery.[39] Queen Elizabeth II was said to maintain her complexion with Eight Hour Cream and to favor a particular shade of Arden Pink lipstick. She continued to grant the royal warrant to Arden across more than six decades.[40]

American First Ladies do not have official warrants to dispense, but their likes and dislikes nevertheless drive consumer purchases. Mamie Eisenhower shared Arden's passion for pink. Arden's 1950s makeup charts contained more pink than usual, in shades such as "Surprise," "Striking," "Pink Perfection," "Pure Pink," "Pink Spark," and "Arden Pink."

"First Lady Pink" appeared in the summer of 1953, thanks to the Textile Color Card Association of the United States (TCCA). The organization standardized colors and anticipated those likely to be popular for industrial and fashion use. The TCCA gained Mrs. Eisenhower's authorization to use the term to describe the exact pink of her inaugural gown. TCCA head Margaret Hayden Rorke predicted it would become an instant hit for everything from dresses to upholstery. She was not far wrong. First Lady Pink, colloquially called "Mamie Pink," took off. Interior designers went wild with pink kitchen appliances, pink bathrooms, pink linens, and pink walls. Product designers followed suit with pink dishes, clocks, vases, and nearly everything else imaginable.[41]

Elizabeth Arden was thrilled that she and the new First Lady shared a favorite color. Arden had decreed a full five years before the Eisenhower inaugural that the forecast was "pink and pretty," but pink never truly went out of style as far as Arden was concerned. Pink Perfection starred in Arden's spring 1953 fashion showing—harmonizing beautifully with her Fashion Floor designs. In 1954, it was "Lido-Venice Pink" and "Parma-Violet."[42] She began to create colors in a "Plus" shade. "Parma-Violet Plus," for example, was one shade darker and sold individually or in a Duet lipstick holder with Parma-Violet. This cue nudged forward the fashion trend of wearing several items of clothing in various degrees of saturation in the same color.[43]

The overall look changed little from 1947 through 1955. Tiny waists and full skirts coexisted with a straight up-and-down silhouette, but both emphasized an hourglass figure. Full corsets, corselets ("merry widows"), high-waist girdles, longline bras, and hip padding helped achieve the shape. Fashions of the 1940s were no-nonsense to help women do the critical work of winning World War II, and skirts were straight because of fabric rationing. Like short hair, the look was appropriate to the crisis. The new decade, however, called for a return to traditional feminine beauty, including longer locks. In the 1950s, when domesticity was prized, Arden huffed that "no girl with short hair has made an advantageous marriage lately!" That was because, she insisted, "men simply don't like short hair."[44]

Helping realize her vision was her newest fashion designer, Count Ferdinando Sarmi. Sarmi left Italy in November 1951 to work with Arden, which he did successfully for nearly eight years. They shared the same love for dresses embellished with feathers, beadwork, and lace. He professed to "make clothes to enhance a woman's beauty or to hide her faults," and Arden approved. Fashion journalists acclaimed his collection, especially the quality of his fabrics and his chic designs.[45]

Also assisting was Fanny Fern Fitzwater, whom Arden hired in 1953 as vice president in charge of her fashion department, a job she maintained until her death in 1966. Fitzwater had been a fashion reporter, illustrator, and educator at Traphagen School of Fashion in New York City and elsewhere.[46] Arden, Fitzwater, and Sarmi together created the Fashion Floor's postwar look. Softer coiffures and makeup, a pronounced waistline, and pastel shades for daytime wear earned praise for their "timeless elegance" and "feminine perfection." Bare shoulders, tightly fitting bodices, the cinched waist, and flowing skirts characterized Sarmi's designs and those whose work echoed his. He used yards of luxurious velvets and imported brocades for winter and frothy, diaphanous fabrics—organzas, chiffons, silk taffetas, shantung—for summer (in florals by 1954). Outspoken in defense of longer hair and shorter skirts, Arden defined her label by this classic ultrafemininity for self-assured women who carried themselves with aplomb. Elizabeth Arden always maintained that "clothes should be functional as well as beautiful." And while she promoted a svelte figure as the healthy ideal, she showed ready-to-wear gowns in sizes up to (today's) fourteen.[47]

The focus on femininity moved Arden to heights of ornamentation. For the 1953 holiday season she sold pink "Fun-Mitts" decorated with "pearls and gold glitter, made to hold that slippery cocktail shaker or to help lift the Yuletide fire log." For gift giving she suggested "a jeweled feather duster," a pearl-encrusted piggy bank, "spangled" velveteen Christmas stockings, and oodles of rhinestone jewelry. Makeup also got the sparkle treatment in gold, silver, and "multicolor." She added glitter to eye shadow, created "Star Twinkle" for sprinkling in the hair and onto bare shoulders, and advised putting her special sequins on one's nails before coating with clear polish. The daring could also place sequins on their lips—over the lipstick but under a gloss—making them "fantastic" but also easily removable in advance of hors d'oeuvres. For fun, she brought back 1920s beauty marks, but this time around made with sequins. Her "glitter-glamour" became all the rage. Other cosmetics companies rushed to copy Arden.[48] She had begun this "star dust" look in January 1951, in conjunction with the makeup she did for Cole Porter's musical *Out of This World*. The Arden evening style included opalescent cosmetics, "glitter" eye makeup on top of an iridescent eye shadow and white eyeliner, two shades of blue mascara, and silver dust brushed into the hair.[49] Virginia Pope called it "very come-hitherish" and "alluring," and loved "the usual glamorous Arden touch."[50]

New product creation was exhilarating: Valencia perfume; Spun-Cream Permanent Wave kit for home perms; the dandruff-eliminating Electric Cap Velva Treatment; a purse-size "pressurized atomizer" with her Blue Grass scent.[51] "For over a year," she promised, she had "worked with my chemists" to invent a novel liquid foundation called Basic Sheen available in six popular shades.[52] A whimsical, accordion-like plastic container she called a "Puff-Puff" filled with Blue Grass–scented dusting powder was meant to be affordable and fun.[53] Interchangeable lipsticks got their own beauty makeover with lovely cases and inexpensive refills.[54] Reminding clients of her international connections, and because of the soft spot she had for Gladys and all things French, Arden brought out a "Napoleonic" compact with a new product called Ardena Invisible Veil makeup.[55] Firmo-Lift for tightening the face and neck (best used with her new "quilted and flowered" "Herbal Chin Strap") had a big transatlantic launch.[56] Gladys and Elizabeth joined Teddy Haslam and Gordon Yates, Arden's European sales manager, in London to meet with nearly one hundred buyers, all of whom were invited to try Firmo-Lift and then the "Méditerranée" makeup line. It was a long, celebratory afternoon with tea, try-ons, and champagne toasts. Another big launch was Creme Extraordinaire, also billed as having years of research behind its whipped texture and wondrous ability to smooth,

nourish, and fight aging. It came in an arresting, updated apothe-
cary's jar.[57]

Watching the baby boom happening around her, Arden released a
children's kit for girls. It was shaped like a circus train and contained
toothpaste and toothbrush, two kinds of bath soap, hand lotion, Blue
Grass Flower Mist (a very light perfume), Velva Cream moisturizer,
Eight Hour Cream, and a clear lip balm.[58] Arden never stopped creating
new beauty kits. Her 1954 holiday ads included ten! They ranged in
price from $10.00 to $177.50.[59] And that was only a portion of the boxes
and cases she stocked. Many she designed herself, and all were beautiful, giftable, and truly convenient because everything one needed came
together in a single, lovely (usually pink-lined) box for travel or dressing
table.

An old idea of hers returned in a flashy promotion. "Two Colors Are
Better Than One" reminded women that lipstick, eye shadow, and face
powder all benefited by being layered.[60] Her two-sided "Italian Duet"
tube (with the ad slogan "1 + 1 = 4") came in eight different lipstick
color combinations.[61] Then she went one better. Her "Byzantine Look"
called for wearing three different colors of eye shadow. The audience at
the "Mosaic of Fashion" show in Dallas loved it.[62] Blue made a comeback,
too, with "Maquillage Bleu." "For the prettiest you, turn blue!" read the
promotion. It worked especially well with pastels and black-and-white
ensembles. One applied "sea blue eye shado, dark blue mascara, dark
blue eyebrow pencil to outline the eyes, and grey pencil to sketch in the
brows." A bluish-pink blush and lipstick completed the look. It "sounds
bizarre but it's pretty," one woman swore. Arden worked with the Paris
cosmetics firm Stendhal and its founder, chemist Roger Thirion, to
create the makeup.[63]

Although she had offered her Joie de Vivre Hormone Cream since
the 1930s, hormone preparations became trendy again. Arden duly reminded customers she had invented hers in "collaboration with scientists and research chemists here and abroad" through "observation and

treatment of thousands of women in her salons all over the world." Adding "Estrogenic Hormones" to her Basic Sheen foundation meant she could sell it for an extra $1.50 a jar.[64]

Science also helped her promote "Pure Red," a color she introduced in 1954. Rapid advances in medicine and technology made scientists the darlings of the decade. Focusing on the chemistry behind the cosmetics capitalized on their social lionization. Her Pure Red magazine ads showed a beaker used as a bud vase with a red liquid at the bottom. One Arden window designer earned Lester Gaba's favor by combining a "hot" look with "cold, clinical laboratory equipment." The artistically displayed mortars and pestles, test tubes, and distillers "epitomiz[ed]" the Cold War era's "love of romantic, dramatic science" and suggested that Pure Red was cutting-edge couture and chemistry combined.[65]

Charles Revson focused on another type of chemistry altogether with his bombshell "Fire and Ice" advertisement. On November 1, 1952, he broke the long-standing barrier between makeup and sex. In the pages of *Vogue*, Revson asked American women some shocking questions:

> What is the American girl made of? Sugar and spice and everything nice? Not since the days of the Gibson Girl! There's a *new* American beauty . . . she's tease and temptress, siren and gamin, dynamic and demure. Men find her slightly, delightfully baffling. Sometimes a little maddening. Yet they admit she's *easily* the most exciting woman in all the world! She's the 1952 American beauty, with a foolproof formula for melting a male! She's the "Fire and Ice" girl. (Are *you*?)

When Arden first opened her doors, makeup suggested dishonesty. Only women with something to hide put on a false face. Downplaying any connection between "painted women" (itself a euphemism for sex workers) and cosmetics was thus Arden's career-long imperative. With one dramatic ad Revson erased that line and proclaimed that the purpose of makeup was "melting a male." It's not that Arden never referenced men in her ads; rather, she emphasized being healthy and getting the Arden look for a wholesome and classic beauty. Even an ad including men and suggesting that a woman's looks were important to men, such as "Frankly, He Was Fascinated," showed a woman in a deeply unsexy uniform: the man's fascination came from the woman's decision to enlist. By contrast, the photograph accompanying Revlon's "Fire and Ice" highlighted every curve of model Dorian Leigh.

The "Fire and Ice" ad spoke to an emergent new woman—not the idealized 1950s housewife. Revlon decreed its makeup was for females "who love to flirt with fire, who dare to skate on thin ice," and asked readers to take a test. If a woman answered "yes" to eight or more of the fifteen questions, she was a "'Fire and Ice' girl." "Do you sometimes feel that other women resent you? . . . Do you love to look *up* at a man? . . . If tourist flights were running, would you take a trip to Mars? Do you close your eyes when you're kissed?"[66] The quiz was distributed at cosmetic counters and featured nationwide in store and window displays, part of Revlon's vast publicity barrage.

The 1950s, although the era of the suburbs and the baby boom, was also the decade of *Playboy* and the "swinging bachelor," of Elvis Presley's hips and James Dean's sultry masculinity. Americans absorbed the results of Alfred Kinsey's sexuality research, which suggested that more people were engaging in more and different kinds of sex than previously imagined. Personal freedom sounded better than domesticity to some freethinkers. Helen Gurley Brown's *Sex and the Single Girl* was still in the future, and there was no agreed-upon social term for the women such men-about-town brought back to their "bachelor pads." Nevertheless, Revson adroitly tapped into a vein of discontent and latent rebellion. The connection between makeup and sex did not sit comfortably with Elizabeth Arden. She was less concerned that Revlon surpassed her in profits and market share, because single women attracted to avowed bachelors living in gadget-filled apartments were never her customer base.

Other competitors nipped at her heels, just enough to keep her sharp and interested in her industry. She knew that winds of change were blowing—but that had been true since she began and they never really stopped. The benefit of being a world-renowned prestige label meant she could afford to sail on securely. As long as she continued to innovate within the look and the brand she had created, she would be fine. More than fine. Seventy-five years old as Dwight Eisenhower sought reelection mid-decade, Elizabeth Arden looked fifty-five and felt thirty-five, sufficiently vigorous to relish whatever challenges lay ahead.

Twenty-Three

Maine Chance Mania

The Eisenhowers were never known for drama. Yet their ano-
dyne Maine Chance visit kicked off a national conversation about
the limits of a First Lady's privacy and kept Elizabeth Arden in
the news. It was unexpected—but not wholly unwelcome—publicity.

The Eisenhower kerfuffle occurred as Arden's visibility was increasing in the Republican Party. In 1956, the GOP gathered in San Francisco to renominate Dwight D. Eisenhower. Arden attended Citizens
for Eisenhower parties and fundraisers. The campaign had an active
women's division led by Iowan Dorothy Houghton, who pinned Eisenhower's immense popularity with wives and mothers on his ending the
Korean War. Just as critical was the party's endorsement of the Equal
Rights Amendment, which included support for women in the military,
farming, and labor, and advocated an end to employment discrimination based on "race, creed, color, national origin, ancestry or sex." More
than five hundred female delegates and alternates attended the 1956
convention; among the most famous was Arden.[1]

Republicans wanted to see and be seen at her parties. She started
planning long before she left New York, inviting six hundred people,

especially "VIP convention-goers," the Eisenhowers, cabinet members, political and military leaders, and bigwig journalists, to a buffet dinner with dancing and a cabaret, in the Mark Hopkins Hotel ballroom.[2] The list "read like a Who's Who in Republican circles," the *Chicago Tribune* marveled. Arden, dressed in "pink, dotted with tiny blue petaled buds," and wearing white gloves, greeted every guest individually. Party crashers stormed the premises, somehow eluding the Pinkerton guards, but newspaper photographers kept their cameras on the dignitaries.[3]

The real thrill was Eisenhower's unanimous renomination. Arden considered him "our dearest national possession."[4] She proudly wore her oversize, jewel-encrusted "I Like Ike" pin, especially to Washington gatherings both public (like the $56-a-plate Eisenhower Day fundraiser) and private (like her "delightful," quiet, corner-table luncheons with the Nixons).[5] Her unfailing support earned her a second official inaugural invitation. We hope, Mamie wrote, "that you will be the personal guest of the President and myself for the various functions (the swearing-in ceremony, the parade, and one of the balls)."[6] Arden accepted gladly.

National attention focused on the inaugural gowns, their colors, and their designers. Second Lady Pat Nixon decided quite early to wear Elizabeth Arden but could disclose neither the style nor the color until Mrs. Eisenhower released such information about her own.[7] For the outdoor swearing-in ceremony, Nixon chose Arden's "rose red suit with a slim sheath skirt and abbreviated jacket" topped by matching hat decked with ostrich feathers. Over it she wore a coat made from the "Afghanistan black lamb pelts" Queen Humaira gave her during the Nixons' 1953 visit to her country. At the four inaugural balls, Pat donned an ice-blue gown chosen with the vice president's help at Arden's Fifth Avenue salon. It was gorgeous: floor-length, with shoulder straps, back and side pleats, a snug waist, and a pearl- and crystal-accented bodice. Mrs. Nixon sported matching satin pumps and costume jewelry also selected from the Arden salon. She completed her

ensemble with a white ermine wrap and elbow-length white gloves.[8] For
Elizabeth Arden, the second inaugural was as thrilling as the first.

The Eisenhowers were popular. Their approval ratings were high,
and citizens, Arden among them, expressed sympathy following the president's heart attack in 1955 and the First Lady's 1957 hysterectomy (although that word was not used publicly then). Americans understood
when Dwight Eisenhower sought relaxation at his favorite spot in Georgia, and when Mamie longed for a rest cure.

Announcing the trip, Press Secretary James C. Hagerty offhandedly
told reporters that the couple would fly to Georgia, where Eisenhower
would golf and hunt quail. Afterward, as Laurence Burd of the *Chicago
Tribune* reported on February 21, "the President may fly to Phoenix,
Ariz., Sunday and drop Mrs. Eisenhower off there for a few days' visit at
Main [*sic*] Chance farm, fashionable estate of Elizabeth Arden, cosmet-
ics maker and race horse owner."[9] It was a social call, Hagerty implied.
A nonstory.

Yet an unattributed front page *Washington Post* headline on the same
date suggested something quite different: "Mamie Hoping to Visit Plush
Phoenix Resort." Further, the article claimed that Arden wasn't in Phoenix. She was at Florida's Hialeah Park racetrack with no plans to leave.
So what was happening?[10]

The trouble began two days later, when reporters rounded on Hagerty
demanding to know why, as they now saw it, the president was using
taxpayer money on an unnecessary seven-hour flight to take his wife to
"a beauty resort." Why hadn't Hagerty told them that Mamie was also
taking along her sister Frances Moore and a friend, Grace Slater? Why
wouldn't Eisenhower just head straight back to Washington and send
the women off on their own? What "justification" could there be for
the loss of presidential time and the expenditure of taxpayer money?
Hagerty, at a complete loss, snapped. "I think when the President of the
United States wants to go any place he wants to with his wife, that is his
business and nobody else's," he barked.

Reporters fought back. They said he had purposefully misled them. Questions flew thick and fast. If it was a social call, why wasn't Elizabeth Arden going to be there? How long would the First Lady stay? What was "Maine Chance Farm" anyway? They thought he meant a horse farm, but now they knew it was really a fat farm. What *exactly* would Mrs. Eisenhower be doing out there—and who would pay for it?

The press secretary grew splenetic. He had no answers. He could not tell them how long the women would remain in Phoenix. He had not heard that Elizabeth Arden was in Florida. He didn't know who was paying. He flatly denied that the First Lady would be taking "weight control courses." When asked point-blank whether Mrs. Eisenhower was there for beauty treatments, the spluttering Hagerty managed to choke out "I don't think she needs any." Rest and sunshine were the goals, he swore. It was "the sharpest exchange" ever between the press secretary and journalists. Hagerty bellowed that they were "out of bounds" for questioning why the president "wants to take Mrs. Eisenhower to Phoenix." Reporters snorted. If this were truly a nonstory, why did Hagerty "blow his top"?[11]

Scrutiny focused on the use of *Columbine III*, an early version of Air Force One. It was 3,624 miles out of the way for Eisenhower to fly the women to Maine Chance. Reporters did the math: chartering a jet to fly that far would cost approximately $12,000—was this what taxpayers would pay?[12] Hagerty couldn't say whether the women would return to D.C. on the *Columbine III*.

Meanwhile, on the same day that most reporters fixated on the use and the cost of the *Columbine*, *The Washington Post* quoted Maine Chance business manager Maydelle Bankston saying that as "guests of Miss Arden" none of the women would pay "any bills." Bankston volunteered that Gladys de Maublanc would divert from visiting her son in Los Angeles to meet the First Lady. Newspapers covered the Eisenhowers' progression in minute detail, and complementary articles about the look, feel, treatments, schedule, personnel, and efficacy of Maine Chance explained how clients could "revitalize themselves in a sugar-coated routine combining Spartan self-improvement with pampered luxury." And, luckily, the Maine Chance building expansion had just been completed, so the brand-new, private, three-bedroom "Garden of Arden" cottage was ready for the First Lady and her companions.[13]

A crowd of one thousand welcomed the Eisenhowers to Phoenix. The official greeting party included the mayor, the publisher of *The Arizona Republic* newspaper, and the state's Republican party leaders. The president headed off to eighteen holes of golf at Paradise Valley Country Club. The women got settled at Maine Chance before Eisenhower joined them for dinner. He departed Phoenix at 11:35 p.m. on the *Columbine*.[14] Hoping to become (sumptuously) embedded journalists, female reporters angled for reservations, but Arden kept them out and guarded her guests behind high walls and vows of staff silence.[15] Protecting Mamie were "21 armed men—six Secret Service agents, six members of the Arizona highway patrol and nine Maricopa County sheriffs deputies," working "around the clock, seven men to each eight-hour shift."[16]

As the gates closed around the First Lady's activities at Maine Chance, speculation and censure swelled. The intimidating *Washington Post* newshound Drew Pearson charged corruption. In addition to the private use of the president's plane, the cost to citizens, and the poor optics of the First Couple relaxing during a recession, Pearson zeroed in on Mamie's companions. Her sister Frances Doud Moore was the wife of George Gordon Moore, then facing accusations of pushing the Federal Communications Commission to grant a television license to a company in which he had an interest. Pearson made two more accusations. Grace Slater's husband, Ellis, was one of Eisenhower's closest friends and advisers, and Pearson insinuated that Slater, a liquor company executive, had a malign power over the president. Finally, Pearson implicated Arden, alleging a quid pro quo: the First Lady would publicize Maine Chance and Arden would donate to the GOP.[17]

Pearson drove Dwight Eisenhower to distraction. But Slater was more concerned about his friends. He penned in his diary that Mamie had never fully recovered from her hysterectomy: "She hadn't been feeling too well since her operation, has taken on some weight in the wrong places and wasn't feeling too well mentally." Additionally, she was worn down worrying about the president's health. Slater had predicted that the cost of the women's travel and stay would earn them bad press, and suggested to Eisenhower that they take a commercial plane instead. But because "Mamie is scared to death of flying" he knew that would never happen. He eventually stopped arguing because he believed that "this trip is needed by Mamie and if she can get into a better frame of mind, it will be good for Ike, too."[18]

Drew Pearson kicked up a firestorm, but not all reporters followed him. Doris Fleeson of *The Boston Globe* asked, with a smidgeon of exasperation and perhaps a touch of female solidarity: "Did They Expect [Mamie] to Take the Bus?"[19] Syndicated columnist Bob Spivack thought faultfinders' writings were a cheap way of getting at the White House. "I think," he wrote, "the boys who travelled along with Ike might have dug up something more substantial than news about Mamie's mud packs."[20]

But mudpacks, paraffin baths, massages, and aquatic aerobic exercises fascinated American women. They demanded details. Maydelle Bankston accommodated this Maine Chance mania to a point: the First Lady spent her initial hours sunning by the pool before retiring to her cottage with its lovely garden view. Mrs. Eisenhower's secretary, Rose Wood, and members of the Secret Service were nearby, housed on-site, where the telephone company had installed a modern switchboard and a private telephone line. Bankston confirmed that Mrs. Eisenhower would be staying two weeks and taking the "regular" course along with the other two dozen guests.[21] This last was not strictly true. Mamie's schedule cards show that she remained late abed—as she usually did— and that while she did take several treatments, including those for weight loss, her evening activities were her own.[22] Reporters who spotted the First Lady at the Valley Presbyterian Church on Sunday heard her decline an offer to join their coffee hour. Maine Chance is "rather strict about meals," she said, laughing.[23]

After the First Lady left, reporters descended on the spa and filled pages with enthusiastic copy. One journalist asked the chauffeur to pause at the Phoenix airport so she could have a last cocktail. "'They all do,' he replied, resignedly. 'I always wait.'" Her bedroom was "big enough to enclose a bungalow" with an original Chagall hanging over a marble fireplace. She could not believe her meals were actually low-calorie or that the women around her dined in Dior and Mainbocher gowns. She enjoyed outings to the local movie theater and playhouse. She extolled the diathermy treatment, the pampering, and the six and a half pounds that came off and stayed off. And the guest who complained loudly about not losing weight—while secretly enjoying a nightly pre-dinner ritual of "drinks in her room"—mightily amused her. Feature articles, like this one in *Look* magazine, with a circulation in the millions, kept the Arden name before Americans young and old.[24]

Suddenly, women wanted it known that they, too, splashed out to go off to Arizona or Maine. The famous—Rosalind Russell, Ava Gardner, Ethel Barrymore, Oveta Culp Hobby, Peggy Goldwater, Zsa Zsa Gabor—and the unknown (wives of rich businessmen, mostly) made sure their Maine Chance visits got into the social columns, as did Arden's fashion industry colleagues.[25] Many women, including the great actors Olivia de Havilland and Audrey Hepburn, let slip that they were devotees of Arden's beauty salons and makeup.[26]

Mamie Eisenhower, rested and tanned, lost five pounds (actually, over six, according to Maine Chance records), and told the public she was "already looking forward to going back."[27] For weeks afterward, stories about the First Lady mentioned her weight loss and the enthusiastic reception of her "new look" at the hands of the Arden experts.[28] In response to this interest, Elizabeth Arden released the Maine Chance diet plan, calculatedly generating more publicity.[29]

The national Maine Chance obsession prompted the Cradle Society to substitute a luncheon straight from Phoenix for its 1958 fundraiser, instead of its usual calorie-rich meal. Green apple soup and molded aspic filet of sole, served without rolls, butter, salt, cream, or fattening desserts, made a wonderful promotion but a less-than-festive occasion. "It's different!" the chairwoman chirped bravely. The Cradle Society did not repeat the experiment in 1959.[30] Nor ever again.

Elizabeth Arden and Mamie Eisenhower maintained their friendship despite the to-do. After her initial visit, the First Lady continued to invite Arden to White House events, and the women worked together for the American Women's Voluntary Service.[31] Arden promised to hold a "permanent niche" for Eisenhower in Phoenix.[32] Indeed, Mamie Eisenhower returned to Maine Chance annually for more than a decade. It was, she said, "the only place I can go where I can really have a vacation."[33]

The episode added fuel to the ongoing national debate as to whether the First Lady was a private citizen or a public figure. The next year, Mamie Eisenhower took the train and paid for herself, though that never placated Drew Pearson.[34] Not to worry, the Eisenhowers told a fretting Arden. They "no longer pay attention to the false accusations appearing in newspapers."[35] While the incident generated criticism of Eisenhower's administration and contributed to the national discussion of the status of the First Lady, Elizabeth Arden had a different response: Mamie's friendship was lovely and her patronage generated indisputably splendid publicity.

A MAJOR CHANGE occurred about the same time in Arden's racing empire. She purchased Crown Crest Farm outside Lexington, added two hundred acres to its five hundred, and renamed it Maine Chance Farm. It had offices for her managers, nine specialized horse barns, sixty-four paddocks, and a mile-long training track. Finally, she owned a single geographical spot for her thoroughbreds, which had heretofore been boarded in various rented stables. At this point she had twelve horses in her "Over $100,000 Club" and had won dozens of races—some of them more than once—including "the Belmont, Pimlico and Arlington Futurities." She earned nearly $1 million racing in the first five years of the 1950s and had high hopes for the future.[36] To this pink-painted "equine Utopia," this "palace of Pegasus," Arden moved her sixty brood mares, two dozen foals, and forty-five yearlings from Leslie Combs's Spendthrift Farm.[37]

Maine Chance Farm was sprawling and luxurious. She tasked a local interior designer with creating a French feel using her racing colors of cerise and blue as accents. Flowers proliferated. Arden's bedroom was pink and spacious, with floor-to-ceiling windows. Her niece Patricia Graham Young, brother Bill's daughter, was by then Arden's closest companion. Still in her aunt's employ, Pat had, as she put it, "learned the beauty business from the bottom floor to the top of the Elizabeth Arden 11-story salon on Fifth Avenue."[38] Divorced from banker Charles W. Young in 1947, Pat lived part of each year at Maine Chance Farm.

The two entertained frequently on the enclosed terrace so guests could look across the white four-board fence into the paddocks. A Louisville reporter described the domain of Elizabeth Arden Graham (as she was known in thoroughbred circles since the Kentucky Derby win) as "elegant and colorful, sophisticated and completely feminine." New York City remained Arden's primary residence, but she spent a great deal of time at her new Kentucky home, hosting friends from her overlapping worlds and becoming a respected breeder.[39]

The purchase of Maine Chance Farm was another step toward Arden's legitimacy among the thoroughbred crowd. For more than twenty-five years, Arden had suffered public excoriation for changing trainers as often as she changed lipstick colors, or hairstyles, or dress lengths (trackside journalists had a lot of fun with that trope throughout the decades). Eventually, she pushed back. In 1956, *The Thoroughbred Record* wrote: "'What some critics have not taken into consideration,' explains Mrs. Graham calmly and with every indication that the matter of trainers is her own business, 'is that quite a few of the men who have been listed at times as Maine Chance trainers have not been men of that caliber at all, but merely stable foremen temporarily put in charge. Yet, our stable has compiled a record of victories that not too many others can match.'"[40]

Later, Arden was clearer: "I know what I want and I know how to communicate what I want and I insist on getting it, else I get a new trainer." She admitted she had "made life miserable for enough trainers and stable people." But she knew her words and her actions had communicated her vision. She would not put up "with nonsense or ignorance." Believing her methods better for her horses, she was unapologetic. At least, she said, she "had the heart to be close to the horses and give them personal attention." Like the women who sought her beauty help, horses were not "machines." Mutual respect, affection, and communication were essential, she insisted, between horse and trainer, and horse and jockey. And especially between owner and trainer.[41] She was tired of being underestimated. A journalist once tested her by asking "what a horse must do to become a great racer." With the speed and economy of a striking rattlesnake, she retorted, "Run fast."[42]

By the mid-1950s, even the most misogynistic sportswriters praised Arden. The *Washington Post* columnist Walter Haight reluctantly concluded that "perhaps, she knows what she is doing."[43] The thoroughbred world came to respect her tenacity, her support for Silent Tom Smith, the high salaries she paid—from stable hand to jockey—her generosity toward track-related fundraisers, her string of victories, and the "admirable equanimity" with which she met setbacks, including the time one of her horses nipped off her fingertip. Arden blamed herself for that mishap. She didn't have it in her to blame her horse.[44]

For several years, Arden had also sold, purchased, and raced horses in Great Britain and Ireland.[45] Although she raced against the queen,

Arden remained friendly with members of the royal family.[46] Before the 1957 Derby, Arden had a private tea with the queen mother, whose autographed photo always perched proudly on the grand piano in her New York penthouse.[47] Arden ran her thoroughbreds at Royal Ascot, in the Epsom Derby, and at Newmarket, and enjoyed the experiences so much that in 1962 she plunked down $200,000 for a home in County Kildare near Curragh Racecourse. A twelfth-century castle, to be precise.

Barretstown Castle sat on five hundred peacock-patrolled acres. Arden planned to breed horses and "pedigree cattle," and to entertain widely.[48] She hired Tony Duquette to create the perfect interiors.[49] He had masterminded Arden salon makeovers since the 1950s and won a Tony Award for his *Camelot* costume designs, but was best known for his lavish—some might say excessive—interior designs that borrowed indiscriminately from all eras, sources, and cultures.[50] "Fantastically, ravishingly baroque," one observer pronounced. "Convention-defying," "chimerical," thought another. His clients would include the Duchess of Windsor, David O. Selznick, and Sharon Stone. Duquette brought in furniture, wallpaper, rugs, and embellishments from all over the world for Barretstown, and made sure to use pinks, greens, and dusty blues to please Arden. Adding to his kaleidoscopic ideas for the castle were two of Arden's: a red front door and pink throughout the stables. Despite the expense, Arden did not spend as much time in Ireland as she had planned, although she seems to have made it there at least once a year.[51] To most of her friends Barretstown Castle appeared the height of ridiculous extravagance. But not to Elizabeth Arden, who defined and enjoyed success in her own way.

Twenty-Four

Rounding Out the Fifties

S till the reigning queen of the global cosmetics industry, Elizabeth Arden reaped the rewards of the postwar consumer economy. Her products were high-priced signifiers of wealth, astutely marketed. Cultural triumphs accompanied her financial rewards. Flowers were named after her; she judged the 1953 Miss America pageant; and she was dubbed an "Immortal" by Boston's important Retail Trade Board.[1] She earned the Bates College Distinguished Service Citation and a second honorary doctorate.[2] The journalism sorority Theta Sigma Phi presented Arden with the "She Walks in Beauty" award for being "the woman who's done most to contribute beauty to other women."[3] Influential television journalist Edward R. Murrow invited Arden to appear on *Person to Person*.[4] The Canadian Women's Press Club flattered her as "one of Canada's most remarkable women." When her hometown begged her to dedicate Dalziel Pioneer Park, she returned to Woodbridge, planted a maple tree, and posed for photographs among her admirers on land that "her father occupied when she was born."[5] Most significant, Arden was the first American woman to win the prestigious Coupe d'Or prize given by the Comité du bon goût français, or, as her trophy read: "the Gold Cup of France for Outstanding Achievement in the Development of Parfum '*Mémoire Chérie*,' the finest fragrance ever created and acclaimed by France."[6]

A most unexpected private honor came when Charles James asked her to be godmother to his son. Jaws discreetly dropped when he wed wealthy Kansan Nancy Lee Gregory, who went into the marriage eyes wide open. "My wife knew I was homosexual," he later attested, and contemporary accounts suggest that everyone else did, too. Despite past tempests, James and Arden maintained their mutual affection. Arden never discussed her religious life with anyone who recorded it, but it seems unlikely that she served as any real spiritual mentor to Charles Junior.[7] Perhaps it was a future payoff, rather than spiritual guidance, that James sought for his son. Insiders knew well that Arden "made this business . . . [and] put the glamour in cosmetics."

Her approach was unorthodox. Her peers called her "the mother of the treatment business" for making not just cleanser, toner, and moisturizer female requisites, but all the additions and spin-offs, too. She was the "goddess" because without her, their line of work would not exist. "In a field where the principal difference between one product and the next is a matter of odor, texture, packaging and price, she has made Elizabeth Arden stand for the utmost in quality and swank," *The Saturday Evening Post* marveled. "There are few in the cosmetic business who won't agree that 'when Arden says a thing will sell, she's always right.' Her knowledge of what women will buy, and how to make them buy it, amounts to genius."[8]

Part of that genius was a never-ending commitment to innovation. In 1957, for instance, Elizabeth Arden theorized that it was time to try making and marketing men's toiletries again. During World War II, soldiers had learned to use "deodorants, foot powders, and pomade for chapped lips." The Fashion Group predicted that they would continue to do so. Their research suggested that men preferred female salesclerks and favored "simple, mannish packaging, utilitarian and not ornamen-

tal."[9] The widespread belief, though, was that most men wanted nothing to do with anything anywhere "near a beauty counter." Arden thus
did not rush in, but let other manufacturers test the theory first. Guerlain and Charbert, among others, sold a men's aftershave and cologne,
and Henri Bendel marketed its own store brand early in the 1950s.

In March 1957, Arden told *Los Angeles Times* beauty reporter Lydia
Lane that "the time has come for men to be more critical of their
appearance—they are competing with women in business more and
more, and I plan to help them with their problem before too long." Helena Rubinstein must have read that article, for twenty-three days later,
she was quoted in the same paper saying that while "the only virgin
field left in the cosmetic industry lies in products for men," she soon
hoped to help men overcome their "shyness" regarding the topic.[10] Cu-
riously, both businesswomen had already invested in men as a market—
more than once.

Like Arden, Rubinstein had tried before. In 1941 (three years into
her second marriage, to Prince Artchil Gourielli), she opened a men's
salon in New York City to sell "toiletries of tomorrow" in her new
Prince and Princess Gourielli line. She began with thirty items, including shaving soap, aftershave lotion, and talc in a line called "Tang."[11] It
was not profitable. In 1954, long after her first men's salon had faded
away but three years *before* she told the press that it was a "virgin field,"
Rubinstein opened a second salon. The Gourielli Men's Shop provided
shaves, manicures, and shoeshines, plus a limited selection of clothing
and accessories. Enticingly, the store offered a wondrous hangover machine: "The sufferer places his head in a clear plastic box, in which a
tray of ice cools the oxygen, and breathes deep."[12]

Arden, who had previously offered little more than suntan lotions to
men, entered the fray in advance of the 1956 holiday season—four
months prior to her Lydia Lane interview. She designed and patented
the much-praised black-and-gold "Arden for Men" bottles and filled
them with shaving cream, aftershave lotion (in mild or astringent),

healing face cream, talc, cologne, toothpaste, deodorant, hair spray, "colorless lip pomade," and sandalwood soaps. They came individually, in gift sets, and in plastic travel-size containers.[13] She threw a large cocktail party for friends and industry acquaintances to celebrate the birth of the new line.[14]

Capitalizing on the media attention, Arden opened a pop-up men's shop. "Half the population of New York made a mad dash for the place, enthusiastically buying everything in sight, even to the handsome sconces on the red burlap walls," one fashion editor exclaimed. Products ranged from the extremely expensive (a $950 mink lining for a man's winter dress coat) to the possibly affordable (one of her famous leather shaving boxes for $50). Catering to the swinging bachelor as well as the settled husband, she presented shoppers with Venetian martini shakers, a Diners Club card holder (for the first-ever credit card), leather jewelry cases, West German ski sweaters, and both volumes of *The Gentleman's Companion: I. Being an Exotic Cookery Book* and *II. Being an Exotic Drinking Book.*[15]

Stepping into the male market made greater business sense for Arden than supermarkets, which were the next big thing. By the mid-1950s, the old butcher shop, bakery, and dry goods store had combined into one large "super market" built near the rapidly growing suburbs. Housewives found it convenient, and so mass-market cosmetic giants like Revlon, Hazel Bishop, Coty, and Toni (owned by Gillette) rushed to put their cosmetics on chain supermarket shelves where a customer could pick up any box on her own. But Elizabeth Arden believed in her trained experts who could instruct and answer questions about her products and their use, and was committed to selling her line in its entirety. She knew from the start that she would never place her products in supermarkets. Piggly Wiggly did not suit Arden glamour.

At the same time, television came fully into its own, appearing in American homes faster and more comprehensively than previously imagined. Hazel Bishop gained national attention by hooking up with General Motors to cosponsor the NBC TV series *This Is Your Life*. Bishop poured a majority of her advertising budget into radio and especially television, the perfect vehicle for supermarket cosmetics. Her profits soared into the millions. This feat, even more than her smudge-free lipstick, became the overnight talk of the industry. Clairol, Toni, and others raced to keep up, channeling massive amounts of money to the medium Arden had long known would be important.[16]

Revlon emerged as the clear victor when it scored the sponsorship of *The $64,000 Question*. Charles Revson initially called the CBS quiz show "crap." He could not have been more wrong. In no time it garnered the highest ratings on television, knocking even *I Love Lucy* from the top spot. Revlon profits zoomed skyward as Bishop's plummeted. But suddenly, a widespread quiz show cheating scandal shocked Americans and Revson was caught up in it. CBS canceled *The $64,000 Question* in 1958. By then, toiletries expert James Bennett concluded, Revlon was the "dominant" cosmetics firm, but "victory came at a cost. The move into television advertising ultimately cheapened the Revlon brand that Charles Revson had worked so hard to make high fashion and glamorous."[17] Revson did not abandon TV, but the whole tawdry game show experience was a cautionary tale to others, including Elizabeth Arden. She remained aloof.

No Arden product was ever sold in the new supermarkets nor did she ever sponsor a costly TV series, but in response to the changing 1950s demographics she broadened her distribution. For example, when the Los Angeles population topped two million, her long, exclusive, and profitable relationship with J. W. Robinson gave way to pragmatism. She placed her complete line into high-class department stores throughout the city. Customers loved the wider availability. Arden had earlier kept pace with California's suburban growth, and downtown expansion was similarly smart.[18]

Arden soon contemplated another experiment: a salon in a shopping center.[19] Shopping centers, also known as "miracle miles," contained a wonderful array of stores in a walkable area. A precursor to malls, most shopping centers were located near the proliferating suburbs, and they facilitated the family togetherness so prized by many Americans. Elizabeth Arden and her executive vice president Carl Gardiner hoped that placing cosmetics, fashions, and treatments close to busy wives and mothers would pay off.

This was part of what *Women's Wear Daily* called Arden's "worldwide expansion program" to move beyond the fifty-two countries where she had salons. Other beauty purveyors sprinted to stay abreast. Arden opened a boutique in her Madrid beauty salon, and Spanish aristocrats came to admire locally made jewelry and "hand-loomed" cocktail skirts in "geometric patterns in brilliant colors."[20] She opened a members-only salon at the private Lyford Cay Club in the Bahamas.[21] New salons in Venice, Dublin, and Kuching, in Malaysia, followed.[22] In New York, she enlarged the Fifth Avenue salon space by moving the "show room and executive offices" to the two top floors of Three East Fifty-Fourth Street.[23]

Successful sales methods received continual analysis and updating because Arden understood she was a pacesetter who lost sight of future trends at her peril. For this reason she formed partnerships with other luxury firms such as Givenchy.[24] Only a very few could afford a $600 18-karat gold compact containing Ardena Invisible Veil powder, made cooperatively with prestige jeweler Black, Starr & Gorham.[25] Renovating salons guaranteed up-to-the-modern-minute luxury in aesthetics and equipment. The Washington, D.C., treatment rooms became "pale, pale pink" and the beauty salon received an arctic blue, white, and gold makeover, complete with hair dryers with transparent "plastic domes, so the ladies can look around and see who their neighbors are."[26] Across the continent, only Tony Duquette's unique interiors would do for her newest California salon.[27]

As economic growth continued through the 1950s, Arden maintained her luxury bona fides in some unusual ways. For the exclusive clientele of Air France's "Fashion Holiday in Europe," a monthlong $2,349 spree on the Lockheed Super Starliner with five-star hotel accommodations in European capitals and stops at all the major design houses, only Arden provided rejuvenating spa treatments.[28] The sole hair salon aboard the sumptuous *Monterey* cruise ship was Arden's.[29] Two other luxury liners, RMS *Windsor Castle* and RMS *Transvaal Castle*, also featured onboard Arden salons.[30] Air India, Qantas, Pakistan International Airlines, and British European Airways carried Arden toiletries for men and women aboard their flights.[31] When New York Airways opened its first helicopter service, the stewardesses (as they were known) were required to have their hair done at the Elizabeth Arden Salon.[32] KLM airlines proudly advertised that their staff learned "make-up from Elizabeth Arden in Holland."[33]

Arden's intimate gatherings with fashion journalists continued even as her product and fashion launches grew ever more extravagant.[34] Each autumn from 1954 through 1963, Arden underwrote the Blue Grass Ball for the Travelers Aid Society of New York. Travelers Aid assisted "travelers, strangers, and newcomers of all ages, sexes, race or creed" including runaways, displaced persons, those caught without funds, or anyone in trouble while traveling. Usually held at the Plaza Hotel, the Blue Grass Ball brought together benevolence, publicity, and glamour at a time when such charity dances were status markers.[35]

It was called the Blue Grass Ball because Blue Grass remained a top seller. Arden brought out a much-anticipated new scented item annually. In 1959, it was the Aqua Spray, a showerhead with a compartment to hold refillable Blue Grass–scented pellets. When the water turned on, it released a "bubble making water softener and the gentlest skin cleanser."[36] Arden for Men Aqua Spray with sandalwood pellets followed.[37]

Other items reflected social changes. Wigs were back in style, combined with false eyebrows made from human hair.[38] Arden sold matching eyelashes, unless a woman preferred her own; then the salon could dye both eyebrows and eyelashes.[39] When the 1960s knocked on the door in 1959, and white lipstick became trendy "for the extremes—the extremely self-assured, the extremely theatrical, the extremely unconventional," Arden filled one end of her Duet lipstick with White Lustre and the other with a color.[40] She resurrected kohl for dramatic eye effects and sold gold and silver eye shadow containing the actual precious metals.[41] Refillable lipstick was now called "Click-Change."[42]

More than a thousand corporations, schools, and institutions from around the world sent their employees to Elizabeth Arden Schools for lessons in posture, beauty, and health.[43] But she continued to place a premium on training for her own workforce. Pharmacists, demonstrators, counter staff, treatment experts, buyers, and the sales force attended regular refresher courses.[44] Occasionally, Arden sent out samples to try at home—2,232 saleswomen received boxes of free products one spring.[45] Employee training remained a priority because it benefited everyone. Arden customers expected a very high level of knowledge and skill, and the better informed her staff, the greater their understanding of and loyalty to the company.

Elizabeth Arden's spectacularly successful partnership with Sarmi concluded at the end of the decade. Together they had resisted the "sack dress," speaking out against the shapeless garment and helping to shorten its moment in the spotlight, and kept American women in the beautiful, floaty frocks they preferred.[46] Headlines suggested it was Arden who "cut" the "Sarmi tie," and he turned to wholesaling expensive fashions.[47]

In Sarmi's absence, Arden convinced not one but four extraordinary Paris couturiers to "design original, exclusive clothes for the Arden salon in New York": Jean Patou, Nina Ricci, Jacques Heim, and Madeleine de Rauch.[48] Arden's "particular pet" was Ricci, whose curvaceous silhouettes the CEO preferred. Pat Nixon, one of Arden's best clients, ordered five dresses during the design quartet's first large showing. Reviewers praised both the "breath-taking" creations and the "newsmaking" display.[49] Arden hired the great Carmel Snow as her chief European buyer.[50] Snow brought back pieces by Hubert de Givenchy, already closely associated with Audrey Hepburn and soon to become Jacqueline Kennedy's beloved designer, and Irene Galitzine, famous for her palazzo pants.[51] Ready-to-wear and custom orders also shared space with American designers in the Arden showroom, known as the dependable source of upmarket, wearable couture.[52]

THE DECADE OF THE 1950s drew to a close with the death of Elizabeth's brother, Bill Graham. Her feelings were complicated. She had followed him to America. They had shared a fierce drive to make something of themselves. His loan and guidance likely helped her start her salon. Eventually they became successful business owners together, educating each other. In the 1930s, Bill conceived the concept of "two-pattern china," a way to convince women to purchase two different settings in two different patterns. Just as Arden taught women to layer and combine their perfume and makeup, Bill taught them to layer and combine their tableware.[53] But Bill had betrayed her. He looked the other way when Tom took up with the demonstrators. Almost as bad, Bill had traveled to Canada at Tom's request to facilitate the official proceedings by signing a legal document confirming the one fact Elizabeth fought to conceal: her birth year. She never really forgave him. Taking Lewis's side cost Bill his relationship with his sister, although she remained close to his daughters.[54] Arden had a global reputation, money to spare, industry recognition, and wide-ranging friends. But she had only one big brother. His death, despite everything, was a bitter and irrevocable break.

Twenty-Five

The Not-Yet-Swinging Sixties

lection season 1960: Elizabeth Arden became caught up in it quite unexpectedly when Jacqueline Kennedy denounced her. The glamorous wife of Democratic presidential candidate John F. Kennedy defended herself from journalists who accused her of dropping a whopping $30,000 a year on clothing by retorting, "I'm sure I spend less than Mrs. Nixon on clothes. She gets hers at Elizabeth Arden, and nothing there costs less than $200 or $300." Besides, she sniffed, "I couldn't spend that much unless I wore sable underwear."[1] The spouse of the Republican presidential contender, Pat Nixon, diplomatically had "no comment about what Mrs. Kennedy wears or what she says. I shop like any American woman, mostly in Washington and off the rack. Everyone knows I am a careful shopper."[2]

A sartorial storm ensued. Jackie Kennedy's fresh and modern look—so different from Mamie Eisenhower's—was the envy of many women. Detractors suggested Kennedy was too highbrow to be a successful First Lady. *Women's Wear Daily* had earlier headlined "Mrs. Pat Nixon Keeps Eye on Clothes Budget" and rationalized that Nixon also knew fashion because she had once worked in Bullock's clothing department.

Inadvertently undercutting their own argument, *WWD* stressed that she always enjoyed "shopping for bargains," seldom selected designer clothes, and wore out the moderately priced ready-to-wear fashions she regularly chose.[3] Other papers differentiated between the two women in that Nixon bought American-made while Kennedy's dresses came from Paris designers.[4] The truth was that both women purchased clothing at Elizabeth Arden—although Nixon was the more consistent client. Former president Harry Truman harrumphed that the subject of what candidates' wives spent on clothing should be none of the public's business. Fashion insiders disagreed. They understood that Kennedy's youth, beauty, and style could be a tremendous boon to the industry, and they deeply appreciated Nixon's frequent proclamations that she was "very happy with American designers and designs."[5] As the topic widened to include the damning suggestion that the candidates mimicked their wives' shopping preferences—John Kennedy purchased most of his clothes abroad while Richard Nixon found his in the United States—the competition helpfully kept the spotlight on the importance of appearance and of the American garment industry.[6]

Resourceful *New York Times* columnist Nan Robertson sought Arden's opinion. Her public relations spokesman, Lanfranco Rasponi, confirmed that Pat Nixon was a long-term customer with "a wonderful figure" and the ability to "wear ready-made clothes." He acknowledged that such off-the-rack styles cost between $150 and $350. Robertson interviewed cagey customers who admitted that "it was possible to find a dress at Miss Arden's for as little as $25."[7] *Life* magazine piled on by showing Kennedy in a $600 Givenchy suit next to a photo of Nixon in her famously frugal "Republican cloth coat."[8]

Elizabeth Arden resurfaced regularly on this topic throughout the summer and fall campaign season as Americans wrestled to define the most desirable qualities in a First Lady, all of them connected to larger concerns about national pride, American-made goods, labor unions, and the necessity of supporting the fashion business. Some of Arden's

clothing was imported and most of it was expensive, but not as costly
as custom-made Parisian gowns. Arden was an American who hired
American garment workers. Her tailors had been unionized since 1952.
The excellent wages she paid her workers were legendary.[9] She wisely
kept mum.

But the woman whose salon was the synonym for expensive good
looks could not attend the convention to see how it played out. She was
nearing eighty, and poor health began to plague her with increasing
frequency. She kept to herself that summer, disappointing Republicans,
who missed her soirees.[10] She did make it to Mamie Eisenhower's farewell party, joining Pat Nixon, Alice Roosevelt Longworth, and other
GOP stalwarts sad to see the cheerful First Lady depart.[11]

John F. Kennedy bested Arden's friend Richard Nixon in the 1960
presidential election. She took comfort in the fact that the new First
Lady was a paragon of style who, along with several other Kennedys,
wore Elizabeth Arden clothing and frequently engaged Arden hairstylists. Kennedy women also wore Arden wigs, which the First Lady reportedly found particularly helpful on trips abroad. She practiced before
wearing them publicly, having learned from her sister-in-law Ethel,
who once wore hers to a party and gasped as it flew right off her head
while she was dancing the Twist![12]

Every couturier, every cosmetic manufacturer, every hairstylist has-
tened to create fashions à la Jackie Kennedy. A 1963 study found that 70
percent of American women closely watched celebrity styles, and that
two fifths of them changed their look to match.[13] Jacqueline Kennedy
was svelte, soft-spoken, multilingual, well-traveled, and self-possessed
in the manner of those born to wealth. Elizabeth Arden forecast "dark"
makeup, influenced by Kennedy's chestnut hair and brown eyes. The
Los Angeles Times explained that "if Miss Arden's prophesy has its way
the white skinned, no color lips, not-long-for-this-world look will give
way to the blooming beauty of tawny skin, pink touched cheeks and
color ripened lips." Arden supplied the cosmetics to create the ashen

complexion, bold eyes, and pale lips and cheeks made famous by Britain's trendiest designer Mary Quant, but she did not love it. Castillo complained to *WWD* that it "look[ed] sick" on women.[14] Kennedy's celebrity promised a return to pastel fashion shades and the understated, more natural beauty on which Arden had built her fame and fortune.

Darker makeup also allowed her to tap into the hottest Hollywood epics, *Lawrence of Arabia* and *Cleopatra*, both set in the Middle East. *Lawrence of Arabia* sparked a resurgence of kohl, bronzing powders, and dramatic eye shadows in deep green and gold, even though the film had virtually no female actors.[15] It did, however, boast a cast of several men considered eminently swoonworthy. Arden's "Sheik" ads cautioned "all members of the chic cult to wear Sheik with caution or you may end up betrothed to a [desert] chieftain."[16] The film's near-global popularity made possible Gladys's presentation to Queen Juliana of the Netherlands, where de Maublanc launched the line and directed a fashion show to demonstrate makeup application and color harmony.[17] In this case, Arden's rule of maintaining a cache of her past cosmetics, in case she had one customer who called for an old favorite, really helped. She was ready for both *Lawrence of Arabia* and the scandalous blockbuster *Cleopatra*, starring the on- and off-screen lovers Richard Burton and Elizabeth Taylor.

Arden was right on trend: "Cleopatra eyes, aided by Elizabeth Arden . . . are rimmed in black, painted with pale blue eye shadow over the entire lid right up to the eyebrows and as far out as the temples." She repackaged her kohl "in an ebony urn." Her Rome salon "turned the Italian mannequins into smart sphinxes, [and] will do the same here for any willing customer," the *New York Times* fashion writer discovered, right down to variations on the Cleopatra coiffure.[18] The film's fashion reverberations continued for months.

In one of the greatest honors of Arden's life, the French government recognized her long and influential contributions with the order of Chevalier de la Légion d'honneur in 1961. It was given "as a token of appreciation by the French for all that she has done to facilitate trade and goodwill in the fields of beauty and couture between France and other countries."[19] Gladys had earned the same award after World War II. Arden told Hedda Hopper she was "just thrilled" about it; her Christmas card photograph for that year was of the moment when Ambassador Hervé Alphand presented her with the Legion of Honor in Washington, D.C.[20]

AGE, THE ULTIMATE ENEMY, seemed finally to catch up to Arden in the 1960s. Progressively frequent bouts of poor health confined her to her oversize, round bed.[21] In September 1960, she missed the Cradle fundraiser for the first time ever.[22] In 1961, she broke her wrist. Another hard blow was Carmel Snow's death that spring. She had not been long with Arden as an employee, but the two women had worked in overlapping fields for almost thirty years. They shared a passionate belief in the importance of holding the line of high fashion. "She led the American woman," Snow's obituary accurately stated, "down the intricately demanding and seasonally shifting paths of style with imagination and taste."[23]

Later that year, Arden's sister Lillian became the first of the four Graham girls to pass away. Lillian had lived in Connecticut, close enough to Manhattan for frequent visits. Like many other family members, Lillian worked for the company. She held an executive job on the cosmetics side for twenty-five years.[24] Another sorrow followed when, in early 1962, longtime friend and trusted associate Teddy Haslam died. He ably ran the European arm of the Arden company for decades. Just before his death, he managed to land a substantial sales order from behind the Iron Curtain.[25] Gordon Yates took over the U.K. division. An employee since 1929, Yates was well positioned to step into Haslam's shoes, but he could never replace Teddy in Arden's heart.[26]

In 1963, after a difficult spell, Arden had her gall bladder removed.

She visited Maine Chance only once in that year, for a brief, three-day stay. Employee Jake Gordon recalled that "most of the staff were frightened to death" of her, because "if she was unhappy, look out." During the drive from the airport, Arden did not converse with Gordon, and he followed the instructions he was given by the spa director to keep both hands on the wheel and to go eighty miles per hour "on the straightaways" because Arden "didn't like to waste time." Gordon put it down to the "idiosyncrasies of an old lady who was accustomed to having her own way," but ill health factored in, too.[27] Nothing was more frustrating than inactivity to a woman used to traveling more than one hundred thousand miles each year, unless it was sickness—a bitter pill for the world's most famous purveyor of good health.[28]

Business worries clouded her horizon. The entire cosmetics industry felt threatened by the FDA's plan to ban seventeen lipstick colors under the Food, Drug, and Cosmetic Act that required all synthetic colors to prove safe in lab tests. Rats reacted badly to some lipstick dyes, so the FDA called for those to be phased out immediately. Since the ruling would affect all lipstick makers, the Toilet Goods Association (TGA) stood up for the producers. The TGA pointed out that for more than a quarter century the dyes had been used without any human becoming ill. While both sides agreed that the current laws needed clarification and amendment, the FDA did not back down.[29] The thought of having to reimagine the hundreds of lipstick colors in Elizabeth Arden's warehouses—all but one of which she had carefully created herself— was enough to keep her under the bedcovers for months.

As was, no doubt, Drew Pearson's 1960 column accusing her of "pulling wires behind the scenes" to slow the regulatory process and thereby "embarrass" the FDA. Arden's power, Pearson wrote, originated, as he had earlier alleged, from a quid pro quo: the inappropriate and free "considerable hospitality" she had provided First Lady Mamie Eisenhower at Maine Chance Phoenix. Arden hit back so hard that Pearson apologized. He held firm, though, to his charge that Arden had granted an improper favor to Mamie because Maydelle Bankston had called the visit complimentary. The fact that "Miss Arden's spokesman in New York now denies the statement of her Phoenix manager" changed nothing in Pearson's mind. The episode made Arden look out of touch and not fully in control of her business.[30]

In between illnesses, Arden moved from racetrack to factory, from factory to salon, from the United States to Europe, overseeing the business, fundraising for charities, and charming interviewers. "Ruler of the first global beauty domain, she proved to be neither a dowager empress nor mysterious high priestess," one wrote with relief. "She's more of a queen mother. Very human. Very warm. And very sensible."[31] A group of reporters asked her how she fit into her day all the activities she suggested for others while also running an international business. Early to bed, early to rise, she insisted, and exercise—in which, she laughed, her dog joined her. Then facial, bath, breakfast, and "telephoning." To the office by 10:00 a.m. for updates from around the world. After lunch, meetings with "chemists, advertising people, then perhaps a trip to her Long Island factory where," Arden beamed, "'I make all my own colors.'" Demonstrating by blending lipstick shades on a pad of white paper, she looked the picture of "a charming woman who truly delights in her work, even the simplest task." One brave journalist broached the topic of marriage: "I'm too busy to think about it," Arden shot back. "With all the rest of my business I wouldn't know how to cope with a husband."[32]

Besides, she called her employees family, an appellation that appeared frequently in Arden company promotional materials. Refresher courses, her letters to her workforce, and her visits to her salons, factories, laboratories, and sales counters built camaraderie. So did the good-natured Arden factory-based soccer teams in Europe. The first international competition occurred as the Italian Arden team met their Swiss counterparts in 1965. An audience of one hundred Arden workers watched the athletes—all stylishly kitted out in uniforms designed with a version of the Arden for Men horse symbol—take the field. Zurich hair-stylist Carl Rappauer scored the winning goal and held aloft the silver victory cup. According to the *Elizabeth Arden News*, the amity behind the soccer tournament "really was a living example of what the words 'Elizabeth Arden Family' mean."[33]

Keeping up with the times had never been difficult for Arden. She adapted easily when the 1960s "youthquake"—as Diana Vreeland named it—began. Arden hired Lenny Newton of Killer Joe Piro's Dance Studio to teach her dinner guests the newest dance mania, the Twist. Her party, in honor of visiting French fashion designer Jean Dessès, "exploded" merrily when "bodies that hadn't turned right or left in twenty years became experts." The event was a great success, and Dessès said he looked forward to introducing the Twist to his Parisian friends.[34] Hedda Hopper joked that afterward she "twisted all over New York—grandest exercise I have ever come across."[35] One month later Arden created a lipstick color she titled "Let's Dance."[36]

The 1960s brought "a real revolution in beauty," *Vogue* declared. Who was part of it? Despite entering her eighties, Elizabeth Arden was chic and cutting-edge with new, smudgy under-eye effects starring her kohl and false eyelashes.[37] Still committed to her trademark understated look, Arden maintained that "make-up misses the point when it is too extreme." She sought the sweet spot between so trendy as to be bizarre and so old-fashioned as to be forgotten.[38] Her initial assistant was painter turned makeup expert Baron Gerard de la Boudinière, imported from Europe to demonstrate imaginative and highly complicated looks for eyes.[39] Her newest French "artistic and technical director of hair styling," M. Norbert, set the tone for fashion-forward 1960s hair.[40] He also developed Arden's "Beauty Passport," a handy set of three annotated drawings—"front, back and profile"—made by the stylist and tucked into a passport holder for the client to carry to any of the fifty Arden beauty salons worldwide. And such jet-setting women could pay for their treatments with "Beauty Checks," pink traveler's checks that could be spent in any Arden salon, obviating the need for local currency.[41]

A different sort of advertising was just starting, and this Arden embraced. She agreed to feature her products in color ads on envelopes carrying salon or department store bills. She eschewed more pedestrian outlets, such as milk cartons, grocery bags, and paperback books.[42] Innovative advertising had its uses, but Arden remained committed to the beautiful and the verbose, spinning out magical tales of a life enhanced by her toiletries or providing application guidance.

Arden went in for another brand-new sales vehicle called Moviematic machines, which looked like televisions. They sat on Arden counters and screened her fifteen-minute film. Saleswomen provided running commentary for the story of a secretary readying for an evening's appointment, from makeup removal through Blue Grass bath, to makeup reapplication. In a cloud of on-screen perfume, she sailed beautifully and happily out the door. As the show ended, the clerks pitched to viewers with a focus on the products featured on the Moviematic.[43]

In a twist on an older idea, Elizabeth Arden's perfumes became an ambient element of the Art Institute of Chicago's benefit exhibition of floral paintings. Arden scents wafted throughout the gallery as visitors viewed the art. It's "Smellovision," the benefit chair chuckled, as he handed out Arden samples to one hundred lucky women.[44]

The foreshock of the 1960s' youthquake was teenagers. From *Mademoiselle* magazine to Fashion Group newsletters, high schoolers stole the glamour headlines. There were twenty-three million teenagers in America in 1963, and that number was increasing. Twenty percent of the cosmetics industry was dedicated to teens because they spent some $300 million on toiletries. Young females were 10 percent of the nation's total population, but they accounted for a quarter of "the total toiletries dollar."[45] The editor of *Seventeen* magazine urged producers and retailers to "think young in everything you do." Don't condescend to teenagers; market to them! She suggested installing a "young cosmetics bar" at every makeup counter so young women could have the joy of experimenting with different colors.[46] One study revealed that girls developed loyalty to a brand between the ages of twelve and fourteen.[47]

An Elizabeth Arden spokeswoman who led makeup classes for young women—as Arden had been doing for many years—knew that teenagers loved learning in one-on-one tutorials: "The individual attention they receive impresses them and makes them feel important." On the other hand, as a wise teen herself observed, "We pay for these courses and when you pay for something yourself, you appreciate it much more."[48] When Bullock's put on a three-part television show for teens and college women, complete with forty female and six male models, plus the era's obligatory folk singers, Arden did all the makeup and gained all the publicity among that important young target audience.[49]

As she had done since the 1930s, Arden also calibrated her treatments to ingenues, and incorporated "young" elements into older ideas, such as adding an instructional record album to her new "Sound of Beauty" box.[50] The companion booklet promised that faithful attention to Arden's advice would "train her hands . . . to form, early and firmly and effortlessly, the good habits that constitute the only beauty insurance there is."[51]

Women made up a third of the workforce by 1960, another figure that rose throughout the decade. While a definable women's movement was still in the future, it germinated underground. President Kennedy created a Commission on the Status of Women in 1961, chaired by Eleanor Roosevelt. The commission released its report in 1963, the same year that Betty Friedan published her groundbreaking book *The Feminine Mystique*. Women in positions of governmental, corporate, and societal power were much more prevalent than when Arden started out. A sweeping sense of sex-based injustice and possibility simmered among women of all backgrounds, ethnicities, and classes. Following the powerful example of the civil rights movement and spurred by the energy of youth, women in the early 1960s asked more insistent questions about their role and status. Shirley Chisholm, Bella Abzug, Dolores Huerta, Ruth Bader Ginsburg, Gloria Steinem, and the members of Women Strike for Peace were among many turning to larger, organized activity. The Equal Pay Act of 1963 kept women's concerns at the top of the nation's consciousness before the National Organization for Women formed in 1966. Arden's entire life attested to her certain belief in the abilities of women, and she could only have been thrilled to see broader institutional support for ideas she personified.

One interesting project to which Arden contributed aimed "to train Moslem girls to be self-supporting." As the head of a global company, she had more experience with international affairs than most Americans and wanted to assist the United Nations Relief and Works Agency as it established the first Vocational and Teacher Training Centre for Girls. The goal was to help young women learn skills leading to self-sufficiency. She flew one of her experts to Jordan to instruct female refugees from what had been, until 1948, Palestine. Arden's representative in Ramallah taught classes that added to the young women's preparation in career fields including "secretaries, clerks, institution managers, preparatory nurses, dressmakers . . . hairdressers and beauticians." Elizabeth Arden pledged to hire "the most proficient" graduate.[52]

Arden's next big designer proved that her trend-detecting abilities were still sharp. She began negotiations with a young man from Lanvin-Castillo named Oscar de la Renta. So impressed was she that she brought him in at the extravagant annual salary of $36,400 in early 1963. Arden's support of de la Renta, like James, Castillo, and Sarmi before him, gave wings to what became an extraordinary career.[53]

Born in 1932 in the Dominican Republic, de la Renta studied painting in Spain, but gravitated to fashion in part with the help of Arden's friend and onetime employee Francesca Lodge. A Parisian apprenticeship began under Cristóbal Balenciaga and concluded with three years as Castillo's tailoring assistant.[54] De la Renta approached Arden after consulting with *Vogue* fashion editor Diana Vreeland. He told her of his desire to enter the lucrative ready-to-wear field. Vreeland famously advised him that the only place he could avoid standing in the shadow of Christian Dior's white-hot fame and escape a boss meddling in his designs was at Arden's. "Go to Arden because you will make your reputation faster," she emphasized. And, de la Renta confirmed, "that is exactly what happened."[55] Arden's unmatched "talent for picking the talented ones" continued, as de la Renta joined the prestigious list of haute couturiers whom Arden selected, sponsored, and turned into legends.[56]

Many great designers became household names in the 1950s and '60s: Balenciaga, Valentino, Galanos, Quant, and Scaasi. Older designers still working, such as Sarmi, Dior, Castillo, and Carnegie, added to the luster of high fashion. De la Renta quickly joined their ranks. His ready-to-wear or custom-made creations could be purchased at Arden's salon. Women who came to her Red Doors for treatments and hairstyling gladly stayed for the fashion shows aimed at the "elegant, conservative, traveled woman-of-the-world . . . rang[ing] from a debutante to a society matron." High-profile Arden clients then included Ethel Kennedy, Patricia Kennedy Lawford, and Happy Rockefeller, New York's First Lady. Women in their twenties and thirties also found de la Renta's designs to their tastes as he crafted graceful, uncomplicated clothing with broad generational appeal.[57]

His first show, in March 1963, demonstrated the range of his vision: "elegantly simple suits and coats," sparkling A-line evening gowns, and "*jeune fille* embroidered organdy party dresses," nearly all in a spectacular color array.[58] The response was overwhelmingly positive. He paints "a summer fashion picture as delicately lovely as a Fragonard or Watteau canvas," one reviewer wrote, describing exactly Arden's lifelong tastes. Suddenly de la Renta creations were the talk of the nation.[59]

As Carmel Snow had done, de la Renta also assisted Arden by selecting designs from Parisian couturiers that Arden's seamstresses copied for her U.S. market.[60] Arden sold other designers, including Vera Maxwell, John Moore, Federico Forquet, and Fira Benenson.[61] But de la Renta was her star. She always made a point of wearing the clothing of her main designer and of featuring only his line at her many benefits. Her 1964 fashion shows were all about de la Renta's obsession with black lace, brocade, and mink. On the Chicago Cradle runway, the clothing was "every bit as well bred," one reporter wrote, "as the woman to whom her clothes appeal."[62] It was Arden who gave "the ladies who lunch" their look.

The pair worked well together, and shared a similar sensibility. De la Renta's reading of his boss's archetype was "romantic, beautiful, ladylike, and serene" even though she was the one who "decrees the length of her hemlines and the cut of her clothes," *The New York Times* sagely observed.[63] It was a rich and rewarding period, but brief. As his accolades, prices, and clientele steadily increased, he looked for another opportunity. In March 1965, he found it at the design studio of Jane Derby.[64]

As de la Renta prepared to leave Arden, she received sad personal news. In the summer of 1964, her niece Beatrice Graham died. Beatrice had enjoyed a brief acting career before marrying, having a child, and devoting herself to her family. Then, less than three months later, Beatrice's sister Virginia passed away. While Arden loved all three of her brother's daughters, she was very close to Virginia. Virginia had been an Arden executive for decades and served as her contact to the Kappa Kappa Gammas.[65] Arden laid both nieces to rest in Sleepy Hollow Cemetery in New York, next to sister Lillian and Virginia's husband, Edward, who had also recently died.[66]

Alongside Arden's grief, business continued. After several months of rumors, a surprising headline read: "Elizabeth Arden and Castillo Reunited."[67] She persuaded him to return because "he is the best there is today in all of Paris." "We are old friends," he agreed, as the first model stepped out to debut his fall and winter collection before an eager audience of four hundred at Arden's salon on Fifth Avenue. "I can never forget what she has done for me. I agreed to design this collection, and the next. After that, we shall have to see," he shrugged, because his Paris showroom still required his presence.[68] Weeks later, Castillo won the *Sunday Times* of London Fashion Award for France, another feather in Arden's cap.[69]

The sixty garments in Castillo's spring show landed well with conservative women "who neither expected nor wanted fashion surprises, and were not handed any." No André Courrèges mods, no miniskirts and boots, no outré couture. Castillo's brightly saturated colors—hot pink, brilliant aquamarine—were enough of a nod to the youth trend. Arden's cosmetic artist, Pablo, and his "Fragile" makeup, perfected by the whimsical handiwork of her hairstylist Imo, matched the flowery spring look. She had created a design dream team that pulled together harmoniously to charm the traditional Red Door customer with just the right amount of edginess.[70]

Pablo smoothed the transfer of genius from de la Renta back to Castillo. Dashing and aristocratic, Count Pablo Manzoni got his start at Rome's Red Door salon when he was seventeen. He moved to Manhattan when he was twenty-four and single-handedly upended the makeup world. Arden called him "the Picasso of eye makeup."[71] His designs were dramatic, shocking. *Vogue* put his "ornamental zebra eye" on the September 1964 cover and his disco look on December's. Soon Pablo extended his craze for "ornamental eyes" to eyelids and eyebrows, which he decked with jewel mosaics, lace, butterfly wings, and peacock feathers (some real, some painted on), in designs that latter-day Goths and steampunk votaries would emulate.[72]

Pablo was *the* fashion story of the year. Women waited in lines to have him create a face for them. Brides wanted his "Fragile" look, society women opted for his big-eyed, "squared" treatment, and night owls clamored for his "switched-on" discotheque makeup with rhinestone rows under, on, and over the eyelid.[73] Because of him, 1964 was the "Year of the Eye." So pervasive and instant was Pablo's effect on fashion that he attracted the world's most stylish women, inspired copycats, and earned extravagant praise. He was a true sensation.

Arden introduced Pablo's disco style when she turned the 1964 New York Couture Week runway fashion show into an electric dance party. She hired "Killer Joe" Piro to teach the fashion reporters the Frug, the Watusi, and the Chicken as Louis Armstrong's "Hello, Dolly!" blared. Arden, smart in de la Renta, urged the amazed audience to their feet. "The new evening life in America heralds a new face," the octogenarian beauty maven decreed, as she showed off her fantastic visagiste.[74]

Customers paid $20 per half hour to learn from Pablo, "an untemperamental, sensible young man who does not believe that sequined eyelids are to be worn in the supermarkets." He loved teaching, had strong opinions about cosmetics, could rave about Arden products with genuine enthusiasm, and took his honors and his prestigious client list in stride. It was quite the roster of stars who made their way to Arden's salon for his makeover: Jackie Kennedy, the Duchess of Windsor, Gloria Vanderbilt, Sophia Loren, Twiggy, Bianca Jagger, Maria Callas, and Raquel Welch.[75]

To assist his artistry, alongside the kohl, desert green lids, and three sets of false eyelashes (which she called "Leap Your Lashes"), Arden devised new colors, such as "Fragile Pink." Sold in a diminutive crate labeled "Fragile—Handle with Care," it came packaged with three other eye shadow colors: pale yellow-green, ivory, and light beige.[76] Augmented with a popular pale blue, Pablo used it to create variations on his subtle, understated Fragile face as he toured her U.S. salons in 1964.[77] His daytime styles were sensationally popular, too, and as they evolved, Arden kept up, selling the cosmetics and colors he used and that women purchased to re-create the look at home.

Despite his youth, in 1965 he won a special Coty Fashion Critics Award—the first ever given "for face design" and "the highest accolade the fashion world bestows." For twenty-three years he was known as Pablo of Elizabeth Arden (he said after he left that his blood had turned pink by that time!), the recognized leader of a growing field of professional makeup artists hired by salons, society women, and celebrities at ever-skyrocketing salaries.[78]

Another brilliant Arden Italian import was hairstylist Imo Ughini. His designs hearkened to the "'sweet' woman of the nineteen-thirties." Imo proclaimed himself sick of long, straight hair that covered the eyes and the nape of the neck. He opted for soft waves, a shorter length, and the abandonment of high bouffants and back-combing. Such coiffures perfectly complemented the Fragile look, as well as Pablo's spring makeup styles: "freshly scrubbed . . . wide-eyed and innocent," in "limpid watercolor shades."[79] What made the covers of fashion magazines, however, were his wild, loopy upsweeps, with braids and curls that looked as though they had been set with soup cans. These dramatic hairdos paired perfectly with de la Renta and Castillo's most avant-garde fashions and the newest wizardry of Pablo: rhinestones, pearls, and gems for shoulders, arms, legs, and toes, in a look straight from *Scheherazade*.[80]

In 1965, Arden was eighty-three, but only admitted to seventy-four.[81] At either age, she didn't remain merely relevant, she set trends. *The New York Times* confirmed her membership in the "In Crowd," the top one hundred "wealthiest, most famous, and most creative people, an enormously influential social, intellectual and cultural elite." Oscar de la Renta was one of four "In" designers. Elisabeth Marbury surely would have been proud to know that Jerome Zerbe, in his *The Art of Social Climbing*, pronounced Arden's the chicest place to purchase clothing. The In Crowd "replaced the Four Hundred, Café Society, and the Jet Set." They raised money, made or supported on-point artistic statements, and were not limited by race, religion, or pedigree.[82]

By way of example, Arden was an early underwriter of Maestro Leopold Stokowski's newly formed American Symphony Orchestra (ASO), whose purpose was to demystify and showcase contemporary classical music. She opened her penthouse for a private concert in order, she said, "to help" the conductor, "a wonderful man," who, by creating the ASO had "done such lovely things for New York." She donated $5,000 (around $50,000 today) for the privilege of having a professional ASO quartet entertain her friends, whom she then encouraged to support the orchestra.[83]

Arden remained, above all else, a savvy and experienced business-woman. She hired innovative designers and pushed their state-of-the-art creations out to *Vogue*, *Cosmopolitan*, and emerging high-fashion magazines, even as she tailored the majority of her clothing to her base. She did not believe, as her friend Andy Warhol predicted, that "clothes will disappear" just because skirts were four inches above the knee and climbing. She took a dim view of middle-aged women wearing mini-skirts, but then, pragmatically, she also had an exercise plan for achieving lovely knees, unlike Avon, Revlon, or Rubinstein.[84] While no photo exists of Arden wearing slacks, she nonetheless sold them and allowed customers to wear them in her salons at a time when women were barred from many restaurants and clubs—including the Jockey Club—for donning pants.[85] She rolled with the times, teaching and selling the Arden look while responding to social and economic changes.

Tennis increased in popularity in the 1960s. Rather than bemoaning the lack of becoming court clothing for women of a certain age, Arden decided to do something about it. She hired professional athlete Virginia Rice Johnson to devise costumes cut for ease of movement with both short and long hemlines, decorated with eyelet and Arden Pink. She opened a Tennis Boutique in her salons and introduced the line to the public at a fashion show where Pablo made up the models in false eyelashes "long enough," *The New York Times* winked, "to replace the old-fashioned visor as sun-shades."[86]

Pica poles—Arden's newest way to grow supple and slender—were invented by a Spanish military officer and favored by Antoinette, Arden's exercise director, who created "dazzling routines" of bending, stretching, lunging, and dipping using two slender, mobile poles attached to a base. The muscle resistance coupled with the movement of the poles, done to music, attracted professional dancers and other athletes interested in grace as well as strength.[87] Picas became all the rage for a time and were evidence of Arden's desire to remain an industry leader in the field of exercise.

Arden constantly updated her male toiletries line. Facial moisturizer and an aerosol hair spray for men were new products in her black-and-gold containers—not, as one young Harvard grad suggested, in a package that looked like a beer can.[88] By 1966, Arden for Men accounted for 12 percent of sales, and, satisfyingly, had "tripled in volume in the last three years."[89]

The Black American middle class expanded after World War II, and the 1950s civil rights movement rendered the nation's inequalities and injustices impossible to ignore. Black activism forced retailers like Elizabeth Arden to pay attention. Nineteen sixty-one was the first year that evidence appears for the presence of African American beauty experts in attendance at Arden's "Fashion Press Week." "Marlene," beauty journalist for *The Pittsburgh Courier*, included two photographs of M. Norbert's hairstyles that she suggested her readers "will be seeing (and trying we hope) this winter." Marlene especially loved Arden's Star Twinkle and her gold, silver, and two-toned "pearly green" eye shadows.[90] In 1963, Cleveland's *Call and Post* showed Arden in smiling conversation with that newspaper's fashion editor, Anita Polk. Polk described the week to her readers in detail, concluding, "Miss Arden was a gracious hostess, and because we have met her numerous times at her 'house,' she requested that we (*Call and Post* Writer) pose with her. She has begun a picture collection of the more than two hundred and fifty editors. You might not believe this. . . . But again, *Call and Post* was the first taken, [and] she asked for it!"[91] Black women certainly bought and used Arden toiletries; stage and screen star Diahann Carroll sought Pablo's artistry at an Arden salon. But societal change was glacial. Naomi Sims, considered the first Black supermodel, did not appear on a mainstream magazine cover in the United States until 1968, two years after Arden's death. Fashion Fair, an upscale cosmetics company created for Black women, began in 1973. Beverly Johnson made *Vogue*'s cover in 1974. Revlon aimed a short-lived cosmetic line at African American women in 1975. Throughout Elizabeth Arden's life, the color line in cosmetics remained every bit as firm as it was in society.[92]

ARDEN WAS BUSY with plans for modernizing her presence on Chicago's Near North Side. She sold the East Walton Place building for $440,000 and paid nearly twice that for property at the corner of North Michigan Avenue and East Superior Street on the city's Magnificent Mile.[93] She intended to build a seventeen-story replacement venue in a two-step process. First, four stories to contain office spaces along with treatment, beauty, and fashion salons, then thirteen stories to be added later.[94] She never took the second step, but the low-slung, striking Indiana limestone building enticed Tiffany and Florsheim to lease space in the Arden Building, while three blocks north the John Hancock Center began its unmistakable one-hundred-story climb into the sky.[95] With her niece Pat at her side, she cut the velvet ribbon opening Remisoff's interiors to view. Chicago boasted a permanent, on-site Arden for Men boutique and a room dedicated, thanks to Pablo's influence, exclusively to eyes. He was there, along with her hippest hair designers, a raft of "opulent" and "elegant" clothing, and an entourage of friends from New York. Close around Arden was the hometown phalanx from the Cradle, returning the support she had so long given the adoption agency.[96]

Her annual European sojourn in the early fall satisfactorily concluded, Arden returned for the 1964 presidential election season pitting Democrat Lyndon Johnson of Texas against Arizona Republican Barry Goldwater. Arden socialized with both political families. Lady Bird Johnson and her daughters were known to purchase the occasional Arden dress, and both Lady Bird and Peggy Goldwater frequented Maine Chance Phoenix. Probably scenting the political winds rightly, and because her health continued precarious, Elizabeth Arden maintained a low profile as either woman as First Lady would bring helpful publicity. When the Johnson landslide materialized, Arden, a houseguest of Democrat Perle Mesta for inauguration week, told reporter Betty Beale that she had voted for LBJ![97]

WITHOUT WARNING, on April Fool's Day in 1965, Helena Rubinstein died. Papers reported her age as ninety-four. Driven to the very end, she was in the office on Monday, fell ill on Tuesday, and passed away on Wednesday. Her company was overseen by the trustees who held the majority of Rubinstein stock, while three long-serving family members took over the day-to-day management of the large corporation.[98] Arden did not attend the funeral. Obituaries mentioned Madame's extensive art collection, the charitable work of the Helena Rubinstein Foundation, and her "intense and much-publicized rivalry" with Arden, repeating old myths about their never having met.[99]

Many years earlier, in 1941, Elaine Brown Keiffer penned a portrait of Rubinstein in *Life* magazine. She claimed that "the rivalry with Arden is the chief spur in Rubinstein's life."[100] The truth of that statement is not borne out by the facts. The competition between the two women was seldom written about during their lifetimes. In their final years and after their deaths, only a small number of people referred to it. Analyzing who was first with a skin care or makeup idea very quickly turns into a caliginous muddle, as all cosmeticians borrow from one another just as often as they rename and repackage their own items and call them new. Truly novel inventions stand out for that precise reason. In fact, the contest between Arden and Rubinstein was only a small part of a larger, industry-wide battle for status, customers, employees, column inches, new products, and influence. The two moguls understood they had much to fear from other luxury lines, such as Lenthéric, Dorothy Gray, and Charles of the Ritz. While Arden and Rubinstein did not closely compete with less expensive brands, still, any woman might pick up a tube of lipstick from Maybelline or Max Factor and find herself willing to try another. Challenges could come from anywhere at any time.

A whispered rivalry was not necessarily a bad thing. If the main goal was to make a profit, then one's name bruited about publicly had potential. A morsel of malevolence, a cantlet of cattiness kept a name and a brand circulating. It was rumored that each called the other "that woman." But then Arden supposedly referred to a number of male cosmetics executives as "that man," too. Keiffer quoted Rubinstein—in a distressing attempt to capture her Polish accent—saying, "Vee haf been at zee same parties, yes . . . but ve haf nevair met—nevair."[101] That is patently untrue. Arden and Rubinstein had attended the small luncheon that launched the Fashion Group. They had served together on committees. And they had dined, well-mannered, at the same table with First Lady Eleanor Roosevelt.

Keiffer's article suggested that the enmity between the two beauty bosses thrived because they poached each other's employees, yet those in the skin care, cosmetics, and fashion fields regularly switched jobs. The ubiquity of this fact caused Arden to write into her divorce papers, Keiffer disclosed, a clause forbidding Tom Lewis to "re-enter the beauty business for five years."[102] That's why, in 1939, Keiffer smirked, Helena Rubinstein immediately hired him. Whether Arden expected any sort of loyalty from the former husband who cheated on her is an open question. He had been, since 1936, president of a start-up called Dubin Laboratories that produced "Vi-Syneral," a vitamin-infused cod liver oil, which was a far step from the new line of men's products that Rubinstein wanted him to oversee—so perhaps she did hire Lewis to needle Arden.[103] A rivalry chiefly spurred creativity. It provided a juicy dinner topic for friends and enemies, mattering not a whit whether the tale was real or imagined. Both women were far more interesting than one-dimensional foils for a catfight.

IN AUGUST 1966, Arden had been schmoozing with the fashion cognoscenti in Paris. In September, she was traveling across the United Kingdom on her annual laborious business tour before returning to France to meet Castillo for lunch after an Yves Saint Laurent fashion show. She squeezed in a visit to Barretstown Castle, but a fall there briefly incapacitated her.[104] Later that month she was one of the beautiful people at the televised opening of the new Metropolitan Opera, joining Cecil Beaton, Ted and Joan Kennedy, Charles Revson, and Estée Lauder, among others. Even First Lady Lady Bird Johnson was there, providing remarks on the "milestone in music" as Leontyne Price starred in Samuel Barber's *Antony and Cleopatra*, controversially directed by Franco Zeffirelli.[105]

In early October, Elizabeth Arden attended a "champagne-brunch-fashion show" at a Cleveland department store to benefit the city's Musical Arts Association.[106] Returning briefly to her New York penthouse, she gathered her grandniece Vicki Graham and zoomed off to California for a benefit for the Maryvale orphanage. "It's a joy to be here," she glowed as the audience prepared to be wowed by Castillo's designs and Pablo's makeup. Sizing her up in her new "Pure Pure Red" lipstick, the *Los Angeles Times* pronounced Arden to be at her "Sparkling Best": "There were elegant fashions on the runway, champagne in silver buckets and beautiful people to enjoy them but the sparkle and bubble were where Elizabeth Arden Graham was," the paper noted. Present as the underwriter for the Orphanage Guild's benefit, Arden was "as spirited as the thoroughbreds she races," her sense of humor intact despite an injured knee. She wore Castillo, of course, but laughingly directed journalists' attention to a pin on her shoulder in the shape of a flower. "This is what I'm really proud of. . . . It was designed by someone I think is in jail now. I don't know how he got the rubies."[107] It was perhaps her last good day. Another tumble reinjured her knee, requiring her to miss the Cradle Society benefit in Chicago on October 12. She sent her regrets and deputized her friend Serge Obolensky and her niece Pat Young to take her place.[108]

Arden's physical stamina was considerable. She somehow got herself to Belmont for what turned out to be one final weekend among the horses that brought her contentment. Once at home, she was uncharacteristically slow to leave her bed. Pat summoned the physician. On Monday, October 17, he admitted Arden to Lenox Hill Hospital, where she succumbed to a heart attack. No one could really believe the news the next day: the ageless, peerless, pathbreaking Elizabeth Arden was dead.[109]

Afterword

The only choice was the "undertaker to the stars," Frank E. Campbell. There, Arden, like the great and the good before her, the celebrities from the arts, business, politics, religion, and sports, lay in discreet but undeniable splendor as mourners paid their respects. Masses of pink flowers filled the funeral parlor's five large rooms. One white floral cross stood out. Its card read: "Ike and Mamie."[1]

Arden's funeral was held at St. James' Episcopal Church, which had been, like Lenox Hill Hospital, a frequent recipient of her largesse. Behind family members from Canada, Europe, California, and New York, one thousand mourners arrayed themselves. Her former husband "Prince" Michael Evlanoff was there, along with stage and screen actors, "bankers and financiers, former diplomats, editors of leading fashion magazines and presidents of the race tracks at which her horses ran." Perhaps nicest of all were what *The New York Times* described as "socially prominent women who regularly visited her salons here and abroad and who had become personal friends."[2]

Encomiums rolled in. "I'm crying for the first time in my life,"

Castillo admitted.[3] "I feel," Charles Revson said, "the industry has lost one of its greatest creators, one of its finest contributors." The head of Charles of the Ritz credited her as "the first to coordinate a complete line of products for the skin and if only for this, she deserved a medal." *Women's Wear Daily* called Arden "one of the greatest of any 20th Century businesswomen." Organizations with which she worked, like the American Women's Voluntary Services and the American Friends of France, recorded their sorrow. Racecourse flags flew at half-mast.[4]

She was buried near family members in Sleepy Hollow Cemetery. It was Elizabeth Arden's final presentation. Located in Tarrytown, then a stylish suburban village fewer than thirty miles from her Manhattan penthouse, the cemetery nestles in hills overlooking the Hudson River. Locals and tourists are drawn today to its undulant, winding paths. In the spring, ancient lilacs and pink azaleas adorn stunning nineteenth-century mausoleums. Spectacular fall colors enhance hauntingly lovely memorials by Augustus Saint-Gaudens and Andrew O'Connor. It would be difficult to imagine a final resting place more beautiful.

Sleepy Hollow is renowned because of the short story by American author Washington Irving. He lived nearby in a home called Sunnyside and lies in an unassuming grave in the cemetery. In 1820, Irving wrote "The Legend of Sleepy Hollow," featuring the Headless Horseman and set in "Tarry Town." Every October, Tarrytown makes much of Irving's ghostly tale, with after-dark graveyard tours, a Halloween parade, a haunted hayride, and a several-thousand-strong jack-o'-lantern "blaze" at the nearby Van Cortlandt Manor.

But for the rest of the year, Sleepy Hollow's fame rests on those buried there. Among the artists and philanthropists are titans of American industry: Andrew Carnegie, Walter Chrysler, William Rockefeller, Ogden Mills, and IBM founder Thomas Watson. Elizabeth Arden chose as her eternal colleagues a constellation of America's wealthiest capitalists. Beneath the breathy voice, the perfume clouds, the yards of designer pink finery, she knew who she was: Florence Nightingale Graham, the tough, uncompromising business genius who built a global company from the ground up—with no formal education and despite naysayers. The successful-by-any-measure entrepreneur who made wearing makeup not just possible, but desirable. Who taught women that self-care was not just indulgence but an aid to achievement. Who insisted that health was the foundation of beauty, but that beauty, ultimately, was power. She changed not just American business but American culture. Elizabeth Arden could have been buried almost anywhere. But she put herself among her equals.

And yet in an inscrutable act of humility—or perhaps reflecting the lived experience of a clear separation between Elizabeth Arden and Florence Nightingale Graham—Arden neither built a monument nor inscribed forever the name that made her famous. The family marker simply states "Graham." In front are five plain stones laid flat amid the well-tended grass. They designate the graves of her sister-in-law, Ada, and Ada's three daughters, Beatrice, Pat, and Virginia. There is also a stone for Martha Brown that records "Born Bellaghy, Ireland, April 22, 1867, died New York, February 5, 1943." Brown appears to have been a maid. Arden shares a marker with her sister. It reads "Lillian Graham, 1877–1961," and underneath is chiseled "Elizabeth N. Graham, 1966." Even in death, Arden kept her age a secret, a pardonable vanity.

A modest Celtic cross stands before the grave of Andrew Carnegie, once the nation's richest man. William Rockefeller, cofounder of global petroleum powerhouse Standard Oil, lies in an imposing, classically inspired mausoleum. Arden felt her business accomplishments entitled her to share their burial ground. Her choice of an unpretentious grave, and a family plot, at that, her avoidance of her business name, the interment of her maid, a fashionable cemetery in a location with which she had no obvious connection—how to understand the mixed messages at the conclusion of her life?

Perhaps it was only this: she had made good; she was grateful to the women of her family. Maybe it was best not to tempt the Deity by gloating overmuch at the end. Understatement had, after all, been her stock-in-trade. She was confident in her success and trusted that Elizabeth Arden would not be forgotten. After a lifetime of hard work, she expected to rest in beauty by her family and alongside her professional peers.

OR PERHAPS THE STORY ENDS another way: with Elizabeth Arden so committed to anti-aging that she believed she would live forever. At her death, her personal and her professional finances, though vast, were in such chaos that they took years to sort out. Initial estimates put her estate in the range of $30 million to $50 million. Arden left $4 million to Gladys, who remained in charge of the business in France, where her son, John (who inherited $1 million from his aunt), also worked.[5] The bulk of Arden's estate, including her art, furniture, and jewelry, went to her niece Patricia Graham Young. Arden left substantial funds to her maid and chauffeur and dictated that $1.3 million be divided among employees who had worked for the company for ten or more years. There were many of them. An internal study found that the average length of service of Arden employees was "over thirty years."[6] Characteristically, Arden made special provisions for her horses, stipulating that mares and their foals must be sold together.[7] Maine Chance Farm became part of the equine and agricultural research program of the University of Kentucky.[8] The two Maine Chance Spas remained open in the years immediately following Arden's demise, but faced increasing competition from newer challengers.[9]

Arden made no firm plans for her company's continuance after her death. Most people thought she would hand over command to Gladys or Pat, but that did not happen. Instead, Carl Gardiner took the helm. Her loyal executive vice president since 1948, Gardiner said he had had "personal contact or telephone conversation with [Elizabeth Arden] every day for 19 years."[10] The two were so close that she left Gardiner a bequest of $250,000. She also left him a financial mess, plus an estimated $35 million corporate tax bill. The first thing Gardiner did was axe Arden's Fashion Floor, putting the tailors and seamstresses out of work. He focused instead on off-the-rack designer garments, cutting prices substantially to encourage purchases. Gardiner then decided to open Arden salons in shopping centers, decrease the number of products available, and promote the men's line more aggressively.[11]

Over the years, the company survived the anti-makeup backlash of the 1970s feminist movement and a succession of corporate takeovers. Eli Lilly came first in 1971, followed by Fabergé in 1987, Unilever in 2003, and then Revlon in 2016. Each maintained the Elizabeth Arden name and capitalized on Arden's reputation for luxury and elegance. Eight Hour Cream and Blue Grass perfume remain on the shelves today, but Red Door is the current signature perfume. Carl Gardiner's presidency set a precedent, lasting over half a century. Not until 2018, when Revlon made Debra Golding Perelman its first female CEO, was a woman finally back in charge of Elizabeth Arden. Covid shuttered the last of the salons, but the Arden brand lives on, more than 110 years after its founding, available in good department stores and through online Red Doors.[12]

FROM THE HUMBLEST OF ORIGINS, pioneering businesswoman Elizabeth Arden grew into a global industry leader. A creative genius at marketing, at timing her innovations, and at brand strategy, she exhibited a strong grasp of the psychology of influence decades before it was studied by business researchers. Her many contributions helped construct the culture of our own time. Before Arden, only sex workers wore makeup. Today, anyone can. Before Arden, rest, relaxation, and taking time for oneself were considered sybaritic, slightly sinful, and the exclusive purview of the rich. The notion that women should slow down and take care of themselves is now part of the broader culture—if still too often ignored. Elizabeth Arden conceived of a holistic understanding of beauty decades before today's superstar influencers like Kate Hudson and Gwyneth Paltrow urged women to watch what they put in and on their bodies. Arden was a lifestyle coach who created a multifaceted business empire echoed in the careers of Jessica Alba, Rachael Ray, and Martha Stewart. Arden's life and work reversed deeply held paradigms. Thanks to her, we know that makeup can be a way to express oneself and that whole-body care leads to greater happiness and success. She brought about these enormous cultural shifts with the ideals she held her entire life. Elizabeth Arden's story thus ends where it began: with her determination, her unwavering belief in her own abilities, and her passionate conviction that every woman deserves to be beautiful.

Acknowledgments

The great Diana Nyad said recently of her career as a marathon swimmer, "It looks like a solitary sport, but it's a team." The same, I happily admit, is true for book writing, and as this project draws to a close, I am glad to acknowledge my sincere thanks to the many people who helped and supported me.

I must begin with my cherished friends Dr. Lewis L. Gould and his marvelous wife, Jeanne Robeson, because it was they who suggested Elizabeth Arden as a topic. For more than forty years Lew Gould has been my teacher, role model, inspiration, and guide. I could ask for no truer North Star.

Fortunate is the scholar with academic colleagues willing to share their time and knowledge. Mine include Michael D. Bailey, Fran Becque, Jeremy Best, Jeff Bremer, Nora Carleson, Catherine Clay, Wayne Duerkes, Robert C. Hale, Martin Holland, Theresa Kaminski, Richard Kehrberg, Heath Lee, Lawrence McDonnell, John Warne Monroe, Einav Rabinovitch-Fox, Dirk Ringgenberg, Alisa Roost, Larry Rudiger, Amy Rutenberg, Lisa Walker, Daniel Weinbren, Timothy Wolters, and Amy Wood. Drs. Julie Courtwright, Pamela Riney-Kehrberg, and I formed a happy and productive writing group. Any errors of interpretation are mine, of course.

Historians depend upon primary sources—often documents in archives—to research, analyze, and write about their subjects. Functioning democracies rest, in part, upon historians writing as accurately, objectively, and dispassionately as possible. By providing access to documents and suggesting collections and research avenues, archivists are essential to this process. When Covid closed archives and stymied travel, they responded heroically, answering frantic emails, locating documents, waiving fees, speeding up delivery, and commiserating. On behalf of all professional historians, thank you.

Thanks especially to Pamela Cruz, who tapped her Society of American Archivists network to confirm my suspicion that there are no public collections of Elizabeth Arden's personal papers. I am grateful to SAA members who responded to her query, especially Ellen Chapman, Garret B. Kremer-Wright, and Lindy Narver.

I also appreciate the work of the following archivists who helped me, either online or in person: Jill Shaw, City of Vaughan, Ontario, Archives & Records Management; Aimee E. Brown, Kathryn A. Martin Library Archives and Special Collections, University of Minnesota, Duluth; Jim Davies, British Airways Museum, British Airways Speedbird Centre, Harmondsworth, United Kingdom; Grace Wagner and Annie Trizna, Special Collections Research Center, Syracuse University; Jena P. Jones and Serena McCracken, Kenan Research Center, Atlanta History Center; Grace Bichler, Division of Rare and Manuscript Collections, Cornell University Library; Micha Broadnax, Library, Information, and Technology Services, Mount Holyoke College; Sylvia Hernandez, The Texas Collection, Baylor University; Anne Price, Townsend Memorial Library, University of Mary Hardin-Baylor; Beth Norvell, Museum at the Parker House and Alumni Engagement, University of Mary Hardin-Baylor; Amanda Nelson, Special Collections & Archives, Olin Library, Wesleyan University; Linnea M. Anderson, Social Welfare History Archives, Elmer L. Andersen Library, University of Minnesota; Natalie Navar Garcia, Lawrence B. De Graaf Center for Oral and Public History, California State University, Fullerton; Craig Wright, Supervisory Archivist, Herbert Hoover Presidential Library; Crystal Toscano, Patricia D. Klingenstein Library, The New-York Historical Society; Rebecca Goldman, Special Collections, Margaret Clapp Library, Wellesley College; Kevin Cason, Tennessee State Library & Archives; David Rose, March of Dimes Archives; Sam Grate, Auburn Cord Duesenberg Automobile Museum, Auburn, Indiana; Paul Ayres, Cadillac & LaSalle Club Museum and Research Center, Dexter, Michigan; Evelina Stulgaityte, Tarlton Law Library, University of Texas at Austin; Susan Gillis, Boca Raton Historical Society & Museum; Martha Tenney, Barnard College Archives & Special Collections; Jessica Guardado, William H. Hannon Library, Loyola Marymount University, Los Angeles; Sophie Denman and Sebastian Wormell, Harrods Company Archive, London; Beth Ann Koelsch, The Betty H. Carter Women Veterans Historical Project, Hodges Special Collections & University Archives, the University of North Carolina, Greensboro; Kristine Krueger, Academy of Motion Picture Arts and Sciences, Margaret Herrick Library, Beverly Hills; Allison Smith, Special Collections, Neilson Library, Smith College; Amber L. Dushman, Department of Records Management and Archives, American Medical Association Library, Chicago; Anna Towlson, Academic Services Group, London School of Economics Library; Sarah Coblentz, Sarah Dorpinghaus, Katie Henning, and Daniel Weddington, Special Collections Research Center, Margaret I. King Library, University of Kentucky; Angela Salisbury, The Irene Lewisohn Costume Reference Library at The Costume Institute, Metropolitan Museum of Art, New York City; Dr. Gaila Sims, Reference and Research Services, Harry Ransom Center, University of Texas at Austin; Katie Young and Charles Wommack, University of Arizona Special Collections; Emma Muntis, Library Services Department, Florida State University/Ringling Museum of Art, Sarasota; Bruce Kirby, Manuscript Division, Library of Congress; Nathalie Proulx, The Dance Archive, Special Collections and Archives, University of Denver; and Paul Jordan and Robin Wheelwright Ness, John Hay Library, Brown University. For interlibrary loan help, thanks to Jeannette Fiedler of the Stoxen Library at Dickinson State University and to Jason Carpenter at Parks Library, Iowa State University.

I am more than usually indebted to Kevin M. Bailey, Dwight D. Eisenhower Presidential Library; Brian C. McNerney, Lyndon B. Johnson Presidential Library; Timothy R. Mottaz, Illinois State Archives; Roda Ferraro and Becky Ryder, Keeneland Library; Kylie Towers Smith, Kappa Kappa Gamma Archives; and Ruth Loughrey and her excellent staff at Unilever Art, Archives and Records Management, in Port Sunlight, United Kingdom.

The following kind people shared ideas, documents, or connections. Bob Curran, former vice president of corporate communications for the Jockey Club, answered horse questions; Canadian historian Dr. Douglas McCalla helped me understand why Arden probably doesn't have a birth certificate; Stillwell & Gladding president Robert Maltese shared information about A. Fabian Swanson; physician and author Dr. Andrew Bamji taught me about

Dr. Harold Gillies; Richard Boursy, research archivist at Yale's Music Library, alerted me to an unexpected Edna Ferber source; and former Arden employee Elinor Pritchard did her best to help me track down company leads.

James Bennett is a beauty industry historian located in western Australia. He has created an astounding website dedicated to, as its name suggests, cosmetics and skin. Full of primary documents, time lines, and helpful histories of business leaders, companies, and products, cosmeticsandskin.com is an extremely valuable source—second only to Bennett himself. In email conversations, he provided answers and asked probing questions. He forwarded photographs and other documents to help me understand his industry. I am deeply grateful to James Bennett for responding so graciously to a stranger's inquiries, for his encouragement, and for the resources he has made freely available.

Interviews with Nancy Wilt, Woman Marine historian and curator of the Women of the Corps Collection, and Kentuckian Kim Ryan, thoroughbred horse owner and trainer, made a palpable difference in my understanding of Arden and her world.

During Covid, several researchers did meticulous work in places I could not visit. Thanks to Samuel Dix (British Airways Heritage Collection, British Airways Museum); Simon J. Judkins (Remisoff Papers, University of Southern California Libraries Special Collections); Sydney Marshall (Gene Frederico Papers, Earle Ludgin Papers, and the Baskin Collection, Duke University Special Collections); and Brian Neumann (Casey and Dudley Families Papers, University of Virginia Library); and to Ashley Harris for laborious printing of online sources at a difficult time.

Special acknowledgments are due to my Iowa State University colleague Joanne Messman, whose sympathetic push strengthened me to write the book proposal. I am grateful to friends and colleagues at Dickinson State University for their warm encouragement, especially Alexa Delbridge, Steven Doherty, Johnna Douthit, Stephen Easton, Sandi Frenzel, Kelly Hyland, Erik Johnson, Sharon Kilzer, Marietta Kovash, Haylie Oberlander, and Michelle Stevier-Johanson. At Iowa State, I benefited from the interest of Dean Amy Slagell, from a Faculty Professional Development Award, and from a Center for Excellence in the Arts and Humanities research grant.

The publishing world lost a towering figure and I lost my very dear agent during this project. Sterling Lord gambled on me almost twenty years ago, and I miss him and his sage advice. Deepest thanks to Laurie Liss at Sterling Lord Literistic for taking me on. At Viking, I appreciate the behind-the-scenes work by Paloma Ruiz and the truly incredible copyediting of Maureen Clark. Thanks to both of you for improving this book. My editor for almost twenty years, the peerless and brilliant Wendy Wolf, will be retired by the time this book is in print. To say that it has been a tremendous honor working with her on three biographies is the sort of understatement of which she generally approves. I count our editor-author relationship as one of the most amazing miracles of my long career. Senior editor at Viking/Penguin Emily Wunderlich has adopted me with overwhelming grace and kindness, for which I am enormously grateful.

A constellation of friends, in and out of the academy, have listened and supported with more sympathy than I deserved. This simple list of names does not adequately express my gratitude: Paula Barnes, Susan Bartsch, Hope Grebner Bibens, Crystal Brandenburgh, Hannah Brennan, Karen Cates, Mary Beth Delaney, Debora Dragseth, Laura Duncan, Jennifer Goedke, Laura Grimm, Robert T. Grimm, Kimberly Hamlin, Clive Hanley, Krissi Jimroglou, Regina Bannan Johnson, Evy Lipecka, Dacey Messinger, Kristie Miller, Annie Moore, Brenda Mottaz, Danielle Nierenberg, Mary Lou Pease, Katie Roeth, Larry Rudiger, Lauren Schwab, Roger Smith, and Kathy Wagoner. The munificent Paige Halpin Smith fed and housed me, gave me a guided tour of Arden's Kentucky, and researched side by side with me at Keeneland.

Even though I am a writer, I truly have no words to express my profound gratitude to six eagle-eyed saints whose unfailingly honest comments immeasurably improved the manuscript: Karen Cates, Simon Cordery, Kristie Miller, Pamela Riney-Kehrberg, Larry Rudiger, and Roger Smith.

My family members are in a category all their own. For computer wizardry, thanks to Simone Cordery-Cotter. For photographic ideas, thanks to Sara Rumens. For unflagging encouragement, thanks to Mary and Ned Cordery, Doug and Larissa Rozek, Sara Rumens and Adam Dix, Susanne Cordery and Joe Antolick, Cormac Cordery-Cotter, and Jill Allardyce.

Using his training in historical musicology, my son, Gareth Cordery, good-naturedly answered questions about music, offered source suggestions, and, being a superb researcher in his own right, conducted essential archival forays for me, digging through the Travelers Aid Society papers in the New-York Historical Society, the World's Fair Collection in the New York Public Library, the Virgil Thomson Papers at Yale University, and the George Antheil Papers at Columbia University. But all that pales in comparison to his bringing into our family *ma belle fille*, Sophie Richard Cordery. With her training in art history, Sophie likewise expertly fielded my questions about Arden and art. Together, they squired me around New York City and Sleepy Hollow Cemetery and celebrated every step of this long process. I am exceedingly grateful for both of them.

First, last, and in everything, Simon Cordery is my partner. He contributed to this project in a thousand vital ways. Although he is also a historian, and a department chair, he gave unstintingly of his time, expertise, patience, and love. To repay him is impossible; to thank him, a joy.

It seems fitting to conclude with this list of women, who, in ways they will never know, taught me about beauty: Paula Barnes, Catherine Miltner Brewer, Mary Burfield Cordery, Sophie Richard Cordery, Julia Durney, Karen K. Gould, Tamela O'Dell Grabb, Annie Lavrut Moore, Gerda Nischan, Mary Lou Pease, Barbara McPherson Rozek, Helen Zielinski Rozek, Larissa Zemstova Rozek, Paige Halpin Smith, and above all, my mother, Agnes May Brewer Rozek.

Notes

PREFACE

1. Pamela Walker Laird, *Pull* (Cambridge, MA: Harvard University Press, 2006), 133, 134.
2. "Beauty Specialist Ready to Advise," *Los Angeles Times*, 21 June 1933, A5. See also Genina Gavin, "And Now It's Television," *The Boston Globe*, 20 June 1948, A7.

CHAPTER 1: BEGINNINGS

1. Susan Tadd was born on 7 December 1844 in Polruan, a fishing village on the Fowey Estuary. She had two brothers, Samuel Tadd Jr. and J. Liberty Tadd. William Graham was born on 1 January 1848 in Symington, South Lanarkshire, Scotland. He had a brother named Adam and a sister named Christine. Marriage license between William Graham and Susan Pearce Tadd, ancestry.com. Susan was twenty-seven and William was twenty-three when they married.
2. The 1881 Canadian census lists William Graham as a peddler. The 1891 census has William Graham, age forty-two, still a peddler, and unmarried.
3. John Benson, "Hawking and Peddling in Canada, 1867–1914," *Histoire Sociale / Social History* 18, no. 35 (1985): 803.
4. The town, sometimes spelled Burrwick, was renamed in 1855.
5. Information on Woodbridge comes from Herb. H. Sawdon, *The Woodbridge Story* (Woodbridge, ON: self-pub., 1960), and from information provided by the City of Vaughan Archives and Records Management Services, including "A Brief History of Woodbridge" (undated, no publisher), "The Origin of the Names 'Burwick' and 'Woodbury,'" and "City of Vaughan: Woodbridge Heritage Discovery Tour" (undated pamphlets).
6. "Elizabeth Nightingale Graham, 1885–1966," *The Thoroughbred Record*, 29 October 1966, 1451. The Queen's Plate (now the King's Plate) is a thoroughbred race in Canada.
7. Love of animals: Kathryn Loring, "She's at Home at the Racing Oval and in the Best Circles," *Chicago Tribune*, 22 September 1957, 6.

Biographical material comes from Alfred Allan Lewis and Constance Woodworth, *Miss Elizabeth Arden* (New York: Coward, McCann & Geoghegan, 1972), chap. 1.
8. Information from the 1901 Canadian census. That census also listed her as being eighteen years old rather than nineteen, and having been born in December 1882 rather than December 1881. Her birth year moved steadily ahead throughout her life. See, for example, 1885 in "Elizabeth Nightingale Graham, 1885–1966," *The Thoroughbred Record*, 1451.
9. Cynthia Baker et al., *Ties That Bind* (Ottowa: Canadian Association of Schools of Nursing, 2012), 4, 7, 8.
10. "Beauty Advisor to Millions, Elizabeth Arden Dies at 82," *The Boston Globe*, 19 October 1966, 2.
11. Simon J. Bronner, "Reading Consumer Culture," in *Consuming Visions*, ed. Simon J. Bronner (New York: W. W. Norton, 1989), 25.
12. Lewis and Woodworth, *Miss Elizabeth Arden*, 38.
13. Toronto had three truss manufacturers in 1903. The largest and oldest firm was Authors & Cox on Church Street. There were too many dentists, real estate agencies, and banks to hazard a guess as to her employers. See 1903 Toronto City Directory: static.torontopubliclibrary.ca/da/pdfs/torontodirec190300mighuoft.pdf.
14. Alma Whitaker, "Sugar and Spice," *Los Angeles Times*, 13 March 1935, 6. The "whiz" quote comes from "'I Am a Famous Woman in This Industry,'" *Fortune*, October 1938, 62.
15. 1910 U.S. Census, ancestry.com.
16. "Dr. Edward Robinson Squibb," *American Druggist and Pharmaceutical Record* 37, no. 10 (12 November 1900): 288. See also W. A. Pearson, "Original and Selected: The Preparation and Testing of Drugs," *The Pharmaceutical Era* 44, no. 8 (August 1911): 336.
17. Lewis and Woodworth, *Miss Elizabeth Arden*, 44–45. Or perhaps Squibb was only a momentary stepping stone. In a 1935 *New Yorker*

profile, Margaret Case Harriman wrote that Arden worked for Squibb for exactly ten days. See Harriman, "Profiles: Glamour, Inc.," The New Yorker, 6 April 1935, 25.

18. Digital Toronto city directories, 1900–1908, Toronto Public Library, torontopublicli brary.ca/history-genealogy/lh-digital-city -directories.jsp.

19. The best information about Eleanor Adair is found on the website Cosmetics and Skin, created by James Bennett, an Australian scientist whose work and interest in the beauty industry came to encompass the history of the field. See cosmeticsandskin.com/companies/adair.php. According to Bennett, Adair opened her London salon in 1900 and her Paris salon in 1902.

20. Annette Blaugrund, Dispensing Beauty in New York & Beyond (Charleston, SC: History Press, 2011), 133.

21. Melanie Gustafson, "The Family and Business Life of Harriet Hubbard Ayer, Culminating in Fights over Her Person and Property," Journal of the Gilded Age and Progressive Era 11, no. 3 (July 2012): 345–404.

22. Harriet Hubbard Ayer, Harriet Hubbard Ayer's Book (Springfield, MA: King-Richardson Company, 1899); Gustafson, "Family and Business Life of Harriet Hubbard Ayer," 346–47.

23. Gustafson, "Family and Business Life of Harriet Hubbard Ayer," 348.

24. "Mrs. E. Adair" ad, Vogue, 2 January 1908, 4. Photo of "Mrs. Adair's Rooms," in "Mrs. Adair Says" ad, Vogue, 17 September 1908, 415. Photos of the Paris salon can be found on Bennett's Cosmetics and Skin website. The salon was located at 15 West Thirty-Ninth Street, near Bryant Park.

25. "An Exposé of a Situation Which Is of Interest to All Women" Adair ad, Vogue, 19 March 1908, 384.

26. "The Culture of Beauty" Adair ad, Vogue, 4 February 1904, vii.

27. The descriptions of Adair's products and services are consistently found throughout her 1903–9 Vogue ads. These quotes are from "Mrs. Adair's Annual Sale," Vogue, 19 August 1909, 249.

28. Raise: Lewis and Woodworth, Miss Elizabeth Arden, 46.

29. Bennett, "Eleanor Adair."

30. Eleanor Huntley Nicholson, "Suspensory Chin Strap or Band," 28 April 1902, GB Patent #190209783A; Eleanor Huntley Nicholson, "A Forehead Bandage or Strap," 28 October 1902, GB Patent #190223540A. For more on women and inventions in the beauty industry, see Kathy Peiss, Hope in a Jar (Philadelphia: University of Pennsylvania Press, 1998), 63.

31. "Mrs. E. Adair" ad, Vogue, 2 January 1908, 4-A.

32. Jessica P. Clark, "'Clever Ministrations': Regenerative Beauty at the Fin de Siècle," Palgrave Communications Online 3, no. 47 (2017): 5.

33. Clark, "'Clever Ministrations,'" 6–7; Bennett, "Eleanor Adair." For electricity used to

remove unwanted hair, see Rebecca Herzig, "Subjected to the Current," Journal of Social History 41, no. 4 (Summer 2008): 867–85.

34. The entire line consisted of Ganesh Eastern Oil, Ganesh Bleachine, Eastern Freckle Remover, Ganesh Hair Cleanser, Ganesh Hair Lotion, Eastern Tonic, Lily Sulphur Lotion, Ganesh Diable Skin Tonic, Eastern Balm Cream, and Beauty Sachets and Liquid Powder, which came in pink and white. Quote is from "Mrs. Adair Says" ad, Vogue, 17 September 1908, 415.

35. "Mrs. E. Adair" ad, Vogue, 5 November 1908, 783; Annual Report of the Bureau of Labor Statistics for the State of New York for the Year Ended September 30, 1912 (Albany: State Department of Labor, 1913), 472–82. In 1910, $2.50 was equal to nearly $83.25 today. All financial conversions in this book come from measuringworth.com, created by the Economic History Association. I used the Purchasing Power Today, the "Real Price as measured by inflating the Consumer Price Index," throughout.
For strap prices, see "An Exposé of a Situation Which Is of Interest to All Women," Vogue, 19 March 1908, 384. On occasion, Adair charged 25 cents for her "free" booklet.

36. Second floor: Hambla Bauer, "High Priestess of Beauty," The Saturday Evening Post, 24 April 1948, 189. Bauer wrote that the rent was $75 a month, just over $2,600 today. All other information on the Graham-Hubbard partnership comes from Lewis and Woodworth, Miss Elizabeth Arden, 47–51. "The Springtime" Hubbard ad, Vogue, 4 December 1909, 1000.

37. "The Springtime" Hubbard ad, Vogue, 4 December 1909, 1000. The full name of the booklet appeared first in an ad in Vogue, 1 June 1910, 69.

38. "Helen of Troy" Hubbard ad, Vogue, 22 January 1910, 58.

39. "Business Troubles," NYT, 16 August 1910, 10. Quotes are from "Fashion's Fads and Fancies," The Washington Post, 21 August 1910, ES7.

40. Hubbard opened her new salon at 505 Fifth Avenue, one slim storefront away from her former partner. "Our Patron's Attention" Hubbard ad, Vogue, 15 October 1910, 65. In Trow's General Directory of the Boroughs of Manhattan and Bronx for 1910, Elizabeth Hubbard is listed at 509 Fifth Avenue (p. 687). In 1911, she is listed at 505 Fifth Avenue under "massage" (p. 730). In the 1913 directory, Elizabeth Arden is listed as the firm located at 509 Fifth Avenue (p. 48).

41. Trow's General Directory of the Boroughs of Manhattan and Bronx, vol. CXXVI ([for the year ending 1 August 1913] 1912), 56.

42. "'I Am a Famous Woman in This Industry,'" 61.

43. Margaret Case Harriman, "Profiles: Glamour, Inc.," The New Yorker, 6 April 1935, 26.

CHAPTER 2: THE BEAUTY CULTURALIST

1. Geoffrey Jones, Beauty Imagined (New York: Oxford University Press, 2010), 66. Before Ar-

den's time, Jeannette Jobbins became Jeannette Scalé became Mrs. Jeannette Pomeroy, "arguably the West End's most enterprising and visible woman retailer, whose [beauty] empire extended across Great Britain and its colonies, from Dublin to Cape Town." See Jessica P. Clark, "*Pomeroy v. Pomeroy,*" *Women's History Review* 22, no. 6 (2013): 879.

2. The phrase is Eric Konigsberg's, in his "Inside 'Mad Men,'" *Rolling Stone,* 16 September 2010, rollingstone.com/movies/movie-news/inside-mad-men-a-fine-madness-175222.

3. See for example, "Deaths," *Baltimore Sun,* 13 November 1912, 6; "Tiny Baltimoreans Help to Save Less Fortunate Babies," *Baltimore Sun,* 15 September 1912, 29.

4. Lloyd Shearer, "Elizabeth Arden Graham," *The Boston Globe,* 28 August 1960, B6. *Elizabeth and Her German Garden* was originally published without the author's name, but by 1910, copies circulated with Elizabeth von Arnim as the author.

5. John F. Sinclair, "Machado Is Not Out of Tangle Yet," *Hartford Courant,* 31 May 1931, A6. Further attesting to the renown of "Enoch Arden," D. W. Griffith released a silent film based on the poem in the summer of 1911. In 1915, Lillian Gish starred in another film version of "Enoch Arden."

6. Shearer, "Elizabeth Arden Graham," B6.

7. Alfred Allan Lewis and Constance Woodworth, *Miss Elizabeth Arden* (New York: Coward, McCann & Geoghegan, 1972), 53.

8. William Leach, "Strategists of Display and the Production of Desire," in *Consuming Visions,* ed. Simon J. Bronner (New York: W. W. Norton, 1989), 121.

9. Initially the pink was the color of her labels. Not until much later did she sell a lipstick called Arden Pink, and she never settled on one consistent shade. If it was pink and she sold it, it could be called Arden Pink.

10. The earliest available version of the booklet is from 1920 and can be found on James Bennett's Cosmetics and Skin website, cosmeticsandskin.com/booklets/arden-quest-20-php. Newer versions appear in various archives. Bennett notes that the booklet was first mentioned in an advertisement in 1911.

11. Elizabeth Arden, *The Quest of the Beautiful* (1920). In 1920, her product list ran to twenty-two pages.

12. For $6,000 from a cousin, see "'I Am a Famous Woman in This Industry,'" *Fortune,* October 1938, 62. For $6,000 from her brother, see "Obituary: Mrs. Elizabeth N. Graham," *The Blood-Horse,* 22 October 1966, 2964. For "less than $1,000," see "Elizabeth Arden Is Dead at 81," *NYT,* 19 October 1966, 1. For $600, see "Elizabeth Arden Is Dead," *The Washington Post,* 19 October 1966, C4. For $100, see Alma Whitaker, "Sugar and Spice," *Los Angeles Times,* 13 March 1935, 6.

13. See, for example, "Money Loaned to Salaried People," *The Washington Post,* 5 January 1910, 10.

14. David W. Baker, "J. Liberty Tadd, Who Are You?," *Studies in Art Education* 26, no. 2 (Winter 1985): 76–77.

15. Ancestry.com. Bill became a naturalized citizen in 1903.

16. "New Incorporations," *NYT,* 23 April 1913, 12. The incorporators (and board of directors) were "William P. Graham, Florence Balaban, and Frederick A. Schabmayer." They leased the site at 104 Fifth Avenue. "Leasing Market Continues Active," *NYT,* 19 October 1913, XX2.

17. "W. P. Graham of Graham & Zenger," *Crockery and Glass Journal* (20 November 1913): 17.

18. "U.S. to Refund Customs Duties," *The New York Sun,* 19 December 1917, 3.

19. Margaret Moore, *End of the Road for Ladies' Mile?* (New York: The Drive to Protect the Ladies' Mile District, 1986), 7.

20. For department stores, including their critics, see William Leach, *Land of Desire* (New York: Vintage, 1993), and Bronner, *Consuming Visions,* especially the chapters by Barton, Lears, Lash, Agnew, and Halttunen.

21. Geral Dean, "Aggressive Boston Advertisers and Their Mediums," *Printers Ink* 36, no. 13 (25 September 1901): 18.

22. "Beauty, Its Wooing and Winning" Arden ad, *Vogue,* 1 November 1910, 91.

23. Gillian Dyer, *Advertising as Communication* (New York: Methuen, 1982), 16, 25.

24. Quoted (censoriously) in Mary Catherine Phillips, *Skin Deep* (New York: Vanguard Press, 1934), 6.

25. Helen Damon-Moore, *Magazines for the Millions* (Albany: State University of New York, 1994); Matthew Schneirov, *The Dream of a New Social Order* (New York: Columbia University Press, 1994); Jennifer Scanlon, *Inarticulate Longings* (New York: Routledge, 1995); and James Landers, *The Improbable First Century of Cosmopolitan Magazine* (Columbia: University of Missouri Press, 2010).

26. Like Ayer, Arden wrote her own ads. For Ayer, see Melanie Gustafson, "The Family and Business Life of Harriet Hubbard Ayer, Culminating in Fights over Her Person and Property," *Journal of the Gilded Age and Progressive Era* 11, no. 3 (July 2012): 358n52. For the *Vogue* quote, see Laird Borrelli-Persson, "*Vogue* at 130," *Vogue,* 7 March 2017, vogue.com/article/vogue-covers-models-facts-history.

27. Elizabeth Arden ad, *Vogue,* 15 October 1910, 82.

28. Rob Schorman, *Selling Style* (Philadelphia: University of Pennsylvania Press, 2003), 36. Arden's next *Vogue* ad announced that "FLORENCE GRAHAM" was "now managing the Elizabeth Arden Establishment at 509 Fifth Avenue." It would not have been clear to readers of this ad whether Florence Graham was Elizabeth

Arden. The eliding of Graham with Arden continued for some time. "Venetian Preparations, Facial Treatments" Arden ad, *Vogue*, 15 November 1910, 77.

29. "Beauty: Its Wooing and Winning" Arden ad, *Vogue*, 1 November 1910, 91.

30. Fannie Hurst, *Imitation of Life*, ed. Daniel Itzkovitz (1933; repr., Durham, NC: Duke University Press, 2004), 145.

31. Elizabeth Arden ad, *Vogue*, 15 October 1910, 82.

32. Bleachine Cream Arden ad, *Vogue*, 15 May 1911, 79.

33. Ardena Skin Tonic in Elizabeth Arden ad, *Vogue*, 15 November 1910, 77. These descriptions were usually printed on the label and in advertisements. See, for example, File of Labels, EA/6/14/1, Elizabeth Arden Ltd. Papers, Unilever Archives, Port Sunlight, UK.

34. Kathy Peiss, *Hope in a Jar* (Philadelphia: University of Pennsylvania Press, 1998), 35. See also pp. 40–43 and 150–51.

35. For the classic explosion of the meaning of beauty, see Naomi Wolf, *The Beauty Myth* (New York: William Morrow, 1991).

36. Ayer's drawing was based on the famous 1800 painting by Jacques-Louis David. For "Helen of Troy," see the "Mrs. E. Hubbard" ads in *Vogue*, 22 January 1910, 58, and 15 April 1910, 110.

37. Lydia Lane, "Elizabeth Arden Lauds L.A. Women," *Los Angeles Times*, 24 March 1954, B1. Lane wrote that Arden penned the sign in lipstick, but Arden told an audience in the 1940s that she asked a nurse to write it on brown paper in red crayon and hang it on her hospital wall during an undated stay for appendicitis. See Elizabeth Arden, "The Call to Perfection," undated speech [1940s], p. 8, Women's Institute of Duluth Records, University of Minnesota, Duluth.

38. Arden as trainer: "'I Am a Famous Woman in This Industry,'" 62; practicing on knees: Katherine Brush, "Out of My Mind," *The Washington Post*, 2 July 1939, A2.

39. "Jessica Ogilvie, 58, of Ogilvie Sisters," *NYT*, 25 October 1943, 15; Ada Patterson, "Story of the Ogilvie Sisters," in *Ogilvie Sisters Care of the Skin* (1931), 20–22, cosmeticsandskin.com/booklets/ogilvie-1931.php. The sisters were Mary Gladys, Elizabeth, Jessica, Anne, Clara, Mabel, and Georgina. They had a brother named William. The millinery shop Gladys owned was on East Twenty-Seventh Street in 1911. In 1912, it had become Ogilvie Modes, and had moved to 28 East Forty-Sixth Street. Georgina joined her by 1914. By 1914, Georgina, Jessica, Gladys, and Clara lived together on West Fifty-Eighth Street. They (at least Jessica and Clara) had previously lived at 515 Lexington Avenue. All information from *Trow's General Directory of the Boroughs of Manhattan and Bronx*.

40. Jones, *Beauty Imagined*, 47, 48. For the history of hairdressing, see pp. 45–52.

41. Jones, *Beauty Imagined*, 51–52; Peiss, *Hope in a Jar*, 67–70. Jones wrote that Walker had "sales of over $1 million by World War I" and that "both Turnbo Malone and Walker were probably millionaires by 1914 and, as a result, were among the first American self-made female millionaires" (51–52). For charitable works, see Julie A. Willett, *Permanent Waves* (New York: New York University Press, 2000), 24–26.

42. "War Bond Fraud Charged," *NYT*, 19 September 1943, 50, suggests that Delaney hired on in 1911. "Miss Florence Delaney," *NYT*, 30 January 1949, 61, is less specific, and states that Delaney "joined the Arden firm in its infancy thirty years ago as a bookkeeper."

43. Hambla Bauer, "High Priestess of Beauty," *The Saturday Evening Post*, 24 April 1948, 189.

44. Richmond Barrett, *Good Old Summer Days* (Boston: Houghton Mifflin, 1952), 42.

45. All information about Bar Harbor is from Stephen J. Hornsby, "The Gilded Age and the Making of Bar Harbor," *Geographical Review* 83, no. 4 (October 1993): 455–68. For 221 families, see p. 456; Vanderbilt's number of rooms, p. 458; Northern landscape, p. 456; *Boston Advertiser* quote, p. 464.

46. Arden ad, *Vogue*, 15 July 1911, 64. See also "Narragansett Pier" ad, *Vogue*, 15 July 1912, 57. Her Narragansett salon was situated in the Hazard Block, newly rebuilt after the 1900 fire. See "Venetian Pore Cream" ad, *Vogue*, 1 September 1912, 93, for salon location.

47. Barrett, *Good Old Summer Days*, 43. See also Arden ads in *Vogue* from 15 July 1912, 57; 1 August 1912, 57; and 15 September 1911, 92. She was in Newport in 1911, but possibly not in the Newport Casino until 1912.

48. Elizabeth Arden ad, *Vogue*, 1 October 1911, 91.

49. "Suffrage Army Out on Parade," *NYT*, 5 May 1912, 1. It is also possible that Arden joined the November 1912 nighttime, torchlit suffrage parade, although no documentary evidence supports this. Blatch's Women's Political Union was located at 46 East Twenty-Ninth Street.

50. The tale of Arden in a suffrage march can be found in Lewis and Woodworth, *Miss Elizabeth Arden*, 60. They claim the May march began just after lunch, but it started at 5:00 p.m. while the November march began at 8:00 p.m.

51. Johanna Neuman, *Gilded Suffragists* (New York: New York University Press, 2017), 3.

52. Neuman, *Gilded Suffragists*, 47.

53. "Society Outside the Capital," *The Washington* Post, 16 January 1911, 7, 9. Quote is found on p. 9, and in Neuman, *Gilded Suffragists*, 118. For an analysis of suffragists and their use of fashion in this era, see Einav Rabinovitch-Fox, *Dressed for Freedom* (Urbana: University of Illinois Press, 2021), chap. 2.

54. This story is apocryphal. In *War Paint*, Lindy Woodhead wrote that "as a badge of courage they wore bright red lipstick" in the 1912

New York City suffrage parade (Hoboken, NJ: John Wiley & Sons, 2003, 98). I have found no evidence for this. Neither has historian Johanna Neuman, who could not locate it in magazines, in newspapers, in "the memoirs of [Harriot Stanton] Blatch, Alva Belmont's unpublished memoirs, or the scholarship of Cooney, DuBois, Flexner, Montgomery, and others" (from her *Gilded Suffragists*, 183n58). I concur with Neuman's conclusion regarding the lack of any evidence for the claim that suffragists wore red lipstick. There is similarly no evidence to suggest that Elizabeth Arden left her salon that day—or any day—to distribute red lipstick to the marchers. Suffrage bling—fans, literature, even "Suffrage sundaes" made with fresh peaches—was occasionally handed out at parades and other events. Lipstick was not. As Arden herself said speaking about a date two years after the parade: "In 1914, lipsticks were in the experimental stage" (from her speech "The Call to Perfection," p. 13).

CHAPTER 3: CHANGING THE FACE OF AMERICA
1. "Off for Europe Today," *NYT*, 13 July 1912, 9; "H. G. Lewis, Banker, Dead," *NYT*, 25 August 1912, 19.
2. Jessica P. Clark, "'Clever Ministrations,'" *Palgrave Communications Online* 3, no. 47 (2017): 4. See also the Epilogue in Clark's "'Beauty on Bond Street'" (Ph.D. diss., Johns Hopkins University, 2012). Jeannette Scalé Pomeroy was not running the business in 1912. For the curious case of how she became separated from the successful business she started, see Clark, "*Pomeroy v. Pomeroy*," *Women's History Review* 22, no. 6 (2013): 877–903.
3. Rubinstein advertised in *Vogue* twice in 1911. Only the May ad was specifically targeted to women going abroad for the London season. Quotes in this paragraph are from "The London Season Cunard" ad, *Chicago Tribune*, 17 May 1911, 19; Rubinstein American *Vogue* ads, 15 May 1911, 59, and 1 June 1911, 51. Her London salon was located at 24 Grafton Street, and her Paris salon at 255 rue Saint-Honoré. Helena Rubinstein had been operating in Paris only since 1909 and in London since 1908.
4. James Bennett's Cosmetics and Skin website is the basis for the biographical information in this paragraph, except for the parental disapproval. That is from Rubinstein's *The Art of Feminine Beauty* (London: Victor Gollancz, 1930), 16. See also Rubinstein's memoir, *My Life for Beauty* (New York: Simon & Schuster, 1966); Michèle Fitoussi, *Helena Rubinstein* (London: Gallic Books, 2010); Patrick O'Higgins, *Madame* (New York: Viking, 1971); Maxine Fabe, *Beauty Millionaire* (New York: Thomas Y. Crowell, 1972); and Lindy Woodhead, *War Paint* (Hoboken, NJ: John Wiley & Sons, 2003).
5. Rubinstein, *Art of Feminine Beauty*, 25, 24, 23.
6. Titus was born Arthur Ameisen in 1870, also in Kraków. When he was twenty-one, he emigrated and became an American citizen. He may

have had a first marriage. He seems to have studied law in Pittsburgh before going to Australia. He is usually given credit for Rubinstein's packaging, her extravagant advertising claims, and some of the emphases of her business. See, for example, Fitoussi, *Helena Rubinstein*, chap. 9. Fitoussi calls Titus Rubinstein's "guide," "as vital to her as the air she breathed" (98). For Asquith, see Rubinstein, *My Life for Beauty*, 44.
7. For increasing the salon, see Arden ad, *Vogue*, 1 April 1913, 116. "Elizabeth Arden Announces Several New and Important Toilet Preparations," *Vogue*, 1 October 1912, 117; mail-order products, "Bleachine Cream, Pore Cream" ad, *Vogue*, 15 October 1912, 115.
8. "Painted Angels at Saratoga," *Godey's Lady's Book*, November 1865, 451.
9. See Karen Halttunen, *Confidence Men and Painted Women* (New Haven, CT: Yale University Press, 1982); Lois Banner, *American Beauty* (New York: Alfred A. Knopf, 1983), 111–17; Jackson Lears, "Beyond Veblen," in *Consuming Visions*, ed. Simon J. Bronner (New York: W. W. Norton, 1989), 91–93.
10. The Marquise de Fanhael, in "How to Be Beautiful," *Vogue*, 6 December 1894, 370, gave the same warning. See also Max Beerbohm, *A Defence of Cosmetics* (1896; repr., New York: Dodd, Mead, 1922), 4–5, 6. Murray Wax, "Themes in Cosmetics and Grooming," *American Journal of Sociology* 62, no. 6 (May 1957): 588–93, provides a brief history of cosmetic deception.
11. Arden ad, *Vogue*, 15 October 1912, 115.
12. Arden ad, *Vogue*, 1 November 1913, 111.
13. Arden ad, *Vogue*, 15 October 1913, 100; Arden ad, *Vogue*, 15 January 1913, 102.
14. "Be Beautiful" Arden ad, *Vogue*, 1 July 1911, 50.
15. Lillian Russell, "Lillian Russell's Beauty Secrets: French and American Women," *Chicago Tribune*, 14 October 1912, 11.
16. Lillian Russell, "Lillian Russell's Beauty Secrets: Good Taste," *Chicago Tribune*, 23 December 1911, 6.
17. Lillian Russell, "Lillian Russell's Beauty Secrets: French and American Women," *Chicago Tribune*, 14 October 1912, 11.
18. Connie Karstens, "A Scientific Showgirl," *Chicago Tribune*, 13 April 1913, G3.
19. Lip Salve: "Birthdays Leave Their Marks" Arden ad, *Vogue*, 1 April 1913, 116; "Rose" Arden ad, *Vogue*, 1 December 1913, 144.
20. Arden ad, *Vogue*, 1 November 1914, 125.
21. Alfred Allan Lewis and Constance Woodworth, *Miss Elizabeth Arden* (New York: Coward, McCann & Geoghegan, 1972), 69.
22. The term is Kristin L. Hoganson's, from her "The Fashionable World: Imagined Communities of Dress," in *After the Imperial Turn*, ed. Antoinette Burton (Durham, NC: Duke University Press, 2003), 73, 76, 78.
23. Hambla Bauer, "High Priestess of Beauty," *The Saturday Evening Post*, 24 April 1948, 189.

24. Jessica Clark uses this phrase to apply to the look created by Jeannette Pomeroy before her business closed in 1905; see *"Pomeroy v. Pomeroy,"* 888.

25. Regina Lee Blaszczyk, *The Color Revolution* (Cambridge, MA: MIT Press, 2012), 199–200.

26. Arden ad, *Vogue*, 1 December 1913, 144. For samples, see 16 April 1914, 91.

27. "Should Women Paint?," *The Baltimore Sun*, 25 August 1912, D6.

28. Geoffrey Jones, *Beauty Imagined* (New York: Oxford University Press, 2010), 64.

29. Roger Boutet de Monvel, "What Says the Man of Woman's Make-Up?," *Vogue*, 15 January 1920, 90.

30. Elizabeth Arden, *The Quest of the Beautiful* (1920), 4.

31. "Remaking the Complexion" Arden ad, *The Washington Post*, 10 December 1916, ES9.

32. Other cities included St. Louis, Omaha, Chicago, Cincinnati, and later Atlanta, Pittsburgh, and Springfield, Missouri.

33. "Venetian Preparations, Facial Treatments" Arden ad, *Vogue*, 15 April 1912, 101. I could not verify this lecture. The Congress of American Women may not have been the name of the organization to which she spoke. That name is more usually associated with the short-lived (1948–50), post–World War II women's rights organization.

34. "The Arden Hydro-Firmo Chin Perfector" ad, *Vogue*, 15 May 1912, 91.

35. As Kathy Peiss lays out, beauty culturalists advertised skin creams and treatments, but not cosmetics until World War I. Arden was unusually early for marketing makeup; see *Hope in a Jar* (Philadelphia: University of Pennsylvania Press, 1998), 105.

36. William J. Enright, "Ad Men Support Consumer Groups," *NYT*, 22 June 1939, 36.

37. "Don't Look Old" Arden ad, *Chicago Tribune*, 24 November 1912, K13, and *The Washington Post*, 24 November 1912, SMA13.

38. Boudoir Box Arden ad, *Vogue*, 1 December 1913, 144; Arden Skin Treatment Box ad, *Vogue*, 15 December 1913, 116.

39. Hambla Bauer, "High Priestess of Beauty," *The Saturday Evening Post*, 24 April 1948.

40. For dates and addresses, see her *Vogue* ads, 1 May 1914, 119, and 1 September 1914, 116. Her 3 January 1915 *Washington Post* ad announced the move to 1147 Connecticut Avenue NW (p. E6).

41. "Elizabeth Arden Announces the Removal of Her Salon to 1147 Connecticut Ave." ad, *The Washington Post*, 3 January 1915, E6, and "Beauty Is One Part Nature and Three Parts Care" ad, *The Washington Post*, 10 January 1915, E11.

42. "Beauty Is One Part Nature and Three Parts Care" ad, *The Washington Post*, 10 January 1915, E11.

43. "Firming the Facial Tissues by Skillful Treatment" ad, *The Washington Post*, 24 January 1915, A9.

44. "A Lenten Opportunity" ad, *The Washington Post*, 7 February 1915, E6.

45. "How to Preserve a Youthful Face" ad, *The Washington Post*, 4 April 1915, ES10.

46. Jones, *Beauty Imagined*, 26–27.

47. Bauer, "High Priestess of Beauty," 189. Bill Graham was on an extended trip to Europe in the summer of 1914.

CHAPTER 4: BUILDING A NATIONAL BEAUTY BRAND

1. The two may have met on Arden's first trip to Europe in 1912 because "Miss Elizabeth Arden" and "T. J. Lewis" were both aboard the *Lapland* en route to Antwerp. Perhaps they encountered each other in one of the Manhattan banks where Tom Lewis worked, or at the Union First Mortgage Company.

2. In the 1900 U.S. Census, Lewis was a "bank examiner" and Henry was a "bank clerk." In the 1905 U.S. Census, Lewis was a "cashier, bank" and Henry was an assistant bank cashier. In 1910, both brothers were listed as "banker." See also "National Reserve Bank," *The Wall Street Journal*, 10 July 1911, 8; "National Reserve Election," *Brooklyn Daily Eagle*, 8 July 1911, 11; "Financial Notes," *NYT*, 8 October 1911, 88; and "Brooklyn Has New Mortgage Company," *The Bankers Magazine*, November 1911, 669. Brother Henry died in 1912. See "H. G. Lewis, Banker, Dead," *NYT*, 25 August 1912, 19. In that article, Tom Lewis is identified as "Treasurer of the Union First Mortgage Company."

3. Lewis's discharge paper lists his birthday as 23 April 1875, and all the census data has him born in that year. His marriage certificate, however, lists him as thirty-eight. If that were true, he would have had to have been born in 1877. He appears to have lied about his age, calling himself thirty-eight instead of forty. They were both residing in Manhattan. He lived at 50 Central Park West and she lived farther north at 302 West Seventy-Ninth Street. For a highly creative narrative of their meeting and courtship, see Alfred Allan Lewis and Constance Woodworth, *Miss Elizabeth Arden* (New York: Coward, McCann & Geoghegan, 1972), chap. 4. In 1914, a Thomas J. Lewis cofounded the Secured Holdings Corporation and took possession of an apartment building fronting on Central Park. See "The Real Estate Field," *NYT*, 4 August 1914, 15.

4. State of New York Certificate and Record of Marriage of Thomas Jenkins Lewis and Florence Nightingale Graham, 29 November 1915, New York City Municipal Archives, Department of Records and Information, New York City. For Houghton, see John W. Leonard, ed., *Men of America* (New York: L. R. Hamersly, 1908), 1229–30, and *First Citizens of the Republic* (New York: L. R. Hamersly, 1906), 217–18. Arden listed her age as thirty-two on the marriage certificate, making her year of birth 1883, except that she was actually born in 1881. In *Miss Elizabeth Arden*, Lewis and Woodworth (p. 80) state that Arden snuck out of the salon without telling anyone and was back,

married, in one hour. In 1948, Hambla Bauer wrote that Arden was out of the office for thirty minutes for the wedding; see "High Priestess of Beauty," *The Saturday Evening Post*, 24 April 1948, 189. For Rockefeller, see Matthew Josephson, *The Robber Barons* (New York: Harcourt, 1934), 48.

5. "Just What I Have Always Wanted" Arden ad, *Vogue*, 1 May 1914, 119.

6. Bauer, "High Priestess of Beauty," 189.

7. Bauer, "High Priestess of Beauty," 189.

8. "Elizabeth Arden Announcing Removal," *Vogue*, 1 September 1915, 115.

9. "The First Christmas Gifts" ad, *Vogue*, 23 November 1929, 100. When she relocated in 1930, she made sure that the new salon door was red: "Vogue's Eye View," *Vogue*, 15 December 1934, 17. A persistent belief that red doors marked churches as a haven may have inspired Arden's choice of color for her salon doors, or the fact that Episcopal churches (long the church of society leaders) often had red doors, but she never wrote or spoke of her reason.

10. Elizabeth Arden, *The Quest of the Beautiful* (1920), 5. *Camera* means "room" in Latin.

11. William R. Taylor, "The Evolution of Public Space in New York City," in *Consuming Visions*, ed. Simon J. Bronner (New York: W. W. Norton, 1989), 297.

12. Elizabeth Arden, *The Quest of the Beautiful* (1927), 6.

13. Elizabeth Arden, *The Quest of the Beautiful* (1920), 5. For a fictionalized version of an Arden Salon, see Fannie Hurst, *Imitation of Life*, ed. Daniel Itzkovitz (1933; repr., Durham, NC: Duke University Press, 2004), 155. Arden and Hurst were friends.

14. *Finance and Industry: The New York Stock Exchange Historical Review* (New York: Historical Publishing Company, 1886), 163. Lewis and Woodworth, *Miss Elizabeth Arden*, 73.

15. JAMA Bureau of Investigation, *Cosmetic Nostrums and Allied Preparations* (Chicago: Bureau of Investigation of the Journal of the American Medical Association, n.d.): 2. This publication is undated but was published sometime after 1925. A Swedish immigrant, Swanson was hired by Stillwell & Gladding as an assistant chemist upon his graduation from Brown University in 1906. Arden made him her chief chemist in 1920.

16. For information on Axel Fabian Swanson, and verification that he did not come to work full-time for Arden until 1920, see his October 1933 Alumni Questionnaire in his biographical file at the John Hay Library, Brown University. See also Louis Kahnweiler v. Stanley M. Chandler and John D. Meddick, Supreme Court Case, google .com/books/edition/Supreme_Court_Appellate _Division/1NWqJjMXCoUC?hl=en&gbpv=1. "Papers on Appeal," 23 March 1920, especially p. 107. On 1 January 1915, Thomas S. Gladding transferred sixty shares of Stillwell & Gladding capital stock to Swanson. Stock certificate in the

Stillwell & Gladding corporate headquarters, thanks to Stillwell & Gladding president Robert Maltese for this information.

17. On 15 September 1915, Arden explained that "commodious laboratories have been added to meet the immense commercial demand for Venetian Preparations, from all over the world." See Arden ad, *Vogue*, 15 September 1915, 131. In interviews later in life, she suggested that she and Swanson worked together in her salon to formulate this cream. See Pat McDonnell, "Grand Duchess of Beauty," n.d., *Long Beach Press Telegram*, Nicolas Remisoff Papers, Collection no. 0199, Special Collections, USC Libraries, University of Southern California.

18. "Skin and Complexion Perfect" Arden ad, *Vogue*, 1 April 1914, 147. In later ads that year, she called it "an exclusive Parisian cream"; see Arden ad, *Vogue*, 1 September 1914, 116, for example. James Bennett, a toiletries expert, wrote that "it was marketed as a powder base which suggests it may have been a type of vanishing cream, possibly a 'snow,'" which gave it "a foamy consistency"; see Bennett, Cosmetics and Skin Care, cosmetsandskin.com/companies/elizabeth-arden.php.

19. All announcements from Arden's *Vogue* ads: Vantie Cream, 15 March 1914, 97; Almond Skin Food, Special Eye Lotion, and Beauty Sachets, 1 April 1914, 147; Bathodomes, 1 May 1914, 119; Orange Skin Food and Ideal Bath Salts, 15 September 1914, 111.

20. All announcements from Arden's *Vogue* ads: New Special Astringent, 15 May 1915, 112; new powder colors and Venetian Special Bleach Cream, 1 August 1915, 77; Venetian Freckle Cream, 15 September 1915, 131; Venetian Hand Cream and Dermatex Depilatory, 1 November 1915, 133; Venetian Atomizer, Verdè Ophelia, Shading Powder, Beauty Box and traveling case, 1 December 1915, 165.

21. Elizabeth Arden ad, *Vogue*, 1 October 1916, 167.

22. For Stern Brothers, see Bauer, "High Priestess of Beauty," 189. Stern Brothers built a new store in 1913 on Fifth Avenue and West Forty-Second Street, very near to Arden's salon. Steinbach Company ad, *Asbury Park Evening Press*, 2 October 1916, 10; Jacobs' Pharmacy ad, *The Atlanta Constitution*, 20 May 1917, 7; Joseph Horne Company ad, *The Pittsburgh Press*, 2 March 1917, 13; Bonwit Teller ad, *The Philadelphia Inquirer*, 23 April 1916, 6; Bonwit Teller & Co. ad, *NYT*, 20 February 1916, 5, and 2 April 1916, 5; and "Specialty Shops," *WWD*, 23 February 1916, 3.

23. "J. W. Robinson Co." ad, *Los Angeles Times*, 25 June 1916, III15.

24. Geoffrey Jones, *Beauty Imagined* (New York: Oxford University Press, 2010), 64.

25. Arden ad, *Vogue*, 15 December 1915, 107.

26. "Mrs. 'X' Called" ad, *Vogue*, 1 February 1916, 115.

27. "Serving Society in Every City" ad, *Vogue*, 15 March 1917, 119.

28. "A Further Talk with Elizabeth Arden" ad, *Vogue*, 15 April 1917, 127.

29. Thomas Jenkins Lewis military discharge record, Adjutant General's Office, Series B0808, New York State Archives, Albany, New York, from ancestry.com. I am indebted to my colleague Timothy Wolters for his help with understanding Lewis's record. For background, see Rebecca Hancock Cameron, *Training to Fly* (Air Force History and Museums Program, 1999), 112; Ross J. Wilson, *New York and the First World War* (Burlington, VT: Ashgate, 2014), especially chap. 5. Laurence M. Burke points out that the army discovered that "the success of journalists, bankers, engineers, lawyers, and men from other non-athletic careers in frontline squadrons demonstrated that athletic ability was not the primary quality in a good pilot"; see "'What to Do with the Airplane?'" (Ph.D. diss., Carnegie Mellon University, 2014), 461. Army aviation was a branch of the Signal Corps until the spring of 1918, when it became the Air Service. For a firsthand view, see Ralph W. Page, "What I Learned at Plattsburgh," *The World's Work* (November 1915): 105–8. For the list of courses offered at Princeton, see "The School of Military Aeronautics," *Princeton Alumni Weekly* XVIII, no. 14 (16 January 1918): 318.

30. "When the Man Who Is Absent" ad, *The Washington Post*, 9 June 1918, F7; "Since Society" ad, *The Washington Post*, 13 May 1917, E9; "The Arden Way" ad, *Vogue*, 1 May 1917, 157; "Wise War-Time Philosophy" ad, *Vogue*, 15 May 1918, 94; "The Charm of Cleverness" ad, *Vogue*, 1 July 1918, 97.

31. "Special Editorial," *Vogue*, 15 November 1917, 12.

32. "Elizabeth Arden in Washington" ad, 12 November 1916, 4; "society leaders": "Remaking the Complexion" ad, 10 December 1916, ES9; "international authority": "Don't 'Veneer' Your Complexion" ad, 25 February 1917, E9; largest clientele: "Elizabeth Arden Will Be in Washington" ad, 4 March 1917, E2, all from *The Washington Post*.

33. Bennett, "Maybelline," cosmeticsandskin .com/companies/maybelline.php; "Note the Big Change" Maybell Labs ad, *Chicago Tribune*, 9 April 1916, 704.

34. "Shoppers' & Buyers' Guide," *Vogue*, 15 August 1916, 6.

35. Bennett, "Dorothy Gray," cosmeticsandskin .com/companies/dorothy-gray.php.

36. Helena Rubinstein, *My Life for Beauty* (New York: Simon & Schuster, 1966), 57–58.

37. "A Famous European 'House of Beauty'" Rubinstein ad, *Vogue*, 15 February 1915, 10.

38. Rubinstein, *My Life for Beauty*, 59.

39. Bennett, "Helena Rubinstein," cosmetic sandskin.com/companies/helena-rubinstein.php.

40. Lewis and Woodworth, *Miss Elizabeth Arden*, 88.

41. "No Woman Believes" ad, *The Washington Post*, 10 June 1917, E9; Arden ad, *Vogue*, 15 July 1917, 68.

42. Bauer, "High Priestess of Beauty," 189.

43. Thomas Jenkins Lewis military discharge record, ancestry.com.

CHAPTER 5: THE NEW WOMAN AND THE ARDEN LOOK

1. See Appendix IV, "Businesswomen by Historical Period," in Carol H. Krismann, *Encyclopedia of American Women in Business*, vol. 2 (Westport, CT: Greenwood Press, 2005), 592.

2. Tom Lewis gave up his job as a stockbroker and went to work for Arden sometime between 8 January and 12 April 1920. The 1920 census, dated 7 January 1920, has him listed as a stockbroker. Arden's passport application, dated 12 April 1920, states he was working in toiletries.

3. Pennsylvania and New Jersey Church and Town Records, 1669–2012, ancestry.com; "Marriage Licenses Issued," *Philadelphia Inquirer*, 5 May 1918, 21. Like her big sister, Gladys grew younger with each official document. She was in her early thirties when she married Baraba.

4. The information about Gladys working for her sister comes from Alfred Allan Lewis and Constance Woodworth, *Miss Elizabeth Arden* (New York: Coward, McCann & Geoghegan, 1972), 93.

5. "Goodwin's Drug Stores" ad, *Hartford Courant*, 16 November 1919, A10.

6. "E. T. Slattery Co." ad, *The Boston Globe*, 17 February 1918, 46.

7. "Sex o'clock" was coined by William Marion Reedy in 1913 in the book review he wrote for the *St. Louis Mirror*. See *Hagar Revelly* ad, *NYT*, 25 May 1913, BR318, and "Sex O'Clock in America," *Current Opinion* 55 (July 1913): 113–14.

8. *Flapper* originally referred to a young woman in her mid-to-late teens, what a later generation would call a sub-deb. She was initially described as thin, self-absorbed, and dressed to stand out. See, for example, Mrs. Henry Symes, "Concerning Health and Beauty," *The Baltimore Sun*, 21 May 1911, W5; Alma Whitaker, "The Feminine Sartorial Debacle," *Los Angeles Times*, 1 August 1911, 117; "Her Share of the Bureau," *The Chicago Defender*, 27 July 1912, 4; Alma Whitaker, "Concerning Smiles," *Los Angeles Times*, 24 September 1911, 114; "Flapper Girl of Ten Years Ago Now Extinct, Say Educators," *The Washington Post*, 27 August 1913, 5. By November 1913, *flapper* was a synonym for *debutante*: "Of What Use Is Slang?," *The Boston Globe*, 2 November 1913, 46. See also Joseph Gustaitis, *Chicago Transformed* (Carbondale: Southern Illinois University Press, 2016), chap. 8.

9. "Risk of Modern Girls," *The Washington Post*, 18 September 1914, 4.

10. Beatrice Hinkle, "New Morals for Old Women and the New Morality," *The Nation*, 19

November 1924, 541. On Hinkle, see Frances Maule Björkman, "The Spread of Drugless Healing," *The World Mirror*, November 1909, 190.

11. "The New Woman" ad, *The Washington Post*, 11 March 1917, 26.

12. All these examples come from the February 1919 issue of *Cosmopolitan*. Winfield Scott Hall wrote *Sexual Knowledge*, and William H. Walling authored *Sexology*.

13. Linda Hall, "Fashion and Style in the Twenties," *The Historian* 34, no. 3 (May 1972): 487.

14. Hall, "Fashion and Style in the Twenties," 488. See also Jill Fields, "'Fighting the Corsetless Evil,'" in *Beauty and Business*, ed. Philip Scranton (New York: Routledge, 2001), 109–40. For the history of the bra, see Jane Ferrell-Beck and Colleen Gau, *Uplift* (Philadelphia: University of Pennsylvania Press, 2002).

15. Rachael Alexander, "Consuming Beauty: Mass-Market Magazines and Make-Up in the 1920s," *IJAS Online* 4 (2015): 3.

16. For Chanel, see Bonnie English, *A Cultural History of Fashion in the 20th and 21st Centuries* (New York: Bloomsbury, 2013), 32–43.

17. Valerie Steele, *Fashion and Eroticism* (New York: Oxford University Press, 1985), 240.

18. Einav Rabinovitch-Fox, *Dressed for Freedom* (Urbana: University of Illinois Press, 2021), 83. Rabinovitch-Fox discusses flappers and fashion in "Dressing the Modern Girl," chap. 3.

19. F. Scott Fitzgerald, *This Side of Paradise* (New York: Charles Scribner's Sons, 1920), 282.

20. Richard L. Strout, "America Goes on a Spree," *The Christian Science Monitor*, 1 June 1977, 14.

21. Helena Rubinstein, *My Life for Beauty* (New York: Simon & Schuster, 1966), 59.

22. Irving Bacheller, "What Is a Gentleman?," *The Delineator*, March 1924, 11.

23. Alexander, "Consuming Beauty," 6. Of course, this was a long process. See Simon J. Bronner, "Reading Consumer Culture," in *Consuming Visions*, ed. Simon J. Bronner (New York: W. W. Norton, 1989), especially p. 25.

24. Steele, *Fashion and Eroticism*, 239.

25. Laura Gurney Troubridge, *Memories and Reflections* (London: William Heinemann, 1925), 118.

26. "Face young": "Turn Back the Clock!" ad, *The Washington Post*, 4 January 1920, 31; "Whatever defects": "The Mystery of Beauty" ad, *The Washington Post*, 21 March 1920, 24; "specialist": "Go to Headquarters!" ad, *The Washington Post*, 8 February 1920, 30.

27. Elizabeth Wilson, *Adorned in Dreams* (New Brunswick, NJ: Rutgers University Press, 2003), 130–31.

28. Regina Kelley, "Skins Must Be Protected from Rapid Sun-Tanning," *The Washington Post*, 28 July 1929, 10.

29. "Now to Look Sunburnt," *Harrods News*, 19 May 1930, 18, Harrods Company Archive, London.

30. "Loveliness Returns Swiftly" ad, *Vogue*, 29 September 1930, 93.

31. "Fashion Turns Color" ad, *Chicago Tribune*, 12 October 1930, H6.

32. Tiki Yates, son of Arden employee Gordon Yates, quoted in Lindy Woodhead, *War Paint* (Hoboken, NJ: John Wiley & Sons, 2003), 140.

33. "Easter Apparel and Novelties" ad, *The Baltimore Sun*, 28 March 1920, 5; "The Quest for the Beautiful" ad, *Chicago Tribune*, 4 April 1920, C4.

34. For an excellent, brief history of traveling salespeople, see Louis P. Cain, "Entrepreneurship in the Antebellum United States," in *The Invention of Enterprise*, ed. David S. Landes, Joel Mokyr, and William J. Baumol (Princeton, NJ: Princeton University Press, 2010). See also S. L. de Gorin, "How to Use the Demonstrator," *Essential Oil Review*, August 1934, 277.

35. Isobel Silden, "Beauty," *Los Angeles Times*, 10 March 1978, H1.

36. "'I Am a Famous Woman in This Industry,'" *Fortune*, October 1938, 145. According to industry analyst Catharine Oglesby, demonstrators made more money than department store saleswomen, plus some (not Arden's) earned a commission. See Oglesby, *Fashion Careers* (New York: Funk & Wagnalls, 1936), 181. The 1924 to 2024 salary comparison uses MeasuringWorth .com's Compensation/Relative Labor Earnings scale.

37. "Beauty for All," *The Mercury* [Hobart, Tasmania], 22 March 1939, 6.

38. De Gorin, "How to Use the Demonstrator," 277–79, 325; Elizabeth Arden "Common Sense Care of the Skin" ad, *Vogue*, 1 May 1912, 71.

39. See, for example, "Ten Personal Questions" ad, *Vogue*, 1 January 1920, 100.

40. "Don't Look Old" ad, *The Washington Post*, 24 November 1912, 13; "Becky Sharp" ad, *The Washington Post*, 6 January 1918, 8. Arden had been promising personal responses since 1912.

41. *Quest of the Beautiful* (1920), cosmeticsand skin.com/booklets/arden-quest-20.php.

42. The Newport salon was probably only open in the summer when the resorts were busiest. See "Trade Notes," *The American Perfumer*, July 1927, 283.

43. According to Arden's passport application on ancestry.com, her "description of applicant" included blue eyes, a straight nose, an oval face, a round chin, brown hair, and dark skin. She stood five feet three inches tall. They planned to visit France, Belgium, and England, for business purposes. She described herself as a toiletries professional. Vouching for her was chemist and 1895 Princeton alum Ralph W. Bailey of Stillwell & Gladding. Gladys's son, John, traveled with her.

44. Pharmaceutical Society of Great Britain, *The Registers of Pharmaceutical Chemists and Chemists and Druggists* (London: 1919), 157.

45. The information regarding the 1920 trip comes from Lewis and Woodworth, *Miss*

Elizabeth Arden, 98–101. The Haslam quote is on p. 101.

46. "Elizabeth Arden Venetian Preparations" ad, *Harrods News*, 6 November 1920, 50, and 11 September 1921, n.p., Harrods Company Archive, London.

47. Lewis and Woodworth, *Miss Elizabeth Arden*, 101–2.

48. "Annonces légales," *Cote de la Bourse et de la banque*, 24 November 1920, 2. The other three people were identified as Mrs. Piatkowska, Mr. Vanson, and Mr. Legendre.

49. Bennett, "Elizabeth Arden, 1920–1930," Elizabeth Arden ad, cosmeticsandskin.com/companies/elizabeth-arden-1920.php. Translation by Gareth Cordery.

50. Lewis and Woodworth, *Miss Elizabeth Arden*, 107–8; "Environment Scents the Status Thing," *The Baltimore Sun*, 9 September 1974, B5. Louis Amic would later work with couturiers—including Schiaparelli in the 1930s—to launch high-fashion perfumes. In the 1940s, Amic headed Roure-Bertrand Fils et Justin Dupont, the world's largest perfume manufacturer. He launched perfumes associated with Balmain, Nina Ricci, and Balenciaga, among others.

51. "Home Again from Paris!" ad, *Vogue*, 1 November 1921, 124; "A 'Fair' Exchange with Paris" ad, *Vogue*, 1 November 1920, 152.

CHAPTER 6: AN EMPIRE OF HEALTH

1. Bill and Ada Graham lived with their daughters on Seventy-Fifth Street. As the decade began, Patricia was thirteen, Virginia twelve, and Beatrice five. For Bill's business travails, see "W. P. Graham," *Crockery and Glass Journal* (23 March 1916): 17; "Acid Fumes Drive Out Fire Fighters," *NYT*, 1 January 1921, 10; "Reimer to Represent Well Known Factories," *Crockery and Glass Journal* (17 February 1921): 38; "New York News," *The Pottery, Glass & Brass Salesman*, 19 January 1922, 29. Bill had been ill in 1918 and again in 1922. For his travels, see "W. P. Graham," *Crockery and Glass Journal* (16 March 1922): 26.

2. The children were Ralph, age twelve, and Laura, age eight. For William's obituary, see "William Graham Is Dead at Age of 80," *Windsor Star*, 14 September 1928. William Graham lived with Christine and her family.

3. Geoffrey Jones, *Beauty Imagined* (New York: Oxford University Press, 2010), 27.

4. "Home Again from Paris!" ad, *Vogue*, 1 November 1921, 124.

5. At Harrods, Haslam had been "Buyer of the Drug Dept." See "Notes from Departments: Drugs," *Harrodian Gazette*, October 1921, 245, Harrods Company Archive, London. Arden grew out of 665 Fifth Avenue. The new factory was located at 212 East Fifty-Second Street, according to "West Side Home Sold," *NYT*, 13 December 1940, 43. "Salvation Army Buys 5 Dwellings," *NYT*, 27 February 1940, 37, stated that Arden also owned 213 through 217 East Fifty-Second Street.

6. According to "The London Salon" (*Elizabeth Arden News*, May 1967, 1, Elizabeth Arden Ltd. Papers, Unilever Archives, Port Sunlight, UK), Arden's salon occupied the entire "house of Merchant Bankers Pybus, Call, Martin and Hale," built in 1811. Other sources suggest that the salon (at the same address) was located above a jewelry firm established there in 1874: Mel Byars, *The Design Encyclopedia* (Hoboken, NJ: Wiley, 1994), 56; "Presentation Casket to the Emperor of Russia," *The Art-Journal* 13 (1874): 240; J. W. Benson ad, *Truth*, 23 May 1889, 985.

7. Margaret Case Harriman, "Profiles: Glamour, Inc.," *The New Yorker*, 6 April 1935, 27.

8. Jessica P. Clark, "'Beauty on Bond Street'" (Ph.D. diss., Johns Hopkins University, 2012), 245.

9. General Power of Attorney agreement, 6 September 1921, Elizabeth Arden Archives, EA/6/26/1/1-15, Unilever Archives. Coach and Horses: See Alfred Allan Lewis and Constance Woodworth, *Miss Elizabeth Arden* (New York: Coward, McCann & Geoghegan, 1972), 110. James Bennett states that the Coach and Horses factory opened in 1923; see "Elizabeth Arden, 1920–1930," cosmeticsandskin.com/companies/elizabeth-arden-1920.php. Hills retired in 1968 after a forty-two-year career with Arden. See "Mr. Hills Retires," *Elizabeth Arden News*, June 1968, 3, Unilever Archives.

10. "Daily Retailing," *WWD*, 8 December 1919, 48. Later, like many of them, she relocated to the Via Parigi, near the private Everglades Club.

11. John F. Eades, "City Planning in West Palm Beach during the 1920s," *Florida Historical Quarterly* 75, no. 3 (Winter 1997): 279; "Big Call Noted for Palm Beach Stores," *WWD*, 8 October 1925, 35; "Christine Finds Demand for Simple White Hats," *WWD*, 14 February 1923, 12.

12. Elsa Maxwell, *I Married the World* (London: William Heinemann, 1955), 82; Raymond B. Vickers, "Addison Mizner," *Florida Historical Quarterly* 75, no. 4 (Spring 1997): 381.

13. Vickers, "Addison Mizner," 381, 383; John Burke, *Rogue's Progress* (New York: G. P. Putnam's Sons, 1975), 190, 189.

14. Marie Dressler, *My Own Story* (Boston: Little, Brown, 1934), 213. Dressler was friends with Anne Morgan and Anne Vanderbilt and had helped them with their American Woman's Association. See "Women's Club Gets $433,400 for House," *NYT*, 17 April 1925, 6. Dressler had starred in Alva Belmont's suffrage play, *Melinda and Her Sisters*, and so trod the boards with Addison Mizner. See Maxwell, *I Married the World*, 82. The two Vanderbilts were William K. Vanderbilt II and Harold S. Vanderbilt.

15. Burke, *Rogue's Progress*, chap. 11; National Park Service, National Register of Historic Places Inventory—Nomination Form: Administration Buildings, 27 June 1985, npgallery.nps.gov/GetAsset/badb2f89-b331-4308-a4dd-88b0a2db182d.

16. "Traveling North & South" ad, *Vogue*, 1 January 1926, 99.

17. For background on the Florida boom, see George B. Tindall, "The Bubble in the Sun," *American Heritage* 16, no. 5 (August 1965), ameri canheritage.com/bubble-sun#2. Quotes about Florida not elsewhere cited come from Tindall.

18. "I Am Very Fond Of" ad, *Vogue*, 15 April 1924, 102.

19. "I've Met Her" ad, *Vogue*, 15 January 1922, 82; "reason for being" quote is from Elizabeth Arden, "The Call to Perfection," undated speech [1940s], p. 7, Women's Institute of Duluth Records, University of Minnesota, Duluth.

20. "Beauty Parlors Bring Prestige Plus Sales to Stores," *WWD*, 31 May 1924, 14.

21. J. W. Robinson ad, *Los Angeles Times*, 13 January 1924, 28, "Beauty Parlors Bring Prestige Plus Sales to Stores," *WWD*, 31 May 1924, 14.

22. "To Remove Superfluous Hair" ad, *Detroit Free Press*, 11 December 1921, 94. Her Detroit salon opened in late November or early December 1921. Detroit was also home to Arden's first chemical and drug manufacturer, Parke-Davis, founded there in 1866. For Parke-Davis, see Milton L. Hoefle, "The Early History of Parke-Davis and Company," *Bulletin for the History of Chemistry* 25, no. 1 (2000): 28–34. See also Charles K. Hyde, "'Detroit the Dynamic,'" *Michigan Historical Review* 27, no. 1 (Spring 2001): 57–73.

23. "Newest Ritz Open," *NYT*, 23 June 1921, 27; "Atlantic City Pageant Will Attract Crowds," *The Baltimore Sun*, 17 July 1921, 10; "Harding Arrives in Atlantic City Today," *Los Angeles Times*, 5 September 1921, 2; "Hotels to Install Radio," *NYT*, 22 January 1922, 26.

24. "Between the Seasons" ad, *Harper's Bazaar*, October 1922, 167. Arden began to include testimonials in her advertisements around this time. See "Aside from the Benefit" ad, *The Washington Post*, 30 January 1921, 40.

25. Elizabeth Arden ad, *Vogue*, 1 June 1921, 99.

26. "Famous Affinities" ad, *Vogue*, 1 April 1922, 138.

27. Bennett, "Elizabeth Arden (1920–1930)," "Will You Do Three Things for Loveliness?," 1923 British Arden ad, cosmeticsandskin.com /companies/elizabeth-arden-1920.php.

28. James Landers, *The Improbable First Century of Cosmopolitan Magazine* (Columbia: University of Missouri Press, 2010), 181–82.

29. 650 retail spots: Bennett, "Elizabeth Arden, 1920–1930."

30. "Notes of the Trade," *American Dyestuff Reporter*, 25 July 1921, 18. Incorporators included Florence Delaney (and F. O'Leary and G. Jones). Arden Chemical Company later became Elizabeth Arden Inc. For earliest use of "Elizabeth Arden Inc.," see Al Chase, "N.Y. Perfumer Buys Site on Walton Place," *Chicago Tribune*, 17 July 1924, 12.

31. A short list of new products included Anti-Wrinkle Cream (1921), Snowdrift Talcum (1921), Crème de France (1922), Ocre Powder (1922), Anti-Brown Spot Ointment (1923), Milk of Almonds (1923), Waterproof Cream (1924), Healing Cream (1926), Spotpruf Cream (1930), No-Shine (1933), Ardena Protecta Cream (1929), and Ardena Bronze (1929). See "Refreshing Lemonies" ad, *The Washington Post*, 22 May 1921, 43. Arden also sold bath salts, soaps, and "puffs," and Savon Kenott toothpaste, imported from France, which debuted in America in 1919. See "Realize This Desire" ad, *Vogue*, 15 April 1919, 130.

32. William Leach, *Land of Desire* (New York: Vintage, 1993), xiii.

33. James Schwoch, "Selling the Sight/Site of Sound," *Cinema Journal* 30, no. 1 (Autumn 1990): 55.

34. "Radio Radiations," *Hartford Courant*, 10 April 1922, 8. The first-ever radio advertisement occurred in the fall of 1922.

35. "Today's Radio Program," *NYT*, 23 May 1922, 22 (*Beauty Talk*), and 6 June 1922, 10 ("How to Care for Sunburn and Freckles"); "Listening In," *The Washington Post*, 20 August 1924, 16 (hot weather).

36. For examples of her talk titles, see "Radio Programs Today," *The Washington Post*, 28 May 1924, 18 ("Health and Beauty"); "Listening In on the Radio," *NYT*, 15 March 1925, XX15 ("Method to Correct or Prevent Wrinkles"); "Today's Radio Program," *Chicago Tribune*, 11 January 1924, 10 ("The Care of the Skin"); "Today's Radio Program," *NYT*, 11 May 1926, 24 ("Beautiful Skin"). For a sense of how really early in the radio game she was, see Donald L. Miller, *Supreme City* (New York: Simon & Schuster, 2014), 301–18.

37. Elizabeth Arden to Mrs. Hyatt, 26 June 1926, Box 174, Lisa Unger Baskin Collection, David M. Rubenstein Rare Book & Manuscript Library, Duke University.

38. "Beauty Comes from Within" ad, *Vogue*, 1 May 1925, 110.

39. "Are You Fat in Spots?" ad, *Vogue*, 15 April 1925, 125.

40. Arden ad, *The Boston Globe*, 3 January 1926, 60.

41. "Summer Demands Particular Care for the Skin," *Vogue*, 15 August 1923, 74. Arden made sure to secure a trademark for the Arden logo she used on the record set and booklets, which she said she'd been using since 1 April 1923. See Ser. No. 187,166, Elizabeth Arden, *Official Gazette of the United States Patent Office*, vol. 321 (8 April 1924): 238.

42. "Exercise with Elizabeth Arden!" ad, *Los Angeles Times*, 13 January 1924, 26; Marcia Vaughn, "The Eternal Feminine," *The Chicagoan*, 21 June 1930, 44. The stationery was referred to as a questionnaire in England.

43. Elizabeth Arden, *Exercises for Health and Beauty* (London: E. Arden, c. 1924), cosmetic sandskin.com/booklets/arden-exercises.php. The

booklet is not paginated. One journalist stated that no woman could purchase the records for home use until she had demonstrated "a certain proficiency" at the exercise routine while at the salon. See "Elizabeth Arden: Queen," *Fortune*, August 1930, 38. For the larger history of exercise, see James F. Stark, *The Cult of Youth* (New York: Cambridge University Press, 2020), chap. 5 (see pp. 165–66 for Arden). The albums and mats could be purchased at Arden salons as well as at many stores that stocked her Venetian line.

44. Lord and Taylor ad, *NYT*, 4 September 1923, 8.

45. See, for example, "Walter Camp's New Way to Keep Fit" ad, *NYT*, 17 April 1921, 56. Camp also set his exercises to music and promised a giveaway of a "portable phonograph" that would play any record album.

46. "I'll Reduce the Weight of Any Woman" Wallace ad, *Chicago Tribune*, 21 November 1920, 25.

47. "Do You Want to Reduce" Wallace ad, *Chicago Tribune*, 25 November 1921, B16; "It's Easy to Get Thin to Music" Wallace ad, *American Magazine*, April 1922, 121.

48. Arden, *Exercises for Health and Beauty*. See also Elizabeth Arden, "Exercises," undated, EA/6/23, Unilever Archives. The exercises were to be repeated until the music stopped, which is why three albums were required.

49. All quotes in the three paragraphs are from Arden, *Exercises for Health and Beauty*.

50. Lady Duff Gordon [Lucile], *Discretions and Indiscretions* (New York: Frederick A. Stokes, 1932), 246.

51. "'Slim Princess[,] Don't Dare Be a Sugar-Baby!,'" *The Baltimore Sun*, 18 November 1923, M3.

52. "Play Hard" ad, *Vogue*, 1 August 1921, 95.

53. Information in this paragraph is based on Dahn E. Salis, "Exercising Authority" (Ph.D. diss., University of Nevada, Las Vegas, 1998), chap. 4; McGovern quote is on p. 72. The Delsarte system called for "aesthetic gymnastics" done with "perfect flexibility" in order for the outer person to reflect one's authentic inner emotions. François Delsarte influenced dancers and stage performers in the late nineteenth century but became broadly popular after the 1886 publication of *The Delsarte System of Expression* by his student Genevieve Stebbins. (Stebbins, New York: Edgar W. Werner Publishing, 1902, quotes from p. 83 and p. 188.)

54. Harriman, "Profiles—Glamour, Inc.," 28–29. Exactly how Arden knew about yoga is not clear. If *The New Yorker* is correct and Arden met the yogis in 1915, this was four years before Anne Vanderbilt (through her daughter) became involved with Pierre Bernard, who had been known as Oom the Omnipotent. For Blanche DeVries and the schools, see Joseph Laycock, "Yoga for the New Woman and the New Man," *Religion and American Culture: A Journal of Interpretation* 23,

no. 1 (Winter 2013), esp. 108, 120. DeVries's school was located on East Fifty-Fourth Street. Unlike Bernard, DeVries, and other confidence men and women, Arden did not ever claim to be something she was not where yoga was concerned. For a biography of Bernard, see Robert Love, *The Great Oom* (New York: Viking, 2010). The avoidance of surgery was so important to Arden that she once named a horse Sir Herbert Barker after the British osteopath who had made a career speaking out against surgeries. See Neil Newman, "From How High to Knockdown," *Turf and Sport Digest*, April 1946, 26.

55. "I've Met Her" ad, *Vogue*, 15 January 1922, 82.

56. "'I Am a Famous Woman in This Industry,'" *Fortune*, October 1938, 63–64.

57. Arden, "Call to Perfection" speech, p. 10.

CHAPTER 7: THE BEAUTY OF FRIENDSHIP

1. Arden's 1920 passport application, ancestry.com; 1920 U.S. Census. At that time, they lived at 471 Park Avenue, and their maids were Aina Tommola from Finland and Elizabeth Hogan from Ireland. The Swedish cook was Maria Westerberg.

2. Janet Leckie, *A Talent for Living* (New York: Hawthorn Books, 1970), 149.

3. Leckie, *A Talent for Living*, 64.

4. William M. Freeman, "Henry Sell Dies," *NYT*, 25 October 1974, 42.

5. Gillian Dyer, *Advertising as Communication* (New York: Methuen, 1982), 45.

6. For the claims, counterclaims, and legalistic pitfalls of testimonials in the 1920s and 1930s, see Kerry Segrave, *Endorsements in Advertising* (Jefferson, NC: McFarland, 2005), esp. chaps. 2–4.

7. Leckie, *A Talent for Living*, 73.

8. "A Painted Face Is Disgusting" ad, *Vogue*, 1 May 1927, 115 (the original was *demodé*); *The Delineator*, June 1927, 61.

9. Undated ad copy [1927], Oversize Posters, Box S103, AMA Department of Investigation Records, American Medical Association Archives, Chicago.

10. "Ebb and Flow," *The Boston Globe*, 1 May 1927, C4.

11. Nixon Waterman, "The Vagaries of Fashion," *The Boston Globe*, 2 September 1927, 18.

12. Benjamin de Casseres, "The First Woman President," *NYT*, 5 September 1920, BRM4.

13. "Ruth Elder's Accomplishment," *Equal Rights* 14, no. 37 (22 October 1927): 3.

14. Leckie, *A Talent for Living*, 86.

15. "These Five Things You Must Do" Arden ad, *The Delineator*, January 1923, 84. Sell went to work for the magazine in 1926.

16. Leckie, *A Talent for Living*, 152. Lewis and Woodworth state that Arden met Marbury when she was brought to a Sunday tea at the latter's home; see *Miss Elizabeth Arden* (New York: Coward, McCann & Geoghegan, 1972), 127.

17. For background, see her memoir, Elisabeth Marbury, *My Crystal Ball* (New York: Boni & Liveright, 1923), and Alfred Allan Lewis, *Ladies and Not-So-Gentle Women* (New York: Penguin, 2000): 267, 268. Marbury was born in 1856.

18. Rosamond Pinchot Diary, 24 January 1933, Rosamond Pinchot Papers, Manuscript Division, Library of Congress.

19. Lewis, *Ladies and Not-So-Gentle Women*, 332.

20. Anne Vanderbilt, recently widowed, moved to 1 Sutton Place, and Mott rebuilt her corner house to suit her. Anne Morgan joined them, at 3 and 5 Sutton Place. The Marbury–de Wolfe home in France was the Villa Trianon in Versailles.

21. Lewis, *Ladies and Not-So-Gentle Women*, 372. In this quote, I have changed Bessy to Bessie. There is no consensus on the spelling of the diminutive. For de Wolfe, see Jane S. Smith, *Elsie de Wolfe* (New York: Atheneum, 1982).

22. Virginia Jeans Laas, ed., *Bridging Two Eras* (Columbia: University of Missouri Press, 1999), 297.

23. *Fortune*, for example, noted that Arden was "frequently seen" at Marbury's Sutton Place home and that "perhaps her greatest friend is Elisabeth Marbury"; see "Elizabeth Arden: Queen," *Fortune*, August 1930, 40.

24. Marbury, *My Crystal Ball*, 157.

25. Information on women in business in this paragraph comes from Angel Kwolek-Folland, *Incorporating Women* (New York: Palgrave, 1998), chap. 4. Only 46 percent of nonwhite women and 31 percent of white women were then employed. Together, they made up only 26 percent of the wage labor force (p. 135).

26. "Elizabeth Arden: Queen," 40.

27. Marbury, *My Crystal Ball*, 41.

28. Laura Troubridge, *Memories and Reflections* (London: William Heinemann, 1925), 241.

29. Lewis and Woodworth, *Miss Elizabeth Arden*, 116, 123–24.

30. "Actors' Fund Luncheon," *NYT*, 2 October 1929, 37. Tom Lewis did not appear in the guest list.

31. Lewis and Woodworth, *Miss Elizabeth Arden*, 124.

32. O. O. McIntyre, "Tomorrow Never Comes," *Austin American-Statesman*, 9 August 1931, 6.

33. Lewis and Woodworth, *Miss Elizabeth Arden*, 126; "Wellington Cross, 88, Dies," *NYT*, 14 October 1975, 40; "Irene Hayes, 79, Florist Here, Dies," *NYT*, 17 September 1975, 48.

34. Arden's list of charities began with the fine arts, hospitals, and women's initiatives, and grew mightily over the decades. For example, in the 1920s: "Comprehensive Apparel Exhibit by Capital Shops," *WWD*, 15 December 1922, 2; "The Nine O'Clock Revue," *NYT*, 29 November 1925, X12; "Social Notes," *NYT*, 25 August 1927, 14;

"$16,458 Given in a Day for Neediest Cases," *NYT*, 24 December 1928, 9.

35. "What Is Going on This Week?," *NYT*, 18 December 1927, N19.

36. Laura Tunbridge, "Singing Translations," *Representations* 123, no. 1 (Summer 2013): 74–75.

37. See, for example, "If You Want a Smooth, Fine Skin" ad, *The Times*, 7 November 1924, 16. Her earliest ad in *Tatler* was May 1922, 48. "Middlesex Hospital Reconstruction Fund," *The Times*, 14 August 1925, 15.

38. Leckie, *A Talent for Living*, 160. See also Lindy Woodhead, *War Paint* (Hoboken, NJ: John Wiley & Sons, 2003), 190. By 1965, both paintings hung in Arden's New York City home. See Douglas J. Roche, "The Elegant Worlds of Elizabeth Arden," *Maclean's*, 20 February 1965, 43. One of the portraits was sold with the company after her death and was hung in Unilever House in London. See Clay Harris, "Mudlark: Not Such a Pretty Picture," *Financial Times*, 5 October 2004. *Management Today*'s 1 May 1995 interview with Sir Michael Perry (Unilever chairman from 1992 to 1996) (managementtoday.co.uk/uk-davidson-interview-sir-michael-perry/article/410453) stated that a "rather coquettish portrait of Arden" hung in his office in 1995. British artist Simon Elwes, most famous for painting portraits of the royal family, reportedly also painted Arden. See Frederick M. Winship, "Paralyzed Hand Shattered Artist's Hope," *The Chicago Defender*, 30 November 1960, 13. The pinnacle of Augustus John's celebrity success came later, in 1939, when he painted Queen Elizabeth The Queen Mother.

39. Lewis and Woodworth, *Miss Elizabeth Arden*, 130.

40. Ariella Budick, "The 'Debussy of the Camera,'" *Financial Times*, 5 January 2018, ft.com/content/28bb1de2-ec96-11e7-b4d1-b2f78612cc4a. Beaton's phrase is sometimes given as "the Debussy of photographers."

41. Philippe Jullian's biographical sketch of de Meyer in *De Meyer*, ed. Robert Brandau (New York: Alfred A. Knopf, 1976), 9.

42. Jullian's biographical sketch in Brandau, *De Meyer*, 10.

43. "An Elizabeth Arden Treatment," *The Delineator*, December 1924, 89. The Ogilvie sisters helped draw traffic to Arden's salon, but by 1925 had relocated in Hubbard's old digs at 505 Fifth Avenue. See "Hairdressers Win Again," *NYT*, 29 April 1925, 3.

44. James Bennett, "Elizabeth Arden, 1920–1930," cosmeticsandskin.com/companies/elizabeth-arden-1920.php; "Voted Beauty Queen of France" Kirk ad, *Chicago Tribune*, 16 June 1929, 7; "Parisian to Texas," *Austin American-Statesman*, 24 April 1927, 1. According to Philippe Jullian, the face was Ira Belin's. See his essay in Brandau, *De Meyer*, 50. In *Miss Elizabeth Arden*, Lewis and Woodworth believe the model was "French

model Cecille Bayless" (p. 113). According to Janet Leckie, who worked with Henry Sell, the face was of a Vionnet model named Roberta, and the whole thing was Sell's idea: he found Roberta, put her in front of de Meyer, and intuited that Arden would love it. See Leckie, *A Talent for Living*, 153–54.

45. Willis Hartshorn, introduction to *A Singular Elegance*, by Adolph de Meyer (San Francisco: Chronicle Books, 1994), 116.

46. Leckie, *A Talent for Living*, 154.

47. Leckie, *A Talent for Living*, 158.

CHAPTER 8: FASHIONING THE AMERICAN WOMAN

1. Elisabeth Marbury, "Sayings of a Wise Woman," *The Delineator*, September 1927, 56.

2. "Exclusive Beauty Shop Specialist Shows Large Group of French Imports," *WWD*, 13 October 1925, 7; "Importance of Black Lingerie Stressed in Elizabeth Arden Imports," *WWD*, 26 October 1926, 45.

3. Diana Vreeland, *D.V.* (New York: Da Capo, 1984), 134–35.

4. Elizabeth Wilson, *Adorned in Dreams* (New Brunswick, NJ: Rutgers University Press, 2003), 102.

5. Linda Hall, "Fashion and Style in the Twenties," *The Historian* 34, no. 3 (May 1972): 488. Seealso Jill Fields, "'Fighting the Corsetless Evil,'" in *Beauty and Business*, ed. Philip Scranton (New York: Routledge, 2001), 109–40, and Jane Ferrell-Beck and Colleen Gau, *Uplift* (Philadelphia: University of Pennsylvania Press, 2002).

6. "For Bewitching Christmas Gifts" ad, *The Times*, 30 November 1925, 14.

7. "For Bewitching Christmas Gifts" ad, *The Times*, 30 November 1925, 14.

8. Arden ad, *Vogue*, 1 December 1922, 88. Babani was the son of Vitaldi Babani, an importer of Asian and Middle Eastern objets d'art and a fashion designer.

9. "To American Women" ad, *NYT*, 18 March 1923, 13.

10. Babani catalogue, undated [1920s], found on Grace E. Hummel's blog at ardenperfumes.blogspot.com/p/babani-perfumes.html.

11. "Every Woman Is a Rainbow of Moods" ad, *The Des Moines Register*, 22 May 1926, 16.

12. "Elizabeth Arden's Very Own Perfume" ad, *NYT*, 20 December 1925, 24.

13. Naomi Lamoreaux, "Entrepreneurship in the United States, 1865–1920," in *The Invention of Enterprise*, ed. David S. Landes, Joel Mokyr, and William J. Baumol (Princeton, NJ: Princeton University Press, 2010), esp. 391; and Margaret B. W. Graham, "Entrepreneurship in the United States, 1920–2000," in *The Invention of Enterprise*, who states that after the 1920s, "the term *entrepreneur* took on a negative connotation, signifying the eccentric individual who was all too likely to be disruptive to the well-integrated organiza-

tion" (p. 403). "Temptation" ad, *Chicago Tribune*, 17 December 1929, 41. See also "Trade Notes: The Babani Line," *The American Perfumer*, December 1927, 585.

14. "To Be Lovely" ad, *NYT*, 2 November 1924, 5; Randall B. Monsen, "The Perfumes of Elizabeth Arden," in Monsen and Baer Inc., *For the Love of Perfume* (Vienna, VA: Monsen and Baer Inc., 1999), 8.

15. Lady Duff Gordon [Lucile], *Discretions and Indiscretions* (New York: Frederick A. Stokes, 1932), 149.

16. Rosina Harrison, *Rose* (1975; repr., New York: Penguin, 2011), 86.

17. "Prices of Paris Clothes Now Higher Than Ever," *NYT*, 24 October 1915, X2. Arden took part in fashion shows whenever and wherever possible. See, for example, her involvement in a Cleveland fashion show: "Lindner's Plan Elaborate Fashion Clinic Sept. 29–30," *WWD*, 22 September 1937, 4.

18. "Unique Exhibition," *NYT*, 29 April 1895, 6; "The Costume Show in Madison Square," *The Illustrated American*, 23 March 1895, 362. For fashion shows, see Caroline Evans, *The Mechanical Smile* (New Haven, CT: Yale University Press, 2013); Alana Staiti, "Real Women, Normal Curves, and the Making of the American Fashion Mannequin, 1932–1946," *Configurations* 28, no. 4 (Fall 2020): 403–31; Jan Whitaker, *Service and Style* (New York: St. Martin's Press, 2006), 141–44.

The nascent film industry put fashion shows on newsreels by 1912. Edna Woolman Chase, who, in 1914, began her powerful, forty-year stint at American *Vogue*, claimed her magazine's World War I–era charitable Fashion Fête created and popularized the fashion show. Michelle Tolini Finamore, *Hollywood before Glamour* (New York: Palgrave Macmillan, 2013), 80–81.

19. Duff Gordon, *Discretions and Indiscretions*, 78.

20. "Race Women Attend Fashion Show," *The Chicago Defender*, 22 August 1914, 1.

21. Paul Poiret, *King of Fashion* (New York: J. B. Lippincott, 1931; London: V&A Publishing, 2009), 78. Citations refer to the V&A Publishing edition.

22. "Elizabeth Arden" ad, *Austin American-Statesman*, 12 August 1928, A5. Grace Doole returned, with a Mrs. T. J. Baier Jr., to "the Elizabeth Arden school in Dallas" in 1931, for another beauty culture course. See "Back from Dallas," *Austin American-Statesman*, 15 February 1931, A1.

23. Elizabeth Arden ad, *The Des Moines Register*, 18 May 1926, 20; "Make an Appointment for Private Consultation" ad, *The Des Moines Register*, 20 May 1926, 19; "Every Woman Has One Particular Point of Beauty" ad, *The Des Moines Register*, 21 May 1926, 28; Elizabeth Arden ad, *Great Falls Tribune*, 31 May 1926, 12. She or another representative returned in November 1926. Elizabeth

Arden ad, *The Des Moines Register*, 21 November 1926, E-3.

24. "'I Am a Famous Woman in This Industry,'" *Fortune*, October 1938, 145; "Sales Gain Reported by Local Stores," *WWD*, 29 September 1927, 10.

25. Edyth McLeod traveled from her base in the New York salon to many parts of the country ("It's Beauty Week," *The Boston Globe*, 15 February 1931, A49). After World War II, McLeod left Arden to become an independent beauty author and columnist. See her *Lady, Be Lovely* (New York: Wilcox and Follett, 1944), *Beauty after Forty* (Garden City, NY: Doubleday, 1949), and *Charm, Beauty, and Personality for Success* (New York: Laurel, 1952), for example. See also "Edyth T. M'Leod," *NYT*, 13 May 1975, 38; Jordan Marsh Company ad, *The Boston Globe*, 6 April 1927, 17; Jelleff's ad, *The Washington Post*, 8 May 1927, S5; Elizabeth Arden ad, *Great Falls Tribune*, 18 May 1927, 12.

26. Janet Leckie, *A Talent for Living* (New York: Hawthorn Books, 1970), 73; Alfred Allan Lewis and Constance Woodworth, *Miss Elizabeth Arden* (New York: Coward, McCann & Geoghegan, 1972), 117.

27. Arden trained and oversaw her treatment staff her entire life. See, for example, "Taking Your Face in Hand," *Vogue*, 15 May 1939, 78–79, 115.

28. Helena Rubinstein, "Manufacturing—Cosmetics," in *An Outline of Careers for Women*, ed. Doris E. Fleischman (Garden City, NY: Doubleday, Doran, 1928), 328, 330.

29. "Cosmetics Made Here Valued at $141,488,000," *NYT*, 6 March 1927, E1.

30. Virginia Pope, "Beauty Trade Ranks as Big Business Now," *NYT*, 20 November 1927, XX4.

31. Dorothy Cocks wrote *The Etiquette of Beauty* (New York: George H. Doran, 1927) and *Help Yourself to Beauty* (New York: Harper & Brothers, 1935). See "Trade Notes: Dorothy Cocks," *The American Perfumer*, August 1927, 346, and Dorothy Cocks advertisement, *The American Perfumer*, February 1931, 126.

32. "Elizabeth Arden Salesgirls' Contest, 1926–1927," 19, EA/6/23, Elizabeth Arden Ltd. Papers, Unilever Archives, Port Sunlight, UK. Hereafter cited as "Salesgirls' Contest."

33. "Salesgirls' Contest," 46.

34. "Salesgirls' Contest," 3, 4.

35. "Salesgirls' Contest," 11, 12.

36. "Salesgirls' Contest," 44, 49.

37. "Salesgirls' Contest," 52.

38. "Miss Elizabeth Arden" ad, *The Washington Post*, 17 November 1922, 7.

39. "Elizabeth Arden Is Coming" ad, *The Washington Post*, 6 April 1927, 7.

40. "Elizabeth Arden Is Coming" ad, *The Washington Post*, 6 April 1927, 7.

41. J. W. Robinson Co. ad, *Los Angeles Times*, 7 April 1927, 9.

42. See, for example, "Curb on Cosmetics Urged by Doctors," *NYT*, 17 May 1927, 7; "To Make Cosmetics Safe for Women," *Los Angeles Times*, 17 August 1927, 20; "Expand the Law," *Austin American-Statesman*, 8 June 1927, 4. Medical journals were another site of warnings regarding cosmetics but were were usually read only by physicians. See, for one example, Alice Carleton, "The Uses and Dangers of Cosmetics," *British Medical Journal* 1, no. 3779 (10 June 1933): 999–1001.

43. Arthur J. Cramp, "The Work of the Bureau of Investigation," *Law and Contemporary Problems* 1, no. 1 (December 1933): 54.

44. "Curb on Cosmetics Urged by Doctors," *NYT*, 17 May 1927, 7. There is a long history of poisons in face creams and cosmetics. See, for example, Kelly Olson, "Cosmetics in Roman Antiquity," *Classical World* 102, no. 3 (Spring 2009): 291–310, and Gwen Kay, *Dying to Be Beautiful* (Columbus: The Ohio State University Press, 2005). Kay states that cosmetics sales played such a small role in the economy that they were left out of the 1906 Pure Food and Drug Act (p. 30).

45. On Cramp, see James Harvey Young, *The Medical Messiahs* (Princeton, NJ: Princeton University Press, 1967), 66–87, and T. Ziporyn, "AMA's Bureau of Investigation Exposed Fraud," *The Journal of the American Medical Association* 254, no. 15 (18 October 1985): 2043. On Cramp's career as evaluated by his peers in the United Kingdom, see "The Work of Dr. Cramp," *British Medical Journal*, 1, no. 3975 (13 March 1937): 565. See also FDA Oral History Interview with Dr. Morris Fishbein, by Charles Jackson, 12 March 1968, fda.gov/media/81547/download.

46. Thomas Lewis to Arthur J. Cramp, 22 October 1930, Box 168, folder 3, AMA Department of Investigation Records, American Medical Association Archives, Chicago. Hereafter cited as AMA Archives. See also Kerry Segrave, *Endorsements in Advertising* (Jefferson, NC: McFarland, 2005), 7–12.

47. Lewis to Cramp, 16 April 1927, Box 168, folder 2, AMA Archives.

48. Lewis to Cramp, 13 April 1927, Box 879, folder 24, AMA Archives.

49. The Journal A.M.A. to Harry V. Spaulding, 28 April 1927, Box 879, folder 24, AMA Archives.

50. The Journal A.M.A. to Marian Laphan, undated [1927], AMA Archives, Box 168, folder 3S. See also The Journal A.M.A. to Edna Lamb, 18 January 1928, AMA Archives, Box 168, folder 3S.

51. Thomas J. Lewis to Arthur J. Cramp, 16 April 1927, Box 168, folder 2, AMA Archives; Susie McKellar, "'Seals of Approval,'" *Journal of Design History* 15, no. 1 (2002): 8; Carolyn Goldstein, *Creating Consumers* (Chapel Hill: University of North Carolina Press, 2012), 201. There is no stand-alone history of the Good Housekeeping Institute. See AMA to William G.

Thuss for evidence that the Good Housekeeping Institute shared its own test results on Arden products with the AMA (Box 169, folder 3, AMA Archives).

52. Undated ad copy [1927], Oversize Posters, Box S103, AMA Archives.

53. Original stories are from Margaret Case Harriman, "Profiles: Glamour, Inc.," *The New Yorker*, 6 April 1935, 28. Quotes are from Donald Jones, *Fifty Tales of Toronto* (Toronto: University of Toronto Press, 1992), 98.

54. Mary Elizabeth Evans's successful home-made candy sales preceded her tearooms. For her story, see Gerald M. Carbone, *Brown & Sharpe and the Measure of American Industry* (Jefferson, NC: McFarland, 2017), 123–25.

55. "New Members, 1931, Original Lists," Box 182, folder 3, Fashion Group International Records, Mss Col 980, New York Public Library Archives & Manuscripts Division, New York City (both Arden's and Rubinstein's names are listed). Hereafter cited as FGIR. The Fashion Group International website includes the original members: fgi.org/about. See also Estelle Hamburger, "The First Fifty Years," Fashion Group International newsletter, Box 151, folder 5, FGIR, but that article does not mention the founders by name. For the restaurant, see "We Record Our Memories of How the Fashion Group Started," *Fashion Group Bulletin*, February 1941, Insert One, Box 144, folder 13, "Newsletters," FGIR. The Fashion Group met informally in 1928, but started officially in 1930.

56. "Business Colleges," *Scientific American*, 18 December 1880, 388–89; see also Steven Conn, *Nothing Succeeds Like Failure* (Ithaca, NY: Cornell University Press, 2019).

57. George French, *20th Century Advertising* (New York: D. Van Nostrand, 1926), 190.

58. "Elizabeth Arden Open 70 Accounts," *WWD*, 14 March 1927, 5; "Even in Old Japan" ad, *The Baltimore Sun*, 13 November 1928, 10. McMann earned a certificate at the NYU School of Commerce in 1912. See *Annual Catalogue, New York University* (New York: New York University, 1912), 209. McMann may have left a position at the Title Guarantee and Trust Company in downtown Baltimore to work for Arden. See "Title Guarantee and Trust Co.," *The Baltimore Sun*, 3 September 1915, 1. According to ancestry .com, McMann sailed from Buenos Aires to New York in September 1924 on the *American Legion*, in August 1926 from Montevideo to New York on the *American Legion*, and from New York to Great Britain in October 1926 on the *France*. For a note about his new job, see "Joins de Markoff," *WWD*, 18 July 1947, 15. The years of his work for Arden are my educated guess.

59. "Para las Arrugas" ad, *Cine-Mundial*, May 1928, 432.

60. "In Europe—Elizabeth Arden" ad, *Chicago Tribune*, 23 October 1928, 37.

61. "Sports Influence Lends Color to German Apparel," *WWD*, 20 November 1928, 10; Maud Lavin, "Ringl + Pit: The Representation of Women in German Advertising, 1929–1933," *The Print Collector's Newsletter* 16, no. 3 (July–August 1985): 90; Lynda J. King, *Best-Sellers by Design* (Detroit: Wayne State University Press, 1988), 84.

62. "Talamini Promoted," *The Drug and Cosmetic Industry*, March 1936, 361.

63. Elizabeth Arden ad, *Asia*, January 1924, 74. For "1,000 smart shops," see "Waterproof Cream" ad, *Asia*, July 1924, 576.

64. "Plaise Chaque Jour Davantage" Arden ad, *Le Figaro*, 18 November 1924, 3. This is the first ad for the salon at the new 2 rue de la Paix address.

65. "A Day of Spring Shopping in the rue de la Paix," *Vogue*, 15 March 1925, 63, 64.

66. "'I Am a Famous Woman in This Industry,'" 63–64.

67. "Large Increase Expected," *The American Perfumer*, January 1926, 626.

68. "The Women Who Pass through the Arden Doorway" ad, *The Washington Post*, 29 October 1922, 34.

CHAPTER 9: EXERCISING MODERN PERFECTION

1. This is a widely reprinted quote attributed to Elizabeth Arden.

2. Al Chase, "N.Y. Perfumer Buys Site on Walton Place," *Chicago Tribune*, 17 July 1924, 12; "Trade Notes," *The American Perfumer*, November 1924, 500; limestone: "The Stone" ad, *Chicago Tribune*, 25 September 1928, 9.

3. "To Clients of My Paris Establishment" Arden ad, *Chicago Tribune*, 5 April 1928, 37; "The Chicagoenne for Face and Figure," *The Chicagoan*, 10 March 1928, 29. Joseph Platt later designed the film sets for *Gone With the Wind* and *Rebecca* and served as a "Decorating Consultant" for the magazine *House & Garden*. See Dianne O. Pierce, "Design, Craft, and American Identity" (master's thesis, History of the Decorative Arts and Design, Cooper Hewitt, 2010), 74. According to the Industrial Designers Society of America, Platt was an artist, a product designer, a magazine cover illustrator, a cofounder of the Society of Industrial Designers, and "a major figure in the artistic community" in the 1930s and 1940s. See "Joseph Platt, FIDSA," idsa.org/profile/joseph -platt.

4. "Where Beauty Is Created in a Setting of Beauty" ad, *The Chicagoan*, 1 March 1933, 51.

5. "Elizabeth Arden's Invitation to the Women of Chicago" ad, *Chicago Tribune*, 24 October 1926, F4.

6. "An Invitation to Meet Elizabeth Arden" ad, *Chicago Tribune*, 10 April 1928, 36. Arden hired Helen M. Sayles away from her job as receptionist at Huldah's Beauty Parlor in the Drake Hotel, where Arden stayed when in Chicago. After

Sayles spent two years at the appointment desk, Arden promoted her to hair salon manager. See "Helen Sayles, Served City's Elite at Elizabeth Arden Hair Salon," *Chicago Tribune*, 8 December 1997, A7. Sayles retired from Elizabeth Arden in 1968. For a photo of the reception room, see "Wings, Keels and Wheels," *The Chicagoan*, 1 July 1933, 74.

7. Arden leased the space from Celia Gould Milne, daughter of Gilded Age industrialist Charles A. Gould. When completed in 1927, the building became the headquarters of the Aeolian organ company. Architects Whitney Warren and Charles Wetmore designed several other New York landmark buildings, including Grand Central Terminal, the Ritz-Carlton (http://npcli brary.org/db/bb_files/2011-Madison BelmontBuilding.pdf), and Biltmore hotels, and the Consolidated Edison Building. Information about the Aeolian Building comes from Jay Schockley, "Aeolian Building," Landmarks Preservation Commission, 10 December 2002, 1–7, https://s-media.nyc.gov/agencies/lpc/lp/2125 .pdf. Arden purchased the building in 1944 and the company sold it in 1969.

8. "Salon for Beauty," *NYT*, 26 January 1930, 154; "Remisoff and the *Chauve-Souris*," *The Christian Science Monitor*, 16 May 1922, 16; Mark Turbyfill, "Nicolas Remisoff: An Intimate Pen Painting of the Artist Who Painted the Town," *The Chicagoan*, January 1932, 33–34, 68–70; Elizabeth Arden to Nicolai Remisoff, telegram, 27 January 1930, Nicolas Remisoff Papers, Collection no. 0199, Special Collections, USC Libraries, University of Southern California. Carpenter was married to classical music composer John Alden Carpenter. They traveled in circles that included Gertrude Stein, Edward Elgar, Langston Hughes, Igor Stravinsky, John Singer Sargent, and Pablo Picasso.

9. Rue W. Carpenter, "Problems in Decoration," *Vogue*, 2 August 1930, 30. See also "Chicago's Distinguished Decorator" Manor House Coffee ad, *Chicago Tribune*, 31 January 1931, 11; Mary Hoyt Wiborg, "A Rare Spirit in Art," *NYT*, 12 December 1931, 18; Howard Pollack, *John Alden Carpenter* (Chicago: University of Illinois Press, 1995), chap. 3.

10. "Opening of New Elizabeth Arden Salons Greeted by Crowds in Formal Afternoon Mode," *WWD*, 22 January 1930, 3.

11. "Salon for Beauty," *NYT*, 26 January 1930, 154.

12. "Salon de Beauté," *Vogue*, 15 March 1930, 81; "Lace Emphasises the Chic of a Bell-Shaped Silhouette," *Vogue*, 26 April 1930, 41–42.

13. "Trade Notes: Elizabeth Arden, Inc., Recently Opened a Beautiful New Salon," *The American Perfumer*, February 1930, 747.

14. "Attractions in the Amusement World," *The Washington Post*, 25 November 1929, 3. Marbury was their agent, and Anne Morgan and Anne Vanderbilt of the American Woman's Association were the patrons supporting their New York concert performance.

15. Karen Halttunen, "From Parlor to Living Room: Domestic Space, Interior Decoration, and the Culture of Personality," in *Consuming Visions*, ed. Simon J. Bronner (New York: W. W. Norton, 1989), 157–90; Marie J. Clifford, "Brand Name Modernism" (Ph.D. diss., University of California, Los Angeles, 1999), esp. chap. 9.

16. "Shopping with Bab," *The Washington Post*, 27 August 1929, 9; "Elizabeth Arden Building," D.C. Historic Sites, historicsites.dcpreservation .org/items/show/173; "Plans for New Building," *The Washington Post*, 15 December 1929, R4. See also "Shopping with Bab," *The Washington Post*, 9 February 1930, S2. Different sources give alternative floor layouts.

17. The comtesse hailed from the Bourbon-Orléans branch of French royalty (descended from the younger brother of Louis XIV). Thanks to my colleague French historian Dr. John Warne Monroe for this information.

18. "Shopping with Bab," *The Washington Post*, 23 February 1930, S2.

19. "Remaking Your Measurements," *Vogue*, 15 January 1957, 112.

20. "Shopping with Bab," *The Washington Post*, 2 March 1930, S2. The exercise equipment list comes from this article.

21. "Exercise Your Right to Beauty," *Vogue*, 29 September 1930, 57.

22. "Exercise Your Right to Beauty, 84.

23. Gretta Palmer, "Beauty through Surgery," *Photoplay*, June 1939, 85–86.

24. "Exercise Your Right to Beauty," 84.

25. "Exercise Your Right to Beauty," 84 (last quote, p. 57). For the Shado-Graph, see "Stand Up for Yourself," *Vogue*, 1 January 1936, 68–69, 78, and Ida Jean Kain, "Your Figure, Madame!," *The Washington Post*, 17 February 1938, X13, which contains specific exercises.

26. "Exercise Your Right to Beauty," 57, 84.

27. Marcia Vaughn, "Body and Soul Business," 31 January 1931, 29. Arden sold the tap dance outfit worn in the studio for home use: "black satin trunks, and orange-yellow blouse, black strap shoes, and white socks that," *Fortune* wrote, "few women could resist"; see "Elizabeth Arden: Queen," *Fortune*, August 1930, 38.

28. "Masculine Type of Dress Seems Definitely Discarded," *Great Falls Tribune*, 19 September 1929, 13.

29. Betty Thornley, "Merrily We Roll Along," *Collier's*, 7 December 1929, 19, 83. For context, see Dahn E. Shaulis, "Exercising Authority" (Ph.D. diss., University of Nevada, Las Vegas, 1998), esp. chap. 4.

30. "Your Beauty Is at Your Fingertips" ad, *NYT*, 10 February 1929, 102.

31. "Grace and Vitality" ad, *NYT*, 27 January 1929, 14; "There are Some Modern Miracles" ad, *Chicago Tribune*, 29 January 1929, 46.

32. Jeffrey L. Meikle, *American Plastic: A Cultural History* (New Brunswick, NJ: Rutgers University Press, 1997), esp. chaps. 1 and 2.

33. "Grace and Vitality" ad, *NYT*, 27 January 1929, 14.

34. "Very Modern, Very Fascinating" ad, *NYT*, 24 February 1929, 104.

35. "Build for Beauty by Plastic Exercise" ad, *NYT*, 13 January 1929, 30.

36. "Figures Rebuilt," *Vogue*, 12 October 1929, 115. Arden also borrowed, intentionally or not, from the Dalcroze dance system that had arrived from Europe just before World War I. Swiss innovator Émile Jaques-Dalcroze used the terms "plastic exercise" and "plastic expression" for his system of movement that also stressed grace and weight loss. See "Dalcroze Eurythmics Have Come to New York," *NYT*, 25 January 1914, 41.

37. "Figures Rebuilt," *Vogue*, 12 October 1929, 115.

38. "Washington Man Sleeps Under Electric Blanket," *The Boston Globe*, 27 November 1927, 12.

39. "Elizabeth Arden Herself" ad, *Chicago Tribune*, 13 January 1929, 7; "An Invitation to Meet Elizabeth Arden" ad, *Chicago Tribune*, 10 November 1927, 33.

40. E. P. Cumberbatch, C. A. Robinson, and F. Howard Humphris, "Discussion on Medical Diathermy," *British Medical Journal* 2, no. 3269 (25 August 1923): 311–12, 314. See also James F. Stark, *The Cult of Youth* (New York: Cambridge University Press, 2020), esp. chap. 4.

41. J. Alexander Mohan, *Vienna Yesterday and Today* (Vienna: Halm and Goldman, 1933), 297, 298. For Last, see Henry M. Kissman, *Views from the Road I Traveled* (Bloomington, IN: Xlibris, 2008), 66; "Dr. Erwin Last," *NYT*, 14 February 1948, 13. For Steinach, see Harry Benjamin, "Eugen Steinach, 1861–1944," *The Scientific Monthly* 61, no. 6 (December 1945): 427–42, and Per Södersten, David Crews, Cheryl Logan, and Rudolf Werner Soukup, "Eugen Steinach: The First Neuroendocrinologist," *Endocrinology* 155, no. 3 (1 March 2014): 688–95.

42. "Elizabeth Arden Is in Chicago Now" ad, *Chicago Tribune*, 12 April 1928, 32.

43. "Arden Muscle-Strapping Treatments" ad, *The Washington Post*, 13 May 1917, 9.

44. "Health and Beauty" ad, *Chicago Tribune*, 11 January 1927, 20.

45. "Elizabeth Arden's Gland Cream" ad, *NYT*, 20 May 1934, 22. By 1938, she had renamed it Joie de Vivre Gland Cream; "Every Woman Can Achieve the Elizabeth Arden Look" ad, *Vogue*, 15 January 1938, 109.

46. One of her newest fashion shows was entitled "Farewell to Age." See "Elizabeth Arden's Gland Cream" ad, *Chicago Tribune*, 21 March 1934, 3; Stark, *The Cult of Youth*, 185.

47. AMA Bureau of Investigation to Mrs. George C. Bleier, 26 October 1936; AMA Bureau of Investigation to Mrs. W. F. Moore, 8 Decem-

ber 1936, both from Box 168, folder 3, "Cosmetics, Correspondence 1921–1937, Elizabeth Arden," AMA Department of Investigation Records, American Medical Association Archives, Chicago. In 1951, she replaced Gland Cream with Special Hormone Cream. See James Bennett, "Elizabeth Arden, 1930–1945," cosmeticsandskin .com/companies/elizabeth-arden-1930.php. For more on gland and hormone creams, see Stark, *The Cult of Youth*, 177–87. Stark places worries about aging bodies in "anxieties over human degeneration and World War One," which were "exacerbated by Depression-era economic hardship and the revitalised physical prowess of Germanic youth" (p. 168). For examples of her ads and prices, see "Elizabeth Arden Tells You How to Wage War on Wrinkles" J. W. Robinson ad, *Los Angeles Times*, 22 January 1937, 9, and Saks Fifth Avenue ad, *NYT*, 10 June 1934, 27. For a discussion of the evolution and use of hormones in beauty products, see Stark, *The Cult of Youth*, chap. 6.

48. James Bennett, "Helena Rubinstein, 1930–1945," cosmeticsandskin.com/companies/helena -rubinstein-1930.php. Bennett states that Rubinstein did not develop one until seven years later.

49. Stark, *The Cult of Youth*, 129.

50. Chandak Sengoopta, *The Most Secret Quintessence of Life* (Chicago: University of Chicago Press, 2006), 92; Bennett, "Radioactive Cosmetics," cosmeticsandskin.com/aba/glowing-com plexion.php, and "Arden Vienna Youth Mask," cosmeticsandskin.com/efe/vienna-youth.php; Lucy Jane Santos, *Half Lives* (New York: Pegasus Books, 2021). Arden introduced the Vienna Youth Mask in 1938.

51. "On the Dressing-Table," *Vogue*, 1 February 1928, 92. The number of Vienna Youth Mask treatments was variously thirty or thirty-two.

52. "What IS Elizabeth Arden's Vienna Youth Mask?" ad, 1930, in Bennett, "Arden Vienna Youth Mask," cosmeticsandskin.com/efe/vienna -youth.php. See also Marcia Vaughn, "The Game of Make-Up," *The Chicagoan*, October 1931, 57. For a positive review of the entire Arden salon experience, see Vaughn, "Lithe Lines for the Leap Year," *The Chicagoan*, January 1932, 58–59.

53. "Dare's Weekly Fashion Letter," *The Washington Post*, 22 December 1929, S9. In fact, Duncan was born in 1877, and Arden on 31 December 1881, so Arden was actually four and a half years *younger* than Duncan.

54. Calculated for 1929, the year she invented it, from measuringworth.com.

55. F. N. Lewis, "Puffy Eye Strap," Patent #1,593,216, 19 January 1923; "Forehead Strap," Patent #1,497,858, 2 March 1923; "Lady's Dressing Case," Patent #1,600,830, 15 October 1924.

56. Margaret Case Harriman, "Profiles: Glamour, Inc.," *The New Yorker*, 6 April 1935, 28.

57. B. Zorina Khan, *The Democratization of Invention* (Cambridge: Cambridge University Press, 2005), esp. chap. 5.

58. "The Trousseau of Princess Marie-Jose of Belgium," *WWD*, 16 December 1929, 3.

59. She appears not to have patented the bandeau. J. W. Robinson ad, *Los Angeles Times*, 15 November 1934, 11.

60. Woodward & Lothrop ad, *The Washington Post*, 21 November 1934, 4.

61. F. N. Lewis, "Bottle" (hand grenade), Patent #98,040, 31 December 1935; F. N. Lewis, "Bottle" (glass hand), Patent #110,870, 16 August 1938. For a history of glass hand vases and bottles, see Marinka Bozzec, "Glass Hand Vases," The Glass Museum On Line, theglassmuseum.com /glasshandvases.htm; "New Products," *The Drug and Cosmetic Industry*, November 1939, 571. More than one version of this Victorian-themed bottle existed, and Arden certainly modeled hers on those. In December 1939, she sold two different versions. See "Shop-Hound Gets a Whiff of Christmas," *Vogue*, 15 December 1939, 78, for the descriptions. See also Monsen and Baer Inc., *For the Love of Perfume* (Vienna, VA: Monsen and Baer Inc., 1999), 14–15, 22–23. Some of Arden's hand bottles were made by Baccarat. She used the hand grenade bottle for more than one perfume as well. See "Night and Day" ad, *Los Angeles Times*, 10 April 1938, D11.

62. F. N. Lewis, "Jewelry Component or the Like," Patent #126,416, 8 April 1941; Monsen and Baer, *For the Love of Perfume*, 19.

63. F. N. Lewis, "Vanity Case," Patent #117,102, 10 October 1939; "Elizabeth Arden's Gilt Harlequin Compact" Bonwit Teller ad, *NYT*, 12 December 1939, 4; "Elizabeth Arden's Famous Harlequin" ad, *NYT*, 7 April 1940, 39, lists the colors. It debuted in 1939 and eventually also came in gold. F. N. Lewis, "Compact" (leaf design), Patent #130,169, 28 October 1941.

64. "Another Elizabeth Arden Triumph" ad, *NYT*, 31 January 1937, 28.

65. For ski kit, see "Boston Women Hear Beauty Talk," *The Boston Globe*, 14 June 1935, 17. All the other inventions can be found on Google Patents under F. N. Lewis.

66. "In the Courts," *WWD*, 23 January 1935, 36.

67. Harry and Katherine Mitchell to Florence Nightingale Lewis, Deed of Sale #06680055, 22 August 1929, Kennebec County Registry of Deeds. She paid $7,500 for the land. See Mortgage #06520220, 22 August 1929, and Discharge #07050112, 5 September 1934, Kennebec County Registry of Deeds. See also "Beauty and Pleasure," *Time*, 6 August 1945. For land purchased from Elsie de Wolfe Mendl, see Deed #06960472, dated 20 October 1933, Kennebec County Registry of Deeds.

68. "New Cottages Building in Augusta Lake Region," *The Boston Globe*, 1 November 1929, 25.

69. At Maine Chance, playwright Eugene O'Neill, for example, kindled a romance with Carlotta Monterey, the actress who would soon replace Agnes Boulton to become his third wife. Jane Scovell, biographer of O'Neill's daughter,

Oona, suggests that this encounter occurred in the summer of 1926, according to Arden's guest book. This cannot be the correct date, as Arden did not purchase the property until 1929. Scovell states that the guest book burned in a fire. See *Oona: Living in the Shadows* (New York: Warner Books, 1998), 51.

70. "New Cottages Building in Augusta Lake Region," *The Boston Globe*, 1 November 1929, 25. Harper, a graduate of New York University, was president of R. G. Harper & Co. in 1923. See R. G. Harper ad, *NYT*, 14 February 1923, 30 The other home was owned by W. E. Smith of Boston.

71. *Northward-Ho!*, 8 August 1914, 31; 15 August 1914, 22; and 22 August 1914, 34; "New York Golfers Win in Maine," *NYT*, 30 August 1914, S4. For education, see Leo Weldon Wertheimer, ed., *The Twelfth General Catalogue of the Psi Upsilon Fraternity* (1917), 52. He was NYU class of 1912.

72. "Curb Stock Drops 25 Points in Hour," *NYT*, 24 September 1929, 47. Harper had been "[a member] of a syndicate which offered the stock to the public." See also Dayton Airplane Engine Company incorporation notice, *NYT*, 26 February 1929, 42.

CHAPTER 10: INVENTING COLOR HARMONY

1. "Search Is Widened in Theft of $64,000," *NYT*, 20 October 1929, N1; "Flees with $63,000 in an Armored Car," *NYT*, 18 October 1929, 1.

2. "Bank Pool to Revive Stocks: 2nd Big Slump; Day's Loss Set at 14 Billions," *Chicago Tribune*, 29 October 1929, 1; "Banker Poorer by Millions: New York Banker Sees Own Stock Fall $18,000,000 in Less Than Week as Bears Work," *Los Angeles Times*, 29 October 1929, 1.

3. Tom Lewis told *The American Perfumer* that their 1929 sales were up 30 percent over 1928, and they expected 1930 sales to be even better across the fifty-eight different countries where Arden products were sold. See "Leaders Expect Good Business," *The American Perfumer*, January 1930, 646–47.

4. Margaret B. W. Graham, "Entrepreneurship in the United States, 1920–2000," in *The Invention of Enterprise*, ed. David S. Landes, Joel Mokyr, and William J. Baumol (Princeton, NJ: Princeton University Press, 2010), 408. Margaret Case Harriman, in "Profile: Glamour, Inc.," *The New Yorker*, 6 April 1935, wrote that Arden just kept expanding after the stock market crash (p. 27).

5. Rosamond Pinchot Diary, undated, folder Jan–June 1933, Papers of Rosamond Pinchot, Manuscript Division, Library of Congress.

6. Antoinette Donnelly, "Lives There a Woman Who Is Happy without Lipstick?," *Chicago Tribune*, 7 March 1938, 19.

7. "Views on 1930's Problems," *The American Perfumer*, January 1931, 671.

8. J. W. Robinson ad, *Los Angeles Times*, 2 April 1924, 9; Arden perfume ad, *NYT*, 5 April 1925, 4.

She offered these different sizes throughout the 1920s and 1930s.

9. "'I Am a Very Famous Woman in This Industry,'" *Fortune*, October 1938, 63–64.

10. Janet Leckie, *A Talent for Living* (New York: Hawthorn Books, 1970), 123.

11. Raye Virginia Allen, *Gordon Conway* (Austin: University of Texas Press, 1997), ix.

12. *The American Perfumer*, February 1930, 752. That's around $11 million today.

13. "If You Should Take a Boat" ad, *Vogue*, 4 January 1930, 101.

14. "Joy" ad, *Vogue*, 12 April, 1930, 171. These perfumes all debuted before the Great Depression, but this series of advertisements was new. See F. N. Lewis, Patent #74,233, 10 January 1928, U.S. Patent Office; "L'Amour d'Elizabeth" ad, *Vogue*, 24 May 1930, 99. She also designed the glass display used when photographed by de Meyer. A 32-ounce bottle sold for $125 in 1930, which would be just under $4,500 today. She utilized the bottle design for more than one perfume.

15. "Dreams" ad, *Vogue*, 1 March 1930, 117.

16. "Love" ad, *Vogue*, 29 March 1930, 97.

17. "One of Edward Burne-Jones's" ad, *Vogue*, 21 June 1930, 81.

18. "$15,374 Added Here for Red Cross Fund," *NYT*, 15 February 1931, 2; Sage-Allen & Company ad, *Hartford Courant*, 3 December 1931, 4; "Company Plans to Aid Jobless," *Los Angeles Times*, 6 December 1931, 14; "Aiding Oklahoma City Needy," *WWD*, 10 December 1931, 25; "Additional Contributions for Unemployed Reported by Emergency Relief Committee," *NYT*, 17 December 1931, 21, and "Additional Contributions to Fund for Unemployed," *NYT*, 27 December 1931, 34.

19. "Relief Plans Discussed at Luncheon," *The American Perfumer*, November 1932, 497; "Job Relief Group Maps Survey Here," *NYT*, 1 September 1931, 4.

20. "It's up to the Women" ad, *NYT*, 7 January 1932, 19. Catt was not mentioned in the *NYT* January advertisement for the full article in the February *Ladies' Home Journal* issue, but her piece "Up to the Women" appears on p. 7, where Arden's article, "Beauty and Optimism," begins.

21. Loring A. Schuler, "It's Up to the Women," *Ladies' Home Journal*, January 1932, 3.

22. Elizabeth Arden, "Beauty and Optimism," *Ladies' Home Journal*, February 1932, 52.

23. Arden, "Beauty and Optimism," 7, 52.

24. See for example, "Make-up Suggestions," *Ladies' Home Journal*, March 1932, 97.

25. "Beauty at Face Value," *Vogue*, 1 July 1932, 60.

26. "Stern Brothers Feature Massage Oil," *WWD*, 6 October 1927, 6.

27. "Manhattan Mortgages," *NYT*, 5 December 1930, 50; "Business Records," *NYT*, 29 August 1931, 27.

28. Harriman, "Profiles: Glamour, Inc.," 26. There is evidence that she owned a warehouse and factory space at 213–217 East Fifty-Second Street, then sold it in 1939 to the Salvation Army, paying cash at the same time for a "four-story factory building at 3809 Forty-Third Avenue, Long Island City." She wanted that to serve as a laboratory and factory. She hired Carl F. Peehl to manage the facility. Then she leased 208 and 210 East Fifty-Second Street to F. J. Newcomb furniture makers and 212 East Fifty-Second Street to upholsterer Philip Bargetzi. "Salvation Army Buys 5 Dwellings," *NYT*, 27 February 1940, 37; "Buys Plant in Queens," *NYT*, 29 June 1939, 43; "Realty Financing," *NYT*, 9 August 1939, 36; "Mrs. Carl A. Peehl," *NYT*, 1 November 1941, 15; "Rents 2 Buildings in Midtown Area," *NYT*, 5 July 1940, 25; "West Side Home Sold," *NYT*, 13 December 1940, 43.

29. "Auction Nets $114,600," *NYT*, 20 September 1930, 34. She sold it for $35,300—around $1.2 million today. It was located on the corner of Fifty-Third Street and Twenty-First Avenue.

30. "Advertising Man Rents Walton Place Penthouse," *Chicago Tribune*, 20 May 1934, 26.

31. "Cosmetic House Leases Building," *NYT*, 5 July 1928, 36; "Building Plans Filed," *NYT*, 5 March 1929, 61; "Elizabeth Arden, Inc., New York," *The American Perfumer*, July 1928, 311.

32. Harriman, "Profiles: Glamour, Inc.," 26.

33. "Views on 1931's Problems," *The American Perfumer*, January 1931, 674.

34. "Elizabeth Arden Adopts Special Contract Aimed at Prevention of Retail Price Cutting," *WWD*, 28 March 1930, 5. See also Grace R. Alker, "Competition by the Department Store," *The American Perfumer*, June 1933, 179–80.

35. "Consignment Sales Grow," *NYT*, 6 March 1932, N18.

36. Francis Chilson, "The Production Man's Diary," *The American Perfumer*, February 1932, 690.

37. "Fifth Avenue at Your Door" ad, *Barnard Bulletin*, 6 October 1931, 2; "Is the College Trade Important? Ask Vassar," *WWD*, 6 May 1932, 6.

38. "Home Making Centre Holds Fashion Shows," *WWD*, 16 April 1930, 8; "Program Issued for Second Week of Picken Course," *WWD*, 15 August 1930, 4.

39. Max Factor May Company ad, *The Baltimore Sun*, 28 September 1930, 6.

40. See, for example, "Events of Interest to the Club Women of the Capital," *The Washington Post*, 9 March 1930, S2, and 16 March 1930, S2; "Apparel Fashion Course for Boston," *WWD*, 3 February 1930, 1; "Discusses Make-Up at Jordan Marsh's," *WWD*, 8 April 1930, 13.

41. See, for one example, "Meet at Filene's Clothes Institute," *The Boston Globe*, 10 October 1931, 3. One or more Arden representatives spoke at this event, which went on through the first half of the 1930s.

42. "Discusses Make-Up at Jordan Marsh's," *WWD*, 8 April 1930, 13.

43. Elizabeth Arden Jelleff's ad, *The Washington Post*, 18 February 1931, 10; "The Triumph of Color in Make-Up" Elizabeth Arden ad, *Vogue*, 15 May 1931, 104. Max Factor sold a "color harmony kit" and chart in the fall of 1929, but his was keyed to "your individual type, and complexion colorings." See "By Special Arrangement with Max Factor" ad, *The Baltimore Sun*, 28 September 1930, 6. Factor meant makeup that harmonized with one's "individual type," an idea Arden always rejected.

44. Elizabeth Arden, "The Call to Perfection," undated speech [1940s], p. 13, Women's Institute of Duluth Records, University of Minnesota, Duluth; "Learn Elizabeth Arden's New Color Science of Make-Up" ad, *NYT*, 13 October 1931, 11.

45. See Charlotte Nicklas, "One Essential Thing to Learn Is Colour," *Journal of Design History* 27, no. 3 (2014): 218–36.

46. "What Make-Up Are You Wearing" ad, *NYT*, 1 March 1931, X14.

47. "The Triumph of Color in Make-Up" ad, *Vogue*, 15 May 1931, 104.

48. "Striking Hues Prevail," *NYT*, 3 May 1925, X10. For examples of makeup matching, see "How to Apply Lipstick," *Chicago Tribune*, 2 January 1927, C3; "How to Achieve Beauty," *The Boston Globe*, 23 July 1927, 17; for time of day, see Lois Leeds, "Milady Beautiful," *The Boston Globe*, 30 August 1929, 26.

49. "The Triumph of Color in Make-Up" ad, *Vogue*, 15 May 1931, 104.

50. "From the Soul," *The New Yorker*, 4 July 1953, 16–18; Regina Lee Blaszczyk, "Chromophilia," *Journal of Design History* 27, no. 3 (2014): 207–8. For the final quote, see "Striking Hues Prevail," *NYT*, 3 May 1925, X10. Blaszczyk's article draws from her excellent book, *The Color Revolution* (Cambridge, MA: MIT Press, 2012). Many sources explain the transition to ready-to-wear and its impact on society. See, for example, Rob Schorman, *Selling Style* (Philadelphia: University of Pennsylvania Press, 2003), where he makes the point that as the wording changed from readymade to ready-to-wear—at the end of the nineteenth century—the emphasis shifted from production to consumption (p. 7). See also Claudia B. Kidwell and Margaret C. Christman, *Suiting Everyone* (Washington, DC: Smithsonian Institution Press, 1974), esp. 165–95.

51. Antoinette Donnelly, "How to Apply Lipstick," *Chicago Tribune*, 2 January 1927, C3. Donnelly predicted, "We're getting to be decidedly clever about color combinations in dress and about knowing the right color of hat, shoes, stockings, and bag to go with the right dress. It won't be long before the colors that go on the face will be thought of, likewise, as component parts of a perfect whole." See also "How to Achieve Beauty," *The Boston Globe*, 23 July 1927, 17; Viola

Paris, "Beauty and You," *The Washington Post*, 24 March 1929, SM7. In 1929, the Tre-Jur cosmetics company sold a compact that came in four different colors to match one's outfit. Inside, though, the powder was all the same shade. Photos of the compacts and the Tre-Jur advertisements can be found on the Collecting Vintage Compacts website, collectingvintagecompacts.blogspot.com/2013 /07/tre-jur-part-3-diversity-and-great.html. Thanks to James Bennett for this information.

52. Marcia Vaughn, "Town Faces and Hairlines," *The Chicagoan*, September 1932, 52.

53. "Arden's Color Chart," *The Drug and Cosmetic Industry*, May 1934, 485.

54. *Printers Ink*, the advertisers' trade magazine, pointed out in 1926, "The ensemble idea [is] a device for increasing the sale of style merchandise to the consumer." Quoted in Blaszczyk, *Color Revolution*, 172.

55. "The Same Woman . . . but with Infinite Variety" ad, *Vogue*, 15 June 1931, 81.

56. *New Fashions from Paris, New Faces by Elizabeth Arden* booklet, undated, EA/6/26/2/4, Elizabeth Arden Ltd. Papers, Unilever Archives, Port Sunlight, UK.

57. "Fashion: Rodier," *Vogue*, 1 February 1926, 14, 122.

58. "Elizabeth Arden's Lipstick Ensemble" ad, *Vogue*, 15 October 1931, 99; "Coordinate Your Face with the New Colors" ad, *Vogue*, 15 November 1931, 99.

59. "Elizabeth Arden Amarillo Combination" ad, *NYT*, 8 November 1936, 34.

60. "Facing the New Colours," *Vogue*, 1 June 1931, 44.

61. "Facing the New Colours," *Vogue*, 1 June 1931, 104. Arden's chief imitator in this was Dorothy Gray, also mentioned in the article.

62. They sold individually for $1.50 or packaged together as the Arden Lipstick Ensemble for $7.50. The first ad carrying the six new names I was able to locate is a Jelleff's ad from 14 June 1931, *The Washington Post*, 15. See James Bennett, "Colour Coordination," cosmeticsandskin.com /efe/colour-coordination.php, for an extremely helpful context.

63. "The Vivid Spring Colours" Jelleff's ad, *The Washington Post*, 18 February 1931, 10.

64. "Lipsticks of the Ensemble" ad, *Vogue*, 15 September 1931, 131. Ellipses used instead of commas in the original.

65. Jelleff's ad, *The Washington Post*, 14 June 1931, S5.

66. "She's Wearing Red" ad, *The Washington Post*, 5 July 1931, S5. Today, the suit would be worth $1,050.

67. Filene's ad, *The Boston Globe*, 17 May 1931, A49; J. W. Robinson Anniversary Sale ad, *Los Angeles Times*, 11 September 1931, 9. Today, $15 would be worth $600.

68. "Several thousand" from "Robinson Says 'Any Hue If the Make-Up's Right,'" *WWD*, 11

November 1932, 11; Arden ad, *Vogue*, 15 April 1932, 9.

69. Jelleff's ad, *The Washington Post*, 3 February 1932, 10; "Beauty and Fashion Show," *WWD*, 18 February 1932, 23.

70. "A. T. Lewis & Son, Denver, Features Sportswear in Hotel Fashion Exhibit," *WWD*, 12 April 1932, 34.

71. "Kansas City Auto Show Features Wash Frock Style Revue," *WWD*, 21 February 1935, 11. For the San Francisco Junior League, Arden hosted the "Face, Figure and Fashion" show at I. Magnin. See "Magnin and Junior League Hold Face, Figure and Fashion Show," *WWD*, 3 November 1932, 11.

72. "Bloomingdale's Holds Beauty, Bathing Suit Show in Swim Shop," *WWD*, 3 June 1932, 2. The emcee was Patricia Cunningham.

73. "'Powder Tints' in Lingerie to Be Promoted to Match Complexion Hues of Cosmetician," *WWD*, 9 August 1932, 33. The company is misspelled here as DeGarcy.

74. Mandel Brothers ad, *Chicago Tribune*, 7 October 1932, 8.

75. Antoinette Donnelly, "Makeup Graduates into Realm of Art," *Chicago Tribune*, 2 July 1931, 24.

76. J. W. Robinson ad, *Los Angeles Times*, 25 August 1932, 9. The box generally included powder, rouge, eye shadow, mascara, and a lip pencil. She initially made eight different boxes and sold them to coordinate with complexion type as well as seasonal fashion colors. In 1932, they sold for $6.25.

77. "My Make-Up Secret" Max Factor ad, *NYT*, 17 September 1933, 30.

78. Ardena trademark: see Ardena, 6 May 1930, U.S. Patent and Trademark Office, tmsearch .uspto.gov/bin/gate.exe? f= doc & state =4808:lp1m87.5.8. Rubinstein quote: "Make-Up News from Paris" Rubinstein ad, *Los Angeles Times*, 14 October 1934, B2.

79. Penny Dade, *All Made Up* (Hendon, UK: Middlesex University Press, 2007), 23.

80. "Beauticians Make New Discoveries," *WWD*, 22 July 1932, 7.

81. John F. Sinclair, "Woman Wins Trade Spurs," *Los Angeles Times*, 2 June 1931, 14. Rubinstein sold the American part of her company. See Geoffrey Jones, *Beauty Imagined* (New York: Oxford University Press, 2010), 105, and Jones, "How Helena Rubinstein Used Tall Tales to Turn Cosmetics into a Luxury Brand," *Cold Call* podcast, Harvard Business School, 14 March 2019, hbswk.hbs.edu/item/how-helena-rubinstein -used-tall-tales-to-turn-cosmetics-into-a-luxury -brand.

82. "Gold Mounted Cine-Kodak Adorns $16,500 Automobile," *International Photographer*, February 1932, 26.

83. "Boston to Present Gift to Famous Flyer Today," *The Boston Globe*, 29 June 1932, 15.

CHAPTER 11: MORE BEGINNINGS, AND ENDINGS

1. Purchase offers: Janet Leckie, *A Talent for Living* (New York: Hawthorn Books, 1970), 161–62; Margaret Case Harriman, "Profile: Glamour, Inc.," *The New Yorker*, 6 April 1935, 27. Leckie wrote that Arden was offered $25 million, while Harriman wrote it was $15 million. For the "Beauty is power" quote, see Elizabeth Arden's early booklet *The Quest of the Beautiful* (n.p., 1923), 6. In the fall of 1932, the Lewises rented a penthouse at 834 Fifth Avenue, across from Central Park. The building had only opened in 1931. Then as now it was known for its luxury; see "Large Suites Are Rented," *NYT*, 13 September 1932, 37.

2. "'I Am a Famous Woman in This Industry,'" *Fortune*, October 1938, 61.

3. Cobina Wright, *I Never Grew Up* (New York: Prentice-Hall, 1952), 230–31.

4. Harriman, "Profile: Glamour, Inc.," 27, 30.

5. "A Beauty Tribute," *Harrods News*, 4 April 1932, n.p., Harrods Company Archive, London.

6. Rosina Harrison, *Rose* (1975; repr., New York: Penguin, 2011), 90.

7. Harrods' Advance Invitation, *Harrods News*, 11 April 1932, n.p., Harrods Company Archive, London. Assisting Haslam, until May 1934, was Robert P. Lewis, "sales manager of the Arden Company in England." See "Robert Lewis Joins Marinello," *The Drug and Cosmetic Industry*, May 1934, 521.

8. "'Blind' Beauty Contest On," *Los Angeles Times*, 15 May 1932, 8.

9. "Elizabeth Arden's Five-Point Plan" ad, *Vogue*, 15 May 1933, 79. In this ad, Arden made an uncharacteristically fantastical claim that the bath could "melt away as much as *twenty pounds* . . . if you're good, and follow directions exactly!" See "Shopping with Bab," *The Washington Post*, 4 March 1930, 8, for another description of the wonders of Arden's paraffin bath.

10. Harriman, "Profiles: Glamour, Inc.," 24.

11. James Bennett, "Paraffin Wax Treatments," cosmeticsandskin.com/cdc/paraffin-wax.php.

12. "'I Am a Famous Woman in This Industry,'" 142.

13. "Ogden Nash's Trick Rhyme Making Hit," *The Boston Globe*, 25 January 1931, B2.

14. Rosamond Pinchot Diary, 28 April 1933, Papers of Rosamond Pinchot, Manuscript Division, Library of Congress.

15. "Mode Show to Feature New Idea," *Los Angeles Times*, 24 October 1932, A8; J. W. Robinson ad, *Los Angeles Times*, 25 and 26 October 1932, 9.

16. Julia Blanshard, "'Kyphosis' or 'Lordosis'?," *Austin American-Statesman*, 22 July 1931, 6.

17. "Heads Down," *Vogue*, 15 November 1932, 57.

18. The White House visitor was Fannie Hurst. See Stella Hershan, *A Woman of Quality* (New York: Crown, 1970), 57.

19. "Maine Democrats Gather for Luncheon," *Hartford Courant*, 26 July 1931, B9, states that ER stayed with Marbury for the weekend. FDR was at a cornerstone laying event. See "Governor to Dedicate State Park Gateway," *NYT*, 22 July 1931, 2.

20. "Elizabeth [*sic*] Marbury Shrine Planned," *The Boston Globe*, 20 August 1933, B7.

21. "Optimistic Maine Democrats Meet," *The Boston Globe*, 7 August 1932, 9.

22. Pinchot Diary, 22 January 1933.

23. Virginia Jeans Laas, ed., *Bridging Two Eras* (Columbia: University of Missouri Press, 1999), 297. "Marbury Funeral to Be Held Today," *NYT*, 24 January 1933, 19; "Dignitaries Honor Elizabeth [*sic*] Marbury," *The Boston Globe*, 25 January 1933, 17; "State and Stage Pay Tribute to Miss Marbury," *Hartford Courant*, 25 January 1933, 4. For the number of observers and limousines, see Alfred Allan Lewis, *Ladies and Not-So-Gentle Women* (New York: Penguin, 2000), 430.

24. Pinchot Diary, 24 January 1933. See also Lewis, *Ladies and Not-So-Gentle Women*, 400.

25. Lewis, *Ladies and Not-So-Gentle Women*, 277–78, 367. See also Cindy S. Aron, *Working at Play* (New York: Oxford University Press, 1999), esp. chap. 7.

26. Wright and her husband lost everything in the 1929 stock market crash. "Cobina Wright, Society Hostess and Hollywood Columnist, Dies," *NYT*, 11 April 1970, 30. See also her memoir, *I Never Grew Up* (New York: Prentice-Hall, 1952), esp. chaps. 17 and 18.

27. "Marbury Memorial Is Planned in Maine," *NYT*, 16 July 1933, N1.

28. "Elisabeth Marbury's Maine Home Purchased by Mrs. T. J. Lewis for a Memorial Shrine," *NYT*, 19 July 1933, 19. See also Lewis, *Ladies and Not-So-Gentle Women*, 435–37.

29. "Getting Away from It All," *Vogue*, 15 May 1933, 81. So enamored was she, that Arden added her voice to a radio chorus for "State of Maine Summer Visitors' Day," alongside Amelia Earhart, Rudy Vallee, Charles Dana Gibson, John D. Rockefeller Jr., and Gene Tunney. See Lloyd C. Greene, "Radio Broadcasts," *The Boston Globe*, 1 September 1933, 33.

30. "Elizabeth [*sic*] Marbury Shrine Planned," *The Boston Globe*, 20 August 1933, B7; Jane Smith, *Elsie de Wolfe* (New York: Atheneum, 1982), 261–62; "Saratoga Luncheon to Honor O'Brien," *NYT*, 5 August 1933, 12; "Mrs. F. D. Roosevelt Greeted at Saratoga," *NYT*, 11 August 1934, 17.

31. Arden ad, *Vogue*, 4 January 1930, 101.

32. "Women in Business: III," *Fortune* 12 (July–December 1935): 81, quoted in Kathy Peiss, "'Vital Industry' and Women's Ventures," *Business History Review* 72 (Summer 1998): 219.

33. "Lady's Day in Louisville," *Time*, 6 May 1946, 60. This is the genesis of the oft-quoted "revolving door" line. It reads, "Her competitors say: 'Work for Elizabeth Arden and live in a revolving door.'"

34. There are many, many examples of employees with decades-long careers, such as chemist Daniel L. Couch, whom she hired in 1929 and who worked for her until his death in 1954 ("Daniel L. Couch, Cosmetic Chemist," *Brooklyn Daily Eagle*, 19 January 1954, 9). Frances Burke worked for Arden for eighteen years ("Frances Burke Joins Bonwit Teller, Boston," *WWD*, 19 September 1947, 10). Fanny Fern Fitzwater managed the fashion department from 1953 until her death in 1966 ("Of Things and People," *WWD*, 23 January 1953, 10). Norman Dahl, who oversaw the Canadian region and also worked in the United States and England, was employed by Arden for sixteen years. He left Arden for two years at Lehn & Fink, and then was president of Prince Matchabelli for just under four years ("Hear Norman Dahl to Leave Matchabelli," *WWD*, 19 May 1948, 14). Executive Leo V. Talamini spent eleven years working for Arden before moving to Prince Matchabelli and then rejoining Arden. (See "Joins Ann Haviland," *WWD*, 7 May 1948, 20; "Appointed by Arden," *WWD*, 30 July 1948, 13.) Noël Madden began with Arden in 1937 and worked for her until his accidental death in 1964 ("Mr. Noël Butler-Madden," *Elizabeth Arden News*, January 1965, 1, Elizabeth Arden Ltd. Papers, Unilever Archives, Port Sunlight, UK). The truth is that the fashion and cosmetics industries were full of men and women who moved around frequently—no company was immune as even a cursory analysis of the business columns of *WWD* proves.

35. Janet Flanner, "Comet," 18 June 1932, in *Profiles from* The New Yorker, ed. Clifton Fadiman (New York: Alfred A. Knopf, 1938), 243.

36. Leckie, *A Talent for Living*, 155. Margaret Thilly took "a quarter grain tablet of phenobarbital," according to Leckie, 153.

37. Leckie, *A Talent for Living*, 154.

38. "Elizabeth Arden: Queen," *Fortune*, August 1930, 40, 41.

39. For double-booking, see Lawrence Schneider to Sheldon Luce, 16 July 1936, MS 3014, Box 78, Papers of Henry R. Luce, Patricia D. Klingenstein Library, New-York Historical Society. Quotes are from Lydia Lane, "Elizabeth Arden Lauds L.A. Women," *Los Angeles Times*, 24 March 1954, B1.

40. Leckie, *A Talent for Living*, 161.

41. Leckie, *A Talent for Living*, 161; Pinchot Diary, 18 October 1933.

42. Pinchot Diary, undated, folder Jan–June 1933.

43. Alfred Allan Lewis and Constance Woodworth, *Miss Elizabeth Arden* (New York: Coward, McCann & Geoghegan, 1972), 153.

44. "Elizabeth Arden: Queen," 41.

45. "Committees of A.M.T.A.," *The American Perfumer*, January 1932, 608. In 1933, Lewis was a member of the Trade Practices Committee: "Committees of the A.M.T.A," *The American Perfumer*, January 1933, 586.

46. For mention of the offer, see Harriman, "Profiles: Glamour, Inc.," 27.

47. Lewis and Woodworth, *Miss Elizabeth Arden*, 150–51.

48. Lewis and Woodworth, *Miss Elizabeth Arden*, 136.

49. "Arden Gets Divorce," *The Drug and Cosmetic Industry*, November 1934, 523. Ellipsis in the original.

50. "T. J. Lewis Leaves Elizabeth Arden," *WWD*, 29 January 1934, 2.

51. "Thomas Lewis Quits Arden," *The Drug and Cosmetic Industry*, January 1934, 72. See also "Lewis Resigns from Arden," *The American Perfumer*, January 1934, 529, which states that Lewis "resigned" on 1 January 1934 and Arden "has assumed charge of the wholesale division" in his absence. In April 1934, Arden hired E. P. Matthiesen to replace Lewis as general manager. Matthiesen had an Ivy League degree and extensive experience in drugstores, perfumes, and cosmetics, including an eight-year stint as sales manager of Houbigant. See "Matthiesen—Arden Manager," *The Drug and Cosmetic Industry*, April 1934, 401. Matthiesen also took Lewis's place on the A.M.T.A. Executive Board: "Fortieth A.M.T.A. Convention," *The American Perfumer*, June 1934, 167.

52. The two friends were Norris Henrotin and David C. Moss, and they set up shop at 40 Wall Street (today, the Trump Building); see "Financial Notes," *NYT*, 18 June 1934, 31. See also "New Firm Formed," *The Wall Street Journal*, 18 June 1934, 4, which described the firm as "security dealers and distributors." See also their ad in the *NYT*, 13 August 1935, 27, and "Other Municipal Loans," *NYT*, 23 October 1935, 33. "Lewis in Investment Business," *The American Perfumer*, June 1934, 196, states that Henrotin and Moss had a background in drugs and cosmetics. The company appears to have still been in business in the 1950s.

Interestingly, Lewis's obituary states that he worked as an executive in the Arden corporation from 1935 until 1944; see "Thomas J. Lewis, 95, Cosmetics Official," *NYT*, 2 January 1979, 20.

53. "'Elizabeth Arden' Sues," *NYT*, 7 October 1934, 32; "Elizabeth Arden Sues to Divorce Her Husband," *Chicago Tribune*, 7 October 1934, 4. Elisabeth Marbury's connections aided Arden one last time by providing her with a divorce attorney, F. Harold Dubord. With his assistance, Arden sued Lewis for divorce on the grounds of "cruel and abusive treatment" and "mental cruelty . . . over a long period of time."

CHAPTER 12: MAINE CHANCES

1. "The Marbury Home in Sutton Pl. Sold," *NYT*, 15 February 1934, 36. Instead, Arden, Eleanor Roosevelt, Rosamond Pinchot, Anne Morgan, and the others planned to "endow and maintain the home in memory of Miss Marbury." For the third plan, see Mark Barron, "New Yorker Today," *The Washington Post*, 18 September 1933, 10.

2. "Coudert Sr. Lauds M'Kee as a Leader," *NYT*, 27 October 1933, 3; "Mrs. F. D. Roosevelt Greeted at Saratoga," *NYT*, 11 August 1934, 17; "Curley in Maine Talk Blames Republicans," *Hartford Courant*, 12 August 1934, C6. This event occurred in August 1934, after Maine Chance Spa was up and running, so she clearly used the spa for at least these two purposes simultaneously for a little while.

3. See Ian Bradley, *Health, Hedonism, and Hypochondria* (New York: I. B. Tauris/Bloomsbury, 2021); David C. Large, *The Grand Spas of Central Europe* (New York: Rowman & Littlefield, 2015); Thomas A. Chambers, *Drinking the Waters* (Washington, DC: Smithsonian Institution Scholarly Press, 2002); Susan Cayleff, *Wash and Be Healed* (Philadelphia: Temple University Press, 1991).

4. "Dear America!" ad, *Vogue*, 1 February 1938, 15.

5. "Summer Siesta: Chez Elizabeth Arden in Maine," *Vogue*, 15 June 1934, 66–67, 78.

6. David Svenson, "Ahead of the Curves," *Portland Monthly*, September 2012, 63–65.

7. "Maine Chance Beauty Lessons for the Young," *Vogue*, June 1951, 131; "Of Things and People," *WWD*, 14 May 1954, 27. In 1954, college students paid only $150 a week. "A Beauty Seminar" Arden ad, *Vassar Chronicle*, 22 May 1954, 6; Dan Hillard interview by Lisa Walker, 20 July 2015, Maine Chance Oral History Project, University of Southern Maine Digital Commons, digitalcommons.usm.maine.edu/mcfinterviews/6.

8. Quimby Robinson interview by Lisa Walker, 23 July 2015, Maine Chance Oral History Project, University of Southern Maine Digital Commons, digitalcommons.usm.maine.edu/mcfinterviews/5.

9. Aquaplaning was a precursor to waterskiing. "Discoveries in Beauty," *Vogue*, 1 July 1936, 80; "It's a Bath in Any Language," *Vogue*, 15 September 1936, 93. See also "Summer Siesta," *Vogue*, 15 June 1934, 66–67, 78.

10. "Arden to Start Fencing Classes," *The American Perfumer*, March 1936, 76. Joseph Fiems began with Arden in March. He took on twice-weekly classes at the New York Red Door Salon in addition to the teaching he did at Bryn Mawr, St. John's, and the Sword Club of Philadelphia. She replaced Fiems with the Olympian at Maine Chance.

11. "Discoveries in Beauty," *Vogue*, 1 July 1936, 80; "An Open Letter from Elizabeth Arden," *Vogue*, 1 November 1936, 103; for Elizabeth Arden Fencing Club, see Wanamaker's ad, *NYT*, 18 November 1936, 26. Nadi's comments are in his memoir, *The Living Sword* (Bangor, ME: Laureate Press, 1995), 309, 311.

12. "Fencing: Its Marked Increase in Popularity," *WWD*, 13 September 1938, 26.

13. Dan Hillard interview.

14. Eric Hooglund, "She Took Chances in Maine," *Belgrade Lakes Association Newsletter*, Summer 2016, 14, belgradelakesassociation.org /Portals/0/PDFs/News%20Letters/2016 %20Summer%20Newsletter.pdf.

15. For an excellent description of the Maine Chance experience by a woman who worked there for several summers in the 1960s, see Lisa Walker interview with Ellie Smerlas, 1 July 2013, https://digitalcommons.usm.maine.edu/mcfinter views/1/.

16. Arden purchased a total of 1,200 acres and used it to augment the spa property, for greenhouses, and for pastureland. Susan McMillan, "Former Elizabeth Arden Estate on Long Pond for Sale," centralmaine.com, 12 June 2014, cen tralmaine.com/2014/06/12/former-elizabeth -arden-estate-on-long-pond-for-sale. For the properties in Mount Vernon and Rome, Maine, that she amassed and deeded to the Elizabeth Arden Corporation, see Deed #08070197, 21 July 1944, Kennebec County Registry of Deeds, kennebec .gov/deeds.

17. Quimby Robinson interview.

18. "Take Your Own Cure," *Vogue*, 15 April 1934, 80–81; "Summer Siesta," *Vogue*, 67, 78. Cups and gowns: "Give Yourself the Maine Chance," *Vogue*, 15 April 1937, 134.

19. Hedda Hopper, *From Under My Hat* (New York: MacFadden, 1963), 204–5.

20. "Elizabeth Arden Is Dead at 81," *NYT*, 19 October 1966, 1.

21. Arden went by several names, serially and overlapping, in the racing world—Mrs. T. J. Lewis, Elizabeth N. Lewis, Elizabeth Arden Lewis, Elizabeth Graham, and Elizabeth Graham Lewis, among others—and her stable was known first as Nightingale Stable (or Mr. Nightingale Stable) before she changed it to Maine Chance Farm, occasionally misspelled as Main Chance.

22. John McEvoy, in "She Added a New Wrinkle to Racing," *Daily Racing Form*, 17 September 1994, 18, wrote that she acquired her first thoroughbred in 1934 at the Saratoga track. Article from the Maine Chance 1970s–90s folder, Keeneland Library. She was certainly frequenting Saratoga before that year. See "Notes of Social Activities in Metropolitan District and Elsewhere," *NYT*, 28 August 1932, 22.

23. This tale first appears in chapter 11 of Alfred Allan Lewis and Constance Woodworth's *Miss Elizabeth Arden* (New York: Coward, McCann & Geoghegan, 1972), and Arden and Riddle knew each other, but the public record neither supports that story nor suggests that they were much together. Arden first purchased show hunters before transitioning to thoroughbreds. See Frank Talmadge Phelps, "The Horse-Loving Cosmetics Queen," *Turf and Sport Digest*, December 1955, 34.

24. First races: "Ha Ha Wins Feature at Belmont Park," *Chicago Tribune*, 20 May 1932 ("How High" won $1,000), 26, and "Aqueduct Entries," *NYT*, 15 June 1932, 24 (did not win). Victories: "Aqueduct Racing Chart," *NYT*, 16 June 1932, 30 ($800); "Closes Strongly to Take Feature," *NYT*, 28 June 1932, 30; Bryan Field, "How High Triumphs by Margin of Head," *NYT*, 21 September 1932, 19. How High won $800 and $1,440. Her jockey, Frank Horn, was accused of "rough riding," and even though How High won the claiming stake, the victory was revoked. "Oakdale Handicap to Garden Message," *NYT*, 29 September 1932, 28.

25. Dark Secret, "Who's Who at Santa Anita Park: No. 12—The Nightingale Stable," *Los Angeles Times*, 24 December 1935, A10; "How High, 15 to 1 Shot, Defeats Field of 3-Year-Olds at Saratoga," *The Baltimore Sun*, 5 August 1933, 12.

26. For R. Pinchot, see "Glidelia Victor in a Nose Finish," *NYT*, 19 May 1933, 24.

27. Bryan Fields, "War Admiral Wins Last Start of the Year," *NYT*, 13 November 1938, 81. She also named a horse Main Chance: "Wise Daughter Winner at Spa," *The Baltimore Sun*, 9 August 1933, 14.

28. "Boxholders Named for Belmont Park," *NYT*, 16 May 1926, S7; "Winooka Arrives for Belmont Race," *NYT*, 6 November 1933, 27. Industrialists such as Wanamakers, Fields, and Replogles.

29. "Beau Peep Whispers," *Los Angeles Times*, 15 December 1935, D1.

30. Quote is from Malvina Lindsay, "Turf Is the Only Life, Says Mary Hirsch, America's Only Woman Horse Trainer," *The Washington Post*, 21 November 1934, 13. Allene Talmey, "Horse Sense: A Sketch of Young Mary Hirsch, the First Woman to Hold a Horse Trainer's License," *Vogue*, 1 August 1936, 54, 88.

31. "Horses of Mrs. Payson and Mrs. Laughlin Will Race as Manhasset Stable in 1934," *NYT*, 5 December 1933, 34; Jack Ryan, "Horse Racing—Sport of Queens," *Family Weekly*, 29 April 1962, 14, 16, Maine Chance File, 1960–65, Keeneland Library. See also Bert Sugar, *Horse Sense* (Hoboken, NJ: John Wiley & Sons, 2003), 47–48, and Steven Crist, "Matriarchs of the Meadow," *NYT Magazine*, 31 March 1985, 36–38, 40.

32. Crist, "Matriarchs of the Meadow," 36.

33. Author interview with Kim Ryan, 19 October 2018, Lexington, Kentucky. See also Tim Layden, "Fifty Years after Diane Crump First Rode in the Kentucky Derby, Women Jockeys Continue the Fight," NBC Sports, 2 September 2020, sports.nbcsports.com/2020/09/02/diane -crump; "The Ladies of the Triple Crown," *Sports History Weekly*, sportshistoryweekly.com/stories /triple-crown-kentucky-derby-secretariat-diane -crump-julie-krone-penny-chenery, 866.

34. Kim Ryan and her husband bought a twenty-acre farm, foaled one hundred horses, but "could never find a trainer who would work with us," she recalled, "because we were outsiders." The Ryans finally trained their own horses, and

they won several stakes races (where owners contribute to the purse) at Keeneland. "They'll take your money," she attested, "but they'll never let you in." Author interview with Ryan. "Admission" vs. "acceptance": Sugar, *Horse Sense*, 46, 49–50.

35. Arch Ward, "In the Wake of the News," *Chicago Tribune*, 13 May 1946, 27.

36. Raymond Brooks, "Horse Racing Bill Nears Vote," *Austin American-Statesman*, 20 March 1933, 1. The legislator was H. H. Ray of Troy.

37. See, for example, "Horse Racing Bill Gains Support," *Austin American-Statesman*, 5 February 1929, 1 (for the opposition of the Woman's Christian Temperance Union and other women's clubs in Texas); "D.C. Federation of Women's Clubs Opposes Racing Bills," *The Washington Post*, 4 March 1934, 5; "220 Vote Opposition," *The Washington Post*, 18 March 1937, 7; "Women in Jersey Oppose Racing Bill," *NYT*, 20 May 1939, 20; "Federation Reports on Biennium," *Los Angeles Times*, 13 May 1945, C1. Women in parent-teacher associations also came out against betting in the 1930s, as they feared that children were spending their pocket money on pari-mutuel betting at the tracks.

38. By the late 1930s, the press often clarified that Elizabeth Graham was Elizabeth Arden. This trend increased through the 1940s. See, for example, Judith Cass, "Fashions and Fancy," *Chicago Tribune*, 8 July 1945, F1: "Mrs. Graham, who as Elizabeth Arden has been responsible for glamorizing countless American women . . . turned up at the track to cheer for some of the entries from her Maine Chance stables," which is from the women's page, not the sports page.

39. Natalie Voss, "Kentucky Farm Time Capsule: Maine Chance Farm," *Paulick Report*, 22 January 2018, "Maine Chance 2000s" folder, Keeneland Library.

40. Jinx Falkenburg and Tex McCrary, "Elizabeth Arden Says Short Hair Keeps Girls from Marrying Well," *The Boston Globe*, 11 March 1950, 11.

41. Elizabeth Conger, "Treat a Woman Like a Horse and a Horse Like a Woman," *Spur*, March/April 1984, 54, Keeneland.

42. Jim Bolus, "Beauty Cream on Racehorses?," *Louisville Times*, 2 May 1982, unpaginated clipping, Maine Chance 1970s–90s folder, Keeneland.

43. McEvoy, "She Added a New Wrinkle to Racing," 18.

44. McEvoy, "She Added a New Wrinkle to Racing," 18.

45. Trainer Mack Miller attested to the olive oil: "They were the best looking horses I ever saw. I never saw such coats in my life. I know the olive oil did it. Most people couldn't afford it, but she did." Miller respected her. See Jim Bolus, "Beauty Cream on Horses?," *Louisville Times*, 2 May 1982, unpaginated clipping from Maine Chance

1970s–90s folder, Keeneland Library. Teaching the trainers is also from Bolus. Arden quote is from Falkenburg and McCrary, "Elizabeth Arden Says Short Hair Keeps Girls from Marrying Well," 11: "My horses use my creams, too, you know—horses are just as sensitive as people." In an interview with Jeane Hoffman, Arden spelled out the rest of her equine treatments: "Mrs. Graham Uses Lotion on Horses," *Los Angeles Times*, 30 January 1955, A19. Sending the physical therapist: see Margaret M. Buhrman, "Elizabeth Arden Expected No One to Grow Old," *The St. Augustine Record*, 23 October 1933, Day File, EA/6/15/1, Elizabeth Arden Ltd. Papers, Unilever Archives, Port Sunlight, UK.

46. Marion E. Altieri, "Elizabeth Arden: Thoroughbred Owner, Breeder, Healer," Equine Info Exchange, 8 June 2017, "Maine Chance 2000s" folder, Maine Chance Papers, Keeneland. Quote is from "Mrs. Elizabeth Graham . . . among Those Who Died," *Sunday Herald-Leader*, 15 January 1967, L-2. See also G. F. T. Ryall, "Women and Horses," *Vogue*, 15 April 1948, 148–49, and Mary Jane Gallagher, "Women-Owners," *Vogue*, 1 June 1958, 114, 152.

47. Conger, "Treat a Woman," 54.

48. "Benning Notes," *The Blood-Horse*, 17 March 1934, 355. The horse, Sir Herbert Barker, did not make the Derby.

49. Paul Lowry, "Arden Nags to Run Here," *Los Angeles Times*, 11 August 1935, 14; Paul Lowry, "World's Greatest Stables Gather at Santa Anita for Opening of Meeting," *Los Angeles Times*, 8 December 1935, 24. Other great thoroughbred owners had established stables at Santa Anita by then, too. Arden's racing pink was called alternately "Cyclamen" or "cerise." See Frederick M. Burlew, *American Racing Colors*, vol. 6, 1945–1965, K–Z, Keeneland. Cyclamen had definitely replaced red before 1945, and it seems to have happened over time rather than all at once.

Arden bought her first broodmare in 1932 and boarded her breeding stock at Combs's Spendthrift Farm in Kentucky until she purchased a horse farm outside Lexington called Maine Chance Farm; see Voss, "Kentucky Farm Time Capsule." Conger states she purchased Maine Chance Farm "in the late 1940s" ("Treat a Woman Like a Horse," 52). The Lexington newspaper the *Herald-Leader* gives 1956 as the date. She leased it with an option to purchase in September 1955 and bought it in January 1956.

50. Howland Blackiston, "Get a Glimpse of This 1935 Cadillac Town Car, Once Owned by Cosmetics Queen Elizabeth Arden," *The Self-Starter* 51, no. 1 (January 2008): 20–21; quote is on p. 20. See also this Carolina Classic Cars YouTube video: youtube.com/watch?v=4_xx6X Uio2E. The gold color was "Bolivian Brown." Arden may have owned the Prince of Wales Duesenberg, or possibly one of two Ladies Berlines, made in 1931 or 1933, and selling for $16,000

then. See "On Her Dressing-Table," *Vogue*, 15 March 1923, 90; Bonhams' 1934 Duesenberg Model J Prince of Wales Berline, bonhams.com /auctions/25593/lot/450; Sam Grate, curator, Auburn Cord Duesenberg Automobile Museum, email to author, 18 December 2020. For the Rolls-Royce, see "Elizabeth Arden, Queen," *Fortune*, August 1930, 47. The Cadillac's $5,709.50 is well over $200,000 in contemporary worth.

51. "Elizabeth Arden: Queen," 40; Rosamond Pinchot Diary, undated, folder Jan–June 1933, Papers of Rosamond Pinchot, Manuscript Division, Library of Congress.

52. Pinchot Diary, undated, folder Jan–June 1933. For descriptions and photographs of the penthouse, see "Background for Beauty," *Vogue*, 15 September 1933, 60–61, and Jennifer Boles, "An Early Thirties Set Piece," *The Peak of Chic*, 11 April 2016, thepeakofchic.blogspot.com/2016/ 04/an-early-thirties-set-piece.html. Her photos come from *House & Garden*, March 1933. Remisoff's Napoleonic soldier is modeled on the 1809 portrait of Prince Boris Yusupov by Antoine-Jean Gros.

53. Pinchot Diary, 3 October 1934.

54. Pinchot Diary, 13 January 1933. The "Pulitzer" Pinchot refers to was probably Ralph Pulitzer, son of Joseph and former president of the Pulitzer Publishing Company. "'Emperor Jones' as Opera, Jan. 7," *NYT*, 28 December 1932, 15. See also Nelson D. Neal, "Hemsley Winfield," *Afro-Americans in New York Life and History* 40, no. 1 (July 2018): 137–51.

55. On Hurst, see her autobiography, *Anatomy of Me* (Garden City, NY: Doubleday, 1958), and Brooke Kroeger, *Fannie* (New York: Random House, 1999).

56. Fannie Hurst to Elizabeth Arden, undated, Papers of Fannie Hurst, Harry Ransom Center, University of Texas at Austin. The original quote is "seems to know no limits."

57. Fannie Hurst to Elizabeth Arden, 3 March 1928, Hurst Papers.

58. Fannie Hurst, *Imitation of Life*, ed. Daniel Itzkovitz (1933; repr., Durham, NC: Duke University Press, 2004), 155, 165, 199.

59. Collie Small, "Gossip Is Her Business," *The Saturday Evening Post*, 11 January 1947, Gen Mss 1122, Series III, Box 148, "Clippings—Hedda Hopper, 1940s & 1950s," Jerome Zerbe Photographs and Papers, Beinecke Rare Book and Manuscript Library, Yale University. Hereafter cited as Zerbe Papers.

60. Arden's intensive training remained part of working for her. Newspapers called it the Elizabeth Arden School.

61. Hopper, *From Under My Hat*, 200–204 ("maharajah" quote from previous paragraph is on p. 200). See also Small, "Gossip Is Her Business," Zerbe Papers.

62. Ilka Chase, *Past Imperfect* (Garden City, NY: Doubleday, Doran, 1942), 183, 184.

63. Clare Boothe Luce, *The Women* (1937; repr., New York: Dramatists Play Service, 1995), 36. The play debuted in 1937.

64. Jennifer Scanlon, "'If My Husband Calls I'm Not Here,'" *Feminist Studies* 33, no. 2 (Summer 2007): 312.

65. "Elizabeth Arden . . . Sole Head of Vast Cosmetic Empire," press release, c. 1955, Press Release File, EA 6/18/4, Unilever Archives, Port Sunlight, UK.

66. For O'Keeffe as an "ardent feminist," see Robert M. Coates, "Abstraction—Flowers," 6 July 1929, in *Profiles from* The New Yorker, ed. Clifton Fadiman (New York: Alfred A. Knopf, 1938), 152. Alfred Stieglitz to Elizabeth Arden, 1 November 1936, YCAL MSS 85, Series 1, Box 3, Alfred Stieglitz/Georgia O'Keeffe Archive, Beinecke Rare Book and Manuscript Library, Yale University. Hereafter cited as O'Keeffe Archive, Yale.

67. Elizabeth Blair, "Newly Uncovered Georgia O'Keeffe Letters Shed Light on Her Greatest Paintings," NPR, 21 March 2019, npr.org/2019 /03/21/705569875/newly-uncovered-georgia -okeeffe-letters-shed-light-on-her-greatest -paintings. The 1936 painting was 70 × 83.5 inches. The scholar is Barbara Bair, who served as Library of Congress manuscript curator.

68. Payment Memorandum, O'Keeffe to Arden, 20 July 1936, O'Keeffe Archive, Yale. Other sources state that Arden paid $10,000, but it is clear from the memorandum that the agreed-upon price was $12,000.

69. Stieglitz to Arden, 26 July 1936, and 22 May 1936, O'Keeffe Archive, Yale.

70. Stieglitz to Arden, 22 May 1936, O'Keeffe Archive, Yale.

71. Pinchot Diary, undated, folder Jan–June 1933.

72. Stieglitz to Arden, 27 April 1936, and 9 May 1936, O'Keeffe Archive, Yale.

73. *Jimson Weed* (1936) is today held by the Indianapolis Museum of Art (collection.imamu seum.org/artwork/51855). For Arden's title, see "Invitation to Play" Arden ad, *NYT*, 31 January 1937, 82. That painting should not be confused with *Jimson Weed/White Flower No. 1*, a smaller painting of a single jimsonweed done by O'Keeffe in 1932. That painting sold for more than $44 million in 2014 and is housed at the Crystal Bridges Museum of American Art in Arkansas (collection.crystalbridges.org/objects/5355/jim son-weedwhite-flower-no-1). It is the highest price ever paid for a painting by a female artist; see sothebys.com/en/auctions/ecatalogue/2014 /american-art-n09229/lot.11.html. Arden named her exercise space the Gymnasium Moderne in 1937.

74. O'Keeffe to David H. McAlpin, 24 December 1936, in Jack Cowart and Juan Hamilton, *Georgia O'Keeffe* (Washington, DC: National Gallery of Art; Boston: Little, Brown, 1987), 221–22.

75. Stieglitz to Arden, 31 May 1939, and Angela Howley to Stieglitz, 3 June 1939, O'Keeffe Archive, Yale. In 1939, Arden purchased a third O'Keeffe painting, *A White Camellia*. Some evidence exists that she also owned a fourth, described by a visitor to her home as "two giant petunia blossoms." Arden paid $4,000 for *A White Camellia*. Its most recent (2012) purchase price was just over $3 million. It is privately held; see sothebys.com/en/auctions/ecatalogue/2012/american-art-n08911/lot.25.html. For the petunia painting, see Charlotte Curtis, "Musicale Offered by Mrs. Graham Includes Quartet," *NYT*, 12 April 1965, 42. For a photo of her with the probable painting, see Marietta McPherson Interview with Elizabeth Arden, September 1955, R11224-1122-2-E, Box 6353, File number: Assignment 5510-5, Library and Archives, Canada, recherche-collection-search.bac-lac.gc.ca/eng/home/record?app=fonandcol&IdNumber=3829696&q=%22Elizabeth%20Arden%22%20and%20Marietta%20McPherson.

76. Arden to Stieglitz, undated, O'Keeffe Archive, Yale.

77. For sale to Lehman Brothers, see Helena Rubinstein, *My Life for Beauty* (New York: Simon & Schuster, 1964), 72–74. Marie J. Clifford, "Helena Rubinstein's Beauty Salons, Fashion, and Modernist Display," *Winterthur Portfolio* 38, no. 2/3 (Summer/Autumn 2003): 86. Clifford's description comes from "On Her Dressing-Table," *Vogue*, 1 May 1915, 82, 84. See also Mason Klein, *Helena Rubinstein* (New Haven, CT: Yale University Press, 2014). *Modern Beauty Shop* quote from Clifford, "Helena Rubinstein's Beauty Salons," 91.

78. See Marie J. Clifford, "Brand Name Modernism" (Ph.D. diss., University of California, Los Angeles, 1999).

79. See John Warne Monroe, *Metropolitan Fetish* (Ithaca, NY: Cornell University Press, 2019). For the exhibition, see H. I. Brock, "Black Man's Art," *NYT*, 5 May 1935, SM10.

80. Carl van Vechten, "On Words and Music," *NYT*, 18 February 1934, X2; Edward Moore, "New Opera Has Fine Music but Lacks Meaning," *Chicago Tribune*, 4 March 1934, 4. The best book about the opera and its cultural significance is Steven Watson, *Prepare for Saints* (New York: Random House, 1998). See also Lisa Barg, "Black Voices/White Sounds," *American Music* 18, no. 2 (Summer 2000): 121–61, and Kara Anne Gardner, review of *Prepare for Saints*, by Steven Watson, *American Music* 19, no. 4 (Winter 2001): 466. The Arden display window was in Bergdorf Goodman.

81. Hopper, *From Under My Hat*, 200–201.

82. "Dance Given for Two Debutantes in Cellophane Setting at Ritz," *NYT*, 9 December 1934, N9. Lawson, a set and costume designer, actor, and technical director, would serve in the Federal Theatre Project and then go to Hollywood to work in the film industry.

83. "Society's Fashion Pageant Lends Rich Color to Setting for Show," *NYT*, 7 November 1935, 29. Jean's father was Frederick Johnson. While Pat and Virginia were not mentioned in the newspaper accounts, it would have been very odd for either sister to have missed Beatrice's debutante ball.

Bill Graham filed for bankruptcy in November 1935. See "Business Records," *NYT*, 16 November 1935, 20. His Graham & Zenger was one of several high-end glassware and china firms to become victims of the Great Depression. See, for context, P. Bradley Nutting, "Selling Elegant Glassware during the Great Depression," *Business History Review* 77, no. 3 (Autumn 2003): 447–78, esp. 478.

84. "Notes of Social Activities in New York and Elsewhere," *NYT*, 9 October 1934, 15; "Debutantes Are Honored," *NYT*, 2 November 1934, 28; "New York Society," *Chicago Tribune*, 3 November 1934, 19; Katie Edwards and Donna Plasket, eds., *The Society of the Four Arts* (West Palm Beach, FL: StarGroup International, 2017), 15, 18; "Debutantes to Be Honored at Supper Dance Tomorrow," *NYT*, 7 December 1934, 30. Gladys married Henri Maublanc de Boisboucher in 1932.

85. Lewis and Woodworth, *Miss Elizabeth Arden*, 163–64, for the Winchell quote and the names of titled guests.

86. F. N. Lewis, "Combined Perfume Container and Stand Therefor," Patent #113,635, 7 March 1939; F. N. Lewis, "Combined Perfume Container and Stand Therefor," Patent #113,636, 7 March 1939; "Gifts from Elizabeth Arden Are Gifts of Beauty!" Jelleff's ad, *The Washington Post*, 4 December 1938, S5. Helena Rubinstein seems not to have used cellophane in her packaging in 1934. This cellophane fad is the reason that Cole Porter's 1934 hit "You're the Top" includes cellophane.

87. Clifford, "Helena Rubinstein's Beauty Salons," 100.

88. "Shop Hound," *Vogue*, 15 December 1936, 74; "Fashion: New Head Dress," *Vogue*, 1 November 1938, 68; Clifford, "Helena Rubinstein's Beauty Salons," 101. Arden used cellophane as a selling point in other products as well, such as the Treasurette Box; see "Beauty for Easter" ad, *Los Angeles Times*, 10 April 1938, D5.

CHAPTER 13: BUSINESS SAVVY DURING HARD TIMES

1. "Elizabeth Arden: Queen," *Fortune*, August 1930, 92. Rosamond Pinchot Diary, 19 March 1933, Papers of Rosamond Pinchot, Manuscript Division, Library of Congress. Industry dominated by men: "Big Beauty Business," *Fortune*, August 1930, 41–43.

2. "Cosmetics: The American Woman Responds," *Fortune*, August 1930, 29. "Junior League" quote is from "Elizabeth Arden: Queen," 37.

3. Janet Leckie, *A Talent for Living* (New York: Hawthorn Books, 1970), 149.

4. "'I Am a Famous Woman in This Industry,'" *Fortune*, October 1938, 58.

5. Elizabeth Arden, "The Call to Perfection," undated speech [1940s], p. 8, Women's Institute of Duluth Records, University of Minnesota, Duluth.

6. "The Depression's Effect on Sales," *The American Perfumer*, August 1934, 288.

7. Margaret Case Harriman, "Profiles: Glamour, Inc.," *The New Yorker*, 6 April 1935, 27.

8. This is a quote from the October issue of *Fortune*, found in "Merchandising News," *The Drug and Cosmetic Industry*, October 1938, 436–37. *Fortune* claimed that Arden sold 108 different products. My count of her extensive product list suggests twice that many. See, for example, "Price List to the Retail Trade," November 1937, GB1752.EA/5/2, Elizabeth Arden Ltd. Papers, Unilever Archives, Port Sunlight, UK.

9. "Price List to the Retail Trade," Elizabeth Arden Sales Corp., May 1936, EA/5/2, Unilever Archives.

10. For Dorothy Gray, see "Notes on Cosmeticians," *Fortune*, August 1930, 43. For Marie Earle, see "M. Coty, Mr. Levy, Beauty's Biggest Business Men," *Fortune*, August 1930, 97. Coty purchased Earle in 1928.

11. "Invitation to Play" ad, *NYT*, 31 January 1937, 82. In 1938, she added the rhumba to her dance classes; see "Tap Dance Your Way" ad, *NYT*, 6 December 1938, 26.

12. "Elizabeth Arden Color Capes" Best & Company ad, *NYT*, 20 September 1936, 7; "An Open Letter from Elizabeth Arden," *NYT*, 11 October 1936, D2; "Why Work at Reducing?" ad, *NYT*, 20 November 1938, 44. The Scotch Hose hydrotherapy treatment was new in the fall of 1938.

13. For the Bicycle Kit, see "New Products," *The Drug and Cosmetic Industry*, April 1936, 494; "Discoveries in Beauty," *Vogue*, 1 July 1936, 80. For the Beach Bag, see Bonwit Teller Arden Beach Bag ad, *NYT*, 22 May 1938, 5. Her Beach Bag was also called Sun Fair Kit; see Jelleff's ad, *The Washington Post*, 21 June 1938, 11. For the perfume pins, see "Elizabeth Arden's Perfume Pins" ad, *NYT*, 19 November 1939, 35. For the automatic lipstick, see "Elizabeth Arden's New Jeweled Compact and Automatic Lipstick!" ad, *Vogue*, 15 March 1934, 106. For the depilatory, see "New Products," *The Drug and Cosmetic Industry*, August 1935, 220. Arden's product debuted in 1935. For the Face Moulding Home Treatment, see "Recast Your Features" Arden ad, *Vogue*, 15 October 1937, 37. For the perfume, see J. W. Robinson "Elizabeth Arden Tuberose" ad, *Los Angeles Times*, 28 September 1933, 9; "On Her Dressing-Table," *Vogue*, 1 October 1933, 61; and for the name confusion, see Fannie Hurst to Arden, 29 December 1935 and 9 November 1936, Fannie

Hurst Papers, Harry Ransom Center, University of Texas at Austin.

14. "A New Smart Case" ad, *The Boston Globe*, 21 July 1937, 3.

15. Leckie, *A Talent for Living*, 149.

16. "Summer Siesta," *Vogue*, 15 June 1934, 78.

17. "On Her Dressing-Table," *Vogue*, 15 March 1934, 84. Le Printemps seems to have been "sponsored" by Arden, and not necessarily inside of her flagship New York City salon. It was located at 3 East Fifty-Third Street, in Manhattan.

18. Elizabeth Arden Presents ad, *Vogue*, 15 March 1936, 14.

19. Elizabeth Arden Presents ad, *Vogue*, 15 March 1936, 14.

20. See, for example, "Elizabeth Arden Presents New Coiffures by Guillaume of Paris" ad, *NYT*, 17 January 1937, 14; "Guillaume Returns to Washington" ad, *The Washington Post*, 11 March 1927, 12; "Guillaume Returns to New York" ad, *NYT*, 18 March 1937, 10; "Guillaume Returns to Chicago" ad, *Chicago Tribune*, 2 April 1937, 24; "Elizabeth Arden Exhibits in Her New Salon de Coiffure" ad, *Los Angeles Times*, 2 May 1937, D9; "Guillaume of Paris Comes to Boston to the New Elizabeth Arden Hair Salon" ad, *The Boston Globe*, 29 November 1938, 15.

21. "Elizabeth Arden Announces the Arrival of Guillaume from Paris" ad, *NYT*, 9 October 1938, 50; "'Guillaume,' Here, Says Up Hair Is a Must for All," *WWD*, 11 October 1938, 5; "'Up-Style' in Hair Called Coming Trend by Parisian," *The Christian Science Monitor*, 30 November 1938, 11.

22. "Elizabeth Arden Announces the Opening of Her New Hair Salon" ad, *Los Angeles Times*, 25 April 1937, D12; "Guillaume Arrives from Paris to Advise Elizabeth Arden Salon," *The Christian Science Monitor*, 1 December 1938, 7.

23. For one stylist's story, see Lyonel Nelson, *From Farm to Fifth Avenue* (Galesburg, IL: self-pub., 2014). Nelson worked for Arden from 1958 to 1970. Arden's acceptance as a leader in coiffures was complete long before she teamed up with Lilly Daché in a Fashion Group luncheon show in 1939. For Daché and Arden, see "High in Front, Low in Back If New Hats Are to Match Hair-Do's," *WWD*, 11 October 1939, 21. Arden invented a Burnt Sugar hair rinse to match her Burnt Sugar makeup, etc. Male hairdressers were not new. According to Geoffrey Jones, in 1896 Paris had "47,640 hairdressers" and "nine-tenths" were men; see *Beauty Imagined* (New York: Oxford University Press, 2010), 47.

24. "Darby Day, Jr., and Wife to Meet in Courtroom Today," *Los Angeles Times*, 28 April 1925, A12; "Princess Mikeladze," *NYT*, 17 November 1969, 47.

25. "Opens Honolulu Salon," *WWD*, 3 June 1938, 10; "Casa Anglo-Brasileira in New Sao Paulo, Brazil, Home," *WWD*, 14 August 1939, 8; "A South American Store," *WWD*, 23 November

1943, 27. Arden products were sold in São Paulo exclusively at the Casa Anglo-Brasileira, later Mappin. For London, see James Bennett, "Elizabeth Arden, 1930–1945," cosmeticsandskin.com /companies/elizabeth-arden-1930.php; Diane K. Bolton, Patricia E. C. Croot, and M. A. Hicks, *A History of the County of Middlesex*, vol. 7 (London: Victoria County History, 1982), 30, british-history.ac.uk/vch/middx/vol7/pp23-30.

26. "Elizabeth Arden," *The American Perfumer*, January 1930, 682.

27. She did the same in Berlin, Rome, South America, and London.

28. For Singapore, see Lucile Quarry Mann Diary Transcript, 27 February 1937, p. 18, Box 7, folder 1, Record Unit 007293, William M. Mann and Lucile Quarry Mann Field Books, 1914–1940, Smithsonian Institution Archives Online (Image #SIA2014-07219).

29. "Answers to Correspondents," *Vogue*, 15 February 1934, 94; Elizabeth Arden ad, *Vogue*, 1 June 1921, 99; "Traveling North or South" Arden ad, *Vogue*, 15 January 1926, 127.

30. Harriman, "Profile: Glamour, Inc.," 27.

31. "New Salon Opens Today," *Los Angeles Times*, 14 January 1936, A8; "Oasis on Wilshire Boulevard" Arden ad, *Los Angeles Times*, 15 July 1936, A6. The three extant salons were in Beverly Hills, West Hollywood, and Westwood.

32. J. W. Robinson ads, *Los Angeles Times*, 10 March 1933, 9; 12 March 1933, B7.

33. Whittaker quotes from Alma Whitaker, "Beauty Expert Lauds Climate," *Los Angeles Times*, 14 March 1933, A6. Dropping to the floor to demonstrate her exercise story is from Whitaker, "Sugar and Spice," *Los Angeles Times*, 13 March 1935, 6.

34. Alma Whitaker, "Suzanne Wood Sells Palatial Villa in France," *Los Angeles Times*, 24 January 1934, A7.

35. Irene Guenther, *Nazi Chic?* (New York: Berg, 2004), chap. 4, esp. 91–92.

36. Alma Whitaker, "Suzanne Wood Sells Palatial Villa in France," *Los Angeles Times*, 24 January 1934, A7.

37. "Elizabeth Arden Opens Her New Doorway to Loveliness" ad, *Los Angeles Times*, 18 June 1933, B5.

38. "The Smartest Corner in Town" ad, *Los Angeles Times*, 19 July 1933, A5; "The New Home of Elizabeth Arden" ad, *Los Angeles Times*, 1 October 1933, F3; "Rambling Reporter," *The Hollywood Reporter*, 20 June 1933, 2. For Adrian's discovery by Irving Berlin, see Catharine Oglesby, *Fashion Careers American Style* (New York: Funk & Wagnalls, 1937), 103–4. The last name is variously spelled Greenburg and Greenberg.

39. Olive Gray, "New Arden Shop Opens for Women," *Los Angeles Times*, 21 June 1933, A5.

40. Mamye Ober Peak, "Reel Life in Hollywood," *The Boston Globe*, 9 June 1933, 31. *Little Women* also starred Francesca's husband as Larry Brooke.

41. "Beauty Specialist Ready to Advise," *Los Angeles Times*, 21 June 1933, A5.

42. "With a Stroke of Genius" Mandel Brothers ad, *Chicago Tribune*, 14 December 1932, 8.

43. Aviation kit ad, *Los Angeles Times*, 25 February 1937, 13; "Discoveries in Beauty," *Vogue*, 15 September 1938, 120; Arden in *Life* magazine ad found on James Bennett, "Airline Amenity Kits," cosmeticsandskin.com/fgf/speedbird.php.

44. J. W. Robinson ad, *Los Angeles Times*, 9 June 1933, 11. Arden even flew a horse in for a race and then flew the horse out again upon its completion—all in the same day! See Herb Ralby, "An Early Morning Van Ride Peps Up Suffolk Downs Horses," *The Boston Globe*, 15 May 1955, C78.

45. "Vienna Visitor to Be Honored," *Los Angeles Times*, 31 March 1934, 4; "Sprightly Costume Dance to Flavor Tea," *Los Angeles Times*, 5 April 1934, A6.

46. "Hauser to Give Lecture on Beauty Food Tonight," *The Boston Globe*, 24 May 1934, 6. She sent no less than Ann Delafield, the head of her Department of Exercise, who led Alice Rouse, Irma Sapper, and Helen Langeloh to wow the audience as they moved in perfect time to tunes from the live orchestra.

47. Catherine Carstairs, "'Look Younger, Live Longer,'" *Gender & History* 26, no. 2 (August 2014): 336.

48. Carstairs, "'Look Younger, Live Longer,'" 334.

49. Bengamin Gayelord Hauser, *Diet Does It* (New York: Coward-McCann, 1944), 1–3.

50. Hauser, *Diet Does It*, 1–3; Peter Kerr, "Gayelord Hauser, 89, Author," *NYT*, 29 December 1984, 26.

51. Carstairs, "'Look Younger, Live Longer,'" 337. Hauser used Bengamin and Benjamin, and Gayelord can be found spelled both with and without the *e*. Historian Catherine Carstairs posits that the *g* in Bengamin and the use of "Gayelord" may have signaled his sexuality.

52. For California move, see Peter Kerr, "Gayelord Hauser, 89, Author," *NYT*, 29 December 1984, 26; "Free Lectures by America's Foremost Teacher of Modern Food and Health" ad, *Hartford Courant*, 15 January 1930, 4.

53. "4 Free Lectures" ad, *The Boston Globe*, 28 October 1932, 44.

54. J. W. Robinson ad, *Los Angeles Times*, 5 May 1933, 9. Hedda Hopper was also appearing there, to "greet her friends personally" at the "Antoine Coiffure Shop where she has her hair dressed daily." Hauser also appeared at the May Company store. See their *Los Angeles Times* ad, 16 May 1933, 6.

55. "Beauty Cocktails Latest in Drinks," *Los Angeles Times*, 3 April 1934, 18. Hauser similarly absorbed, repackaged, and called his own Elsie de Wolfe Mendl's ideas about aesthetics and design.

56. Hauser, *Diet Does It*, 115–16.

57. Carstairs, "'Look Younger, Live Longer,'" 339. Bengamin Gayelord Hauser, *Eat and Grow Beautiful* (New York: Faber & Faber, 1939).

58. Carstairs, "'Look Younger, Live Longer,'" 340.

59. Carstairs, "'Look Younger, Live Longer,'" 341. Gayelord Hauser, *Look Younger, Live Longer* (New York: Farrar, Straus, 1950).

60. Unspecified author to the AMA, 21 July 1928, Box 323, Bengamin Gayelord Hauser Correspondence File, AMA Department of Investigation Records, American Medical Association, Chicago. Hereafter cited as Hauser, AMA.

61. The Journal A.M.A. to John Kremer, 9 April 1925, Hauser, AMA.

62. 1926 Hauser lecture pamphlet, Hauser, AMA.

63. Paul W. Conant to K. B. Wilson, 2 April 1929, Hauser, AMA.

64. "Garbo's Gayelord," *Time*, 16 February 1942, 60.

65. "Hauser Is Coming!" ad, *Los Angeles Times*, 10 January 1935, 16; "Food Expert at May's," *Los Angeles Times*, 16 January 1935, 3; Jill Davies, "Fad Diets—Health Implications," *Nutrition and Food Science*, 1 October 1994, 23.

66. "Eat and Be Beautiful," *Vogue*, 15 June 1935, 57, 76, 78. Quote is from p. 57.

67. "Sorry If You Couldn't Get In" Hauser ad, *Los Angeles Times*, 11 October 1936, A5.

68. "3 Free Lectures" Hauser ad, *The Washington Post*, 13 March 1938, M15. In this ad, Hauser described himself as "Formerly Dietetic Director of Elizabeth Arden's 'Beauty Farm.'"

69. Alice Hughes, "A Woman's New York," *The Washington Post*, 26 December 1939, 9.

70. Hedda Hopper, "Hedda Hopper's Hollywood," *Los Angeles Times*, 14 June 1939, 12; Hedda Hopper, "In Hollywood," *Hartford Courant*, 29 October 1947, 10. Hauser was in Europe to study post–World War II malnutrition.

71. Morris Fishbein, "Modern Medical Charlatans: II," *Hygeia* 16, no. 2 (February 1938): 113–15. Quote is from p. 114.

72. "Lindner's Plan Elaborate Fashion Clinic Sept 29–30," *WWD*, 22 September 1937, 4.

73. "National Costumes of Many Countries Are Worn by Dolls," *WWD*, 13 April 1932, 3–4; "Shop-Hound," *Vogue*, 15 June 1932, 61. They were created by Polish artist Jeanne Lebedeff, who modeled them on the ethnographic exhibits in Paris's Trocadéro Museum. Bonwit Teller ad, *NYT*, 5 December 1932, 5. See also "Elizabeth Arden's Foreign Ambassadors" ad, *Hartford Courant*, 11 June 1933, 9, and "Will Give Beauty Talks in Six Languages at Filene's," *The Boston Globe*, 25 April 1932, 10. The six languages spoken by Stella Harding, Sonja Allanmeyer, and Rita Gradini were Swedish, Russian, Italian, French, Spanish, and German. See Woodward & Lothrop ad, *The Washington Post*, 4 May 1932, 7. "Elizabeth Arden's Beauty Ambassadors" ad, *Chicago Tribune*, 17 October 1932, 5, states there were thirty dolls

"of the 57 countries in which Elizabeth Arden's Beauty Preparations are the key to beauty." See J. W. Robinson ad, *Los Angeles Times*, 25 February 1934, B8.

74. Lester Gaba, *The Art of Window Display* (New York: Thomas Y. Crowell, 1952), 11.

75. Gaba, *The Art of Window Display*, 11.

76. On the Gaba Girls, see "They've Come to Live at Bloomingdale's" ad, *NYT*, 20 May 1934, 14; Janet Mabie, "Beautiful, but Dummies," *The Christian Science Monitor*, 27 November 1935, 5; and Gaba, *The Art of Window Display*, esp. pp. 10–12. Alana Staiti, who has a Ph.D. from Cornell University in Science & Technology Studies, considers Gaba's mannequins in part a reaction against surrealist window displays, and puts them in the context of a narrowing definition of beauty ideals. See her "Real Women, Normal Curves, and the Making of the American Fashion Mannequin, 1932–1946," *Configurations* 28, no. 4 (Fall 2020): 403–31.

77. "Wanamaker's First Spring 1934" ad, *NYT*, 19 February 1934, 16; "Wanamaker Spring Fashion Showing," *WWD*, 21 February 1934, 3.

78. "Elizabeth Arden's Beauty Theatre" ad, *NYT*, 14 January 1934, 3.

79. "Beauty Gossip," *Vogue*, 15 February 1934, 84.

80. There were three different types of puppets, according to Eleanor H. Rich, who created the puppets' clothing: "miniature heads, the marionettes and the eighteen inch mannikins." See "On and Off the Campus," *Barnard College Alumnae Monthly*, March 1934, 4. Rich's quote is from "They Write Us," *Barnard College Alumnae Monthly*, April 1934, 16.

81. "If You Have a Dry Skin" ad, *The Boston Globe*, 7 February 1934, 9; "You Must See Them!" ad, *Chicago Tribune*, 26 February 1934, 6; "Elizabeth Arden's Puppets" ad, *Los Angeles Times*, 26 February 1934, A7; G. Fox & Co. ad, *Hartford Courant*, 15 April 1934, 6; "Arden Uses Marionette Window," *The American Perfumer*, April 1934, 90; "You Must See Them!" Younkers ad, *Des Moines Register*, 6 June 1934, 18. See also John Bell, "Gertrude Stein's Identity: Puppet Modernism in the U.S.," *TDR* 50, no. 1 (Spring 2006): 87–99, esp. pp. 89, 90.

82. "As We Go to Press," *What's On the Air*, June 1931, 6.

83. "The Career Woman's Blind Spot—Daytime Radio," *Fashion Group Bulletin*, May 1938, 3, 9, 4, Box 144, folder 10, Fashion Group International Records, Mss Col 980, New York Public Library Manuscripts & Archives Division, New York City.

84. "Station Accounts," *Broadcasting*, 1 February 1932, 19.

85. Class of 1921, *Vassar Quarterly*, July 1934, 302; "New Arden Radio Program," *The American Perfumer*, May 1934, 135. The show debuted on 24 April 1934.

86. "Beauty-duty" quote, "Elizabeth Arden Speaks from New York Tonight" I. Magnin ad,

Los Angeles Times, 24 April 1934, 2. For Knickerbocker, Margaret Case Harriman, "Profiles: Dolly and Polly, Billy and Cholly—II," *The New Yorker*, 23 October 1937, 26.

87. Damon Runyon, "The Brighter Side," *The Austin American-Statesman*, 13 December 1937, 4.

88. "Elizabeth Arden Has a Message for You" ad, *NYT*, 8 May 1934, 27; "Elizabeth Arden's Radio Program," *NYT*, 15 May 1934, 24; "Lizzie Arden Extends," *Variety*, 15 May 1934, 37.

89. "Elizabeth Arden's Radio Program," *NYT*, 22 May 1934, 19.

90. See, for example, "Two Important Reminders" Arden ad, *NYT*, 29 May 1934, 16; "Elizabeth Arden on the Air Tonight" J. W. Robinson ad, *Los Angeles Times*, 29 May 1934. 9. Quote is from Harriman, "Profiles: Dolly and Polly, Billy and Cholly—I," *The New Yorker*, 16 October 1937, 23.

91. Harriman, "Profiles: Dolly and Polly, Billy and Cholly—II," 26; Eve Brown, *Champagne Cholly* (New York: E. P. Dutton, 1947), 144; "Maury Paul, Noted as Society Writer," *NYT*, 18 July 1942, 13. Brown's book provides a window into Paul's vanity, egoism, and addiction to luxury.

92. "Cholly in the Flesh," *Variety*, 29 May 1934, 36.

CHAPTER 14: MARKETING VALUE

1. "On Her Dressing-Table," *Vogue*, 24 November 1930, 94; "On Her Dressing-Table," *Vogue*, 1 September 1934, 86.

2. "The Magic of Eight Hour Cream," *Adweek*, undated, adweek.com/brand-marketing/the-skin-cream-that-celebrities-swear-by-was-created-by-a-nurse-nearly-90-years-ago.

3. "On Her Dressing-Table," *Vogue*, 24 November 1930, 94; "Elizabeth Arden Answers," *Los Angeles Times*, 18 February 1934, B10; "On Her Dressing-Table," *Vogue*, 1 March 1931, 81; "Opening of New Salon, Presentations of Summer Items Cosmetic Features," *WWD*, 14 June 1935, S113; "Snow Maiden" ad, *Chicago Tribune*, 7 February 1937, 17; Elizabeth Arden ad, *Vogue*, 1 June 1939, 85.

4. "Eight Hour Cream," *Elizabeth Arden News*, June 1965, 3, Elizabeth Arden Ltd. Papers, Unilever Archives, Port Sunlight, UK.

5. "Can You Bear to Wait" Arden ad, *Vogue*, 15 December 1934, 68. Sprayed in salons: Hedda Hopper, *From Under My Hat* (New York: Mac-Fadden, 1963), 202.

6. "The French Relief Fund," *The American Perfumer*, October 1921, 368.

7. For Fragonard and Fuchs, see Maison Fragonard, "About Us: A Family Story," usines-parfum.fragonard.com/en/about-us/a-family-story. Monsen and Baer Inc., *For the Love of Perfume* (Vienna, VA: Monsen and Baer Inc., 1999), 17–19, 22, 72. For the perfume industry in the 1930s, see "The Lure of Perfumes," *Fortune*, August 1930, 32–35.

Blue Grass–scented nail polish: Arden ad, *NYT*, 4 April 1948, 54.

8. Elizabeth Arden to Nicolai Remisoff, 21 August 1935, Nicolas Remisoff Papers, Collection no. 0199, Special Collections, USC Libraries, University of Southern California. For the ad, see *Vogue*, 1 November 1935, 16b.

9. It debuted in a slightly ornamented version of the square bottle she had earlier designed for her perfume quartet. See F. N. Lewis, "Perfume Bottle," Patent #74,233, granted 10 January 1928; "On Her Dressing-Table," *Vogue*, 1 September 1934, 86. For new bottles and items, see, for example, F. N. Lewis, "Combined Bottle and Base Therefor," Patent #110,871, 11 June 1938; F. N. Lewis, "Jewelry Component or the Like," Patent #126,416, 26 October 1940; F. N. Lewis, "Brooch Pin," Patent #126,982, 6 May 1941; "Winner! Elizabeth Arden's Blue Grass Horse Pin" Arden ad, *NYT*, 4 May 1941, 51; "Blue Grass Charger Is Now a Perfumed Pin" Marshall Field ad, *Chicago Tribune*, 14 May 1941, 13; "Blue Grass: Our Own Prize Dress That's Come In First" Bonwit Teller ad, *NYT*, 6 May 1941, 6; Elizabeth Arden dress ad, *Vogue*, 1 May 1941, 61; for guest soap, see "Discoveries in Beauty," *Vogue*, 1 May 1948, 192.

10. "Quality Means *Economy*" ad, *Chicago Tribune*, 19 March 1933, 10. Ellipsis in original title replaced with a comma.

11. "You Have Helped Me" ad, *NYT*, 26 March 1933, 2. Ellipsis in original.

12. "Powder" ad, *NYT*, 2 April 1933, 2.

13. "Loveliness with Economy" ad, *Vogue*, 15 April 1933, 87.

14. "The Only 'Beauty Gift'" ad, *NYT*, 12 March 1933, 2.

15. "Care for Your Skin Daily" ad, *Chicago Tribune*, 20 April 1939, 19.

16. Leroy Fairman, "The Vogue of the 'Treatment,'" *The American Perfumer*, April 1930, 82. For example, as late as 1938, a course of twelve Intra-Cellular Mask treatments cost $100, or just under $4,500 today. See "Beauty Laughs at Birthdays!" ad, *Chicago Tribune*, 6 March 1938, G4.

17. She created the lipstick herself, and prevailed upon her chemist, A. Fabian Swanson, to let her try it on him. See Margaret Case Harriman, "Glamour, Inc.," *The New Yorker*, 6 April 1935, 26.

See Mandel Brothers ad, *Chicago Tribune*, 10 July 1931, 9; Arden ad, *Vogue*, 1 December 1931, 99; and "Have You Your Quota of Lipstick" Wanamaker ad, *NYT*, 4 April 1932, 18. Ads for an indelible lipstick first appeared in *The New York Times* in 1881 and ran very infrequently through 1885, billed as a "secret beauty" product in that era when makeup was synonymous with prostitution. The phrase does not appear there again until 1924. *Vogue* mentioned indelible French lipstick—no company name noted—just once in 1913, and then not again until 1922. Two years after Arden, in 1924, the Armyne Company released its version, then Guerlain. Others rapidly followed.

18. Maybelline ad, *NYT*, 22 November 1925, RPA5; "To Beautify Eyes" Arden/Robinson ad, *Los Angeles Times*, 20 July 1933, 9; "No Woman Need Fear for Her Beauty" Rubinstein ad, *Los Angeles Times*, 6 July 1934, A5; "Tattoo Your Eyelashes" Tattoo ad, *Vogue*, 1 January 1936, 78; "Don't Be a Chrysanthemum!" Kurlash ad, *Vogue*, 15 November 1937, 193; "Be Sun Fair" Arden ad, *Vogue*, 1 June 1938, 98. Helena Rubinstein's first *Vogue* advertisement was "Cosmetic Classics," *Vogue*, 15 September 1940, 110–11. For a history of mascaras, including how they became more water-resistant, see James Bennett, "Cake Mascara," cosmeticsandskin.com/cdc/block-mascara.php, and "Liquid and Cream Mascara," cosmeticsandskin.com/ded/liquid-cream-mascara.php.

19. "With Hats 'Off the Face'" ad, *Chicago Tribune*, 28 September 1930, 21; "Internationalia," *Vogue*, 1 June 1932, 95. See also "Latest Paris Cable," *Vogue*, 15 April 1932, II.

20. "Making-Up to the New Clothes," *Harrods News*, 13 March 1933, 20, Harrods Company Archive, London.

21. "Beige and Pimento Make-Up" Bonwit Teller ad, *NYT*, 1 August 1937, 5.

22. "Loveliness with Economy" ad, *Vogue*, 15 April 1933, 87; Marcia Vaughn, "Boudoir Tidings," *The Chicagoan*, April 1933, 73. A smaller, companion "Debutante" Beauty Box sold for less than her regular-size beauty boxes. See "Are You Looking for Ideas for Christmas Gifts?" ad, *The Chicagoan*, 1 December 1933, 11.

23. "Dear Elizabeth Arden" ad, *Vogue*, 15 June 1933, 55; "Stand Tall and Look Slender" ad, *NYT*, 12 June 1938, 44.

24. The first gift certificates appeared in the 1890s but were rare. Not until the 1930s did they become more commonly offered by merchants. Arden was among the early adopters. See Mandel Brothers ad, *Chicago Tribune*, 4 December 1898, 40; "Give Beauty This Christmas" Arden ad, *The Washington Post*, 16 December 1936, X16.

25. "Cosmetic Bargain Promotions," *The Drug and Cosmetic Industry*, January 1939, 40, 42; "Elizabeth Arden Products 20% Off" Best & Co. ad, *NYT*, 24 June 1938, 7.

26. "Store to Show Mural," *NYT*, 13 October 1935, N4; "Capital to See Clara Thomas' Famous Mural," *The Washington Post*, 28 November 1935, 15; "Beauty of the Ages," *Vogue*, 15 October 1935, 50; "'Beauty' Mural Exhibited," *NYT*, 15 October 1935, 10; Photo spread, *NYT*, 20 October 1935, RP9; "Mural of Beauties through Ages Shown by Saks-Fifth Avenue," *WWD*, 15 October 1935, 3; "Ageless Beauty Is Mural Theme," *Chicago Tribune*, 27 October 1935, E14. Newspapers gave those dimensions, but the pamphlet that traveled with the mural listed it as 65 feet in length, 10.5 feet tall, and made of fourteen separate panels. *A Pageant of Beauty* pamphlet, ASC/B/B11 Friends and Benefactors Records, RG07, Mount Holyoke College Special Collections, aspace.fivecolleges.edu/repositories/2/resources/460.

27. Arden's work with college women was extensive and included campus appearances, talks, and makeup demonstrations, donations for campus improvements, advertisements in college newspapers, "college clinics" at department stores in college towns, and toiletries and kits aimed at college students.

28. Mary Bradley [?] to Gertrude V. Bruyn, 7 October 1936, and *A Pageant of Beauty* pamphlet, ASC/B/B11 Friends and Benefactors Records, RG07, Mount Holyoke College Special Collections, aspace.fivecolleges.edu/repositories/2/resources/460. The mural was valued at $10,000 for insurance purposes. See also Mary Wick, "Pageant of Beauty Is Shown in Dwight Hall," *The Mount Holyoke News*, 30 October 1936, 1; and "A Pageant of Beauty," *The American Perfumer*, November 1935, 82. Thomas is no longer remembered today, but she was well-known in her time. See "Clara Thomas, 79, Muralist, Is Dead," *NYT*, 27 April 1970, 33; and "James F. Fargo, 80, Financier, Is Dead," *NYT*, 20 June 1937, N7. In 1951, RLS Shops—which seems to have been medical offices—on East Sixtieth Street in Manhattan exhibited the Thomas mural in the garden space. See "Diverse Paintings in Galleries Here," *NYT*, 14 May 1951, 25.

29. Frances Mangum, "Expert Exposes Illusions on Beauty Traditions," *The Washington Post*, 22 January 1935, 13.

30. "Heims Are Guests at Luncheon Here," *The Boston Globe*, 13 December 1937, 7.

31. Coronation Red: see Arden ad, *NYT*, 27 September 1936, N5; Royal Make-Up: see "Coronation Harmony" Arden ad, *Chicago Tribune*, 4 April 1937, G7; "Royal Lipstick" ad, *NYT*, 13 April 1937, 11. The enamel case came in four different colors. Arden actually introduced Coronation Red nine months before the event.

32. May Birkhead, "Americans in London Stay Up Late at Coronation Fetes," *Chicago Tribune*, 12 May 1937, 5; Hope Ridings Miller, "Mrs. Emil Hurja Found Excitement in Coronation," *The Washington Post*, 1 June 1937, 16; Alice Hughes, "A Woman's New York," *The Washington Post*, 3 July 1937, 13.

33. Elizabeth Arden to Alfred Stieglitz, 23 July 1936, MSS 85, Box 3, folder 54, Series I, Alfred Stieglitz/Georgia O'Keeffe Archive, Beinecke Rare Book and Manuscript Library, Yale University.

34. "NRA Campaign Here to Use No Coercion," *NYT*, 8 August 1933, 5. The quote was from Isabel Leighton, head of the women's division. In another article, those on the list were described as "women volunteer workers" gathered together

by Emma Dot Partridge, chairman of the Consumers NRA Campaign, whose job was "to conduct the consumer canvass"; see "Socialists Balk at NRA Campaign," *NYT*, 5 September 1933, 3.

35. "Cosmetic Houses and NRA," *The Drug and Cosmetic Industry*, September 1933, 276.

36. Catharine Oglesby, *Fashion Careers American Style* (New York: Funk & Wagnalls, 1936), 123. Catharine Oglesby's first name is frequently misspelled Catherine.

37. "Advertising News and Notes," *NYT*, 9 April 1938, 20.

38. See, for example, "Miss Johnson Arden Adv. Mgr.," *The Drug and Cosmetic Industry*, June 1935, 743; "Elizabeth Arden's Advertising," *NYT*, 7 April 1937, 46; "Mrs. Quimby Joins Serwer," *WWD*, 13 February 1939, 23; and "Helen Cornelius to Join Elizabeth Arden in Promotional Post," *WWD*, 5 April 1938, 1. It seems likely that Arden employed a number of different advertising agents or firms simultaneously. See "A Revised Directory of National and Regional Radio Advertisers," *Broadcasting*, 1 July 1935, 62, and "Radio Advertisers," *Broadcasting*, 15 August 1936, 43.

39. "The Art of Beauty," *Mercury* [Hobart, Tasmania], 13 December 1934, 5; "Beauty Specialist," *South Western Times* [Bunbury, Australia], 27 October 1934, 9; "Arriving Today," *The Tribune* [Philippines], 28 September 1937, 5.

40. "Deaths: Scantlebury—Mignon," *NYT*, 6 March 1952, 31. Scantlebury took up her D.C. post in 1941.

41. B. J. Perkins, "Helen Cornelius Resigns from Elizabeth Arden," *WWD*, 25 August 1939, 9; "London Fashion Group Hears U.S. Promotion Activities Lauded," *WWD*, 9 August 1939, 3.

42. "Miss de Mille Exits Fashion Stage in Style," *WWD*, 10 January 1966, 1, 16.

43. Edyth Thornton McLeod, *How to Sell Cosmetics* (New York: The Drug and Cosmetic Industry, 1937). For outright theft of ideas, see especially her chapters on color matching ("we have found a new keynote in make-up, that of harmonizing the face with fashion" [p. 67]), on powder ("It is a clever idea in selling to suggest that your client use two shades of powder" [p. 51]), and the way she describes beauty overall: "There is romance and research in every bottle and jar that finds its way to your counter and finally comes to rest on milady's dressing table" (p. 14). In 1935, McLeod left Arden ("McLeod Joins Associated," *The Drug and Cosmetic Industry*, August 1935, 237) and by 1937 she had become a cosmetic industry consultant ("Talking about Ourselves," *Fashion Group Bulletin*, October 1937, p. 2, Box 144, folder 9, Fashion Group International Records, Mss Col 980, New York Public Library Archives & Manuscripts, New York City).

44. Margaretta Byers, *Designing Women* (New York: Simon & Schuster, 1938). For personality types, see chap. 9.

45. "Elizabeth Arden Is Dead at 81," *NYT*, 19 October 1966, 1, 47.

46. "Community Fund but $9000 Behind 1937 Figure," *The Boston Globe*, 3 February 1938, 1. "Highest Salaries for 1935 Are Listed," *NYT*, 7 January 1937, 28; "Highest Salaries Paid in Nation in 1936 Are Listed by House Committee," *NYT*, 9 January 1938, 44. Her salary went from $75,000 in 1935 to $50,000 in 1936. There is no evidence that she cut her employees' salaries.

47. "Business Leaders Act on Welfare Aid," *NYT*, 21 October 1933, 7; "Relief Demands Found Unabating," *NYT*, 4 November 1933, 4; "Civil Leaders Seek $4,000,000 to Augment Family Relief Here," *NYT*, 19 October 1933, 1; "$4,147,034 Raised for Family Relief," *NYT*, 16 December 1933, 1. She raised $1,500 in the first month: "Family Fund Total Nearing $1,000,000," *NYT*, 24 November 1933, 8. "$2,721,144 Is Raised for Family Relief," *NYT*, 7 December 1933, 28; "Gifts to the Family Welfare Fund," *NYT*, 5 January 1933, 22; "Generous Response to Welfare Drive," *WWD*, 29 November 1934, 1–2.

48. "Red Cross Drive Opens Here Nov. 11," *NYT*, 5 November 1933, N1; "Red Cross Sees Gain in Roll-Call Results," *NYT*, 25 November 1933, 17; "Red Cross Aides Named for Drive," *NYT*, 4 November 1934, N7; "O.D. Young Sounds Call for Red Cross," *NYT*, 8 November 1936, N10; "Chairmen Chosen in Red Cross Drive," *NYT*, 7 November 1937, 52; "Red Cross Names Group Chairmen," *NYT*, 3 November 1940, 4. Arden chaired in 1933, 1934, 1936, 1937, and 1940.

49. "Activities of Women's Clubs," *Hartford Courant*, 6 March 1936, 13; "Woman's Club Plans 14-Story Dwelling," *The Christian Science Monitor*, 26 April 1922, 3; "Miss Morgan Reports on Club Activities," *NYT*, 22 April 1931, 23.

50. Anne Petersen, "Week Dedicated to Woman's Advance in Business Begins Today," *NYT*, 9 October 1938, 53.

51. "Elizabeth Arden Kills Mythical Person Theory," *Los Angeles Times*, 24 March 1935, 22. See, for example, "New York Mardi Gras for Paralysis Fund," *Hartford Courant*, 26 January 1941, A12.

52. In California, Arden toured a local Assistance League chapter and committed to helping two young girls afflicted with infantile paralysis. See Hedda Hopper, "Hollywood Highlights," *Movie Classic*, July 1936, 63. Two years later, Hopper reported that Arden was still caring for the children. See her "Society Bureau Opens Barred Doors to Lens," *Los Angeles Times*, 18 September 1938, C1.

53. "Lack $400,000 in Final Lap," *The Boston Globe*, 8 February 1937, 1; "Speers Aids Fight on Tuberculosis," *NYT*, 23 October 1940, 48.

54. The scope of Arden's charitable giving is broad and deserves its own study. Evidence for her philanthropy is easily found in newspapers.

CHAPTER 15: NEW DIRECTIONS

1. "Arden Buys DeLong," *The Drug and Cosmetic Industry*, May 1935, 599; "Chatter," *Variety*, 10 April 1935, 60.

2. "Design Contract Let for Make-Up Studios," *Los Angeles Times*, 19 May 1935, 32. Arden made Burt Chose managing director and put Charles Weekes in charge of product development. See "Hollywood Makeup Company Purchased," *Los Angeles Times*, 30 March 1935, 1; "New Cosmetics Plant Planned by Miss Arden," *Los Angeles Times*, 8 May 1935, 2; "Weekes Joins Arden," *The Drug and Cosmetic Industry*, July 1935, 93.

3. Tip Poff, "That Certain Party," *Los Angeles Times*, 31 March 1935, 1; Marshall Kester, "Outdoor Recreation Favored by Guests at Hidden Valley Ranch Rendezvous," *Los Angeles Times*, 31 March 1935, B7; Tip Poff, "That Certain Party," *Los Angeles Times*, 7 April 1935, 1.

4. Sylva Weaver, "Writers' Club Thronged by Film Notables at Gala Revel for Artists' Fund," *Los Angeles Times*, 7 April 1935, B9.

5. "H'Wood Powder Puff War," *Variety*, 10 July 1935, 3, 67.

6. "H'Wood Powder Puff War," *Variety*, 10 July 1935, 3; James Bennett, "House of Westmore," cosmeticsandskin.com/companies/westmore .php; and Christina Benson, "The Westmores of Hollywood," westmoresofhollywood.com.

7. "Arden's New Nuchromatic Make-Up," *The Drug and Cosmetic Industry*, July 1935, 57; "Stage and Screen Make-Up by Elizabeth Arden," *The Drug and Cosmetic Industry*, September 1935, 329, 361; Robare ad, *Hollywood Filmograph*, 28 April 1934, 5. See also "Cosmetic Business Control Is Being Fought, *Hollywood Filmograph*, 28 April 1934, 1, 7, and James Bennett, "Arden Screen and Stage Make-up," https://cosmeticsandskin.com /bcb/arden-screen-stage.php. Soon Arden dropped "Nuchromatic" and more consistently advertised it as "Elizabeth Arden's Stage and Screen Make-Up."

8. Thorpe W. Deakers, "Hollywood and Its Cosmetic Industry," *The Drug and Cosmetic Industry*, November 1935, 611. For an example of a demonstrator, see "Elizabeth Arden Stars Again!" ad, *Chicago Tribune*, 19 February 1937, 21.

9. Michelle Tolini Finamore, *Hollywood before Glamour* (New York: Palgrave Macmillan, 2013), 7.

10. "Short Subject Reviews: Broadway Gossip," *The Film Daily*, 10 November 1933, 12.

11. Sibley, Lindsay & Curr ad, *The Christian Science Monitor*, 30 March 1933, 4; "Scarbrough's Invites You to Attend," *Austin American-Statesman*, 2 April 1933, A3.

12. "Scarbrough's Invites You to Attend," *Austin American-Statesman*, 2 April 1933, A3; "You Are Invited" ad, *Los Angeles Times*, 2 April 1933, B10.

13. Larry Wolters, "Our Miss Brooks at Home," *Chicago Tribune*, 18 October 1953, E30. "News of the Screen," *NYT*, 30 March 1937, 20; "A Pretty Tale," *Boxoffice*, 3 April 1937, 20. This film seems not to have been made.

14. *Steps to Loveliness* ad, *Winnipeg Tribune*, 23 January 1933, 8. Whitney's obituary credits him with creating the first Technicolor short film: "John Hay Whitney Dies at 77," *NYT*, 9 February 1982, A1. For Whitney, see E. J. Kahn, *Jock* (Garden City, NY: Doubleday, 1981), esp. chap. 8. On Arden and Whitney, see James Bennett, "Pan-Cake Make-Up," cosmeticsandskin.com/bcb /cake.php, and "Elizabeth Arden, 1930–1945," cosmeticsandskin.com/companies/elizabeth -arden-1930.php.

15. "It Could Happen to YOU!" ad, *Modern Screen*, July 1937, 25.

16. William E. Celestin, "The Keller-Dorian Three-Color Process," *International Photographer*, June 1936, 29.

17. "Arden Plans New British Plant," *The American Perfumer*, April 1936, 79; "Screen Make-Up Factory," *The Film Daily*, 28 February 1936, 8; "Arden to Expand in Britain," *The Drug and Cosmetic Industry*, May 1936, 668.

18. "250G Elizabeth Arden Suit over Theatrical Makeup," *Variety*, 28 April 1937, 3. Several actors used Arden's makeup, even when the entire cast did not. See "The Prisoner of Zenda" Woodward & Lothrop ad, *The Washington Post*, 21 October 1937, 5. Cast members in *Ebb Tide* (1937), *Tovarich* (1937), *The Adventures of Tom Sawyer* (1938), and *The Great Waltz* (1938) used Arden's makeup. For *Tom Sawyer*, see MOMA Press Release, undated, MOMA Press Release Archive, moma.org/momaorg/shared/pdfs/docs/press_ar chives/420/releases/MOMA_1937_0060_1937 -12-17_371217-44.pdf.

19. "'Revolutionary Make-Up' Used in Color Picture" clipping, undated [6 August 1937, 16], attached to Marcia Connor to "The President" [Grover Whalen], 9 August 1937, Box 446, folder 4, New York World's Fair 1939 and 1940 Incorporated Records, Mss Col 2233, New York Public Library Archives & Manuscripts Division, New York City. Hereafter cited as World's Fair NYPL.

20. For the lack of success of Arden's film makeup, see Bennett, "Arden Screen and Stage Make-up," https://cosmeticsandskin.com/bcb/arden -screen-stage.php, and "H'Wood Powder Puff War," *Variety*, 10 July 1935, 3. For Nuchromatic Screen & Stage Make-up still for sale, see "Make-Up for the Camera," *Vogue*, 15 June 1941, 39. Arden brought out a Special Camera Kit packed with Nuchromatic makeup ("Discoveries in Beauty," *Vogue*, 15 June 1941, 68).

21. Alice Hughes, "A Woman's New York," *The Washington Post*, 16 April 1938, X11; "Crochet Wizard Wins by a Scallop," *NYT*, 2 May 1939, 25.

22. "Cosmetics," *Fashion Group Bulletin*, June 1938, 9, Box 144, Fashion Group International Records, Mss Col 980, New York Public Library Archives & Manuscripts Division, New York City. Hereafter cited as FGIR.

23. Telecast Red debuted in May 1939. Volney D. Hurd, "Television Test at Fair Reveals Marked Advance," *The Christian Science Monitor*, 2 May 1939, 1; Alfred D. Charles, "Gotham Raises Curtain on Its World's Fair," *The Baltimore Sun*, 1 May 1939, 1; "Charity Ball Tonight Features Television," *NYT*, 15 December 1939, 31; "Program Telecast at Charity Dance," *NYT*, 16 December 1939, 18. The Television Ball benefited the Goddard Neighborhood Center.

24. First two quotes from "Introducing Elizabeth Arden's Telecast Red" Bonwit Teller ad, *NYT*, 14 January 1940, 41. Third quote from "Elizabeth Arden Presents Telecast Red" ad, *Vogue*, 15 March 1940, 109. See also Marshall Field ad, *Chicago Tribune*, 25 January 1940, 7, and "Elizabeth Arden Telecast Red" ad, *NYT*, 25 February 1940, 8. For a longer description of the Telecast Red line, see Ida Chapman, "The Beauty Box," *Hartford Courant*, 4 March 1940, 9.

25. "Television Calls for New Make-Up," *Los Angeles Times*, 28 June 1936, C4; Lee Shippey, "The Lee Side," *Los Angeles Times*, 25 July 1936, A4; Philip K. Scheuer, "Town Called Hollywood," *Los Angeles Times*, 17 January 1937, D1.

26. "Death Beckons to Max Factor," *Los Angeles Times*, 31 August 1938, 1.

27. "Blind Movie Fans 'Watch' Film Making," *Hartford Courant*, 23 July 1939, A7. For an excellent explanation of television makeup, with photographs, see James Bennett, "Max Factor and Television," cosmeticsandskin.com/aba/max-and-the-tube.php.

28. "Tonight—KMTR" ad, *Los Angeles Times*, 30 October 1936, A19.

29. "Mutual's New Accts," *Variety*, 8 December 1937, 28. There's some question as to whether the show was an hour or thirty minutes in length, despite the title.

30. "Elizabeth Arden on NBC," *Broadcasting*, 15 September 1937, 21; "Network Accounts," *Broadcasting*, 15 September 1937, 70; "Studio Shows Dominate," *Variety*, 6 October 1937, 29.

31. "Offer George Fischer for Arden Account," *Variety*, 9 March 1938, 29.

32. Eddie [sic] Duchin for Arden," *Motion Picture Daily*, 30 September 1937, 13.

33. "Elizabeth Arden Will Speak Tonight" ad, *Los Angeles Times*, 22 February 1938, 12; "Eddie [sic] Duchin for Arden," *Motion Picture Daily*, 30 September 1937, 13; NBC Blue Network ad, *Broadcasting*, 1 October 1937, 25; for the booklet, see "Lights! Camera! Action! Beauty!" ad, *Photoplay*, February 1938, 83.

34. "Music of Romance," *Radio Daily*, 1 October 1937, 5.

35. The prize was likely Arden advice and products. "Beauty and Romance," *Broadcasting*, 1 February 1938, 82. The answers could be no more than two hundred words in length.

36. "'Cinderella' Contest," *Radio Daily*, 2 February 1938, 5.

37. "Cosmetic Offers," *Broadcasting*, 1 March 1938, 66.

38. But she never lost her affection for her friend. In 1937, Arden purchased 4 Sutton Square, where she had spent so many happy hours with Bessie. It was an investment property, one she leased initially to Anne Morgan's relative Pierpont M. Hamilton. See "Manhattan Mortgages," *NYT*, 23 March 1932, 39; "Rents Sutton Sq. Home," *NYT*, 12 October 1937, 45; "In East Side Deal," *NYT*, 9 August 1940, 28; "Manhattan Transfers," *NYT*, 22 July 1944, 25; "C. E. Gilbert Sells Sutton Square Home," *NYT*, 6 April 1949, 51. By 1944, Arden seems no longer to have owned the property; see "Sutton Square House Leased," *NYT*, 22 May 1943, 23.

39. The United States of America before Federal Trade Commission in the Matter of Elizabeth Arden, Inc., [15 May 1937], Box 15, folder 1, Walton H. Hamilton Papers, Tarlton Law Library, University of Texas, Austin, Texas. See also "Complaint against Elizabeth Arden," *The Wall Street Journal*, 20 May 1937, 12. Quantity discounts were legal, as long as they were offered to all retailers fairly (i.e., proportionally) and if they made cost savings sense to the retailer. The problem came from preferential *and unfair* treatment. See P. J. B. Crowley, "Equal Price Treatment under the Robinson-Patman Act," *University of Pennsylvania Law Review* 95, no. 3 (February 1947): 337–38. See also "Cosmetic Companies Get FTC Complaint," *NYT*, 18 May 1939, 38, for the charges against Coty and Arden.

40. Lindley quoted in Crowley, "Equal Price Treatment under the Robinson-Patman Act," 306. For the list of cosmetics and other firms, see H. C. Hallam, "The Robinson-Patman Act," *The Drug and Cosmetic Industry*, May 1940, 552, 555; and "Bourjouis & Hudnut Amended Complaints" and "Arden & Coty Amended Complaints," both in *The Drug and Cosmetic Industry*, June 1939, 739.

41. "Cosmetics," *Fashion Group Bulletin*, March 1937, 4, Box 144, FGIR.

42. Crowley, "Equal Price Treatment under the Robinson-Patman Act," 334.

43. FTC Press Release, 6 January 1939, Box 168, Folder Cosmetics, Arden, Elizabeth, Special Data, AMA Department of Investigation Records, American Medical Association Archives, Chicago; "F.T.C. Stipulations," *The Drug and Cosmetic Industry*, February 1939, 196; "Agree to Stop Cosmetic Claims," *NYT*, 7 January 1939, 29.

44. "Cease and Desist," *National Association of Broadcaster (NAB) Reports*, 18 June 1936, 1372.

45. T. Lyddon Gardner, "The Cosmetic Industry," *Journal of the Royal Society of Arts* 110, no. 5076 (November 1962): 901.

46. "Attacks on Food and Drug Act Arouse Women to Support It," *The Christian Science Monitor*, 22 March 1939, 2.

47. See Jennifer Frost, *Hedda Hopper's Hollywood* (New York: New York University Press, 2011).

48. "Backing of Mayor Won by Benvenga," *NYT*, 1 November 1939, 15.

49. "AFA Meet Slates First Code Airing," *Broadcasting*, 15 June 1939, 10; "Ad Federation Will Hear Walter Hoving," *WWD*, 16 June 1939, 27; "George Sokolsky, Columnist, Dies," *NYT*, 14 December 1962, 16.

50. "Advertising Federation of America," *Variety*, 17 May 1939, 24; "Arrivals," *Variety*, 12 April 1939, 2.

51. "'I Am a Famous Woman in This Industry,'" *Fortune*, October 1938, 58–65, 142, 145–46, 152, 154.

52. "Neiman-Marcus Issue Honored Designer List," *WWD*, 14 August 1939, 1; "To Get Neiman-Marcus Awards," *NYT*, 24 August 1939, 32; "2,000 at Neiman-Marcus Fashion Exhibit, Presentation of Awards," *WWD*, 12 September 1939, 1. American fashion designers Hattie Carnegie and Clare Potter, men's hat creator John Cavanagh, and Janet May of Carlin Comforts were also honored. Arden could not be there in person. She may have sent Henry Sell to accept for her.

53. Inez Robb, "'Met' Opening to Find New Faces in Circle," *The Washington Post*, 1 December 1940, S4; "Lists of Opera Boxholders," *NYT*, 17 November 1941, 22.

54. "Advertising Medal Goes to Thomson," *NYT*, 16 February 1939, 40.

55. Ron Magliozzi, "'Crazy with the Wind': The 'Gone with the Wind' World Premiere Campaign Scrapbook," *MoMA* 18 (Autumn–Winter 1994): 33.

56. Cape Cod: "At Saratoga," *WWD*, 3 August 1939, 29. North Wales Club: Nina Carter Tabb, "The Hunt Country," *The Washington Post*, 4 December 1939, 12. Art opening: Lucius Beebe, "This New York," *The Washington Post*, 22 October 1939, AM1. Marcus: "Will Honor H. S. Marcus at Dinner May 11," *WWD*, 15 April 1941, 2; "250 Leaders from 17 Trades on Dinner Committee for H. Stanley Marcus Testimonial," *WWD*, 30 April 1941, 4; "Marcus Dinner to Spotlight Style Trends," *WWD*, 8 May 1941, 8. Helena Rubinstein was never mentioned in any of the articles about Marcus. Clifton Fadiman, ed., *Profiles from The New Yorker* (New York: Alfred A. Knopf, 1938), 329–41. Margaret Case Harriman wrote Arden's, which ran in the 6 April 1935 issue.

57. "New Styles Decree Nails Must Match Hues of Lip Rouge," *The Washington Post*, 13 December 1937, 11; "Price List to the Retail Trade," November 1937, p. 12, GB1752.EA/5/2, Elizabeth

Arden Ltd. Papers, Unilever Archives, Port Sunlight, UK; "Sequin Make-Up" ad, *NYT*, 26 September 1937, 7L.

58. For example, "Keep Your Face in the Pink," *Vogue*, 1 May 1938, 66–67; "Cyclamen" ad, *Vogue*, 1 May 1938, 113; Best & Co. Arden Sky Pink ad, *NYT*, 6 June 1938, 5; Bonwit Teller Elizabeth Arden ad for Paquin's pink, *NYT*, 15 May 1938, 4; "Take to the Roofs," *Vogue*, 1 June 1938, 30 (for Arden and Paquin). Cyclamen Color Harmony Boxes debuted in September 1937, but they contained several different shades of makeup. She began naming lipstick, rouge, and nail polish Cyclamen by January 1938.

59. She had been doing this since she first created her color harmony. For the 1938 version, see "Complexion Colors" ad, *NYT*, 18 September 1938, 4.

60. "Spring Hosiery Colors Accent Trend to Soft, Clear Ranges," *WWD*, 18 November 1938, 10; "Shoes Selling with Manufacturers," *WWD*, 25 November 1938, 4; "Palter DeLiso Borrows Elizabeth Arden's Cosmetic Colours for Kidskins," *NYT*, 18 December 1938, 5; "Match Your Southern Accessories to Your Make-Up in Elizabeth Arden Colors," *Chicago Tribune*, 19 December 1938, 14; "Vivacious Cosmetic Colors in Kidskins by Palter DeLiso," *Chicago Tribune*, 8 January 1939, F2. For girdles, see "Sky Blue Pink for Your New Treo Girdles" Saks Fifth Avenue ad, *NYT*, 14 April 1939, 7. Tie-ins will grow more elaborate, but never wane in popularity. See, for example, "Color Promotion Ties In Hose with Perfume for Easter," *WWD*, 11 March 1955, 24.

61. See, for example, "British Sweaters in Lipstick Colors," *WWD*, 5 June 1939, 15.

62. "Color Affiliates" ad, *Vogue*, 1 September 1940, 16; "A White Season Is Forecast by Glove Importer in South," *WWD*, 12 January 1940, 11, lists Hodge millinery, Koret bags, D'Liso [*sic*] shoes, Kislav gloves, and Stroock woolens. "Color Affiliates Preview Tuesday," *WWD*, 19 January 1940, 14, lists Norman Blum gloves, Koret handbags, Stroock fabrics, Hodge millinery, Deliso [*sic*] shoes. In 1940, Color Affiliates added Delman Inc., and Mallinson Fabrics. See "Color Groups Unanimous on Soft, Warm, Deep Accessory Tonings," *WWD*, 12 July 1940, 10.

63. "Lipstick Hats," *WWD*, 13 March 1941, 18.

64. "Type, Price, Variety in Hats Shown in Current Retail Ads," *WWD*, 28 February 1940, 21.

65. Woodward & Lothrop ad, *The Washington Post*, 14 February 1940, 5.

66. Preliminary Meeting of Fashion Council, [1937], Box 445, folder 3, World's Fair NYPL. There seems to have been a meeting in June as well, and Arden's niece Virginia Graham Wobber, who was working for her in the 1930s, appears to have attended that meeting. See also Luisina Silva, "New York Fashion Industry Goes

to the Fair" (master's thesis, City University of New York, 2014), 17–18. For the name, see S. L. Mayham, "I have checked with . . . ," 15 March 1939, Box 171, folder 15, World's Fair NYPL.

67. S. L. Mayham to Norman Dahl, 6 December 1938, Box 446, folder 18, World's Fair NYPL.

68. *The Story of the Westinghouse Time Capsule* (East Pittsburgh, PA: Westinghouse Electric & Manufacturing Company, undated [1939]), 20.

69. "Copper Pink and Luster Blue Interior for World's Fair 'World of Fashion' Building," *WWD*, 31 May 1940, 1, 43; "Doorway to Beauty" ad, *Vogue*, 1 May 1939, 107.

70. "Fair Faces," *WWD*, 1 August 1939, 3.

71. "Wednesday IADM Day at World's Fair," *WWD*, 23 June 1939, 7.

72. "Elizabeth Arden's New School" ad, *NYT*, 5 November 1939, 26. "Maine-Chance-in-Town" ad, *Vogue*, 1 March 1940, 103; "Latest News" Arden ad, *NYT*, 19 October 1938, 33. She also used "Maine-Chance-in-Town" to refer to an individualized experience, priced depending upon the client's needs.

73. "For Women in Business," *NYT*, 30 April 1939, 53.

74. "Dance Your Way to Beauty" ad, *NYT*, 27 November 1938, 40.

75. "Elizabeth Arden's Quick Make-Up Kit" Marshall Field ad, *Chicago Tribune*, 9 November 1938, 21; "Daily Rituals," *WWD*, 18 November 1938, 4.

76. Elizabeth Arden ad, *NYT*, 2 February 1941, 38.

77. "Bonwit Fashion Tour of South America Will Not Accept Orders," *WWD*, 5 December 1938, 23.

78. "Harrods (Buenos Aires) Sticks to Quality Goods despite Import Trouble," *WWD*, 3 June 1940, 5.

CHAPTER 16: WAR BEGINS IN EUROPE

1. "Elizabeth Arden in Paris," *Vogue*, 15 April 1939, 130–31; "Paris Cotton Against a New Paris Décor," *Vogue*, 15 April 1939, 82–83; "Fashion Flashes from Paris," *WWD*, 20 January 1939, 1. For Vertès, see "Marcel Vertès," in Richard R. Brettell, *Nineteenth- and Twentieth-Century European Drawings in the Robert Lehman Collection* (Princeton, NJ: Princeton University Press, 2002), 382.

2. "La Mode et la Beauté," *Le Journal*, 4 April 1939, 8.

3. B. J. Perkins, "Glimpses of Paris," *WWD*, 12 April 1939, 4.

4. Alfred Allan Lewis and Constance Woodworth, *Miss Elizabeth Arden* (New York: Coward, McCann & Geoghegan, 1972), 202–3.

5. SS *Queen Mary* manifest, arriving New York City 6 April 1939, 5, ancestry.com. The *Queen Mary*'s maiden launch occurred in 1936.

6. "Elizabeth Arden Sells Gas Mask Bag and Service Kit in Britain," *WWD*, 29 August 1939, 1.

7. "Central European Notes," *WWD*, 13 October 1938, 23; B. J. Perkins, "Glimpses of Paris," *WWD*, 23 April 1939, 4.

8. Lesley Blanch, "London Life—Under Arms," *Vogue*, 15 October 1939, 62, 110, 111; quotes on p. 62. Wealthy Americans in England could often afford to import goods difficult to find otherwise, and U.S. military bases overseas carried many products available almost nowhere else in Great Britain. See Lynne Olson, *Citizens of London* (New York: Random House, 2011).

9. B. J. Perkins, "Paris Firms Cite Need for Prompt Payment from U.S.," *WWD*, 7 September 1939, 1.

10. "Fashion Flashes from Paris," *WWD*, 29 September 1939, 1.

11. "'War Creates Its Own Fashions,' Say Leading London Retailers," *WWD*, 25 September 1940, 1.

12. Edna Woolman Chase, Speech to Fashion Group luncheon, 27 September 1939, 32, Speeches and Transcripts, Box 73, Fashion Group International Records, Mss Col 980, New York Public Library Archives & Manuscripts Division, New York City. Hereafter cited as Chase Speech, September 1939. Collection hereafter cited as FGIR.

13. "Fashion Flashes from Paris" and "4 Manchester Stores Pool Deliveries," *WWD*, 22 September 1939, 1, 7. Both quotes are found on p. 7.

14. Chase Speech, September 1939, 31.

15. "Elizabeth Arden's Gauzy Gas Masks Pack into Handbag," *WWD*, 29 September 1939, 1. For an interesting overview of the decoration of gas mask holders, see historian Mats Fridlund's "Keep Calm and Carry One: The Civilian Gas Mask Case and Its Containment of British Emotions," in *Boxes: A Field Guide*, ed. Susanne Bauer, Martina Schlünder, and Maria Rentezi (Mattering Press, 2019), matteringpress.org/books /boxes.

16. "Functional Accessories," *WWD*, 22 September 1939, 5; "What Europe Does about Gas Masks," *WWD*, 20 October 1939, 20.

17. Chase Speech, September 1939, 30.

18. Rebecca Arnold, *The American Look* (New York: I.B. Tauris, 2009), 24–25. For one example of the Fashion Group's work, see "Ten Committees Listed for Staging 'Fashion Futures—American Edition,'" *WWD*, 16 November 1937, 28. And for more on the Fashion Group, see Arnold, *American Look*, 93–101, and Einav Rabinovitch-Fox, *Dressed for Freedom* (Urbana: University of Illinois Press, 2021), esp. 117–29.

19. "Fashion Flashes from London," *WWD*, 27 October 1939, 2.

20. "London War Notes," *Vogue*, 1 November 1939, 73.

21. "Fashion Flashes from London," *WWD*, 26 April 1940, 1; "'Brittania' and 'Marianne' Unite in a New Shawl," *WWD*, 7 June 1940, 19.

22. "London War Notes," *Vogue*, 1 November 1939, 72.

23. Janet Leckie, *A Talent for Living* (New York: Hawthorn Books, 1970), 159–60. Lewis and Woodworth second this point of Arden's preparedness (*Miss Elizabeth Arden*, 207).

24. "Presenting Stop Red" Arden ad, *NYT*, 5 March 1939, 2; "Color Affiliates" Marshall Field ad, *Chicago Tribune*, 2 August 1940, 2. For Stop Red quote, see I. Magnin ad, *Los Angeles Times*, 12 January 1940, 3. For Schoolhouse quote, see "Schoolhouse Red" Arden ad, *Vogue*, 1 October 1940, 105. For Cinnabar quote, see Robinson's ad, *Los Angeles Times*, 27 August 1940, 11.

25. "Measuring Up," *WWD*, 30 January 1940, 3. The waist size depended on one's height.

26. "What Are These New Slenderizing Treatments?" Arden ad, *NYT*, 23 June 1940, 3. For "equatorial bulges," see "Can You Bare It?" Arden ad, *NYT*, 14 July 1940, 3.

27. "Makeup, Exercises, Featured at Ritz Luncheon Showing," *WWD*, 24 January 1940, 9; "Debutante Models Display New Styles," *NYT*, 24 January 1940, 16.

28. "12 Models on Way for Exhibit in U.S.," *WWD*, 28 March 1940, 5.

29. "Information Wanted," *The Times*, 1 July 1940. I am indebted to Dr. Daniel Weinbren for this source.

30. For background, see Anne Sebba, *Les Parisiennes* (New York: St. Martin's Press, 2016).

31. "Bond Street Retailers Launch Fighter Fund," *WWD*, 22 August 1940, 36.

32. Talks by Louise Macy and Elizabeth Penrose, 26 June 1940, Fashion Group International Speeches, Box 73, folder 8, FGIR. For Schiaparelli's account of this, see her memoir *Shocking Life* (1954; repr., London: V&A Publishing, 2018), 116–17.

33. Schiaparelli, *Shocking Life*, 114.

34. "Cosmetics," *Fashion Group Bulletin*, May 1941, 8, Box 144, folder 13, "Newsletters," FGIR.

35. Edward Drayton, "Morale Is a Woman's Business," *WWD*, 18 December 1941, 32.

36. "Go Ahead!," *Cosmopolitan*, January 1943, 131.

37. "Morale in Wartime England," *Fashion Group Bulletin*, December 1941, Insert Two, Box 144, folder 13, FGIR. "Make Do and Mend" was a government slogan that became popular after Great Britain instituted clothing rationing. Even in December 1941, however, the speaker told the Fashion Group that seamstresses were in such short supply that women were teaching (or reminding) themselves how to sew. See also Penny Dade, *All Made Up* (Hendon, UK: Middlesex University Press, 2007), 32.

38. For the auction, see "Apparel Contributed to Raise Funds for British War Relief," *WWD*, 6 August 1940, 35. See several articles in the *Fashion Group Bulletin*, July 1941, Box 144, folder 13, FGIR. The clothing donation was for Bundles for Britain and is mentioned on Insert Two of that issue. See also the December 1941 *Fashion Group Bulletin* for more examples.

39. "Contributors to the Committee to Aid the Allies," *NYT*, 11 March 1941, 10; "Benefits Slated at Palm Springs," *Los Angeles Times*, 19 February 1941, A7. This was for Bundles for Britain. See also "Help England," *WWD*, 1 October 1940, 4; "Reception Is Held by French Relief," *NYT*, 10 May 1941, 19; "Frenchwomen Hold a Spring Fair Today," *NYT*, 15 May 1941, 20.

40. "Hold Your Chin High" Arden ad, *The Washington Post*, 9 February 1941, A2; "Merchandise on Sale in Stores March 17," *WWD*, 26 February 1941, 10; "Broad Publicity Drive to Tell BAAC Story," *WWD*, 26 February 1941, 11.

41. The American Friends of France, *Spécialités de la Maison* (New York: H. Wolff, 1940). Arden's recipe is found on p. 113. See also Schiaparelli, *Shocking Life*, 142–48.

42. Christy Fox, "Pygmalion to Draw Society Tonight," *Los Angeles Times*, 10 February 1941, A5; "City's Easter Parade Will Rival Fifth Ave.," *Los Angeles Times*, 19 February 1941, A6; Museum of Modern Art Press Release, 26 July 1941, MOMA Press Release Archive Online: moma.org/momaorg/shared/pdfs/docs/press_archives/720/releases/MOMA_1941_0057_1941-07-23_41723-56.pdf. "Dinner Nov. 29 for Los Angeles Home," *WWD*, 3 November 1941, 2; "Debutantes Give Help to Cotillion," *NYT*, 12 October 1941, D1; "Debutantes Feted at Diamond Ball," *NYT*, 25 October 1941, 18; "'Dramatic Contrast' Important Lesson in Saks-34th St. 'Spring Fashion School,'" *WWD*, 12 March 1940, 6.

43. "Through the Looking Glass," *Glamour*, August 1940, 73.

44. "About Dresses for Daytime," *WWD*, 21 February 1941, 3; "Summer Clearance" Arden ad, *NYT*, 16 July 1941, 7.

45. "Make-Ups Keyed to Jewels Launched by Elizabeth Arden," *WWD*, 11 October 1940, 2; "Cosmetics and Perfumes Color Costume," *WWD*, 27 October 1940, 8.

46. "Few Chicago Stores Bid for Visitors' Trade," *WWD*, 17 July 1940, 6.

47. "City Celebrations Attended by 8,000," *NYT*, 31 January 1939, 10.

48. Marcia Winn, "Food Runs Out at Big Luncheon for Women Visitors," *Chicago Tribune*, 25 June 1940, 7.

49. Christine Sadler, "Women Share Convention Spotlight," *The Washington Post*, 25 June 1940, 1.

50. "Republicans Get $772,275 Gifts Here," *NYT*, 1 November 1940, 21.

51. "They Will Vote for the Republican Standard Bearer," *NYT*, 4 November 1940, 12.

52. "GOP Mock Convention Is Tuesday," *Hartford Courant*, 5 June 1938, A8; "Women's Republican Club of State Names Ticket in Mock Convention," *The Boston Globe*, 16 May 1940, 13. Katherine Howard, who played Arden in 1940, was the spouse of former Massachusetts congressman Charles P. Howard.

53. The organizers were scrambling. Mary Lewis, fashion director for the fair, cut the cost of exhibiting in half. See Mary Lewis form letter, 16 March 1949, Box 444, folder 16, New York World's Fair 1939 and 1940 Incorporated Records, Mss Col 2233, New York Public Library Archives & Manuscripts Division, New York City. Hereafter cited as World's Fair NYPL. See also "'World of Fashion' Building Draws Acclaim at Opening," *WWD*, 3 June 1940, 1, 6.

54. "Fashion: Straight from the American Openings," *Vogue*, September 1, 1940, 49.

55. Christa Molinaro, "Dressing the World of Tomorrow" (master's thesis, SUNY Fashion Institute of Technology, 2020), 23.

56. "Elizabeth Arden Display Sale of Cosmetics," "Elizabeth Arden at the World of Fashion," and "The Elizabeth Arden 'Isle of Beauty' Exhibit" press releases, all undated [1940], Box 1823, folder 2, World's Fair NYPL. For the World's Fair Box, see Amos Hiatt to Edward E. Warner, 10 May 1939, and for the smaller box, see G. Franklin to H. A. Flanagan, 15 June 1939, Box 829, folder 6, World's Fair NYPL.

57. "Opportunities in Fashion," *Vassar Miscellany News*, 22 January 1941, 2.

58. "Join Elizabeth Arden's Beauty Career Classes" Arden ad, *Los Angeles Times*, 12 August 1941, A6.

59. Sleek Hair Remover: AMA to Joe Phillips, 7 March 1942, Box 168, folder 5, "Cosmetics, Arden, Elizabeth, Correspondence, 1941–1945," AMA Department of Investigation Records, American Medical Association Archives, Chicago. Hereafter cited as AMA Archives. For Ardena Sensation Cream, Joie de Vivre, and Ardena Skin Lotion, see FTC Press Release, 9 September 1941, Box 168, folder 2, "Cosmetics, Arden, Elizabeth, Special Data," AMA Archives.

60. AMA Bureau of Investigation to Catherine Gosney, 15 February 1941, Box 168, folder 4, "Cosmetics, Arden, Elizabeth, Correspondence, 1938–1940," AMA Archives.

61. "Boston Parley to Discuss U.S. Fashion Role," *WWD*, 3 September 1940, 1.

62. The five hundred industry executives who gathered also heard from Firestone, Swift, Walt Disney, and *New York Times* CEOs. Arden's talk was the closing session, Tuesday, 8 October, in the afternoon. Her topic was "Fashions in the Cosmetics Business." See "Boston Conference on Distribution to Set Attendance Record," *The Boston Globe*, 3 October 1940, 24. See also "Boston Conference on Distribution Opens Oct. 7," *The Boston Globe*, 8 September 1940, A22; "Fashion Group to Give Cocktail Party at Boston Parley," *WWD*, 20 September 1940, 33.

63. "'Economic Police' to Act, Distribution Conference Told," *The Boston Globe*, 9 October 1940, 1, 5. Arden quote is on p. 5.

64. "U.S. Will Finally Learn to Create, Sara Pennoyer Holds," *WWD*, 9 October 1940, 6;

"Luncheon Guests at Distribution Conference," *The Boston Globe*, 9 October 1940, 5.

65. Gladys became a naturalized French citizen in 1942. See "Lois et Décrets," *Journal officiel de l'Etat française*, 2 August 1942, 2671, gallica.bnf.fr/ark:/12148/bpt6k9613616d#.

66. Edna Ferber to Constance Collier, 27 January 1941, folder 956, Hedda Hopper Papers, Margaret Herrick Library, Academy of Motion Picture Arts and Sciences, Beverly Hills, California.

67. Christy Fox, "Society Treks Home after Busy Holidays," *Los Angeles Times*, 2 January 1941, F5; Louella O. Parsons, "Close-Ups and Long-Shots of the Motion Picture Scene," *The Washington Post*, 10 January 1941, 7; "Chatterbox," *Los Angeles Times*, 10 January 1941, A6; "Beauty and Britain," *WWD*, 25 April 1941, 3; Edwin Schallert, "Kate Smith Proffered Lead in 'Navy Blues,'" *Los Angeles Times*, 4 April 1941, 14.

68. Leonard Lyons, *The Washington Post*, 19 May 1941, 14. William Haines was set designer, composer George Antheil wrote the film's score, and Will Jason directed. For Antheil, see "Orchids to Charlie by George Antheil," *Catalog of Copyright Entries*, n.s., vol. 36, pt. 3, *Musical Compositions* (Washington, DC: Library of Congress Copyright Office, 1941), 1320. Antheil's memoir does not mention the experience; *Bad Boy of Music* (Garden City, NY: Doubleday, Doran, 1945).

69. Mayme Ober Peak, "Most Photographed Face," *The Boston Globe*, 15 June 1941, A53; Edwin Schallert, "Carole Lombard Likely Star of 'Mating Call,'" *Los Angeles Times*, 20 June 1941, A10.

70. "Barring of Women from Pilot Training Rapped," *Los Angeles Daily News*, 29 July 1941, 13. See also "News about Earl Blackwell Is Received from New York," *Atlanta Constitution*, 25 August 1941, 13.

71. Hedda Hopper, "Hedda Says," *Pittsburgh Press*, 28 April 1941, 17.

72. "Daytime First Aid Classes Begin This Morning," *The Washington Post*, 11 July 1940, 11. List from "Service Uniform for Women Shown," *NYT*, 25 September 1941, 22. For Saxer, see Arlene Dahl, "How Expert Keeps Film Stars Slim," *Chicago Tribune*, 26 March 1958, A4.

73. "Mrs. Davie to Lead Volunteer Women," *NYT*, 17 September 1941, 9.

74. "Beauty for Defense" Arden ad, *Chicago Tribune*, 17 November 1941, 16. All of her major salons taught this class. By August 1941, Hudnut DuBarry Salon offered a "Physical Preparedness Program" under the direction of former Arden exercise expert Ann Delafield; see "Success School" Hudnut DuBarry ad, *NYT*, 5 August 1941, 3.

75. "Queen Inspects U.S. Gifts," *NYT*, 27 April 1940, 4; Jessie Arndt Ash, "Headquarters Opened Here to Train Volunteers in Case of Flood, Quake, Fire or War," *The Washington Post*, 2 June 1940, S6; "Service Unit Maps Organization

Plan," *The Washington Post*, 1 July 1940, 10. For Arden's further involvement, see, for example, "A.W.V.S. Will Hold Style Show Oct. 17," *NYT*, 16 September 1951, 107; "Style Show, Luncheon Oct. 13 Planned by American Women's Voluntary Group," *NYT*, 14 September 1954, 31; and "Style Show to Aid Women's Unit Today," *NYT*, 13 October 1954, 24. Her support continued to her death. See, for example, "Annual Luncheon of the A.W.V.S. Scheduled Oct. 4," *NYT*, 13 September 1961, 52. Much of her service—including all of her AWVS hands-on volunteer work—she did under "Mrs. E. Graham Lewis" rather than Elizabeth Arden. She was not interested in taking advantage of the war in this way to make sales.

Arden also made a first aid kit that contained none of her toiletries and no decorations. It was strictly for first aid. A photo of her "24 Unit Kit" can be seen here: liveauctioneers.com/item /152950085_ww-ii-first-aid-kit-by-elizabeth -arden.

76. "Industrialist Says Women Entering More into Business World," *The Christian Science Monitor*, 8 October 1941, 21.

77. "Business Women Challenging Men," *NYT*, 8 October 1941, 18.

78. "My First Break," *Los Angeles Times*, 22 May 1949, F12. See also Philippe Halsman, *The Frenchman: A Photographic Interview* (New York: Simon & Schuster, 1949). Quote is from Carolyn Abbott, "Exotic and Demure in Make-Up," *The Washington Post*, 3 April 1942, 17.

79. "Victory Red" Arden ad, *Vogue*, 15 September 1941, 109. For the pamphlet, see James Bennett, *Victory Red*, cosmeticsandskin.com/booklets /arden-victory.php.

80. La Guardia quote is from "Army Officer Praises Discipline and Spirit," *The Boston Globe*, 18 November 1941, 28; sartorial quote is from "Today in Society," *The Boston Globe*, 18 November 1941, 17.

81. "Vesper George School," *The Boston Globe*, 23 November 1941, B39.

CHAPTER 17: BEAUTY AND MORALE

1. "226 Concerns Here Have German Units," *NYT*, 9 November 1930, N12.

2. "Carlson-Klee," *Hartford Courant*, 25 July 1932, 7; Edwin J. Geiges, *Alumni Record of Wesleyan University 1831–1970*, 10th ed. (Middletown, CT, 1971), 294; Wesleyan University *Olla Podridas* Yearbook (Albany, NY: Fort Orange Press, 1928), 66, 233, Wesleyan University Special Collections and Archives, Middletown, CT. See also Pat DiGeorge, *Liberty Lady* (Vero Beach, FL: Beaver's Spur Publishing, 2016), 50.

3. Alma Whitaker, "Suzanne Wood Sells Palatial Villa in France," *Los Angeles Times*, 24 January 1934, A7. Arden took her out of Germany in March 1933.

4. For excerpts from several Nazi leaders about the role of women, see George L. Mosse, ed.,

Nazi Culture (New York: Grosset & Dunlap, 1966), 39–47.

5. *Fashion Group Bulletin*, November 1934, Box 144, folder 16, 6, Fashion Group International Records, Mss Col 980, New York Public Library Archives & Manuscripts Division, New York City. Hereafter cited as FGIR.

6. Günter Berghaus, "Girlkultur: Feminism, Americanism, and Popular Entertainment in Weimar Germany," *Journal of Design History* 1, no. 3/4 (1988): 205.

7. In December 1936, Scott-Williams appears to have been back in the United States. See her letter to Constance Dudley, Box 1, Papers of the Casey and Dudley Families, Special Collections, University of Virginia, Charlottesville.

8. Otto D. Tolischus, "The Nazis Recant on Woman's Place," *NYT*, 30 January 1938, 61. "*Kueche, kinder, kirche*" translates to kitchen, children, church.

9. For an excellent analysis of the role of cosmetics in Nazism, including a comparison between Arden's German and North American ads, see Yvonne Barbara Houy, "Of Course the German Woman Should Be Modern" (Ph.D. diss., Cornell University, 2002). The point about Goebbels is from p. 194. For an important analysis of German fashion during World War II, see Irene Guenther, *Nazi Chic?* (New York: Berg, 2004). Among elite female Nazis, makeup wearing had never gone out of style. Such women made their own rules. Eva Braun, Hitler's mistress, used Arden face creams and lipstick. See Harry Sions, "Berchtesgaden: Hitler's Mountain Retreat," *Yank: The Army Weekly*, 22 June 1945, 4, and Becky E. Conekin, "'Magazines Are Essentially about the Here and Now. And This Was Wartime,'" in *Gender, Labour, War and Empire*, ed. Philippa Levine and Susan R. Grayzel (New York: Palgrave Macmillan, 2009), 132.

Fashion plate Magda Goebbels also preferred Arden makeup and skin care products, as did former actress Emma Goering. One Elizabeth Arden employee, Gerda Daranowsky Christian, quit her Red Door job to become Hitler's "best secretary." See John Toland, *Adolf Hitler* (Garden City, NY: Doubleday, 1976), 733; quote is on p. 743.

10. Leonard Lyons, "The *Post*'s New Yorker," *The Washington Post*, 27 July 1937, 16, and 28 July 1937, 12. Göring was almost never seen in photos without his World War I Pour le Mérite medal.

11. "Memorandum for Mr. A. M. Thurston," 6 October 1941, Elizabeth Arden FBI File, Federal Bureau of Investigation Records: The Vault Online, vault.fbi.gov/Elizabeth%20Arden. Hereafter cited as EA FBI File. For Thurston, see Ray Batvinis, "A Thoroughly Competent Operator," FBI Studies Online, October 2017, fbistudies .com/2017/10/30/a-thoroughly-competent -operator-former-fbi-sa-arthur-thurston.

12. For *Die Dame*'s history and usage by the Nazis, see Christiane Nickel, "Fashion in the Third Reich" (master's thesis, SUNY Fashion Institute of Technology, 2011).

13. Elizabeth Lewis to [Name blacked out] at the *Daily Mirror*, 8 March 1941, EA FBI File. The date of this letter might actually have been 8 March 1942, which is the date J. Edgar Hoover used to refer to it in his letter of 23 April 1942 to "Special Agent in Charge," EA FBI File.

14. Department of Justice, Request for Records Disposition Authority, 26 August 1996, NARA Online: archives.gov/files/records-mgmt/rcs/schedules/departments/department-of-justice/rg-0065/n1-065-96-001_sf115.pdf. For Arden as an SSC, see unsigned memo to the Special Agent in Charge, mailed 23 April 1942, and Memo for D. M. Ladd, 1 May 1942, EA FBI File.

15. Steve Hewitt, *Snitch* (New York: Continuum/Bloomsbury, 2010), 82–83; Sam Staggs, *Inventing Elsa Maxwell* (New York: St. Martin's Press, 2012), 4; Don Rhodes, *Ty Cobb: Safe at Home* (Guilford, CT: Lyons Press, 2008), 141–42.

16. For a fascinating example of an Arden salon director simultaneously working as an Allied spy in the center of Rome, see historian Ladislas Farago's *Burn after Reading* (New York: Walker, 1961), 164–65.

17. "Training and Requirement for Women Factory Workers," *Fashion Group Bulletin*, May 1942, 1, FGIR; Kathleen McLaughlin, "Woman War Workers," *NYT*, 3 January 1943, A41.

18. Mary-Elizabeth Parker, "Is Beauty Worth Half a Billion?," *NYT*, 20 December 1942, SM25.

19. Lydia Lane, "Feminine Role in National Defense Starts at Beauty Shop, Says Expert," *Los Angeles Times*, 18 February 1942, B16.

20. Ann Dean, "Beauty of the Nation's Women Most Important Wartime Factor," *The Boston Globe*, 19 April 1942, B9.

21. Maxine Bartlett, "Personal Appearance Aids Morale," *Los Angeles Times*, 15 May 1942, B20.

22. For a larger discussion of how wartime messages constrained and punished women who—in society's opinion—took the admonition to be beautiful for the boys too far, see Marilyn E. Hegarty, *Victory Girls, Khaki-Wackies, and Patriotutes* (New York: New York University Press, 2008), esp. chap. 5.

23. "Fashion in America Now," *Vogue*, 1 February 1942, 50, 123.

24. "Do Not Foster Obsolescence, Warns H. Stanley Marcus," *Fashion Group Bulletin*, March 1942, 1–4; Mills quote is from "Cosmetics," p. 4, FGIR. Mills joined Arden in 1941 at $15,000 per year. See Florence N. Lewis to Ruth Mills, 1 July 1941, Box 2, Ruth Mills and Elizabeth Mills Family Papers, Tennessee State Library & Archives, Nashville.

25. "Sen. Smith Isn't Convinced, Apparently, That Ruffle-Rationing Will Win the War," *Austin American-Statesman*, 2 June 1942, 1.

26. "Walk—and **Like** It" Arden ad, *NYT*, 15 November 1942, 53; "Hands of Today" Bonwit Teller ad, *NYT*, 25 October 1942, 37.

27. "Faces of Today" Bonwit Teller ad, *NYT*, 18 October 1942, 50.

28. "Elizabeth Arden Shop" Stearns ad, *The Boston Globe*, 30 October 1942, 20.

29. "Tone of Fashion's New 'Dress Parade,'" *WWD*, 14 January 1943, 47; "Blueprints for Beauty," *Vogue*, 1 January 1943, 66; "Blueprint for a Bright Future" Arden ad, *Vogue*, 1 January 1943, 69. For the booklet, see Elizabeth Arden, *Efficiency Plan, General Maintenance*, Rich's Department Store Collection, hc.MSS 791f, undated [1946–1953], Kenan Research Center, Atlanta Research Center.

30. Martha Parker, "The Beauty Quest," *NYT*, 29 July 1943, 22.

31. "Plumed Parade Stirs Crowds on Fifth Avenue," *NYT*, 7 May 1919, 3.

32. "Feather Red Is Launched by Designers," *The Christian Science Monitor*, 21 January 1942, 15; "Contest in Spring Cosmetics—Gay Bright New Red," *WWD*, 23 January 1942, 12. Arden was inconsistent with the name. Sometimes she used Feather Red and sometimes Red Feather.

33. This was a revisiting of the Greek myth of Pygmalion, who fell in love with Galatea, the statue of the ideal woman that he created. "Galatea Moderne," *WWD*, 21 November 1941, 3; "Pygmalion Magic!," *Los Angeles Times*, 4 December 1941, A6; "'Galatea' Manikins at Filene's Become Beauteously Alive Today," *The Boston Globe*, 23 January 1942, 16.

34. "It's New . . . It's Trim . . . It's Essential" Arden ad, *NYT*, 25 January 1942, 5.

35. "Sir Galahad Coiffure" ad, *NYT*, 25 October 1942, 38.

36. "Winged Psyche" Arden ad, *Los Angeles Times*, 20 December 1942, D6.

37. "Morale-Inventory for Fashion Industry and Individual 'Take the Folly Out of Fashion,'" *Fashion Group Bulletin*, February 1942, 1, 3–5 (quote is on p. 4), FGIR. "Clip Top" Arden ad, *The Boston Globe*, 11 February 1942, 19. For more on British *Vogue* in wartime, see Conekin, "Magazines Are Essentially about the Here and Now," 116–38.

38. Elizabeth Arden advertisement, *Vogue*, 1 January 1945, 94.

39. "The Miracle of Susan" Arden ad, *The Boston Globe*, 5 February 1942, 15. The commas after "days" and "work" are ellipses in the original.

40. "Defense Dividends for Busy Women," *The Boston Globe*, 24 February 1942, 13.

41. "Republican Business Women Get Pointers on 'Victory Grooming,'" *The Boston Globe*, 25 February 1942, 2; "What Price Physical Fitness?," *Vogue*, 15 May 1942, 88–89.

42. Virginia Pope, "Woman's Day during Time of War Is Dramatized at Style Show Here," *NYT*, 11 February 1942, 24; "Make-Up, War, Home Costumes Suggested for Woman of Today," *WWD*, 11 February 1942, 3; "Lenora Corbett," *Vogue*, 1 April 1942, 59. Final quote is from Carolyn Abbott, "Exotic and Demure in Make-Up," *The Washington Post*, 3 April 1942, 17. For a searing analysis of the connection between the stage and fashion in America, see Marlis Schweitzer, *When Broadway Was the Runway* (Philadelphia: University of Pennsylvania Press, 2009).

43. Hedda Hopper, "Hedda Hopper's Hollywood," *Los Angeles Times*, 29 April 1942, 13. "All" is an overstatement.

44. Andrea Nouryeh, "The Stage Door Canteen: The American Theatre Wing's Experiment in Integration (1942–45)," in *Experiments in Democracy*, ed. Cheryl Black et al. (Carbondale: Southern Illinois University Press, 2016), 269–70.

45. J. W. Robinson ad, *Los Angeles Times*, 10 February 1938, 13.

46. "British Women Taught to Handle Weapons," *The Christian Science Monitor*, 18 September 1942, 14. WHD units worked at times in conjunction with the Home Guard.

47. It took 240 pairs of stockings' worth to make one parachute in 1942. "Stretching the Supply," *WWD*, 30 October 1942, 12; "What Is That Clever Elizabeth Arden Preparation?," *Chicago Tribune*, 29 June 1932, 16. In 1932, it was tinted Protecta Cream marketed for legs. See also Anne Sebba, *Les Parisiennes* (New York: St. Martin's Press, 2016), 115.

48. Nickel, "Fashion in the Third Reich," 12. Ricci opened her shop in 1932.

49. Sebba, *Les Parisiennes*, 151. Information about Paris in this paragraph is from Sebba, chap. 4.

50. For evidence that the Paris Arden salon remained open into the spring of 1944, see "Nazi-Paris Shortwave Strong on Couture Names, Shy on Style News," *WWD*, 25 April 1944, 3.

51. "War Held Challenge to Buyers," *WWD*, 21 January 1942, 15.

52. "Cosmetics," *Fashion Group Bulletin*, November 1942, 4, FGIR.

53. "War Held Challenge to Buyers," *WWD*, 21 January 1942, 15.

54. See, for example, "War's Horrors Need Not Include Shiny Nose, Lack of Beauty Aids," *NYT*, 5 March 1942, 19, and "Cosmetics," *Fashion Group Bulletin*, April 1942, 5, FGIR.

55. "Saks-Fifth Avenue Features Compacts," *WWD*, 29 December 1927, 5; "Elizabeth Arden's Perfume Pins" ad, *NYT*, 19 November 1939, 35; "Have an Elizabeth Arden Refill for Your Lipstick," *NYT*, 30 July 1942, 3.

56. Elizabeth Arden lipsticks Franklin Simon ad, *NYT*, 20 September 1942, 20; "A Lipstick of Distinction" Arden ad, *The Boston Globe*, 6 December 1942, B22. See also Sydney B. Self,

"Bottled Beauty," *The Wall Street Journal*, 14 January 1943, 1.

57. For Haslam, see "British Adjusting Cosmetics Supply," *NYT*, 27 October 1942, 30. See also Tania Long, "Cosmetics Benefit Morale in Britain," *NYT*, 28 April 1942, 18.

58. Sydney B. Self, "Bottled Beauty," *The Wall Street Journal*, 14 January 1943, 1.

59. "9th Annual Fashion Congress Opens Today," *WWD*, 22 April 1942, 16.

60. "13 Best Dressed Women," *The Boston Globe*, 22 March 1942, B7; quote is from "Best-Dressed Women, within Means, Selected," *The Washington Post*, 22 March 1942, 1. Arden won in the category of businesswomen.

61. "Elizabeth Arden Gives Lecture on 'Loveliness,'" *The Boston Globe*, 8 April 1938, 14.

62. Cobina Wright, *I Never Grew Up* (New York: Prentice-Hall, 1952), 230.

63. "Mrs. E. G. Lewis Becomes a Bride," *NYT*, 31 December 1942, 9. "Stanley C. Notts Hosts in Florida," *NYT*, 30 January 1942, 16. See also "Michael Evlanoff," *NYT*, 10 May 1972, 50.

64. "Mrs. E. G. Lewis Becomes a Bride," *NYT*, 31 December 1942, 9; "Prince Evlanoff and Bride on Honeymoon," *The Washington Post*, 5 January 1943, B4. See also New York Marriage Licenses, 28 December 1942, vol. 11, New York City Municipal Archives, New York City Records and Information Services. The date of the wedding, according to this document, was the twenty-eighth. Most newspapers put the wedding on the thirtieth.

65. "Elizabeth Arden Becomes the Bride of Prince Evlanoff," *Atlanta Constitution*, 3 January 1942, 36; "Prince Evlanoff and Bride on Honeymoon," *The Washington Post*, 5 January 1943, B4.

66. The only thing that seems certain about their ages is that Evlanoff was younger than Arden. Accounts of their age difference range wildly. Evlanoff's obituary states that he was seventy-six at his death, making him born in 1896 or in 1897. See "Michael Evlanoff," *NYT*, 10 May 1972, 50.

67. D. M. Ladd memo to J. Edgar Hoover, 8 July 1943, EA FBI File. Alfred Allan Lewis and Constance Woodworth, in *Miss Elizabeth Arden* (New York: Coward, McCann & Geoghegan, 1972, pp. 222–23), state that Michael Evlanoff was Nobel's "secretary" and "help[ed] him to escape from Russia during the Revolution," but Nobel died in 1896, about a decade before the Russian Revolution. Evlanoff did write two books about Nobel: *Nobel, Prize Donor* (Ada, MI: Revell, 1943) and, with Marjorie Fluor, *Alfred Nobel* (Los Angeles: Ward Ritchie Press, 1969).

68. D. M. Ladd memo to J. Edgar Hoover, 8 July 1943, EA FBI File. Hoover was apparently unavailable, so she spoke with his aide.

69. "Elizabeth Arden talking," handwritten notes, MS 327, Box 7, File 15, Ada Peirce

McCormick Papers, University of Arizona Special Collections, Tucson.

70. "Elizabeth Arden Seeks Divorce," *The Boston Globe*, 3 February 1944, 13; "Court May Hear Arden Divorce Suit This Week," *The Boston Globe*, 4 February 1944, 7; "Elizabeth Arden Obtains Divorce," *The Boston Globe*, 8 February 1944, 12. For the gossip, see Lewis and Woodworth, *Miss Elizabeth Arden*, 222–26. For another take on Evlanoff, by the granddaughter of a woman whom Evlanoff courted, see Kathryn Harrison, *Seeking Rapture* (New York: Random House, 2003), 30–33.

CHAPTER 18: "FOR BEAUTY ON DUTY"

1. "For Beauty on Duty," from "Elizabeth Arden's Barracks Box" Marshall Field's ad, *Chicago Tribune*, 17 February 1943, 17.

2. Linking patriotism with advertising was not a new idea. See Rob Schorman, "Remember the *Maine*, Boys, and the Price of This Suit," *The Historian* 61, no. 1 (Fall 1998): 119–34, and his *Selling Style* (Philadelphia: University of Pennsylvania Press, 2003), chap. 4.

3. "Style Show Will Aid Navy Relief," *The Washington Post*, 22 February 1942, S2.

4. "Benefit Renamed 'Fashion and Fun,'" *NYT*, 25 February 1945, 34.

5. Lindy Woodhead, *War Paint* (Hoboken, NJ: John Wiley & Sons, 2003), 185–86.

6. "War Bond Fraud Charged," *NYT*, 19 September 1943, 50. For Delaney's titles, see her obituary, "Miss Florence Delaney," *NYT*, 30 January 1949, 61. Gladstone was "convicted on grand larceny charges" and disbarred. See "Two Lawyers Disbarred," *NYT*, 6 May 1944, 9. He stole $8,320.

7. Leisa D. Meyer, *Creating G. I. Jane* (New York: Columbia University Press, 1996), esp. the prologue and chap. 1.

8. Mattie E. Treadwell, *The Women's Army Corps* (Washington, DC: Government Printing Office, 1953), 186–87.

9. "Women Marines," *Life* 16, no. 13 (27 March 1944), 81. There was an inherent tension between Holcomb's statement and the fact that the women were Marines only in relation to the definitive, male Marine. See Zayna N. Bizri, "Recruiting Women into the World War II Military" (Ph.D. diss., George Mason University, 2017), 71–72.

10. Katherine A. Towle, "Lady Leathernecks," *Marine Corps Gazette* 30, no. 2 (February 1946): 3. For an insider's view of the USMCWR, see Katherine A. Towle, "Administration and Leadership" Oral History, conducted by Harriet Nathan, Bancroft Library, University of California, Berkeley, 1970.

11. For a list of the jobs, see Pat Meid, *Marine Corps Women's Reserve in World War II* (Washington, DC: U.S. Marine Corps, 1964), app. A, 85–87, and Towle, "Lady Leathernecks," 4. For WAC jobs, see Fjeril Hess, *WACS at Work* (New York: Macmillan, 1945).

12. "WAAC Uniform Is Secret, but Undies Aren't," *Chicago Tribune*, 20 May 1942, 9.

13. For an analysis of the effect of Mainbocher's design on the WAVES themselves, see Kathleen M. Ryan, "Uniform Matters," *Journal of American Culture* 37, no. 4 (December 2014): 419–29.

14. Col. Mary V. Stremlow, *Free a Marine to Fight* (Washington, DC: U.S. Marine Corps, 1994), 17. See also Meid, *Marine Corps Women's Reserve*, 21–26.

15. Stremlow, *Free a Marine to Fight*, 15–20.

16. Author interview with Nancy Wilt, Marine veteran and curator of the Women of the Corps Collection, Kerrville, Texas, 23 January 2019. Hereafter cited as WOC Collection.

17. Wilt interview. For the patent, see "Montezuma Red," *The Official Gazette of the United States Patent Office*, vol. 559, no. 4 (22 February 1944), 548, and *Catalog of Copyright Entries*, pt. 4, 39, nos. 1–2 (1944), 112.

18. Meid, *Marine Corps Women's Reserve*, 24.

19. Woodhead, *War Paint*, 287.

20. Linda Cates Lacy, *We Are Marines!* (n.p.: Tar Heel Chapter, NC1, Women Marines Association, 2004), 93.

21. Faye Shumway Oral History, 11 May 2007, conducted by Kira A. Gentry, Center for Oral and Public History, California State University, Fullerton. Quote is found on p. 25 of the transcript.

22. Wilt interview. Marines wore Montezuma Red into the mid-1960s, even after several uniform redesigns. See Marjorie Rutherford, "Marines Go Soft," *The Boston Globe*, 29 May 1966, 1.

23. "Montezuma Red" Saks ad, *NYT*, 23 April 1944, 17.

24. "Montezuma Red" Arden ad, *Vogue*, 15 April 1944, 115; earlier ad in the *Chicago Tribune*, 9 April 1944, E5, and same day in the *NYT*, 28.

25. Nancy Wilt, "Elizabeth Arden and the Women Marines," n.d., WOC Collection.

26. Shumway Oral History, 5.

27. Meid, *Marine Corps Women's Reserve*, 24.

28. "Greetings Women Marines!" Arden ad, *NYT*, 16 February 1945, 6.

29. Donated by Arden: Wilt interview.

30. *Montezuma Red*, WR pamphlet, undated; newspaper clipping ("Women Marines are not required . . ."), undated, both from WOC Collection.

31. Virginia Graham Wobber to Captain Gretchen Thorp, 21 August 1943, RG 112, Professional Administrative Service Women's Health and Welfare Unit, 1941–1944, Box 243, Records of the Office of the Surgeon General (Army), NARA, Washington, DC.

32. Wobber to Thorp, 21 August 1943, NARA.

33. Hairstyles and descriptions are from Elizabeth Arden, *On-the-Double*, 1943, PAM 2011.464, Published Collections Department, Hagley Museum and Library, Wilmington, DE, digital .hagley.org/pc. See also Martha Parker, "G.I.

Coiffures," *NYT*, 3 October 1943, SM30; Meyer, *Creating G.I. Jane*, 154–55; and Amanda M. Willey, "Fashioning Femininity for War" (Ph.D. diss., Department of History, Kansas State University, 2015).

34. Women Marines Association, "Women Marines History," womenmarines.org/wm-history.

35. "New York City Offers Numerous Privileges for Nurses," *The Army Nurse* 1, no. 10 (October 1944), 10, Women Veterans Historical Project Online, University of North Carolina at Greensboro, gateway.uncg.edu/wvhp. Almira J. McNaboe, "Career Women Give Services to the Services," *The Key*, February 1945, 59, Kappa Kappa Gamma Historical Archives Online, kappa.historyit.com. Hereafter cited as KKG Archives.

36. Quote is from Harriette Silver Scott, "Marine Landed," *The Key*, February 1944, 37, KKG Archives; "Mrs. Edward H. Wobber," *NYT*, 13 October 1964, 43; Laura O. Miller, "New York Fashion Mart Features History-Making Glitter Numbers," *Indianapolis News*, 30 July 1943, 18. The 1940 census lists Wobber as "Advertising Writer," ancestry.com.

37. See, for example, mention of Margaret Thilly, "a New York Kappa who handles [Arden's] advertising" in Virginia Cluff Forsythe, "New York Kappas' Service Center Is Something," *The Key*, April 1943, 81; and Virginia Conner, "the decorator chosen by Elizabeth Arden to do the powder room" in New York, from "Chapter Letters—New York," *The Key*, April 1943, 162, KKG Archives.

38. Janet Butler Munch, "Making Waves in the Bronx," CUNY Lehman College Academic Works Online, 1993, 9, academicworks.cuny.edu/cgi/viewcontent.cgi?article=1228&context=le_pubs.

39. "New York City Offers Numerous Privileges for Nurses," *The Army Nurse*, 10, Women Veterans Historical Project online, UNC Greensboro.

40. See, for example, Phebe Gage Hayslip, "Portland: Shares First Postwar Veterans' Club," *The Key*, October 1945, 263–65, KKG Archives.

41. "Service Women's Center" poster, *Plan for Elizabeth Arden Lounge in Service Women's Centers*, pamphlet, c. 1944, and Almira Johnson McNaboe, "Service Women Shared Founders' Day Tea," *The Key*, December 1944, 301. See also "Columbus Center Adds to Kappa Memories of Historic Hotel," *The Key*, February 1944, 43; "Denver Center . . . Rates with Ranks Since March Opening," *The Key*, October 1944, 240; "WAVES in K.C. Get Powder Bar Harbor," *The Key*, October 1944, 240–41; and Cordelia See, "St. Louis Kappas Open Center in 'Y,'" *The Key*, December 1943, 337–39. All from KKG Archives.

42. Helen Snyder Andres, "Seattle: Arden Powder Room Sponsored in New Club," *The Key*, October 1945, 266, KKG Archives.

43. Anna Jo Davis, "Arden Powder Bar Opened in El Paso USO," *The Key*, December 1944, 296, KKG Archives.

44. Betty Mudd, "Dayton Service Women's Club Gets Powder Room," *The Key*, October 1945, 256–58, KKG Archives.

45. Ruth G. Haskell, *Helmets and Lipstick* (New York: G. P. Putnam's Sons, 1944), 130.

46. "Biltmore Center Rounds Off Year of Service," *The Key*, February 1944, 47; Alice Burrows, "Biltmore Center Adds 'Liberty' Tours," *The Key*, October 1943, 291. See also the photograph of Arden visiting the Phoenix USO lounge with the Arden powder room KKG sponsored, in *The Key*, October 1965, 268. All from KKG Archives.

47. "Parties Are Just Desserts to Two-Year-Old," *The Key*, April 1945, 119, KKG Archives.

48. Shumway Oral History, 16.

49. "Elizabeth Arden's Barracks Box" Marshall Field ad, *Chicago Tribune*, 17 February 1943, 17; "Elizabeth Arden's 'Service Kit'" B. Altman's ad, *NYT*, 14 February 1943, 24.

50. Ida Chapman Heris, "Two New Beauty Items for the Traveler," *Hartford Courant*, 21 August 1941, 13.

51. Elizabeth Arden Filene's ad, *The Boston Globe*, 15 March 1943, 3. After two decades with Arden, Wedekind used her promotion to move on to general manager of Marie Earle Products. See "It's New," *WWD*, 11 July 1946, 16. She set up her own business for a short time before taking a job with Lenthéric as head of packaging and research. See "Miss M. Wedekind Sets Up Own Office," *WWD*, 21 January 1949, 11; "Business Notes," *NYT*, 26 January 1950, 43; "Three Executives Leave Lenthéric, Inc.," *WWD*, 25 January 1950, 2; and "New on Lenthéric's Executive Staff," *WWD*, 27 January 1950, 10.

52. "Right Face" Arden ad, *NYT*, 14 March 1943, 20.

53. "It's Happening to You" Arden ad, *Vogue*, 15 March 1943, 89.

54. "Frankly, He Was Fascinated" Arden ad, *Vogue*, 15 January 1943, 81. The comma after "woman" is an ellipsis in the original.

55. Andrew Bamji, *Faces from the Front* (Solihull, UK: Helion, 2017), 168, 171.

56. Reginald Pound, *Gillies* (London: Michael Joseph, 1964), 82.

57. Pound, *Gillies*, 146.

58. "History of Skin Camouflage," British Association of Skin Camouflage, skin-camouflage.net/scwp/index.php/history-of-skin-camouflage.

59. Quotes from Wilt, "Elizabeth Arden and the Women Marines," WOC Collection.

60. Irene Brion, *Lady GI* (Novato, CA: Presidio Press, 1997), 164.

CHAPTER 19: THE END OF WORLD WAR II

1. Laurence Wilkinson, "Duke Held in Paris Red Cross Round-Up," *Daily Express*, 6 March 1944, 4.

2. Sarah Helm, *Ravensbrück* (New York: Anchor Books, 2015), xvii–xviii.

3. Anne Sebba, *Les Parisiennes* (New York: St. Martin's Press, 2016), 199 (de Gaulle quote), 202 (d'Alincourt quote).

4. "Hommage aux femmes résistantes," *Le Petit Journal*, 14 March 2018, lepetitjournal.net/31 -haute-garonne/e31t-toulousain/2018/03/14 /hommage-aux-femmes-resistantes.

5. "American Countess Tells of Aid to Fliers," *NYT*, 8 October 1944, 11.

6. Peter Hore, *Lindell's List* (Stroud, UK: The History Press, 2016), 190 (date and number of women), 169 (quote).

7. "Viscountess de Maublanc Is Dead at 87 in Paris," *NYT*, 12 December 1970, 33.

8. Hedda Hopper, "Looking at Hollywood," *Chicago Tribune*, 25 February 1944, 16. Ada's husband was Frederick C. McCormick.

9. "Elizabeth Arden Entertained at Boyd Hearthstone," *The Key*, April 1944, 81; "Chapter and Alumnae News: Delta Epsilon," *The Key*, April 1944, 175, Kappa Kappa Gamma Historical Archives Online, kappa.historyit.com. Hereafter cited as KKG Archives. The Delta Epsilon chapter from Rollins College celebrated Arden at a tea on 16 January 1944.

10. She purchased the Aeolian Building that housed her Manhattan salon. The first floor was a store selling Arden products, gifts, and her burgeoning clothing department. The next five floors were dedicated salon space, while others held Arden offices. She rented out at least one space to the madly creative shoe, jewelry, and apparel designer Steven Arpad. See "Arden Interests Buy Control of Building," *NYT*, 9 March 1944, 28; "Lease Fills 689 Fifth Ave.," *NYT*, 2 April 1944, RE1; "Fully Occupied," *NYT*, 2 April 1944, RE1.

11. "Elizabeth Arden Reported Opening Apparel Department," *WWD*, 19 June 1944, 1.

12. "Elizabeth Arden" want ad, *WWD*, 21 June 1944, 32.

13. Elizabeth Wilson, *Adorned in Dreams* (New Brunswick, NJ: Rutgers University Press, 2003), 3.

14. Quotes from Michèle Gerber Klein, *Charles James* (New York: Rizzoli, 2018). Quotes are on pp. 4, 7, 9, and viii; Klein's assessment is on p. 78.

15. Woolf quote is from Klein, *Charles James*, 8. Dior and Balenciaga quotes are from Jan Glier Reeder, *Charles James* (New York: Metropolitan Museum of Art/Yale University Press, 2014), 8. For Chanel and Schiaparelli, see Laura Jacobs, "Gowned for Glory," *Vanity Fair*, November 1998, vanityfair.com/news/1998/11/charles-james -couture.

16. Klein, *Charles James*, 79.

17. Klein, *Charles James*, 79.

18. Klein, *Charles James*, 80.

19. "Fashions Coming Along," *Vogue*, 1 July 1944, 57, 58.

20. "Marlene Dietrich," *Vogue*, 1 October 1944, 126.

21. "Charles James Re-creates Dress Silhouettes Keyed to 'A New Posture,'" *WWD*, 5 May 1944, 3; Simpson quoted in Klein, *Charles James*, 83; "Posture Fashions Shown," *NYT*, 5 May 1944, 14.

22. "On Elizabeth Arden's New Fashion Floor," *Vogue*, 15 December 1944, 54.

23. Jan Gore, *Send More Shrouds* (Barnsley, UK: Pen & Sword Military, 2017). The book is unpaginated.

24. Odette Fabius, *Un lever de soleil sur le Mecklembourg* (Paris: Albin Michel, 1986), 159–60. Fabius describes Jones as "a chief of the I.S. in Paris," but as there was no "I.S.," I assume she means the Secret Intelligence, or, in French, the Intelligence Secrète. Thanks to Annie Moore and Simon Cordery for help with the French translations.

25. "Benefit Renamed 'Fashion and Fun,'" *NYT*, 25 February 1945, 34; "Women Will Open War Fund Campaign," *NYT*, 24 September 1944, 34. Arden contributed $750 to the Greater Boston United War Fund in November 1944 ("W. Lynn Vet Gets Fund's Prize-of-Day," *The Christian Science Monitor*, 11 November 1944, 4). For the high school assembly, see "Freshness Emphasized," *The Washington Post*, 30 May 1945, 9.

26. "Vittel," *Holocaust Encyclopedia*, U.S. Holocaust Memorial Museum, encyclopedia.ushmm .org/content/en/article/vittel. The August release date is from "American Countess Tells of Aid to Fliers," *NYT*, 8 October 1944, 11. See also Hore, *Lindell's List*, 180.

27. American Red Cross, Historical Reports and Monographs—Staff Section Reports, File #538, ancestry.com, fold3.com/image /290389077.

28. Gladys confirmed: "American Countess Tells of Aid to Fliers," *NYT*, 8 October 1944, 11. Legion of Honor: "Viscountess de Maublanc Is Dead at 87 in Paris," *NYT*, 12 December 1970, 33. See also "Légion d'honneur: Défense nationale, Le général de Linares grand-crois," *Le Monde*, 10 November 1954, 7. It is difficult to know whether the Arden salon closed after Gladys and Solange were imprisoned. See "Ingenious Parisian Women Found Still Retaining Chic despite War's Havoc," *WWD*, 29 August 1944, 2. That article states that "beauty salons are doing a land office business. Such famous face parlors as Elizabeth Arden's have reopened."

29. Leonard Lyons, "Loose Leaf Notebook," *The Washington Post*, 28 February 1945, 3. Lyons reported that Gladys was expected in the United States in March 1945. In a letter to Ada McCormick, Arden states that Gladys arrived in May 1945. See Arden to McCormack [*sic*], 7 June 1945, MS 327, Box 7, File 15, Ada Peirce McCormick Papers, University of Arizona Special Collections, Tucson.

30. Bill Hart, "AMC Store Representatives View Television Show," *WWD*, 2 October 1944, 1, 22.

31. "Full-Color Television Effective Selling Medium," *Fashion Group Bulletin* 11, no. 6 (October 1945), 1, Fashion Group International Records, Mss Col 980, New York Public Library Archives & Manuscripts Division, New York City.

32. Quoted in Lindy Woodhead, *War Paint* (Hoboken, NJ: John Wiley & Sons, 2003), 289.

33. "Elizabeth Arden Shows Collection of Distinguished Custom Clothes," *WWD*, 31 October 1944, 3. With Robert Rothschild and Madame Ruspoli de Gramont (later Hugo) Arden opened the Hugo Art Gallery in 1945. See Brooks Jackson Oral History Interview, 22 March 1976, Smithsonian Archives of American Art online, aaa.si.edu/collections/interviews/oral-history -interview-brooks-jackson-12916.

34. Eugenia Sheppard, "Halston's Sick of Everyone Looking Alike," *Hartford Courant*, 28 January 1970, 11E. Other sources suggest that James created his "Loop-a-Loop" scarf in 1933; see Reeder, *Charles James*, 33.

35. "New Designs Open Arden Fashion Floor," *NYT*, 31 October 1944, 16.

36. Barbara E. Scott Fisher, "Elizabeth Arden Now Presents Clothes Designed for the New American Figure," *The Christian Science Monitor*, 1 November 1944, 12.

37. Fisher, "Elizabeth Arden Now Presents Clothes Designed for the New American Figure," 12.

38. Klein, *Charles James*, 81.

39. Fisher, "Elizabeth Arden Now Presents Clothes Designed for the New American Figure," 12.

40. Martha Parker, "Trim Figure," *NYT*, 12 November 1944, 37.

41. Miss Cusack to Elaine Whitelaw, memorandum, 12 January 1945, Series 3: Fashion Show, Folder: Fund Raising, Planning & Arrangements, March of Dimes Archives, Arlington, Virginia. Coty made "a substantial contribution to the Drive for the privilege of doing makeup at the Fashion Show." For the creation and goals of the New York Dress Institute (and its group of all-male founders and committee members), see "N.Y. Dress Promotion Plan Is Underway," *WWD*, 10 March 1941, 1, 28, and Rebecca Arnold, *The American Look* (New York: I.B. Tauris, 2009), 139–40.

42. Klein, *Charles James*, 87. For the gown, see "Style Finds Its Voice," *New York World-Telegram*, clipping, 25 January 1945, from Series 3: Fashion Show, 1945–1970, "Fashion Show—Publicity" Folder, March of Dimes Archives. Both Arden and James would remain committed to the March of Dimes fashion shows—just not together.

43. Klein, *Charles James*, 85.

44. Michael Botwinick quoted in Elizabeth Ann Coleman, *The Genius of Charles James* (New York: Brooklyn Museum/Holt, Rinehart and Winston, 1982), 7.

45. Klein, *Charles James*, 87. James and Arden garnered publicity when his gowns were worn in Broadway plays, too. See, for example, "Drama in Clothes Worn at Last Night's Fulton Theatre Opening," *WWD*, 8 February 1945, 3.

46. Interview of Charles James re Elizabeth Arden, 14 August 1972, Subseries IV.C. Institute of Sound 1960s, Box 147, folder 19, Charles James Papers, The Costume Institute's Irene Lewisohn Costume Reference Library, Metropolitan Museum of Art, New York City. For a long list of the women for whom he designed, see "Clients of Charles James," Box 109, folder 9, Charles James Papers, Lewisohn Costume Reference Library.

47. Charles James to Elizabeth Arden, 16 April 1964, Box 50, folder 5, Corr. A–F, 1963–1964, Charles James Papers, Lewisohn Costume Reference Library.

48. The complaint was the same as before: discriminating among retailers by providing demonstrators to some but not others. See Federal Trade Commission Release, 7 October 1944, Order 3153, in Cosmetics, Arden, Elizabeth, Special Data, Box 168, folder 2, AMA Department of Investigation Records, American Medical Association Archives, Chicago; *Annual Report of the Federal Trade Commission for the Fiscal Year Ended June 30, 1945* (Washington, DC: Government Printing Office, 1945), 44; "Cosmetic Maker Cited by FTC," *The Washington Post*, 7 October 1944, 12; Louise Overacker, "American Government and Politics: Presidential Campaign Funds, 1944," *American Political Science Review* 39, no. 5 (October 1945): 915.

49. "What About the Service Women's Centers?," *The Key*, October 1945, 265, KKG Archives.

50. Phebe Gage Hayslip, "Portland: Shares First Postwar Veterans' Club," *The Key*, October 1945, 263–65; quote is on p. 265. See also "Six Service Centers Keeping Things Alive: If Honolulu's Closes, Then There'll Be Five!," *The Key*, February 1946, 43. Both from KKG Archives.

51. Helen McCreery, "Denver Bows Out: Read This Resume in the Past Tense," *The Key*, December 1945, 354. Sally Goepp Herrick, "Honolulu Contributes 'One for the Book,'" *The Key*, December 1945, 356, 357, 358. For the formal appreciation of KKG's national organization, see Almira Johnson McNaboe, "Center's Closing Ends Gallant Record," *The Key*, December 1945, 360–62. All from KKG Archives.

52. "Winged Victory" Robinsons' ad, *Los Angeles Times*, 15 January 1945, 5.

53. Marshall Field ad, *Chicago Tribune*, 9 September 1945, 21; "'American Claret,' First Postwar Accessory Color Coordination," *WWD*, 1 September 1945, 5.

54. Marshall Field ad, *Chicago Tribune*, 9 September 1945, 21.

55. C. M. Reckert, "Corporate Profits Down 1.3% in 1945," *NYT*, 13 May 1946, 41.

56. "Paris Not to Dim Style Center Here," *NYT*, 2 September 1944, 14.

CHAPTER 20: THE HORSEWOMAN

1. Geoffrey Jones, "Blonde and Blue-Eyed?," *Economic History Review* 61, no. 1 (2008): 131. See also Kathy Peiss, "Educating the Eye of the Beholder," *Daedalus* 131, no. 4 (Fall 2002): 101–9.

2. Jones, "Blonde and Blue Eyed?," 136.

3. "Helena Rubinstein Opening New Headquarters in London in January," *WWD*, 10 June 1949, 12. This article states that she had been operating her business out of her home.

4. Emily Clark, *Innocence Abroad* (New York: Alfred A. Knopf, 1933), 109.

5. Although Arden designed and patented a dress and a girdle, she never aspired to or pretended to be a fashion designer. Elizabeth Arden "Dress," Patent #130,469, 18 November 1941, and "Foundation Garment," Patent #2,327,310, 17 August 1943. The girdle patent was filed on 25 August 1942. "Elizabeth Arden Didn't Like Modern Fashions—So She Started Her Own Line," 17 March 1950, hand-dated, unidentified clipping from University Archives Clippings Files/Graham, Florence Nightingale—Alumni Papers, Special Collections Research Center, Syracuse University. Among the designers she hired were John Moore and Mark Mooring. See "Lumber Industry Loss Fashion World's Gain," *Austin American-Statesman*, 24 April 1958, B11, and "American Made-to-Order Collections," *Vogue*, 1 October 1946, 155. Moore designed for Marilyn Monroe and created Lady Bird Johnson's 1965 inaugural gown; see "John Moore, 68, Fashion Designer," *NYT*, 31 August 1996, 27.

6. "Reports on Paris," *WWD*, May 1945, 1.

7. "March of Dimes Show Attracts 3,000," *WWD*, 23 January 1946, 1; "Tailored Elegance, by Castillo, for Elizabeth Arden Fashions," *WWD*, 21 February 1946, 1; "Castillo Draped Hip, Birdwing Pleat, Ornamental Capelets at Elizabeth Arden Dressmaker Showing," *WWD*, 21 February 1946, 3; Virginia Pope, "Simple Elegance Marks New Styles," *NYT*, 21 February 1946, 18. Castillo quote is from "You'll Be 'Lovely to Look At,'" *The Washington Post*, 17 March 1946, S3. The show raised an estimated $15,000 to $20,000 for the March of Dimes. See Virginia Pope, "Fashion Pageant Aids Dimes March," *NYT*, 23 January 1946, 20.

8. Virginia Pope, "Castillo Shows Third Collection," *NYT*, 27 February 1947, 24.

9. See, for example, "Arden Presents New Drama Lip, Nail Color," *WWD*, 11 September 1946, 75; "A Crimson Foil for Fall Fashions," *WWD*, 12 September 1946, 3; "You'll Be 'Lovely to Look At,'" *The Washington Post*, 17 March 1946, S3.

10. "Mainly about People," *Austin American-Statesman*, 29 December 1946, A3.

11. "Castillo to Design for Elizabeth Arden," *WWD*, 3 October 1945, 2; "Paris Designer Here," *NYT*, 18 October 1945, 16; Mary Brooks Picken and Dora Loues Miller, *Dressmakers of France* (New York: Harper & Brothers, 1956), 117.

12. "Lady's Day in Louisville," *Time*, 6 May 1946, 62. See also James Hill, "A Thoroughbred Era Ends with Main [sic] Chance Sale," *Lexington Herald*, 5 January 1967, Maine Chance 1967, Jan–Jul clipping file, Keeneland Library.

13. "Fire at Belmont Park Kills 3 Show Horses Prized by Rich Owner," *The Boston Globe*, 4 March 1937, 20; "Fire Kills Prize Horses," *NYT*, 4 March 1937, 5.

14. Peter Quennell, *The Marble Foot* (London: Collins, 1976), 230.

15. Cobina Wright, *I Never Grew Up* (New York: Prentice-Hall, 1952), 231.

16. "Woman Turf Trainer Lands Big Time Job," *Chicago Tribune*, 9 April 1940, 20; "Society Matron Is Now Big Time Horse Trainer," *Hartford Courant*, 9 April 1940, 16. Feustel worked for Arden from 1937 to late 1939.

17. "Noted Turfwoman Dies in Auto Crash," *NYT*, 10 December 1940, 27; "Mrs. Bosley Dies in Auto Crash: Ranking Woman Horse Trainer," *The Washington Post*, 10 December 1940, 1. See also Bill Bennings, "At the Post," *The Washington Post*, 10 December 1940, 24. The first two articles suggest that Bosley worked for Arden, and then did not, and then returned to Arden. When Bosley's husband, John, died in 1951, newspapers suggested that he—or they—had trained Arden's horses—not Elizabeth. See "John Bosley Jr., 66, Trainer of Horses," *NYT*, 13 October 1951, 12.

18. Kyle Williams, "Tom Smith: His Horses Spoke for Him," *Washington Thoroughbred*, 58, no. 8 (August 2004): 660. Both from Tom Smith File, Keeneland Library. All the horse-specific journals cited in this chapter are from the Keeneland Library.

19. "Obituary: Tom Smith," *The Blood-Horse*, 12 February 1957, 38.

20. Don Grisham, "[John] Wozneski Believes in Rog 'n' John," unidentified clipping, Tom Smith File.

21. Elizabeth Conger, "Treat a Woman Like a Horse and a Horse Like a Woman," *Spur*, March/April 1984, 52. Smith quote is from "Beauty & Pleasure," *Time*, 6 August 1945, 63.

22. "Mrs. Elizabeth N. Graham, 81, Succumbs in New York Hospital," *Daily Racing Form*, 19 October 1966, from Maine Chance, 1966: Death of Mrs. Arden File, Keeneland Library.

23. "Mrs. Elizabeth N. Graham, 81," *Daily Racing Form*, 19 October 1966.

24. "Jet Pilot's Derby Victory Vindication for Mrs. Graham," *The Baltimore Sun*, 5 May 1947, 19.

25. Conger, "Treat a Woman Like a Horse," *Spur*, 53; Williams, "Tom Smith: His Horses Spoke for Him," 658, Tom Smith File. Combs quote is from Conger, 53. For earnings, see Neil Newman, "From How High to Knockdown," *Turf and Sport Digest*, April 1946, 45.

26. "Tom Smith and His Atomizer," *The Blood-Horse*, 17 November 1945, 1108, 1009.

27. See the Jockey Club's "About" page, jockeyclub.com/Default.asp?section=About&area=0.

28. Milton C. Toby, "Silent Tom's Atomizer," *The Blood-Horse*, 25 May 2017, online and unpaginated, bloodhorse.com/horse-racing/features/silent-toms-atomizer-221653.

29. "Tom Smith and His Atomizer," *The Blood-Horse*, 1007, Tom Smith File.

30. Alex Bower, "The Smith Hearing in New York," *The Blood-Horse*, 22 December 1945, 1360, 1361. For Arden's tests, see "Hearing for Tom Smith," *The Blood-Horse*, 1 December 1945, 1188, Tom Smith File. The universities were Cornell, Northwestern, and the University of Pennsylvania.

31. Bower, "The Smith Hearing in New York," *The Blood-Horse*, 1363.

32. Bower, "The Smith Hearing in New York," *The Blood-Horse*, 1367 (agreeing with Gold), 1364 (quote). Buckingham said he had treated the pets of every president from Theodore Roosevelt to Harry Truman.

33. "Tom Smith and His Atomizer," *The Blood-Horse*, 1109.

34. Bower, "The Smith Hearing in New York," *The Blood-Horse*, 22 December 1945, 1365.

35. Bower, "The Smith Hearing in New York," 1367. This event was covered extensively in thoroughbred magazines, racing journals, and newspapers with columns devoted to horse racing and sports. Bower's article is a fine summary of the daily press. Milton Toby's 2017 *Blood-Horse* piece, "Silent Tom's Atomizer," puts the Smith accusation in a larger context of doping in the racing industry. See also "Hearing for Tom Smith," *The Blood-Horse*, 1 December 1945, 1188, and William H. P. Robertson's *The History of Thoroughbred Racing in America* (New York: Bonanza Books, 1964), chap. 56, for an examination of the Smith case and its connection to tighter regulations and a cleaner sport.

36. Joe H. Palmer, "Maine Chance Farm May Start Four Colts in Kentucky Derby," clipping, 22 March 1946, Maine Chance File, Keeneland Library.

37. Today the Pimlico Futurity is the Laurel Futurity. Paul Lowry, "Knockdown, Star Pilot One-Two in Derby," *Los Angeles Times*, 24 February 1946, A5. Star Pilot took second place in that Santa Anita Derby. For trainer, see "Maine Chance Farm's Knockdown Captures $100,000 Santa Anita Derby," *The Baltimore Sun*, 24 February 1946, SP4.

38. "Pronounced Derby Swing to Hampden; Arlington Blaze Is Fatal to 23 Horses," *Daily Racing Form*, undated clipping, 1946, Maine Chance File; "Fire Kills 25 Horses," *Austin American-Statesman*, 2 May 1946, 1. Other papers claim there were as many as eighteen stable hands involved. See "Probes Begun in Track Fire," *The Baltimore Sun*, 3 May 1946, 16. "Costliest Fire in Turf History Destroys 23 Elizabeth Arden Horses Valued at $500,000," *The Boston Globe*, 3 May 1946, 11.

39. "Costliest Fire in Turf History," *The Boston Globe*, 11.

40. "At Racing Board's First Meeting," *Chicago Tribune*, 18 June 1941, 22. Williams quote from "Double Probe of Race Stable Fire Is Opened," *Chicago Tribune*, 3 May 1946, 32.

41. "Costliest Fire in Turf History," *The Boston Globe*, 11.

42. Arch Ward, "In the Wake of the News," *Chicago Tribune*, 3 May 1946, 31.

43. "23 Young Maine Chance Racers Die in $500,000 Arlington Park Blaze," *NYT*, 3 May 1946, 29.

44. "Track Officials Cleared," *NYT*, 7 May 1946, 33.

45. "Maine Chance Fire," *The Blood-Horse*, 11 May 1946, 1142–43. This article lists the names of the horses lost.

46. "Probe Absolves Arlington Park in $500,000 Fire," *Chicago Tribune*, 7 May 1946, 22.

47. "Admits Blame in Fire Fatal to 23 Horses," *Chicago Tribune*, 5 May 1946, A3. See also "Horse Fire Guilt Traced," *NYT*, 5 May 1946, S4.

48. "Board Blames 23 Horse Fire on Watchman's Negligence," *The Washington Post*, 7 May 1946, 11.

49. "Sheridan Bruseaux Resigns from Bachelor Boys Club," *The Chicago Defender*, 17 November 1923, 4. He was "chief investigator for Frank J. Loesch and the special grand juries of 1928 and 1929." For that, see "Sheridan Bruseaux, Crime Investigator, Opens Office," *Chicago Tribune*, 22 February 1940, 17.

50. "Cleared in Fire at Race Track," *The Chicago Defender*, 18 May 1946, 11.

51. "Track Officials Cleared," *NYT*, 7 May 1946, 33. See also "Probe Absolves Arlington Park in $500,000 Fire," *Chicago Tribune*, 7 May 1946, 22.

52. "New Quiz Opened on Shooting Laid to Louis' Trainer," *Chicago Tribune*, 17 November 1935, 3.

53. "Costliest Fire in Turf History," *The Boston Globe*, 11.

54. Bill Henry, "By the Way," *Los Angeles Times*, 3 August 1946, A1.

55. "25 Horses Die in Chicago Track Fire," *Los Angeles Times*, 21 October 1948, C4.

56. Hedda Hopper, "Looking at Hollywood," *Los Angeles Times*, 9 May 1946, A3. *Time* identified her on the 6 May 1946 cover as "Elizabeth Arden: A Queen Rules the Sport of Kings," with horses at the starting gate in the background. Any fiction of a separation between Elizabeth Arden and Elizabeth N. Graham ended with that cover.

57. Grantland Rice, "Jet Pilot Winner of 73rd Kentucky Derby," *The Baltimore Sun*, 4 May 1947, 1.

58. Alex Bower, "Mud, Uncertainty, a Waving Whip," *The Blood-Horse*, 10 May 1947, 304; Keene Daingerfield Jr., "Yielding to the Annual Temptation," *The Thoroughbred Record*, 10 May 1947, 11. "Eric Guerin Used 'Hand Ride All the Way' on Victorious Jet Pilot," *The Baltimore Sun*, 4 May 1947, 2. Guerin was under contract to another

owner, who kindly released him when Arden's first-choice jockey pulled out because his wife was ill. See "Eric Guerin Used 'Hand Ride.'"

59. "Go, go, go," from "Ladies Day in Louisville," *Time*, 6 May 1946, 60; Smith quote: Alex Bower, "Mud, Uncertainty, a Waving Whip," *The Blood-Horse*, 304. Arden quote: "Jet Pilot's Derby Victory Vindication for Mrs. Graham," *The Baltimore Sun*, 5 May 1947, 19.

60. Cover photo, *The Thoroughbred Record*, 10 May 1947.

61. "Tom Smith Confident of Jet Pilot's Chances," *The Baltimore Sun*, 4 May 1947, 2; "Skinner to Auction 1947 Kentucky Derby Trophy," *Science Letter*, 12 May 2009, 3782; Bob Considine, "Phalanx 2nd, Faultless Close 3d in Thriller," *The Washington Post*, 4 May 1947, M1. Tom Smith died in January 1957, always, in Elizabeth Arden's mind, her best and favorite trainer. They had parted ways by then, but remained friends. See "Tom Smith Dies; Trained Seabiscuit," *The Washington Post*, 24 January 1957, D4.

CHAPTER 21: "BEAUTY IS POWER"

1. Peggy Preston, "Arden Adds Dressmaker to Name Synonymous with Beauty," *The Washington Post*, 2 August 1949, B5; Genina Gavin, "And Now It's Television," *The Boston Globe*, 20 June 1948, A7.

2. *WWD* began printing the Retail Advertising Index in July 1947. In most weeks, Arden was far above all other brands. In the half year from June through December 1947, for example, Arden topped the chart with 735,044 lines of advertising. Next was Coty, with 660,782; then Revlon, with 630,799; then Rubinstein, with 511,306; and Gray, with 390,132. See "Branded Toilet Goods for Women Advertising Index," *WWD*, 30 January 1948, 12.

3. "Hear Arden Cosmetic Business to Be Sold," *WWD*, 14 April 1947, 35; "No 'For Sale' Sign at Elizabeth Arden," *WWD*, 18 April 1947, 17.

4. Preston, "Arden Adds Dressmaker," *The Washington Post*, B5.

5. Gavin, "And Now It's Television," *The Boston Globe*, A7.

6. "Women of Achievement Chosen," *The Washington Post*, 9 November 1948, B4; "D.P. Change Asked by Jewish Women," *NYT*, 12 January 1950, 30; Rebecca Blake, "The Pink Look Is the Look for 1951," *The Boston Globe*, 5 January 1951, 26; "Women in Business Get Honor Scrolls," *NYT*, 17 October 1950, 29. "Prophetic": "Shingled Hair Out, Says Arden," *The Washington Post*, 2 September 1949, C2; Peggy Preston, "Prettiness Is Keynote of Fashion," *The Washington Post*, 14 April 1948, B3.

7. Mary Van Rensselaer Thayer, "To Feel Right, Look Right, Says Miss Arden as She Does a Spot of Modelling," *The Washington Post*, 7 April 1948, B6.

8. Mary Van Rensselaer Thayer, "Legislators Go Soaring," *The Washington Post*, 9 April 1948, C5.

9. Elisabeth Marbury, *My Crystal Ball* (New York: Boni & Liveright, 1923), 41.

10. Arden donated time, products, and money for five decades. Her list of charities was extremely broad. Sometimes she gave as Elizabeth Arden, and sometimes less publicly as Elizabeth Graham. The information about her largesse in the paragraphs that follow comes primarily from newspapers nationwide.

11. Arden loved classical music, both symphonic and operatic. She underwrote the work of orchestras and music education, and was actively and consistently involved with the Musicians Emergency Fund benefits until her death. For Tulsa, in addition to newspaper coverage, see Walter H. Helmerich to Hedda Hopper, 7 November 1957; Memo re: Board of Directors of Tulsa Philharmonic Society, 23 November 1957; and Invitation to Hedda Hopper to Meet Elizabeth Arden, n.d., folder 543, Hedda Hopper Papers, Margaret Herrick Library, Academy of Motion Picture Arts and Sciences, Beverly Hills, California.

12. "Preview of Film to Aid Music Fund," *NYT*, 18 March 1955, 30.

13. Information on donations to colleges comes from the schools' own newspapers, such as *The Mount Holyoke News*. See also Elizabeth Brothers to R. Brinkley Smithers, 9 May 1966, RG 08, Box 1, Mount Holyoke College Friends and Benefactors Records, Mount Holyoke College Archives and Special Collections Online, aspace.fivecolleges.edu/repositories/2/resources/460.

14. "Elizabeth Arden: Legend in Beauty," *Palm Beach Life*, August 1962, 50, EA/6/15/1, Elizabeth Arden Ltd. Papers, Unilever Archives, Port Sunlight, UK.

15. Lou Stillman's gym had a reputation for being purposefully filthy, so this may have been ironic, too. "Open Pore Tycoon Says Old-Timers Worked Hardest; Pugs Won't Train Now," *Austin American-Statesman*, 7 June 1948, 14.

16. Charles Poore, "Books of the Times," *NYT*, 21 December 1950: 27.

17. "Warsaw Group Aims to Define Aggression," *NYT*, 22 November 1950, 8; "The World," *NYT*, 26 November 1950, E2. The East German representative was Otto Zweig.

18. Billy Rose, "Pitching Horseshoes," *The Boston Globe*, 28 August 1947, 14.

19. Aleister Crowley, "The Jungle of Elizabeth Arden," in *Olla: An Anthology of Sixty Years of Song* (London: W. A. Guy, Ltd., 1946), 40. Thanks to Gareth Cordery for bringing this poem to my attention.

20. Ilka Chase, *Past Imperfect* (Garden City, NY: Doubleday, Doran 1942), 223–24. Chase also wrote a venomous novel titled *In Bed We Cry*, with a protagonist probably based on Arden.

21. "On the Lighter Side of the Capital," *Nation's Business*, 1 May 1946, 118.

22. "On the Radio Today," *NYT*, 1 December 1947, 42. Arden was a guest on various shows with

some regularity. See "Air Attractions," *Boston Globe*, 16 May 1950, 21, for her guest appearance on Louise Morgan's television program *Beauty Jubilee*.

23. "Tribune Style Show Winners Are Described," *Chicago Tribune*, 8 October 1948, B1.

24. "Mayor Meets Fashion Trade on Plans for City's Jubilee," *WWD*, 13 May 1948, 4. It was a brainstorming session to see how New York's important garment and fashion industries could join the celebration of the consolidation of the five boroughs.

25. "Gibson-Girl Styles Revived at Benefit," *NYT*, 11 March 1948, 36.

26. "Frederick & Nelson to Fete Style Leaders," *WWD*, 27 March 1946, 6; "Off for Frederick & Nelson Fashion Show," *WWD*, 12 April 1946, 38.

27. "Elizabeth Nightingale Graham," from the University Archives Clippings Files/Graham, Florence Nightingale—Alumni Papers, Special Collections Research Center, Syracuse University.

28. "Elizabeth Arden Fashion Show to Benefit S.U. Fund," 9 March 1950, and "Elizabeth Arden Shows Fashions," 8 May 1940; "Elizabeth Arden Didn't Like Modern Fashions—So Started Her Own Line," 17 March 1950, hand-dated clippings from University Archives Clippings Files/Graham, Florence Nightingale—Alumni Papers, Special Collections Research Center, Syracuse University. It was the Beta Tau chapter of KKG.

29. "Miss Florence Delaney," *NYT*, 30 January 1949, 61; Elizabeth Arden to friend Theresa Helburn, 28 February [1949], YCAL Mss 436, Ser. 1, Box 17, folder 271, Theatre Guild Archive, Beinecke Rare Book and Manuscript Library, Yale University; "As a Tribute," *NYT*, 31 January 1949, 4. For Arden quote, see Jinx Falkenburg and Tex McCrary, "Elizabeth Arden Says Short Hair Keeps Girls from Marrying Well," *The Boston Globe*, 11 March 1950, 11.

30. "Music Sorority to Meet," *NYT*, 29 June 1946, 22; "BPW Members Will Meet in Convention," *The Washington Post*, 10 April 1948, B4. For Arden quote, see Genevieve Reynolds, "Foreign Affairs Thought Instead of 'Tricks' Advised," *The Washington Post*, 11 April 1948, C4.

31. "Dewey Completes Council of Women," *NYT*, 21 October 1945, 32; Mary Van Rensselaer Thayer, "Lively Feminine Trio Runs Campaign Show at Dewey Headquarters," *The Washington Post*, 20 June 1948, S1; "State Council Members Listed," *WWD*, 9 March 1960, 10. *Why Do You Look So Nice?*, #2763, Box 4, Jane Hedges Todd Papers, Division of Rare and Manuscript Collections, Cornell University.

32. Alfredo Graham, "Applying for a Job?," *The Pittsburgh Courier*, 19 May 1962, 13. See also "Guide to Grooming," *NYT*, 10 June 1963, 34. The new title was *The Order of Your Appearance* (Jane Hedges Todd Papers, #2763, Box 4, Division of Rare and Manuscript Collections, Cornell University).

33. Jessie Ash Arndt, "Women's Council Advances Small Business," *The Christian Science Monitor*, 16 November 1963, 16.

34. Mary Van Rensselaer Thayer, "Vandenberg Loses Way," *The Washington Post*, 23 June 1948, B3.

35. Thayer, "Vandenberg Loses Way," B3, and "Video-Wise Democrats Will Likely Sod Sad Sam's Scintillating Dome," *The Washington Post*, 11 July 1948, L1.

36. "FTC Opposed Review on Demonstrator," *WWD*, 7 April 1947, 2.

37. "Denies Unfair Use of Demonstrators," *NYT*, 13 November 1940, 42. For the earlier attack on demonstrators, see "No Demonstrators?," *Drug and Cosmetic Industry*, January 1937, 56, 84.

38. "Demonstrator Issue Up to Highest Court," *WWD*, 7 March 1947, 19.

39. "May Appeal Ruling in Cosmetics Case," *NYT*, 12 June 1946, 37.

40. "Hope Seen for End of Ambiguous Law," *NYT*, 3 August 1947, 35; "FTC Toilet Goods Conference on Demonstrators Forecast," *WWD*, 18 June 1946, 9; "Demonstrators—Pros and Cons," *WWD*, 27 December 1946, 14.

41. "Demonstrators—Pros and Cons," *WWD*, 27 December 1946, 14; "Are Demonstrators Irreplaceable?," *WWD*, 3 January 1947, 13; "Demonstrators Indispensable in Cosmetic Departments," *WWD*, 10 January 1947, 21.

42. "Cosmetics Tax Cut of 10% Anticipated," *WWD*, 31 December 1946, 31.

43. "FTC Suddenly Drops Action in Arden Case," *WWD*, 25 July 1947, 1. Elizabeth Arden Inc., Elizabeth Arden Sales Corporation, and Florence N. Lewis all petitioned. The Supreme Court refused to hear her appeal on 14 April 1947.

44. "Demonstrator Issue Up to Highest Court," *WWD*, 7 March 1947, 19. The other firms were Bourjois, Charles of the Ritz, Coty, Elmo, Richard Hudnut, and Primrose House.

45. "Digging up Scarecrows," "Coty Head, FTC in Class on Demonstrators," *WWD*, 9 May 1947, 46; "Violation of Law by Coty Is Denied," *NYT*, 9 May 1947, 37.

46. "Hope Seen for End of Ambiguous Law," *NYT*, 3 August 1947, 35.

47. "Manufacturers Take Rebuffs Pleasantly, Says Pittsburgh," *WWD*, 20 February 1948, 30.

48. "Demonstrators Discontinued at Neiman-Marcus," *WWD*, 5 March 1948, 15.

49. For "more than doubled," see "Of Things and People," *WWD*, 30 October 1953, 12. "Doubled-Sales Recipe: Opalescent Make-Up," *WWD*, 28 May 1954, 29. In 1958, Arden demonstrators were still making headlines for their weeklong stay in department stores such as Garfinckel's and Fox's. See "Spring's the Fashion and Style's on the Calendar," *The Washington Post*, 23 March 1958, F3; "Beauty Consultants at G. Fox This Week," *Hartford Courant*, 17 February 1958, 9.

50. Bruce Lambert, "Carl Gardiner, 88, a Former President of Elizabeth Arden," *NYT*, 15

August 1933; quote is from Lindy Woodhead, *War Paint* (Hoboken, NJ: John Wiley & Sons, 2003), 333.

51. "Arden Beauty" Woodward and Lothrop ad, *The Washington Star,* 6 September 1949, B8.

52. "A&S Expects 5,000 Reservations for Arden Salon Classes," *WWD,* 10 June 1949, 12. Press release and photos from Box 8, folder 11, Frances Bemis Papers, Sophia Smith Collection of Women's History, Smith College Special Collections, Smith College, Northampton, Massachusetts.

53. "A&S Reports Arden Promotion Asset to Store, Department," *WWD,* 17 June 1949, 9.

54. "Classes in Beauty," *The Washington Post,* 12 September 1949, B3; Peggy Preston, "Beauty School Opens," *The Washington Post,* 20 September 1949, B3.

55. "Classes Draw Capacity Crowds," *WWD,* 8 May 1953, 13.

56. "Arden Classes Set," *WWD,* 21 July 1950, 10. See also "Response Good to Scruggs 'Face and Figure School,'" *WWD,* 24 April 1953, 14, and Jane Cahill, "Arden School of Beauty Scores at Strawbridge's," *WWD,* 30 October 1953, 11.

57. "Paine's of Boston Opens First-Time Cosmetics Dept." and "Beauty Fair Week in Boise Termed Highly Successful," *WWD,* 1 November 1946, 8.

58. B. Altman ad, *NYT,* 10 March 1949, 12; Elizabeth Arden Eye-Stopper ad, *NYT,* 23 March 1949, 14. It sold for $3 and came with two refills.

59. "Discoveries in Beauty," *Vogue,* 1 March 1948, 244; "It's New!," *WWD,* 20 February 1948, 30.

60. Ann Dean, "Easy Way to Lose Weight," *The Boston Globe,* 9 August 1949, 8.

61. "The New Woman, the New Complexion" Arden ad, *The Washington Post,* 11 March 1917, 26; "Easy Way to Counteract Blackheads," *The Boston Globe,* 12 January 1949, 20.

62. Elizabeth Arden ad, *Los Angeles Times,* 31 October 1943, D2. For children, see "Elizabeth Arden Announces" ad, *NYT,* 25 January 1949, 3.

63. "Superior 6950?" Arden ad, *Chicago Tribune,* 20 March 1944, 19. For an example of the class at Neiman-Marcus, see "Elizabeth Arden Presents Her Teen-Age School of Beauty for Daily Skin Care," *WWD,* 30 April 1948, 15.

64. "Salons, Personnel in Market Spotlight," *WWD,* 9 September 1949, 11; "Elizabeth Arden to Open New Salon," *WWD,* 18 June 1948, 19. The address was 550 Sutter Street. The success of the pool at her Phoenix Maine Chance spa, opened in 1947, led to her incorporating a pool in her new San Francisco salon.

65. "Bonnets of Our Times," *Vogue,* 15 March 1946, 144 (Churchill). The Alain Roure ad proclaimed their new French collection included "designs of such couturieres as Worth and Elizabeth Arden"; see his ad in *WWD,* 10 June 1947, 6.

66. "American Made-to-Order Collections," *Vogue,* 1 October 1946, 155.

67. "Made-to-Order Collections in the U.S.A.," *Vogue,* 1 April 1946, 146. For "fashionable, but timeless," see "American Dressmaker Collections," *Vogue,* 1 October 1946, 270.

68. "Elizabeth Arden in Wholesale Apparel Field," *WWD,* 3 June 1949, 1; "Neckline Fantasy at Arden," *WWD,* 15 June 1949, 3.

69. Peggy Preston, "Arden Adds Dressmaker to Name Synonymous with Beauty," *The Washington Post,* 2 August 1949, B5; Barbara E. Scott Fisher, "Influences of Many Countries Help Set Style Pace at New York Showing," *The Christian Science Monitor,* 18 July 1949, 10. Forty dollars in today's money is around $750.

70. "Not to Be Worn before 6 P.M.," *The Washington Post,* 25 September 1949, S4.

71. "Fashions by the Sea Endorse Both Brief Shorts and Full Skirts," *NYT,* 29 May 1948, 18. For Mooring, see "Boa Constrictors Don't Bother, Just Rock," *Austin American-Statesman,* 26 August 1951, C9; "Mark Mooring, 71, Fashion Designer," *NYT,* 13 January 1971, 42; "M. Mooring Resigns as Arden Designer," *WWD,* 15 July 1952, 41. Mooring joined with another former Arden employee, Ann Sadowsky, to create ready-to-wear separates. See "Ann Sadowsky Returning to Wholesale Field," *WWD,* 28 April 1953, 32.

72. "Top Name Designers Create Housecoats to Sell at $16.95," *WWD,* 20 January 1949, 23.

73. "Fashion Fair Makes Debut Tomorrow," *WWD,* 11 June 1947, 5; "Fashion Prizes to Be Given," *Los Angeles Times,* 17 August 1948, B4. Castillo won the Neiman-Marcus Award for Distinguished Service in the Field of Fashion that Arden had won in 1939.

74. Virginia Pope, "Glamour Is Added to Fall Fashions," *NYT,* 10 September 1947, 33.

75. "Castillo Out at Elizabeth Arden," *WWD,* 5 June 1950, 34.

76. "The Bigelow-Weston Wedding," *Vogue,* 1 July 1950, 58–59.

77. "Castillo to Design for Jeanne Lanvin," *WWD,* 16 September 1950, 8.

78. "The Elizabeth Arden Collection" ad, *NYT,* 21 August 1950, 3.

79. "'Old' Paris Models Counting Wrinkles," *NYT,* 16 July 1964, 35.

80. Rea Seeger, "More Fashions Displayed in Press Preview Parade," *Chicago Tribune,* 13 July 1951, A1.

81. Rebecca Blake, "What's New in Fashion," *The Boston Globe,* 6 December 1951, 21. The resort line was shown in several places, including at the Boston Hadassah Silver Anniversary Donor luncheon.

82. Virginia Pope, "Castillo Designs a Fabric Fantasy," *NYT,* 24 February 1949, 27.

83. "Christian Dior's Corolla Silhouette," *WWD,* 13 March 1947, 1.

84. "Skirt Choice in Villa Zigmund Imports," *WWD,* 10 September 1947, 3.

85. Rich's Department Store Collection, hc. MSS 791f, undated [1946–1953], Kenan Res-

earch Center, Atlanta Research Center. The exercise director was not named: Ann Dean, "Reducing No Longer Luxury Even for Grandma," *The Boston Globe*, 14 March 1948, A7.

86. For the Guêpìere Treatment and Heim, see "Paris Firms Begin Wasp Waist 'Treatments,'" *WWD*, 9 October 1947, 8; "You Get It (the New Look) by Taking It Off," *WWD*, 10 October 1947, 13.

87. "Le Carnet du Jour," *Le Figaro*, 11 March 1948, 2; "Global Cosmetics," *The Wall Street Journal*, 13 November 1950, 1.

88. "Arden Schedules Oct. Opening for Coiffure Department in Paris," *WWD*, 10 September 1948, 12; "Shingled Hair Out, Says Arden," *The Washington Post*, 2 September 1949, C2.

89. Glenn Fowler, "China Turns Beauty-wise," *WWD*, 9 September 1949, 2.

90. "French Perfumes Reported Recapturing Mexican Market," *WWD*, 17 December 1948, 9; "Publicity Problems in Latin America Told to Ad Women," *WWD*, 18 October 1939, 29. For Iraq, "Of Things and People," *WWD*, 31 July 1953, 8; Heinrich Harrer, *Seven Years in Tibet* (London: Rupert Hart-Davis, 1953), 126; Lester Gaba, "Lester Gaba Looks at Display," *WWD*, 11 May 1948, 55; "Elizabeth Arden Opens Zurich Salon," *WWD*, 21 November 1952, 10; "Arden Beauty School Opens in Johannesburg," *WWD*, 26 March 1948, 32. There, Marie Weber Ball was the trainer.

91. "Promotions, TV Get Spotlight in Market," *WWD*, 29 April 1949, 10. In 1949, South Africa did cut back on imports, causing a steep decline in availability.

92. "Cosmetic Expert Is Miss Arden's Niece," *The Sydney Morning Herald*, 20 October 1947, 7. This article, mistakenly, I have concluded, suggested that Patricia Graham married Philip Keen and went to Australia to help him with the business there.

93. "It All Began in a Flying Boat," *Elizabeth Arden News*, October 1965, 2, Unilever Archives.

94. B. Altman ad, *NYT*, 9 June 1949, 7; Jordan Marsh ad, *The Boston Globe*, 16 June 1949, 17; Saks ad, *NYT*, 26 June 1949, 17; Jelleff's ad, *The Washington Post*, 2 July 1949, B3; Wanamaker ad, *NYT*, 4 June 1950, 80.

95. See, for example, *BOAC Cabin Service* (British Overseas Airways Corporation, 1963); *Sydney—by BOAC* (London: Page Bros., 1962). Both from the British Airways Museum, British Airways Speedbird Centre, Harmondsworth, UK. The Sydney salon opened in 1955. See p. 3 of "News Letter—June 1955," EA/6/15/1, Elizabeth Arden Ltd. Papers, Unilever Archives. For training, see "It All Began in a Flying Boat," *Elizabeth Arden News*, Unilever Archives.

CHAPTER 22: MAINE CHANCE PHOENIX
1. Elizabeth Arden to Ada McCormick, 6 July 1944, MS 327, Box 7, File 15, Ada Peirce McCor-

mick Papers, University of Arizona Special Collections, Tucson.

2. Elizabeth Arden to Hedda Hopper, 11 April 1963, folder 616, Hedda Hopper Collection, Special Collections, Margaret Herrick Library, Academy of Motion Picture Arts and Sciences, Beverly Hills, California; Sondra Gottlieb, "Slimming in Arizona with the Very Rich," *Maclean's*, 1 October 1974, archive.macleans.ca/article/1974/10/1/slimming-in-arizona-with-the-very-rich.

3. "Discovery in Beauty: Underwater Exercise," *Vogue*, 1 October 1954, 146–47.

4. Evelyn Manners, "Arizona Maine Chance," *Harper's Bazaar*, September 1949, reprint, Box 2, A70-11, White House Social Office, Personal Files of Mamie Doud Eisenhower, Dwight D. Eisenhower Presidential Library, Abilene, Kansas. Hereafter cited as DDEPL.

5. Eleanor Roosevelt, "My Day," 21 March 1946, Eleanor Roosevelt Papers Project, George Washington University, erpapers.columbian.gwu.edu/my-day.

6. "Take Another Chance," *Vogue*, 1 October 1947, 208, 210.

7. Sylvia Porter, "Your Money's Worth: 'Maine Chance'—a Loser," *The Cincinnati Post*, 29 January 1962, Elizabeth Arden: Maine Chance, 1960–1965 clipping file, Keeneland Library.

8. Martha Weinman Lear, "A Greenhouse for Wilted Women," *NYT*, 19 June 1966, 211.

9. "Hemlines Are Uneven in Castillo Designs," *WWD*, 26 February 1948, 3; "Yellow from All Directions," *WWD*, 28 February 1946, 3; "One of a Pair of Beauties," *WWD*, 5 September 1947, 16.

10. Hambla Bauer, "High Priestess of Beauty," *The Saturday Evening Post*, 24 April 1948, 27.

11. Norma Lee Browning, "Laud Fashions at Preview of *Tribune* Show," *Chicago Tribune*, 7 October 1949, A1. Both Eisenhowers and Arden were guests of *Tribune* owner Colonel Robert McCormick.

12. "Citizens for Eisenhower-Nixon, List of Contributions of $1,000 to $5,000 from . . . August 20, 1952 to December 23, 1952," Box 1, Citizens for Eisenhower Contributors folder, Dwight D. Eisenhower Papers, Presidential: Campaign Series, DDEPL. In that four-month period, Arden contributed $1,900, or approximately $31,000 today. Arden Company Newsletter no. 3, 1952, EA/6/15/1, Elizabeth Arden Ltd. Papers, Unilever Archives, Port Sunlight, UK.

13. Elizabeth Arden to Mamie Eisenhower, undated, and Mamie Eisenhower to Elizabeth Arden, 10 July 1952, Box 2, A70-11, White House Social Office, Personal Files of Mamie Doud Eisenhower, DDEPL.

14. According to Stephen C. Wood, 1940 was the first year that political conventions were televised. See "Television's First Political Spot Ad Campaign: Eisenhower Answers America," *Presidential Studies Quarterly* 20, no. 2 (Spring 1990): 280.

15. Josephine Ripley, "Convention Color," *The Christian Science Monitor*, 9 July 1952, 18; Christine Sadler, "Senator Smith, Maine, Boomed for 2nd Place," *The Boston Globe*, 8 July 1952, 1; Dorothy Chandler, "Convention Chatter," *Los Angeles Times*, 10 July 1952, B1; Elizabeth Arden telegram to the Eisenhowers, 30 June 1952, and Eisenhower reply telegram, 2 July 1952, Box 2, White House Social Office, Personal Files of Mamie Doud Eisenhower, DDEPL; "From the Society Notebook," *Chicago Tribune*, 3 July 1952, A1.

16. Wood, "Television's First Political Spot Ad Campaign," 269.

17. Genina Gavin, "And Now It's Television," *The Boston Globe*, 20 June 1948, A7; Hedda Hopper, "Looking at Hollywood," *Los Angeles Times*, 15 June 1948, 23.

18. "Television: Buyers and Sellers," *Fashion Group Bulletin*, September 1948, 3, 4, Box 145, folder 3, Fashion Group International Archives, Mss Col 980, New York Public Library Archives & Manuscripts Division, New York City. Hereafter cited as FGIR. The luncheon was held in July 1948.

19. "Fashion on TV," *The Boston Globe*, 30 October 1949, A2.

20. "Store TR Show Found Boosting Fashion Sales," *WWD*, 2 March 1950, 1. Hudson's in Detroit also had a television program, *Fragrance, Beauty and You*. The store interviewed industry representatives. Tussy was the first interview. Elizabeth Arden—probably one of her representatives—was the focus of the second show. "Hudson's to Start TV Series Tomorrow," *WWD*, 22 May 1950, 43.

21. "TV: Muddled Picture," *NYT*, 3 June 1951, 144.

22. "Number of TV Households in America: 1950–1978," The American Century online digital archives, Washington and Lee University.

23. G. Maxwell Ule, "Your New Consumer: How Women Have Changed in the Last 10 Years," *Fashion Group Report*, 21 May 1954, 2, FGIR. In 1954, the average American watched five hours of television a day.

24. "On Television," *NYT*, 18 January 1951, 36; "Television Highlights," *The Washington Post*, 7 January 1952, B9.

25. NBC television ad, *NYT*, 25 August 1954, 42; "Of Things and People," *WWD*, 16 July 1954, 22. Actress Arlene Francis promoted Arden's Sleek Hair Remover. The two women both assisted with the 1946 March of Dimes Fashion Show. See Virginia Pope, "Fashion Pageant Aids Dimes March," *NYT*, 23 January 1946, 20.

26. Woodward & Lothrop ad, *The Washington Post*, 23 January 1951, B6.

27. See, for example, "Of Things and People," *WWD*, 12 September 1952, 10, and "Television Ads Highly Successful in Boosting Volume, Detroit Store Finds," *WWD*, 14 December 1951, 12.

28. Elizabeth Arden to Mamie Eisenhower, 4 December 1952 (Anniversary Only), Box 2, White House Social Office, Personal Files of Mamie Doud Eisenhower, DDEPL.

29. Dorothy Dix, "Men Who Used to Run from Spinster Now Run after Her," *The Boston Globe*, 17 February 1948, 15.

30. Elizabeth Arden to Mamie Eisenhower, 4 December 1952, and Mamie Eisenhower to Elizabeth Arden, 5 January 1953, Box 2, White House Social Office, Personal Files of Mamie Doud Eisenhower, DDEPL.

31. "Mrs. Eisenhower Brings Bangs into High Fashion," *Hartford Courant*, 13 July 1952, B15; "U.S. Women Copy Hairdo of Mrs. Eisenhower," *Los Angeles Times*, 2 March 1953, A1.

32. "Styles in Balance?: Hairdressers Chide First Lady on Bangs," *Los Angeles Times*, 26 February 1953, 30; Dorothy McArdle, "'I'll Stick to the Bangs,' Says Mamie," *The Boston Globe*, 8 August 1954, A7.

33. "Bangs across the Sea," *The Boston Globe*, 14 January 1957, 2.

34. Elizabeth Arden to Mamie Eisenhower, 20 February 1953, Box 2, White House Social Office, Personal Files of Mamie Doud Eisenhower, DDEPL. The nine-step drawings and the written instructions are attached.

35. Elizabeth Arden to Mamie Eisenhower, 20 March 1953, Box 2, White House Social Office, Personal Files of Mamie Doud Eisenhower, DDEPL; "Mamie Hoping to Visit Plush Phoenix Resort," *The Washington Post*, 21 February 1958, A1.

36. Evelyn Hayes, "Fashions and Foibles," *The Washington Post*, 8 November 1954, 22. "Christmas 1954," Arden London Newsletter, December 1954, EA/6/15/1, Elizabeth Arden Ltd. Papers, Unilever Archives, Port Sunlight, UK.

37. Quotes in these two paragraphs are from Arden London Newsletter, June 1953, EA/6/15/1, Unilever Archives. For Mesta's party, including a partial guest list, see Perle Mesta, *Perle: My Story* (New York: McGraw Hill, 1960), 185–88. The Arden-Mesta friendship seems to have continued throughout the decade, regardless of party affiliation. See, for one example, "Sunday Lunch," *The Washington Post*, 3 February 1958, B3. For Arden's newest "Coronation Pink" and corporate tie-ins, see James J. Nangle, "News of the Advertising and Marketing Fields," *NYT*, 24 May 1953, F8.

38. Ernestine Carter, "Mum Is the Word Now on the Princess' Dress," *NYT*, 3 May 1960, 47.

39. Tim Heald, *By Appointment* (London: Queen Anne Press, 1989), 44, 297, 313.

40. Hannah Coates, "The Story behind a Classic Beauty Product That's Fit for the Queen," *British Vogue*, 5 June 2022. The queen mother awarded Arden her royal warrant at some point before 1963. Queen Elizabeth II awarded hers in early 1963. See "We are proud . . . ," *Elizabeth Arden News*, April 1963, 1, Unilever Archives.

41. "From the Soul," *The New Yorker*, 4 July 1953, 16–18; Peggy Preston, "Prettiness Is Keynote of Fashion," *The Washington Post*, 14 April

1948, B3. See also "The Prevalence of Pink," *Vogue*, 1 June 1954, 54–59.

42. "It's New!," *WWD*, 4 January 1954, 20; "Parma-Violet" Arden ad, *Vogue*, 15 October 1954, 145.

43. "'Perfection Pink' Theme with 'Feminine Elegance,'" *WWD*, 12 March 1953, 3. See Virginia Pope, "Fashions Feature Fluid Silhouette," *NYT*, 12 March 1953, for a photo of one bicolor Pink Perfection gown from a showing that featured Pink Perfection makeup. Duet lipstick came out in 1952.

44. Jinx Falkenburg and Tex McCrary, "Elizabeth Arden Says Short Hair Keeps Girls from Marrying Well," *The Boston Globe*, 11 March 1950, 11. "Marital Status of the Population of the United States, by States: 1960," *1960 Census of Population Supplementary Reports*, 11 September 1961, Series PC(S1)-12 (Washington, DC: Bureau of the Census), 1.

45. Quote is from "Fashion: Bugles, Bangles & All Woman," *Time*, 25 June 1965. On Sarmi, see Elisa V. Massai, "The Tempestuous Decade," *WWD*, 27 December 1960, 12; "Count Sarmi to Be in N.Y. Thursday," *WWD*, 6 November 1951, 46; Rea Seeger, "Choice Models Designed by Sarmi of Italy," *Chicago Tribune*, 18 November 1951, E3. Sarmi was never Arden's sole designer. She showed and sold the work of others in her shops. See "Custom Made—Curved to the Figure," *WWD*, 16 September 1953, 3; Dorothy O'Neill, "Fashions: Young Designers Win Early Accolades," *NYT*, 19 November 1953, 39; and Virginia Pope, "California, New York Designers Present Creations at Coast Show," *NYT*, 23 March 1954, 22. Loretta G. Scannell of *Town & Country* took credit for Sarmi meeting Arden. See her Letter to the Editor, *WWD*, 25 October 1966, 19.

46. "Of Things and People," *WWD*, 23 January 1953, 10. See also "Fanny Fern Fitzwater," Missouri Remembers website, and Cassidy Zachary, "Ethel Traphagen: American Fashion Pioneer," *Fashion Studies Journal*, 27 February 2018, fashionstudiesjournal.org/5-histories/2018/2/27/ethel-traphagen-american-fashion-pioneer.

47. "Elizabeth Arden at War with Shingled Bob," *WWD*, 19 January 1950, 3; "With Bravo from the Men" Arden ad, *Chicago Tribune*, 22 January 1950, 14; Evelyn Hayes, "Arden Presents Collection: Applause and Sigh Greet Style Parade," *The Washington Post*, 17 March 1954, 30.

48. "Many Odd Whimsies Are Among Gift Items," *NYT*, 10 December 1953, 69; "Of Things and People," *WWD*, 4 December 1953, 8; "Glitter in the Arden Boutique," *WWD*, 11 December 1953, 14; "Nth Degree of Change," *Vogue*, 15 October 1952, 57–58; Evelyn Hayes, "Sparkle Is Clue to Holiday 'Look,'" *The Washington Post*, 31 December 1953, 16. *Vogue* gave Arden credit for coming up with the sequin ideas; see "Discoveries in Beauty: July," *Vogue*, 1 July 1954, 92.

49. Rebecca Blake, "Tricky Accessories to Adorn Spring, Summer Fashions," *The Boston Globe*, 11 January 1951, 1; "Arden Mannequins Wore 'Star Dust' Waves in Hair," *WWD*, 14 March 1952, 12; "People Are Talking About," *Vogue*, 1 April 1951, 140–41.

50. Virginia Pope, "Come-Hither Look Is Arden Feature," *NYT*, 16 March 1951, 28. See also "Arden's Opalescent Look Debuts," *WWD*, 18 September 1953, 8; "Doubled-Sales Recipe: Opalescent Make-Up," *WWD*, 28 May 1954, 29.

51. Ann Dean, "Beauty Hints," *The Boston Globe*, 12 November 1958, 13 (for Valencia); Ann Dean, "Unique Way to Apply Luxury Perfume," *The Boston Globe*, 15 December 1954, 26.

52. "Sales of Arden Home Wave Off to Good Start," *WWD*, 14 April 1950, 11; "It's New," *WWD*, 28 April 1950, 16; Ann Dean, "Effective Way to Counteract Falling Hair," *The Boston Globe*, 16 February 1951, 31: "Striking" Arden ad, *Vogue*, 1 March 1951, 207; "Tautening Lotion," *WWD*, 26 February 1951, 12; "Discoveries in Beauty for Mrs. Exeter," *Vogue*, 1 September 1951, 230; Ann Dean, "New Type of Makeup Stirs Beauty World," *The Boston Globe*, 3 October 1952, 34; "The Loveliest Liquid Foundation of All Time!" Arden ad, *Vogue*, 15 October 1952, 119.

53. "It's New!," *WWD*, 8 May 1953, 13.

54. "It's New!," *WWD*, 24 September 1954, 28.

55. Ann Dean, "New Make-Up Gives Veil-Like Quality to Skin," *The Boston Globe*, 16 February 1954, 6.

56. "Discoveries in Beauty for Mrs. Exeter," *Vogue*, 1 September 1951, 230.

57. "New Cream Is Extraordinary," *Hartford Courant*, 8 February 1958, 5.

58. Evelyn Hayes, "Ribbon and Tinsel Make a Real Gift," *The Washington Post*, 1 December 1953, 28. For the content list, see "Fragrance Manufacturers Say," *WWD*, 16 October 1953, 8.

59. "Yours—for a Beautiful Christmas" Arden ad, *Vogue*, 1 December 1954, 10–11. The ten boxes were a train case, a fitted travel case, the Elegante Beauty Box, the Globe-Trotter Case, the World Traveller Beauty Box, the Weekender Beauty Box, the On Dit Beauty Bath Box (with her On Dit fragrance introduced in 1946), the New Beauty Carryall, the Beauty Case, and the Introductory Beauty Box. All her holiday ads included a dizzying number of gift items. Holiday 1954 had color photographs of well over fifty.

60. "Two Colors Are Better Than One" Arden ad, *Vogue*, 15 March 1952, 131; Ann Dean, "New Make-Up Technique Gives Flattering Tone," *The Boston Globe*, 16 July 1952, 22.

61. "Sheer Genius!" Arden ad, *WWD*, 2 May 1952, 10.

62. "Success Story—New Byzantine Look by Elizabeth Arden," *WWD*, 17 September 1954, 30.

63. Patty Cavin, "Alert Mother to Save Scent of the Essence," *The Washington Post*, 4 May 1954, 43; "Blue Make-Up Sounds Bizarre but It's Pretty," *The Boston Globe*, 16 May 1954, C84;

"Make-Up Says Blue in Two Languages," *WWD*, 30 April 1954, 32. The comma between "you" and "turn" is an ellipsis in the original.

64. "Keep Youthful Skin with Special Arden Hormone Cream" ad, *Los Angeles Times*, 8 September 1952, 29; "Arden Offers New Hormone Cream," *WWD*, 30 November 1951, 9; Ann Dean, "New Type of Makeup Stirs Beauty World," *The Boston Globe*, 3 October 1952, 34; "A Wholly New Concept in Make-Up," *Los Angeles Times*, 19 November 1952, B5.

65. Lester Gaba, "Fashions in Display," *WWD*, 14 September 1954, 20; "Pure Red" Arden ad, *WWD*, 24 September 1954, 27.

66. "Fire and Ice" Revlon ad, *Vogue*, 1 November 1952, 28, 29. The photograph is on p. 28 and the test is on p. 29.

CHAPTER 23: MAINE CHANCE MANIA

1. Christine Sadler Coe, "The Ladies May Swing Vote to Ike," *The Washington Post*, 26 August 1956, F1; "Republican Party Platform of 1956," The American Presidency Project Online, UC Santa Barbara, presidency.ucsb.edu/documents/republican-party-platform-1956.

2. "Party Guest Lists Hit Four Figures," *The Washington Post*, 3 August 1956, 33. The party was on Tuesday night, 21 August 1956.

3. Muriel Bowen, "She Is Scheduling Sinatra," *The Washington Post*, 9 August 1956, 47; "G.O.P. Gives Party That's a Challenge," *Chicago Tribune*, 22 August 1956, 7; Christine Sadler Coe, "Mamie Stars at Pageant," *The Washington Post*, 23 August 1956, 33; Hedda Hopper, "Work, Play Combined in Convention City," *Los Angeles Times*, 24 August 1956, 24.

4. Elizabeth Arden to Mamie Eisenhower, 29 September 1955, Box 2, folder A70-11, White House Social Office, Personal Files of Mamie Doud Eisenhower, Dwight D. Eisenhower Presidential Library, Abilene, Kansas. Hereafter cited as DDEPL.

5. Ruth Wagner, "Miss Arden Bows into Town," *The Washington Post*, 26 September 1956, 27; "Cabinet Members to Attend Dinner for Ike Friday," *The Washington Post*, 11 October 1956, 66; "Today's Events," *The Washington Post*, 12 October 1956, 46; Dorothy Kilgallen, "Suggested Role for Rita: Rita," *The Washington Post*, 20 December 1956, C6. For "delightful" see Elizabeth Arden to Patricia Nixon, 20 December 1956, Patricia Ryan Nixon Collection, PPS 271, folder "December 1965," Richard Nixon Presidential Library and Museum, Yorba Linda, California. Thanks to Heath Lee for this document.

6. Mamie Eisenhower to Elizabeth Arden, 21 December 1956, Box 2, A 70-11, White House Social Office, Personal Files of Mamie Doud Eisenhower, DDEPL.

7. "Color of First Lady's Gown for Inaugural Kept Secret," *Los Angeles Times*, 3 January 1956, A1; Ruth Wagner, "White Gowns, Long Gloves for Inaugural," *The Washington Post*, 6 January 1957, F1. When news did leak out, Arden was quick to reassure Nixon that it was not she who did it. See Elizabeth Arden to Patricia Nixon, 20 December 1956.

8. Marie Smith, "Pat Nixon Picks Patriotic Colors," *The Washington Post*, 16 January 1957, B1; Annette Culler Ward, "Trio of Inaugural Ensembles Announced by Mrs. Nixon," *WWD*, 16 January 1957, 4. For a color photo of the dress, see "People Are Talking About," *Vogue*, 15 April 1957, 83.

9. Laurence Burd, "Fight to Bar Depression, Ike Tells 11 Governors," *Chicago Tribune*, 21 February 1958, 9.

10. "Mamie Hoping to Visit Plush Phoenix Resort," *The Washington Post*, 21 February 1958, A1.

11. William Knighton Jr., "Ike and Wife to Visit Arizona Beauty Camp," *The Baltimore Sun*, 23 February 1958, 1. See also Ellis D. Slater, *The Ike I Knew* (n.p.: Ellis D. Slater Trust, 1980), especially p. 169. The original quote was "blew his top."

12. Edward T. Folliard, "Ike to Return North via 3000-Mile Trip," *The Washington Post*, 23 February 1958, 1.

13. "Mamie Hoping to Visit Plush Phoenix Resort," *The Washington Post*, 21 February 1958, A1; "Resort Says Mamie Won't Be Charged," *The Washington Post*, 23 February 1958, A2; "Beauty Mecca Resembles Rare Jewel Set in Desert," *The Washington Post*, 23 February 1958, A2. For Gladys's arrival, see Hedda Hopper, "Brazzi, Krasner Doing Own Film," *Los Angeles Times*, 28 February 1958, 6.

14. "Ike Flies to Arizona, Plays Full Golf Round," *The Boston Globe*, 24 February 1958, 17; "The President's Appointments, Sunday, February 23, 1958," DDEPL, eisenhowerlibrary.gov/sites/default/files/research/online-documents/presidential-appointment-books/1958/february-1958.pdf.

15. "Mamie Is A-Sittin' in the Arizona Sun," *The Washington Post*, 26 February 1958, C5.

16. "The First Lady: Behind the Curtain," *Time*, 10 March 1958, content.time.com/time/subscriber/article/0,33009,863054,00.html.

17. Drew Pearson, "Public's Opinion Affects Ike Less," *The Washington Post*, 26 February 1958, D9. For his brief diary entry on the topic, see Tyler Abell, ed., *Drew Pearson Diaries, 1949–1959* (New York: Holt, Rinehart and Winston, 1974), 437–38.

18. Slater, *The Ike I Knew*, 175.

19. Doris Fleeson, "Did They Expect Her to Take the Bus?," *The Boston Globe*, 25 February 1958, 14.

20. Robert G. Spivack, "Watch on the Potomac," *The Chicago Defender*, 26 February 1958, A4.

21. "Mamie's High-Class Hideaway," *Life*, 10 March 1958, 54; "Resort Calls Mamie Guest, Not Customer," *Chicago Tribune*, 25 February 1958, 17; "What Mamie's Going Thru on Arizona Beauty

Ranch," *Chicago Tribune*, 26 February 1958, 1; "Mamie Is A-Sittin' in the Arizona Sun," *The Washington Post*, C5; "Resort Says Mamie Won't Be Charged," *The Washington Post*, 23 February 1958, 2.

22. Maine Chance Farm schedule cards, Mamie Doud Eisenhower Papers, Scrapbooks and Albums, 1894–1979, Box 13, DDEPL.

23. "Mamie Almost Incognito," *The Washington Post*, 3 March 1958, B3.

24. Eleanor Harris, "Reducing at $500 a Week," *Look*, 29 April 1958, 35–44. Quotes are from pp. 35 and 43. The very positive article was also excerpted in *Reader's Digest*, reaching even more Americans.

25. Hazel A. Washington, "This Is Hollywood," *The Chicago Defender*, 10 March 1958, 17; Eleanor Page, "May Festival Plans Warm Up Cold Day," *Chicago Tribune*, 28 January 1961, S11; Leonard Lyons, "Lyons Den," *The Chicago Defender*, 21 February 1961, 1; Marie McNair, "Town Topics," *The Washington Post*, 21 February 1961, D6.

26. Hedda Hopper, "Olivia Signs to Play 'Lady in a Cage,'" *Chicago Tribune*, 3 December 1962, B23; Herb Lyon, "Tower Ticker," *Chicago Tribune*, 12 October 1960, 18; Eugenia Sheppard, "Cherished and Wanted," *Hartford Courant*, 16 May 1961, 13; Gloria Emerson, "Co-Stars Again," *NYT*, 8 September 1965, 54. Audrey Hepburn wore Arden's Silver Jonquil lipstick.

27. "Mamie, More Slender and Tanned, Gets Warm Welcome in Cold Capital," *The Boston Globe*, 12 March 1958, 1.

28. Marie Smith, "Trim First Lady Is in the Pink—in All Green," *The Washington Post*, 13 March 1958, C1.

29. "Elizabeth Arden's Maine Chance Diet" clipping, *House & Garden*, undated, Dwight D. Eisenhower Papers, Post-Presidential, 1961–69, Augusta–Walter Reed Series, Box 6, Recipes, Menus, Gift Catalogues folder, DDEPL.

30. Judith Cass, "Passavant 'Sailors' Have Fling Ashore," *Chicago Tribune*, 13 September 1958, 19; for quote, see Mary Middleton, "Women Plan May Benefit for Hospital," *Chicago Tribune*, 25 March 1958, A4. For the green apple soup recipe, see "Apples at Health Core, Elizabeth Arden Says," *Los Angeles Times*, 21 April 1966, E11.

31. "Dinner Opens White House Social Season," *Chicago Tribune*, 12 December 1958, 2. For the AWVS, see "Aides Are Listed for Fete to Help Women's Group," *NYT*, 25 September 1960, 90; "Women's Group Announces Aides for Fete Oct. 10," *NYT*, 12 August 1962, 75; "Training Agency Will Give Lunch at St. Regis Roof," *NYT*, 13 October 1965, 50. For Eisenhower's volunteering, see Marilyn Irvin Holt, *Mamie Doud Eisenhower* (Lawrence: University Press of Kansas, 2007), 33.

32. Mamie Eisenhower to Elizabeth Arden, 2 July 1958, and Arden to Eisenhower, 8 July 1958, Box 2, A70-11, White House Social Office, Personal Files of Mamie Doud Eisenhower, DDEPL.

33. Ann Sonne, "Ex-First Lady's Desert Party Cooling Oasis," *Los Angeles Times*, 27 January 1967, D1; "First Lady Begins Beauty Regimen," *The Washington Post*, 8 March 1960, B7.

34. Drew Pearson, "Mamie's Jaunt Costly to Public," *The Washington Post*, 27 February 1959, D13; Drew Pearson, "Lease of Planes Helpful to Chalk," *The Washington Post*, 4 March 1959, D13. After she left the White House, Mamie Eisenhower also traveled to Phoenix by car. See, for example, "Mrs. Eisenhower Visits Beauty Spa," *The Washington Post*, 7 March 1964, 18.

35. Mamie Eisenhower to Elizabeth Arden, 16 February 1960, Box 2, A70-11, White House Social Office, Personal Files of Mamie Doud Eisenhower, DDEPL. Arden wrote Eisenhower about a Pearson "Washington Merry-Go-Round" column from the 3 March 1960 issue of *The Washington Post* suggesting that Arden tried to use her closeness to Mamie Eisenhower to influence the Food and Drug Administration. She denied it. Pearson also reported in that column that Eisenhower actually did pay for her stays at Maine Chance in 1958 and 1959. Clipping in Box 23, Folder "MDE Trips-Phoenix, March 1960 (2)," R. L. Schulz Records, 1948–1961, DDEPL.

36. Len Tracy, "It Sprang Full-Blown into Being," *The Thoroughbred Record*, 19 May 1956, 12, 13, 22. Arden had a photo wall of all of her $100,000-winning horses. See Jinx Falkenburg and Tex McCrary, "Elizabeth Arden Says Short Hair Keeps Girls from Marrying Well," *The Boston Globe*, 11 March 1950, 11.

37. J. H. Ransom, "A Queen Leads in the Sport of Kings," in *Who's Who in Horsedom*, vol. 9 (Lexington, KY: Ransom Publishing, 1957), 51. See also Tracy, "It Sprang Full-Blown into Being," *The Thoroughbred Record*, 12, 13, 22. Several reports note that she painted her horse barns Arden Pink. See, for example, Charlotte Curtis, "Turf Set Out for Belmont Ball," *Chicago Tribune*, 4 June 1965, C1.

38. Hugh J. McGuire, "Maine Chance Farm's Equine Population Numbers over 135," *Daily Racing Form*, 13 May 1957, Maine Chance clipping file, Keeneland Library. "Cosmetic Expert Is Miss Arden's Niece," *Sydney Morning Herald*, 20 October 1947, 7, suggests that Pat worked for Arden in Australia.

39. Sue McClelland Thierman, "A House of Feminine Gender," *Courier-Journal Magazine*, 12 May 1957, 16–18, Maine Chance clipping file, Keeneland Library; "300 Honor Mrs. Graham at KTBA Annual Dinner," *Daily Racing Form*, 1 May 1958, Keeneland Library.

40. Tracy, "It Sprang Full-Blown into Being," *The Thoroughbred Record*, 22.

41. Whitney Bolton, "Mrs. Graham a Woman Who Wants Things Done Her Way," *The Morning Telegraph*, 3 May 1958, 33.

42. "Advertising Club to Hear Noted Woman Columnist," *The Chicago Defender*, 16 April 1966, 21.

43. Walter Haight, "Horses and People," *The Washington Post*, 10 September 1957, A24.

44. Arden was involved with the increasing numbers of fundraising events in the postwar years. See, for example, Marie McNair, "Ball's Starting Gait Speedy," *The Washington Post*, 3 November 1957, F2; Marie McNair, "SRO Sign Out for International Ball," *The Washington Post*, 19 October 1958, F6; Marie McNair, "International Set Sees Nine Nations' Dozen Finest Run," *The Washington Post*, 12 November 1959, C17; "Aides Are Listed by Belmont Ball for June 8 Event," *NYT*, 29 May 1962, 24; "Belmont Ball Listed June 1 at the Waldorf," *NYT*, 24 February 1966, 31; "Flamingo Ball: Extravagant Barn Dance at Hialeah Race Course," *NYT*, 4 March 1966, 29. The Belmont Ball began in 1951 and Hialeah's Flamingo Ball in 1965. For the fingertip episode, see "Jewel's Reward Bites Owner," *Hartford Courant*, 14 March 1959, 14A. For blame, see Elizabeth Arden to Mamie Eisenhower, 25 March 1959, White House Social Office, Box 2, A 70-11, Personal Files of Mamie Doud Eisenhower, DDEPL; Elizabeth Arden to Hedda Hopper, 1 April 1959, folder 616, Hedda Hopper Collection, Special Collections, Margaret Herrick Library, Academy of Motion Picture Arts and Sciences, Beverly Hills, California.

45. "Chance Farm [*sic*] Ships Seven Yearlings to 'Newmarket,'" *The Chicago Defender*, 30 September 1963, A27; Ransom, "A Queen Leads in the Sport of Kings," 49.

46. Muriel Bowen, "Horses High among the Queen's Hobbies," *The Washington Post*, 17 September 1957, B5; Chuck Connors, "Connors Corner," *Daily Racing Form*, 3 June 1957, and Vernon Morgan, "Favored Crepello Gains Clever Victory in 178th Epsom Derby," *Daily Racing Form*, 6 June 1957, Keeneland Library.

47. Alison Adburgham, "Elizabeth Arden, Ruler of a Far-Flung Empire," *The Guardian*, 7 June 1957; Douglas J. Roche, "The Elegant Worlds of Elizabeth Arden," *Maclean's*, 20 February 1965, 43.

48. "Elizabeth Arden Buys Old Irish Castle, Estate," *Chicago Tribune*, 6 June 1962, 4; Betty MacNabb, "Names Make News," *Austin American-Statesman*, 20 June 1962, 3.

49. Hutton Wilkinson, Tony Duquette, and Wendy Goodman, *Tony Duquette* (New York: Abrams, 2009), 300. See also Julie V. Iovine, "Tony Duquette, a Decorator of Fantasy, Is Dead at 85," *NYT*, 14 September 1999, B9.

50. Elaine Wrightman, "Tony Duquette," *House Beautiful*, September 2022; Sarah Medford, "Blithe Spirit," *Town & Country*, December 2007; Wilkinson, Duquette, and Goodman, *Tony Duquette*, 169. For the *Camelot* designs, see Hutton Wilkinson, Tony Duquette Studios, tonyduquette.com.

51. "The Feminine Touch," *Hartford Courant*, 29 December 1962, 3; Eugenia Sheppard, "Never

a Dull Moment," *Hartford Courant*, 7 June 1962, 30; "Horsemen," *The Blood-Horse*, 6 July 1963, 35.

CHAPTER 24: ROUNDING OUT THE FIFTIES

1. Mary C. Sekman, "Flowers," *NYT*, 4 March 1951, 255; Ruth M. Peters, "The Evolution of Perennials," *NYT*, 16 March 1952, 45; "Pink Elizabeth Arden Rose," *Elizabeth Arden News*, September 1964, 1, Elizabeth Arden Ltd. Papers, Unilever Archives, Port Sunlight, UK. The famous British horticulturalist Harry Wheatcroft created the Elizabeth Arden Rose. For the beauty pageant, see "Meet the Judges Who Will Pick Miss America 1953," *Official Yearbook of the Miss America Pageant*, September 1952, 22, Hagley Digital Archives, digital.hagley.org/1972430 _1952#page/22/mode/2up; "52 Girls to Compete in 26th Annual Miss America Contest," *The Baltimore Sun*, 31 August 1952, 4. For the industry award, see "Distribution Hall of Fame to Include 140 'Immortals,'" *WWD*, 23 September 1953, 2; "Distributors' 'Hall of Fame,'" *The Boston Globe*, 8 November 1953, B6; "Distribution Experts Honored," *The Christian Science Monitor*, 23 September 1953, 16; Edwards Park, "How a Boston Conference Grew to International Importance," *The Boston Globe*, 17 October 1954, 36.

2. Lou Brown, "Bates Sponsors Convocations for Seniors, Guests," *The Bates Student*, 23 May 1958, 1, 4; "N.E. Colleges Gird for 'Big June Day,'" *The Christian Science Monitor*, 3 June 1958, 6. Nasson College awarded the honorary degree in 1958; see nasson.org/honorary-degree-recipients.html.

3. "San Franciscan Wins Theta Sigma Phi Award," *Los Angeles Times*, 23 March 1954, B1; Hedda Hopper, "Vic Mature Sought as 'Ben Hur' Star," *Los Angeles Times*, 19 March 1954, A8; "Elizabeth Arden Honored as Beauty-Bestower," *WWD*, 26 March 1954, 12.

4. Donald Kirkley, "Look and Listen," *The Baltimore Sun*, 22 April 1954, 12. An illness meant Arden had to decline Murrow's invitation.

5. "Christmas 1954," Arden London Newsletter, December 1954, EA/6/15/1, Elizabeth Arden Ltd. Papers, Unilever Archives, Port Sunlight, UK, and Donald Jones, *Fifty Tales of Toronto* (Toronto: University of Toronto Press, 1992), 98. Arden had long attended Women's National Press Club events in the U.S. See, for example, Marie McNair, "Can't Stop the Party Whirl," *The Washington Post*, 22 May 1954, 36.

6. For "first American woman," see Lindy Woodhead, *War Paint* (Hoboken, NJ: John Wiley & Sons, 2003), 371. Arden's perfume debuted in 1955 and she won the Gold Cup in 1959. "The Judgment of Paris" Arden ad, *Vogue*, 1 December 1959, 49. Ann Dean, "Beauty Hints," *The Boston Globe*, 6 December 1955, 21. This article states that limited quantities of Mémoire Chérie were available from Paris. It was more widely available in the United States in 1956. The committee "represents French industry, art, commerce and

government. The cup is presented to persons or organizations that have contributed to the prestige of France." See "French Give Ohrbach's Award for Good Taste," *Los Angeles Times*, 29 June 1959, 21.

7. For the James quote, see Judith Thurman, "Dressing Up," *The New Yorker*, 5 May 2014, newyorker.com/magazine/2014/05/05/dressing-up-3. Nancy was two decades younger than James. They divorced in 1961. James earned his own honors that decade: a Coty in 1950 and the Neiman-Marcus Award in 1953.

8. Hambla Bauer, "High Priestess of Beauty," *The Saturday Evening Post*, 24 April 1948, 27. Quote from previous paragraph also from Bauer, 27.

9. "Cosmetics: Men's Toiletries," *Fashion Group Bulletin*, October 1945, 4, Fashion Group International Records, Mss Col 980, New York Public Library Archives & Manuscripts, New York City. Hereafter cited as FGIR.

10. Lydia Lane, "Elizabeth Arden Lauds L.A. Women," *Los Angeles Times*, 24 March 1957, B1; Lydia Lane, "Look, Men: Mme. Rubinstein Says You're Being Neglected," *Los Angeles Times*, 16 April 1957, A5.

11. Frank Ewing, "Pretty Blondes with Soft Hands Pat Beauty onto Manly Maps in Swanky Salon," *Austin American-Statesman*, 25 September 1941, 1. In 1954, Rubinstein tried again with a men's salon: "A Saffron Vest with the Shampoo, Sir?," *NYT*, 16 November 1954, 32. For "thirty items," see "Gourielli" Rubinstein ad, *Vogue*, 1 April 1942, 13; "Introducing Gourielli" Rubinstein ad, *The Baltimore Sun*, 15 March 1942, CS4. Artchil Gourielli died in 1955. See "Prince Artchil Gourielli," *WWD*, 25 November 1955, 19.

12. "A Saffron Vest with the Shampoo, Sir?," *NYT*, 32.

13. See undated Arden for Men pamphlets with photos of the product line, from "Leaflets," EA/6/5, Elizabeth Arden Ltd. Papers, Unilever Archives. Matching patents: F. N. Lewis, "Talcum Powder Container," Des. 110,872, 16 August 1938, and "Cake of Soap," Des. 110,971, 23 August 1938. "It's New," *WWD*, 30 November 1956, 18; Ann Dean, "Beauty Hints," *The Boston Globe*, 6 December 1957, 30.

14. "Arden for Men," *Carrefour*, 18 December 1957, 13; Theresa Helburn to Elizabeth Arden, 31 December 1956, YCAL Mss 436, Series 1, Box 17, folder 271, Theatre Guild Archive, Beinecke Rare Book and Manuscript Library, Yale University.

15. Eleanor Nangle, "Creates Line of Toiletries Just for Men," *Chicago Tribune*, 14 January 1957, B13. Charles H. Baker Jr., *The Gentleman's Companion* (New York: Crown, 1946). For the transient nature of the store, see "Gifts Only for Men Sold in New Shop," *NYT*, 5 December 1956, 46; "Shop Talk," *NYT*, 16 November 1957, 15; "Beauty Roundup," *The Washington Post*, 17 November 1957, F16; "Elizabeth Arden Spells Christmas" ad, *Vogue*, 1 December 1957, 34–35.

16. Hodge Love, Grace Gaynor, and Kay Torrey, "Your Customers' New Shopping Habits," *Fashion Group Report*, May 1952, 1–4, Box 145, folder 7, FGIR; T. A. Wise, "Beauty Battle," *The Wall Street Journal*, 16 July 1952, 1; "Pathos Being Worked Over Extensively on Television," *Hartford Courant*, 15 December 1952, 20 (for Bishop and *This Is Your Life*); James Bennett, "American Lipstick Wars," cosmeticsandskin.com/efe/lipstick-wars.php.

17. Bennett, "American Lipstick Wars," cosmeticsandskin.com/efe/lipstick-wars.php.

18. "Broader Arden Distribution in Los Angeles Gets Consumers' OK," *WWD*, 30 November 1951, 13. See also "Arden Keeps Outlets Few, Sales Up on West Coast," *WWD*, 5 May 1950, 11.

19. "Elizabeth Arden to Open Boutique, Salon in Phoenix," *WWD*, 19 July 1963, 6; Samuel Feinberg, "From Where I Sit," *WWD*, 20 November 1953, 13.

20. "Elizabeth Arden to Move," *WWD*, 19 August 1956, 19; "Arden Cosmetics Further Proof It's a Small World," *WWD*, 8 March 1951, 21; "Madrid Letter," *WWD*, 14 December 1956, 5; Dorothy Kilgallen, "Noel Coward Bows Out of Rehearsal," *The Washington Post*, 14 January 1956, 19.

21. "Two Places on the Warm Islands—Full-Scale Beauty," *Vogue*, 1 March 1961, 178.

22. "Elizabeth Arden Salons," *Elizabeth Arden News*, December 1962, 1, Unilever Archives.

23. "Elizabeth Arden to Move," *WWD*, 19 August 1956, 19.

24. "Celadon Makeup—Tranquil, Enigmatic," *WWD*, 29 July 1955, 5; "Eye Appeal," *WWD*, 29 January 1958, 5.

25. "Old-Fashioned Compacts Have Taken a 'Powder,'" *NYT*, 11 February 1958, 26.

26. "On the Avenue There's a New Look," *The Washington Post*, 14 August 1960, F14.

27. Christy Fox, "Feline Fantasy, Cupid Vie for Our Town's Attention," *Los Angeles Times*, 5 March 1958, 1; Hedda Hopper, "Young Actress Starred in Her Second Film," *Chicago Tribune*, 11 December 1957, B14; "1,100,000 Building to Rise on Beverly Hills Site," *Los Angeles Times*, 5 August 1956, E22.

28. "Gossipy Memo on Travel," *Vogue*, 1 July 1959, 106.

29. William W. Yates, "King Neptune's South Sea Court Convicts 'Polliwogs,'" *Chicago Tribune*, 25 October 1959, E1.

30. "Elizabeth Arden Salons," *Elizabeth Arden News*, December 1962, 1, Unilever Archives.

31. "One More Proof," *Elizabeth Arden News*, April 1963, 1, Unilever Archives; "New Good Move for Travellers: Australia," *Vogue*, May 1, 1964, 96.

32. Charlotte Curtis, "Stewardess Will Serve on 'Copter," *NYT*, 14 June 1962, 26.

33. KLM ad, *Vogue*, 1 May 1963, 103.

34. Marilyn Hoffman, "Meet Manhattan," *The Christian Science Monitor*, 3 March 1959, 8.

35. Information on Arden's role in the Blue Grass Ball and her election as an honorary board member can be found in the Records of the Travelers Aid Society of New York, 1917–1979, MS 635, New-York Historical Society, New York City, esp. Series I, Boxes 3, 4, and 6. Quote is from "Meeting of Terminal Committee, 20 May 1947," Series I, Box 3, folder 2. See also the Andy Warhol–designed invitation to a Blue Grass party, liveauctioneers.com/item/152780959_andy -warhol-design-invitation-for-elizabeth-arden.

36. Eleanor Nangle, "New Spray for Shower Is Heavenly," *Chicago Tribune*, 6 March 1959, B16.

37. Ann Dean, "Has Father Tried Sandalwood Soap?," *The Boston Globe*, 14 June 1960, 21. By 1963, Arden for Men included twenty different items. See "The Vanity Box: Even the Men Are Getting Scent," *Hartford Courant*, 14 December 1963, 8.

38. "Perle Mesta Has Fun at Party," *The Washington Post*, 22 June 1958, F5; Mary Van Rensselaer Thayer, "Queen Mother Takes Stitch in Time for Kneeler," *The Washington Post*, 30 March 1958, F1. Wigs continued to be very popular into the 1960s. "False Brows Shaped to Structure of Bone," *NYT*, 7 May 1959, 40; Eleanor Nangle, "New Fast Seller: Fake Eyebrows," *Chicago Tribune*, 18 May 1959, C10; "Choose Your Own Winged Eyebrows," *The Washington Post*, 31 May 1959, F17.

39. Gloria Emerson, "Beauty and the Beach," *NYT*, 2 July 1960, 9.

40. "Try White Lipstick for Effect," *The Washington Post*, 31 May 1959, F17.

41. "Of Things and People," *WWD*, 20 May 1955, 32; "Discoveries in Beauty," *Vogue*, 1 May 1955, 147. She also sold "Chair," which was a mixture of gold and silver.

42. "New Fashion: 'Click-Change'" Arden ad, *Vogue*, 15 September 1957, 65; "Your Lips Speak the Last Word in Fashion" Arden ad, *Vogue*, 1 January 1959, 139.

43. "Elizabeth Arden Schools," *Elizabeth Arden News*, December 1962, 3, Unilever Archives. See also Art Buchwald's humorous column regarding TWA employees sent to Arden's Beauty School: "Masculine Intruder in Beauty Salon Finds Hostesses Hard at Work Keeping Pretty," *TWA Skyliner*, 6 March 1952, 6.

44. "Schools," *Elizabeth Arden News*, June 1964, 2, and "1965 Refresher School," *Elizabeth Arden News*, June 1965, 1, Unilever Archives.

45. Barbara Curry to All Road Staff, July [1963], and Barbara Curry to Cosmetic Buyer, 1963, EA/6/15/1, Elizabeth Arden Ltd. Papers, Unilever Archives. The samples were sent out in 1963.

46. The sack dress "makes a fool of a woman," Arden stated, and "men loathe it." See "Chemise Designers Called 'Little Boys,'" *The Baltimore Sun*, 19 February 1958, 3. Sarmi said clothing should "make a woman look feminine, pretty, and nice"; see Marilyn Hoffman, "Custom Designs Shown," *The Christian Science Monitor*, 18 March 1957, 10. Barbara Cox, "Sack? In Paris It's Unraveling," *Los Angeles Times*, 23 February 1958, D4; Evelyn Livingstone, "Fashion Group's Show Is Really a Circus," *Chicago Tribune*, 26 February 1958, B3; Marilyn Hoffman, "Sack Spurned," *The Christian Science Monitor*, 17 March 1958, 6. Even Castillo agreed: Bernadine Taub, "'Saque' Is for Secretaries, Castillo Asserts," *WWD*, 29 March 1958, 5.

47. "Arden Cuts Sarmi Tie," *NYT*, 7 January 1959, 26; "Sarmi Forms New Better Dress Firm," *WWD*, 12 February 1959, 6; "Sarmi Plans Own Business," *WWD*, 12 January 1959, 27.

48. "Four Paris Couturiers Will Design for Arden," *NYT*, 2 September 1959, 33. *WWD* stated that the four designers would produce only the fall and winter collections, and after that, she would choose designs from a larger number of artists; see "Arden Line by 4 Couturiers," *WWD*, 2 September 1959, 59. The first was a Nina Ricci gown displayed at the Cradle fashion show that Arden sponsored: "Column Slim Gown," *Chicago Tribune*, 17 September 1959, C3.

49. "Four French Couturiers Design Original Styles for a Salon Here," *NYT*, 28 September 1959, 39; Elizabeth Bernkopf, "Elizabeth Arden Brings Paris Originals to Hub," *The Boston Globe*, 15 October 1959, 30.

50. John Fairchild, "Cardin Outstanding as Paris Lines Open," *WWD*, 26 January 1960, 1; Fairchild, "Balenciaga Retains Top Position as Big Ordering Starts in Paris," *WWD*, 3 February 1960, 1.

51. "Stay-at-Homes Put on Dramatic Airs," *NYT*, 25 November 1959, 24; J. W. Cohn, "Peak Fall Retail Promotion Due for Fashion Imports," *WWD*, 20 July 1959, 24. In 1962, Arden was still purchasing Galitzine's garments—far beyond palazzo pants by then. See "Eye on the Markets," *WWD*, 1 March 1962, 40.

52. Gloria Emerson, "Feminine Enchantment Is Captured in Paris Adaptations," *NYT*, 18 March 1960, 28.

53. Harriet B. Blackburn, "China Patterns Mingled," *The Christian Science Monitor*, 10 February 1958, 6.

54. Woodhead, *War Paint*, 196. "American Foreign Service Report of the Death of an American Citizen, William P. Graham," Berlin, Germany, 24 March 1959, ancestry.com.

CHAPTER 25: THE NOT-YET-SWINGING SIXTIES

1. Nan Robertson, "Mrs. Kennedy Defends Clothes," *NYT*, 15 September 1960, 1.

2. "Clothes Debate Closed on Candidates' Wives," *Austin American-Statesman*, 16 September 1960, 3; Winzola McLendon and Marie Smith, "Elizabeth Arden or Balenciaga?," *The Washington Post*, 16 September 1960, 1.

3. Annette Culler, "Mrs. Pat Nixon Keeps Eye on Clothes Budget," *WWD*, 22 July 1960, 1.

4. Marilyn Bender, "Pat Nixon: A Diplomat in High Heels," *NYT*, 28 July 1960, 31; Marie Smith, "Pat's a Political Partner Seeking 'Greatest Role of All,'" *The Washington Post*, 31 July 1960, F3; Doris Fleeson, "Jackie's Glamour Now a Campaign Issue," *The Boston Globe*, 4 September 1960, 51; Whitney Walton, "Jacqueline Kennedy, Frenchness, and French-American Relations in the 1950s and Early 1960s," *French Politics, Culture & Society* 31, no. 2 (Summer 2013): 34–57, esp. 39.

5. "Nominees Wives in Lively Tilt over Cost of Clothes," *Chicago Tribune*, 16 September 1960, D4.

6. Bill McPherson, "They're Hanging Haberdashery on That Political Battle Line," *The Washington Post*, 19 September 1960, B3; Eugenia Sheppard, "Candidate Wives Head Style Ticket," *Los Angeles Times*, 28 September 1960, 1.

7. Nan Robertson, "She Shops Like Any Woman, Mrs. Nixon Replies on Clothes," *NYT*, 16 September 1960, 16.

8. "That Fancy Fashion Fuss," *Life*, 26 September 1960, 18–21.

9. "NLRB Orders Vote at Elizabeth Arden," *WWD*, 10 October 1952, 43; "AFL Union Certified at Elizabeth Arden," *WWD*, 15 December 1952, 28.

10. Inez Robb, "Youth Hold Spotlight at Convention," *Austin American-Statesman*, 27 July 1960, 4.

11. Marie McNair, "Pink Party Is Farewell Frosting," *The Washington Post*, 30 November 1960, C3.

12. Winzola McLendon, "Trip Won't Ruffle Hair of Her Head," *The Washington Post*, 21 February 1962, D2; "Eye," *WWD*, 24 June 1966, 27.

13. Joseph E. North, "The Cosmetics and Toiletries Industry," *Financial Analysts Journal* 19, no. 1 (January–February 1963): 41–42.

14. Julie Byrne, "Don't Look Now, but Dark Woman in Future Is . . . You!," *Los Angeles Times*, 10 January 1963, C1; "Antonio Del Castillo," *WWD*, 7 May 1963, 2.

15. Marilyn Hoffman, "'Lawrence' and 'Oliver!' Set Gay Young Trends for Chic Spring Wear," *The Christian Science Monitor*, 18 February 1963, 10.

16. "Sheik" ad, *Vogue*, 15 January 1963, 22.

17. "Madame la Vicomtesse de Maublanc" *Elizabeth Arden News*, January 1964, 1, Elizabeth Arden Ltd. Papers, Unilever Archives, Port Sunlight, UK.

18. "'V' Shape Cuts Caper in Florence," *Los Angeles Times*, 18 January 1962, 1; "Land of Nile New Source for Fashion," *NYT*, 20 January 1962, 14; "The Vanity Box," *Hartford Courant*, 24 February 1962, 6; "Ancient Egypt Captured in New Look," *NYT*, 25 January 1962, 47.

19. "Elizabeth Arden Gets Award from France," *NYT*, 3 November 1961, 38.

20. Elizabeth Arden to Hedda Hopper, 30 November 1961, and Arden Christmas card, folder 616, Hedda Hopper Papers, Special Collections, Margaret Herrick Library, Academy of Motion Picture Arts and Sciences, Beverly Hills, California. Hereafter cited as Hopper Papers, AMPAS.

21. "Stars Like Big Beds in Odd Shapes," *Chicago Tribune*, 9 September 1962, H4.

22. Mary Middleton, "Bids $2,000 for Gown at Cradle Fete," *Chicago Tribune*, 22 September 1960, G4.

23. "Top Arbiter of Fashion Dies at 73," *Hartford Courant*, 9 May 1961, 4; "Greats of Fashion Attend Last Rites for Carmel Snow," *WWD*, 11 May 1961, 10.

24. "Lillian Graham Is Dead," *NYT*, 2 October 1961, 31.

25. "Deaths," *NYT*, 27 March 1962, 31; Michael Glennie, "Trade Fair," *The Spectator*, 2 June 1961, 310.

26. "Mr T. Gordon Yates," *Elizabeth Arden News*, October 1971, 1–2, Unilever Archives.

27. Jake Gordon interview by Lisa Walker, 15 June 2015, Maine Chance Oral History Project, University of Southern Maine Digital Commons, digitalcommons.usm.maine.edu/mcfinter views/2.

28. See Edna Ferber to Elizabeth Arden, 23 September 1963, Schubertiade Music & Arts, schubertiademusic.com/cloudsearches/find; "Carol Says," *WWD*, 20 September 1963, 7; Elizabeth Arden to the Eisenhowers, 21 November 1963, Principal File A to An 1963, A65-16, Box 33, Office of Dwight D. Eisenhower, Dwight D. Eisenhower Presidential Library; "The Eye," *WWD*, 18 October 1963, 21. For the one hundred thousand miles, see Douglas J. Roche, "The Elegant Worlds of Elizabeth Arden," *Maclean's*, 20 February 1965, 43.

29. John Osmundson, "Color Threat to Lipsticks Hit by Trade," *NYT*, 17 April 1959, 18; "Lipstick Makers to Fight Ban," *Chicago Tribune*, 21 November 1959, D3; "Lipstick Firms Decry U.S. Ban on Colors," *The Baltimore Sun*, 21 November 1959, 1.

30. "Reprieve on Color Order Won by Lipstick Industry," *Hartford Courant*, 31 January 1960, 28; Drew Pearson, "Dawson Halted Drug Price Probe," *The Washington Post*, 28 January 1960, B15; Drew Pearson, "Orders Upset Navy Band Survivors," *The Washington Post*, 3 March 1960, D19. Pearson investigated Arden on topics ranging from her donations to the Republican Party to her culpability regarding the 1937 FTC cosmetics rulings. See the folder "Arden, Elizabeth" in the Drew Pearson Papers, LBJ Presidential Library and Museum, Austin, Texas.

31. Mary Cooke, "She Rules an Empire of Beauty," *Sunday Advertiser*, 8 January 1961, Day File, EA/6/15/1, Elizabeth Arden Ltd. Papers, Unilever Archives.

32. Cooke, "She Rules an Empire of Beauty," Unilever Archives.

33. "McCarthy Turns Reporter," *Elizabeth Arden News*, October 1965, 4, Unilever Archives. The newsletter was begun in 1963.

34. Hedda Hopper, "Fonda Sure Bet to Play 'Cardinal'" (Hopper incorrectly identified Killer Joe Piro as Killer Jones), *Los Angeles Times*, 13 November 1961, C14.

35. Hedda Hopper to Elizabeth Arden, 27 November 1961, folder 956, Hopper Papers, AMPAS.

36. Fay Hammond, "Holiday Gala Inspires Visions of Style Plums," *Los Angeles Times*, 5 December 1961, 1.

37. "The Beauty Shake-Up," *Vogue*, 15 September 1960, 194.

38. Eleanor Nangle, "'Peace Rose' New Color," *Chicago Tribune*, 10 October 1960, D1.

39. Eleanor Nangle, "Eye Beauty Expert Just Like Painter," *Chicago Tribune*, 31 October 1960, B4.

40. "He Teaches Clients to Coif Up," *Los Angeles Times*, 11 October 1960, 1.

41. "Beauty Passport Aids Travelers," *NYT*, 4 December 1961, 52; Eleanor Nangle, "Christmas Gift Idea: Beauty Checks," *Chicago Tribune*, 19 December 1961, 4. They sold in books of $25, $50, and $100.

42. Peter Bart, "Advertising: Battle over Runless Stockings," *NYT*, 11 June 1962, 48.

43. "Moviematic Promotion," *Elizabeth Arden News*, April 1963, 4, Unilever Archives.

44. Eleanor Page, "Sweet Floral Scent to Accompany Art," *Chicago Tribune*, 6 May 1960, D1.

45. North, "The Cosmetics and Toiletries Industry," 41; Mary Burt Holmes, "Teen-Agers Work Hard for Beauty," *NYT*, 25 April 1961, 30.

46. Kay Corinth, "The Young Look Show," *FGI Bulletin*, 14 February 1962, Box 146, folder 9, Fashion Group International Records, Mss Col 980, New York Public Library Archives & Manuscripts Division, New York City. Hereafter cited as FGIR.

47. "Brand Loyalty among Girls Said to Form at Age 12–14," *WWD*, 24 July 1964, 12.

48. Holmes, "Teen-Agers Work Hard for Beauty," 30.

49. "Coast TV Shows Expected to Draw Much B-T-S Activity," *WWD*, 22 August 1962, 25.

50. "Hawaiian Look Available Here in Bright Styles," *NYT*, 1 August 1961, 26.

51. Eleanor Nangle, "Learn How to Use Beauty Kit—from Record," *Chicago Tribune*, 18 September 1961, B9; Mary Burt Baldwin, "A Natural Look Is Urged in Teen-Agers' Make-Up," *NYT*, 8 November 1962, 64.

52. Mary van Rensselaer Thayer, "Jordan Refugee Girls Offered New Hope at Training Center," *The Washington Post*, 23 December 1962, F3.

53. Eugenia Sheppard, "Hand-Painted Pants," *Hartford Courant*, 4 December 1962, 9; "The Eye," *WWD*, 4 January 1963, 8. In contrast to *WWD*, the *NYT* states that de la Renta's first collection with Arden was held in the spring of 1962. See "New York Now Lures Designers from Paris," *NYT*, 30 August 1963, 14. For his salary, see Cathy Horyn and Enid Nemy, "Oscar de la Renta Who Clothes Stars and Became One, Dies at 82," *NYT*, 20 October 2014, 1. His salary would be near to $405,000 today.

54. "Carol Says," *WWD*, 23 October 1963, 10.

55. Bernadine Morris, "Diana Vreeland, Editor, Dies," *NYT*, 23 August 1989, 1.

56. Ruth Wagner, "A New Star to Be Shown," *The Washington Post*, 2 March 1963, C3.

57. Bernadine Morris, "Arden Styles Balance Austerity and Extravagance," *NYT*, 5 March 1964, 28.

58. Ruth Wagner, "A New Star to Be Shown," *NYT*, 29 March 1963, C3.

59. "Oscar de la Renta's Fashion Winners," *Los Angeles Times*, 21 May 1963: C1. Elizabeth Bernkopf, "It Was a Long Night at the Opera," *The Boston Globe*, 16 April 1963, 22; Eugenia Sheppard, "The Heyday of Everything," *Hartford Courant*, 21 May 1963, 33.

60. "The Eye," *WWD*, 13 April 1964, 1.

61. Virginia Lee Warren, "Few Shops Put Stress on Size 18," *NYT*, 11 July 1964, 12; Farnsworth Fowle, "Fira Benenson, Fashion Designer," *NYT*, 24 October 1977, 32; "Eye," *WWD*, 13 October 1965, 10.

62. Evelyn Livingstone, "This Clothing Has Breeding and a Dash of High Fashion," *Chicago Tribune*, 20 October 1964, B1; Kay Loring, "A Make-Up Expert Has a Busy Day," *Chicago Tribune*, 22 October 1964, C7.

63. Marilyn Hoffman, "Arden Couture," *The Christian Science Monitor*, 18 November 1965, 10; Bernadine Morris, "Arden Fashions Are Sleek by Day, Lavish at Night," *NYT*, 18 February 1965, 37.

64. "De la Renta's 7th Avenue Debut Is a Hit," *NYT*, 11 June 1965, 34.

65. "Mrs. Edward H. Wobber," *NYT*, 13 October 1964, 43. Virginia Graham Wobber died of heart failure. See her death certificate on ances try.com.

66. "Mrs. B. G. Van Breems," *NYT*, 26 July 1964, 56. Edward passed away in 1961, the same year as Lillian.

67. Gloria Emerson, "Elizabeth Arden and Castillo Reunited," *NYT*, 1 September 1965, 33.

68. Marilyn Hoffman, "Paris Touch Added to New York Fashions," *The Christian Science Monitor*, 27 September 1965, 6.

69. "Castillo Wins *Sunday Times* Award," *Elizabeth Arden News*, October 1965, 2, Unilever Archives. James Galanos won for the United States.

70. Enid Nemy, "A Pretty Spring at Arden," *NYT*, 24 March 1966, 45; Marilyn Hoffman, "Of Fashion without Fads," *The Christian Science Monitor*, 1 April 1966, 16.

71. "Arden is said to have referred to her protégé as the 'Picasso of eye makeup'": See Laird Borrelli-Persson, "Remembering Pablo Manzoni, the Original 'Make-Up Man' and One of Fashion's Brightest Stars," *Vogue*, 10 March 2022, vogue.com/article/obituary-pablo-manzoni-makeup-artist. Also see "Elizabeth Arden's Face Designer Pablo," *Elizabeth Arden News*, January 1966, 1, Unilever Archives.

72. Covers, *Vogue*, 15 September and 1 December 1964; "Eye View of Wonders," *Vogue*, 1

December 1964, 187–91. Lanfranco Rasponi speculated that since clothing design had become so simple, the focus had to go somewhere else: hair and makeup. For his explanation of the rise of superstar hair and makeup stylists, see his *The International Nomads* (New York: G. P. Putnam's Sons, 1966), esp. 150–56.

73. Angela Taylor, "'Switched-On' Make-Up Lights Up Discotheques," *NYT*, 21 August 1964, 32; "Beauty Bulletin," *Vogue*, 1 October 1964, 150.

74. Peg Zwecker, "The Eyes Have It—the Disco Look," *The Washington Post*, 10 July 1964, B9; see Susan J. Tonery, "The Gay Divorcee 'Lives' the Late Show," *Hartford Courant*, 10 July 1964, 15; Anita L. Polk, "Couture Week Sees C-P Fashion Editor Do 'Frug' at Gamble Benedict Mansion," *Call and Post*, 18 July 1964, 4B. For more on Piro, see Charles L. Mee Jr., "Discotheque Man," *NYT*, 9 January 1966, 216.

75. Angela Taylor, "Women Seek His Help to Get a Natural Look," *NYT*, 26 April 1965, 37; Rosemary Feitelberg, "Celebrity Makeup Artist Pablo Manzoni Dies at 82," *WWD*, 3 March 2022, wwd.com/eye/people/celebrity-makeup-artist -pablo-manzoni-dies-at-1235118256.

76. Carolyn Bengtson, "Go Away Wrinkles," *Austin American-Statesman*, 2 April 1964, 8; Eleanor Nangle, "New Spring Make-Up," *Chicago Tribune*, 17 March 1964, B5.

77. Angela Taylor, "Style Trends Were Started by the Young," *NYT*, 1 January 1965, 23; Eugenia Sheppard, "Pablo Calls It the Fragile Look," *Hartford Courant*, 5 March 1964, 24.

78. Taylor, "Women Seek His Help to Get a Natural Look," *NYT*, 37; Catherine Brewster, "Make-Up Optimism," *The Baltimore Sun*, 29 December 1965, B2. For pink blood, see Lisa Anderson, "Good Looks," *Chicago Tribune*, 19 June 1985, F8. Also see "A Touch of Sable," *Time*, 10 June 1966, 69; Eugenia Sheppard, "Pablo Puts Their New Faces On," *Corpus Christi Caller-Times*, 12 March 1964, 30. For the Coty Award, see "Beauty Bulletin," *Vogue*, 15 September 1965, 152 (for quote), and Joan Cook, "Coty Jury Votes Special Citations but No Winners," *NYT*, 30 June 1965, 26. For the Coty AFC Award, see "Fashion Critics Cite Designers," *Hartford Courant*, 14 October 1965, 33.

79. Angela Taylor, "'Sweet' Look Foreseen by Italian Hairdresser," *NYT*, 7 October 1964, 56; "The Accessories: The Beauty Part," *WWD*, 4 December 1964, 17.

80. "Jewels Abundant," *Vogue*, 1 December 1965, 176–79; "The Face of Fall," *WWD*, 3 June 1966, 22. Arden's next makeup artist find was George Masters, who also became visagiste to Hollywood stars.

81. Charlotte Curtis, "Fun Night: Danny Kaye Helps Raise $40,000 for Philharmonic," *NYT*, 30 March 1965, 42.

82. Sherman L. Morrow, "The In Crowd and the Out Crowd," *NYT Sunday Magazine*, 12–14, 16, 18–19. Quotes from p. 12. Jerome Zerbe, *The Art of Social Climbing* (Garden City, NY: Doubleday, 1965), 46.

83. Charlotte Curtis, "Musicale Offered by Mrs. Graham Includes Quartet," *NYT*, 12 April 1965, 42.

84. "Beauty Requires a Knee-Knack," *Hartford Courant*, 17 February 1966, 45.

85. "Where the Pants Go," *WWD*, 16 May 1966, 30; "Pants Verboten in Chic Spots in Capital," *WWD*, 18 April 1966, 6.

86. "Tennis Fashions Have Femininity," *NYT*, 10 June 1965, 42; "New Tennis Fashions Flattering, Graceful," *The Boston Globe*, 15 July 1965, 31. Arden's tennis line also became the centerpiece of tennis-related charitable events. See Bud Collins, "Breeze Costs Sedgman Match," *The Boston Globe*, 15 July 1965, 49, for example.

87. "New Beauty Tips," *Vogue*, 1 May 1961, 191; Eleanor Nangle, "S-T-R-E-T-C-H with Pica Sticks," *Chicago Tribune*, 19 November 1961, E1.

88. "Big Names, Big Panel," *FGI Newsletter*, April 1965, 12, Box 147, Fashion Group International Papers, FGIR; "New Hairsprays Designed for Men," *NYT*, 23 March 1966, 36.

89. Angela Taylor, "The Big Gamble in Cosmetics," *NYT*, 4 January 1966, 31.

90. Marlene, "Fashions for M'Lady," *The Pittsburgh Courier*, 14 October 1961, 15.

91. Anita L. Polk, "Editors See New Arden Color," *Call and Post*, 24 August 1963, 8C.

92. Blanche Van Hook, "Social Events of the City," *Call and Post*, 13 September 1941, 4B; Betty Guy, "You Can Be Lovelier," *Call and Post*, 9 February 1952, 3C.

93. James M. Gavin, "Plan Office Building on N. Michigan," *Chicago Tribune*, 15 January 1963, B4.

94. James M. Gavin, "Tall Office Building Set for N. Side," *Chicago Tribune*, 29 May 1963, C7; "Begin Work Soon for New Arden Salon," *Chicago Tribune*, 11 July 1964, 5; "Home of Elizabeth Arden," *Chicago Tribune*, 20 September 1964, F3. Each new story had a slightly different number of planned floors.

95. "Tiffany's Inks Lease for Chicago Branch," *WWD*, 19 October 1965, 31; "Space Leased by Florsheim in Arden Building," *Chicago Tribune*, 23 October 1965, C5; "Bergdorf to Open Chicago Store," *NYT*, 9 November 1965, 61; "Billion Dollars in 8 Years!," *Chicago Tribune*, 29 August 1965, E1.

96. Pablo and Imo were her stylists, and the designer was Castillo. Eleanor Nangle, "Elegance Marks Finery Shown at Salon Opening," *Chicago Tribune*, 17 December 1965, C21; Nangle, "If the Painting . . . ," *Chicago Tribune*, 2 May 1966, B2; Sue Smith, "Plans for Princeton Show Told," *Chicago Tribune*, 16 December 1965, D1; Sue Smith, "Guest List Is Impressive at Style Salon Opening," *Chicago Tribune*, 17 December 1965, C19.

97. Betty Beale, "Parties All over the Capital," *The Boston Globe*, 24 January 1965, 52; Eugenia

Sheppard, "Ask the Policeman What to Wear to the Ball," *Hartford Courant*, 12 January 1965, 17. For Lady Bird at Maine Chance, see Marian Christy, "'Health Farm' Offers an Escape Hatch: Pampering the Super-Rich," *The Boston Globe*, 29 November 1970, A34.

98. "Helena Rubinstein, 94, Dies," *The Baltimore Sun*, 2 April 1965, 15.

99. "Helena Rubinstein Dies Here at 94," *NYT*, 2 April 1965, 1.

100. Elaine Brown Keiffer, "Madame Rubinstein," *Life*, 21 July 1941, 39.

101. Keiffer, "Madame Rubinstein," 39. Another article that characterized theirs as a so-called rivalry was "The Pink Jungle," *Time*, 16 June 1958, 88–95.

102. Keiffer, "Madame Rubinstein," 39.

103. "Lewis Heads Dubin Labs.," *Drug and Cosmetic Industry*, June 1936, 813.

104. "The Norbert Set," *WWD*, 23 September 1966, 10; "Eye," *WWD*, 27 September 1966, 24. For lunch with Castillo, see "Features," *WWD*, 3 October 1966, 15. For Barretstown and the fall, see Lindy Woodhead, *War Paint* (Hoboken, NJ: John Wiley & Sons, 2003), 410. Woodhead's chronology does not align with newspaper coverage, however.

105. Carol Bjorkman, "Features," *WWD*, 19 September 1966, 10; Lady Bird Johnson, Press Release for the Opening of the Metropolitan Opera House Special Television Program, 25 September 1966, Mrs. Johnson—Speeches, Reference File, LBJ Presidential Library, discoverlbj .org/item/ref-ctjspeeches-19660925-1830.

106. "Cabbages and Kings," *Call and Post*, 8 October 1966, 2B.

107. Anne Sonne, "Miss Arden at Sparkling Best," *Los Angeles Times*, 8 October 1966, B1. See also Fay Hammond, "Social Set, Fashion Glitter at Champagne Benefit," *Los Angeles Times*, 8 October 1966, B1.

108. Sue Smith, "Cradle Unit Benefits by Arden Show," *Chicago Tribune*, 12 October 1966, C2.

109. "Elizabeth Arden Is Dead at 81: Made Beauty a Global Business," *NYT*, 19 October 1966, 1. For other details, see Woodhead, *War Paint*, 412. Arden died on Tuesday, the eighteenth. Her birth year remains unprovable as I cannot locate a birth certificate. In the June 1900 census, her birth year was 1875. In the 1906 census it was 1881. On a 1914 White Star Line passenger list, it was 1880. One year later, on her first marriage certificate, it was 1884. Her brother's statement regarding her birth year may or may not have been correct, and his reason for traveling to Canada to file the official paperwork was connected to his sister's unhappiness with him regarding his infidelity with her treatment girls, according to Woodhead.

AFTERWORD

1. Gregory Jaynes, "About New York: 90 Subdued Years of Funerals for the Famous," *NYT*, 8

June 1988, B1; Kay Loring, "Front Views & Profiles," *Chicago Tribune*, 25 October 1966, B4.

2. "Elizabeth Arden Honored by 1,000," *NYT*, 22 October 1966, 26.

3. "A Life of Beauty Ends," *WWD*, 19 October 1966, 8.

4. "A Life of Beauty Ends," *WWD*, 8; AWVS, "Graham—Elizabeth Arden," *NYT*, 20 October 1966, 43; Mrs. John E. Roosevelt [Helen Daae], "Graham—Elizabeth Arden," *NYT*, 19 October 1966, 47.

5. Trixie Belmont, "Ambition," *The Baltimore Sun*, 1 December 1966, B7; "Beauty-Fashion Tycoon, Elizabeth Arden, Dies at 84," *The Baltimore Sun*, 19 October 1966, A17. John Baraba was identified in newspapers as John Graham, and in 1968 he had taken "an important executive position with Elizabeth Arden in South America." That occurred at the same time Gladys de Maublanc appointed Telford M. Allen as CEO and general manager of Arden's French company. See "Vicomtesse Henri de Maublanc," *Elizabeth Arden News*, January 1968, 1, Elizabeth Arden Ltd. Papers, Unilever Archives, Port Sunlight, UK.

6. Lindy Woodhead, *War Paint* (Hoboken, NJ: John Wiley & Sons, 2003), 416. For her obituary in the thoroughbred world, see "Elizabeth Nightingale Graham, 1885–1966," *The Thoroughbred Record*, 29 October 1966, 1451, and "Mrs. Elizabeth N. Graham," *The Blood-Horse*, 22 October 1966, 2964–65; "Elizabeth N. Graham Succumbs at 81," *Daily Racing Form*, 19 October 1966, all from Maine Chance 1966, Death of Mrs. Arden file, Keeneland Library.

7. "Arden Estate Estimated at $50 Million," *Chicago Tribune*, 28 October 1966, 22; Joseph Egelhof, "Set Elizabeth Arden Estate at 50 Millions," *Chicago Tribune*, 28 October 1966, 3; Douglas Robinson, "Elizabeth Arden's Will Is Filed," *NYT*, 28 October 1966, 31; "Heiress: Arden Niece Beneficiary," *Austin American-Statesman*, 28 October 1966, 20; "Arden Family, Employes Slice $40 Million Pie," *WWD*, 28 October 1966, 20.

8. "Why Maine Chance?," *The Open Door*, University of Kentucky Alumni Association, Maine Chance 1967, Jan–Jul Clipping File, Keeneland. The trustees authorized $2 million for the 721 acres. Jim Miller, "Maine Chance Being Developed for Ag Use," *Kentucky Kernel*, 4 February 1969, 1–2, Maine Chance Farm and University of Kentucky Collections, Special Collections Research Center, Margaret I. King Library, University of Kentucky.

9. Maine Chance in Maine was sold in 1969. See "Another Maine Chance Farm, This One in Maine, Is Sold by Graham Estate," *Lexington Sun*, 28 September 1969, Maine Chance 1969, Mar–Dec Clipping File, Keeneland Library. In 1970, Maine Chance Phoenix was still going strong. See Marian Christy, "'Health Farm' Offers an Escape Hatch: Pampering the Super-Rich," *The Boston Globe*, 29 November 1970, A34.

10. "Elizabeth Arden Chooses President and 6-Man Board," *NYT*, 11 November 1966, 60. Charles M. Bliss became chair. Bliss was chairman of the Bank of New York. Quote is from "An Interview with Mr. Gardiner," *Elizabeth Arden News*, May 1967, 5, Unilever Archives. See also "Ardent Dedication," *WWD*, 17 February 1967, 10–11.

11. "Custom Change," *WWD*, 18 November 1966, 32; Isadore Barmash, "Elizabeth Arden," *NYT*, 20 December 1966, 65.

12. In 2014, according to *Cosmetic Executive Women*, there were more than twenty-five Red Door spas offering treatments, including the newest at 200 Park Avenue South in New York City; see Aubree Mercure, "New Arden Outpost Represents Spa of Future," *CEW*, 7 January 2014, cew .org/beauty_news/new-arden-outpost-represents -spa-of-future. Covid finally closed the last remaining spas. See Allison Collins, "Coronavirus Closure: Former Elizabeth Arden Red Door Spa Files for Liquidation," *WWD*, 20 March 2020, www.com/ beauty-industry-news/ beauty -features/coronavirus-closure-elizabeth-arden -red-door-spa-bankrupt-1203544011. Perelman is still in charge of Revlon at the time of writing.

Bibliography

ARCHIVAL COLLECTIONS

A. Fabian Swanson Biographical File. John Hay Library Special Collections. Brown University, Providence, Rhode Island.

Ada Peirce McCormick Papers. University of Arizona Special Collections, Tucson, Arizona.

Alfred Stieglitz/Georgia O'Keeffe Archive. Beinecke Rare Book and Manuscript Library. Yale University, New Haven, Connecticut.

Alumni Records and *Olla Podridas* Yearbook. Wesleyan University Special Collections and Archives. Wesleyan University, Middletown, Connecticut.

Barnard College Periodicals. Barnard College Digital Collections. digitalcollections.barnard.edu /collections.

Bengamin Gayelord Hauser Correspondence File. American Medical Association Department of Investigation Records. American Medical Association Archives, Chicago, Illinois.

British Airways Heritage Collection. British Airways Speedbird Centre, Harmondsworth, United Kingdom.

Brooks Jackson Oral History Interview, 22 March 1976. Smithsonian Archives of American Art. aaa.si.edu/collections/interviews/oral-history -interview-brooks-jackson-12916.

Charles James Papers. The Costume Institute's Irene Lewisohn Costume Reference Library. Metropolitan Museum of Art, New York City.

Charles Luckman Papers. Archives and Special Collections. William H. Hannon Library. Loyola Marymount University, Los Angeles, California.

City of Vaughan Archives and Records Management Services. Vaughan, Ontario, Canada.

Drew Pearson Papers. Lyndon Baines Johnson Presidential Library and Museum, Austin, Texas.

Dwight D. Eisenhower Papers. Dwight D. Eisenhower Presidential Library and Museum, Abilene, Kansas.

Earle Ludgin Papers. David M. Rubenstein Rare Book & Manuscript Library. Duke University, Durham, North Carolina.

Elizabeth Arden FBI File. Federal Bureau of Investigation Records: The Vault Online. vault.fbi .gov/Elizabeth%20Arden.

Elizabeth Arden Letter to Mrs. Hyatt. Lisa Unger Baskin Collection, David M. Rubenstein Rare Book & Manuscript Library. Duke University, Durham, North Carolina.

Elizabeth Arden Ltd. Papers. Unilever Archives, Port Sunlight, United Kingdom.

Fannie Hurst Papers. Harry Ransom Center. University of Texas, Austin, Texas.

Fashion Group International Records, Mss Col 980. New York Public Library Archives & Manuscripts Division, New York City.

Faye Shumway Oral History. Center for Oral and Public History. California State University, Fullerton, California.

Frances Bemis Papers. Sophia Smith Collection of Women's History. Smith College Special Collections. Smith College, Northampton, Massachusetts.

Gene Federico Papers. David M. Rubenstein Rare Book & Manuscript Library. Duke University, Durham, North Carolina.

George Antheil Papers. Rare Book and Manuscript Library, Columbia University, New York City.

Graham, Florence Nightingale—Alumni Papers. Special Collections Research Center. Syracuse University, Syracuse, New York.

Harrods Company Archive, London, United Kingdom.

Hedda Hopper Papers. Special Collections, Margaret Herrick Library. Academy of Motion Picture Arts and Sciences, Beverly Hills, California.

Henry R. Luce Papers. Patricia D. Klingenstein Library. New-York Historical Society, New York City.

Historical Health Fraud and Alternative Medicine Collection. American Medical Association Archives, Chicago, Illinois.

Jane Hedges Todd Papers. Division of Rare and Manuscript Collections. Cornell University, Ithaca, New York.

Jerome Zerbe Photographs and Papers. Beinecke Rare Book and Manuscript Library. Yale University, New Haven, Connecticut.

Kappa Kappa Gamma Historical Archives Online. kappa.historyit.com.

Keeneland Library, Lexington, Kentucky.

Kennebec County Registry of Deeds Online, Augusta, Maine. kennebec.gov/deeds.

Lady Bird Johnson—Speeches, Reference File. Lyndon Baines Johnson Presidential Library and Museum Online. discoverlbj.org/item/ref-ctj speeches-19660925-1830.

Lucile Quarry Mann Diary Transcript. William M. Mann and Lucile Quarry Mann Field Books, 1914–1940. Smithsonian Institution Archives Online. transcription.si.edu/project/7518.

Maine Chance Farm and University of Kentucky Collections. Special Collections Research Center. Margaret I. King Library. University of Kentucky, Lexington.

Mamie Doud Eisenhower Papers. Dwight D. Eisenhower Presidential Library and Museum, Abilene, Kansas.

March of Dimes Archives, Arlington, Virginia.

Mount Holyoke College Friends and Benefactors Records. Mount Holyoke College Archives and Special Collections Online. aspace.fivecolleges.edu/repositories/2/resources/460.

New York City Municipal Archives. New York City Records and Information Services, New York City.

New York State Archives, Albany, New York.

New York World's Fair 1939 and 1940 Incorporated Records, Mss Col 2233. New York Public Library Archives & Manuscripts Division, New York City.

Nicolas Remisoff Papers. Special Collections. University of Southern California Libraries, University of Southern California, Los Angeles.

Papers of the Casey and Dudley Families. Special Collections, University of Virginia, Charlottesville.

Published Collections Department Online. Hagley Museum and Library, Wilmington, Delaware. digital.hagley.org/pc.

Records of the Office of the Surgeon General (Army). National Archives and Records Administration, Washington, DC.

Records of the United States Marine Corps. National Archives and Records Administration, Washington, DC.

Records of the War Department General and Special Staffs. National Archives and Records Administration, Washington, DC.

Rich's Department Store Collection. Kenan Research Center. Atlanta History Center, Atlanta, Georgia.

Rosamond Pinchot Papers. Manuscript Division. Library of Congress, Washington, DC.

Ruth Mills and Elizabeth Mills Family Papers, 1869–1997. Tennessee State Library & Archives, Nashville, Tennessee.

Ruth King Garrett Interview. University of North Carolina at Greensboro Special Collections Online. libcdm1.uncg.edu/cdm/singleitem /collection/WVHP/id/4293/rec/2.

Shirley M. Tillson Letters. Women Veterans Historical Project Online. University of North Carolina at Greensboro. gateway.uncg.edu/wvhp.

Syracuse University Clippings Files and Photograph Collection. Special Collections Research Center. Syracuse University, Syracuse, New York.

Theatre Guild Archive. Beinecke Rare Book and Manuscript Library. Yale University, New Haven, Connecticut.

Travelers Aid Society of New York Records. New-York Historical Society, New York City.

Virgil Thompson Papers. Gilmore Music Library. Yale University, New Haven, Connecticut.

Walton H. Hamilton Papers. Tarlton Law Library. University of Texas, Austin, Texas.

Women's Institute of Duluth Records (S2374). University of Minnesota, Duluth, Minnesota.

SELECTED PERIODICALS
The American Perfumer
Barnard College Alumnae Monthly
Barnard College Bulletin
The Blood-Horse, Keeneland Library
Broadcasting
The Chicagoan
Chicago Tribune
The Christian Science Monitor
Crockery and Glass Journal
Daily Racing Form, Keeneland Library
The Drug and Cosmetic Industry
Elizabeth Arden News, Unilever Archives
Essential Oil Review
The Film Daily
Fortune
Hartford Courant
The Key, Kappa Kappa Gamma
Los Angeles Times
Motion Picture Daily
The New York Times
Radio Daily
The Thoroughbred Record, Keeneland Library
Time
Turf and Sport Digest, Keeneland Library
Variety
Vogue
The Washington Post
Women's Wear Daily

PRIMARY SOURCES
Abell, Tyler, ed. *Drew Pearson Diaries, 1949–1959*. New York: Holt, Rinehart and Winston, 1974.

Aldrich, Amey. *Fifty Years Ago: Early Days of the Cosmopolitan Club*. Stamford, CT: Overbrook Press, 1959.

American Friends of France. *Spécialités de la maison*. New York: H. Wolff, 1940.

Antheil, George. *Bad Boy of Music*. Garden City, NY: Doubleday, Doran, 1945.

Arden, Elizabeth. "Beauty and Optimism." *Ladies' Home Journal*, February 1932.

Askinson, George W. *Perfume and Cosmetics: Their Preparations and Manufacture*. New York: Norman W. Henley, 1915.

Ayer, Harriet Hubbard. *Harriet Hubbard Ayer's Book: A Complete and Authentic Treatise on the Laws of Health and Beauty*. Springfield, MA: King-Richardson, 1899.

Beerbohm, Max. *A Defence of Cosmetics*. Reprint, New York: Dodd, Mead, 1922. First published 1896.

Benjamin, Harry. "Eugen Steinach, 1861–1944: A Life of Research." *The Scientific Monthly* 61, no. 6 (December 1945): 427–42.

Braggiotti, Gloria. *Born in a Crowd*. New York: Thomas Y. Crowell, 1957.

Brion, Irene. *Lady GI: A Woman's War in the South Pacific*. Novato, CA: Presidio Press, 1997.

Brown, Eve. *Champagne Cholly: The Life and Times of Maury Paul*. New York: E. P. Dutton, 1947.

Byers, Margaretta. *Designing Women: The Art, Technique, and Cost of Being Beautiful*. New York: Simon & Schuster, 1938.

Carleton, Alice. "The Uses and Dangers of Cosmetics." *British Medical Journal* 1, no. 3779 (10 June 1933): 999–1001.

Chambers, Bernice G., ed. *Keys to a Fashion Career*. New York: McGraw Hill, 1946.

Chase, Ilka. *In Bed We Cry*. Garden City, NY: Doubleday, Doran, 1945.

———. *Past Imperfect*. Garden City, NY: Doubleday, Doran, 1942.

Clark, Sue A., and Edith Wyatt. *Making Both Ends Meet: The Income and Outlay of New York City Working Girls*. New York: Macmillan, 1911.

Cocks, Dorothy. *The Etiquette of Beauty*. New York: George H. Doran, 1927.

———. *Help Yourself to Beauty: A Modern Woman's Practical Guide*. New York: Harper & Brothers, 1935.

Cosmetic Nostrums and Allied Preparations. Chicago: Bureau of Investigation of the Journal of the American Medical Association, n.d.

Coutant, Frank R. "Research as an Aid to Pricing and Production." *American Marketing Journal* 1, no. 3 (July 1934): 119–24.

———. "Understanding the Consumer—Research as an Aid to Pricing and Production." *The Management Review* 23, no. 6 (June 1934): 163–70.

Cramp, Arthur J. "The Work of the Bureau of Investigation." *Law and Contemporary Problems* 1, no. 1 (December 1933): 51–54.

Crowley, P. J. B. "Equal Price Treatment under the Robinson-Patman Act." *University of Pennsylvania Law Review* 95, no. 3 (February 1947): 306–43.

Cumberbatch, E. P., C. A. Robinson, and F. Howard Humphris. "Discussion on Medical Diathermy." *British Medical Journal* 2, no. 3269 (25 August 1923): 311–18.

De Meyer, Adolph. *A Singular Elegance: The Photographs of Baron Adolph de Meyer*. San Francisco: Chronicle Books, 1994.

Downing, John Godwin. "Cosmetics—Past and Present." *The Journal of the American Medical Association* 102, no. 25 (23 June 1934): 2088–91.

"Dr. Edward Robinson Squibb." *American Druggist and Pharmaceutical Record* 37, no. 10 (12 November 1900): 288.

Dressler, Marie. *My Own Story*. As told to Mildred Harrington. Boston: Little, Brown, 1934.

Duff Gordon, Lucy [Lucile]. *Discretions and Indiscretions*. New York: Frederick A. Stokes, 1932.

"Elizabeth Arden: Queen." *Fortune*, August 1930.

Evlanoff, Michael. *Nobel, Prize Donor: Inventor of Dynamite, Advocate of Peace*. Ada, MI: Revell, 1943.

Evlanoff, Michael, and Marjorie Fluor. *Alfred Nobel: The Loneliest Millionaire*. Los Angeles: Ward Ritchie Press, 1969.

Fabius, Odette. *Un lever de soleil sur le Mecklembourg: Memoires*. Paris: Albin Michel, 1986.

Fadiman, Clifton, ed. *Profiles from* The New Yorker. New York: Alfred A. Knopf, 1938.

Fashion Group. *The Keys to a Fashion Career*. New York: McGraw-Hill, 1946.

Finance and Industry: The New York Stock Exchange Historical Review. New York: Historical Publishing Company, 1886.

First Citizens of the Republic. New York: L. R. Hamersly, 1906.

Fishbein, Morris. "Modern Medical Charlatans: II." *Hygeia* 16, no. 2 (February 1938): 113–15.

Flanner, Janet. "Inside Ravensbrück: A Survivor Shares Her Experiences." *The New Yorker*, 27 April 1945. newyorker.com/magazine/1945/05/05/letter-from-paris-inside-ravensbruck.

Fleischman, Doris E. *An Outline of Careers for Women: A Practical Guide to Achievement*. Garden City, NY: Doubleday, Doran, 1928.

French, George. *20th Century Advertising*. New York: D. Van Nostrand, 1926.

Gaba, Lester. *The Art of Window Display*. New York: Thomas Y. Crowell, 1952.

———. *On Soap Sculpture*. New York: Henry Holt, 1935.

Gardner, T. Lyddon. "The Cosmetic Industry." *Journal of the Royal Society of Arts* 110, no. 5076 (November 1962): 892–903.

Halsman, Philippe. *The Frenchman: A Photographic Interview*. New York: Simon & Schuster, 1949.

Harrer, Heinrich. *Seven Years in Tibet*. London: Rupert Hart-Davis, 1953.

Harriman, Margaret Case. "Profiles: Glamour, Inc." *The New Yorker*, 6 April 1935, 24–30.

Harrison, Rosina. *Rose: My Life in Service to Lady Astor* [1975]. New York: Penguin, 2011.

Haskell, Ruth G. *Helmets and Lipstick: An Army Nurse in World War Two.* New York: G. P. Putnam's Sons, 1944.

Hauser, Bengamin Gayelord. *Diet Does It.* New York: Coward-McCann, 1944.

———. *Eat and Grow Beautiful.* New York: Faber & Faber, 1939.

———. *Look Younger, Live Longer.* New York: Farrar, Straus, 1950.

Hauser, Bengamin Gayelord, and Ragnar Berg. *Dictionary of Foods.* New York: Tempo Books, 1932.

Hess, Fjeril. *WACS at Work: The Story of the "Three B's" of the AAF.* New York: Macmillan, 1945.

Hoefle, Milton L. "The Early History of Parke-Davis and Company." *Bulletin for the History of Chemistry* 25, no. 1 (2000): 28–34.

Hopper, Hedda. *From Under My Hat.* New York: MacFadden, 1963.

Hurst, Fannie. *Anatomy of Me: A Wonderer in Search of Herself.* Garden City, NY: Doubleday, 1958.

———. *Imitation of Life.* Edited by Daniel Itzkovitz. Durham, NC: Duke University Press, 2004. First published 1933.

"'I Am a Famous Woman in This Industry.'" *Fortune,* October 1938.

Keiffer, Elaine Brown. "Madame Rubinstein." *Life,* 21 July 1941, 36–40 and 43–45.

Kissman, Henry M. *Views from the Road I Traveled: Segments of an Autobiography.* Bloomington, IN: Xlibris, 2008.

Koller, Theodor. *Cosmetics: A Handbook of the Manufacture, Employment and Testing of All Cosmetic Materials and Cosmetic Specialties.* London: Scott, Greenwood & Son, 1920.

Laas, Virginia Jeans, ed. *Bridging Two Eras: The Autobiography of Emily Newell Blair, 1877–1951.* Columbia: University of Missouri Press, 1999.

Lambert, Eleanor. *World of Fashion: People, Places, Resources.* New York: R. R. Bowker, 1976.

Lauder, Estée. *Estée: A Success Story.* New York: Random House, 1985.

Leonard, John W., ed. *Men of America.* New York: L. R. Hamersly, 1908.

Luce, Clare Boothe. *The Women.* New York: Dramatists Play Service, 1995. First published 1937.

Maine Chance Oral History Project. University of Southern Maine Digital Commons. digitalcommons.usm.maine.edu/mcfinterviews.

Marbury, Elisabeth. *My Crystal Ball.* New York: Boni & Liveright, 1923.

Marie, Grand Duchess of Russia. *A Princess in Exile.* New York: Viking, 1932.

Marietta McPherson Interview with Elizabeth Arden (Photograph), September 1955. R11224-1122-2-E, Box 6353, File number: Assignment 5510-5. Library and Archives, Canada. recherche-collection-search.bac-lac.gc.ca/eng/home/record?app=fonandcol&IdNumber=3829696&q=%22Elizabeth%20Arden%22%20and%20Marietta%20McPherson.

Maxwell, Elsa. *I Married the World.* London: William Heinemann, 1955.

McDonough, Everett G. *The Truth about Cosmetics.* New York: The Drug and Cosmetic Industry, 1927.

McGrory, Mary. *The Best of Mary McGrory: A Half-Century of Washington Commentary.* Edited by Phil Gailey. Kansas City, MO: Andrews McMeel, 2006.

McLeod, Edyth Thornton. *Beauty after Forty.* Garden City, NY: Doubleday, 1949.

———. *Charm, Beauty, and Personality for Success.* New York: Laurel, 1952.

———. *How to Sell Cosmetics.* New York: The Drug and Cosmetic Industry, 1937.

———. *Lady, Be Lovely: A Guide to Beauty, Glamour, and Sex Appeal.* New York: Wilcox and Follett, 1944.

Mesta, Perle. *Perle: My Story.* New York: McGraw Hill, 1960.

Miller, Hiram E., and Laurence R. Taussig. "Cosmetics." *The Journal of the American Medical Association* 84, no. 26: 1999–2002. doi: 10.1001/jama.1925.02660520027012.

Mitford, Jessica. *Poison Penmanship: The Gentle Art of Muckraking.* New York: Alfred A. Knopf, 1979.

Mohan, J. Alexander. *Vienna Yesterday and Today.* Vienna: Halm and Goldman, 1933.

Morris Fishbein Oral Interview Transcript. Conducted by Charles Jackson. U.S. Food and Drug Administration Online, 12 March 1968. fda.gov/media/81547/download.

Mosse, George L., ed. *Nazi Culture: Intellectual, Cultural and Social Life in the Third Reich.* New York: Grosset & Dunlap, 1966.

Nadi, Aldo. *The Living Sword: A Fencer's Autobiography.* Bangor, ME: Laureate Press, 1995.

Neal, Nelson D. "Hemsley Winfield: First African American Modern Dancer Contracted by the Metropolitan Opera." *Afro-Americans in New York Life and History* 40, no. 1 (July 2018): 137–51.

Nelson, Lyonel. *From Farm to Fifth Avenue: How I Became a Stylist to the Rich & Famous at the World's Most Exclusive Salon.* Galesburg, IL: self-published, 2014.

"New York City Offers Numerous Privileges for Nurses." *The Army Nurse* 1, no. 10 (October 1944). Women Veterans Historical Project Online, University of North Carolina at Greensboro.

Nigel, Simeone, ed. *The Leonard Bernstein Letters.* New Haven, CT: Yale University Press, 2013.

North, Joseph E. "The Cosmetics and Toiletries Industry." *Financial Analysts Journal* 19, no. 1 (January–February 1963): 39–50.

Obolensky, Serge. *One Man in His Time: The Memoirs of Serge Obolensky.* New York: McDowell, Obolensky, 1958.

Odlum, Hortense. *A Woman's Place: The Autobiography of Hortense Odlum.* New York: Charles Scribner's Sons, 1939.

Oglesby, Catharine. *Fashion Careers American Style*. New York: Funk & Wagnalls, 1936.

Overacker, Louise. "American Government and Politics: Presidential Campaign Funds, 1944." *American Political Science Review* 39, no. 5 (October 1945): 899–925.

Pearson, W. A. "Original and Selected: The Preparation and Testing of Drugs." *The Pharmaceutical Era* 44, no. 8 (August 1911):'335–37.

Pharmaceutical Society of Great Britain. *The Registers of Pharmaceutical Chemists and Chemists and Druggists*. London: 1919.

Phillips, Mary Catherine. *Skin Deep: The Truth about Beauty Aids—Safe and Harmful*. New York: Vanguard Press, 1934.

Picken, Mary Brooks, and Dora Loues Miller. *Dressmakers of France: The Who, How and Why of the French Couture*. New York: Harper & Brothers, 1956.

Poiret, Paul. *King of Fashion: The Autobiography of Paul Poiret*. London: V&A Publishing, 2009. First published 1931 by J. B. Lippincott.

Quennell, Peter. *The Marble Foot: An Autobiography, 1905–1938*. London: Collins, 1976.

Ransom, J. H. *Who's Who in Horsedom*, vol. 9. Lexington, KY: Ransom Publishing, 1957.

Rasponi, Lanfranco. *The International Nomads*. New York: G. P. Putnam's Sons, 1966.

Roche, Douglas J. "The Elegant Worlds of Elizabeth Arden." *Maclean's*, 20 February 1965, 20–21, 43.

Rubinstein, Helena. *The Art of Feminine Beauty*. London: Victor Gollancz, 1930.

———. *My Life for Beauty*. New York: Simon & Schuster, 1966.

Ryan, Kim. Interview by author, 19 October 2018. Lexington, Kentucky.

Schiaparelli, Elsa. *Shocking Life: The Autobiography of Elsa Schiaparelli*. London: V&A Publishing, 2018. First published 1954.

Slater, Ellis D. *The Ike I Knew*. N.p.: Ellis D. Slater Trust, 1980.

Steiner, Lee R. *Where Do People Take Their Troubles?* New York: Houghton Mifflin, 1945.

The Story of the Westinghouse Time Capsule. East Pittsburgh, PA: The Westinghouse Corporation, [1939].

"Tadd, J. Liberty." *American Art News* 15, no. 34 (16 June 1917): 4.

Tadd, J. Liberty, and W. Schlich. "Cantor Lectures: Elementary Art Education." *The Journal of the Society of Arts* 49, no. 2545 (30 August 1901): 725–36.

Thornley, Betty. "Merrily We Roll Along. *Collier's*, 7 December 1929, 19, 73.

Thoroughbred Racing & Breeding: The Story of the Sport and Background of the Horse Industry. N.p.: Thoroughbred Racing Association of the United States, 1945.

Towle, Katherine A. "Administration and Leadership" Oral History. Conducted by Harriet Nathan. Bancroft Library, University of California, Berkeley, 1970.

———. "Lady Leathernecks." *Marine Corps Gazette* 30, no. 2 (February 1946): 3–7.

Troubridge, Laura. *Memories and Reflections*. London: William Heinemann, 1925.

U.S. Marine Corps Historical Branch. "Marine Corps Women's Reserve in World War II." Washington, DC: Historical Branch, G-3 Division, 1968.

Vail, Gilbert. *A History of Cosmetics in America*. New York: Toilet Goods Association, 1947.

Veblen, Thorstein. *Theory of the Leisure Class*. New York: Macmillan, 1899.

Vreeland, Diana. *D.V.* New York: Da Capo, 1984.

Wilt, Nancy. Phone interview by author, 23 January 2019.

Women Veterans Historical Project Oral Interviews. University of North Carolina at Greensboro. gateway.uncg.edu/wvhp.

"The Work of Dr. Cramp." *The British Medical Journal* 1, no. 3975 (13 March 1937): 565.

Wright, Cobina. *I Never Grew Up*. New York: Prentice-Hall, 1952.

Zerbe, Jerome. *The Art of Social Climbing*. Garden City, NY: Doubleday, 1965.

SELECTED SECONDARY SOURCES

Alexander, Rachael. "Consuming Beauty: Mass-Market Magazines and Make-Up in the 1920s." *IJAS Online* 4 (2015).

Allen, Margaret. *Selling Dreams: Inside the Beauty Business*. New York: Simon & Schuster, 1981.

Allen, Raye Virginia. *Gordon Conway: Fashioning a New Woman*. Austin: University of Texas Press, 1997.

Arnold, Rebecca. *The American Look: Fashion, Sportswear and the Image of Women in 1930s and 1940s New York*. New York: I.B. Tauris, 2009.

Aron, Cindy S. *Working at Play: A History of Vacations in the United States*. New York: Oxford University Press, 1999.

Ash, Mary Kay. *Mary Kay*. New York: Harper Perennial, 1981.

———. *Miracles Happen: The Life and Timeless Principles of the Founder of Mary Kay, Inc.* New York: Harper Perennial, 1994.

Baker, Cynthia, et al. *Ties That Bind: The Evolution of Education for Professional Nursing in Canada from the 17th to the 21st Century*. Ottawa: Canadian Association of Schools of Nursing, 2012.

Baker, David W. "J. Liberty Tadd, Who Are You?" *Studies in Art Education: A Journal of Issues and Research* 26, no. 2 (1984): 75–85.

Bamji, Andrew. *Faces from the Front: Harold Gillies, The Queen's Hospital, Sidcup and the Origins of Modern Plastic Surgery*. Solihull, UK: Helion, 2017.

Banner, Lois. *American Beauty*. New York: Alfred A. Knopf, 1983.

Barg, Lisa. "Black Voices/White Sounds: Race and Representation in Virgil Thomson's *Four Saints in Three Acts*." *American Music* 18, no. 2 (Summer 2000): 121–61.

Barrett, Richmond. *Good Old Summer Days: Newport, Narragansett Pier, Saratoga, Long Branch, Bar Harbor.* Boston: Houghton Mifflin, 1952.

Barthes, Roland. *The Language of Fashion.* New York: Oxford, 2004.

Batvinis, Ray. "A Thoroughly Competent Operator: Former SA Arthur Thurston, 1938–1944." FBI Studies Online, October 2017. https://fbistudies.com/2017/10/30/a-thoroughly-competent-operator-former-fbi-sa-arthur-thurston.

Bauer, Susanne, Martina Schlünder, and Maria Rentezi, eds. *Boxes: A Field Guide.* Mattering Press, 2019. matteringpress.org/books/boxes.

Beauty Queens: Elizabeth Arden. Directed by Elia Hershon and Roberto Guerra. RM Production for Channel 4 TV, 4 January 1988.

Belk, Russell W., and Richard W. Pollay. "The Good Life in Twentieth Century US Advertising." *Media Information Australia* 46 (November 1987): 51–57.

Bell, John. "Gertrude Stein's Identity: Puppet Modernism in the U.S." *TDR* 50, no. 1 (Spring 2006): 87–99.

Bennett, James. Cosmetics and Skin, cosmeticsandskin.com.

Benson, John. "Hawking and Peddling in Canada, 1867–1914." *Histoire Sociale / Social History* 18, no. 35 (1985): 75–83.

Berghaus, Günter. "Girlkultur: Feminism, Americanism, and Popular Entertainment in Weimar Germany." *Journal of Design History* 1, no. 3/4 (1988): 193–219.

Billings, Victoria Chipman. "Altered Forever: A Woman's Elite and the Transformation of American Fashion Work and Culture, 1930–1955." Ph.D. diss., University of California, Los Angeles, 1990.

Bizri, Zayna N. "Recruiting Women into the World War II Military: The Office of War Information, Advertising, and Gender." Ph.D. diss., George Mason University, 2017.

Black, Cheryl, et al., eds. *Experiments in Democracy: Interracial and Cross-Cultural Exchange in American Theatre, 1912–1945.* Carbondale: Southern Illinois University Press, 2016.

Blackiston, Howland. "Get a Glimpse of This 1935 Cadillac Town Car, Once Owned by Cosmetics Queen Elizabeth Arden." *The Self-Starter* 51, no. 1 (January 2008): 20–22.

Blaszczyk, Regina Lee. "Chromophilia: The Design World's Passion for Color." *Journal of Design History* 27, no. 3 (2014): 203–17.

———. *The Color Revolution.* Cambridge, MA: MIT Press, 2012.

Blaugrund, Annette. *Dispensing Beauty in New York & Beyond.* Charleston, SC: History Press, 2011.

Bloodgood, Edith Holt, ed. *First Lady of the Lighthouse: A Biography of Winifred Holt Mather.* New York: The Lighthouse & the New York Association for the Blind, [1953].

Blower, Brooke L. *Becoming Americans in Paris: Transatlantic Politics and Culture between the World Wars.* New York: Oxford University Press, 2011.

Boles, Jennifer. "An Early Thirties Set Piece." *The Peak of Chic,* 11 April 2016. thepeakofchic.blogspot.com/2016/04/an-early-thirties-set-piece.html.

Bolton, Diane K., Patricia E. C. Croot, and M. A. Hicks. *A History of the County of Middlesex,* vol. 7. London: Victoria County History, 1982. british-history.ac.uk/vch/middx/vol7/pp23-30.

Borrelli-Persson, Laird. "Remembering Pablo Manzoni, the Original 'Make-Up Man' and One of Fashion's Brightest Stars." *Vogue,* 10 March 2022. vogue.com/article/obituary-pablo-manzoni-makeup-artist.

———. "*Vogue* at 130." *Vogue,* 7 March 2017. vogue.com/article/vogue-covers-models-facts-history.

Bradley, Ian. *Health, Hedonism, and Hypochondria: The Hidden History of Spas.* New York: I.B. Tauris/Bloomsbury, 2021.

Brandau, Robert, ed. *De Meyer.* New York: Alfred A. Knopf, 1976.

Brandon, Ruth. *Ugly Beauty: Helena Rubinstein, L'Oréal, and the Blemished History of Looking Good.* New York: HarperCollins, 2011.

Brands, H. W. *Masters of Enterprise.* New York: Free Press, 1999.

Breaking Codes, Breaking Barriers: The WACS of the Signal Security Agency, World War II. Fort Belvoir, VA: U.S. Army Intelligence and Security Command, 2001.

Brettell, Richard R. *Nineteenth- and Twentieth-Century European Drawings in the Robert Lehman Collection.* Princeton, NJ: Princeton University Press, 2002.

Brodowsky, Pamela, and Tom Philbin. *Two Minutes to Glory: The Official History of the Kentucky Derby.* New York: Collins, 2007.

Bronner, Simon J., ed. *Consuming Visions: Accumulation and Display of Goods in America, 1880–1920.* New York: W. W. Norton, 1989.

Bundles, A'Lelia. *On Her Own Ground: The Life and Times of Madam C. J. Walker.* New York: Scribner, 2002.

Burke, John [Richard O'Connor]. *Rogue's Progress: The Fabulous Adventures of Wilson Mizner.* New York: G. P. Putnam's Sons, 1975.

Burke, Laurence M. "'What to Do with the Airplane?': Determining the Role of the Airplane in the U.S. Army, Navy, and Marine Corps, 1908–1925." Ph.D. diss., Carnegie Mellon University, 2014.

Burton, Antoinette, ed. *After the Imperial Turn: Thinking with and through Nation.* Durham, NC: Duke University Press, 2003.

Caldwell, Helen Marie. "The Development and Democratization of the American Perfume Market, 1920–1975." Ph.D. diss., University of Connecticut, 1995.

Cameron, Rebecca Hancock. *Training to Fly: Military Flight Training, 1907–1945.* Air Force History and Museums Program, 1999. media.defense.gov/2010/Dec/02/2001329902/-1/-1/0/training_to_fly-2.pdf.

Carbone, Gerald M. *Brown & Sharpe and the Measure of American Industry.* Jefferson, NC: McFarland, 2017.

Carstairs, Catherine. "'Look Younger, Live Longer': Ageing Beautifully with Gayelord Hauser in America, 1920–1975." *Gender & History* 26, no. 2 (August 2014): 332–50.

Carter, Ernestine. *With Tongue in Chic.* London: Michael Joseph, 1974.

Case, Carole. *The Right Blood: America's Aristocrats in Thoroughbred Racing.* New Brunswick, NJ: Rutgers University Press, 2001.

Cayleff, Susan. *Wash and Be Healed: The Water-Cure Movement and Women's Health.* Philadelphia: Temple University Press, 1991.

Cecil, Matthew. *Hoover's FBI and the Fourth Estate: The Campaign to Control the Press and the Bureau's Image.* Lawrence: University Press of Kansas, 2014.

Chambers, Thomas A. *Drinking the Waters: Creating an American Leisure Class at Nineteenth-Century Mineral Springs.* Washington, DC: Smithsonian Institution Scholarly Press, 2002.

Christgau, John. *The Gambler and the Bug Boy: 1939 Los Angeles and the Untold Story of a Horse Racing Fix.* Lincoln: University of Nebraska Press, 2007.

Clark, Jessica P. "'Beauty on Bond Street': Gender, Enterprise, and the Establishment of a British Beauty Industry, 1850–1919." Ph.D. diss., Johns Hopkins University, 2012.

———. *The Business of Beauty: Gender and the Body in Modern London.* London: Bloomsbury, 2020.

———. "'Clever Ministrations': Regenerative Beauty at the Fin de Siècle." *Palgrave Communications Online* 3, no. 47 (2017).

———. "*Pomeroy v. Pomeroy:* Beauty, Modernity, and the Female Entrepreneur in *Fin-de-Siècle* London." *Women's History Review* 22, no. 6 (2013): 877–903.

Clifford, Marie J. "Brand Name Modernism: Helena Rubinstein's Art Collection, Femininity, and the Marketing of Modern Style, 1925–1940." Ph.D. diss., University of California, Los Angeles, 1999.

———. "Helena Rubinstein's Beauty Salons, Fashion, and Modernist Display." *Winterthur Portfolio* 38, no. 2/3 (Summer/Autumn 2003): 83–108.

———. "Working with Fashion: The Role of Art, Taste, and Consumerism in Women's Professional Culture, 1920–1940." *American Studies* 44, no. 1/2 (Spring/Summer 2003): 59–84.

Coleman, Elizabeth Ann. *The Genius of Charles James.* New York: Brooklyn Museum/Holt, Rinehart and Winston, 1982.

Conn, Steven. *Nothing Succeeds Like Failure: The Sad History of American Business Schools.* Ithaca, NY: Cornell University Press, 2019.

Corson, Richard. *Fashions in Makeup: From Ancient to Modern Times.* London: Peter Owen Publishers, 2003.

Cowart, Jack, and Juan Hamilton. *Georgia O'Keeffe: Art and Letters.* Washington, DC: National Gallery of Art; Boston: Little, Brown, 1987.

Crane, Diana. *Fashion and Its Social Agendas: Class, Gender, and Identity in Clothing.* Chicago: University of Chicago Press, 2000.

Cronin, Anne M. *Advertising Myths: The Strange Half-Lives of Images and Commodities.* New York: Routledge, 2004.

Curran, Jeanne. "USM Professor Seeks Memories, Memorabilia about the Maine Chance Spa in Mount Vernon," 12 June 2013. College of Arts, Humanities, and Social Sciences, University of Southern Maine. usm.maine.edu/college-of-arts-humanities-social-sciences/usm-professor-seeks-memories-memorabilia-about-maine-chance-spa-mount-vernon.

Dade, Penny. *All Made Up: 100 Years of Cosmetics Advertising.* Hendon, UK: Middlesex University Press, 2007.

Damon-Moore, Helen. *Magazines for the Millions: Gender and Commerce in the* Ladies' Home Journal *and* The Saturday Evening Post, *1880–1910.* Albany: State University of New York, 1994.

Da Silva Lopez, Teresa, and Mark Casson. "Entrepreneurship and the Development of Global Brands." *Business History Review* 81, no. 4 (Winter 2007): 651–80.

Davies, Jill. "Fad Diets—Health Implications." *Nutrition & Food Science*, 1 October 1994, 22–24.

Delano, Page Dougherty. "Making Up for War: Sexuality and Citizenship in Wartime Culture." *Feminist Studies* 26, no. 1 (Spring 2000): 33–68.

DiGeorge, Pat. *Liberty Lady: A True Story of Love and Espionage in WWII Sweden.* Vero Beach, FL: Beaver's Spur Publishing, 2016.

Dootson, Kirsty Sinclair. "'The Hollywood Powder Puff War': Technicolor Cosmetics." *Film History: An International Journal* 28, no. 1 (2016): 107–31.

Douglas, Mary, and Baron Isherwood. *The World of Goods: Towards an Anthropology of Consumption.* New York: Penguin, 1980.

Drachman, Virginia G. *Enterprising Women: 250 Years of American Business.* Chapel Hill: University of North Carolina Press, 2002.

Dyer, Gillian. *Advertising as Communication.* New York: Methuen, 1982.

Eades, John F. "City Planning in West Palm Beach during the 1920s." *Florida Historical Quarterly* 75, no. 3 (Winter 1997): 276–88.

Eco, Humberto, ed. *History of Beauty.* New York: Rizzoli, 2004.

Edwards, Katie, and Donna Plasket, eds. *The Society of the Four Arts*. West Palm Beach, FL: StarGroup International, 2017.

Eldridge, Lisa. *Face Paint: The Story of Makeup*. New York: Harry N. Abrams, 2015.

"Elizabeth Arden Building." DC Historic Sites Online. historicsites.dcpreservation.org/items /show/173.

Ellenberger, Allan R. *The Valentino Mystique: The Death and Afterlife of the Silent Film Idol*. Jefferson, NC: McFarland, 2005.

English, Bonnie. *A Cultural History of Fashion in the 20th and 21st Centuries: From Catwalk to Sidewalk*. New York: Bloomsbury, 2013.

Evans, Caroline. *The Mechanical Smile: Modernism and the First Fashion Shows in France and America, 1900–1929*. New Haven, CT: Yale University Press, 2013.

Fabe, Maxine. *Beauty Millionaire: The Life of Helena Rubinstein*. New York: Thomas Y. Crowell, 1972.

"Fanny Fern Fitzwater." Missouri Remembers Online. missouriartists.org/person/morem164.

Farago, Ladislas. *Burn after Reading: The Espionage History of World War II*. New York: Walker, 1961.

Ferrell-Beck, Jane, and Colleen Gau. *Uplift: The Bra in America*. Philadelphia: University of Pennsylvania Press, 2002.

Finamore, Michelle Tolini. *Hollywood before Glamour: Fashion in American Silent Film*. New York: Palgrave Macmillan, 2013.

Fitoussi, Michèle. *Helena Rubinstein: The Woman Who Invented Beauty*. London: Gallic Books, 2010.

Forty, George. *U.S. Marine Corps Handbook, 1941–1945*. Stroud, UK: Sutton, 2006.

Frost, Jennifer. *Hedda Hopper's Hollywood: Celebrity Gossip and American Conservatism*. New York: New York University Press, 2011.

Gamber, Wendy. "Gendered Concerns: Thoughts on the History of Business and the History of Women." *Business and Economic History* 23, no. 1 (Fall 1994): 129–40.

———. "A Gendered Enterprise: Placing Nineteenth-Century Businesswomen in History." *Business History Review* 72, no. 2 (Summer 1998): 188–217.

Garelick, Rhonda L. *Mademoiselle: Coco Chanel and the Pulse of History*. New York: Random House, 2015.

Garvey, Ellen. *The Adman in the Parlor*. New York: Oxford University Press, 1996.

Gavenas, Mary Lisa. *Color Stories: Behind the Scenes of America's Billion-Dollar Beauty Industry*. New York: Simon & Schuster, 2002.

Geers, Alexie, and Helen Tomlinson. "A Magazine to Make You Beautiful: *Votre Beauté* and the Cosmetics Industry in the 1930s." *Clio: Women, Gender, History* 40 (2014): 226–46.

Ginger, Nolan. "Savage Mind to Savage Machine: Techniques and Disciplines of Creativity,

c. 1880–1985." Ph.D. diss., Columbia University, 2015.

Goldstein, Carolyn. *Creating Consumers: Home Economists in Twentieth-Century America*. Chapel Hill: University of North Carolina Press, 2012.

Gore, Jan. *Send More Shrouds: The V1 Attack on the Guards' Chapel 1944*. Barnsley, UK: Pen & Sword Military, 2017.

Gould, Lewis L. "First Ladies and the Press." *American Journalism* 1, no. 1 (1983–84): 47–62.

Green, Annette. *Spritzing to Success with the Woman Who Brought an Industry to Its Senses*. Indianapolis: Dog Ear, 2018.

Guenther, Irene. *Nazi Chic? Fashioning Women in the Third Reich*. New York: Berg, 2004.

Gundle, Stephen. *Glamour: A History*. New York: Oxford University Press, 2008.

Gustafson, Melanie. "The Family and Business Life of Harriet Hubbard Ayer, Culminating in Fights over Her Person and Property." *Journal of the Gilded Age and Progressive Era* 11, no. 3 (July 2012): 345–404.

Gustaitis, Joseph. *Chicago Transformed: World War I and the Windy City*. Carbondale: Southern Illinois University Press, 2016.

Hall, Linda. "Fashion and Style in the Twenties: The Change." *The Historian* 34, no. 3 (May 1972): 485–97.

Halttunen, Karen. *Confidence Men and Painted Women: A Study of Middle-Class Culture in America, 1830–1870*. New Haven, CT: Yale University Press, 1982.

Hansen, Peer Henrik. *Second to None: U.S. Intelligence Activities in Northern Europe, 1943–1946*. St. Louis: Dordrecht, 2011.

Harrison, Kathryn. *Seeking Rapture: Scenes from a Woman's Life*. New York: Random House, 2003.

Heald, Tim. *By Appointment: 150 Years of the Royal Warrant and Its Holders*. London: Queen Anne Press, 1989.

Hegarty, Marilyn E. *Victory Girls, Khaki-Wackies, and Patriotutes: The Regulation of Female Sexuality during World War II*. New York: New York University Press, 2008.

Helm, Sarah. *Ravensbrück: Life and Death in Hitler's Concentration Camp for Women*. New York: Anchor Books, 2015.

Hernandez, Gabriela. *Classic Beauty: The History of Makeup*. Atglen, PA: Schiffer, 2017.

Hershan, Stella. *A Woman of Quality*. New York: Crown, 1970.

Herzig, Rebecca. "Subjected to the Current: Batteries, Bodies and the Early History of Electrification in the United States." *Journal of Social History* 41, no. 4 (Summer 2008): 867–85.

Hewitt, Steve. *Snitch: A History of the Modern Intelligence Informer*. New York: Continuum/ Bloomsbury, 2010.

Hill, Daniel Delis. *Advertising to the American Woman*. Columbus: Ohio State University Press, 2002.

"History of Skin Camouflage." British Association of Skin Camouflage. skin-camouflage.net /scwp/index.php/history-of-skin-camouflage.

Hoefle, Milton L. "The Early History of Parke-Davis and Company." *Bulletin for the History of Chemistry* 25, no. 1 (2000): 28–34.

Hoganson, Kristin. *Consumers' Imperium: The Global Production of American Domesticity, 1865–1920.* Chapel Hill: University of North Carolina Press, 2010.

Holloway, Camara Dia. "Lovechild: Stieglitz, O'Keeffe, and the Birth of American Modernism." *Prospects* 30 (October 2005): 395–432.

Holt, Marilyn Irvin. *Mamie Doud Eisenhower: The General's First Lady.* Lawrence: University Press of Kansas, 2007.

Hood, John. *Selling the Dream: Why Advertising Is Good Business.* Westport, CT: Praeger, 2005.

Hore, Peter. *Lindell's List: Saving British and American Women at Ravensbrück.* Stroud, UK: The History Press, 2016.

Hornsby, Stephen J. "The Gilded Age and the Making of Bar Harbor." *Geographical Review* 83, no. 4 (October 1993): 455–68.

Houlbrook, Matt. "'The Man with the Powder Puff' in Interwar London." *The Historical Journal* 50, no. 1 (March 2007): 145–71.

Houy, Yvonne B. "'Of Course the German Woman Should Be Modern': The Modernization of Women's Appearance during National Socialism." Ph.D. diss., Cornell University, 2002.

Hyde, Charles K. "'Detroit the Dynamic': The Industrial History of Detroit from Cigars to Cars." *Michigan Historical Review* 27, no. 1 (Spring 2001): 57–73.

Johnson, Louise Clair. *Behind the Red Door: How Elizabeth Arden's Legacy Inspired My Coming-of-Age Story in the Beauty Industry.* Columbus, OH: Gatekeeper Press, 2021.

Jones, Donald. *Fifty Tales of Toronto.* Toronto: University of Toronto Press, 1992.

Jones, Geoffrey. *Beauty Imagined: A History of the Global Beauty Industry.* New York: Oxford University Press, 2010.

———. "Blonde and Blue-Eyed? Globalizing Beauty, c. 1945–c. 1980." *Economic History Review* 61, no. 1 (2008): 125–54.

———. "How Helena Rubinstein Used Tall Tales to Turn Cosmetics into a Luxury Brand." *Cold Call,* 14 March 2019. Harvard Business School. hbswk.hbs.edu/item/how-helena-rubinstein-used-tall-tales-to-turn-cosmetics-into-a-luxury-brand.

"Joseph Platt, FIDSA." Industrial Designers Society of America. idsa.org/profile/joseph-platt.

Josephson, Matthew. *The Robber Barons.* New York: Harcourt, 1934.

Kahn, E. J. *Jock: The Life and Times of John Hay Whitney.* Garden City, NY: Doubleday, 1981.

———. *The World of Swope.* New York: Simon & Schuster, 1965.

Kay, Gwen. *Dying to Be Beautiful: The Fight for Safe Cosmetics.* Columbus: The Ohio State University Press, 2005.

Kessler-Harris, Alice. "Ideologies and Innovation: Gender Dimensions of Business History." *Business and Economic History* 20 (1991): 45–51.

Khan, B. Zorina. *The Democratization of Invention: Patents and Copyrights in American Economic Development, 1790–1920.* Cambridge: Cambridge University Press, 2005.

Kidwell, Claudia, and Margaret C. Christman. *Suiting Everyone: The Democratization of Clothing in America.* Washington, DC: Smithsonian Institution Press, 1974.

King, Lynda J. *Best-Sellers by Design: Vicki Baum and the House of Ullstein.* Detroit: Wayne State University Press, 1988.

Kirkpatrick, Jerry. *In Defense of Advertising: Arguments from Reason, Ethical Egoism, and Laissez-Faire Capitalism.* Westport, CT: Quorum Books, 1994.

Klein, Mason. *Helena Rubinstein: Beauty Is Power.* New Haven, CT: Yale University Press, 2014.

Klein, Michèle Gerber. *Charles James: Portrait of an Unreasonable Man.* New York: Rizzoli, 2018.

Krismann, Carol H. *Encyclopedia of American Women in Business,* vol. 2. Westport, CT: Greenwood Press, 2005.

Kroeger, Brooke. *Fannie: The Talent for Success of Writer Fannie Hurst.* New York: Random House, 1999.

Kwolek-Folland, Angel. *Engendering Business: Men and Women in the Corporate Office, 1870–1930.* Baltimore: Johns Hopkins University Press, 1994.

———. *Incorporating Women: A History of Women and Business in the United States.* New York: Palgrave, 1998.

Lacy, Linda Cates. *We Are Marines!: Stories of Women Marines by Women Marines, World War I to the Present.* N.p.: Tar Heel Chapter, NC1, Women Marines Association, 2004.

Landers, James. *The Improbable First Century of Cosmopolitan Magazine.* Columbia: University of Missouri Press, 2010.

Landes, David S., Joel Mokyr, and William J. Baumol, eds. *The Invention of Enterprise: Entrepreneurship from Ancient Mesopotamia to Modern Times.* Princeton, NJ: Princeton University Press, 2010.

Large, David C. *The Grand Spas of Central Europe: A History of Intrigue, Politics, Art, and Healing.* New York: Rowman & Littlefield, 2015.

Lavin, Maud. "Ringl + Pit: The Representation of Women in German Advertising, 1929–1933." *The Print Collector's Newsletter* 16, no. 3 (July–August 1985): 89–93.

Laycock, Joseph. "Yoga for the New Woman and the New Man: The Role of Pierre Bernard and Blanche DeVries in the Creation of Modern Postural Yoga." *Religion and American Culture: A*

Journal of Interpretation 23, no. 1 (Winter 2013): 101–36.

Leach, William. *Land of Desire: Merchants, Power, and the Rise of a New American Culture.* New York: Vintage, 1993.

Lears, T. Jackson. *No Place of Grace: Antimodernism and the Transformation of American Culture, 1880–1920.* Chicago: University of Chicago Press, 1981.

Leckie, Janet. *A Talent for Living: The Story of Henry Sell, an American Original.* New York: Hawthorn Books, 1970.

Levine, Philippa, ed. *Gender, Labour, War and Empire: Essays on Modern Britain.* New York: Palgrave Macmillan, 2009.

Lewis, Alfred Allan. *Ladies and Not-So-Gentle Women.* New York: Penguin, 2000.

Lewis, Alfred Allan, and Constance Woodworth. *Miss Elizabeth Arden: An Unretouched Portrait.* New York: Coward, McCann & Geoghegan, 1972.

Ley, Sandra. *Fashion for Everyone: The Story of Ready-to-Wear, 1870s–1970s.* New York: Charles Scribner's Sons, 1975.

Longinotti-Buitoni, Gian Luigi, with Kip Longinotti-Buitoni. *Selling Dreams: How to Make Any Product Irresistible.* New York: Simon & Schuster, 1999.

Love, Robert. *The Great Oom: The Improbable Birth of Yoga in America.* New York: Viking, 2010.

Lowry, Beverly. *Her Dream of Dreams: The Rise and Triumph of Madam C. J. Walker.* New York: Vintage, 2004.

Magliozzi, Ron. "'Crazy with the Wind': The 'Gone with the Wind' World Premiere Campaign Scrapbook," *MoMA* 18 (Autumn–Winter 1994): 32–34.

Marsh, Madeleine. *Compacts and Cosmetics: Beauty from Victorian Times to the Present Day.* Barnsley, UK: Pen & Sword, 2014.

Marshall, Mary. *Great Breeders and Their Methods: Leslie Combs II and Spendthrift Farm.* Neenah, WI: Russell Meerdink, 2008.

McKellar, Susie. "'Seals of Approval': Consumer Representation in 1930s' America." *Journal of Design History* 15, no. 1 (2002): 1–13.

Meid, Pat. *Marine Corps Women's Reserve in World War II.* Washington, DC: U.S. Marine Corps, 1964.

Meikle, Jeffrey L. *American Plastic: A Cultural History.* New Brunswick, NJ: Rutgers University Press, 1997.

Meyer, Leisa D. *Creating G.I. Jane: Sexuality and Power in the Women's Army Corps during World War II.* New York: Columbia University Press, 1996.

Miller, Donald L. *Supreme City: How Jazz Age Manhattan Gave Birth to Modern America.* New York: Simon & Schuster, 2014.

Miskill, Peter. "Cavity Protection or Cosmetic Perfection: Innovation and Marketing of Toothpaste Brands in the United States and Western Europe, 1955–1985." *Business History Review* 78, no. 1 (Spring 2004): 29–60.

Molinaro, Christa. "Dressing the World of Tomorrow: Fashion at the 1939–1940 New York World's Fair: An Exhibition." Master's thesis, SUNY Fashion Institute of Technology, 2020.

Monroe, John Warne. *Metropolitan Fetish: African Sculpture and the Imperial French Invention of Primitive Art.* Ithaca, NY: Cornell University Press, 2019.

Monsen and Baer Inc. *For the Love of Perfume: The Perfumes of Elizabeth Arden.* Vienna, VA: Monsen and Baer Inc., 1999.

Moore, Margaret. *End of the Road for Ladies' Mile?* New York: The Drive to Protect the Ladies' Mile District, 1986.

Mower, Sarah. *Oscar: The Style, Inspiration and Life of Oscar de la Renta.* New York: Assouline, 2002.

Munch, Janet Butler. "Making Waves in the Bronx: The Story of the U.S. Naval Training School (WR) at Hunter College." CUNY Lehman College Academic Works Online, 1993. academicworks.cuny.edu/cgi/viewcontent.cgi?article=1228&context=le_pubs.

Neuman, Johanna. *Gilded Suffragists: The New York Socialites Who Fought for Women's Right to Vote.* New York: New York University Press, 2017.

Nicholson, James C. *The Kentucky Derby: How the Run for the Roses Became America's Premier Sporting Event.* Lexington: University Press of Kentucky, 2012.

———. *Never Say Die: A Kentucky Colt, the Epsom Derby, and the Rise of the Modern Thoroughbred Industry.* Lexington: University Press of Kentucky, 2013.

Nickel, Christiane. "Fashion in the Third Reich." Master's thesis, SUNY Fashion Institute of Technology, 2011.

Nicklas, Charlotte. "One Essential Thing to Learn Is Colour: Harmony, Science and Colour Theory in Mid-Nineteenth-Century Fashion Advice." *Journal of Design History* 27, no. 3 (2014): 218–36.

"Number of TV Households in America: 1950–1978." The American Century Digital Archives, Washington and Lee University. americancentury.omeka.wlu.edu/items/show.

Nutting, P. Bradley. "Selling Elegant Glassware during the Great Depression: A. H. Heisey & Company and the New Deal." *Business History Review* 77, no. 3 (Autumn 2003): 447–78.

O'Higgins, Patrick. *Madame: An Intimate Biography of Helena Rubinstein.* New York: Viking, 1971.

Olson, Kelly. "Cosmetics in Roman Antiquity: Substance, Remedy, Poison." *Classical World* 102, no. 3 (Spring 2009): 291–310.

Olson, Lynne. *Citizens of London: The Americans Who Stood with Britain in Its Darkest, Finest Hour.* New York: Random House, 2011.

Pallingston, Jessica. *Lipstick.* New York: St. Martin's Press, 1999.

Peiss, Kathy. "Educating the Eye of the Beholder: American Cosmetics Abroad." *Daedalus* 131, no. 4 (Fall 2002): 101–9.

———. *Hope in a Jar: The Making of America's Beauty Culture*. Philadelphia: University of Pennsylvania Press, 1998.

———. "Making Faces: The Cosmetics Industry and the Cultural Construction of Gender, 1890–1930." *Genders* 7 (Spring 1990): 365–491.

———. "'Vital Industry' and Women's Ventures: Conceptualizing Gender in Twentieth Century Business History." *Business History Review* 72 (Summer 1998): 219–41.

Pierce, Dianne O. "Design, Craft, and American Identity: Russel Wright's 'American Way' Project, 1940–1942." Master's thesis, Cooper Hewitt, 2010.

Piper, Henry Dan. "Fitzgerald's Cult of Disillusion." *American Quarterly* 3, no. 1 (Spring 1951): 69–80.

Pollack, Howard. *John Alden Carpenter: A Chicago Composer*. Chicago: University of Illinois Press, 1995.

Potter, David. *People of Plenty: Economic Abundance and the American Character*. Chicago: University of Chicago Press, 1954.

Pound, Reginald. *Gillies: Surgeon Extraordinary*. London: Michael Joseph, 1964.

Rabinovitch-Fox, Einav. *Dressed for Freedom: The Fashionable Politics of American Feminism*. Urbana: University of Illinois Press, 2021.

Rantisi, Norma M. "The Ascendance of New York Fashion." *International Journal of Urban and Regional Research* 28, no. 1 (March 2004): 86–106.

Reeder, Jan Glier, and Harold Korda. *Charles James: Beyond Fashion*. New York: Metropolitan Museum of Art/Yale University Press, 2014.

Rhodes, Dan. *Ty Cobb: Safe at Home*. Guilford, CT: Lyons Press, 2008.

Robertson, William H. P. *The History of Thoroughbred Racing in America*. New York: Bonanza Books, 1964.

Ronald, Susan. *Condé Nast: The Man and His Empire*. New York: St. Martin's Press, 2019.

Rust, Daniel. *Flying across America: The Airline Passenger Experience*. Norman: University of Oklahoma Press, 2009.

Ryan, Kathleen M. "Uniform Matters: Fashion Design in World War II Women's Recruitment." *Journal of American Culture* 37, no. 4 (December 2014): 419–29.

Salis, Dahn E. "Exercising Authority: A Critical History of Exercise Messages in Popular Magazines, 1925–1968." Ph.D. diss., University of Nevada, Las Vegas, 1998.

Santos, Lucy Jane. *Half Lives: The Unlikely History of Radium*. New York: Pegasus, 2021.

Sawdon, Herb. H. *The Woodbridge Story*. Woodbridge, ON, Canada: self-published, 1960.

Scanlon, Jennifer. "'If My Husband Calls I'm Not Here': The Beauty Parlor as Real and Representational Female Space." *Feminist Studies* 33, no. 2 (Summer 2007): 309–34.

———. *Inarticulate Longings: The Ladies' Home Journal, Gender, and the Promises of Consumer Culture*. New York: Routledge, 1995.

Schneirov, Matthew. *The Dream of a New Social Order: Popular Magazines in America, 1893–1914*. New York: Columbia University Press, 1994.

Schockley, Jay. "Aeolian Building." Landmarks Preservation Commission, 10 December 2002. npclibrary.org/db/bb_files/2011-Madison BelmontBuilding.pdf.

Schorman, Rob. "Remember the *Maine*, Boys, and the Price of This Suit." *The Historian* 61, no. 1 (Fall 1998): 11934.

———. *Selling Style: Clothing and Social Change at the Turn of the Century*. Philadelphia: University of Pennsylvania Press, 2003.

Schweitzer, Marlis. "'The Mad Search for Beauty': Actresses' Testimonials, the Cosmetics Industry, and the 'Democratization of Beauty.'" *The Journal of the Gilded Age and Progressive Era* 4, no. 3 (July 2005): 255–92.

———. *When Broadway Was the Runway: Theater, Fashion, and American Culture*. Philadelphia: University of Pennsylvania Press, 2009.

Schwoch, James. "Selling the Sight/Site of Sound: Broadcast Advertising and the Transition from Radio to Television." *Cinema Journal* 30, no. 1 (Autumn 1990): 55–66.

Scovell, Jane. *Oona: Living in the Shadows; a Biography of Oona O'Neill Chaplin*. New York: Warner Books, 1998.

Scranton, Philip. *Beauty and Business: Commerce, Gender and Culture in Modern America*. New York: Routledge, 2001.

Sebba, Anne. *Les Parisiennes: How the Women of Paris Lived, Loved, and Died under Nazi Occupation*. New York: St. Martin's Press, 2016.

Segrave, Kerry. *America Brushes Up: The Use and Marketing of Toothpaste and Toothbrushes in the Twentieth Century*. Jefferson, NC: McFarland, 2010.

———. *Endorsements in Advertising: A Social History*. Jefferson, NC: McFarland, 2005.

Sengoopta, Chandak. *The Most Secret Quintessence of Life: Sex, Glands, and Hormones, 1850–1950*. Chicago: University of Chicago Press, 2006.

Shaulis, Dahn E. "Exercising Authority: A Critical History of Exercise Messages in Popular Magazines, 1925–1968." Ph.D. diss., University of Nevada, Las Vegas, 1998.

Shuker, Nancy. *Elizabeth Arden: Beauty Empire Builder*. Woodbridge, CT: Blackbird Press, 2001.

Silva, Luisina. "New York Fashion Industry Goes to the Fair." Master's thesis, City University of New York, 2014.

Skinner, Joan S. *Form and Fancy: Factories and Factory Buildings by Wallis, Gilbert & Partners, 1916–1939*. Liverpool: Liverpool University Press, 1997.

Smith, Jane S. *Elsie de Wolfe: A Life in the High Style*. New York: Atheneum, 1982.

Smith, Ralph Lee. *The Health Hucksters*. New York: Thomas Y. Crowell, 1960.

Södersten, Per, David Crews, Cheryl Logan, and Rudolf Werner Soukup. "Eugen Steinach: The First Neuroendocrinologist." *Endocrinology* 155, no. 3 (1 March 2014): 688–95.

Sowers, Richard. *The Kentucky Derby, Preakness and Belmont Stakes: A Comprehensive History*. Jefferson, NC: McFarland, 2014.

Staggs, Sam. *Inventing Elsa Maxwell: How an Irrepressible Nobody Conquered High Society, Hollywood, the Press, and the World*. New York: St. Martin's Press, 2012.

Staiti, Alana. "Real Women, Normal Curves, and the Making of the American Fashion Mannequin, 1932–1946." *Configurations* 28, no. 4 (Fall 2020): 403–31.

Stark, James F. *The Cult of Youth: Anti-Ageing in Modern Britain*. New York: Cambridge University Press, 2020.

Steele, Valerie. *Fashion and Eroticism: Ideals of Feminine Beauty from the Victorian Era to the Jazz Age*. New York: Oxford University Press, 1985.

Stewart, Mary Lynn. *For Health and Beauty: Physical Culture for Frenchwomen, 1880s–1930s*. Baltimore: The Johns Hopkins University Press, 2001.

Strasser, Susan. *Satisfaction Guaranteed: The Making of the American Mass Market*. New York: Pantheon, 1989.

Stremlow, Mary V. *Free a Marine to Fight: Women Marines in World War II*. Washington, DC: U.S. Marine Corps, 1994.

———. *A History of the Women Marines, 1946–1977*. Washington, DC: Government Printing Office, 1986.

Strum, Rebecca W. "Elisabeth Marbury 1856–1933: Her Life and Work." Ph.D. diss., New York University, 1989.

Sugar, Bert. *Horse Sense: An Inside Look at the Sport of Kings*. Hoboken, NJ: John Wiley & Sons, 2003.

Sussman, Peter Y., ed. *Decca: The Letters of Jessica Mitford*. New York: Alfred A. Knopf, 2006.

Sussman, Warren. *Culture as History: The Transformation of American Society in the Twentieth Century*. New York: Pantheon, 1984.

Tedlow, Richard. *New and Improved: The Story of Mass Marketing*. New York: Oxford University Press, 1990.

Tindall, George B. "The Bubble in the Sun." *American Heritage* 16, no. 5 (August 1965). americanheritage.com/bubble-sun.

Toland, John. *Adolf Hitler*. Garden City, NY: Doubleday, 1976.

Treadwell, Mattie E. *The Women's Army Corps*. Washington, DC: Government Printing Office, 1953.

Tunbridge, Laura. "Singing Translations: The Politics of Listening between the Wars." *Representations* 123, no. 1 (Summer 2013): 53–86.

Van Beck, Todd W. *The Genius of Frank E. Campbell: How One Man Changed Funeral Service and Unwittingly Set the Stage for Movie Stars*. Scotts Valley, CA: CreateSpace, 2018.

Vickers, Raymond B. "Addison Mizner: Promoter in Paradise." *Florida Historical Quarterly* 75, no. 4 (Spring 1997): 381–407.

Vinikis, Vincent. *Soft Soap, Hard Sell: American Hygiene in an Age of Advertisement*. Ames: Iowa State University Press, 1992.

Walton, Whitney. "Jacqueline Kennedy, Frenchness, and French-American Relations in the 1950s and Early 1960s." *French Politics, Culture & Society* 31, no. 2 (Summer 2013): 34–57.

Watson, Steven. *Prepare for Saints: Gertrude Stein, Virgil Thomson, and the Mainstreaming of American Modernism*. New York: Random House, 1998.

Wax, Murray. "Themes in Cosmetics and Grooming." *American Journal of Sociology* 62, no. 6 (May 1957): 588–93.

Welters, Linda, and Abby Lillenthun, eds. *The Fashion Reader*, 2nd ed. New York: Berg, 2011.

Whitaker, Jan. *Service and Style: How the American Department Store Fashioned the Middle Class*. New York: St. Martin's Press, 2006.

Wilkinson, Hutton. Tony Duquette Studies, tonyduquette.com.

Wilkinson, Hutton, Tony Duquette, and Wendy Goodman. *Tony Duquette: More Is More*. New York: Abrams, 2009.

Willett, Julie A. *Permanent Waves: The Making of the American Beauty Shop*. New York: New York University Press, 2000.

Willey, Amanda M. "Fashioning Femininity for War: Material Culture and Gender Performance in the WAC and WAVES during World War II." Ph.D. diss., Kansas State University, 2015.

Wilson, Elizabeth. *Adorned in Dreams: Fashion and Modernity*. New Brunswick, NJ: Rutgers University Press, 2003.

Wilson, Ross J. *New York and the First World War: Shaping an American City*. Burlington, VT: Ashgate, 2014.

Wolf, Naomi. *The Beauty Myth: How Images of Beauty Are Used against Women*. New York: William Morrow, 1991.

Women Marines Association. "Women Marines History." womenmarines.org/wm-history.

Wood, Stephen C. "Television's First Political Spot Ad Campaign: Eisenhower Answers America." *Presidential Studies Quarterly* 20, no. 2 (Spring 1990): 265–83.

Woodhead, Lindy. *War Paint: Madame Helena Rubinstein & Miss Elizabeth Arden*. Hoboken, NJ: John Wiley & Sons, 2003.

Wrightman Fox, Richard, and T. J. Jackson Lears, eds. *The Culture of Consumption: Critical*

Essays in American History, 1880–1980. New York: Pantheon, 1983.

Young, James Harvey. *The Medical Messiahs: A Social History of Health Quackery in 20th Century America.* Princeton, NJ: Princeton University Press, 1967.

Zachary, Cassidy. "Ethel Traphagen: American Fashion Pioneer." *Fashion Studies Journal,* 27 February 2018. fashionstudiesjournal.org/5-histories /2018/2/27/ethel-traphagen-american-fashion -pioneer.

Zeitz, Joshua. *Flapper: A Madcap Story of Sex, Style, Celebrity, and the Women Who Made America Modern.* New York: Crown, 2006.

Ziporyn, T. "AMA's Bureau of Investigation Exposed Fraud." *The Journal of the American Medical Association* 254, no. 15 (18 October 1985): 2043.

Index

Credits

INSERT 1

p. 1: From the collection of the author

p. 2: (top and bottom) Süddeutsche Zeitung Photo/Alamy

p. 3: Artepics/Alamy

p. 4: Courtesy of the Canadian National Exhibition Association Archives

p. 5: (top) Alamy, (bottom) Adolph de Meyer/Wikimedia

p. 6: (top) University of Southern Maine, "Ardena Muscle Oil by Elizabeth Arden [View Front]" (2019). *Farm Ephemera*, 16, via CC BY-NC-ND 4.0, (bottom) Mirco de Cet/Alamy

p. 7: (top) Sasha/Hulton Archive/Getty Images, (bottom) Alfred Eisenstaedt/Shutterstock

p. 8: Longley Studio, University of Southern Maine, Digital Commons via CC BY-NC-ND 4.0

p. 9: (top) Library of Congress, Prints & Photographs Division [LC-DIG-ggbain-30596], (bottom) From the Thurston Zachow Family Collection, University of Southern Maine, "Maine Chance Farm Christmas Card" (1933). *Farm Ephemera*, 4, Digital Commons via CC BY-NC-ND 4.0

p. 10: (top, middle) Alfred Eisenstaedt/Shutterstock, (bottom) Bettman/Getty

p. 11: (top) Alfred Eisenstaedt/Shutterstock, (bottom) Alan Fisher/Library of Congress, Prints & Photographs Division [LC-USZ62-123247]

p. 12: Neil Baylis/Alamy

p. 13: (top) From the collection of the author, (bottom) Helen E. Hokinson/ The New Yorker Collection/The Cartoon Bank

p. 14: From the collection of the author

p. 15: Alamy

p. 16: From the collection of the author

INSERT 2

p. 1: Kappa Kappa Gamma Archives

p. 2: (top, bottom) Kappa Kappa Gamma Archives

p. 3: Hulton Archive/Getty

p. 4: (top) f8 archive/Alamy, (bottom) Chicago History Museum/Alamy

p. 5: (top) Keeneland Library Meadors Collection, (bottom) Leonard McCombe/Life Picture Collection/Shutterstock

p. 6: Leonard McCombe/Life Picture Collection/Shutterstock

p. 7: (top) Leonard McCombe/Life Picture Collection/Shutterstock, (bottom) MediaPunch Inc./Alamy

p. 8: (top) Keeneland Library Morgan Collection, (bottom) copyrighted © 2024 by Daily Racing Form, LLC, and Equibase Company. Reprinted with permission of the copyright owner.

p. 9: (top) Gottscho-Schleisner Collection, Library of Congress, Prints & Photographs Division [LC-G613-73477], (bottom) Mondadori/Getty Images

p. 10: (top) Catherine Bliss Enslow Papers, Marshall University, (bottom) Boris Carmi/Meitar Collection/National Library of Israel/The Pritzker Family National Photography Collection via CC BY 4.0

p. 11: Trevor Whyte Photography

p. 12: (top) Frank Monaco/Shutterstock, (bottom) Toni Frissell, Look Magazine Photograph Collection, Library of Congress, Prints & Photographs Division

p. 13: (top) Keeneland Library Meadors Collection, (bottom) Morgan Collection/Getty Images

p. 14: Wikimedia Commons via CC0 1.0

p. 15: (top) Donald Stampfli/RDB/ullstein bild via Getty Images, (bottom) Potter/Express/Hulton Archive/Getty Images

p. 16: St. Louis County Historical Society